CHRONOLOGY HIGHLIGH

n 624, Arabian leader and priestess Hind al Hunnud leads her tribe, he Quraish, against Muhammad in the Battle of Badr.

Empress Jito rules Japan from 686 to 697.

Chinese painter Lady Li creates the major genre of monochrome ink bamboo painting c. 925.

| 501–1000 |

apanese poet and novelist Murasaki Shikibu writes *Genji Monogatari Tale of Genji*), arguably the world's first novel, in 1004.

Norse explorer Gudrid Karlsefni urges and participates in a failed oyage of colonization to the new land of Vinland (North America).

oltec queen Xochitl falls in battle while leading a battalion of women nto the field c. 1116.

| 1001–1200 |

ueen Zabel becomes ruler of Lesser Armenia in 1219.

orotea Bocchi is appointed to the chair of medicine and moral hilosophy at the University of Bologna in 1390.

n June 20, 1397, the Union of Kalmar makes Queen Margrethe the le ruler of Denmark, Sweden, and Norway.

| 1201–1400 |

ench warrior and saint Joan of Arc is executed on May 30, 1431.

1492, Spanish Queen Isabella funds the first expedition of Columbus the Americas.

ueen Elizabeth I establishes Trinity College in Dublin in 1591.

| 1401–1600 |

dy Deborah Moody founds the first English settlement in Kings unty on New York's Long Island in 1643.

therine Duchemin submits a still life, *Basket of Flowers on a Table*, to e French Académie Royale in 1663, and becomes the first woman mitted.

June 1678, Elena Lucrezia Cornaro Piscopia, through the University Padua, becomes the first woman to earn a Ph.D.

| 1601–1700 |

ntinued inside back cover)

CHRONOLOGY
OF
WOMEN'S HISTORY

CHRONOLOGY
OF
WOMEN'S HISTORY

Kirstin Olsen

Greenwood Press
Westport, Connecticut • London

Library of Congress Cataloging-in-Publication Data

Olsen, Kirstin.
    Chronology of women's history / Kirstin Olsen.
       p. cm.
    Includes bibliographical references and index.
    ISBN 0–313–28803–8 (alk. paper)
    1. Women—History—Chronology. I. Title.
  HQ1121.047   1994
  305.4′09—dc20   93–50542

British Library Cataloguing in Publication Data is available.

Library of Congress Catalog Card Number: 93–50542
ISBN: 0–313–28803–8

First published in 1994

Greenwood Press, 88 Post Road West, Westport, CT 06881
An imprint of Greenwood Publishing Group, Inc.

Printed in the United States of America

The paper used in this book complies with the
Permanent Paper Standard issued by the National
Information Standards Organization (Z39.48–1984).

10 9 8 7 6 5 4

Chronology Highlights compiled by Karen E. Davis.

For Emily
so that she may know her mothers

Contents

Acknowledgments

This book was written during a pregnancy and the first months of my daughter's life. It seems a fitting circumstance in which to write about the history of women, but it was also very stressful. Several people helped by researching, babysitting, and murmuring sympathetically at appropriate moments; without them, the cliché is true: this book would not have been possible. Chief among them were my mother, Nancy Olsen, whose help was invaluable and given at great personal inconvenience; my father, Brian Olsen, who managed to overcome his fear of blood and icky things to be present at the delivery of my baby; my husband, Eric Voelkel, who takes fathering very seriously; my sister, Erica Olsen, whose friendship sustained me through some rough moments; and Dave Mackie. Thanks also to Jeanne Beatty DeSana and Jim DeSana; the Spiny Norman crew: Vince and Lori Bocchino, Dan Levin, Brian Ehrmantraut, Moana Kutsche, Tom Kessler, Jane Johnson, and especially Naomi Andrews and Alyson Collins; and the satellites of the Troublemakers' Table, who smoothed the path while I taught, wrote, and incubated simultaneously: Jack Johnson, Tim Kelly, Kathy Hansell, Gerald Renouf, Elisabeth Stitt, Jim Johnson, Valerie Sacks, Anna Friebel, Tom Scully, Pat Blanar, Don Knapp, Ray Jimenez, Sandy Briley, Meg McClintock, Judy Angelo, Freddie Lee, Carolyn McVeigh, Tracy Murphy, Jeanie Wallace, and Mary Alice Callahan.

Introduction

This book lists some of the landmarks in women's history from 20,000 B.C. to 1993. It is by no means an exhaustive list of all women's accomplishments, but it does make an effort to be inclusive. The reader will find entries from every inhabited continent and from a variety of fields of endeavor. Most chapters have ten categories:

1. *General Status and Daily Life.* Here the reader will find information on women's legal status with regard to marriage, children, widowhood, chastity, infidelity, divorce, remarriage, property rights, and crimes against women such as rape, infanticide, and spousal abuse. Other topics covered in this category include divisions of labor, general opportunities for women, typical duties, freedom of movement, etiquette, dress, housework and home economics, life expectancy, average number of children, average age at marriage, sexual habits, contraception, abortion, diet, cosmetics, and the general attitudes of various cultures toward women. Women famous or infamous for reasons unrelated to one of the other categories (e.g., a notorious murderer or a woman who rescued drowning sailors) are also included here.

2. *Government, the Military, and the Law.* This category discusses women who were members of the governmental establishment: political leaders, royalty, royal consorts and First Ladies, warriors or leaders of warriors, legislators, lawyers, bureaucrats, diplomats, government spies, law enforcement and corrections officers, and judges. The dates on which various women achieved suffrage are listed here, while the fight for suffrage (since it is outside the establishment) appears in category 6.

3. *Literature and the Visual Arts.* This category lists women's accomplishments in poetry, fiction, drama, journalism (as reporters—publishers are found in category 7), diaries, letters, architecture, painting, sculpture, decorative arts and crafts, cartooning, and photography. Museum curators and founders and artists' models are also listed here.

4. *Performing Arts and Entertainment.* This category includes women's accomplishments in music, opera, theater, movies, radio and television (including broadcast news), stand-up comedy, and dance.

5. *Athletics and Exploration.* Here the reader will find explorers and travelers (and their publications), aviators, early colonists, organizers of athletic groups, athletes of all kinds, and players of sports (like chess) that may not necessarily be primarily physical in nature.

6. *Activism.* This category is reserved for social reform outside the government establishment: feminism, civil rights, pacifism, suffrage, social reform, temperance, philanthropy, and all women's organizations not devoted to one of the other categories (e.g., the General Federation of Women's Clubs is listed here, while the Society of Women Engineers is found in category 8). Publications are listed here only if they are specifically designed to promote reform rather than to serve as analyses or scholarly studies.

7. *Business and Industry.* This category includes entrepreneurs, managers, labor leaders, occupational safety experts, inventors, and general information on women's wages and participation in the work force. Women who commit (often) illegal acts for profit, such as prostitutes and thieves, are also listed here.

8. *Science and Medicine.* This category includes the fields of mathematics, chemistry, physics, geology, paleontology, biology, botany, zoology, genetics, medicine, anatomy, physiology, and astronomy. The reader will find information on scientific publications and organizations, as well as details on women's health care.

9. *Education and Scholarship.* This category includes educators, educational reformers, social scientists, art historians, literary critics, the foundation of women's schools and colleges, admission of women to universities and scholarly organizations, and all nonfiction publications except those that qualify for categories 3, 6, 8, or 10.

10. *Religion.* This category includes religious leaders, clergy, religious authors, theologians, saints, and other religious figures.

For the sake of clarity and continuity, women are discussed under the names by which they are best known, even if at that particular time they have not yet adopted the pseudonym or married name under which they will become famous. George Sand, therefore, is listed as George Sand even before she becomes a writer under that name; and the author of *Uncle Tom's Cabin*, born Harriet Beecher, is listed as Harriet Beecher Stowe even before her marriage.

Most women are identified by nationality and occupation whenever they appear (e.g., U.S. author Mary E. Wilkins Freeman), but some well-known women (e.g., Susan B. Anthony, Marie Curie) or women who appear in numerous entries are so identified only in their first entries.

Acronyms

Acronyms are used after the first mention of a major organization.
Some acronyms used frequently in this book are listed below:

AAU	Amateur Athletic Union
AAUW	American Association of University Women
ACDWF	All-China Democratic Women's Federation
ACE	American Cinema Editors
ACLU	American Civil Liberties Union
AFL-CIO	American Federation of Labor-Congress of Industrial Organizations
AFT	American Federation of Teachers
AMA	American Medical Association
ANC	African National Congress
AP	Associated Press
ASWPL	Association of Southern Women for the Prevention of Lynching
AWSA	American Woman Suffrage Association
BBC	British Broadcasting Corporation
DAR	Daughters of the American Revolution
EEOC	Equal Employment Opportunity Commission
EPA	Environmental Protection Agency
ERA	Equal Rights Amendment
HUAC	House Un-American Activities Committee
HUD	Housing and Urban Development
IEEE	Institute for Electrical and Electronics Engineers
ILGWU	International Ladies' Garment Workers' Union
ILO	International Labor Organization
IOC	International Olympic Committee
IWW	International Workers of the World
KKK	Ku Klux Klan
LPGA	Ladies Professional Golf Association
LWV	League of Women Voters
MoMA	Museum of Modern Art
NAACP	National Association for the Advancement of Colored People
NACW	National Association of Colored Women
NASA	National Aeronautics and Space Administration
NAWSA	National American Woman Suffrage Association
NCNW	National Council of Negro Women
NOW	National Organization for Women
NWSA	National Woman Suffrage Association
SNCC	Student Non-Violent Coordinating Committee
SWE	Society of Women Engineers
SWG	Society of Woman Geographers
TUC	Trades Union Congress

UMW	United Mine Workers
UN	United Nations
USSR	Union of Soviet Socialist Republics
WAC	Women's Army Corps
WASPs	Women's Air Force Service Pilots
WAVES	Women Accepted for Voluntary Emergency Service
WCTU	Women's Christian Temperance Union
WILPF	Women's International League for Peace and Freedom
WSPU	Women's Social and Political Union
WTUL	Women's Trade Union League
YWCA	Young Women's Christian Association

The Chronology

Prehistory to 3000 B.C.*

General Status and Daily Life

20,000–10,000 Cro-Magnon humans live in migratory hunting-gathering tribes. Women tend to live less long than men and are probably less numerous, perhaps due to female infanticide—female babies in many later cultures will be killed at birth because they are valued less than boys.

The division of labor is not absolute when it comes to finding food. Women as well as men participate in cooperative hunts and hunt small animals; when game is scarce, men help to gather plants. Women carry burdens, cook, clean, and care for children. They are probably responsible for the invention of pottery. Population increases rather slowly, for several reasons: women's life expectancy is low, so childbearing years are few; lactation and malnutrition inhibit fertility; and resources are often scarce.

As social organization increases, taboos regarding incest and menstruation develop. It is possible that the menstrual cycle itself becomes a cause of human advancement, as a certain amount of abstract thinking is required to track cycles. Puberty rites for girls are developed, with boys' rituals often mimicking girls' loss of blood.

10,000–9000 The Neolithic (New Stone) Age begins in Asia. Societies develop many of the skills, tools, and structures associated with civilization: agriculture, domestication of animals, ladders, chisels, pulleys, levers, millstones, fishhooks, wheels, axes, hoes, looms, saws, brooches, needles, dyes, cloth weaving, surgery, bonesetting, organized religion, monarchies, written language, number systems, laws, taxes, artificial shelters, villages, tanning, scrapers, awls, mortars and pestles, and cosmetics. Many of these innovations (even if one lists only those considered stereotypically "feminine") are doubtless the work of women.

Once humans begin to settle in villages, some societies become matrilocal (in which husbands move to their wives' tribes or homes) and patrilocal (in which the reverse is true). Women are more powerful in matrilocal societies. Some societies are monogamous, with one husband and one wife in each family unit; some are polygynous, with a man taking more than one wife; some are polyandrous, with a woman taking more than one husband. Sometimes marriage takes place by capture or purchase. In some places, women are killed or transferred like property upon the husband's death. Women still live shorter lives than men and rarely live past thirty.

7000–6000 Paleo-Indians in the Americas are gradually replaced by settled groups living in caves, in hide tents, or under cliffs. They develop agriculture, milling stones, weaving, rituals, ornaments, and basketry. In various parts of the world, goats, sheep, pigs, and cattle are domesticated. In Egypt, face powder and eye paint are invented.

5000 Villages and pottery are common in the Near East. In the Americas, the lands that will become the Maya empire have been settled. The Mesopotamians build the first cities, and the Neolithic advances spread to Northern Europe, reaching the British Isles around 4000 B.C.

4000 The fashionable Egyptian woman wears green eye shadow, blue-black lipstick, red rouge, red henna stains on her fingers and feet, and blue and gold accents on her breast veins and nipples. The eye shadow, sometimes made iridescent by crushed beetle shell, is applied to

---

*All dates in this chapter are approximate. Information about this period is largely speculative; scholars have had to make guesses based mostly on fragmentary fossil records, artifacts, and analogies to modern-day hunting and gathering societies.

upper and lower lids, and the eyes and lashes are heavily lined with kohl, a dark paste moistened by saliva and applied with a stick. If the eyebrows do not naturally meet above the nose, the space will be filled in with kohl.

4000–3000 Women begin brewing beer in Egypt.

3000 In China, fingernail varnish is worn by both men and women. In Egypt, men and women stain their fingers and nails with henna.

3000 Skin creams, skin oils, and moisturizers are developed in the Near East. Aging skin is treated by sleeping six nights "in a facial paste of milk, incense, wax, olive oil, gazelle or crocodile dung, and ground juniper leaves." Egyptian women bathe in scented baths and anoint their hands with one perfume and their feet with another.

Government, the Military, and the Law

Most Neolithic cultures are male-dominated; some North American tribes, like the Iroquois and Seneca, will develop powerful political roles for women as well.

Literature and the Visual Arts

Women probably participate in many of the crafts of this time: pottery, weaving, basketry, and tanning. There is also no evidence that all cave painters and sculptors are male.

Performing Arts and Entertainment

Judging from the attribution of this achievement to goddesses in some parts of the world, women may be the inventors of musical instruments.

4000–3000 Occupations for women in Egypt include dancer and acrobat.

Business and Industry

Women are indispensable to early agriculture. They are probably also the first sowers and collectors of seeds and the inventors of many agricultural tools such as digging sticks, hoes, and plows. As towns develop, women often become the traders in the family. However, much of the control of agriculture and trade is co-opted by men in the Neolithic period.

Science and Medicine

As gatherers, women are probably the inventors of the first medicines.

Education and Scholarship

4000 The first known inscription is carved on a Goddess temple at Erech (Uruk), Sumeria.

Religion

25,000–15,000 Small sculptures of women are carved throughout Europe and the Middle and Near East. The figures are usually faceless, with exaggerated breasts, hips, and bellies. They may be religious icons associated with fertility, early examples of erotica, or simply attempts at portraiture. Women may be worshiped at this time for their ability to give birth. In some cultures, women are believed to become pregnant not because of sexual intercourse, but because they are invaded by spirits or because they have eaten a particular type of food.

7000 The first goddess shrines are built in Jericho.

6000 In Çatal Hüyük, Turkey, forty goddess shrines exist in thirty-two acres. The goddess is sometimes depicted as a young woman, sometimes as a mother, and sometimes as an old woman.

4000 Goddess figurines are made in Neolithic India. In the Middle East, the fertility cult of Innana (elsewhere known as Ishtar and Astarte) is strong; huge temples are built to the goddess at Uruk.

3000–2000 B.C.

General Status and Daily Life

Most Sumerian houses are made of straw, clay, and reeds, with earthen floors; water is drawn from wells and carried by women to the house. The woman retains control of her dowry, has equal rights over her children, and can own slaves and transact business. However, her legal rights are not unlimited. She can be sold by her husband, put to death for adultery (though the same is not true of her husband), and divorced if barren or drowned for refusing to bear children.

In Egypt, polygyny is replaced by monogamy. Women

use metal mirrors.

Girls throughout the Near East marry at about eleven or twelve years of age.

In most parts of the world, female slaves are subject to the master's sexual whims.

In Babylon, a woman accused of adultery must swim the Euphrates to prove her innocence. Trial marriage is permissible, but the woman must wear an identifying symbol to show that her status is lower than a legal wife's. Marriage is arranged by parents, with the groom offering a bride-price and the parents reciprocating with a larger dowry. Parents who cannot afford a good dowry sometimes sell their daughters at auction. A man can divorce his wife by giving back her dowry and saying, "You are not my wife." Legitimate causes for divorce include barrenness, adultery, incompatibility, and poor housekeeping. A woman cannot do the same; in fact, if she does, she is to be drowned. A woman can leave her husband's home, keeping her property and dowry, but only if she can prove that he has been cruel and that she herself is an exemplary wife. The Babylonian wife's duties include care of children, fetching water, grinding grain, cooking, spinning, weaving, and cleaning. Upper-class Babylonian women are segregated in certain parts of the house and let out only when accompanied by an entourage.

c. 2350 Polyandry is outlawed in Sumeria.

c. 2450–2880 The *Maxims of Ptah Hotep* gives this advice to Egyptian husbands: "Love thy wife at home as is fitting. Fill her belly; clothe her back. Ointment is the prescription for her body. Make her heart glad as long as thou livest. She is a profitable field for her lord. Thou shouldst not contend with her at law, and keep her from gaining control. . . . Her eye is her stormwind."

c. 2000 The Laws of Eshnunna (near present-day Baghdad) discuss bride-money, or the price paid by a prospective groom to his father-in-law. According to others of these laws, a man who rapes the virgin fiancée of another man is condemned to death, adultery by a married woman is punishable by death, and a willing fugitive from his village has no claim to his wife when he returns. A man who seduces or rapes another's female slave must pay a fine to her owner of one-third of a mina of silver. By comparison, the fine for biting off another man's nose is a full mina of silver.

Government, the Military, and the Law

2852 In China, according to legend, Fu Hsi becomes king; he and his educated wife introduce painting, music,

writing, net fishing, and silk cultivation to China.

Literature and the Visual Arts

c. 2300 Sumerian poet Enheduanna, the world's first known poet, is born. A daughter of King Sargon I and a priestess of Innana, the Sumerian love goddess, she praised the goddess for her formidability in battle and superiority to lesser gods.

c. 2200 According to legend, the art of painting is invented in China by Lei, sister of Emperor Shun.

Performing Arts and Entertainment

Egyptian women work as singers and musicians.

Business and Industry

Women run shops in the Near East, particularly wine shops.

Egyptian women work as maids, hairdressers, spinners, weavers, porters, cooks, brewers, wet nurses, water carriers, lamp tenders, businesswomen, importer-exporters, and landowners.

c. 3000 Chinese empress Se Ling-she invents silk cultivation; she will later be deified as the goddess of the silkworm.

Education and Scholarship

Some women serve as scribes in Egypt.

Religion

Babylon has temple prostitutes, whose services glorify the goddess. The everyday woman also makes a sacrifice to Ishtar; once in her life, she goes to the temple and remains there until a man offers to have sex with her. She must take the first man who offers, regardless of who he is. When she has discharged this duty to the goddess, she is free.

Egyptian women work as diviners, magicians, and priestesses.

c. 3000–2501 Sumerians worship the Mother Goddess Innin. Goddess worship is found also in Egypt, Phoenicia, and Scandinavia and often involves nudity, dancing, and the use of drugs.

c. 2500–2001   Egyptians worship Isis and Osiris; Ishtar is the goddess of love in the Near East.

2000–1000 B.C.

General Status and Daily Life

In Greece, women spin, weave, embroider, and wash the clothes. They are bought in marriage, usually with oxen. The husband can legally take concubines and expose his children at birth, leaving them to die or be taken in by the childless; children of slave women and their masters are usually considered freeborn.

In the Americas, women care for children and gather and prepare food. Some societies are matrilineal, charting descent through the mother rather than the father. Early Mayan women wear hide sandals and clothing woven of cotton or sisal. They eat a varied diet of maize, beans, squash, manioc, wild berries, fruits, nuts, and meat from deer, peccaries, tapirs, monkeys, turkeys, iguanas, and fish.

Jewish family life is marked by an acceptance of concubinage and polygamy.

Egyptian women can own and bequeath property. Property descends through the female line. Large families are common, and infanticide is forbidden. Egyptian wives are often beaten, judging from fracture evidence in skeletons; their arms are often broken in a way consistent with shielding the head from a blow. Egyptian women pursue love affairs aggressively and propose to men; girls are often sexually active at ten years old.

c. 1850   In the first known written reference to contraception, Egyptian texts describe contraceptive suppositories made of honey and crocodile dung.

c. 1727   Babylon's Code of Hammurabi allows women to own property, even after marriage. Wives and daughters may inherit property, and in some cases, they are required to inherit, so that they may adequately provide for minor sons. Many laws discuss the inheritance of dowries, which becomes especially complicated in cases of multiple wives, slave and free wives, and so on. Polygyny, in one form or another, is rather common. Childless wives are likely to provide their husbands with female slave concubines to produce the wanted children. A man may also take a second wife if his first is chronically ill, but he is still required to support and care for the first wife.

An adulterous wife and her lover are to be tied together and drowned; the woman may be saved from this fate if her husband wishes, but the lover may be pardoned only by the king. A woman accused by her husband but not caught in the act can exonerate herself by swearing her innocence, though a related law says she should throw herself into the river for her husband's sake. If the husband is taken captive and his wife moves in with another man, she is to be drowned, unless she would have starved without a man's support.

A woman can divorce her husband for cruelty. A woman who hates her husband enough to deprive him of sex may be released from her marriage, but only if she is entirely blameless and her husband has talked against her "greatly." In case of divorce, the woman often receives custody of the children and a generous financial settlement, especially if she is a lay priestess. Widows have extensive lifetime rights to their husbands' property.

Raping another man's virgin fiancée results in death for the man and no punishment for the woman. A man who has sex with his daughter is exiled; a mother and son who have sex are burned alive. A man who has sex with his daughter-in-law is drowned; if he has sex with his foster mother, he is thrown out of the house. If a wife arranges the death of her husband for the sake of another man, she is impaled. Causing a woman to have a miscarriage results in a fine, scaled according to the woman's status. If the woman dies as a result, and she is upper-class, the guilty party's own daughter can be killed in retribution.

c. 1600   Egyptian contraceptives include lint soaked in acacia and honey and placed against the cervix. This actually does work to some extent; the lint pad acts as a barrier, and acacia tips produce lactic acid, which is an effective contraceptive.

1596   In Egypt, women sometimes shave their heads and wear elaborate headdresses. The wigs are topped with cones of perfumed fat, which melt in the heat and give off pleasant odors.

Government, the Military, and the Law

In the Americas, women hold more power in agricultural than in hunting societies, especially if land is passed from mother to daughter; they can be chiefs in some tribes and are especially powerful among the Algonkian, Navajo, and Iroquois peoples.

1500–1000   China's Shang dynasty is supposedly descended from "a mother made pregnant by a bird's egg that fell from heaven."

1482   Egyptian Queen Hatshepsut (b. 1503), daughter

of Thutmose I and aunt of her successor Thutmose III, dies. Depicted as a bearded man in statues and reliefs, she held the title of pharaoh and will be buried in the Valley of the Kings, not the Valley of the Queens. During her reign, she fought battles against the Nubians, expanded trade, and patronized the arts during extensive periods of peace and prosperity. She also installed impressive obelisks at the temple of Karnak and sponsored exploration of the area around the Red Sea.

c. 1390 Teye, wife of Amenhotep III, patronizes art and architecture.

c. 1200 According to tradition, the Amazons, a race of women warriors from Northern Anatolia on the Black Sea, besiege Athens.

1194–1184 According to tradition, the Greeks besiege Troy. Queen Penthesilea leads the Amazons into battle for the Trojans; she is killed by Achilles. Mycenaean Queen Clytemnestra and her lover Aegisthus kill her husband, Agamemnon, as he returns from the Trojan War.

1154–1123 In China, the vicious Chou Hsin rules. His wife Ta-ki is renowned for her cruelty as well, roasting the condemned alive.

c. 1125 The Israelites are led in part by a judge, prophet, and heroine named Deborah. She gives the order to attack the Canaanites in the Battle of Taanach, and she predicts that the victory will belong to a woman. The Canaanite leader, Sisera, is indeed killed by a Kenite woman named Jael, giving the Israelites the victory.

Literature and the Visual Arts

c. 1790–1745 Akkadian poet and princess Inib-sarri composes verses about her unhappy marriage. Her sister Eristi-Aya also writes poetry.

13th century In Egypt, many erotic love songs are written by women; one speaks of climbing through a window to seduce men, and another writes, "O my handsome darling! I am dying to marry you and become the mistress of all your property."

Performing Arts and Entertainment

In Thebes, women are musicians and often entertain at parties.

In Egypt, women work as dancing girls, musicians, and acrobats. They play drums, tambourines, flutes, and stringed instruments.

Athletics and Exploration

In Crete, women hunt and participate in the bull-dance, an acrobatic show in which athletes leap over the back and horns of a live bull.

Women in Egypt sometimes accompany hunts, but they do not actually participate in the kill. They swim, juggle, and play some type of ball game (perhaps as part of a performance), but there is little evidence of their participation in any organized competitive sport.

Business and Industry

In Sparta, much of the land is owned by women.

In Arabia, women own the flocks, with husbands in charge only of pasturing.

Among the Monomini Indians, some women own as many as 1,200 or 1,500 birch-bark boats.

Egyptian women who lend their husbands money can legally charge interest.

c. 2000 Some Mesopotamian perfumers are women.

c. 1727 The Code of Hammurabi mentions women working as secular prostitutes (*harimtu*), wine sellers, and priestesses. Women winesellers who charge unfairly for their wares are to be drowned; those who allow their establishments to be frequented by criminals are also to be executed. A woman who leaves her husband to run a business may be divorced without alimony or demoted to second wife, on the grounds that businesswomen neglect the home and embarrass the husband.

Science and Medicine

c. 2000 A Mesopotamian woman writes a chemistry text.

c. 1550 In Egypt, the oldest known medical text describes ways to induce labor: applying peppermint to the genitals, plastering the abdomen with a mixture that includes sea salt and clean wheat, and using vaginal suppositories made of fennel, incense, garlic, sert-juice, salt, and wasp's dung.

c. 1500 Women study at the medical school at Heliopolis, Egypt.

c. 12th century Annals record a Greek physician named Agamede, an herbalist, daughter of the king of the Epeans.

Religion

The Canaanites worship the goddesses Asherah, Astarte, and Anat, who are associated with both fertility and war. Other areas, including Egypt and Cyprus, worship incarnations of Ishtar or Isis.

c. 1727 Babylonian temple women include priestesses, sacred prostitutes (*qadishtu*), and prostitutes of the goddess Ishtar (*ishtaritu*). The right of women to practice the rites of their mothers is respected, though the penalties for misbehavior are severe; a nun who enters a wine shop is to be burned to death.

c. 1500 In Malta, goddess worship is commemorated by "a seven-foot statue of the goddess, her belly obesely pregnant over pear-shaped legs of massive stone" into which flows the "blood of slaughtered victims in a deep vessel symbolic of the divine vagina."

1500–600 Most Chinese shamans are women; perfumed and clad in elaborate robes, they perform rites to bring rain. Early Chinese kings derive their authority from their supposed ability to mate with rain goddesses.

Mid-14th century Nefertiti, Egyptian queen and wife of Akhenaton, embraces her husband's new cult of Aten, later rejecting it. After his death, she helps reinstate the cult of Amon, whom Aten replaced.

12th century The biblical songs of Miriam and Deborah are written.

1000–701 B.C.

General Status and Daily Life

In Assyria, women who have abortions are impaled on stakes, and their bodies are not buried. Prostitution is regulated by the state. Women are veiled in public and are expected to be sexually faithful to their husbands; no such fidelity is expected of the husbands.

c. 1150–250 The Pentateuch (the first five books of the Old Testament) is written down. It contains several strictures against women. For example, a "woman's word stands only if her husband or father do not disagree with her; otherwise, their views prevail." Male babies are worth five shekels, female only three; men are worth fifty shekels, women only thirty. Concubinage is common, and a man who rapes a virgin can avoid punishment by paying a fine to her father and then marrying her. Prostitutes are sometimes burned to death, while their customers are not penalized. Lot's virtue is

exemplified by his willingness to throw his two virgin daughters to a mob in order to spare his male guests the same fate. During menstruation, women (and anything they touch) are considered impure. A woman who bears a son is unclean for seven days and barred from the temple for thirty-three; a woman who bears a daughter is unclean for fourteen days and barred from the temple for sixty-six.

1000–221 In the Chou era, women are sold publicly in China.

900 Queen Isimkheb of Egypt wears wigs so heavy that she has to have helpers to keep her from tipping over. Wigs are worn in both Assyria and Egypt by the rich.

9th–8th centuries Athenian women in mourning march naked in funeral processions.

753–716 Rome's King Romulus mandates the rearing of all male children and all first-born females. In *confarreatio* (the most binding form of Roman marriage, reserved for patricians and dissolvable only by the complicated *diffareatio*), the wife shares all her husband's possessions and sacred rites. Wives get the death penalty for adultery or drinking wine and can be divorced for adultery, making duplicate keys to the house, or the use of contraceptives or abortifacients. They can also be divorced for other reasons, but in those cases the husband loses part of his estate to the wife (who must sacrifice it to the grain goddess Ceres). A man who sells his wife becomes a human sacrifice, and a daughter-in-law who strikes her husband's father becomes a sacrifice to his gods.

c. 716 Rome's King Numa Pompilius orders that if a pregnant woman dies, she cannot be buried until the child is removed from her uterus.

Government, the Military, and the Law

According to tradition, Italian warrior Camilla of the Volscians fights Aeneas and his Trojan refugees. She is supported by woman warriors Larina, Tulla, and Tarpeia.

1000–221 China's Chou dynasty is supposedly descended from a woman who became pregnant when she stepped into a massive divine footprint.

c. 1000 According to legend, a nation of Amazons rules Libya, training women to fight and rule and relegating child care to the men. Queen Myrine leads 30,000 Amazons against the Gorgon women's army, defeating it and going on to conquer much of Arabia.

c. 961–922 King Solomon of Israel is visited on a

trade mission by the Queen of Sheba, ruler of the Sabeans (in what is now Yemen). Sabaea has a formidable economy due to its control of important trade routes.

843 Athaliah, widow of King Jehoram of Judah, becomes queen in her own right; she is deposed and executed in 837. Her reign is marked by political terror—she murders all of royal blood who might oppose her—and religious change, as she places Ba'al and Yahweh on equal terms. She is replaced on the throne by a son of Ahaziah's who escaped her purge.

811–807 Queen Sammuramat (Semiramis) serves as regent of Assyria for her son Adad-Nirari III. Influential in both politics and religion, she develops irrigation systems and leads military expeditions.

c. 800 Phoenician Queen Dido founds the African city of Carthage, later committing suicide to avoid marriage to a local chief, Iarbas.

Early 8th century According to tradition, the twin founders of Rome, Romulus and Remus, are the illegitimate sons of a Vestal Virgin, Rhea Silvia. Abandoned at birth, they are nursed by a she-wolf (*lupa*). It is possible that this may be a reference to Acca Larentia, a local woman nicknamed "Lupa," who takes the boys in after they are abandoned.

8th century Legend says that King Yu of China lights all the signal fires of the city to please a capricious concubine; the defense forces rush in to protect the city, and she is indeed amused at their consternation when they find no enemy massed before the walls. However, when the real invasion comes, the forces do not respond to the flares, and the city falls.

753 Rome is founded. The male settlers, according to tradition, steal and rape women from the neighboring Sabine tribe; the Sabine men march on Rome, capturing the Capitoline hill through the treachery of a woman named Tarpeia. (Later, the Tarpeian rock, from which Rome's traitors are hurled, will be named for her.) However, the Sabine women rush into the middle of the battlefield, pleading with their old husbands not to kill their new ones, and Romulus and the Sabine leader Tatius become co-rulers.

738 Arab queen Zabibi, fighting against the Assyrians, is conquered and made a vassal. She is succeeded by Queen Samsi, who is also defeated by the Assyrians.

Athletics and Exploration

776 At the first recorded Olympic Games, women are banned as athletes and spectators.

Business and Industry

In Crete women work as merchants, traders, sailors, farmers, charioteers, and hunters.

Religion

In Crete, women work as priestesses of the Goddess.

During this era, the sacred Hindu texts, the Vedas, begin to be written; they will take their present form by about 500 B.C. Several Indian women contribute to the Vedas, including Opala, Ghosha, Viswabara, and Indrani.

c. 1000 The document known to biblical scholars as the "J" strand is recorded. One of several independent narratives that combine to make up the Old Testament, the J strand is believed by some scholars to have been written by a woman.

c. 1000–901 The oldest extant Olympian temple, the Temple of Hera, is built in Greece.

922–915 King Rehoboam rules Judah, the southern kingdom of divided Israel. His favorite wife, Maacah (mother of his son Abijah, king 915–913), worships the fertility goddess Asherah. She gets her husband and son to favor toleration of pagan rituals, ritual prostitution, and homosexuality. Regent for King Asa from 913, she is deposed by him, and her religious policies are reversed.

869–850 Jezebel of Tyre, wife of Israel's King Ahab, worships the Tyrian gods Ba'al Melqart and Asherah. She continues to do so after her marriage, as is customary for foreign wives. She then tries to institute Ba'al as the official court god, a relatively popular move in a country that is about half-Canaanite anyway. To a large extent, she succeeds; the ruling class (with the lukewarm exception of Ahab) becomes Ba'alist, and prophets of Ba'al and Asherah get official recognition. Eventually, however, she begins persecuting Yahwists and incurs hostility, especially from the prophet Elijah, who begins preaching against her. Ultimately, she is murdered, along with her Tyrian court. Meanwhile, Ahab's sister Athaliah introduces Ba'alism to the court of Judah in Jerusalem, where the idea is even less popular than in Israel.

716–673 Numa Pompilius is king of Rome; he dictates that concubines be forbidden to touch the altar of Juno, the Roman goddess of marriage.

700–401 B.C.

General Status and Daily Life

In Persia, polygamy is legal; menstruation is considered one of the evil things created by the Prince of Darkness, Ahriman, along with crime, sodomy, vermin, snakes, darkness, ants, and winter.

Greek women wear cork heels for height, use cloth bands as brassieres, and sometimes dye their hair blond. Oil of mastic is used as an antiperspirant, and different scents are employed for different parts of the body—palm oil for the face and chest, marjoram for the hair, thyme for the knees and throat, mint for the arms, and myrrh for the legs. Rich women bathe once or twice a day, but most others apply oil to the skin and scrape it off with a strigil, or a curved blade.

Abortion and infanticide are practiced in Greece; girls are more often exposed at birth (abandoned to death or possible adoption) than boys.

In Athens, women cannot vote or hold public office.

Greek men marry at about thirty, women at about fifteen. Betrothal takes place between the groom and the bride's father, with the bride not necessarily present. Then a feast takes place at the bride's house, with men and women segregated. The veiled bride is taken to the groom's house and carried across the threshold, where she is received by his family and gods. The guests sing songs and celebrate outside the room until the consummation of the marriage is announced. The fact that women prepare and purchase love potions at this time implies that some romantic importance is attached to marriage, and many husbands and wives erect funerary monuments to each other, with touching tributes to the departed spouse's virtues.

Male adultery bears no penalty, though in a wife it is grounds for divorce. Female sterility is grounds for divorce as well; if the husband is sterile, custom requires that one of his relatives impregnate his wife for him. A man can divorce a wife simply by sending her away. Divorce can also take place by mutual consent; a woman can ask the government for a divorce on the grounds of cruelty.

Women cannot make contracts or contract debts above a trivial sum and cannot sue anyone in court; any action they influence can be declared void. They may make visits or see plays veiled and accompanied by servants or relatives, but at home they are not even supposed to be seen at a window. They eat their meals with the family, unless male guests arrive; then women go to the rear of the house to eat. At the *symposion*, however, a type of formal dinner, no free women are permitted, only *hetairai* (courtesans) and entertainers.

7th century Spartan leader Lycurgus institutes rigid military discipline in that Greek city. Women, though they receive little education, are expected to participate in running, wrestling, javelin, and discus, in the hope that fit mothers will produce strong warriors. Partly because of this training and partly because the men are often at war, Spartan women have more freedom of movement and legal rights than other Greek women. They are the only Greek women who do not engage in wool working. Their clothing is also simpler. Laws forbid them to wear jewelry, perfumes, cosmetics, expensive headdresses, and colored clothes. Girls are expected to march naked at public functions, so that any bodily defects can be spotted and corrected. Men are expected to marry at thirty, women at twenty; the marriage is arranged, and then there is a mock "capture" of the bride, during which she is expected to resist. Divorce is rare.

594 Athenian lawmaker Solon levies a fine of one hundred drachmas on men who rape free women, limits the size of dowries and size of women's wardrobes, and confines women to their homes at night. He also outlaws the selling of one's children into slavery but makes an exception for daughters who have lost their virginity.

c. 500 In China, men can sell their wives and children. Women rarely eat with their husbands. Remarriage for widows is uncommon, with wives sometimes committing suicide on a husband's death.

c. 500 In Rome the wife is in the legal position of a daughter, but she is not confined like the Athenian woman and serves as hostess at dinner, even when male guests are present.

5th century A papyrus from Elephantine, Egypt, contains the first extant marriage certificate, recording the trade of six cows for a fourteen-year-old bride.

5th century In Athens, a man finding his mother, wife, concubine, sister, or daughter having illicit sex can kill her lover with impunity. Widows have the right to reclaim their dowries but inherit none of the husbands' property.

Government, the Military, and the Law

Greek courtesan Thargelia spies for the Persians by questioning the Athenian statesmen who are her clients.

c. 687 Lydian king Candaules is killed in a plot by his wife and his bodyguard, Gyges.

6th century Etruscan leader Lars Porsenna takes Roman hostages, including a young woman named Cloelia. She escapes, steals a horse, and swims across the Tiber River back to Rome. The Romans return her, but Porsenna is so impressed by her feat that he frees all the hostages.

578 The wife of Roman king Lucius Tarquinius Priscus, Tanaquil, is well educated; when he is assassinated, she secures the throne for their son-in-law, Servius Tullius.

529 Scythian queen Tamyris of the Massagetae defeats and kills Persian ruler Cyrus the Great in battle. He asked her to marry him, and when she refused to give up control of her lands, he attempted to invade them, slaughtering many of her soldiers and kidnapping her son during a truce. She told him, "Give me back my son and get out of my country with your forces intact, and be content with your triumph over a third part of the Massagetae. If you refuse, I swear by the sun our master to give you more blood than you can drink."

514 Harmodius, Aristogeiton, and others join in a conspiracy against the Athenian dictator Hippias; afterward, Harmodius's mistress, the courtesan Leaena, is questioned and tortured to death after refusing to answer the questions put to her. When pressed, she bites off her own tongue and spits it at the torturers.

510 Roman noblewoman Lucretia is raped by a relative of King Tarquinius Superbus, Sextus Tarquinius, who resents her virtue. She then commits suicide after begging for revenge. Her husband and a nephew of the king lead a revolt, ousting the king and establishing a republic.

494 Cleomenes of Sparta besieges Argos. The poet Telesilla encourages the Argive women to arm themselves and defend the walls, which they do successfully. The women killed in the battle are buried with honor, and the surviving women are allowed to build a memorial statue; as late as the second century A.D., an annual cross-dressing festival will mark the date of the battle.

c. 490 Roman general Marcius Coriolanus turns traitor and allies with the Volscians against Rome. The noblewomen of the city, led by the matron Valeria, appeal for help to Coriolanus's mother, Volumnia, and his wife, Vergilia, who convince him not to attack the city. In the subsequent rejoicing, the women are hailed as saviors and offered anything they wish by the Senate; they ask for a temple to be built to the Fortune of Women.

Sept. 29, 480 At the Battle of Salamis, Persian sea captain Artemisia of Halicarnassus (the world's first recorded female naval commander) distinguishes herself despite the defeat of Persian king Xerxes' forces. Before the battle, she prophetically, but unsuccessfully, warns Xerxes not to challenge the Greeks at sea; during the

battle, she is pursued by one of the Greeks (who, after her daring rescue of the body of Xerxes' brother at the Battle of Marathon, have offered a reward of 10,000 drachmae for her capture) and, in order to escape, rams one of the Persian ships, fooling the Greeks into thinking she is an ally and fooling Xerxes into thinking she has sunk a Greek ship.

c. 450 In Athens, Milesian *hetaira* Aspasia opens a school of rhetoric and philosophy for wellborn women. Political leader Pericles falls in love with her, agrees to a divorce from his wife, and lives with Aspasia. She encourages the arts, philosophy, and education for women; the philosopher Socrates marvels at her intellect and credits her with teaching him eloquence and with writing at least one major speech of Pericles'. She is accused of impiety in 432 by Pericles' political enemies; he defends her tearfully in court, obtaining a dismissal of the charges, but doing so at the cost of his political career.

Literature and the Visual Arts

Greek women engage in a great deal of wool working, becoming skilled in this craft. Girls participate in wool-carding contests with items such as black-figured vases as prizes.

c. 612 Greek poet Sappho of Lesbos is born. Her nine books of poems discuss women's lives, peaceful social rituals and country life, love, and jealousy. Her erotic poems to other women, combined with the name of her island home, will give rise to the term *lesbian*. An educator of young women, she is among the first poets to write about personal experience, and her meter and stanza structure will be imitated in her own lifetime and for many centuries afterward. Plato calls her the Tenth Muse; she is so famous that people simply refer to her as the Poetess. She writes about 12,000 lines of verse, of which only about 600 will survive to the twentieth century.

5th century? Corinna of Tanagra, Boeotia, is a poet.

c. 450 Greek poet Praxilla writes lyrics noted for their powerful images and sensuality.

Athletics and Exploration

It is likely (if much later observations can be extrapolated backward) that teenage girls wrestle each other in Gambia's Diola tribe, with the winner sometimes marrying the winner from the boys' competition. Among the Yala of Nigeria and the Njabi of the Congo, men and women sometimes wrestle each other. In Melanesia, women box each other. In North

America, Indian women probably play stickball and other games.

Some Etruscan acrobats are women.

6th century According to legend, women's games are held in Greece one month before each Olympic Games. The women's festival, the Heraia, was established by sixteen women to honor the goddess Hera.

Business and Industry

Greek women work as laundresses and weavers, often creating profitable textile businesses.

In Greece, the prostitutes of lowest status and price are the *pornai*, at the port of Piraeus, whose houses are marked with a phallic symbol; men enter the house for an obol (a coin worth one-sixth of a drachma, which, in turn, is worth about a bushel of wheat) and inspect mostly naked women, who can be hired out for a week, a month, or more. Next up are the *auletrides*, the flute-players, who perform music and dancing at parties and may provide sexual services as well. Finally there are the *hetairai*, the companions. Often well educated, they are barred from all temples but that of Aphrodite Pandemos.

Some *hetairai* achieve great fame, including Clepsydra, who times her appointments with an hourglass; Themistonoe, who plies her trade until she is bald and toothless; and Gnathaena, who charges 1,000 drachmas for one night with her exceptionally well educated daughter.

Science and Medicine

Socrates' mother is a midwife. The delivery of children is almost exclusively a female profession and will remain so throughout Europe for two millennia.

Education and Scholarship

Greek girls are educated at home in reading, writing, arithmetic, spinning, weaving, embroidery, singing, dancing, and the playing of a musical instrument.

Late 6th century The Pythagorean school of Greek philosophy includes at least three notable women: Aristoclea, a tutor of Pythagoras; philosopher, mathematician, and physician Theano, Pythagoras's wife, who keeps his school open after his death; and Damo, Pythagoras's daughter, who works for women's education.

5th century Diotima of Mantinea, a priestess, is a teacher of Socrates. A non-citizen of Athens, she exploits this apparent disadvantage to circumvent laws keeping Athenian women restricted to their houses. Arguing in favor of women's education, she acts on her beliefs by moving freely about the city to teach women in their own homes.

5th century Greek female philosopher Perictyone writes *On Wisdom*.

5th century Greek philosopher Lasthenia of Mantinea studies with Plato and Speusippus.

Religion

Though severely restricted in their everyday lives, Greek women feature prominently in the mythology of the society. The Greek pantheon includes Hera, queen of the gods and the patron of married women; Hestia, goddess of the hearth; Aphrodite, goddess of love; Artemis, goddess of the moon, hunting, and virginity; and Athena, goddess of war and wisdom and the patron goddess of Athens. Many minor deities are also female, including Themis (law), Dike (justice), and Aphaea (hunters and fishermen).

Ecstatic religions flourish in Greece. Especially popular among women, these religions include the cult of Eleusis, which focuses on worship of the harvest goddess Demeter and involves such secrecy that its rites will never be entirely uncovered by twentieth-century scholars. In October, Athenian women celebrate Demeter in a ritual involving phallic symbols and an exchange of obscenities. Also popular is the cult of Dionysus, the god of wine and revelry. Maenads are women who worship Dionysus in frenzied rites, occasionally killing men or beasts by tearing them apart and engaging in ritual cannibalism.

Religious ceremonies throughout the year involve women. Besides the festival of Demeter in October, there is a September initiation rite for the cult of Eleusis, an October festival of Dionysus called the Oschophoria, a ritual in December in which women (especially those of "dubious virtue") plant terracotta phalluses, and springtime festivals of Athena and Artemis. Every year, the statue of Athena is bathed, clothed, and presented with offerings of dried figs by Athenian women.

6th century The priestesses of the Delphic oracle, often consulted on matters of national importance, reach the apex of their power.

6th century The temple of Artemis at Ephesus in Asia Minor, considered one of the Seven Wonders of the Ancient World, is built.

6th century Wealthy Indian courtesan Ambapali retires, donates her mango groves to the Buddha, becomes his disciple, and achieves the status of arhat, or holy one. Few men become arhats, and even fewer women; the only higher level is the achievement of nirvana (the end of the cycle of suffering caused by continual reincarnation), and it is believed in the Buddha's day that women are incapable of achieving nirvana at all. They must be content with being as holy as possible in the hope of being reborn as men—and then they can try to reach nirvana. The Buddha only permits women to join his *sangha* (monastic order), only shortly before his death.

c. 500 Of the three major temples on Rome's Capitoline hill, two are devoted to goddesses: Minerva (the Roman equivalent of Athena) and Juno (the Roman Hera). Also, a round temple of Vesta (the Roman Hestia) stands in the center of the Forum and houses relics and a sacred eternal flame. This Vestal temple is staffed by virgin priestesses, who serve for a term of thirty years, learning their duties for ten years, serving for ten, and teaching their successors for ten. The Vestal Virgins have several special privileges. They can make wills in their fathers' lifetimes and have no legal guardians; they have the fasces, the symbol of Roman authority, carried before them when they go out in public; if they meet accidentally with a condemned criminal, his sentence is remitted; and offenses against them can be punished by death. Discipline is strict. The Vestals are whipped for minor offenses and buried alive for breaking their vows of chastity. The first two, Gegania and Verenia, were selected by King Numa Pompilius, who ruled from 715 to 673.

400–101 B.C.

General Status and Daily Life

Greek and Roman fathers can expose deformed or female babies, abandoning them to die or to be raised by any sympathetic passerby.

A Roman woman simply receives a feminine form of her clan's name, for example, Claudia or Julia. If she has a sister, the two may be distinguished from each other by nicknames. Women cannot testify in court, cannot inherit their husbands' property, and may not inherit more than 100,000 sesterces from anyone. However, Vestal Virgins are allowed to leave their property to women, regardless of how much is involved, and daughters can still be left up to half the father's estate.

There are several different types of Roman marriage. Women married *cum manu* are given into the power of their husbands and cannot secure a divorce (though their husbands may divorce them), while those married *sine*

manu remain under their fathers' authority. A *sine manu* marriage requires little in the way of formal ceremony and can be ended by either party, but there are three types of *cum manu* marriage: *confarreatio* (a complicated religious ceremony reserved for patricians, almost impossible to sever by divorce), *coemptio* (bride-purchase), and *usus* (common-law marriage, sealed by cohabitation for a year). Minimum legal age of marriage is twelve for girls and fourteen for boys, though many are betrothed much earlier. The marriage is sealed with the breaking of a straw, the signing of a contract, a gift of an iron ring to the wife, the lifting of the wife over the husband's threshold, the wearing of a mutual yoke, and the wife's acceptance of her husband's gods and name. A man who catches his wife in adultery can legally kill her; a woman with an adulterous husband has no legal recourse.

Upper-class Egyptian women lose power, but the lower classes maintain certain matriarchal elements. In some cities, like Alexandria, women have much freedom of movement; many retain some political influence.

Persian women are held in purdah or seclusion, and upper-class married women are not even allowed to see their own fathers or brothers. Concubines and lower-class women have more freedom. A common saying of the time goes, "Men do not pray for daughters, and angels do not reckon them among their gifts to mankind." Abortion is punished by death.

In Greece, a woman's dowry is paid by her male guardian. Complex regulations govern the repayment of dowry in case of noncompletion of the marriage, divorce, or the death of either spouse. In some parts of the Hellenistic world, there are limits on how much a father may give his daughter as dowry and how much of it she retains in case of divorce.

4th century Women in Greece cannot engage in most monetary transactions and may own no property besides clothes, jewelry, and slaves. While working-class women have some freedom of movement, upper-class women, especially in Athens, live in single-sex seclusion for most of their lives. In the *gynaeceum*, or women's quarters, girls are educated in household tasks—spinning, weaving, cooking, and the management of slaves. They are married in their early teens, often to men they have never seen. They rarely leave their own homes except for religious festivals and visits to other women, and then they are attended by servants or relatives. When her husband has male guests, the wife eats in the back rooms.

4th century A Roman woman can be left to another man in her husband's will. Women cannot form legal contracts for anything greater than the value of a bushel of barley.

331 In Rome's first notable poisoning case, a slave woman accuses several patrician matrons of murdering statesmen; two of them, Cornelia and Sergia, are compelled by the court to drink their concoctions and die as a result. In the resulting public panic, more than 170 matrons are condemned.

3rd century Roman statesman Publius Sempronius Sophus divorces his wife for attending public games without obtaining permission.

2nd century Chinese women paint sharp-pointed eyebrows to replace the ones they have shaved off.

2nd century Rome's Second Punic War results in a shortage of male heirs and leaves more property in the hands of women. Adult women are required to have legal guardians, but these are often guardians now in name only.

2nd century Roman women care for boys till age seven and girls till marriage; they breast-feed their children and often suckle the slaves' children as well as their own to foster siblinglike devotion to the young masters.

2nd century Roman patrician Gaius Sulpicius Gallus divorces his wife for appearing in public with her head uncovered: "The law prescribes for you my eyes alone to which you may prove your beauty."

2nd century Fertility is much prized in Rome, and Cornelia, mother of two prominent statesmen and center of a brilliant intellectual circle, is held up as an example, since she has twelve children. Infant mortality is high; of her twelve children, only three survive to adulthood. She is perhaps most famous for her response to a matron who was showing off her expensive jewelry. Cornelia called for her two sons and said, "These are my jewels."

Government, the Military, and the Law

4th century Persian queen mother Parystais becomes renowned for her cruelty. She has her son's wife Statira poisoned, arranges his next marriage to his own daughter Atossa, gambles with him for the life of a slave and then has the slave flayed, and delights in torture. She once has a condemned man stretched on the rack, pierced through the eyes, and killed by the pouring of molten lead into his ears.

4th century Women in Germany lead tribes and troops of warriors.

270 Greek-Macedonian ruler Arsinoe (b. c. 316) dies. She married the king of Thrace and got his son by a previous wife executed to make way for her own sons.

Later she fled to Egypt, ousted her brother's wife (another Arsinoe), married him, and ruled with him from 279 until her death. She appeared on the coinage, dominated their joint rule, and was worshiped as a goddess.

246 Antiochus II Theos of Syria is murdered by his wife Berenice, sister of Ptolemy III. Conflict arises between Berenice and Queen Laodice, Antiochus's repudiated first wife. In about the year 101, another powerful Berenice will marry her uncle Ptolemy X and become his co-ruler.

216 After the battle of Cannae between Rome and Carthage, Roman survivors reach Canusium and are sheltered and fed by a wealthy Apulian woman, Busa, who also gives them clothing and money. After the war, the Senate formally honors her for her generosity, which must have been extensive, since nearly 10,000 fugitives took refuge in Canusium.

210 Two Capuan women are recognized by the Senate because they helped Rome in its wars against Carthage. Vestia Oppia is recorded as offering sacrifices and prayers for Roman victory, while ex-prostitute Pacula Cluvia "secretly supplied needy prisoners with food." They are luckier than most other Capuan women, who, for their Carthaginian sympathies, are sold into slavery.

203 Masinissa, king of Maesulia, encounters the beautiful Carthaginian captive Sophonisba and promises to keep her safe from the Roman men. To do so, he marries her on the same day he meets her and is chided by the Roman authorities for his hasty and passionate act. Fearing that they will take her from him anyway despite his promise, he sends her a messenger bearing poison, which she accepts, telling the messenger, "I accept this bridal gift—a gift not unwelcome if my husband has been unable to offer a greater one to his wife." "They were proud words," says the Roman historian Livy, "and no less proudly she took the cup and calmly drained it with no sign of perturbation."

195–180 Empress Lu rules China. Cruel and ruthless, she has all political rivals killed and arranges for a romantic rival to be thrown into a cesspool after having her ears and eyes removed.

c. 101 Egyptian queen Berenice marries her uncle Ptolemy X and becomes his co-ruler.

Literature and the Visual Arts

Late 4th century Aristodama of Smyrna becomes known for her poetry.

365 Greek artist's model Phryne (b. 410) dies. She posed for Apelles and Praxiteles and was the first woman allowed to dedicate a statue of herself at Delphi.

Praxiteles, grateful to her for agreeing to pose for a statue of Aphrodite, once offered her any statue in his workshop; she tricked him into thinking his workshop was on fire, then chose the statue he seemed most anxious to save and gave it to her hometown of Thespiae. She once offered to rebuild the walls of Thebes in exchange for her name on the rebuilt walls; the Thebans refused. On another occasion, she was accused of sacrilege for appearing naked at a festival of Aphrodite. At her trial, her nude body was exposed to the jury, resulting in her acquittal.

353 Mausolus of Halicarnassus in Asia Minor dies. His widow Artemisia builds him a gigantic monument, considered one of the Seven Wonders of the Ancient World.

Early 3rd century The Greek poet Erinna of Telos dies at the age of nineteen. She is best known for her 300-verse poem *The Distaff*, which reflects nostalgically on her relationship with her childhood friend Baucis, who is taken from her first by marriage and then by death.

3rd century Female poets of the Greek world include Anyte of Tegea and Nossis of Locri. In about 290, Anyte of Arkadia is noted for her quatrains.

Late 3rd century Greek poet Korinna of Boeotia, praised by Plutarch, beats Pindar in five poetry competitions. Pindar, not a particularly good loser, calls her "a pig," and his supporters blame her victories on "ignorant judges."

117? Chinese poet Cho Wen-chün (b. 179?) dies.

c. 110 Chinese poet Hsi-Chün is married to the old chief of the Wusun near Sinkiang, far from her childhood home. He sees her only twice a year and then cannot communicate with her because neither speaks the other's dialect. In her poetry, she laments the marriage.

Performing Arts and Entertainment

Greek working-class women are often trained as musicians and dancers and hired out as entertainers for parties.

Athletics and Exploration

Early 4th century Cynisca of Sparta erects a statue to memorialize her victory in a horse race. She probably did not compete directly; the recognized winners of equestrian races at this time are the owners, not the drivers, of the chariots. Other horse and chariot-race victors of this era include Bilistiche of Magnesia, a

hetaira (mid-3rd century); Aristoclea of Larisa (early 2nd century); and the daughters of Polycrates of Argos (c. 194–182), Zeuxo, Encrateia, and Hermione.

Activism

195 Roman women successfully demand the repeal of the Oppian Law (215), which forbids women to own more than half an ounce of gold, wear multicolored dresses, or drive chariots in town. Despite the efforts of their husbands, the matrons crowd the Forum, blocking the streets and receiving reinforcements from nearby towns and villages.

Business and Industry

Many Greek women are slaves. Some are taught specialized crafts and can earn money to buy their freedom, but female slaves are less likely to be artisans and more likely to be domestics. Female slaves are also at the mercy of their masters' sexual desires, and there is no legal recourse for a slave who does not wish to submit to the master's advances.

Free women work as nurses, grocers, wet nurses, sesame seed sellers, wool workers, harpists, horse tenders, perfume vendors, *aulos* players, cloak sellers, unguent boilers, honey sellers, shoe sellers, frankincense sellers, salt vendors, and tumblers. Some work as prostitutes, occasionally becoming quite famous. Lais of Corinth asks 10,000 drachmas for one night with the orator Demosthenes and refuses the sculptor Myron's offer of all he possesses but gives herself to the philosopher Diogenes for a pittance. She donates generously to public works and is given a magnificent tomb at her death. The *hetaira* Metiche, however, is not noted for her generosity but for her devotion to punctuality; she is nicknamed Clepsydra, "water clock," because she uses such a device to time her customers' visits. Thaïs of Athens rises highest of all through her charms, becoming the lover of Alexander the Great, urging the burning of Persepolis, and finally marrying Ptolemy I and becoming queen of Egypt.

Science and Medicine

4th century Athenian physician Agnodice becomes the first woman gynecologist, posing as a man in order to practice her profession. Jealous competitors, seeking to discredit her, accuse her of seducing her patients. At her trial, she reveals her sex; the charge of seduction is withdrawn, but she is charged instead with practicing a man's profession. However, she is acquitted after several of her patients appear and testify in her behalf, and she is permitted to continue practicing medicine. Female practitioners are important in Greek life, as many wellborn women refuse, for modesty's sake, to be examined by male doctors. Most women consult midwives instead, who are exclusively female.

4th century Greek scientists dispute the role of the woman in reproduction. Aristotle theorizes that the woman passively provides the fetus with nourishment and substance, while the male provides the active energy that brings the child to life. (He is more accurate on the subject of contraceptives, recommending the use of olive oil on the cervix, which does have a slight contraceptive effect.) Hippocrates believes that the woman's body provides more than simple nourishment to the fetus, but he maintains that "stronger sperm" will result in a male child. He does not object to mechanical means for inducing an abortion; in one case, he tells a patient "to jump up and down, touching her buttocks with her heels at each leap" about seven times. He believes drinking a thick mixture of beans and water will act as a contraceptive for a year.

Education and Scholarship

Early 4th century Greek philosopher Arete of Cyrene flourishes, writing over forty works (none of which survive) and teaching philosophy for thirty-five years. She is credited with educating 110 philosophers.

c. 350 Greek philosopher Axiothea of Philus, one of two female pupils of Plato, dresses as a man in order to study with Plato and Speusippus.

3rd century Athenian philosopher Hipparchia, student of Crates, bullies her parents into letting her marry him. She adopts men's dress and becomes his constant companion, even at dinner parties. She defeats Theodorus the Atheist in philosophical discourse by saying, "If an action cannot be called wrong when done by Theodorus, it could not be called wrong when done by Hipparchia. Therefore, if Theodorus does nothing wrong when he hits himself, Hipparchia does nothing wrong when she hits Theodorus." She brags that she has spent her life on education rather than wasting it in weaving.

2nd century In Rome, wealthy women are being educated better than before and receiving an education similar to that of men.

Religion

Greek women are important in many rites, including the Thesmophoria, a two-week Athenian festival of Demeter. The celebration is open to all freeborn women of good character; it involves nine days of rigorous chastity followed by several days of processions, sacrifices, special meetings run by two female "presidents," fasts, and ritual obscenity. Achaian women celebrate the

Mysia, a seven-day celebration in honor of Demeter Mysia; the fourth day is restricted to women only, and not even male animals are permitted to be present.

Women are also important as priestesses and prophets. In Plato's time, women prophesy in "a state of divine frenzy" at Zeus's oracle at Dodona and Apollo's at Delphi. At the oracle of Apollo Deiradiotes in Argos, the priestess drinks the blood of a lamb once a month to achieve her frenzy. Most notable among the priestesses is the Delphic prophetess, or Pythia. She is a virgin (originally young until one of the Pythias was seduced, and then the office fell instead to women over fifty). The petitioner offers an animal as sacrifice; if the omens are auspicious, the Pythia burns laurel leaves and barley flour in a sacred flame and, dressed like Apollo, takes her seat on a three-legged stool over a rift in the earth that serves as the heart of the oracle. She exhibits a frenzied, trancelike state, and a prophet interprets her ravings. Priestesses like the Pythia are usually chosen by lot; Athenian priestesses, usually wellborn women, have some civic rights and can sign legal documents and plead before public councils.

Roman women worship Venus in April and celebrate the Matronalia on March 1. The Matronalia, a celebration of virtuous marriage, is marked by gifts from husbands to wives, gifts from lovers to young women, and feasts given by wives for their female slaves. Another women's festival is the Matralia of June 11, on which matrons offer cakes and a garland to the goddess Mater Matuta and pray for the welfare of their sisters' children.

4th century In Cyrene, new brides and pregnant women are expected to make a sacrifice to Artemis. In Epidaurus, women with medical problems visit and sometimes sleep in the temple of Asclepius. There is a widespread belief, especially among women, in love potions and curses.

c. 400–200 A Roman priest must usually be married and may lose his post if his wife dies; women can be priestesses in some temples.

Late 3rd–2nd centuries Chinese emperors send expeditions in search of such deities as the Queen Mother of the West, believed to reside in Central Asia and to distribute largesse and immortal status to those who locate her. She rules a heavenly world that is sometimes indicated by a white tiger.

216 Two Vestal Virgins, Opimia and Floronia, are punished for unchastity. One commits suicide; the other is subjected to the ritual form of execution for this crime: burial alive. Floronia's lover is beaten to death by the *pontifex maximus*, the chief religious official of Rome.

205–204 During the Punic Wars, the desperate Romans consult the Sibylline Books, ancient oracular texts said to have been composed by a woman. The books reveal that if Magna Mater (Cybele, the Mother Goddess of Asia Minor) is worshiped in Rome, the Carthaginian enemy will be defeated. Accordingly, a black stone, believed to hold the spirit of the goddess, is brought to Rome. The ship bearing it becomes mired in the mud of the Tiber River, but the Vestal Virgin Claudia frees it, reportedly by the strength of her virtue. The stone is then received by all the matrons of Rome, who carry it through the streets, where the people burn incense and present the goddess with gifts. The worship of Cybele continues to spread after this ceremony of welcome, though the Romans remain suspicious of the Great Mother's self-emasculated priests. Every April the *Megalesia*, a festival of games in honor of the goddess, is celebrated. Eventually, the worship of Cybele will spread from Asia Minor to the Celtic lands of Western Europe.

100–1 B.C.

General Status and Daily Life

About 10% of Roman women are married by age twelve; most marry at thirteen or fourteen. On the eve of her wedding, a Roman woman sacrifices her childhood toys to the Lares, or the household gods of her family. Most marriages are arranged, often for political reasons, in the upper class, and they are easily dissolved. Some ambitious young men marry four or five times, changing wives as quickly as they change alliances. Marriage *cum manu*, in which complete legal control over the wife is given to her husband, is becoming less common. Roman widows cannot marry until ten months after a husband's death. This is the last century in which Roman husbands can legally kill their wives at once if they catch them in an adulterous act.

Celtic women are usually not married without their permission. Girls often marry as early as twelve. Each partner brings a marriage portion to the union and adds to it each year in equal proportion; if one dies, the other retains his or her share of the profits. Celtic women, unlike Romans and Germans, can own personal property after marriage. Divorce is easy for both parties; a Welshman can divorce his wife if she insults him by saying, "Shame on your beard." Polygyny and perhaps even polyandry exist in Celtic lands, with names sometimes derived matrilineally. Trial one-year marriages are accepted.

Greek historian Diodorus Siculus reports that Egyptian men are expected to obey their wives. He quotes from an Egyptian marriage contract: "I bow before your rights as

wife. From this day on, I shall never oppose your claims with a single word."

A popular textbook for women in China is *Lienü zhuan* (*Biographies of Virtuous Women*). Such handbooks, which emphasize female virtues like loyalty and chastity, will remain popular for hundreds of years.

Chinese husbands and wives are often buried together in joint graves, sometimes with their children, if any have predeceased them. Rich women are buried with their household goods, wooden or clay figures, puppets, carriages, furniture, and jewelry. The tomb walls are elaborately painted with pleasant scenes. Poor women are buried with less pomp and sometimes not at all.

92 A marriage contract from Alexandria, Egypt, specifies that the wife, Apollonia, will be obedient and chaste. She must not "spend night or day away from the house" without the knowledge of her husband, Philiscus; she is also forbidden "to ruin the common household or to bring shame upon Philiscus." In return, she has an equal share in all their property. Philiscus must maintain her financially and may not "bring home another wife . . . a concubine or boy-lover, nor . . . beget children by another woman while Apollonia is alive nor . . . maintain another house of which Apollonia is not mistress, nor . . . eject or insult or illtreat her nor to alienate any of their property with injustice to Apollonia." Apollonia can retrieve her dowry and separate from Philiscus; if he does not return her dowry, he shall be liable for the dowry plus one-half its value.

18 In Rome, women must be divorced if they commit adultery. They are banished and deprived of one-third of their property, one-half of their dowry, and the right to remarry. If a husband does not publicize his wife's crime within sixty days, he can be charged with pandering, and her punishment becomes the responsibility of her father. If the father does not prosecute, any citizen may accuse her. There is no penalty for a man's adultery, and he may legally have sex with his female slaves (whether or not they consent) unless he damages their value or encourages them to plot against his wife.
  In his own house or his son-in-law's, a father can kill his daughter's illicit lover. A husband can kill his wife's lover only if he finds the lover in his house, and he cannot kill his wife unless he actually catches her in the act in his house. However, husbands who kill adulterous wives under other circumstances are usually treated with leniency. Men who commit incest are banished. Women who commit incest are not banished unless they have also committed adultery as a result.

18 Roman emperor Augustus mandates marriage for men under sixty and women under fifty. The unmarried have limited inheritance rights and may not attend public festivals. Widows and divorced women must remarry within six months or lose any financial benefits. Unmarried or childless women cannot inherit property if it will raise their worth above 50,000 sesterces and cannot inherit at all after age fifty. Women worth at least 20,000 sesterces are taxed to varying degrees until they marry and have three children. Women with three children are allowed to wear an identifying piece of clothing; they also have certain legal freedoms not granted to most wives, and this condition is known as the *ius trium liberorum*. The law is not a great success, for many reasons. Conservatives dislike the freedom given to mothers of three children, and the law is irregularly enforced and often circumvented. People with friends in high places (like Augustus's wife Livia, who had only two children) can receive the *ius trium liberorum* through political influence rather than dutiful reproduction.

Government, the Military, and the Law

Lady Feng, concubine of Emperor Yüan, throws herself between the emperor and an escaped bear from a wild animal show. She then directs the guards to kill it. Her story will be related for centuries as an example of dutiful loyalty.

Celtic women serve as warriors, and the women of Gaul are especially feared by Roman soldiers: "Swelling her neck, gnashing her teeth, and brandishing sallow arms of enormous size she delivers blows and kicks like missiles from a catapult."

Phile becomes the first female *stephanophorus* (crowned magistrate) in Priene, providing at her own expense a water system for the city.

89 Ptolemy X of Egypt is dethroned; his wife and co-ruler, Queen Berenice II, tries unsuccessfully to help him regain his power by force. He dies in 88, and she marries his successor, the reinstated Ptolemy IX. When Ptolemy IX dies in 80, she tries to rule in her own right, refusing to marry the Roman-backed Ptolemy Alexander. He has her killed, and the people of Alexandria, who loved her, kill Ptolemy Alexander in revenge.

78 Salome Alexandra is queen of Judea, ruling until 69. She makes peace with the Pharisees.

77 Roman defendant Amasia Sentia defends herself in court, securing her own acquittal and earning the title *androgyne*, "because she bore a man's spirit under the appearance of a woman."

63 The failed coup d'état of Roman statesman Catiline is foiled in part by Fulvia, mistress of one of the conspirators, who spreads the news of her lover's strange behavior and boasting. Sempronia, wife of a consul, supports Catiline. She is described by her contemporaries as reckless, daring, aggressively sexual, prodigal with money, ruthless, faithless, well educated, witty, charming, and poetically gifted.

48 Roman senator's wife Gaia Afrania dies. She enjoyed bringing lawsuits and annoyed many by her insistence on arguing the cases herself rather than relying on a male advocate.

47 Queen Anula becomes ruler of Sri Lanka, reigning until 42.

44 Marcus Brutus, with others, plans the assassination of Julius Caesar. Brutus's wife Porcia, daughter of Cato, senses that he is troubled but hesitates to press him for the reason without testing her own courage and discretion. Therefore, she gives herself a deep wound in the thigh with a knife used to cut fingernails. She becomes ill as a result, and seeing Brutus concerned for her pain, she tells him what she has done and why. She then asks him to tell her his plans, saying, "I know that men think women's natures too weak to be entrusted with secrets, but surely a good upbringing and the company of honorable men can do much to strengthen us, and at least Porcia can claim that she is the daughter of Cato and the wife of Brutus."

Daughter of Cato or not, Porcia is heavily burdened by her advance knowledge of the plot. On March 15, the day of the assassination, she is frantic with worry and questions people coming from the Forum about Brutus's welfare. At last she collapses, and although she eventually recovers, the rumor that she is dead reaches Brutus. (She will eventually commit suicide in 42 by swallowing live coals.)

43 Lepidus, Mark Antony, and Julius Caesar's nephew Octavian establish Rome's Second Triumvirate. Antony's ambitious and decisive wife Fulvia (d. 40) suddenly becomes powerful, sparing the riches of a man who helped her and arranging the decapitation of one who had refused to sell her a coveted villa. A number of men condemned to death by the triumvirs are saved by their wives. Acilius's wife bribes the soldiers to find him a safe ship out of the country; Antius' wife hides him inside a bag of clothes and ships him to the coast; Rheginus's wife hides him in a sewer; Coponius's wife gains his safety by sleeping with Antony.

37–34 Herod the Great is king of Judea; he has his wife Mariamne executed for treason, then goes half mad with guilt. When Mariamne's mother organizes a new plot against him, he has the new conspirators executed as well.

30 Queen Cleopatra VII of Egypt (b. 69) dies. She was deposed in 49 by her brother-husband Ptolemy XIII but regained the throne with the help of her lover, Roman general Julius Caesar. She followed him to Rome with their son Caesarion, returning to Egypt after his assassination in 44. In 41, she seduced one of Caesar's successors, Mark Antony, who helped her eliminate another political rival, her sister Arsinoe. He awarded her the titles Queen of Kings and the New Isis; granted the lands of Armenia, Parthia, Media, Cyrenaica, Libya, Syria, and Cilicia to their three children; expressed a desire in his will to be buried near her; gave her a 200,000-scroll library at Pergamum; and neglected his duties in displaying his love for her.

In 32, Antony's co-ruler Octavian (Augustus) declared war on Cleopatra in an effort to subdue Antony. She furnished 200 ships for the prosecution of the war but lost the decisive Battle of Actium on September 2, 31, when her ship fled the fighting, followed by Antony's. She negotiated unsuccessfully with Octavian, who was determined to exhibit her in a humiliating triumphal procession. She tried to kill herself with a knife and then a hunger strike and finally smuggled into her quarters an asp, a poisonous snake that dispatched her and her two handmaids, Iras and Charmian.

17 Queen Dynamis of Bosphorus (d. 7 or 8) assists in a revolt against her husband King Asander, then seizes power herself and issues her own coinage. She is forcibly married to King Polemo of Pontus but flees and raises an army, fighting Polemo and marrying a new husband of her own choosing. When Polemo dies in 8, she seizes power again, becoming a Roman client-queen and thus a favored ally of Rome.

12 Octavia, sister of Roman emperor Augustus and second wife of Mark Antony, dies. She kept peace between her brother and her husband from the time of her marriage in 40 until war erupted in 32; Antony's mistreatment of her helped to turn Roman opinion against him. He divorced Octavia in 32, but she remained loyal to him and, after his suicide in 31, raised his children by Cleopatra and by Fulvia, his first wife.

Literature and the Visual Arts

Roman poet Sulpicia writes love poems to "Cerinthus," whose true identity has never been determined. She is the only Latin woman poet of the classical period whose works survive.

c. 100 Roman artist Iaia of Cyzicus paints and engraves ivory, becoming the foremost painter and sculptor of her day. A lifelong virgin, she worked faster and commanded higher fees than either of the top two male painters of the time.

c. 48–6 Chinese poet Lady Pan, a second-rank concubine of Emperor Ch'eng, writes a poem called *Regret* or the *Round Fan Poem*, which saves her from exile after the emperor discards her for the dancing girl Chao Feiyen.

Activism

42 The members of Rome's Second Triumvirate (Mark Antony, Octavian, and Lepidus) tax 1,400 of Rome's richest matrons; the women appeal unsuccessfully to Antony's wife, Fulvia, and converge on the Forum. A consul's daughter, Hortensia, is chosen as their representative and argues successfully before the triumvirs for a reduction of the tribute. She points out that women have no political power and should therefore not be required to contribute their possessions to the state. The number of women involved is reduced to 400, and men who own more than 100,000 denarii are to make up the difference.

Business and Industry

Roman women often own and manage property.

Science and Medicine

Several Greek women achieve fame as midwives and physicians in this century. Among them are Elephantis, renowned for her midwifery and treatment of baldness; midwife and physician Laïs, an opponent of Elephantis on the use of drugs and an inventor of several "cures" for rabies, fevers, and infertility; midwife Olympias of Thebes, an expert on herbs, especially abortifacients and contraceptives; midwife Salpe of Lemnos, who claims to be able to cure numbness, sunburn, rabies, fevers, and barking dogs; and physician Sotira, admired by Pliny.

Education and Scholarship

Most women (and most men) in China are illiterate.

Religion

In Rome, women are central to the festival of the Bona Dea (Good Goddess). The Vestal Virgins are still powerful, and men of importance often leave their wills in the keeping of the Vestals. Isis worship is the most widespread and popular religion in the Roman Empire and will remain so until the triumph of Christianity. Isis, the Egyptian mother goddess, is revered in Spain, Asia Minor, North Africa, and Germany.

Korea has female shamans, who serve as healers, prophets, and priestesses who bring rain and blessings.

58 Altars of Isis are destroyed in Rome.

4 Mary gives birth to Jesus in Judaea.

1−100

General Status and Daily Life

Greek marriage includes an animal sacrifice to Hera and the shaving of the bride's head. Plutarch reports that women are so sheltered in Greek society that some have borne two or three children without ever seeing their husbands during the day. One husband asks his wife why she has never told him of his bad breath; she replies, "I thought all men smelt like that."

Unwanted Roman daughters are often abandoned at the Columna Lactaria; any babies found there are spared and fed by the state. Abandoned girls are also sometimes taken in by brothel keepers and raised as prostitutes.

Roman women are expected to marry in their teens. Most marriages are still arranged, with the daughter having little say in the matter. The strict morality of the Roman Republic, however, is loosening. Adultery is common. Upper-class women no longer nurse their own children but hire wet nurses instead. Contraception is still rather primitive. The Greek gynecologist Soranus recommends that the woman pull back a little when the man ejaculates, then squat and sneeze to expel the semen, and wipe the vagina. As chemical contraceptives he lists olive oil, honey, cedar resin, white lead, myrtle oil, moist alum, wool as a barrier, ground pomegranate peel, dried figs, and oil of roses. For abortion, he recommends vigorous exercise, diuretics, wine, spicy food, sitting in "a bath of a decoction of linseed, fenugreek, mallow, marsh mallow, and wormwood," bleeding, and vaginal suppositories. He warns against "separating the embryo by means of something sharp-edged, for danger arises that some of the adjacent parts be wounded."

In China's Han period (202 B.C.–A.D. 220), peasants generally cannot afford concubines and are monogamous by necessity; wealthy men are often polygamous. In rich families, the wife takes female attendants with her to her new home; they sometimes serve as concubines, later being released to marry. The emperor has fourteen grades of concubines, many of whom have duties other than sexual ones. Women of the imperial court never call the emperor by name; they hand him items on a tray rather than risk the offense of touching him. Favored imperial concubines can get good government posts for their male relatives, but the most powerful woman of all is the empress. When a Han emperor dies, his widow selects a new successor from his clan. Sometimes she deliberately chooses a weak successor so that her own clan can rule him through a regent.

Government, the Military, and the Law

Women in Pompeii, Italy, post graffiti endorsing political candidates.

c. 6 Erato is queen of Armenia in her own right but is quickly deposed.

9 The Kushite kingdom is rebuilt by King Natakamani, who shares power with the Queen Mother, Candace, until his death in 15.

29 Livia Drusilla, Roman empress and wife of Augustus Caesar, dies. She performed works of charity, helping orphans and dowerless brides, and was given the title "Augusta" (sacred, magnificent) by the Senate. Politically powerful, she stopped at nothing to place her son Tiberius on the throne after the death of Augustus, even perhaps arranging for the deaths of his rivals Agrippa and Germanicus, and exercising great influence over her imperial offspring. Tiberius was not grateful for her intervention, however, and avoided her as much as possible and even moved out of Rome in 26 to escape her control. Upon her death, he ignores the provisions of her will and refuses to succumb to the popular clamor to have her deified. Her grandson Claudius will finally declare her a goddess.

31 Roman emperor Tiberius almost dies in a plot against him by his most trusted aide, Sejanus; women play crucial roles in various aspects of the conspiracy. Tiberius is saved by a warning given him by his sister-in-law Antonia at the risk of her own life. Sejanus's daughter is condemned but cannot be legally executed because she is a virgin, so she is raped first, then strangled. Sejanus's ex-wife Apicata writes a letter implicating Antonia's daughter Livilla (who in 23 helped Sejanus, her lover, to poison her husband, Tiberius's son Drusus), then kills herself; Livilla is charged with treason but starves herself rather than come to trial.

Oct. 18, 33 Roman noblewoman Agrippina I, granddaughter of Augustus and mother of nine children, including Emperor Caligula and Agrippina II (mother of Nero), commits suicide in exile by starving herself to death. A longtime opponent of Emperor Tiberius, she plotted against him and spread the rumor that he had ordered the poisoning of her husband, Germanicus, a possible contender for the throne. She also implicated a woman in the alleged murder: Plancina, a general's wife notorious for her habit of reviewing cavalry exercises and for her friendship with Martina, a well-known poisoner.
    Agrippina's continued machinations led Tiberius to banish her in 29. Some now claim he encouraged or forced her suicide. Tiberius accuses her posthumously of adultery; the historian Tacitus says of these charges, "Actually, Agrippina knew no feminine weaknesses. Intolerant of rivalry, thirsting for power, she had a man's

preoccupations." Her death is closely followed by Plancina's suicide.

35 Queen Sivali rules Sri Lanka.

39 Chinese invaders rape Vietnamese noblewoman Trung Trac and murder her husband. Trung and her sister, Trung Nhi, lead the first Vietnamese rebellion against Chinese rule, fighting for three years before they are defeated and commit suicide. Their army of 80,000 soldiers and 36 women generals includes such notable women as the pregnant Phung Thi Chinh, who gives birth in the middle of a battle and then fights her way to safety.

48 Roman empress Messalina (b. 22), wife of Emperor Claudius, is executed for marrying one of her lovers. Soldiers break into her chambers, where her mother, Domitia Lepida, is counseling her to "make a decent end." She holds a dagger to her throat, then her chest, but cannot summon up the courage to commit suicide and is slain by a soldier. Claudius, at dinner, is informed that she is dead; he does not ask how and continues with his banquet.

In 49, Claudius marries his niece Agrippina II, who exercises a "rigorous, almost masculine despotism." She immediately begins scheming on behalf of her son by a previous marriage, Lucius Domitius Ahenobarbus (Nero). Although Claudius's daughter Octavia is already betrothed, Agrippina arranges for her fiancé, a military hero, to be discredited—ironically, for incest—so that Octavia can marry Nero in 53. Thus she begins to maneuver Nero ahead of Claudius's own son Britannicus in the succession; she is backed by those who fear reprisals for their part in Messalina's death.

51 British king Caractacus seeks refuge with Queen Cartimandua, leader of the Yorkshire Brigantes; she hands him over to the Romans.

53 The Queen Mother of the Korean kingdom of Koguryo serves as regent for her son King T'aejo.

54 Roman empress Agrippina II poisons her husband, Claudius, and has Nero proclaimed emperor by the Guard. Agrippina continues to exercise strong influence over Nero and has her image stamped on the imperial coinage. However, in 55 Nero begins neglecting both his wife and his mother for a slave mistress, Acte. Agrippina schemes to replace Nero with Claudius's son Britannicus, but Nero has Britannicus poisoned, and Agrippina barely escapes execution for treason after she is accused by two dependents of her onetime friend Junia Silana. She defends herself with vigor, saying, "Junia Silana has never had a child . . . so I am not surprised she does not understand a mother's feelings! For mothers change their sons less easily than loose women change their lovers." Agrippina not only avoids condemnation but convinces Nero to exact revenge on Silana and her

followers, who are variously exiled or executed.

59 Poppaea Sabina (d. 65), Emperor Nero's new mistress, encourages him to get rid of both his wife, Octavia, and his mother, Agrippina (b. 15), taunting him with being controlled by these women. Nero orders that a boat be built with a breakaway section to give the impression of an accidental shipwreck. According to this plan, Agrippina will drown, and Nero will play the part of the bereaved son, ordering temples and elaborate rites in her memory.

However, the ship does not collapse in quite the way intended and sinks gradually rather than abruptly. Agrippina's female companion, Acerronia, calls out, "I am Agrippina! Help, help, the emperor's mother!" and is bludgeoned to death by the conspirators; Agrippina wisely stays silent and swims to safety despite a wounded shoulder. However, armed soldiers soon arrive at her home. Agrippina, realizing they are executioners, tells them to strike her in the womb first.

61 King Prasutagas, leader of Britain's Iceni tribe, dies, leaving his wife, Boudica, as regent for their two daughters. Rome confiscates all of the late king's estates. Boudica's daughters are raped, and Boudica herself is publicly flogged. Boudica, described as "tall, and grim-faced in appearance with piercing eyes and a harsh voice," rebels and gets other tribes to follow her, leading her troops southward in the last great act of resistance to Roman rule.

Her first target is Camulodunum (Colchester), which she attacks with 120,000 troops. She kills about 2,500 Roman soldiers. Next she attacks Londinium (London), killing thousands of settlers. Roman historian Dio Cassius says of the British attackers, "They hung up naked the noblest and most distinguished women and then cut off their breasts and sewed them to their mouths . . . Afterwards they impaled the women on sharp skewers run lengthwise through the entire body." In all, the British kill about 70,000 Romans.

Next, Boudica sacks Verulamium (St. Albans); most citizens, warned of the fate of the other two cities, have already fled. The attack gives the Romans time to find favorable terrain; in the ensuing battle, 80,000 Britons and 400 Romans are killed. Boudica dies soon afterward, probably by poisoning herself. Another female British leader, Queen Cartimandua of the Brigantes, remains loyal to the Romans during the uprising and is rewarded nine years later with Roman assistance in holding her crown.

62 Roman emperor Nero divorces Octavia and marries Poppaea Sabina, who has the popular Octavia accused of adultery with a slave and banished. The crowds in Rome riot in favor of Octavia, replacing Poppaea's statues with hers. Octavia is, at the age of twenty, now sent to the island of Pandateria. On June 9, she is ordered to commit suicide but, terrified, resists. She is bound by soldiers and her veins opened; when this proves ineffective, she is suffocated and her severed head sent to Poppaea. Poppaea marries Nero a few days later.

65 A conspiracy to kill Nero is encouraged and partially organized by a freed slave woman named Epicharis. Betrayed, she denies any involvement and refuses to name her accomplices, even after being tortured and branded. The torturers, angry "at being defied by a woman," are particularly brutal to her, and she hangs herself to avoid confessing any names or details.

65 Roman author Seneca is ordered by Nero to commit suicide. Seneca's wife, Pompeia Paulina, vows to die with him. They open the veins in their arms, but Nero orders the soldiers bearing the death order to prevent Pompeia's demise, so they bind her wounds. The incident is reminiscent of another in 42; when Caecina Paetus was ordered to commit suicide, his wife Arria Paeta stabbed herself in the chest and handed him the knife, saying, "It does not hurt."

Sept. 18, 96 Empress Domitia, with military assistance, assassinates her husband Domitian.

Literature and the Visual Arts

Women in the Greek and Roman worlds write poetry and paint in this era. Pliny refers to the works of artists such as Timarete, who painted an image of Diana; Irene, a portraitist; Aristarete, who painted an image of Asclepius; and Olympias.

Performing Arts and Entertainment

Women act and sing in Greece and Rome. In Greece, women participate in lyre contests. In Rome, women can be mimes, but to do so they must allow themselves to be classified as prostitutes, and their performances often rely on sexual innuendo or bodily exposure.

Athletics and Exploration

Roman women lift weights and swim to stay in shape.

Greek women participate in single-course races at the Pythian Games, the Nemean Games, and the Isthmian Games. Women race in armor and participate in chariot races. They can also be gymnasiarchs, in charge of the local gymnasium, although the office is really an honorary post, and the gymnasiarch is expected to spend her own money on official philanthropy.

Three athletic sisters from Tralles in Asia Minor win footraces. Tryphosa wins at the Pythian Games in

Delphi and becomes the first woman to win a footrace at Corinth's Isthmian Games. Hedea and Dionysia also win various races.

66 Men and women from Ethiopia fight in Rome as gladiators. Women captives, especially from Germany, are often sent to the arena under Emperors Nero and Domitian.

80 Women fight beasts at the opening of Rome's Colosseum.

86 Roman emperor Domitian establishes a Greek-style competition of artists and athletes, the quadrennial Agon Capitolinus. At first it features, among other events, a girls' footrace.

Activism

Alexandria has at least one women's club.

43 Junia Theodora, a Roman resident of Corinth, is commended on a public monument for her philanthropy by the people of Patara, Lydia. Many women of the time provide money to repair old buildings and temples.

Business and Industry

Some Roman women follow the unusual trade of poisoner. Locusta is a talented professional poisoner who arranges the deaths of Claudius and Britannicus; Nero so admires her skills that he arranges for her to take on apprentices.

There are about 3,000 *hetairai* in Greece.

Roman emperor Caligula taxes prostitutes at a high rate, even after they give up the profession to marry. Prostitutes must register with the state and wear the toga, a masculine garment, instead of the stola worn by respectable women. However, some "respectable" women actually register as prostitutes to avoid being prosecuted for adultery. Prostitutes are often found in the Temple of Isis.

Roman women work as textile manufacturers, shopkeepers, seamstresses, hairdressers, pedagogues, stenographers and secretaries, wool weighers, weavers, maids, fish sellers, porters, vegetable and grain dealers, and slaves.

Science and Medicine

At about this time, Aspasia, a Greek physician, develops the technique of moving the fetus from the breech position before birth.

Women in Europe work as physicians, midwives, and wet nurses.

1st or 2nd century Alexandrian chemist Mary the Jewess, also sometimes called Maria or Miriam, invents the double boiler, known for centuries as a *bain-marie* and the prototype for the autoclave; the *tribikos*, a still that may be the first distillation device; and the *kerotakis*, a device for creating and capturing the gaseous forms of metals.

Education and Scholarship

In Rome, girls go to school from ages seven to fourteen. They study grammar, Greek, Latin and Greek literature, music, astronomy, history, mythology, philosophy, and dancing.

Epidaurian scholar Pamphile writes thirty-three books of history and "many epitomes of histories and other books, about controversies, sex, and many other things."

Religion

Many women achieve status in their communities as priestesses. Lycian priestess Lalla is honored by a public monument. Pompeiian priestess Eumachia, wealthy and well respected, builds a headquarters for the fullers' guild and has a statue built in her honor. Mamia, another priestess, builds a temple. Flavia Ammon of Phocaea is "high priestess of the temple of Asia in Ephesus, president, twice *stephanephorus*, priestess of Massilia, [and] president of the games."

The Roman emperors encourage worship of the goddesses Isis and Cybele.

Virgin martyr, healer, and cave-dwelling hermit St. Thecla of Iconium lives in Asia Minor.

By now it is standard practice for a Jewish man's morning prayers to thank God "who has not made me a woman." Women thank God for making them "according to thy will."

Most of Korea's shamans, who pray for rain, heal the sick, and divine the future, are women.

24 Rome's Vestal Virgins have reserved seats at the theater. Priests' wives, heretofore married *cum manu* (with complete power given to their husbands) automatically, are given the same marital options as other women.

c. 30 Salome, stepdaughter of Israeli tetrarch Herod

Antipas, dances for him. As her reward, goaded by her mother, Herodias, she requests the head of John the Baptist.

30 Jesus of Nazareth is executed. His followers include Mary Magdalene, who, according to tradition, is the first to receive news of his resurrection.

c. 70 Veleda is an unmarried Celtic prophetess who sometimes serves as an intermediary for the city of Cologne.

101–200

General Status and Daily Life

In Roman Egypt, a childless widow cannot inherit more than one-fourth of her husband's estate; if they have children, she cannot inherit more than any of her sons. Roman women worth more than 20,000 sesterces are taxed one percent of it per year while unmarried. Roman women worth more than 50,000 sesterces cannot inherit anything if they are single and childless. It is difficult for a Roman woman to bequeath any property.

In China, artisans' and merchants' wives help their husbands with their work. Peasant women care for the silkworms, make textiles from hemp and silk, make sandals, brew liquor, and preserve food. In summer they wash out old clothes, make new ones, and dye silk. On New Year's Day, all lesser members of the family, including women, pay their respects to the family patriarch.

India's Tamil kingdoms are matriarchal to some extent, with children tracing their ancestry matrilineally (through the mother). Parts of Tamil lands will remain matrilineal until the nineteenth century.

Women in China shave off their eyebrows and paint curved, arching ones above the natural eyebrow line.

In the African city of Leptis, new brides are to be impressed with the proper respect for their mothers-in-law by enacting an old ritual: "On the day after her marriage the bride sends to her husband's mother and asks her for a pot. She does not give it and says that she hasn't got one."

By the end of this century, free Roman women over twenty-five have de facto control over their property. Most women marry by *usus*, separating from husbands three nights a year to maintain control over their property. Abortion is illegal, and abortionists are banished and fined; they are executed if the woman dies.

2nd to 4th centuries Biologically, a normal ratio of live births is 100 female to 105 male. In Roman Egypt it is just that, but exposure of girls elsewhere results in adult ratios that are greatly skewed. In Roman Spain there are 100 women to every 126 men; in Rome itself, 100 women to 131 men; and in Roman Italy and Africa, 100 to 140.

Government, the Military, and the Law

107 Ngan-ti becomes boy-emperor of China, with the real power belonging to Dowager Empress Deng.

147-168 Chinese emperor Huandi, himself controlled to a great extent by a dowager empress, limits the power of female regents by increasing the power of palace eunuchs. He dies in 168 without a declared successor; Empress Dou is declared dowager and selects the new emperor, twelve-year-old Lingdi. Dou then tries to execute nine of Huandi's former concubines, succeeding in killing only one. She supports her father, Dou Wu, in an attempted coup against the palace eunuchs. The eunuchs and the new emperor win the power struggle; Dou Wu commits suicide, and Empress Dowager Dou is imprisoned.

182 Lucilla, daughter of Roman emperor Marcus Aurelius and sister of the corrupt Emperor Commodus, attempts unsuccessfully to have Commodus assassinated. She is exiled to Capri. Commodus is assassinated in 192 in a plot furthered by his lover Marcia.

197 King Kogukch'on of the Korean kingdom of Koguryo dies. His widow chooses one of his brothers as successor, then marries the new king. It is customary in Koguryo for a man to marry his older brother's widow.

Literature and the Visual Arts

Roman poet Melinno composes sapphic verses in Greek.

Mid-2nd century Chinese poet Hsü Shu writes poetic letters in response to poems from her absent husband Ch'in Chia.

Performing Arts and Entertainment

Greek women work as harpists and lyrists.

Women in South India perform with traveling troops of actors. Two later epics set at about this time record the amorous antics of two such women, Madavi and her daughter Manimegalai, who later become Buddhist nuns.

Athletics and Exploration

According to a spectator, the Heraia, or Greek women's games, features girls' footraces for various age groups. The winners get olive wreaths and sections of the sacrificial cow.

154 Seia Spes wins a footrace for magistrates' daughters at the Sebasteia in Naples.

Activism

Women's clubs exist in various parts of the Roman world, usually for the purpose of organizing religious or burial rites.

Business and Industry

In Greece, women work as salt vendors, concubines, and even gilders. Some women are apprenticed to craftspeople; for example, one girl is apprenticed to a weaver for four years, at increasing pay in each successive year, with eighteen days off per year for sickness and festivals.

Science and Medicine

At about this time, Greek midwife Metrodora writes *Extracts from the Works of Metrodora Concerning the Diseases of Women*.

Women in many parts of the world work as physicians, and all midwives are female. Many midwives begin the trade as slaves and continue it after being freed.

Cappadocian male doctor Aretaeus claims that the uterus can wander or float out of place, moving toward pleasant smells and away from nasty ones and causing choking, sleepiness, loss of speech, vertigo, knee problems, headaches, problems with veins in the nose, heartburn, pulse irregularities, and death. This myth of the floating uterus will be believed by most medical practitioners for hundreds of years.

Education and Scholarship

In his sixth satire, Roman author Juvenal attacks women

for their thorough educations. He is horrified at the thought that some of them can even quote Virgil.

Beruriah of Jerusalem is a philosopher. She is cited in the Talmud as correcting her husband, Rabbi Meir; she tells him to pray, not for the death of sinners, but for their repentance.

115 Chinese scholar, mathematician, astronomer, poet, and historian Ban Zhao (Pan Chao, b. c. 45) dies. She wrote poetry, essays, a continuation of the *History of the Han Dynasty*, and *Nu Chien* (*Advice for Women*, 106), which advises women to be submissive and domestic.

Religion

Women are priestesses of Demeter at Eleusis; in Athens, girls go through a puberty rite in which they present gifts to Athena.

Roman emperor Commodus, among his other atrocities, orders some Isis-worshiping women to commit suicide by beating themselves with pinecones. His persecutions have little effect, however, and Isis remains the Roman world's most popular deity.

In India, several Hindu deities are worshiped, and each god has his female aspect or consort. Brahma has Sarasvati, a goddess of the arts; Vishnu has Lakshmi, goddess of good luck. The sensual Krishna, an aspect of Vishnu, has many loves, but chief among them is the divine milkmaid Radha. Siva is found in company with various mother goddesses, including kind and bountiful Parvati, virtuous Sati, dangerous and aggressive Kali, and demonic Durga.

Women in the early Christian church are expected to be especially modest and good, so as to set a fine example for the pagans. They veil themselves in church to avoid distracting the men and angels; Saint Jerome advocates their cutting off their hair entirely. They do not wear cosmetics, jewelry, or wigs. Abortion and infanticide are banned. Celibacy and virginity are considered preferable to marriage. Divorce is permitted only when a Christian is married to a pagan; homosexuality and remarriage are discouraged.

177 French slave Blandina is martyred at Lyons. Accused with other Christians of incest and cannibalism, she is tortured but says only, "I am a Christian, and we do nothing vile." Finally, she is bound in a bag and thrown to a bull to be gored to death.

185 Roman empress Julia Domna introduces the Syrian goddess Tanit to Rome as Caelestis Dea.

200 Aemilia Aureliana, a goddess worshiper, erects a carving to commemorate "her act of sexual service" to her deity, indicating that her mother and grandmother have done likewise.

201–300

General Status and Daily Life

In legal marriage, Roman children have their father's rank (slave/free, patrician/plebeian); if they are illegitimate, they have their mother's rank. Children of slave women are also slaves unless the woman is free for part of the time between conception and birth. In many cases, a freeborn woman who lives with a slave becomes a slave herself.

Upon a wife's death, her husband keeps one-fifth of her dowry for each living child she has borne and returns the rest to her father; if the father is dead, the husband keeps it all. In divorce, the woman can sue for recovery of the dowry, though the husband is entitled to keep some of it if the divorce is her fault or her father's. A divorced woman, if pregnant, must announce the fact and submit to an examination by five midwives within 300 days, or the child cannot be recognized as her ex-husband's.

In India, texts recommend that a bride be one-third of her husband's age; a bride of eight and a groom of twenty-four is one approved pairing. Child brides may be married early, but they do not live with the husband until about age twelve, and consummation proceeds slowly. The husband is expected to refrain from even kissing his wife for at least ten days.

Women in Persia may marry against their parents' wishes. Dowry, polygyny (particularly where the first wife is infertile), and concubinage are common. Men may divorce their wives for adultery; women may divorce their husbands for cruelty or desertion. Wives are generally relegated to separate, secluded quarters within the home. Infanticide, abortion, and adultery are heavily penalized.

Germanic Goths marry within their own communities when possible. When this is not possible, they kidnap brides from nearby communities, assisted by a strong male friend or "best man."

Government, the Military, and the Law

211 Roman emperor Septimius Severus dies; Caracalla succeeds. His mother, Julia Domna, opposes him and tries to replace him with his younger brother Geta. Geta is stabbed in 212 at the behest of Caracalla and dies in Julia Domna's arms; Caracalla continues to trust his mother with high office, placing her in charge of Rome's domestic affairs while he conducts military campaigns. Intelligent and powerful, Julia Domna patronizes scholars, philosophers, and scientists, including Athenaeus and Galen. When Caracalla is killed by his soldiers in 217, Julia Domna starves herself to death.

218-222 Elagabalus becomes Roman emperor with substantial help from Julia Maesa (d. 226), sister of Julia Domna and mother of Julia Soaemias and Julia Mamaea. He enters Rome, sharing the triumphal procession with Maesa and his mother, Julia Soaemias; Soaemias indulges her sexual passions and runs the Senaculum, or little Senate, a women's court that addresses questions of dress, jewelry, precedence, and etiquette. Maesa becomes effective head of the Roman government. Recognizing that Elagabalus's sexual, financial, and religious excesses are growing unpopular, she distances herself from him and from Soaemias, allying with her other daughter, Julia Mamaea, to place Mamaea's son, Alexander Severus, on the throne. Soaemias tries to rebel, but the Praetorian Guard receives bigger bribes from Maesa and Mamaea, kills Elagabalus and Soaemias, and proclaims Severus emperor in 222. Maesa and Mamaea rule Rome wisely through Severus until 235, when Severus and Mamaea are murdered by the army.

221 Chinese empress Chen is deposed and commits suicide.

247 Japanese queen Himiko declares war on her neighbor, Kunukoko, in southern Japan. Her ally, China, refuses military aid. Himiko is deposed and killed shortly afterward by her brother, who cannot maintain order. Peace is finally restored by the accession of Himiko's daughter Iyo.

c. 248 Vietnamese rebel Trieu Au (Trieu Thi Trinh) leads 1,000 soldiers against the Chinese, waging more than thirty battles. When her brother tries to stop her, she replies, "I want to rail against wind and tide, kill the whales in the ocean, sweep the whole country to save the people from slavery, and I have no desire to take abuse." She is eventually defeated and commits suicide.

266 Queen Zenobia becomes regent of Palmyra, a Roman client-state with important trade significance, for her son Vaballathus Athenodorus. She is renowned for her beauty and her taste for masculine pursuits; she is fond of hunting and riding into battle on horseback or marching on foot instead of being borne in a litter or chariot. Furthermore, she can hold her liquor, as she demonstrates in meetings with foreign envoys and Syrian generals. She speaks Latin, Egyptian, and Syriac; writes history; studies literature and philosophy; and patronizes artists, poets, scholars, and architects.

In 269, hoping to take advantage of temporary weakness on the part of Rome, she seizes Syria and most of Egypt. In 270 she extends her territory to Cappadocia and Bithynia, giving her control of several crucial Roman trade routes. She begins gradually to break her ties to Rome and by 272 is minting her own coinage, a clear sign to Rome that she seeks independence. Rome sends troops to quell her rebellion, and she is defeated in significant battles at Antioch and Emesa. Undaunted, she retreats to Palmyra and begins negotiating her surrender, fleeing in the midst of negotiations to seek help from Persia. Captured, she abandons her independent stance, blaming her rebellion on the men around her. In 274 she is taken to Rome and exhibited in triumph as a captive, then is given a villa on the Tiber River. She later marries a Roman senator and enjoys herself thoroughly as head of one of Rome's principal intellectual circles, dying soon afterward.

291 Since 176, royal consorts' clans in the Korean kingdom of Koguryo have been quite powerful.

Literature and the Visual Arts

Chinese artist and calligrapher Lady Zhao, wife of the ruler of the Wu state, illustrates topographical maps to help her husband plan military campaigns.

239? Chinese poet Ts'ai (Cai) Yen (b. 162?) dies. A captive of the Huns for twelve years, she is the first important Chinese woman poet whose life is reasonably well documented. She succeeded her scholar-father Cai Yong as a great calligrapher.

Performing Arts and Entertainment

Rome has actresses, including one Bassilla.

Science and Medicine

Alexandrian alchemist Cleopatra publishes *Chrysopeia (Gold-Making)*, a text that will remain in use throughout the Middle Ages.

Religion

St. Agatha, a virgin martyr, dies. According to legend, she was a noblewoman pursued by a man named Quintian, who, failing to corrupt her, had her tortured until she died. One of these tortures was the severing of her breasts. She will often be depicted in later art carrying her breasts on a platter, and their shape will lead her to become known as the patron saint of bell makers.

203 Carthaginian martyrs St. (Vibia) Perpetua and St. Felicity die. Perpetua, a young mother of good family, has several religious visions while in prison and refuses pleas from her father to renounce her faith. Felicity, who is pregnant when arrested, gives birth in jail, her pain mocked by guards who say that it is nothing compared with what she will endure in the arena. (The baby is adopted by another Christian.) The two women, along with several other martyrs, are thrown to wild beasts and defend each other against the attacks. They are finally slain with swords, but Perpetua is not killed by the first blow and directs the blade herself on the next thrust.

249 Alexandrian deaconess St. Apollonia is martyred by a rioting mob. Her teeth are knocked out, and she is threatened with burning. Praying, she walks willingly into the flames. Later, her sufferings will lead those with toothaches to pray to her for relief.

259 Roman African martyr St. Marian, after being tortured but refusing to yield her faith, is executed in a mass beheading as part of the persecutions of Emperor Valerian.

260 The most sacred temple in Japan, a shrine to the goddess Izanami, is built. Izanami is considered the creator of Japan, of thirty-three gods, and of many natural formations.

301–400

General Status and Daily Life

Indian women in this period often have more liberty than in other parts of the world. In some cases, they are allowed to choose their own husbands. Romantic love is acknowledged and respected. Wives are expected to know how to sing, sew, clean, play music, make necklaces and artificial flowers, and dance. They should also be conversant with sorcery, cockfighting, ram fighting, gambling, and weapons use. Some women use contraceptives, inserting into the vagina *ghee* (clarified butter), honey, seeds, and rock salt dipped in oil.

Roman emperor Constantine passes a law allowing men to divorce their wives while preserving the right to remarry and keep the wives' dowries. Just causes for such a divorce include adultery, procuring, and poisoning. If the husband is willing to release the dowry and refrain from remarrying for two years, he can obtain a divorce for much less cause.

Perpetual guardianship of women ends in the Eastern

Roman (Byzantine) Empire.

Government, the Military, and the Law

Some Mayan women, like the Woman of Tikal, are powerful and even rise to rulership.

373–380 Syrian queen Mawia leads her armies against Phoenicia, Palestine, and the fringes of Egypt. She defeats Roman armies but later agrees to lend Rome troops to fight the Goths.

Literature and the Visual Arts

Chinese concubine T'ao-yeh (Peach Leaf) writes poetry on a round fan, probably in response to letter poems from her lover, the painter and writer Wang Hsien-chih.

347 Japanese empress and poet Iwa no Hime dies.

350 Chinese artist Wei Shuo (b. 272), better known as Wei Furen or Wei Fu-Jen, a founder of the art of calligraphy and teacher of the male master calligrapher Wang Xizhi, dies.

Performing Arts and Entertainment

A shortage of female oboists and singers leads to riots and fights between prospective clients in Athens, Greece.

Athletics and Exploration

Spanish nun Etheria makes a pilgrimage to Jerusalem and writes a record of her travels.

Sicilian women probably engage in several sports, including the javelin and discus, jumping, running, and ball games.

Science and Medicine

399 St. Fabiola, a Roman nurse, doctor, hospital founder, and the first known woman surgeon, dies.

Religion

c. 304 In widespread persecution of Christians, several women become martyrs. At Salonika, three women named Agape, Chionia, and Irene are burned alive after refusing to participate in a sacrifice for the health of Emperor Diocletian. Agape and Chionia are condemned immediately, but Irene is spared until forbidden Christian books are discovered in her possession. She is placed naked in a brothel to humiliate her and to encourage her to renounce her faith, but she keeps her virtue, so she is condemned and her books burned.

Other martyrs include Yugoslavian St. Anastasia, Numidian St. Crispina (a mother of several children), and Natalia, whose husband, Adrian, is jailed and condemned after professing his faith. She is forbidden to see him in prison but slips in dressed as a boy. After his execution, she tries unsuccessfully to throw herself into his funeral pyre. Another martyr is Sicilian St. Lucy. According to legend, she is saved miraculously from molestation in a brothel and death by fire, only to be executed by being stabbed in the throat. Later she will be invoked against diseases of the eyes.

Some of the victims are quite young. Twelve-year-old Spanish virgin St. Eulalia is killed for scolding a Roman official helping to carry out persecutions of Christians. Roman St. Agnes, probably only twelve or thirteen years old, is also martyred. Fifteen-year-old St. Pelagia of Antioch throws herself off the roof of a building to avoid being raped by soldiers.

326 Helena, mother of Roman Emperor Constantine, reports her discovery of the Holy Cross and Holy Sepulchre.

c. 340? Slave girl Nino, who brought Christianity to Russian Georgia, dies. According to legend, she was sold to a Georgian owner and became popular for her goodness and her skill as a healer in the name of Christ. She got the king to convert, to build a church, and to send for Christian clergy to spread the new faith.

c. 350 Deities in India include Hariti, protectress of children.

379 St. Macrina the Younger (b. c. 327) dies in Cappadocia. The granddaughter of St. Macrina the Elder and the daughter of St. Emmelia, she succeeded her mother as head of a convent in Pontus on the River Iris.

384 Pagan women, unlike Christian ones, can become powerful within more than one branch of worship. Roman matron Aconia Fabia Paulina, for example, is an "initiate of Ceres and the Eleusinian [mysteries], initiate of Hecate at Aegina, tauroboliata, hierophant." She is also listed as "Initiate at Eleusis to the god Iachhus, Ceres and Cora, initiate at Lerna to the god Liber and Ceres and Cora, initiate at Aegina to the two goddesses, tauroboliata, priestess of Isis, hierophant to the goddess Hecate, and initiate in the rites of the Greek Ceres."

387 North African laywoman St. Monica (b. c. 331) dies. The mother of St. Augustine, she encouraged him to become more religious, resorting at times to tactics that were more like bullying than encouragement.

394 Roman emperor Theodosius abolishes the Vestal Virgins.

401–500

General Status and Daily Life

The Talmud, or compilation of Jewish legal commentary, which will remain the basis of Jewish law and scholarship for the next 1,400 years, recommends marriage for women at fourteen, for men at eighteen. Fathers are required to amass a dowry for each daughter.

The Talmud accuses women of talking too much: "Ten measures of speech descended to the world; women took nine, men one." One rabbi believes that "a hundred women are equal to only one [male] witness." Women's earnings are the property of their husbands. Polygamy is permitted, though there is dispute as to how many wives a man may have; adultery is punishable by death.

Divorce can be arranged by mutual consent or by the husband's will, but not by the wife alone. Hillel maintains that a man may divorce his wife for "anything unseemly"; Akiba says he may divorce her simply because he finds another woman more attractive. A man may also divorce a wife who talks loudly, spends too much time talking to men, or appears in public with her head uncovered. Divorce procedures, however, are complicated, and the practice is frowned upon.

In pre-Islamic Arabia, women sometimes practice polyandry, taking as many as ten husbands or having children with several men (in some systems, the woman chooses the men; in other systems, her one legitimate husband chooses them for her). A Bedouin woman can divorce her husband simply by moving her tent.

Government, the Military, and the Law

In this century, Chinese heroine Hua Mu-lan takes her father's place in the army and fights bravely for twelve years disguised as a man.

410 Alaric's Visigoths sack Rome. Galla Placidia (c. 388–November 27, 450), daughter of Emperor Theodosius I, is taken hostage by the Visigoth leaders. She is forcibly married to Alaric's successor, Athaulf, in 414 and to Roman general Constantius (later, Emperor Constantius III) in 417, becoming regent of the Western

Empire in 425.

414 Byzantine princess St. Pulcheria (399–453) becomes regent for her brother Theodosius II. She will rule the Eastern Empire for thirty-three years, continuing her influence even after his majority and marriage and opposing the religious doctrines of Nestorianism and Monophysism. When Theodosius II dies in 450, she becomes Empress. For political reasons, she takes a husband, the general Marcian, but she is deeply religious, and the marriage is never consummated.

478 Royal consorts' clans in the Korean kingdom of Paekche have been quite powerful since 345.

493 Burgundian princess Clothilde (470–545) marries Clovis I, king of the Franks. Within a few years she manages to convert him to Christianity. After his death, she tries unsuccessfully to quell resulting civil conflict.

Literature and the Visual Arts

c. 464 Chinese poet Pao Ling-hui flourishes.

Late 5th–Early 6th centuries Chinese sisters Liu (wife of Wang Shu-ying; her first name is not known) and Liu Ling-hsien write poetry. Liu Ling-hsien's husband, Hsü Fei, dies in 524, and she writes a funerary prayer that is so good that Hsü Fei's father gives up trying to write one himself. She also writes some poems to her husband and possibly to her husband's mistress.

Performing Arts and Entertainment

Chinese poet and professional singer Meng Chu flourishes.

Business and Industry

450 Visigothic law legalizes public whipping and nostril slitting for prostitutes.

Science and Medicine

415 Greek-Egyptian mathematician and philosopher Hypatia (b. c. 370) is killed by a mob at the instigation of Cyril, patriarch of Alexandria, who considers her neo-Platonic principles threatening to Christianity. She is dragged from her chariot, and the flesh is stripped from her bones. A teacher of geometry, algebra, astronomy, and philosophy at the Neoplatonic School of Alexandria,

Hypatia wrote texts on mathematics and astronomy (including the thirteen-volume algebraic text *Arithmetica*, a commentary on Diophantine algebra, a commentary on Ptolemy's *Almagest*, and one of the last works on conic sections until the seventeenth century) and invented an astrolabe, a planisphere, a water-distilling machine, and the first instrument for measuring the specific gravity of liquids.

Education and Scholarship

Feb. 27, 425 Byzantine empress Eudoxia helps to establish Constantinople's first university.

Religion

In Central America, deities include the Water Goddess, Chalchiuhtlicue.

At about this time, Alexandrian prostitute St. Mary the Egyptian converts to Christianity and becomes a notable penitent.

404 Roman matron St. Paula (b. 347) dies. She was a close friend of St. Marcella (325–410), who founded a religious sisterhood and associated with St. Jerome but refused to be intellectually bullied by him.
   The founder of a pilgrims' hospice and women's and men's communal houses in Bethlehem, Paula learned Greek and Hebrew to further her religious studies. Paula became known for her self-mortification and her large gifts to charity, which worried her mentor, St. Jerome, and left her daughter St. Eustochium (c. 368–c. 419) in debt. Eustochium succeeds her mother as head of her Bethlehem women's community.

July 25, c. 408 Byzantine deaconess St. Olympias (b. c. 366), a follower of St. John Chrysostom, dies. A wealthy widow, she gave large sums to charity.

c. 412 Byzantine nun St. Euphrasia (b. c. 382) dies. She gave all her goods to the poor and subjected herself to a lifetime of penances and long fasts.

439 Roman aristocrat and laywoman St. Melania the Younger (b. c. 383), granddaughter of St. Melania the Elder (d. 410), dies. Married against her will, she depleted her fortune through charitable enterprises and the freeing of her slaves; when her family complained about her behavior to Emperor Honorius, he supported Melania. She established three women's religious communities in Africa and Palestine.

458 Convents have become such convenient places to dispose of "extra" daughters that Roman emperor Majorian must forbid the practice of forcing young women into the religious life.

c. 500 French saint Geneviève (b. c. 420), patroness of Paris, dies. She was noted for her dedication to prayer, her charitable works, and her pleas for leniency on behalf of captives to Frankish leaders Chilperic and King Clovis.

c. 500 The Buddhist age begins in China. The new religion's inclusion of women as almost-equals is a radical departure from current custom, but Chinese culture will shape Buddhism just as Buddhism shapes the culture; many passages from Buddhist scriptures are subtly altered to reflect the subordinate position of Chinese women.

501–600

General Status and Daily Life

In the Byzantine Empire, the Justinian Code (529–534) allows men to divorce their wives for adultery, silence about plots against the state, plotting or allowing others to plot against his life, unauthorized public appearances with other men, visits away from home (except to her parents) without consent, visits to public places such as the amphitheater without consent, and getting an abortion. A wife can divorce her husband for treason, plotting against her life, ordering her to commit adultery, falsely accusing her of adultery, and living with another woman.

Men cannot be accused of adultery for having sex with known prostitutes; slaves cannot sue for adultery at all; anyone who profits from or assists adultery can be tried as an adulterer. A father can kill both his daughter and her lover if he finds them engaged in a sexual act in his house or his son-in-law's house. Adultery is punishable by death for men, by restriction to a convent for women. A man may kill his wife's lover if he finds them together at home or in a tavern after warning her three times. Byzantine girls often marry very young and move into their husbands' houses, but they cannot legally consummate the marriage until the age of twelve.

A man guilty of rape is executed, and his belongings are confiscated and given to his victim. A free woman who becomes an actress may be repudiated by her husband. A guardian who rapes or seduces his female ward is banished, stripped of his property, and tried as a rapist. A guardian cannot marry his female ward once she is grown unless it is decreed in her father's will. A wife's property cannot be confiscated to pay her husband's debts. If a woman has an affair with a slave, she and the slave are put to death.

In Germany, a newly married woman receives a *morgengabe* (morning gift) from her husband on the day after their marriage. This is sometimes quite valuable; Chilperic I gives his bride Galswintha the towns of Limoges, Bordeaux, Cahors, Béarn, and Bigorre as her *morgengabe*.

The fine for raping a freeborn Frankish woman is 62.5 solidi, about the same fine that a man must pay for marrying someone other than his betrothed. Abducting and raping a woman authorize the man to marry her and pay her bride-price. If the abduction does not result in sexual intercourse, the abductor must pay a fine or be turned over to the parents, who are allowed to castrate him.

Salic law charges twice as much *wergild* (the fee for harming or killing a person, paid to the family to avoid a blood feud) for the murder of a fertile woman as for a man, but women are kept under perpetual male guardianship. There is no penalty for male adultery, but adulterous women are executed. A man may divorce his wife at any time. Penalties are prescribed for various sexual offenses: fifteen denarii for immodestly stroking a woman's hand, thirty-five for her upper arm, forty-five for her "unwilling bosom."

Bedouin girls can be buried alive at birth by paternal command. They are bought in marriage at the age of seven or eight.

516 Burgundian law gives a woman the right to be her children's guardian and to inherit her father's property if she has no brothers.

c. 550 Among the Maya, children have beads suspended between their eyes and boards strapped to their heads to achieve the desirable characteristics of crossed eyes and a flat, slanted forehead. Earlobes, lips, and one nostril are pierced for the wearing of decorative jewelry; the very rich sometimes have their teeth inlaid with stone. Women braid and ornament their hair. The body is sometimes enhanced with perfumes, body paints, tattoos, or decorative scars.

At five, a girl is given a red shell on a string, to be hung from her waist as a symbol of virginity. It is removed at twelve during a puberty rite. An old woman serves as godmother to the girls being initiated. On a day determined to be lucky, evil spirits are expelled from the site of the ritual, and the girl's head is covered with a white cloth. She is tapped nine times with a bone, and water is used to anoint her forehead, face, and the spaces between her fingers and toes. The cloth is then removed, and gifts are given to the old men who run the ceremony. The girl takes one puff from a pipe, and her mother removes the red shell from her waist. Feasting, drinking, and gifts of cloth for the guests follow.

Girls learn from their mothers to cook and to spin and weave cotton. They also learn proper behavior; a modest woman, passing a man, will lower her eyes, turn her back, and step out of his way. She should be a virgin at marriage. Nonvirgins are ridiculed and whipped, their wounds rubbed with pepper. The average woman will spend her life in a one-room, thatch-roofed house of stone or earth, equipped with pottery, gourd dishes, woven bags, baskets, stone tools, and equipment for grinding corn.

Men usually marry at about eighteen, women at fourteen or fifteen. There are extensive incest taboos, including a prohibition against marrying anyone with the same paternal family name. The marriages are arranged by the parents, usually through a matchmaker who serves as an agent for the groom and helps to negotiate the amount of the dowry. Once married, the wife should not eat, drink, or have long conversations with her husband; she must never laugh at him and must not dance with him except at certain festivals. Custom requires that the new husband spend three to six years living with his in-laws and working for his wife's father. Divorce can be obtained by a simple declaration on the part of either husband or wife, and there is no bar to remarriage after divorce or widowhood. Marriages after the first, however, are less elaborate; the couple simply moves in together and holds a feast for friends.

Rich men may be polygynous, and many choose to keep slaves as concubines, but most marriages are monogamous. Mayan women are reputed to be extremely jealous and can be violent if they suspect infidelity. Of course, penalties for their own lapses are severe; in some cases, the offended husband can kill his wife's lover by dropping a large stone on his head. Rape is punishable by death.

597 King Ethelbert of Kent dictates the fines to be paid to a man for sexual misconduct with a woman in his protection, including thirty shillings for a free woman, six shillings for a farmer's maid, and twelve shillings for a nobleman's maid. Divorce by mutual consent is legal. When a man dies, his widow inherits half his property if she has borne him living children.

Government, the Military, and the Law

525 Byzantine emperor Justinian passes a special law permitting him to marry the lowborn dancer and mime Theodora (497–June 28, 548). At his accession in 527, she becomes empress, sitting in his council and effectively co-ruling the Empire, though she is careful always to apologize for speaking of affairs of state. She supports building projects, engages in diplomacy, purchases the freedom of unwilling prostitutes, and enacts laws giving women greater rights in divorce, inheritance, and dowry matters.

In 532, during Constantinople's Nika Revolts, Theodora shames Justinian into holding onto his throne, though his first impulse is to flee to safety. She says proudly, "If I had no safety left but in flight, I still would not flee. Those who have worn the crown should never survive its loss. . . . Caesar, if you wish to flee,

well and good, you have the money, the ships are ready, the sea is clear. But I shall stay. I love the proverb: [Imperial] Purple is the best winding sheet."

Aug. 30, 526 Italian Ostrogoth Amalasuntha, said to have "wisdom and regard for justice in the highest degree," becomes regent for her ten-year-old son Athalaric. After Athalaric's death, she is forced to marry her cousin Theodahad, who orders her strangled on April 30, 535.

567 Merovingian king Chilperic has his wife Galswintha strangled to please his concubine Fredegund (d. 597). Frankish king Sigebert, husband of Galswintha's sister Brunhilda, declares war on Chilperic, but Fredegund has him assassinated and Brunhilda captured. Brunhilda, however, escapes and becomes an able regent for her son Childebert II. The enmity between Fredegund and Brunhilda will result in nearly forty years of war.

In 584, Chilperic is murdered, possibly by Brunhilda's agent. Fredegund becomes regent for their son and conspires unsuccessfully to kill Brunhilda. According to one source, when her would-be assassin returns to report his failure, she has his hands and feet cut off. However, in 614 Brunhilda is betrayed to Fredegund's son Lothair II, who tortures her for three days and has her dragged to death by a horse.

590 Chinese warrior Lady Feng raises a force to support the Imperial army. Dressed as a soldier, she travels with the troops but does not command them.

593 Suiko (d. 628) becomes the first known Japanese empress in her own right. She is a pawn of the strong male reformer Shotoku Taishi.

Literature and the Visual Arts

A Chinese author known as the Fairy of Wuhsing, probably an entertainer of some kind, writes love poetry to an official named Hsieh Lan.

c. 540 Chinese poet Shen Man-yüan flourishes.

Late 6th century Iraqi poet Al-Khirniq writes Arabic elegies for her murdered husband Bishr ibn 'Amr.

Religion

At the beginning of this century, Rome's Christian emperors suppress all goddess worship and close the temples.

Byzantine empress Theodora builds a home for reformed prostitutes; some inmates are so bored that they kill themselves. She adopts the Monophysite theology abhorrent to the papacy and encourages tolerance for heretics.

Korean women are often priestesses; in fact, the Korean word *shamman*, or religious leader, has always been associated only with women and will remain so until the next century.

c. 6th century Lady Sa is the first female convert to Buddhism in the Korean kingdom of Silla.

c. 523 Irish abbess and saint Brigid (b. c. 450), sometimes called "the Mary of the Gael," dies. Sold into slavery in childhood, she converted her master to Christianity, was set free by the king of Ulster for her piety, and founded the first women's religious community in Ireland.

543 Italian maiden St. Scholastica (b. c. 480), sister of St. Benedict and founder (c. 530) of a convent near Monte Cassino, dies.

c. 550 In Maya religion, young unmarried women serve the temples and care for sacred fires. Ix Chel is the goddess of childbirth, and women who die in childbirth go (like warriors slain in battle, sacrificial victims, priests, and suicides by hanging) to eternal paradise.

587 Frankish queen St. Radegund (b. 518) dies. Forced at about the age of twenty to marry King Lothair I, she left him after he killed her brother and turned to religion, building the Holy Cross abbey at Poitiers (557) and forcing an archbishop to make her a church deacon.

589–590 Princesses Clotild and Basina, residents at the Convent of the Holy Cross at Poitiers, become angry at Abbess Leubovera, who treats them "as though we were not kings' daughters but the offsprings of low serving-women." Clotild gets forty nuns to rebel and leave the convent in protest. She also complains to civil and religious authorities and hires "a gang of thieves, slayers of men, adulterers, and criminals of all kinds." A group of church leaders, trying to excommunicate the rebels, is attacked by this hired band, which then seizes nearby church lands.

The ruffians attack Leubovera's followers; they seize Leubovera and are given orders to kill her if any rescue attempt is made. However, Leubovera is rescued, and more armed conflict ensues. Clotild and her ally Basina argue and develop separate factions; the revolt is put down at last, and Clotild and Basina are censured, but due to intervention by their powerful friends and relatives, they are fully restored to the church within a few months.

589 Queen Theodelinda helps to convert the Lombards to Christianity.

594 Empress Suiko encourages the spread of Buddhism in Japan with her order to build Buddhist temples throughout the nation.

594 Arab prophet Muhammad, twenty-five, marries the forty-year-old Khadija (c. 564–619), a wealthy widow and his employer. She will encourage him to act upon his religious visions and will remain his only wife until her death twenty-six years later. She is the mother of Fatima (606–632), who will found the Fatimid dynasty of caliphs.

601–700

General Status and Daily Life

England begins 1,000 years of publicly punishing women as "scolds."

One item in the midwife's apparatus for a Chinese labor bed is a box of ashes for smothering unwanted girl babies.

Islam's Koran allows women to attend services at the mosque, to hold jobs, to control money, and to inherit and bequeath property. It bans female infanticide. A woman must consent to her own marriage, does not need her parents' consent to marry, and cannot be willed as property to another man. The groom, not the bride, provides the dowry, and a wife can divorce her husband by returning the dowry to him. Reconciliation is encouraged in cases of marital strife, and although a man may divorce his wife by verbally rejecting her three times, these declarations must be made at one-month intervals, to give him time to consider his decision. Muhammad urges Muslims to respect their mothers.

However, the Koran calls menstruating women "a pollution" and forbids them to have sex. A daughter inherits half as much as a son, cannot rule, and is encouraged to stay at home. Men are allowed up to four wives and can divorce their wives for almost any reason. A woman is obliged to obey her husband lest he "banish her to a bed apart, and scourge her." The woman who pleases her husband goes to paradise after she dies.

614 Merovingian king Lothair II orders that a woman may not be married against her will. Of course, not many women—or men—defy their parents, who typically arrange all marriages.

Government, the Military, and the Law

c. 7th-8th centuries The Celtic epic *Táin Bó Cualinge* (*The Cattle Raid of Cúchulainn*) is recorded. One of the dominant characters is Queen Medb (Maeve) of Cruchan, a beautiful, powerful, wealthy warrior woman. Women are active in Irish armies until the seventh century, when they are evicted from the military. Instead of warriors, they will be victims and prizes, like the Ulster ladies who, conquered by Cúchulainn, bare their chests and raise their skirts in defeat "so as to expose their secret places."

c. 7th-8th centuries Totonac women near Veracruz, Mexico, are depicted as shield-bearing warriors with large headdresses.

624 Arabian leader and priestess Hind al Hunnud leads her tribe, the Quraish, against Muhammad in the Battle of Badr. Her father, uncle, and brother are killed, but she continues a guerrilla campaign after the Islamic conquest. In 625, she is one of fifteen women who accompany troops to a battle near Medina, inspiring the army with their songs. She exults over the body of Hamza, who killed her father, chews Hamza's liver, and makes jewelry from his skin and nails.

628–632 Persia has twelve rulers, including two women, Puran and Azarmidokht.

632 Because no male heirs are available in the main line of inheritance, Queen Sondok becomes the sole ruler of the Korean kingdom of Silla. She rules until 647, fighting the neighboring kingdom of Paekche, suppressing rebellion, sending students to be educated in China, and presiding over the completion of Buddhist temples and Asia's oldest observatory. She is revered for her ability to anticipate events. Sondok's successor is her cousin Chindok, who will rule until 654, strengthening royal authority and establishing closer ties to T'ang China.

639–642 In the Muslim conquest of Egypt, Muhammad is assisted by warrior women such as Nassiba bint Kaab and Om Solayem bint Malhan.

649 Chinese emperor T'ai Tsung dies, and, according to tradition, all of his concubines are sent to a convent. However, one of them, Wu Chao (b. 625), forms a liaison with T'ai Tsung's successor, Kao Tsung, who flaunts tradition by bringing her back. Within a few years, she disposes of Kao Tsung's childless wife and amasses significant political power, removing all who oppose her. When Kao Tsung dies in 683, she deposes and exiles his successor, Chung, replacing him with her more compliant second son Jui.

In 690, she formally seizes power, declaring herself "Holy and Divine Emperor." Her reign is marked by sustained peace, ambitious building projects, bureaucratic reforms, and partronage of the arts. She conquers Korea, negotiates with Tibet and Turkey, makes Buddhism the state religion, and makes the period of mourning equal for mothers and fathers.

Mid-7th century The Taika reforms bar women from government posts in Japan.

656 Aishah (613–678), favorite wife of Muhammad, leads troops in a rebellion against the Caliph Ali at the Battle of the Camel. She loses and is returned to her home in Medina. Aishah married Muhammad when she was only ten; after his death she became a powerful political, military, and theological leader and was one of the originators of Sunni Islam.

680 Bathild (b. c. 630), English-born queen of the Franks, dies. In 641, she was captured by pirates, sold as a slave, and eventually married to the Frankish king Clovis II. Upon Clovis's death in 657, she became regent for their son Lothair III and worked to abolish the slave trade. She also founded the Abbey of Corbie and the convent at Chelles, to which she was forced to retire when the nobles removed her from the regency in 665.

686–697 Empress Jito rules Japan.

698 Berber warrior al-Kahina ("the Diviner") dies in battle in North Africa. She led a successful scorched-earth campaign against Byzantine and Arab armies.

Literature and the Visual Arts

The seventh century is notable for the work of Arab female poets, especially Al-Khansa (b. 575). A favorite poet of Muhammad, she is especially adept at elegies, which she writes in memory of her brothers, killed in battle. In the latter part of the century, Iraqi poet Laila Akhyaliyya writes poems to her lover, the leader of a band of thieves.

Irish poet Liadan flourishes.

c. 659 Indian queen Vidya writes poetry in Sanskrit. She is followed by several Indian women poets whose work is harder to date, including Sila, Mahodahi, and Vallana.

Activism

Asma, a poet living in Medina at the same time as Muhammad, is killed by one of his followers for writing verses that criticize the Prophet. She is stabbed through the chest with a sword with such force that she is pinned to her bed.

Religion

In India, the Hindu sect known as Tantrism is taking shape. Tantrism draws on ancient worship of mother goddesses, and many of its rituals focus on *shakti* (female spiritual power).

England develops the institution of the double monastery, a community with both male and female members, run by a female superior.

616 Saxon queen Bertha, also sometimes called Adilberga, dies. The Frankish wife of King Ethelbert of Kent, she brought a Christian priest to England with her upon her marriage and managed to convince her husband to convert. Her efforts to convert the Saxons were aided by Pope Gregory and St. Augustine.

Mid-7th century St. Salaberga of Laon, France, founds seven churches.

659 French abbess St. Gertrude of Nivelles (b. 626) dies. She became abbess of a monastery established by her mother, Itta, and was succeeded by her niece; her sister was St. Begga (d. 693).

c. 676 English abbess St. Ethelburga (Æthelburh) of Barking dies. The abbess of Barking in Essex, she was praised for her piety by the Venerable Bede.

679 English abbess St. Etheldreda (also known as Audrey, b. c. 630) dies. The daughter of an East Anglian king, she married twice but maintained her virginity, a policy that annoyed her second husband greatly. He released her from her marriage vows, and she became a nun, establishing a monastery at Ely. Held in great reverence in her own time and afterward, she had a hymn to her written by Bede, and the site of her community at Ely drew many pilgrimages. She was succeeded as abbess by her sister St. Sexburga; another sister, St. Ethelburga (Edelburge, Aubierge, d. 665), became abbess of Faremoutiers-en-Brie.

680 English abbess St. Hilda of Whitby dies. In 649 she became abbess of a convent at Hartlepool, and in 657 she established and ran a double monastery at Whitby, where she encouraged scholarship. She supported the Celtic party against the Roman party in disputes over religious practice and served as an adviser to both rulers and common people. She influenced the careers of many prominent figures of the time, including a saint, five bishops, and the poet Caedmon.

684 Merovingian noblewoman Aldegund dies. As a young woman, she refused all offers of marriage until her parents stopped trying to find her a husband. She founded a convent at Maubeuge and had twelve religious visions in which sacred relationships are likened to human passions. Her family included eight saints: her parents, Walbert and Bertilia; her brother-in-law; her sister, St. Waudru (Waldetrudis, d. c. 688), who founded a convent; and Waudru's four children.

c. 700 English abbess St. Mildred dies. She led the convent at Minster in Thanet founded by her mother, the Kentish princess Ermenburga. Her sister Mildburga was also a saint, and her mother, sister Mildgytha, and aunt Ermengytha led lives of exceptional holiness as well.

c. 700 English abbess St. Werburgh, daughter of King Wulfhere and St. Ermenilda, dies. Her burial site will be a popular destination for pilgrimages until destroyed by Henry VIII in the mid-sixteenth century.

701–800

General Status and Daily Life

European kitchens begin to feature turnspits, an innovation that will last for over 1,000 years.

Lombard law bans marriage of girls younger than twelve. Lombards sometimes give female slaves as gifts to the Catholic church.

Due to high rates of death in childbirth, Merovingian women in Normandy live shorter lives than men, dying on average at about thirty or forty. Female hermits, whose diet is better and who do not have to worry as much about childbearing, live to about 67.

The Franks impose fines for providing potions that result in sterility.

In Islamic societies, most women marry by age twelve, with the match arranged by the parents. The groom provides a dowry, which is the bride's to keep throughout the marriage and after the divorce, if any. If she is found to be unsatisfactory after a brief examination of her face on the wedding night, he may send her back to her parents immediately.

Female slavery is common in Morocco.

Mid-8th century Islamic women begin to be veiled and secluded in purdah.

785 Saxon law makes a widow the ward of her dead husband's male relatives.

Government, the Military, and the Law

Forceful Saxon queen Cynethryth, wife of King Offa II of Mercia, is the only Queen Consort in English history to issue her own coinage.

705 Empress Wu Chao, China's only female ruler in her own right, is deposed and dies. She reduced government expenditures but increased corruption and despotism. Legends were told of her autocratic nature; one claimed that she commanded all the flowers of her garden to bloom in the dead of winter. All obeyed but the peony, and she was so angry at its disobedience that she banished it to a remote province. Her successors, Emperors Zhongzong and Ruizong, will be dominated until 712 by two powerful women, Empress Wei and the Taiping Princess.

724 Caliph Yezid II dies of grief after the accidental choking death of his beloved slave girl Habiba. In 717, after becoming caliph, he was asked by his wife if there was anything left for him to desire. He replied, "Habiba." His wife summoned the girl, gave her to Yezid, and retired forever to the harem.

756 Chinese concubine Yang Guifei dies, strangled by the emperor's chief eunuch at the behest of the mutinous imperial bodyguards. The concubine of Emperor Ming Huang's eighteenth son, she was loved by both Emperor Xuanzong and his Tatar courtier An Lu-shan, who rebelled against the emperor in 753. Grief-stricken, the emperor (a grandson of Wu Chao) abdicates.

758 Japanese empress Koken, ruler since 749 and a promoter of the cult of filial piety, abdicates. She will return to power, renamed Shotuku, from 764 to 770.

765–780 Lady Manwol of the Korean kingdom of Silla serves as regent for her son King Hyegong.

780 Byzantine empress Irene become regent for her son Constantine VI. She rules ably, making peace with the Ottoman Caliph al-Mahdi, ending the unpopular iconoclastic policies of her predecessors, and showing generosity to monks, who have suffered persecution and robbery at the hands of previous emperors. When Constantine comes of age in 790, Irene does not yield power to him, so he deposes and exiles her. However, he recalls her in 792 and makes her his co-ruler. In 797 she rebels against Constantine and has him blinded. She becomes the first woman to rule the Byzantine Empire in her own right and takes the title "basileus" (king). She reduces taxes, sponsors public works, and distributes charity, becoming popular with the common people.

786 Ottoman Caliph al-Hadi is smothered by his mother, Arabian queen Al-Khaizuran (d. 790), to make way for her younger son, Harun al-Rashid. Al-Khaizuran was sold as a slave girl to al-Mahdi and freed when he became caliph of Baghdad. She became a powerful political figure, especially after his death.

Literature and the Visual Arts

Several Asian poets flourish during this time period, including the Chinese courtesan Chao Luan-luan and the Japanese noblewomen Lady Otomo of Sakanone and Lady Kasa. Poems by women are also included in a famous Japanese anthology, the *Man'yoshu*.

In the Ottoman Empire, Scheherazade allegedly saves her life with words, keeping her murderous husband at bay with her tales of *One Thousand and One Nights*.

701 Japanese poet and princess Oku (b. 661) dies.

Athletics and Exploration

721 Princess Libousa founds the city of Prague.

Business and Industry

Many Christian women, starting for the Holy Land as pilgrims, become prostitutes on the way. Prostitution is still the most lucrative occupation for ordinary women.

Education and Scholarship

Chinese women of the T'ang dynasty (618–907) learn music and dancing. Many write poetry.

Religion

712 Iraqi mystic and poet Rabia al-Adawiyya (d. 801) is born. Celibate and ascetic, she will be freed from slavery for her piety and devote herself to charitable works. She writes in Arabic of the futility of hatred ("My love for God leaves me no room for hating Satan") and of the satisfactions of faith ("O God! Give to Thine enemies whatever Thou hast assigned to me of this world's goods, and to Thy friends whatever Thou hast assigned to me in the life to come; for Thou Thyself art sufficient for me"). She is associated with many miracles; her sect, Sufism, gives fairly equal opportunities to men and women.

c. 735 English abbess St. Frideswide, patron saint of the city and university of Oxford, and founder of a convent in Oxford, dies.

752 Japanese empress Koken publicly proclaims her devotion to Buddhism.

780 English abbess St. Lioba (b. c. 700) dies. She was sent to Germany as the leader of thirty nuns to assist St. Boniface of Credition in spreading the faith and building religious communities; she became an adviser to bishops and other leaders and served as abbess of the highly successful convent of Tauberbischofsheim. Among the other nuns in St. Boniface's influential mission were St. Walburga (d. 779?) and her sister St. Winebald (d. 761). When Winebald died, Walburga became the new head of the double monastery at Heidenheim; after her own death, Walburga's corpse was moved to Eichstätt on May 1, thereafter known in Germany as Walpurgisnacht.

787 Byzantine Empress Irene calls the Second Council of Nicaea to settle a divisive dispute over the worship of sacred images, or icons, establishing relative peace in the church once more. The convocation of 350 bishops supports icon worship.

801–900

General Status and Daily Life

Until the eleventh century, families in Japan are matrilocal; the husband moves in with his wife's family or has a separate household and visits his wife periodically. The upper classes become patrilocal first, and the peasants follow suit centuries later.

c. 900 The *Boke of Saxon Leechdoms* offers this rather painful and odorous contraceptive advice: "Take a fresh horses turd, lay it in hot gledes [coals], make it reek strongly between the thighs up under the raiment, that the woman may sweat much."

Government, the Military, and the Law

802 Influential West Saxon queen Eadburgh accidentally kills her husband when he drinks the poison she prepared for one of his enemies. She becomes unpopular and flees to Charlemagne, who makes her an abbess until she is cast out of the convent for "scandalous behavior."

802 Byzantine empress Irene (b. c. 753), the first woman to rule the empire in her own right, is deposed and exiled. Popular with the people and a just ruler, she is hated by the military and by the iconoclasts, who disapprove of her tolerant religious policies. She is banished to Lesbos and becomes a seamstress, dying penniless in 803.

803 Abbasa, sister of Caliph Harun al-Rashid, is executed at his command. She fell in love with a Persian, Jafar; Harun gave them permission to marry as long as they met only in his presence, lest Abbasa's pure Arabian blood be mingled with a Persian's. When she disobeys and bears Jafar two sons, Harun kills her and her sons.

831 Arabian queen Zubaidah, wife of Harun al-Rashid, dies. A patron of poets and musicians, she commissioned gardens in Baghdad, improved trade routes, and mediated a peaceful settlement of the civil conflict following Harun al-Rashid's death.

833 Frankish king Louis the Pious is overthrown by his sons; his second wife and co-ruler, Judith (d. 840), mother of their rival half-brother Charles the Bald, is jailed and her hair shorn. Judith appeals to the nobility and the clergy to oppose the rebels and is returned to her husband after two of his sons repent.

842 Byzantine empress Theodora, widow of Emperor Theophilus, becomes regent for her son Michael III, ruling until 856 and ending the iconoclastic persecutions of her husband.

862 Lothaire II of Lorraine divorces Queen Theutberga and marries his mistress, Waldrada, by bribing church officials. Theutberga appeals to Pope Nicholas I, who excommunicates the corrupt prelates and orders Lothaire to return to his lawful wife.

887 Chinsong becomes queen of the Korean kingdom of Silla. She is the sister of the previous ruler, King Chonggang. She will rule until 897 and will be accused of incompetence and promiscuity. Her reign is a difficult one, marked by an almost empty treasury, a series of tax revolts, and a strong challenge for power from a wealthy landlord.

891 Frankish queen Engelberge rules jointly with her husband Louis II, running the court at Ravenna, negotiating with nobles and the pope, and helping to conduct military campaigns.

Literature and the Visual Arts

At some point during the T'ang dynasty, which lasts from the seventh to the tenth centuries, Chinese sculptor Miss Yan carves a complex *Auspicious Lotus Mountain* out of sandalwood. She presents it to the emperor and is awarded gold, silk, and the title "Ingenious Lady."

831 Chinese poet Hsüeh T'ao (b. 768) dies. A "singing girl" at the imperial court, she was noted for her beauty and talent and was one of the two most important women poets of the T'ang Dynasty (the other being Yü Hsüan-chi). She wrote about 500 poems.

c. 840 Byzantine Greek poet Kasia, founder of a convent, writes "Mary Magdalene," later a part of the Holy Week services of the Eastern Orthodox church.

868 Chinese poet, courtesan, concubine, and Taoist nun Yü Hsüan-chi (b. c. 843) is executed (probably unjustly) for beating her maid to death. Her poems are highly symbolic yet clear and full of intense emotion.

Nov. 841–843 Dhouda, a woman in southern France, composes a book of advice for her teenage son; it is the only prose work by a ninth-century European woman that will survive to the twentieth century.

880 Japanese poet Ono no Komachi (b. 834) dies. The beautiful daughter of the lord of Dewa, she wrote erotic poetry and died a beggar.

Business and Industry

In China, courtesans cater to T'ang officials.

801 Charlemagne outlaws prostitution.

Education and Scholarship

Frankish emperor Charlemagne's daughter Gisela is noted for her intellectual attainments and her pleasure in studying "the stars in the stillness of the night."

Religion

851 Spanish martyrs Flora and Mary are beheaded in Córdoba. Flora was denounced as a Christian by her Muslim brother, whipped, and released; she and Mary then went to the magistrate and gave themselves up again. They were jailed, threatened with being sold into prostitution, and finally executed.

852 Spanish Christians Natalia and Liliosa, with their husbands, profess their faith during a persecution of Christians by the Muslim Emir Abd ar-Rahman II. They appear unveiled in public and are arrested and beheaded.

853 Spanish martyr Columba of Córdoba dies, beheaded for declaring to the Moorish magistrate that Muhammad was a false prophet. Her body is thrown into the Guadalquivir River.

855 According to legend, a female cleric who has been masquerading as a man becomes pope upon the death of Leo IV. She is allegedly discovered to be a woman in 858 when she gives birth during a church procession and is immediately stoned to death. She will be known to eight centuries of church tradition as "Pope Joan."

901–1000

General Status and Daily Life

Anglo-Saxon law permits seven-year trial marriage; Scottish law permits one-year trial marriage. The woman keeps her own name and family affiliations until the union is formalized.

According to Saxon law, a man who commits adultery must pay a fine to the wronged husband and buy him a new wife. A Saxon man may sell his wife and children as slaves.

Foot-binding begins at the Chinese court. Feet are bound from the age of five or eight to the age of thirteen or fifteen, with the goal of forming a stump three inches long. The foot does not stop growing, even when tightly bound in cloth, so the four small toes are made to curl under the foot, while the bones in the arches are bent upward and eventually broken. The painful feet are numbed by propping them on a board or placing them under someone else's body. Side effects include permanent circulatory problems, gangrene, cutting of the undersides of the feet by the small toenails, an unpleasant odor, and atrophy of the leg muscles. Standing on bound feet is painful; walking is difficult; running is impossible. Over the next several centuries, the procedure will be passed down through the classes until it is rare indeed to see even a servant or farm woman without bound feet. Only ethnic minorities will refuse to bind women's feet.

902 Japanese women pluck out their eyebrows and draw new, thinner ones higher than the natural eyebrow line. They whiten their faces with powder and blacken their teeth.

Government, the Military, and the Law

918 Korean noblewoman Lady Yu convinces her husband to participate in a coup d'état that will make him the first king of the Koryo dynasty. She hides herself while the plotters discuss their plan with him, then emerges and says, "It is an ancient tradition to raise a banner of revolt against a tyrant. Even I, a mere woman, cannot help being aroused by the arguments made by these generals. How can you, a great military leader, hesitate?" She fixes his wavering resolve by fetching his armor on the spot.

June 918 Queen Aethelflaed (b. c. 870), known as the "Lady of the Mercians," dies. Ruler of Mercia after her husband's death in 911, she constructed buildings and fortifications and improved the military. She attacked the Danes, conquering Derby and Leicester, uniting much of England. Aethelflaed refused to have intercourse with her husband again after one experience with the pain of childbirth.

945 Russian princess Olga (860–969), widow of Prince Igor I, becomes regent and begins executing hundreds in retaliation for her husband's murder, scalding the chief conspirators to death. She will remain regent until 964, ruling ruthlessly and later devoting herself so completely to religion that she is made the first Russian saint of the Orthodox church. She will help convert her grandson Vladimir I to Christianity, resulting in the conversion of his subjects as well.

951 In the turmoil over the Italian succession after the death King Lothair, his widow, Adelaide (c. 931–999), is imprisoned. King Otto I of Germany rescues and marries her. In 962, when Otto is crowned emperor, she is crowned empress. After Otto's death in 973, Adelaide remains powerful for twenty years, guiding the reigns of her son and grandson, Otto II and Otto III.

963 Byzantine emperor Romanus II dies, perhaps with a little nudge from his wife Theophano, who secures the throne for her lover, Nicephorus. In 969, she takes a new lover, John Tzimisces, and helps him assassinate Nicephorus and seize the throne. He rewards her with repudiation and banishment.

975-981 Honae, wife of Korean king Kyongjong, helps him rule.

Mar. 18, 978 The stepmother of Britain's king Edward the Martyr murders him so that her own son, Ethelred, may rule. She offers him a cup, then stabs him with a dagger.

983 Otto II dies; his widow, Theophano (d. 991), titles herself "imperator augustus" and defends the crown for her son against various would-be usurpers, with help from her mother-in-law, Empress Adelaide.

Literature and the Visual Arts

10th–11th centuries Japanese poet Izumi Shikibu, the mistress of two princes, writes several poems in an epistolary diary to and from her lover.

c. 10th century Indian poet Andal, a priest's daughter, writes devotional poetry to Krishna.

10th century In Norway, an unknown woman composes the *Wise Woman's Prophecy*, an epic that relates the history of the world and makes predictions for the future.

Early 10th century Chinese empress Jin Feishan is an accomplished painter. Chinese artist Huang Chonggu excels in the "Four Accomplishments": zither playing, chess, calligraphy, and painting.

c. 925 Chinese artist Lady Li, a captive taken in war, creates the major genre of monochrome ink bamboo painting. This art form, which she was inspired to create by seeing the shadows of bamboo on a moonlit night, consoles her in her captivity.

932 Irish poet Lady Uallach dies.

938? Japanese poet Lady Ise (b. 875?) dies. A lady-in-waiting to an imperial consort, she bore a son to Emperor Uda and daughter to Uda's son Prince Atsuyoshi. She is considered one of the Thirty-Six Poetic Geniuses of Japan. She was a competitor in the Teiji-in poetry match of 913 and had 173 of her poems included in imperial anthologies.

Mid-10th century Chinese artist Miss Geng, a Taoist adept, alchemist, conjurer of spirits, painter, calligrapher, and poet, plies her various trades at the palace in Nanking. Another artist of the same period, Miss Tong, paints religious figures and studies with court artist Wang Qihan. Her painting *Six Recluses* is included in an imperial collection.

961 The palace of al-Zahra is completed southwest of Córdoba, Spain. It is named for the woman who envisioned it and suggested its construction: Zahra, favorite wife of Caliph Adb-er-Rahman III.

970 Ende, a medieval artist, completes the first known manuscript illumination by a woman.

972 German author Hroswitha of Gandersheim (b. c. 935) dies. A Benedictine nun, she wrote six Latin comedies, works on mathematics, narrative poems, hagiography, verse history, and a life of the Virgin Mary, making her the first German poet, the first German woman author, and the first modern European playwright. Her plays deal with virgin martyrs, torture, converted prostitutes, and the lives of the saints and will remain virtually unknown until 1500, but, once discovered, her *Lapse and Conversion of Theophilus* will serve as the inspiration for *Faust*.

Business and Industry

In the Middle Ages in Tibet, Nicaragua, Melanesia, Burma, Congo, Cameroon, and Nigeria, women run all or most of the trade and control the marketplaces.

Religion

Minor Chinese deity Tian Hou (Ma Zu) is worshiped as a patroness of fishermen, sailors, and sea traders on the coast of Fujian Province. She is based on "Aunt Lin," a local woman who looked after mariners. Tian Hou will later become a major deity and be awarded the title "Empress of Heaven."

904 Roman noblewoman Marozia, daughter of a papal official, gets her lover installed as Pope Sergius III. In 914, her mother, Theodora, secures the election of Pope John X. The family's influence continues for decades; In 931, after having John X thrown into prison, Marozia gets the papal seat for John XI, allegedly her son by Pope Sergius III. In 955, her grandson (through her son Alberic) will become Pope John XII.

968 German queen St. Matilda (b. c. 895) dies. Wife of King Henry I and mother of King Otto I and St. Bruno, she was mistreated both by Otto and by her favorite son, Henry, who complained that she gave too much to charity.

984 English nun St. Edith (Eadgyth) of Wilton (b. 961?) dies. An illegitimate daughter of King Edgar and a woman named Wulfrida, she was raised in a convent and refused to become an abbess, preferring a life of humble obedience.

988 Vladimir I of Russia converts his realm to Christianity so that he may marry Anna, sister of the Byzantine emperor Basil II, whose dowry is the fertile Crimea. Anna's influence opens Russia to Byzantine culture.

1001–1100

General Status and Daily Life

In Europe, the *droit de seigneur* or *ius primae noctis* allows a feudal lord to deflower any of his female serfs, though usually her father is permitted to pay a fine to exempt his daughter from this institutionalized rape. Upper-class women sometimes have their marital fidelity ensured by chastity belts. These metal barriers cover the genitalia, leaving only a small opening for excretion and menstruation. In England, forced marriage and the sale of women are so common that the invader Cnut of Denmark is forced to pass laws against these practices.

Oddly enough, women have a relatively favorable position in one European society usually stereotyped as barbarous and cruel. Viking society is hardly a paradise for women—polygyny does exist among the wealthier men, and women are perpetually under the thumb of husband or father, but Viking women have a certain measure of protection in a society that values family ties above all else. An offense against a woman is likely to be avenged in blood by her relatives.

In Viking society, a woman's parents find her a husband, who usually pays for the privilege of marrying her; the prospective bride may reject her parents' candidate, but she may not find one of her own. If she does marry against the will of her family, her husband becomes an outlaw, subject to execution by the woman's relatives. A Viking man may divorce his wife at any time, but if he does so without good cause, he is likely to be killed by her family. Women's opinions are often valued, and they are not secluded in women's quarters within the house. A woman is entitled to one-third of her husband's belongings and to one-half of them after twenty years of marriage.

During this period, Japanese women blacken their teeth, wear face powder and lipstick, and shave off their eyebrows.

Early 11th century An Anglo-Saxon marriage contract explains that the groom will give his bride "a pound's weight of gold," two tracts of land, "30 oxen and 20 cows, and 10 horses and 10 slaves."

Early 11th century When a woman gives birth in Japan, all her attendants wear white, and all the furnishings are draped with white as well.

1016 England's penalty for adultery is exile for men and the severing of nose and ears for women.

Government, the Military, and the Law

Moroccan Queen Zineb An Nefzouia is influential.

1008 The Toltec teritory of Topiltzin is defended by women warriors as well as by men.

1028 Byzantine noblewoman Zoë (d. 1050) becomes empress, ruling with her sister Theodora (d. 1056) during the nominal reigns of four emperors, three of them Zoë's husbands. The sisters attack corruption, confiscating embezzled funds and temporarily ending the sale of offices. When Zoë dies, Theodora retires to a convent, returning to rule after the death of Constantine IX in 1055.

1035 Saxon noblewoman Aelgifu (c. 1010-c. 1040), mistress of Cnut of Denmark and regent of Norway on behalf of her son Sweyn, is deposed after the cruelty of her rule enrages the people. She will return to a position of power in 1037, when she gets the English throne for her other son, Harold Harefoot.

1046 Italian countess Matilda of Tuscany (also known as Matilda of Canossa, d. July 15, 1115) is born. At age six, she inherits lands in the Apennines and Alps. Better educated than most European nobles of her day, Matilda learns martial skills as well as embroidery, becoming adept with axe, sword, spear, and pike; she also learns German, French, Italian, and Latin. She will be a successful military commander and a lifelong defender of the papacy, leading her troops into battle with the cry, "For St. Peter and Matilda!"

1052 Yemeni queen Arwa (d. 1137), whose husband, Sultan Al-Mukarram, turned most of his duties and power over to her, is born. Noted for her encouragement of agriculture and trade, she will also avenge her father-in-law's murder and build a new capital at Jiblah. When Al-Mukarram dies in 1091, she will marry his successor, Saba, to maintain her power.

1066 While William the Conqueror attacks England, his wife Matilda rules his duchy of Normandy. Her daughter Adela will rule the territory after William's death, even though Adela's husband, Stephen, as a man, is the official heir.

1067 Byzantine empress Eudocia becomes regent, ruling for four years. She marries and crowns Romanus IV, only to depose, jail, and blind him when he proves an incompetent general.

1083–1094 Lady Yi (Queen Sasuk), wife of Korean king Sonjong, helps him rule.

1084 Yemeni queen Arma (b. 1028), a patron of the arts and a powerful political figure, dies.

1090 Lombard princess Sichelgaita dies. The wife of a mercenary, she often fought at her husband's side. At one skirmish she rallied her fleeing troops, calling, "How far will ye flee? Stand, and quit you like men!"

1099–1102 Jimena, widow of Spanish warrior El Cid, rules the city of Valencia.

Literature and the Visual Arts

c. 11th century Chinese aristocrat and painter Cao Zhongwan has five of her paintings in an imperial palace collection: *The Peach Blossom Stream, Willow Bank,*

The Smartweed Embankment, Geese in the Snow, and *Herding Sheep.* Critics admire her for her ambitious and difficult subject matter.

In the tenth and eleventh centuries, European embroiderers are often upper-class women, like Queen Elgiva, wife of English king Edward the Confessor, and Queen Gisela (d. 1031), embroiderer of Hungary's coronation robe. They are usually highly regarded; in the eleventh century, the abbey of Ely gives embroiderer Ealdswith an entire village in which to carry on her trade. Women in China also embroider, sometimes copying the images found in paintings. The work is delicate, "using . . . needles as thin as hair."

China has several female painters, most of whom are instructed by male relatives. They include the younger sister of Li Chang, the third daughter of master bamboo painter Wen Tong, and Miss Xie, who is praised for taking care of her family obligations first and only then turning to the study of ancient texts and the creation of calligraphy and ink paintings.

Spanish-Arabic poet Walladah bint al-Mustakfi, daughter of the caliph of Córdoba, writes love poems and runs a literary salon.

1001–1004 Japanese poet and novelist Murasaki Shikibu (c. 978–c. 1031) writes the *Genji Monogatari* (*Tale of Genji*), arguably the world's first novel.

1013 Japanese writer Sei Shonagon (b. c. 966), best known for her guide to court life, *Makurano Soshi* (*Pillow Book*), dies.

1041 *Waka* poet Akazome Emon (b. c. 957), lady-in-waiting at the imperial court, dies. (*Waka* is a form of Japanese verse with five lines and thirty-one syllables, with the syllables arranged 5/7/5/7/7.) She publishes an anthology of 600 poems entitled *Akazome Emon Shu,* and 93 of her poems are included in imperial anthologies.

c. 1070 English women, possibly led by Queen Matilda, design and construct the Bayeux "Tapestry," a wool embroidery on linen that records some of the great historical events of the time and that will be of enormous value to historians for its renderings of the Norman Conquest of England.

Late 11th century Spanish slave girl Rumaykiyya is so talented a poet that the Caliph marries her for her verses.

Performing Arts and Entertainment

Some of Korea's court musicians are women. They

sing, dance, play instruments for the king and his guests, and participate in public ceremonies. They are often lowborn and usually beautiful, and they are sometimes expected to provide sexual services to government officials and foreign dignitaries.

Athletics and Exploration

Norse explorer Gudrid Karlsefni urges and participates in a failed voyage of colonization to the new land of Vinland (North America). When warriors from a local tribe attack, they are frightened away by Erik the Red's illegitimate daughter Freydis, who exposes a breast and slaps her sword against it.

Activism

1080 Anglo-Saxon heroine Godgifa (b. c. 1040, better known as Lady Godiva) dies. The wife of Leofric, earl of Mercia, she allegedly rode naked through the streets of Coventry in exchange for a reduction in the townspeople's taxes.

Business and Industry

Women in Korea work as seamstresses and servants at the royal court.

Science and Medicine

c. 1097 Italian physician Trotula, a famous teacher at the University of Salerno, dies. She published *Diseases of Women* and was innovative in her focus on good diet, exercise, and hygiene. Her treatments included medicinal baths, bleeding, herbal compounds, lancing, a new technique for repairing perineal tears, and support for the perineum during labor to prevent tears. Her works will remain popular in manuscript and print for 700 years.

Education and Scholarship

Viking girls are taught housework, singing, and ale brewing. Some learn to play musical instruments.

According to legend, Chinese imperial concubine Hu Yuxiu invents Nüshu, the woman's script of Hunan province. Used until the twentieth century, the special writing is used only by women and is often used to record ideas to be kept secret from men.

Religion

The Viking pantheon contains numerous goddesses as well as gods.

Islamic scholars attribute to Eve's disobedience the following disabilities of woman: menstruation, childbirth, marriage to a stranger, pregnancy, powerlessness over her destiny, lesser inheritance rights, unequal divorce rights, polygyny, the covering of her head indoors, the lesser weight given her testimony in court, her inability to go outside unchaperoned, unequal participation in religious rituals, inability to become a ruler or judge, a waiting period before remarriage after widowhood or divorce, and only one type of merit compared to 999 types for men.

Early 11th century King Hyonjong of Korea bars women from becoming Buddhist nuns or donating money to temples and shrines.

1093 Scottish queen St. Margaret (b. c. 1045) dies. Married in 1070 to King Malcolm III of Scotland, she influenced the Scottish church, cared for orphans and the poor, and co-founded an abbey at Dunfermline with her husband.

1101–1200

General Status and Daily Life

Widows are vulnerable in European society. In theory, a woman is protected financially by her dowry—a quantity of money, land, or goods given to her at the time of her marriage. If her husband dies, the dowry, or widow's portion, sometimes helps to sustain her. (Sometimes it becomes the property of her children, but her children are bound in turn to provide for her; English law guarantees her a seat by the fire for as long as she lives.) Dowry is standard practice throughout Europe by mid-century. Fathers sometimes complain about having to provide their daughters with dowries, but in fact the dowry serves as a substitute for inheritance, enabling the father to pass his land and property mostly intact to his oldest son; the dowry is almost never as large as the daughter's fair share of his property would be.

In many cases, however, the system does not work very well. Many widows' portions are not large enough to keep women out of poverty, and widows form a disproportionate percentage of the poor. Even rich widows have worries. In England, they are in the protection of the king, who often takes their money or forces them to remarry against their wishes. Widows sometimes pay fines to the Crown to avoid having their bodies and wealth transferred to a royal favorite (or to someone who has bribed the king). Heiresses with dead parents are also under the guardianship of the king and are similarly abused. King John of England, for example, annuls his marriage to Isabella of Gloucester, who becomes a royal ward and is sold as a wife in 1214 to the earl of Essex for 20,000 marks.

The feudal system thus leaves women at the mercy of men. However, it also elevates aristocratic women in the cult of courtly love, or chivalry. In the typical example of courtly love, a knight falls in love with a beautiful, unattainable, married lady. He loves her passionately, serves her with unquestioning obedience, and, in the end, dies loving her, though their affair is never consummated in the flesh. Courtly love creates an unrealistic image of women and reinforces the idea that they can be admirable only for beauty and chastity, but, at the same time, it does represent an improvement in the general view of women. Any praise for women is to be valued when most of what is said about them is negative and dismissive; a typical example is Odo of Cluny's assessment, "To embrace a woman is to embrace a sack of manure."

In parts of France, *mulieres rixosas* (brawling women) are exhibited in cages, then mutilated or drowned.

A Chinese guidebook for heads of families says, "Sometimes people's sons are not capable and they have to depend on their daughter's families for support, even their burials and sacrifices falling to their daughters. So how can people say that having daughters is not comparable to having sons?"

Korean women have inheritance rights almost equal to those of men. Women are considered marriageable at about the age of thirteen. A good Korean wife is expected to cook, sew, weave, educate her daughters, contribute to the education of her sons, manage the family finances, and participate in rituals of ancestor worship. She must please her mother-in-law or else be banished from her husband's house. A woman may be divorced for disobeying her husband's parents, being unable to produce a son, committing adultery, exhibiting jealousy, having a hereditary disease, talking too much, or stealing. If she is widowed, she is expected not to remarry, though many widows do.

1140 The *Decretum* of Gratian, an influential compilation of ecclesiastical law, makes it infanticide to abort a female fetus after sixty-six days or a male fetus after forty days.

c. 1200 Engagement rings come into fashion in Europe.

Government, the Military, and the Law

1109 Urraca (b. c. 1080) becomes ruler of the Spanish province of Aragon, fighting with her brother Alfonso and ruling until 1126.

1114 English princess Matilda, daughter of Henry I, marries German emperor Henry V. She becomes popular with the German people, but in 1125 her husband dies, so she returns to England to be groomed as her father's heir (Henry I's only legitimate son, William, died in a shipwreck in 1120). Henry, rightly perceiving that a female ruler will face special difficulties, forces his council to swear oaths of loyalty to her in 1125 and 1127.

c. 1116 Toltec queen Xochitl falls in battle while leading a battalion of women into the field.

June 17, 1128 Matilda of England marries Geoffrey Plantagenet of Anjou, whose lands border English possessions in Normandy. As German emperor Henry V's widow, she is far above Geoffrey in status, and their son will be popularly known as Henry FitzEmpress.

1130 Theresa, widow of Count Henry of Burgundy, dies. Her dowry upon marriage included a territory called Portugal, and she fought her entire adult life to establish it as an independent nation. She did not succeed, but she made it possible for her son to do so. Perhaps because of her patriotism, Portuguese legends feature a fictional woman named Deuladeu Martins, a giant warrior responsible, through her fearsome deeds, for Portugal's independence.

1131 Princess Constance becomes co-ruler of Antioch, reigning until 1163.

Dec. 1, 1135 Henry I of England dies; despite the oaths of loyalty he demanded for his daughter Matilda, the nobles declare his nephew Stephen king instead. Matilda and her husband, Geoffrey, are declared "aliens," much to the anger of the ambitious, intelligent Matilda, who has, according to one contemporary, "the nature of a man in the frame of a woman." A prolonged civil war ensues.

Feb. 1141 Matilda becomes ruler of England for a short time, though she is never officially crowned and refers to herself as *Domina Anglorum* (leader of the English) rather than *Regina* (queen). Her arrogance alienates the people, and she is driven from London before her coronation can take place. Later in the year, hunted by Stephen's forces, she escapes from Devizes to Gloucester dressed as a corpse. In 1142 she escapes from Oxford Castle by descending from the castle on a rope. She leaves England in 1147 and dies January 30, 1167.

c. 1143 Mexican warrior queen Coyolxauhqui is dethroned by invaders. She is said to be the daughter of the Earth Mother Coatlícue.

Easter 1146 Eleanor of Aquitaine (1122–April 1204), holder in her own right of vast lands and Queen of France through her marriage to Louis VII, offers the services of her vassals in the Second Crusade. From 1147 to 1149 she will accompany her husband on the crusade, leading an army of 300 women to fight and to nurse the wounded.

During the crusade, she presses for an annulment of her marriage, despite the opposition of the pope and of Louis, who tries to have her kidnapped. She obtains the annulment in March 1152 and two months later marries the future King Henry II of England, son of Matilda. She is lucky to reach the wedding; on her way, she is twice almost abducted by nobles planning to rape her, marry her, and lay claim to her vast lands.

When Henry inherits the throne in 1154, Eleanor gets the right to collect her own tax, "the queen's gold," from the English. Matilda serves as an influential and effective Queen Dowager, wisely advising Henry in 1155 not to invade Ireland.

1160 Queen Mélisande of Jerusalem (b. 1105) dies. A patron of the arts and founder of an abbey, she was co-ruler with her husband and then her son, struggling with both for supremacy.

Sept. 24, 1180 Byzantine empress Maria becomes regent for her son Alexius. In 1182, a rebellion against her will force Alexius to authorize her execution.

1184 King Giorgi III of Georgia dies, and his daughter and co-ruler Tamara becomes sole ruler. She is not, however, proclaimed queen, but king (*Mepe*), as there is no word for a female ruler in the Georgian language. In 1187, she marries George Bogolyubski. Promiscuous and obnoxious, he publicly reproaches her with barrenness, and she exiles him with a generous separation settlement. In 1191 he will return and lead a nobles' rebellion; failing, he will be exiled again, only to try and fail again in 1200. Tamara's second marriage will produce two children.

c. 1186 Crusader aristocrat Agnes of Courtenay (b. c. 1136) dies. She gained power through her own marriages, the marriages of her children, and her control of her grandson, Baldwin V, becoming virtual ruler of Jerusalem herself from 1180 to 1184.

1189 Henry II of England dies; his son Richard becomes king, and Henry's wife, Eleanor of Aquitaine, imprisoned since 1173 for supporting a rebellion, is freed. She immediately declares an amnesty for prisoners. During Richard's extensive absences from England, she will rule as regent, defending his interests against his brother John. When he is captured during the

Crusades, it is she who will successfully negotiate his release and reconcile him to John afterward. Eleanor will remain vital and interested in politics until her death; at the age of seventy-seven, she will raise an army to defend her lands in Aquitaine from King Philip Augustus of France.

1193 France's king Philip Augustus marries Ingeborg of Denmark for her dowry and after one day of marriage imprisons her for twenty years so that he may live with his favorite, Agnes of Meran.

1197 Queen Lilavati becomes ruler of Sri Lanka, reigning until 1200.

Literature and the Visual Arts

Notable poets of this century include Japanese Lady Horikawa, an attendant to Empress Dowager Taiken; and French author Marie de France, who composes poetry at the court of England's king Henry II. Her lyric poems of love and adventure made her one of the principal women writers of the Middle Ages. She was best known for her heroic *Lais*, her satirical verse fables collected c. 1180 as *Isopet*, and her translation *L'espurgatoire Seint Patriz* (c. 1190)

Chinese women often seek to buy paintings by other women. Many female artists specialize in flower painting; landscape painting is held in higher esteem and is generally more closed to women, both by social conditioning and by the limitation to travel that bound feet constitute.

1130 German manuscript illuminator Diemud, a nun in the convent of Wessobrun, dies. She copied and illustrated forty-five books, including a Bible.

Mid-12th century Chinese textile maker Zhu Kerou (also known as Zhu Qiang) creates silk tapestries of flowers, birds, figures, rocks, and trees. Her designs are considered quite valuable and are collected by the rich.

c. 1151 Chinese poet, book collector, painter, and calligrapher Li Ch'ing-chao (Li Qingzhao, b. 1084) dies. A major poet, she wrote six volumes, only fifty poems of which will survive to the twentieth century. She was a principal practitioner of the Tz'u verse form, a type of poetry most often written by female folksingers.

c. 1156 Indian poet and ascetic Marula writes verses in Sanskrit.

c. 1160 Frau Ava of Melk becomes one of Germany's first women poets.

May 16, 1163 or 1164 French letter writer Héloïse (b. c. 1101) dies. Although she was an abbess and a scholar, she is chiefly remembered for the passionate letters she wrote to her lover, Abelard. The two fell in love, and Abelard was castrated by Héloïse's angry relatives. Both of the lovers entered religious orders, but Héloïse never quite resigned herself to their fate.

c. 1200 Chinese poet and painter of plum blossoms and bamboo Zhu Shuzhen (Chu Shu-chen), one of the two most important women poets of the Song dynasty, dies, and her parents burn her poems. Fortunately, her friends have copies of many of her works.

Performing Arts and Entertainment

Women become troubadours in the courts of Europe, contributing to the development of courtly love and chivalry. These women, composing and performing their songs of love, include Beatriz Countess of Die (b. c. 1140), Fibors, Almucs de Castlenau, Maria de Ventadorn, Lady Caranza, Alamanda, Lady Alais, Azalais de Porcairages (b. c. 1140), and Lady Iselda.

Athletics and Exploration

In England and France, female and male peasants play "folk football," a rowdy predecessor of soccer. Sometimes teams of married women compete against teams of spinsters. Women also play stoolball, an ancestor of cricket and baseball. Young girls run races at fairs for prizes of cloth or clothing.

Business and Industry

Many prostitutes follow the Crusaders, often offering their services as a gift to God.

In China, women work at the preparation of silk.

Twelfth-century Chinese courtesans are expected to be familiar with music, poetry, calligraphy, chess, needlework, dancing, and painting. Those who are particularly beautiful and talented may be purchased from their brothels by clients and taken on as concubines or secondary wives.

1161 Henry II of England passes ordinances concerning prostitution. According to the new laws, women cannot be held in brothels (or "stews," so called because they derived from bathhouses) unwillingly or be charged more than fourteen pence a week for rent; they may sit in doorways but may not "solicit or throw stones at passers-by." Stew holders cannot employ pregnant women or nuns, operate during religious festivals, or lend more than six shillings, eight pence to women in

their employ. Weekly inspections will be held to check for disease or women being held against their will.

Science and Medicine

At about this time, the uterus is believed by Western doctors to have seven chambers: three which produce boys, three which produce girls, and one which produces hermaphrodites. Other doctors, including most Arabic authorities, believe in only two uterine cavities.

Byzantine princess Anna Comnena (b. 1090) cofounds the medical school of Constantinople.

c. 1151–1161 German writer Hildegard of Bingen writes two scientific treatises. In *Causae et Curae*, she analyzes the causes and treatment of forty-seven diseases, making astute observations about diabetes, the circulatory system, and women's reproductive health. In *Physica*, she describes different types of plants, animals, and rocks, giving the medical uses of nearly 300 varieties of herbs.

Education and Scholarship

Byzantine princess Anna Comnena is one of the few women historians before modern times. Her fifteen-book prose poem about her father's reign, the *Alexiad*, provides information about many aspects of the Byzantine Empire, including the lives of women.

Religion

As reverence for the courtly lady increases in the secular world of Europe, so reverence for the Virgin Mary increases in the religious world. During the twelfth century, mariolatry becomes an increasingly popular and officially accepted part of the Catholic church, and in some places Mary, as an accessible intermediary between God and humanity, is accorded more worship than Christ. Only a few theologians attempt, in vain, to halt this rising tide of Mary-worship

Indian poet Mahadevi dies in her twenties. The wife of a local king, she left him to become a naked ascetic, worshiping the god Siva.

Women embrace the Cathar or Albigensian heresy, which denies the Trinity, the Catholic church, and the bodily nature of Christ; women cannot be Cathar bishops, but they can be *perfecti*, or ministers, and they are a majority of the Cathars' followers.

c. 1123 English mystic Christina of Markyate devotes herself to a religious life despite the opposition of her parents, who beat her and threaten to throw her out of the house. Her parents conspire to conclude a betrothal for her, bribing the local bishop to sanction the arrangement, and her mother encourages the prospective bridegroom to rape her. Christina escapes this horror by hiding behind some cloaks hung on the wall, and eventually she escapes the house by disguising herself as a man.

1125 The first Cistercian convent is founded.

1134 The French dual-sex monastery of the Premonstratensians expels its female members, saying, "We..., recognizing that the wickedness of women is greater than all the other wickedness in the world, and that the poison of asps and dragons is more curable and less dangerous to men than the familiarity of women, have unanimously decreed for the safety of our souls, no less than for that of our bodies and goods, that we will on no account receive any more sisters to the increase of our perdition, but will avoid them like poisonous animals."

1148 An ecclesiastical commission verifies that German mystic, scholar, convent founder, and abbess Hildegard of Bingen (d. 1179), known as "the Sibyl of the Rhine," is a divinely inspired prophet. She is currently at work on a record of her visions, *Scivias* (short for *Scito vias Domini*—know the ways of the Lord). Pope Eugenius III writes to Hildegard, after reading parts of the *Scivias*, "We are filled with admiration, my daughter . . . for the new miracles God has shown you in our time, filling you with his spirit so that you see, understand, and communicate many secret things." She completes *Scivias* in 1151; her subject matter, often discussed in erotic terms, ranges from the Creation (where she perceives the Creator as female) to Judgment Day.

Hildegard's other works include *Liber vitae meritorum* (*The Book of the Merits of Life*, 1161); *Liber divinorum operum* (*Book of Divine Works*, 1173), in which she describes visions of the interrelationships of humans and the universe; books on the Gospels and the Benedictine Rule; hagiographies; seventy-four musical works, including hymns and the first European opera; poems; and a new "language" that combined elements of German and Latin.

Hildegarde was often involved in church politics and helped organize support for the Second Crusade. An adviser to, or correspondent of, four popes, two emperors, King Henry II of England, Eleanor of Aquitaine, and St. Bernard of Clairvaux, she told Frederick Barbarossa, "Take care that the Highest King does not strike you down because of the blindness which prevents you from governing justly."

1195 German abbess and artist Herrade of Landsberg dies. She founded two religious communities and a hospital and supervised the composition of the *Hortus*

deliciarum (*Garden of Delights*), a 324-page collection of stories, philosophy, poetry, and songs.

1201–1300

General Status and Daily Life

The Catholic church's age of consent for marriage is twelve for girls and fourteen for boys. Royal children are sometimes married much earlier, even as young as three. Divorce (really, annulment) is rare and is usually granted only for a problem with age, consent of the parties or their parents, or consanguinity.

Wife beating is common in Europe and is endorsed by the church as the loving husband's means of correcting his wife's faults. The *Customs of Beauvais*, a French legal code, says, "Provided he neither kills nor maims her, it is legal for a man to beat his wife when she wrongs him." In Spain, a man may kill his wife or fiancée and her lover if she is unfaithful. In parts of Europe, it is believed impossible for a woman to conceive a child without experiencing sexual pleasure, so if a woman claims she has been raped, she is not believed if a pregnancy results.

However, women do have some rights. Englishwomen are recorded as owning and leasing land, making wills, and acting on their own behalf in courts. Sons are sometimes known by their mothers' names rather than their fathers'. In some parts of France, daughters inherit land equally with sons. English widows have rights to one-third to one-half of their husbands' property.

Noblewomen's duties include arranging the stabling of horses; arranging repairs; purchasing carts, shoes, wine, and hose; managing as many as sixty servants; supervising meals for as many as 500 guests; making charitable gifts; tending the sick of the neighborhood and household; and hiring messengers. A noblewoman may conduct lawsuits, run the estates, settle tenant disputes, or borrow money. To help her learn obedience, good manners, and the running of a household, she will usually be sent at the age of six or seven to live with another noble family, and her parents will in turn accept someone else's daughter as an apprentice in nobility.

Middle-class city housewives rise at dawn, buying freshly slaughtered fowl or rabbits, salt, vinegar, pepper, sugar, honey, bread, milk, oil, wine, fish, cheese, sausage, onions, fruit, and eels. They supervise the cooking, washing, and cleaning, the making of soap, the care of furs, and the gardening. Peasant women cook, clean, milk cows, prepare flax, feed the fowl, shear sheep, make cheese and butter, grow vegetables, spin, weave, sow, reap, plow, thresh, rake, winnow, and thatch.

Childbirth is extremely risky and surrounded by superstition. A woman who wants a boy is encouraged to lie on her right side at night; there are several other superstitions about discovering or influencing the sex of a child. Until a woman recovers from labor, she is considered unclean and may not cook, serve food, or touch holy water. Once she has recovered, she is "churched," a ceremony in which she goes to church holding a lighted candle and is blessed by the priest. If she dies in childbirth, another woman will be churched in her place. Superstitious significance is placed upon the first person seen by the woman as she leaves the church after this ceremony.

Upper-class Mongol men are often polygynous; the chief wife usually holds favored status, and sometimes only her children are considered truly legitimate.

In China, female infanticide is common and accepted. Girls are expected to be chaste, shy, and obedient. Couples often do not meet until the wedding. Men are technically monogamous, but those who can afford it often keep concubines.

Jewish male scholar Maimonides writes about the *onah*, or the man's duty to keep his wife sexually happy: "Men who are healthy and strong, who do not have an occupation that drains their strength, but eat, drink, and stay at home, have their *onah* every night. Physical laborers, if they work in the city where they live, have their *onah* twice a week . . . . people who learn Torah have an *onah* of once a week because the learning of Torah drains one's strength . . . a woman can prevent her husband from leaving town on business so as not to miss her *onah*. So too, she may prevent him from changing jobs, which will lessen the frequency of her *onah*."

1204 Infanticide is common in Italy. Pope Innocent III establishes a foundling hospital in Rome for illegitimate children, prompted by a spate of dead infants netted by local fishermen.

1215 England's Magna Carta ends the king's power to arrange the forced remarriage of wealthy widows, but widows still are often deprived of wardship of their own children; that privilege is given (or sold) to a man, who may misappropriate the child's inheritance. Sometimes a woman is able to buy her own child's wardship or sue for it through the courts.

1231 Mongol China begins nearly a century of demanding a tribute of Korean women to be forcibly married to its soldiers. At first, vulnerable women like criminals' widows are sent, but eventually even upper-class women will be selected. One young woman of good family, Miss Hong, will become the focus of a

struggle between her father and Princess Cheguktaejang, the Mongol wife of Korea's king. Hong's father tries bribery and shaving her head to enable her to escape forced marriage, but the princess responds by having Hong beaten with chains and turned over to a Mongol husband. Korean families react to such incidents by marrying their daughters early (often younger than twelve) or hiding them from government agents trained to find candidates for forced marriage.

Late 13th century Chinese morality guides list point values for good and bad acts; demerits for sexual crimes include 50 for raping a prostitute, 500 for raping a wife, and 1,000 for raping a widow or a virgin. Fewer demerits are applied for the rape of a servant. Having sex with a prostitute earns 20 demerits. Having sex with a Buddhist nun earns 500. Keeping too many concubines and wives earns 50. Showing favoritism to a woman in one's harem earns 10, unless it causes her to be rude, in which case the penalty is 20.

Government, the Military, and the Law

At about this time, Peruvian leader Mana Ocllo, after conquering surrounding lands and establishing Inca power with her seven siblings, marries her brother Manco Copac and founds the Inca ruling dynasty.

Mongol women sometimes engage in warfare.

During the reign of King John (1199–1216), Nicoli Delabair serves as high sheriff of Lincolnshire, England.

1202 Queen Kalyanavati becomes ruler of Sri Lanka, reigning until 1208.

1209 Sri Lankan queen Lilavati, who ruled from 1197 to 1200, is restored to the Sri Lankan throne, ruling until 1210. She will rule again from 1211 to 1212.

Jan. 18, 1212 Queen Tamara of Georgia dies. She reigned twenty-four years, overcoming foreign aggression and rebellions led by her ex-husband. Like many adept leaders of the day, she kept her nobles in line by means of occasional wars and obligatory court attendance during peacetime. She was an able military strategist who was often greeted by her troops with the cry, "To our king!"

Tamara is succeeded by her eighteen-year-old son, Giorgi IV. He dies soon afterward, however, and is followed on the throne by Tamara's daughter Rusudani, who rules until the Mongol invasion of 1236. Rusudani, like her mother, is proclaimed king, not queen.

1219 Queen Zabel becomes ruler of Lesser Armenia, reigning until 1226.

Nov. 8, 1226 Blanche of Castile (d. November 1252), granddaughter of Eleanor of Aquitaine, becomes regent of France for her son Louis IX. She quickly secures the loyalty of most of the nobles, then raises an army to defeat the few who rebel. Later she will fight Henry III of England, the archbishop of Rouen, a mob of religious fanatics, and the bishop of Beauvais in their various attacks on the French monarchy. Even after Louis's majority, she will serve as an adviser and as his regent while he is away on a crusade. During the reign of this "wisest of all women of her time," says a contemporary, "all good things came to the realm of France."

1236 Eleanor (1215–1275), daughter of King John of England, meets Simon de Montfort. They fall in love, but he is French and not royal. Furthermore, Eleanor, disappointed with her first marriage at age nine, has taken a vow of chastity. All in all, it seems unlikely that the current King, her brother Henry III, will consent to the match. Therefore, she feigns pregnancy in 1238 and argues that she must marry immediately to prevent a scandal.

1239 Bettisia Bozzidini is named to the Juridical Chair at the University of Bologna, a position she will hold until 1249.

1240 Indian leader Raziyya Sultana, ruler of Delhi and a renowned warrior since 1236, is deposed after weathering several rebellions. In jail, she marries one of her jailers, Altuniyya. She convinces him to help her regain power; they march to Delhi but are met and killed on October 13 by Hindu troops. She was the first woman to rule a Muslim state in her own right and the only Muslim woman to rule in India.

1241 Mongol khan Ögedei dies; his widow serves as regent during the following political upheaval until 1246.

1248 Mongol khan Güyük dies; his widow serves as regent and is executed when her family fails to seize power.

1249 The caliph of Baghdad dies while preparing to defend his lands against the French. His wife, Shagrat al-Durr, who has already acted as his regent, hides his body and forges orders. Under her leadership, the Arab armies defeat and capture Louis IX of France; she then reveals her husband's death and is named Sultan by the army, later abdicating and marrying her successor, Aibak. She has him murdered in 1257 and is beaten to death in retaliation in 1258.

1257-1259 Eleanor de Montfort blocks a treaty with the French because of her dissatisfaction with the way her dower lands have been mishandled. She claims she is owed twenty-seven years of income from the land, and

she yields and signs the treaty only after her brother Henry III gives her ten manors as compensation. In 1264 she is alienated completely from Henry after her husband, Simon de Montfort, is killed in a treasonous rebellion; she spirits money and hostages out of the country but is captured and forced, with her daughter, to enter a convent.

c. 1294 Chabi, wife of Kublai Khan, helps govern China in the final years of his life.

Literature and the Visual Arts

Authors in or about this century include French traveling poet Barbe de Verrue; Chinese poet Wang Ch'ing-hui, an imperial servant captured by Kublai Khan's Mongols, who writes about her captivity; and Hadewijch, the most important Dutch literary figure of the Middle Ages. As for the visual arts, there are a few women sculptors working in Paris; Sabina von Steinbach reputedly works on the façade of Strasbourg Cathedral; and Italian Isabella Cunio may be the inventor of wood-block engraving.

Chinese ink-flower painter Madame Bao is praised by a master artist: "Monk Ding paints the flowers skillfully but the branches are roughly done, Liu Mengliang has good ideas but his technique is insufficient, yet among women there is Madame Bao, who has been able to preserve her master's method."

1201 Japanese poet and Buddhist nun Princess Shikishi dies.

1239–1241 Henry III of England employs an embroiderer named Mabel, whose work is well paid and highly esteemed. Many women, especially upper-class women, work as embroiderers for kings and churches.

1271 Donzella of Bologna is one of the few women illuminators of manuscripts in Europe.

1292 Thomasse, an illuminator and tavern keeper, lives in Paris. There are seven other female illuminators of manuscripts working in the city.

Performing Arts and Entertainment

Women troubadours or "trobairitz" in France include Castelloza of Auvergne, Isabella, and Clara d'Anduza of Languedoc.

There is at least one woman minstrel in Stratford-upon-Avon, England. Women in England also perform as acrobats, singers, and dancers.

Christmas 1296 English acrobat Matilda Makejoy performs for Edward I.

Business and Industry

European women work as laundresses, wet nurses, and servants. They are also engaged in "bye industries," the thirteenth-century equivalent of part-time jobs, in which they produce cloth or food and sell it for extra money.

If a woman wishes to work at a skilled trade, she must join a guild, which controls who may learn the craft. Lowest on the guild ladder are the apprentices, who trade their labor for education in a trade. The time involved may be extensive; female embroiderers's apprentices serve about six years. Once apprentices have learned the craft, they become journeymen, and when they have their own establishments, they become masters. Most guilds do not admit women as full members, but many allow the wives, widows, or daughters of guild members to practice their craft. In Lübeck, Germany, a guild widow can pass membership to her new husband if she remarries. There are even some guilds that are exclusively female.

In Hangchow, China, there are three classes of prostitutes. The lowest-paid are often prisoners and cater to the poor and the military. Next up on the scale are the women of the wine houses, patronized by government officials and others of similar status. Highest of all are the teahouse women. The teahouses have high entrance fees and elaborate entertainment; the women tend to be well educated, or at least well trained.

Genoan merchant Mabilia Lecavella becomes wine merchant to the king of France.

Mongol women often manage the family's livestock.

In many parts of Germany, women can own property and engage in trade.

1254 Louis IX of France rules that any prostitute who continues her trade after a warning shall be exiled from her parish and deprived of her possessions.

1227 The Order of St. Mary Magdalene for reformed prostitutes is authorized.

1270 In Paris, a woman may engage in trade with her husband's consent.

1274 Several women in London, including Isabella Buckerel, are prominent wool merchants.

1285 Twenty women in Douai, Flanders, complain to the authorities about the man for whom they have been doing piecework. Like many employers of the time, he has been cheating them of their earnings by overcharging them for materials and reimbursing them with inferior goods.

1296 English brewer Agnes de Hagemon falls into tub of hot mash and is scalded to death; the Crown sells the beer at a profit.

Science and Medicine

1220 The University of Paris bans women from practicing medicine.

1226–1257 Benedictine nun Euphemia is abbess of Wherwell Abbey in England. She is responsible for the construction of an infirmary, made especially sanitary by a subterranean watercourse, which carries away waste.

1292 Some women in Paris are barber-surgeons. Eight women are listed as doctors. Doctors, who diagnose illnesses and prescribe medications, are held in considerably higher esteem than surgeons, who merely cut bodies (and often hair as well).

Education and Scholarship

Saxon law dictates that women are to inherit any books in the family, as they are the only ones who read them.

In Europe, noblewomen become ambassadors of culture, patronizing the arts, encouraging courtly love, and spreading (through marriage) poetry and song from court to court throughout Europe. Wealthy girls are educated at home by tutors or in convents by nuns. They learn basic book knowledge, embroidery, and music.

Religion

Catholic convents offer women opportunities for learning and work unavailable in many places in pre-Christian times, but women are still denied positions of leadership within the church. During this century, abbesses grow gradually less powerful, and movements within the church that offer new roles for women, like the Cathar or Albigensian heresy, are firmly suppressed.

One of these new movements is the group known as the Beguines, a wandering, unofficial mendicant order. The Beguines frighten the male establishment for several reasons: they take no formal vows, they move freely in the world rather than being cloistered in a convent, and they preach and interpret Scripture. The response is a frantic effort to force the Beguines into nunneries and limit the powers of women already in convents. Early in the century, Pope Innocent III ratifies bans against women's preaching, hearing confessions, and accepting the vows of novices. By the end of the century, only a few convents will remain out of the control of local bishops.

Within the convent, the power structure is clearly organized. The superior (a woman of social stature who usually rules for life) maintains discipline, the subprioress or treasuress performs administrative functions, the chantress supervises church services, the sacrist maintains religious supplies such as candles and vestments, the fratress supervises furnishings, the chambress supervises clothing and bedding, the cellaress oversees farming and food, the kitcheness oversees the cooking, the infirmaress cares for the sick, and the mistress of novices instructs young aspiring nuns.

Many nuns, particularly those of noble birth, circumvent the rules and purpose of the community, owning personal property, sleeping in their own rooms rather than communally, and eating "meat in cliques by twos and three in their chambers," where they are waited upon by their own private servants. Instead of remaining cloistered, they go to the markets to buy necessities, conduct legal business connected with monastic lands, and receive visitors.

Indian poet Mukta Bai, a beggar in her youth, writes theological and philosophical poems.

1204 The most famous Cistercian convent in Europe, France's Port Royal, is founded.

1207 Italian pilgrim and visionary St. Bona of Pisa (b. c. 1156) dies. She dedicated herself to God at the age of ten and made her first pilgrimage, to Jerusalem, at fourteen. On her way back to Italy she was captured by pirates, jailed, and rescued. She then made the first of nine 1,000-mile pilgrimages to Compostela, eventually becoming an official guide of the Knights of Saint James along that route.

1210 The abbess of the powerful Cistercian convent of Las Huelgas in Spain begins performing priestly functions.

1212 St. Francis and St. Clare of Assisi (c. 1194–1253, canonized 1255) draw up a rule for the order of "Poor Clares," whose vow of poverty is considered quite controversial. The commission of the Poor Clares, who live entirely on alms and have the most rigorous rule of any sisterhood, will be confirmed by Pope Innocent III in 1216.

1231 Hungarian mystic St. Elizabeth of Thuringia (b. 1207) dies. After an unhappy marriage at thirteen, widowhood at twenty, and harsh treatment by her brother-in-law thereafter, she became the spiritual disciple of a rigorous, even sadistic, cleric. Meekly submitting to his physical and verbal chastisement, she led a life of extreme austerity, nursing the sick, caring for the poor, and making clothes for the needy. She will be canonized in 1235.

1243–1244 French noblewomen Blanche de Laurac and Esclarmonde defend the castle of Montségur, the last refuge of Albigensian heretics. Women have embraced the Cathar or Albigensian heresy, which denies the Trinity, the Catholic church, and the bodily nature of Christ; women cannot be Cathar bishops, but they can be *perfecti*, or ministers. When the castle finally surrenders, the defenders are offered generous terms and light penance if they renounce their heresy, death by burning if they do not. Two hundred Cathars, male and female, choose burning.

1250 German mystic and Beguine Mechthild of Magdeburg (c. 1207–c. 1294), "hailed" by the Holy Spirit in about 1219, begins *Das Fliessende Licht der Gottheit* (*The Flowing Light of the Godhead*), a collection of spiritual poems and prose narratives. She writes to "God, You Who burn in Your desire! / O God, You Who melt in union with Your beloved! / O God, You Who rest on my bosom, without You I cannot be!" and refers to God as "my Father by nature, / My Brother by His humanity, my Betrothed by love."

1266 French abbess Odette de Pougy, superior of the abbey of Notre-Dame-aux-Nonnains, blocks construction of a church on the abbey's land in Troyes. Even though the project is the brainchild of Pope Urban IV, she defends her convent's land with an armed band, frightening the workers and destroying the building. Her continued resistance will result, in 1268, in the excommunication of her entire convent.

Aug. 29, 1268 Belgian abbess Beatrice of Nazareth, calligrapher, illuminator, and author of *The Seven Manners of Love* (b. 1200), dies. As a young woman, she was noted for the austerities to which she subjected herself: waking in the middle of the night to sing the Holy Office, sleeping on thorns, fasting, and performing self-flagellation. She became a novice over the objections of her abbess, who feared for her health.

1270 Nun and saint Margaret of Hungary (b. 1242) dies. Daughter of King Bela IV of Hungary, she refused to marry the king of Bohemia, preferring seclusion and self-mortification in a convent.

1278 Italian domestic servant St. Zita (b. c. 1218), patron of maidservants, dies. A weaver's maid, she became known for her charitable works and good deeds.

1293 Pope Boniface VIII's bull *Periculoso* mandates the complete enclosure and isolation of nuns, requiring them to be "altogether withdrawn from public and mundane sights." The bull, however, is never really enforced. In Lincoln, England, the nuns of one convent actually chase the bishop bearing it out of the gates and throw the papal order at his head.

1297 Italian penitent St. Margaret of Cortona (b.

1247) dies. The mistress of a nobleman and an unwed mother, she turned to an austere and religious life as a Franciscan tertiary (lay) sister. Increasingly secluded from the world, she converted many sinners.

1300 There are 700 Cistercian convents in Europe.

1301–1400

General Status and Daily Life

In England, peasant women's marriages are arranged by their parents. The boundary between betrothal and actual marriage is vague, especially in rural areas. Unlike their noble counterparts, peasant women are likely to marry in their twenties rather than their teens and are likely to be personally acquainted with their future spouses. If the prospective bride is not freeborn, her parents must ask the local lord's permission for her to marry and must pay the lord a fee for the privilege. If she marries outside the village, they must pay an additional fine. Typical peasant dowries in France include clothing, bed linens, chests, and money.

Widows may be cared for directly by their children, indirectly by a pension called a "corrody" (in which a sum is paid to a monastery to bring her food and perhaps such items as firewood, clothing, candles, and livestock), or by their own efforts; some take over their late husbands' lands quite effectively.

Obedience is considered a European woman's chief virtue. The good wife is advised, with regard to her husband, to "go out of the house or stay in it, as he commands, and if he forbids it, do not visit even your father or mother or any of your kin." If she transgresses, penalties are severe. In some Italian towns, women who commit adultery are publicly whipped and then exiled. An English law allows men to beat their wives for the purpose of "lawful and reasonable correction." Women are seen as dangerous and sexually insatiable; the vice of lust is usually depicted as female.

Frenchwomen begin taking their husbands' names, but in wealthy families with daughters only, a son-in-law may be required to take his wife's name to perpetuate the line. Surnames are still fairly new, and women throughout Europe still often keep their birth names upon marriage.

English wives are often not allowed to make wills, even with their husbands' permission.

Women in Mali shock foreign travelers with their freedom and their bare breasts.

1329 English law grants old women the right to glean whatever they can from mown fields before the land is used as animal pasture.

1343–1396 Florence, Italy, passes seven sets of sumptuary laws to limit women's wardrobes.

1351 England's Treason Act makes it a crime of petty treason for a wife to kill her husband, since he is her sovereign lord.

Government, the Military, and the Law

Many Korean kings marry Mongol princesses, who, due to their powerful political backing, are often the dominant partners in the marriages. They have a strong influence on court etiquette and policy. Some, like Tognyong (regent 1344-1351), even rule. Many have great freedom of movement; one makes eighty-seven trips, including eight back to Yüan China.

In Paris, if a man cannot serve his curfew (night watch), his wife is expected to serve it for him.

Portugal's "Padeira" ("Baker") of Aljubarrota becomes famous for her militancy against Spain.

1316 Salic Law, which prevents women from inheriting the one piece of land which serves as a family's ancestral seat, is interpreted to mean that women cannot inherit the throne either.

Sept. 24, 1326 Queen Isabella of England, known as "the She-Wolf," and her lover, Roger Mortimer, arrive in England at the head of an army of mercenaries. In 1327, they depose, imprison, and execute her husband, King Edward II. Over the next three years they will grow increasingly unpopular with the people, with their regency marked by extravagance and abuse of power. In 1330, Isabella's son Edward III forces her into a convent and hangs Mortimer.

1333 Italian lawyer and scholar Novella D'Andrea dies. Her father, a law professor at the University of Bologna, sometimes allowed her to give lectures for him, though she was forced to speak from behind a curtain so as not to distract the students with her beauty. Her sister Bettina (d. 1335) was a lawyer and a professor at the University of Padua.

1338 Scottish countess Black Agnes, countess of Dunbar, fends off an English siege of her castle for months until the attackers give up. Directing the defense, she often stops to insult and laugh at the besiegers.

1355 Portuguese noblewoman Inés de Castro is

murdered by King Affonso because his son Pedro's affection for Inés nearly blocked one diplomatic marriage and now jeopardizes another. In 1357, Pedro will become king, exhume Inés's body, crown her queen, and rebury her.

1366 Korean empress Ch'i of China, who rose from ordinary concubine to imperial tea server to imperial favorite to mother of the heir to powerful empress, is driven from power after nearly thirty years as a major figure in Chinese politics.

1369 German countess Margaret Moutash (b. 1318) dies. She expelled her husband from her lands in the Tyrol, rebelled against the pope, and remarried against church law after getting a secular annulment.

1382 Queen Joanna I of Naples (b. 1326), who sold Avignon to the papacy in 1348, is strangled at the order of her fourth husband. She murdered her first husband in 1347, only to be driven out of Naples by his brother in 1348.

1383 Fernando I of Portugal dies. His widow, Leonora, who married Fernando despite the fact that she was already married to another man, becomes regent for her daughter Beatriz. Fearing a proposed Castilian marriage for Beatriz, the people, led by Don João (son of Pedro and Inés de Castro), rebel and defeat the Castilian army in 1385.

1384 Jadwiga (1374–1399), patron of artists, musicians, and scholars, and re-establisher of the University of Krakow, is crowned "king" of Poland. In 1386, she marries Grand Duke Jagiello of Lithuania, uniting the two kingdoms, winning Lithuania to Christianity, and forming an alliance against the knights of the Teutonic Order.

1395 Maria of Anjou, ruler of Hungary since 1382 and a patron of trade and the arts, dies.

June 20, 1397 The Union of Kalmar makes Queen Margrethe (1353–1412) the sole ruler of Denmark, Sweden, and Norway. Regent of Denmark through her father's death (1375) and of Norway through her husband's (1380), she became ruler in her own right after her son's death, being proclaimed "mistress and ruler" of Denmark in August 1387 and "Norway's mighty Lady and rightful Master" in February 1388. She added Sweden to her possessions in 1389. She immediately begins consolidating royal power and privileges. The union of all three countries will last until 1523, and the union of Sweden and Norway will last until 1814.

Literature and the Visual Arts

Indian poet Jana Bai writes verses in the Marathi language.

In China, painting is an avocation of the scholar-gentry, and women pursue art freely within the home. Others learn to paint because they are taught by male relatives who are professional artists. Both courtesans and empresses become renowned for their skill in the genteel art of painting.

1319 Painter and calligrapher Guan Daosheng (b. 1262), the most famous female calligrapher and painter in Chinese history, dies. Emperor Renzhong commissioned works of calligraphy from her. She painted figures, landscapes, plum blossoms, and orchids but was best known for her bamboo; she invented a new way of representing young bamboo in mists after rain, and she helped to reintegrate bamboo into landscapes after bamboo painting had become a separate genre. Her bamboo has a delicate, feathery appearance. In 1310, she wrote, "To play with brush and ink is a masculine sort of thing to do, yet I made this painting. Wouldn't someone say that I have transgressed? How despicable, how despicable."

1342–1347 Painter Marie de Sainte-Katherine is active in Lille.

1358 History first records the work of Bourgot, a famous manuscript illuminator. She is working for Yolande of Flanders and will later work for Charles V and the duke of Berry.

May 1399 Italian-French writer Christine de Pisan (b. 1365), Europe's first professional woman author, writes *L'Epistre au Dieu d'Amours* (*Letter to the God of Love*), sparking a fierce debate over the misogyny of Jean de Meung's poem *The Romance of the Rose*. She is the only woman to attack de Meung in this, one of the great literary debates of the fourteenth century.

1400 Christine de Pisan writes *Le Debat de deux amans*, a debate between two lovers who have found varying success in love; *Le Livre du dit de Poissy*, recounting a visit to a wealthy Dominican convent; and the first portion of *Le Livre de la Mutacion de Fortune* (*The Book of the Changes of Fortune*), a work that will take her three years to complete and which will contain over 23,000 verses.

Performing Arts and Entertainment

1321 Eight members of the Paris minstrels' guild are women.

Sept. 1322 Edward II of England is entertained by Yorkshire singers Agnes the Redhaired and Alice of Whorlton; he pays them four shillings.

Business and Industry

Many European women work as domestic servants, arranging furnishings, tending fires, setting the table, cooking, cleaning, and buying such staples as wine. Italian female servants, including wet nurses, earn about twelve florins a year.

Some girls are apprenticed to trades, swearing not to marry, drink, reveal the master's secrets or steal from him "more than six pence a year during the term." Many a woman, thus apprenticed, carries on her trade after marriage, even if different from her husband's. When doing business, she is considered by law a *femme sole*, not subsumed in her husband's legal identity, though this precaution is largely for the husband's protection.

In various places, women work as spinsters (the suffix *-ster* is feminine in English, and many common English family names derive from a woman's occupation, e.g., Brewster for a female brewer, Baxter for a bakester or female baker, and Webster for a female weaver). They are involved in most aspects of cloth production and use, becoming glovers, girdlers, haberdashers, purse makers, cap makers, weavers, embroiderers, silk and linen weavers, dyers, fullers, laundresses, spinners, and lace makers. Women are responsible for so many phases of cloth production, in fact, that the female side of the family becomes known as the distaff side, and an unmarried woman is called a spinster.

Women also work as butchers, chandlers, cobblers, skinners, bookbinders, gilders, painters, spicers, goldsmiths, peddlers, innkeepers, farmers, farriers, merchants, nurses, fishers, net makers, mustard makers, moneylenders, money changers, cutlers, leather workers, belt makers, cooks, hucksters (retailers) of food and goods from the countryside, saddlers, coppersmiths, pewtersmiths, and blacksmiths. Some women do construction work, hauling stones, sand, water, and bricks; cleaning latrines; digging ditches; and preparing thatch, moss, and bracken for roofs. In England, both men and women brew beer, but women often predominate and sometimes serve as the village ale taster, who upholds brewing standards. Most guilds do not allow women full privileges, but women sometimes circumvent the guilds, working illegally at their trades.

Female peasants in Germany spin, prepare flax and hemp, wash clothes, and dig for beets. Some farmers are women who hold land in their own right.

Queen Philippa, wife of England's Edward III, establishes the Norwich wool industry.

Many European cities open public brothels.

c. 1318 English merchant Rose of Burford sells items to those as lofty as Queen Isabella. When her partner-husband dies with a large loan outstanding to the Crown,

Rose makes five petitions asking for repayment, finally suggesting that she be allowed to recoup the money by not paying customs duties. With this decided advantage over her competitors, she continues to work as a wool merchant until at least 1323.

1347 Queen Joanna I of Naples builds a special new brothel section of Avignon and moves all prostitutes into it. Called the Maison de Débauche, it features weekly medical inspections and a female supervisor. It is closed on Fridays and holy days. Pregnant prostitutes are required to deliver their babies, who are then educated at Joanna's expense.

1351 In England, women who find employment for servants earn one shilling, sixpence for placing a chambermaid, two shillings for a nurse. The "recommendress" is found in other parts of Europe as well.

1364 Agnes, an English cutler's wife, takes one Jusema as apprentice, promising to "feed and clothe her and not beat her with a stick or knife."

1368 English silk manufacturers, who are almost entirely female, petition the Crown to end unfair competition from Continental silk makers.

1372 In London, women's assistance to guild members and artisans is so widely accepted that wives of leather dyers swear to the calling with their husbands. Except for wives and daughters of craftsmen, however, women are excluded from male guilds. Widows are often expected to carry on the husband's trade, and apprentices and tools are often left to them in wills.

1380 In Oxford, England, women are admitted to only twelve of ninety-three listed trades.

1388 A law in Florence, Italy, requires prostitutes to wear bells "so that the token of their shame should enter into eye and ear."

1397 Cologne has forty guilds, three of them all female, twenty-eight dual-sex. Women on their own or as widows of members can belong to the guilds for woodworking, metalworking, leatherworking, needle making, and blacksmithing.

Science and Medicine

In Italy, Abella, a teacher of medicine, is an instructor in Salerno and writes *De atrabile* and *De natura seminis humani*. Physician Mercuriade also teaches at the University of Salerno. In about 1318, Alessandra Giliani is a dissector and anatomy assistant at the University of Bologna.

Cecilia of Oxford is the official surgeon of Queen Philippa, wife of Edward III of England.

Women are fewer than 2% of doctors in France and England; women are mostly involved with medicine as part-time herbalists and midwives. Their work is informal and probably lower in pay and status.

From 1273 to 1410, there are twenty-four women doctors in Naples, Italy.

Early 14th century Wisewoman Geralda Codines operates in Barcelona, reading urines (which the episcopal court allows her to do) and chanting charms (which the court tries in vain to stop).

1322 German physician Jacoba Felicie is tried in Paris for practicing without a license; six witnesses testify that she is more skilled than the university doctors. She defends herself as knowledgeable and women doctors as necessary to the modesty of female patients, but she is found guilty and barred from practice. Also censured and barred from practice are Joanna, a "lay sister but a married woman"; Belota the Jewess; and Margaret of Ypres, a surgeon. Over the next nine years, several other women will be indicted in Paris for practicing medicine without a license.

Mid-14th century Italian teacher of medicine at Salerno Rebecca Guarna writes about fever, urine, and embryology; she is also recognized as a distinguished herbalist.

1381 Jewish female doctor Floreta attends the queen of Aragon.

1389 Over the next century (until 1497), there will be fifteen licensed female doctors in Frankfurt, Germany, three of them Jewish. Jewish women, throughout the Middle Ages, are more likely than Gentiles to be doctors.

1390 Women in London are pushed out of the medical profession by a new licensing procedure that requires a university education.

1390 Dorotea Bocchi is appointed to the chair of medicine and moral philosophy at the University of Bologna, replacing her father. She will hold this professorship for forty years.

Education and Scholarship

Many male writers in Europe object strongly to the idea of women's being allowed to read and write, especially below the noble ranks, lest they read romances and write love letters. Poor girls sometimes go to local elementary schools; girls of the gentry and upper bourgeoisie are sent to convents or great households for their training. Nuns generally charge high fees for education and take few pupils but often fail to provide a rigorous education. Girls in convent schools are usually taught religion, reading, singing, spinning, and needlework. Ladies are expected to learn the social graces: falconry, chess, storytelling, conversation, and music.

Italy has quite a few women schoolteachers, though they are still very much in the minority and are usually paid less than men.

At about this time, three female scribes, Allegra, Flandina, and Uliana, are active in Bologna.

1338 In Florence, Italy, about 9,000 children are taught to read in primary schools, with perhaps 10% of these being female, but the boys alone can go on to further education, where they learn mathematics and perhaps logic and Latin.

1380 There are at least twenty-one female schoolteachers in Paris.

Religion

German theologian Katharina Zell-Schützin flourishes.

Korea has female shamans who attend court and become involved in political intrigues.

In a typical English convent, nuns rise at 2 A.M. for Matins, sleep three hours, then wake again at 6 A.M. for Prime, which is followed by a light breakfast of bread and ale. Other offices through the day include Tierce, Sext, None, and Vespers. Dinner is eaten at noon, while one nun reads aloud. Supper is eaten after Vespers. Agricultural or intellectual labor is performed for about five hours in the middle of the day. Compline, the next religious office, occurs at 7 P.M. in winter and 8 P.M. in summer. Then the sisters go to sleep. Silence is observed at most times, with a sign language used instead of speech. For example, a nun who wants milk will "draw her little finger in the manner of milking."

Obedientiaries perform certain important functions, making sure that the food, clothing, and religious paraphernalia of the convent are in proper supply. Nuns produce their own vegetables, beer, dairy products, and bread; they buy fish, salt, and spices. Most convents are small, with only twenty to thirty members. Funds are short due to bad management, external demands, damage, and insufficient endowment. Boredom leads gradually to the relaxation of religious services; education slips, with nuns losing their knowledge first of Latin and then of French. Nuns are often scolded for vanity, dancing, and keeping pet dogs (as well as rabbits, squirrels, monkeys, and birds).

1302 German nun and mystic St. Gertrude of Helfta (b. 1256), also known as Gertrude the Great, author of *Exercitia spiritualia septem* and *Legatio divinae pietatis*, dies.

1306 A religious text, the *Mirror of Simple Annihilated Souls*, by Beguine Marguerite Porete, is condemned by the Bishop of Cambrai, publicly burned in Valenciennes, and barred from use on pain of excommunication. The book stresses the soul's individual surrender to faith and love, rather than a need for sacraments and clergymen. Porete is arrested for heresy on April 3, 1310, and given the option of recanting. She refuses, saying, "This Soul replies to nobody, unless she wishes to . . . whoever calls this Soul does not find her, and so her enemies have no reply from her." On May 31, the Inquisition turns her over to the secular authorities, and on June 1, she is burned.

1310 The Beguines, a lay order of women who discuss theology, perform charitable works, and refuse to marry, are condemned and excommunicated by the church. The members are "single women over thirty," wearing "black dresses and veils," who have spread through Belgium, France, and Germany. They serve a one-year novitiate followed by a minimum of six years in the sisterhood; some beg, while others make cloth to support themselves. Some members of the established church think of them as no more than "idle, gossiping vagabonds" who refuse to obey men. Many Beguines are accused of heresy and tortured or burned.

c. 1313 Tirolean domestic servant St. Notburga (b. c. 1265), who was fired from her post for giving the poor leftovers intended for the pigs, dies.

1324 Alice Kyteler, the richest woman in Kilkenny, Ireland, is accused of witchcraft, probably over a property dispute. She defies the religious authorities and ultimately flees to safety in England, though her maid Petronella de Meath is burned at the stake.

1336 Portuguese queen St. Elizabeth (also known as Isabel, b. 1271) dies. She was married, unhappily, at the age of twelve to the unfaithful King Denis of Portugal, who imprisoned her after she attempted to reconcile him to their rebellious son Alfonso. She found her solace in religion, establishing a Poor Clare convent and retiring to a religious life after her husband's death in 1325. However, she remained politically active; in 1336, shortly before her death, she succeeded in making peace between her son, Alfonso IV of Portugal, and his neighboring monarch, Alfonso XI of Castile.

1341 Italian founder St. Juliana Falconieri (b. 1270), who refused to marry and in 1304 established a community of tertiary sisters in Florence, dies.

1350 England has 3,500 nuns. Convent membership will decline in England throughout this century and the next.

1372 French religious leader Jeanne Dabenton, a prominent member of a heretical sect called the Brethren of the Free Spirit, is burned to death in Paris.

July 23, 1373 Swedish saint Bridget (b. c. 1303, canonized 1391) dies. An adviser of popes on both religious and political issues, she dictated a book about Christ's sufferings. One of her eight children, Catherine of Vadstena (d. 1381), was also revered as a saint, though she was never officially canonized. In 1370 Bridget founded the Order of the Holy Savior, informally known as the Bridgetines.

Late 14th century Indian mystic and poet Lal-Ded, a follower of Siva, becomes famous for her spiritual poetry and ecstatic dancing.

Apr. 29, 1380 Italian mystic St. Catherine of Siena (b. 1347), who cut her hair as a girl to discourage potential suitors, dies. She nursed the sick, humbling herself by touching, kissing, and even drinking the pus from their abscesses. In 1375, she mediated a Florentine conflict and induced Pope Gregory XI to move the papacy from Avignon back to Rome. In 1378, after the death of Gregory, she supported Pope Urban VI in the Great Schism.

1389 English heretic clergywoman Alice Dexter, with two men, leads a congregation in Leicester.

c. 1400 French theologian Mary of Valenciennes publishes an account of divine love that terrifies local church authorities because it is well argued, unorthodox, and written in French rather than Latin (and thus available to a wide audience).

1401–1500

General Status and Daily Life

An anonymous English poem of this century laments,

> A woman is a worthy thing:
> They do the washe and do the wringe;
> 'Lullay, Lullay,' she dothe thee synge
>   And yet she has but care and woe.
>
> A woman is a worthy wight:
> She serveth a man both daye and nyght;
> Therto she putteth all her might,
>   And yet she hathe but care and woe.

The fifteenth-century woman has many sources of "care and woe." Upper-class women have only two possible destinies, marriage or the convent, and their parents decide which it will be. If it is marriage, the parents choose the groom. In the middle of the century, Englishwoman Elizabeth Paston insists on choosing her own husband; her parents respond by allowing her no visitors and having her "beaten once in the week or twice, and sometimes twice on a day, and her head broken in two or three places." Especially rich young women may be married while they are still infants; the age of consent is seven, though the marriage can be repudiated (but seldom is) by boys up to fourteen and girls up to twelve. Dower can be collected by a widow as young as nine. Russian wives are segregated in a separate part of the household and can be sold as slaves to pay a man's debts. Everywhere in Europe, wife beating is common and accepted.

European wives have numerous duties. Peasants' wives help at harvest times, raise children, prepare and preserve food, and tend cows and poultry. Artisans' wives assist them in their crafts. Wives of feudal lords are responsible for entertaining, baking, brewing, raising and harvesting crops, butter and cheese making, candle making, salting and storing of meat, spinning and weaving cloth, marketing for whatever is not made at home, supervising the dairy and other domestic animals, and assuming their husbands' duties in case of death or absence.

In Metz, women guilty of infanticide are nailed to stakes, decorated with images of their dead children, and burned to death.

In West Africa, men hunt, fish, and care for livestock; women tend crops, raise children, prepare food, weave, and engage in trade.

Ironing in Europe is done with a flat iron heated in the fireplace and often soiled by soot from the fire. Richer households have irons with interior compartments for holding hot coals.

In Florence, Italy, women usually marry by eighteen; men usually marry in their early thirties.

The Korean government works to enforce Confucian principles and to limit women's freedom of movement. Women are forbidden to visit temples or to attend any funerals but those of close relatives, for fear that they will use religious activities as an excuse to socialize. Widows are discouraged from remarrying. A code of laws collected in 1485 forbids women participation in outdoor games and feasts; those who disobey are subject to a hundred lashes. Women must get permission from a male guardian to engage in any social activity. They may not venture outdoors in daylight except in special circumstances; they are, however, allowed to go out between 9 P.M. and 2 A.M., when men are restricted by

a curfew. Women of all classes must cover their faces outdoors.

1427 Women head 15.6% of all households in Florence.

1466 Dowry is standard in all social classes in Europe, and girls who cannot afford a dowry are sometimes provided one by philanthropists. In an upper-class marriage, the dowry can be quite substantial. One Italian bride brings as her marriage portion 2,500 florins, fourteen dresses decorated with gold and jewels, headdresses, various gems and jewelry, and twenty rings.

c. 1470 The duchess of Brunswick dies. She once lamented, "I have lived here in this castle like an anchoress in a cell. What delights or pleasures have I enjoyed here, save that I have made shift to show a happy face to my servants and gentlewomen? I have a hard husband (as you know) who has scarce any care or inclination towards women. Have I not been in this castle even as it were in a cell?"

Government, Military, and the Law

Senegalese female chiefs and warriors fight against the intrusions of Europeans into their territory. According to oral tradition, there have been quite a number of female rulers along the Gambia River.

Lalla Aziza is a powerful tribal leader in Morocco.

John Baker is "grand sergeant to the monarch" of England, which means that it is his job to hold the king's head if the king gets seasick. When Baker dies, he leaves this post to his daughter.

European camp followers, often the wives of soldiers, travel with the army, sometimes making up as much as one-fifth of the total force in the field. They make camp, collect fuel, cook, wash, nurse the wounded, dig trenches, bury the dead, clean the latrines, and serve as prostitutes.

Attacked by invaders, the women of Tlatelolco in Mexico form a battalion to give the male warriors time to prepare for battle. They march onto the battlefield naked, slapping their stomachs, displaying their breasts, and squirting milk at the invading army. The invaders, confused, do not harm them but simply capture them.

In parts of West Africa, there are separate political and religious hierarchies for men and women, with a woman overseeing women's affairs. In some places, rule is inherited through the female line.

Women in the Ottoman sultan's harem are sometimes

trained in sewing, embroidery, harp playing, and singing. Sometimes they are given as special presents to favored courtiers, who are expected to free and marry them.

1414 Joanna II becomes queen of Naples in her own right. She will marry three times, banishing one husband and murdering another. When her adopted heir threatens to depose her, she disowns him and leaves her throne to another, sparking a civil war upon her death in 1435.

1429 Joan of Arc (b. c. 1412), an intelligent, illiterate peasant girl from Champagne, is told by the voices of saints that she must help the heir to the throne, the Dauphin Charles VII, against the English. She convinces a local lord (who earlier sent her back to her father for "a good slapping") to take her to the Dauphin and identifies Charles in a crowd, despite the fact that he is humbly dressed. After testifying before church officials and being verified a virgin by the ladies of the court, she is accepted as divinely inspired and given money for her mission by Queen Yolande, mother-in-law of the Dauphin. Cutting her hair and adopting men's clothes, she acquires a horse, a suit of armor, and a banner and goes to raise the English siege of Orléans.

She arrives in Orléans with provisions on April 29. The people take hope, follow her commands, and worship her fervently. In defending the town, Joan takes an arrow in the shoulder, returning to battle as soon as the wound is dressed. She is compassionate as well as valiant; shortly after the end of the siege, she sees a Frenchman kill an English prisoner and dismounts to hold and comfort the dying man until a priest arrives. However, on some matters she is fiercely vengeful. She makes her troops give up their concubines, and when, on one occasion, she finds prostitutes among the troops, she kills one with a blow so strong that it breaks her sword. On May 8, she rides at the head of the French army at the Battle of Orléans, a decisive French victory. By summer, she has so inspired the French and frightened the English that she is able to secure the surrender of Meung and Troyes by her very presence. Wounded by crossbows in the neck and the thigh, she is noted for her bravery and skill with artillery.

May 24, 1430 Joan of Arc goes to Compiègne to raise a siege but is captured and sold to the English. Charles VII, whose coronation she arranged, abandons her to her fate. Imprisoned for nine months and tried for witchcraft and heresy, she remains witty and resolute through several interrogations, then yields, rejecting the validity of her religious visions in exchange for a sentence of life imprisonment. Her return to male clothing, however, is seen as a sign of recidivism, and she is considered a relapsed heretic. On May 30, 1431, she is condemned at Rouen and burned at the stake as a witch. Her conviction is overturned by the church in 1456.

1445 Henry VI of England marries Margaret of Anjou (1430–1482), who is criticized for her ambition, accused of running the country, and rumored to have committed adultery with Edmund Beaufort, duke of Somerset. When the paternity of her son is called into question, she defends him with fierce devotion and works to have him placed on the throne. A story intended to prove her maternal fervor says that, accosted in the woods by a brigand, she volunteered herself to be killed but insisted that the bandit protect "the child, your future king, your king's only son, I make you to-day the stomach of my child; I appoint you to be his breast; I make you his father and mother." The bandit reportedly fell to her feet weeping and promised to safeguard the heir to the throne with his life.

In 1460, Margaret kills Richard, duke of York, Henry VI's main rival for power. Margaret is presented with his head, decorated with a paper crown. In 1461 she liberates Henry VI from imprisonment, but her armies are soon defeated by Edward IV's, and she flees to Scotland. In 1471, she raises another army but is defeated and captured at Tewkesbury. Her son and husband are killed, ending her dynastic ambitions.

1459 Persian-Afghan queen Gauhar Shad (b. c. 1378), a patron of the arts and a builder of mosques, is executed for her part in a political power struggle.

c. 1460 Bokenham Castle, the home of Alice Knyvet, is claimed by the Crown. When the king's men come to claim it, Knyvet appears from a tower, where she has armed herself with "slings, parveises, fagots, timber and other armaments of war." She says, "Maister Twyer ye be a Justice of the Peace. I require you to keep the peace, for I will not leave possession of this castle . . . and if ye being to break the peace or make any war to get the place of me, I shall defend me, for liever had I in such wise to die than to be slain when my husband cometh home, for he charged me to keep it." The king's commissioners retreat.

1468–1476 Korean Queen Mother Chonghi Taebi serves as regent for Kings Yejong and Songjong until she is deposed in the midst of controversy over a woman's exercising such power.

1470 At the siege of Beauvais, French heroine Jeanne Laisne "Hachette" leads a troop of women armed with hatchets against the Burgundian attackers, raising the siege and capturing the enemy flag. She will be honored by Louis XI and by generations of Beauvais citizens, who will hold an annual march in her honor in which the women march before the men.

1474 After a two-year struggle for power, Venetian Caterina Cornaro (1454–1510) becomes sole ruler of Cyprus; she will work for years to keep Cyprus free of conflicts between Venice and Turkey. Neutrality will fail, however, and on March 14, 1489, she will be forced to abdicate and sell her island nation to Venice. Returning to Italy, she will turn her home at Asolo into a haven for scholars and artists.

1474 The king of Castile, Henry IV, dies; his half-sister Isabella (b. 1451) confiscates the treasury and declares herself queen. She is married to one of the two possible rivals, Ferdinand of Aragon, and quickly defeats another, Henry's illegitimate daughter Juana. Spain is unified in 1479 under the joint rule of Ferdinand and Isabella, though Castile is considered the heart of the new country, and Isabella dictates that Ferdinand must live in Castile, leave it only with her permission, and never wage war without her consent.

Isabella, sometimes referred to by her troops as "King Isabella," is active in the wars between Spain and the Muslim kingdoms of the Iberian peninsula; she and Ferdinand capture the last Muslim stronghold, Granada, on January 2, 1492. Praised for her "masculine strength of mind," Isabella also builds an impressive library and commissions a Latin-Castilian dictionary, in part to prevent women from needing a man's help in translation.

1477 Mary of Burgundy (1457–March 27, 1482) inherits the Burgundian throne and later prevents an attempted French seizure of the Low Countries.

1483 Caterina Sforza (b. 1462), married to a son of Pope Sixtus IV in 1477, defends her husband's lands against aggressors from Venice. Seven months pregnant, she leads the defenders, wearing a sword and cursing freely at the troops. In 1499, she is declared a "daughter of iniquity" by Pope Alexander VI, who gives her lands of Imola and Forlì to his illegitimate son Cesare Borgia. She resists the usurpation, refusing to yield the fortress of Ravaldino even after the surrounding town has surrendered.

Aug. 30, 1483 Louis XI of France dies. His daughter Anne of Beaujeu (1461–1522) becomes regent for her thirteen-year-old brother, Charles VIII. She will rule well for eight years, curbing the state budget, partially remitting poll taxes, pardoning many prisoners and exiles, and defeating rebellious nobles in the Guerre Folle (Foolish War).

1485 Margaret Beaufort, mother of Henry VII of England, is instrumental in helping him overcome his rivals and ascend the throne.

1491 Anne of Beaujeu arranges the marriage of Charles VIII to Anne of Brittany (1477–1514), who patronizes writers and artists and works to reform the court's morals. The marriage unites Brittany, which Anne has ruled since the age of eleven, and France. After Charles's death, Anne will be forced to marry the next French king, Louis XII.

Literature and the Visual Arts

Some of the principal art patrons of the Renaissance are women, like Isabella d'Este (b. 1474) of Ferrara, Italy, whom poet Niccolò da Correggio calls "the first lady of the world." Venetian aristocrat Giovanna Dandolo patronizes writers and encourages early printing presses.

Women are also artists and writers as well as patrons. In Spain, Florencia del Pinar writes lyric poetry. In France, Italian author Christine de Pisan (d. c. 1430) composes autobiographical works like *L'Avision* (1405) and poetry like *La Mutacion de Fortune* (*The Changes of Fortune*, November 1403), an ambitious work of 23,636 lines. She also writes *Le Livre du chemin de long estude* (1402–1403), a verse work describing a trial of the earth's faults in a Court of Reason; *The Book of the City of Ladies* (1404), which celebrates women's virtues and describes the lives of famous and virtuous women from history; *Le Livre des Trois Vertus* (also known as *Le Trésor de la Cité des Dames* or *The Treasure of the City of Ladies*, 1405), which discusses the duties of women in each class; and the poem *Le Ditié de Jehanne d'Arc* (1429), the only known work praising Joan of Arc written in the warrior's lifetime. Pisan is the first European woman to support herself as a writer. She also employs women when possible, hiring Anastaise, a woman illuminator, to illustrate some of her manuscripts.

1431–1438 English mystical writer Margery Kempe tells the story of her search for a religious life in *The Boke of Margery Kempe*, the oldest extant autobiography in English.

1454 The Bruges painters' guild's membership is 12% female.

1463 Italian Franciscan abbess St. Caterina of Bologna (b. 1413) dies. A visionary and a talented calligrapher and minaturist, she also wrote prose and poetry.

1476 Simonetta Catteano, Florentine child-bride celebrated for her golden-haired beauty and painted repeatedly by Sandro Botticelli, most notably in his *Birth of Venus*, dies at the age of twenty.

1500 Welsh poet Gwerfyl Mechain (b. c. 1460) dies.

Performing Arts and Entertainment

Early 15th century Court jester Madame d'Or performs for Philip the Good, Duke of Burgundy.

Athletics and Exploration

In Europe, upper-class women hunt and hawk. Margot of Hainault is a celebrated tennis player.

1442 German towns sometimes hold races for women.

1454 A footrace for prostitutes is held in Augsburg, Germany; a similar event will take place four years later in Pernes, France. Prostitutes' races are fairly common, though they are often simply an excuse for harassment; men find it amusing to insult and trip the racers.

1486 The prioress of England's Sopwell convent publishes the *Boke of St. Albans*, a guide to hunting, falconry, and armor.

May 1, 1486 Spanish queen Isabella grants Columbus an audience at the Alcazar in Córdoba. She rejects his plan for a voyage but appoints a commission to study his idea and agrees to finance his journey in 1492. In 1498 she authorizes the emigration of thirty Spanish women to the new American colonies.

1493 Venice, Italy, holds its first annual regatta for peasant women.

Activism

Holy Week 1401 Women in Nuremberg, Germany, arrange food, clothing, and shelter for lepers.

Business and Industry

European women are involved in a variety of trades, especially those related to cloth manufacture. In fact, the British silk industry is almost entirely run by women in the fifteenth century, and during the reign of Edward IV, at least one woman is a Merchant of the Staple, which grants her the right to export wool to Calais. Women produce most French women's clothing and table linen.

In Strasbourg, women work as blacksmiths, goldsmiths, wagoners, grain merchants, gardeners, tailors, and coopers. Women belong to the merchant guilds in Arles. In England, merchant Alice Chester becomes prosperous trading wool, wine, iron, and oil to places like Flanders and Spain. In some English guilds such as the York and London barber-surgeons' guilds and the Bristol dyers' guild, women are allowed to become full members. Some women even become involved with business indirectly, as patrons. Venetian aristocrat Giovanna Dandolo, for example, stimulates the Burano lace industry and encourages early printing presses.

However, the vast majority of women are involved in a few traditional and poorly paid jobs: laundress, servant, and manual laborer. Domestic service will remain the principal occupation for European women till the 1930s. Even the best-paid servants find that their work makes unreasonable demands on them. For example, Florentine wet nurses in good homes can make up to twenty florins per year; they are among the highest-paid domestic servants. But the wet nurses' own children sometimes suffer as a result of this system; some are put to nurse on goats, while others are abandoned or slowly starve as the employer's child is favored. Manual laborers are not required to sacrifice their children directly, but the low wages earned by women take their toll nonetheless. Male laborers in Florence earn about 15 soldi a day, while women earn only 7. A bushel of wheat costs 15 soldi, and a small house rents for 375 soldi per year.

Many desperate women turn to prostitution, which offers much higher pay. Prostitutes work for about twenty years on average. Few get rich, though the highly educated courtesans of Renaissance Italy can command astronomical fees for a night's entertainment.

Many European cities operate public brothels.

Women in Africa's Upper Guinea and Senegal coast regions are often wealthy traders, dealing directly with Europeans and being treated with respect by Africans and Europeans alike. Many own slaves and sumptuous clothing and jewelry.

1407 English girls are sometimes apprenticed to trades, sometimes when they are as young as three years old. Urban parents often bequeath their daughters money for either a dowry or apprenticeship fee, much as rural parents leave money as dowry for a husband or a convent. Usually, when apprenticed, the girl is taught by the master's wife, not the master himself.

1414 A church council to end the Great Schism is attended by 1,500 prostitutes; one is said to make 800 ducats for one night's work.

1455 English silk women petition the Crown to prevent competition from Lombard silk makers; they will do so again in 1482. They mention that silk making and silk crafts "be and have been crafts of women...of time that no mind runneth to the contrary." There are currently more than 1,000 women in London earning their living from this trade, but there is no female silk guild, despite women's preponderance in the trade.

1456 Silkwomen in Cologne, Germany, secure government restrictions on unlicensed spinners.

1461 Bristol weavers complain that women are becoming apprenticed to the trade against the rules of the guild, thus resulting in unemployment for male weavers; weavers are restricted from training any more women in the craft.

1484 Margaret Paston (b. 1423), English landowner and businesswoman, dies. While her husband was away at Parliament, she ran his malt and wool business, attended to legal affairs, ran the family, and twice defended the house and lands from armed bandits.

1497 Austrian businesswoman Barbara Fugger dies. Her skillful management of the family textile business made her son Jacob one of the wealthiest men in the Holy Roman Empire and allowed him to become banker to its rulers, the Hapsburgs.

1500 Goldsmith Drutgin van Caster becomes an artisan to Holy Roman Emperor Maximilian.

1500 Twelve thousand of Venice's 100,000 residents are prostitutes.

1500 In Frankfurt, Germany, women have been employed in 201 occupations since 1320; 65 of these are exclusively female.

Science and Medicine

German women submit medical theses at universities.

Jewish women often serve as doctors, with their practices not necessarily limited to female patients.

Women are fewer than 2% of doctors in France and England (and probably the rest of Europe); they are mostly herbalists and midwives rather than full-time professionals. Their work is probably lower-paid but often more reliable than that of the male medical establishment.

Women in France acquire midwives' licenses after being examined by local medical practitioners. A midwife must also get authorization to baptize dying infants. Specialization of any kind, especially in midwifery, brings a medical practitioner lower status.

1406 A system for training female doctors is established in Korea; many women, for modesty's sake, refuse to be treated by male doctors, so medicine women are regarded as necessary for the health of the female population. Trainees learn Chinese, nursing, medicine, midwifery, and acupuncture, though their studies often progress slowly because their families need their labor at home.

1421 English surgeons petition Parliament to limit the medical practices of women, "who possessing neither natural ability nor professional knowledge, make the gravest possible mistakes (thanks to their stupidity) and very oft kill their patients; for they work . . . in a casual fashion, nor are they thoroughly acquainted with the cause or even the names of the maladies which they

claim that they are competent to cure."

1422–1423 Costanza Calenda of the University of Naples is the first university-trained female doctor in Western history.

1435 Female doctors in Korea are paid in rice twice a year by the government. Skillful healers are rewarded by the government, but many patients are still reluctant to trust their expertise. In most cases, they make calls accompanied by male doctors; the woman conducts the examination, and the man issues a prescription for treatment.

1440 Roman noblewoman Francesca Bussi dei Ponziani (b. 1384), later canonized as St. Francesca Romana, dies. Founder of a charitable society, the Oblates of Tor de' Oliveto, she served as an informal doctor to her family, servants, neighbors, and friends and also nursed strangers as well. Refusing all medical treatment herself, she healed her patients by touch, prayer, and drugs or referred them to other practitioners; she refused to make charms or to recommend Jewish doctors.

1485 Charles VIII of France forbids women to work as surgeons.

1494 A law in Freiburg, Germany, bans the practice of abortion or infanticide by midwives.

1500 Swiss pig gelder Jakob Nufer performs, on his wife, the first recorded cesarean in which the mother lives.

Education and Scholarship

Upper-class English girls are taught to read, sometimes in convent schools, sometimes while in service at the houses of other well-to-do families.

Italy has quite a few women schoolteachers, though they are still very much in the minority and are usually paid less than men.

French author Christine de Pisan writes *Le Livre des fais et bonnes meurs du sage Roy Charles V* (*The Book of the Deeds and Good Customs of Charles V*, 1404), a manual on good government; *Le Livre du corps de policie* (*The Book of the Body of Policy*, 1406–1407), which contains advice to rulers, soldiers, and the common people on their duties and proper spheres; *Le Livre des fais d'armes et de chevalrie* (1410), a book of instruction for knights; *Le Livre de la paix* (1412–1414), a guidebook to ruling a country written for the Dauphin; *Lamentation on the Evils of Civil War* (1410), an open letter to the people of France; and *Letter of the Prison of Human Life* (c. 1417), composed to console Marie of

Berry for the death or imprisonment of most of her family.

1404 There is at least one female teacher of Latin grammar in England.

1409 Italian teacher Ursa runs a Venetian girls' school.

1438 Italian classicist Isotta Nogarola (1418–1466), known as the "Divine Isotta" for her brilliance, and her scholar sister Ginevra (c. 1417–1468) are accused of promiscuity and incest and forced to flee to Verona to pursue theological works in isolation. It is likely that the charges have been manufactured to drive the sisters from secular, "masculine" studies and into the more acceptably feminine sphere of religion. Isotta will write a *Dialogue on Adam and Eve* (*De pari aut impari Evae atque Adae peccato*, 1451) and an *Oration on the Life of St. Jerome* (*Oratio in laudem beati Hieronymis*, 1453).

1448 Margaret of Anjou, queen of England, establishes Queen's College, Cambridge.

1456 A male schoolteacher in Überlingen, Germany, complains that a female teacher is so good that some of his male pupils are beginning to attend her school. He sues successfully to have her pay him "three schillings per year for every boy that she teaches, because my own income has been diminished."

c. 1465–1469 Onorata and Tadea are teachers of girls in Verona.

1471 Portuguese princess Isabella, wife of Philip the Good of Burgundy, dies. She patronized scholars and translated Xenophon from the Greek.

1475 Korean queen Sohei publishes *Naehun* (*Moral Education for Women*) to popularize tales of virtuous ladies and provide instruction in speech, filial piety, marriage, family relations, and thrift. It is the first book of etiquette for women published in *han'gul*, the new Korean alphabet.

Religion

Two Spanish nuns are burned to death for engaging in lesbian acts.

1400–1600 An estimated two witches per day are executed in Germany.

1409 One Chinese goddess is Tian Hou, originally a simple patroness of fishermen, but now considered a benevolent celestial concubine.

1443 English mystic Julian of Norwich (b. 1342) dies.

1447 French nun St. Colette, born Nicolette Boylet, dies. In 1406 she received authorization to reform the order of the Poor Clares and return it to its original severity of rule. Although she at first met with opposition, she eventually succeeded, founding several new convents in the process.

1468 The papacy exempts witchcraft from the normal limits on torture of the accused.

1485 Korean law dictates that female shamans must stay out of the capital city; if found, they will be punished. This and future regulations discouraging female shamans and fortune-tellers are mostly ineffective. Almost every large town or city has a chief female shaman, some of whom are received at court.

1486 *Malleus Maleficarum* (*Hammer of Witches*), by German monk Jacob Sprenger, outlines the habits of witches. It repeats rumors of the *vagina dentata* and says that witches sometimes collect men's severed penises. The *Malleus Maleficarum* also claims that women, as the weaker sex, are more likely to fall prey to satanic influences.

1490 Italian mystic and saint Catherine of Genoa (1447–1510) becomes matron of the Pammatone Hospital. An extremely devout woman who goes to communion daily and fasts frequently, she has devoted herself to nursing the sick and even tends to plague victims.

1501–1600

General Status and Daily Life

Average age at marriage for women is twenty-five in England, twenty in some parts of France. Legal age of consent in England is twelve for girls. Some European women retain their birth names after marriage. Wives are commonly instructed to address their mates as "husband," rather than by endearments or their first names.

Russian women of high birth are sequestered in the *terem* (women's quarters). Husbands are advised to beat even good wives "but nicely, in secret, and in a polite fashion, avoiding blows of the fist which cause bruises." An ambassador to Russia writes, "A woman is considered honorable only when she lives at home and never goes out . . . . Very seldom is she permitted to go to church, and still more seldom to see friends, except when she is elderly and will not attract suspicion."

A Korean woman does not have a name of her own; she is known, at various times of her life, as so-and-so's daughter, wife, or mother. Once married, she is never supposed to enter her father's house again, which means that if her husband discards her, she has nowhere to go. Marriages are arranged by parents, often when the prospective bride and groom are mere children, though the bride is usually a few years older than her spouse. The bride does not see her husband until the wedding night, and she may not show affection for him in public. Indeed, she is hardly allowed to show him affection in private, at least at first; on the wedding night, her female relatives observe the consummation of the marriage through holes in the paper doors. Her conduct is carefully observed. She must not speak to her husband, even if he asks her questions, and she must not move unless guided by him.

Men and women are strictly segregated within the house. A woman can expect strict filial piety from her son, especially after she becomes a widow; loyalty to both of one's parents is strongly rewarded by society and by the government. Weddings are extremely expensive, and in some families the cost prohibits some daughters from marrying or ruins the family financially. Women can inherit equally with their brothers.

In England, women who transgress the bounds of acceptable feminine behavior are punished for their boldness; a woman found guilty of "scolding" (a crime that can include anything from frank criticism to loud and abusive language) is tied to a chair or "ducking stool" suspended from a beam and dunked repeatedly in the nearest body of water. The ducking stool will survive well into the eighteenth century.

1532 Holy Roman Emperor Charles V bans lesbian acts; the penalty is death by burning. Infanticide is also made a capital crime.

1543 The first shotguns arrive in Japan; metalworker Yatsuita, ordered to copy the devices, trades his own daughter to a Portuguese armorer in exchange for lessons.

1545 Turkish harem women wear a chemise and pair of loose trousers, covered with a floor-length cloak. Outdoors the body will be covered with a shapeless tunic called a *feradge*, and the face will be concealed behind a veil.

1555 Sir Anthony Fitzherbert's *A Boke of Husbandrye* outlines the duties of a wife: "milk the kine, suckle thy calves, strain up the milk . . . get corn and malt ready for the mill to bake and brew . . . make butter and cheese when thou may, serve thy swine both morning and evening . . . take heed how thy hens, ducks, and geese do lay." Linen, flax, and hemp must be "weeded, pulled, watered, washed, dried, beaten, braked, hatchelled, spun, wound, wrapped and woven." The linen is then used to

"make sheets, tablecloths, towels, shirts, smocks, and other such necessaries." A wife must know how to prepare wool and "to winnow all manner of corns, to make malt, wash and wring, to make hay, to shear corn, and in time of need to help her husband to fill the muck wain or dung cart, drive the plough, to load . . . corn, and such other. Also to go to the market, to sell butter, cheese, milk, eggs, chickens, capons, hens, pigs, geese, and all manner of corn. And also to buy all manner of necessary thing belonging to the household, and to make a true reckoning and account to her husband what she hath received and what she hath paid."

1570 More than 8% of women age thirty-one to forty in Norwich, England, have been deserted by their husbands.

1578–1615 Fourteen women in Nuremberg, Germany, are drowned or beheaded for infanticide.

1588 Pope Sixtus V calls all abortions murder.

1598 Mothers of illegitimate children in Devonshire, England, are whipped.

Government, the Military, and the Law

Women of Mexico's Chichimeca tribe are renowned for their bravery in battle and are highly respected by the men of their nation.

Indian leader Chand Bibi, princess of Deccan, leads troops in battle against the Moghuls.

Moroccan queen Sida Al El Horra attacks Portuguese and Spanish ships with her fleet and becomes "Caliph of the Sultan" through her marriage to the Moroccan king.

Wives and concubines of the Ottoman emperor are "couched" with him on a rotating schedule, to prevent jealousy and strife. Records are kept of each woman's encounters with the Sultan to verify the legitimacy of her children. Competition for couching is fierce, and circumvention of the schedule is severely punished; Gülfem Kadin, one of Suleiman the Magnificent's wives, is executed for selling her couching appointment to another member of the harem.

c. 1502 Lucrezia Borgia (1480–June 24, 1519), illegitimate daughter of Pope Alexander VI, marries her third husband, Alfonso d'Este, future Duke of Ferrara. On her journey to her new husband, she is accompanied by 180 retainers, 150 mules carrying her trousseau (including a dress worth over $150,000), and five bishops. Lucrezia has been horribly slandered by her enemies and accused of incest, adultery, and other crimes. However, once she is married to Alfonso, Lucrezia begins gradually to free herself of her family's political intrigues, becoming a highly religious woman and a patron of the arts and serving as regent of Ferrara in Alfonso's absence.

Nov. 26, 1504 Queen Isabella of Castile dies. She ruled independently of her husband, Ferdinand of Aragon, reducing the power of the aristocracy, patronizing scholars and artists, expelling 170,000 Jews from Spain through the Inquisition, driving Muslims from Iberia, and fighting next to her husband in battle, taking her five children with her as she traveled through her realm. In theory, her daughter Juana is now queen, but in practice, Isabella's husband, Ferdinand, still rules Castile. By 1506, Ferdinand will be in complete control of Spain; after the death of Juana's husband, Philip the Fair, Ferdinand has her declared insane and imprisoned. Juana will become known as "la Loca" (the Mad) and will continue to be imprisoned by her son, Charles V, after his accession.

1509 Isabella d'Este (1474–1539), wife of Francesco Gonzaga, ruler of Mantua, Italy, saves the city from invasion after he is captured. When he dies in 1519, she will become regent for their son.

1509 Italian noblewoman Caterina Sforza dies. Well educated, vain, beautiful, and defiant, she took many lovers and became famous for wreaking bloodthirsty vengeance on her enemies. When her children were held hostage as a result of a political conflict, she boasted that she could make more children. She was eventually defeated in battle, however, by Pope Alexander VI's illegitimate son Cesare Borgia, who captured and raped her in 1500. She was later released, but her lands were not returned.

Feb. 18, 1516 After her first five children died in the womb or shortly after birth, Spanish-born Queen of England Catherine of Aragon (1485–Jan. 1536), daughter of Ferdinand and Isabella and first wife of Henry VIII, gives birth to her only surviving child, Princess Mary Tudor.

Nov. 8, 1519 The Spanish conquistador Cortés arrives in the Aztec capital. Soon afterward, he will take as his mistress Malinal (1502 or 1505–1550), a slave of the Aztecs known variously as Doña Marina and La Malinche. She serves as a translator, an intermediary, and, according to some, a traitor: she warns the Spaniards of an impending attack at Cholula, preventing them from being massacred. In 1522, she gives birth to Cortés's son; in 1524, she travels with Cortés to quell a rebellion in Honduras.

1524 Venezuelan Aldonza Manrique becomes governor of the island of Margarita, a post she inherits from her father and will hold for about sixty years.

Aug. 1529 The Peace of Cambrai, a treaty between France and the Hapsburgs, is signed and becomes known as the Paix de Dames, because both signing agents are female. Charles V's proxy is his aunt, Margaret of Austria (1480–1530); the French signatory is Louise of Savoy, Duchesse d'Angoulême (1476–1531). Mother of author Marguerite of Navarre and of King Francis I, Louise served as regent in 1515–1516 and 1525–1526, negotiated Francis's release after he was captured in battle, and enriched herself from the public coffers.

1533 Henry VIII's desire to divorce Catherine of Aragon (for her failure to produce a male heir) and marry his mistress, Anne Boleyn (b. 1507), results in the break of England from the Catholic church. Henry marries Anne, who gives birth on September 7 to a daughter, Elizabeth Tudor, the future Queen Elizabeth I.

May 19, 1536 Henry VIII's wife, Anne Boleyn, who has fallen out of favor, is beheaded, consoling herself that it will not be painful: "I have heard say that the executioner is very good and I have a very little neck." The next day Henry marries his third wife, Anne's lady-in-waiting Jane Seymour. Jane will be queen for little more than a year, dying in October 1537 after giving birth to Edward, the long-awaited male heir to the throne.

1540 Henry VIII marries his fourth wife, Anne of Cleves (1515–1557), then quickly has the marriage annulled on July 9 and marries Anne Boleyn's young cousin Katherine Howard on July 28. Howard will be beheaded for treason on February 13, 1542, after it is discovered that she has had lovers other than the King. Henry marries his sixth and last wife, Catherine Parr (1512–1548), in 1543.

1540–1541 Spanish soldier's wife Beatriz Hernández helps to defend the new settlement of Guadalajara, fighting the Indians with a fierceness barely restrained by her male companions. She repeatedly urges that the town be moved to a more defensible location.

1541 Roxelana, wife of sultan Suleiman the Magnificent, breaks tradition by moving the harem into the sultan's own home, where the actual business of government takes place. This new proximity to power results in a political ascendancy of harem women that will last until 1687. Roxelana brings with her one hundred ladies-in-waiting, a personal dressmaker, and a number of slaves. A former slave, she is the first legal wife of a sultan in more than a hundred years. Ultimately, she will become one of the most powerful figures in the Ottoman Empire, forcing the executions of her enemies and elevating her friends.

June 24, 1542 Spanish conquistadores are attacked along a huge South American river by female archers and name the river "Amazon" after the warrior women of Greek legend.

c. 1550 Among the powerful Native American leaders of the time is the "Lady of Cofitachique," who rules several villages in what will later be known as South Carolina.

July 6, 1553 Edward VI of England dies, setting aside Henry VIII's will (which specifies that Edward's Catholic half-sister Mary Tudor is the next heir) and naming his Protestant cousin, Lady Jane Grey, as his successor. He is encouraged to do so by his powerful advisers, not for religious reasons but because they feel that the teenage Jane, who has been intimidated all her life by her family, will be easier to control than the adult, embittered, and opinionated Mary. To further control Jane, she is married in Edward's last weeks of life to Guildford Dudley, son of Edward's most influential and ambitious adviser, the duke of Northumberland.

Jane is proclaimed queen on July 10, but the increasingly popular Mary is proclaimed queen on July 19, and Lady Jane Grey leaves the throne with obvious relief. Mary, entering London in triumph in August, announces her hope for an English return to Catholicism but promises tolerance for those who follow their consciences.

On February 12, 1554, Jane (b. 1537) is beheaded in the Tower of London after Mary concludes that the would-be queen is too volatile a focus for rebellion. Jane goes to her death calmly, with "her countenance nothing abashed, neither her eyes anything moistened with tears."

Mar. 17, 1554 Following a rebellion by Thomas Wyatt, Elizabeth Tudor, Mary I's half-sister, is confined in the Tower of London. Taken, despite her protests, through the Traitor's Gate, she proclaims, "Here landeth as true a subject, being prisoner, as ever landed at these stairs." In May she is removed from the Tower and in 1555 permitted to return to her own house at Hatfield, though still a prisoner.

1555 Mary Tudor, already unpopular for her marriage to Philip II of Spain, makes heresy illegal and begins burning Protestants, becoming known as a result as "Bloody Mary." She will execute about 300 in all, including 55 women. This is a bad year for the Queen in other ways as well; childless, she believes for a time that she is pregnant. In late April, rumor has it that Mary has delivered a prince; a *Te Deum* is sung and bells are rung. But her condition turns out to be dropsy instead.

1558 Scotsman John Knox publishes *The First Blast of the Trumpet Against the Monstrous Regiment of Women*, which claims that the rule of women like Mary Tudor, Mary Stuart of Scotland, and Elizabeth Tudor is unnatural and unholy.

1558 Sultana Roxelana, wife of Suleiman the Magnificent, dies. She became Suleiman's favorite and managed to oust his first wife, Gülbahar, his other women, his grand vizier Ibrahim, and finally his heir, Prince Mustafa, the rival of her own sons. After her death, she is replaced as Suleiman's most trusted adviser, not by her sons, but by her daughter, Mihrimah.

Jan. 1, 1558 Convinced to wage a war against France by her husband, Philip II of Spain, Mary I of England loses Calais, the last of England's holdings in France. Mary proclaims, "When I am dead and opened, you shall find 'Calais' engraved on my heart." She dies November 17, naming her half-sister Elizabeth as her successor.

Jan. 1559 The House of Commons urges Elizabeth to marry. The decades to follow will see the English people anxiously hoping for an heir, Elizabeth delaying any promise of marriage, and half the eligible royalty of Europe (including Eric of Sweden and Henri of Anjou) seeking to acquire England through matrimony with its queen. Elizabeth expresses her desire to remain a virgin but continues to negotiate with prospective husbands, keeping their governments friendly and thus preserving peace.

Elizabeth's romantic impulses are satisfied in quite another fashion. Always susceptible to flattery, she takes several favorites in turn, including Robert Dudley, earl of Leicester, Sir Walter Raleigh, and the earl of Essex.

July 10, 1559 Henri II of France dies while jousting. His widow and sometime regent, Catherine de Medici (1519–January 5, 1589), forces his mistress, Diane de Poitiers (1499–1566), to return all the money he gave her and to leave the court. Francis II is now king, and his wife Mary Stuart, Queen of Scots (b. 1542), is now queen of France as well. To complete her empire, she also lays claim to the throne of England through her grandmother Margaret Tudor (sister of Henry VIII of England and wife of James IV of Scotland), an ambitious move that displeases Queen Elizabeth. Francis II dies in 1560; Catherine de Medici declares herself regent, ruling until 1570. Mary Stuart returns to her native Scotland, a stranger to its ways, language, and religion.

1561 Maham Anaga, the nurse of Indian Moghul ruler Akbar, arranges to have his regent stabbed. Until 1562 she enjoys great power over the young ruler, but then she falls from favor.

1565 Korean Queen Mother Munjong Taebi dies. She became regent in 1545 for her twelve-year-old son and continued to exercise political influence for the next twenty years.

1565 Mozambique's touchy relations with Portugal are represented by the conflict between the first wife of the king of Munhumuptapa, who favors the Portuguese trade, lives among Christians, and calls herself the mother of the colonists, and the king's second wife, who prefers the Muslims and who would rather exclude the Portuguese.

May 15, 1567 Mary, Queen of Scots, marries the earl of Bothwell, one of the probable conspirators in her first husband Henry Darnley's murder. The marriage is received with outrage by the Scots, who have never quite warmed to Mary. She is imprisoned on July 24, 1567; under duress, she abdicates in favor of her son, one-year-old James VI. In 1568, she escapes and flees to England, where Queen Elizabeth imprisons her.

1568 In India, Rajput women at the fortress of Chitor burn themselves alive rather than be captured by the Moghul emperor Akbar.

1573 Dutch shipwright Kenau Hasselaer (1526–c. 1588) helps defend the city of Haarlem during a siege.

1576 Nigerian queen Amina (b. 1560) takes the throne. A daughter of Queen Bakwa Turunku, she is already known as a formidable warrior who has refused to marry any of her suitors. For the next twenty years, she will concentrate her efforts on conquest and expansion.

1576 Shah Tah-masb of Iran dies; his daughter, Parikhan-Khanum, influential during her father's reign, secures the succession for one of her brothers and deposes him later when he ceases to be ruled by her. She is later assassinated at the behest of the new ruler's wife.

1576 Incan princess Beatriz Clara Coya (b. c. 1558) marries Spaniard Oñez de Loyola, and the two are sent to govern Chile.

1583 Sultana Baffa is strangled in her bed. A Venetian by birth, she was kidnapped by pirates and sold to the sultan's harem, where she became known as Safiye and quickly rose to power. Her influence over Murad IV kept Venetian ships safe from Turkish depredations, and her influence continued during the reign of her son Mehmed III. Other nations recognized her power, and Catherine de Medici and Elizabeth I negotiated with her.

Feb. 8, 1587 Mary, Queen of Scots, is beheaded by order of her cousin Queen Elizabeth. The last straw was the Babington plot, the last in a long string of intrigues to overthrow Elizabeth in favor of Mary. Mary clearly had a hand in some of these plots, though it is unclear that Elizabeth has the right to try or condemn a fellow monarch.

Aug. 1588 Fearing attack from Spain, Elizabeth I addresses the troops at Tilbury, refusing to heed cautions that she could easily be assassinated by one of the soldiers. She says, "I know that I have the body of a weak and feeble woman, but I have the heart and stomach of a King, and of a King of England, too." A Spanish armada attacks in September and is defeated with few English losses; Elizabeth's popularity soars.

1592–1599 During the Japanese invasion of Korea, 356 women kill themselves rather than be raped by the invaders. The entertainer Kyewolhyang, a gifted singer and dancer, performs for the Japanese general Konishi Yukinaga, gets him to fall in love with her, then kills him while he sleeps. Ashamed of having entertained him at all, even for such a patriotic purpose, she insists upon being beheaded for complicity with the enemy.

1593 Irish pirate Grace O'Malley (Grainne Mhaol, b. 1530) is brought barefoot and ragged before Queen Elizabeth at Greenwich. A dreaded enemy of England, O'Malley was called in 1577 "a notorious woman in all the coasts of Ireland."

Literature and the Visual Arts

16th–17th centuries Chinese calligrapher, poet, painter, and embroiderer Xing Cijing becomes well-known for her delicately outlined religious figures.

1503–1507 Arguably the most famous portrait subject in history, Lisa del Gioconda (Mona Lisa) sits for her portrait by Leonardo da Vinci, a painting that her husband ultimately refuses to accept or to pay for.

1514 Dutch poet Sister Bertken (b. 1427?), an Utrecht nun whose poems are full of biblical allusions, dies.

1515 Mystical Spanish poet Teresa de Jesùs is born.

1518 Elizabeth Talbot, countess of Shrewsbury (d. 1608), is born. Better known as "Bess of Hardwick," she will serve as caretaker to the imprisoned Mary, Queen of Scots, and will be best remembered for her construction of a number of historic and beautiful estates.

1530 Italian sculptor Properzia de Rossi (b. c. 1490) dies. She was described as "skilled not only in household matters, . . . but in infinite fields of knowledge, so that not only women but men too were envious. She was beautiful and played and sang better than any other woman in the city at that time."

1539 Italian noblewoman Isabella D'Este dies. An enthusiastic patron of the arts, she commissioned translations of Plutarch and Philostratus and encouraged many artists and writers, including Titian, Da Vinci, Raphael, Castiglione, Ariosto, Tasso, Michelangelo, Jan van Eyck, Mantegna, and Perugino. The poet Bembo said he "desired to serve her and please her as if she were pope."

1545 Manuscript illuminator Susanna Horenbout (b. 1503) dies. She once sold a drawing of Jesus to Albrecht Dürer, who was amazed "that a woman can do so much."

Nov. 1546 Flemish miniaturist Levina Teerlinc (c. 1520–1576) is granted an annual salary of forty pounds per year at the English court, a higher fee than the famous portraitist Holbein's. Famous in England (where she is the country's greatest miniaturist from 1543 to the 1570s) and the Netherlands, she will work for every English monarch from Henry VIII to Elizabeth I.

1547 Italian poet Vittoria Colonna (b. 1490) dies. The center of a brilliant artistic circle, she wrote love sonnets to her husband while he was away conducting military campaigns, composed elegies for him after his death, and sent 143 sonnets to her close friend Michelangelo.

1547 Italian courtesan and scholar Tullia d'Aragona (1510–1556) publishes the poetry collection *Rime*.

Dec. 21, 1549 Marguerite of Navarre (b. 1492), author of letters, poetry, a spiritual guide entitled *The Mirror of the Sinful Soul*, and *The Heptameron* (published posthumously in 1558), dies. Her court offered refuge and support for Protestant clerics and writers, including Dolet, Marot, and Rabelais. She is considered by many to be the mother of the French Renaissance.

1551 Korean artist Sin Saimdang (b. 1504) dies. Noted for her paintings of grapes and grasshoppers, she was also a poet, embroiderer, calligrapher, and scholar of Confucian literature and history.

1554 Italian artist Sofonisba Anguissola (d. November 16, 1625), the best-known woman artist of her time, paints her first known work, a *Self-Portrait*. Self-portraits will become Anguissola's trademark; one of the most famous, painted in 1561, will show her playing the spinet under the observation of a dour old chaperone. Another of her self-portraits will inspire Irene of Spilimbergo (1540–1560) to become an artist.

Apr. 25, 1566 French lyric poet, linguist, salon hostess, and musician Louise Labé (b. 1525) dies. She was a skilled equestrian and archer who fought on horseback for the Dauphin against Spain. She was nicknamed "la belle Amazone" for her fighting ability and "la belle Cordière" for her marriage to a rope maker.

1569 Chinese poet Huang O (b. 1498), one of the few noncourtesans of her day to write erotic poetry, dies.

1573 Indian poet Mira Bai (b. 1498) dies. India's best-known woman poet, she married a prince when she was eighteen and after his death survived a poisoning attempt by a local king angry at her rebellious religious views. Her poetry is notable for its mystical and erotic handling of religious subjects.

Mid-late 16th century Chinese painter Miss Qiu is active. She often paints figures of upper-class women and creates pictures to accompany calligraphy, or studies of Guanyin (Buddha) in delicate gold outlines on black paper.

1587 or 1588 Suor Plautilla Nelli (b. 1523), a nun and artist who began as a miniaturist and copyist and eventually designed altarpieces for prominent patrons, dies.

1589 Korean scholar and poet Ho Nansolhon (b. 1563), author of about 140 poems in Korean and Chinese, dies. She was one of the greatest writers of *kasa*, a genre somewhere between prose and lyric poetry, in which verses are composed of pairs of four-syllable phrases.

1594 Flemish painter Clara Peeters, who will help to invent the genre of still life, is born.

Performing Arts and Entertainment

1544 Korean *kisaeng* (woman entertainer) Hwang Chin-i (b. c. 1506) dies. She was beautiful and witty, a talented poet and singer whose charms seduced even a noted Buddhist monk. She was particularly noted for her *sijo*, poems with three-line, fourteen-to-sixteen-syllable stanzas. *Kisaeng* are skilled dancers and singers. Those in the lower ranks of the *kisaeng* are part-time or full-time prostitutes, but the top-rank *kisaeng* are artists only. Like the courtesans of ancient Greece or medieval Japan and China, they have much more freedom of movement and expression than "respectable" women and are treated almost as comrades by the men they entertain.

Mid-16th century Jane Bold is a jester in the courts of Henry VIII and Mary I of England.

Late 16th century Court jester Mathurine amuses Marie de Medici and Henri IV of France with her political and religious humor.

1580 Laura Peverara, Anna Guarini, and Livia d'Arco are professional musicians at the court of Duke Alfonso d'Este. They are joined in 1583 by Tarquinia Molza (b. 1542), also a talented poet, astronomer, and mathematician, who makes more than twice as much per year as the duke's choirmaster and has rooms in the palace.

Athletics and Exploration

During the Spanish conquest of Mexico, María de Estrada rides into battle with her conquistador husband, killing Mexican warriors with her lance and earning a land grant of two towns for her bravery in leading a charge. In the battle for Tenochtitlán, Beatriz Bermúdez, another soldier's wife, puts on armor and threatens to kill any man who retreats. Isabel Rodrigo nurses the wounded and earns the title "doctor" and the right to practice medicine in the new colony.

1528 Ten Spanish women accompany their husbands on an exploratory mission in the Gulf of Mexico. When their husbands are lost on a journey ashore, they spend a year searching for them before settling in Veracruz and remarrying.

1535 Spanish-Argentinian colonist Isabel de Guevara accompanies an exploratory mission by Pedro de Mendoza. She is one of the first settlers in the new town of Buenos Aires. There are other women in the early settlement as well; according to Isabel, they save the small town by cooking, cleaning, nursing, and performing the traditionally masculine jobs (standing watch, defending the town against attack, and drilling the soldiers) when famine and disease kill or incapacitate many of the men.

1552 St. Andrew's Golf Club is established in Scotland. Among its patrons is Mary, Queen of Scots, probably the first woman golfer.

Aug. 18, 1587 Virginia Dare, daughter of two of Sir Walter Raleigh's 177 Roanoke colonists, is the first English child born in the New World. She, along with the rest of the colony, will disappear within three years, never to be found.

1598 About 130 women join an expedition from Mexico to New Mexico. Among them are Luisa Robledo and Doña Eufemia, who help to defend the colonists against Indian attack by organizing rooftop defense units.

Activism

1572 After the Saint Bartholomew's Eve massacre of Huguenots (Protestants) in France, Louise de Coligny and other women open their homes and lands to refugees.

1577 Prominent Italian courtesan Veronica Franco petitions the government of Venice for a prostitutes' shelter that will admit the women's children as well.

1580 English philanthropist Catherine Willoughby, duchess of Suffolk, dies. She donated funds to Protestant hospitals in Germany and Italy and provided aid to more than 1,000 German religious refugees.

Business and Industry

Aztec women work as tailors, weavers, spinners, manuscript illuminators, cooks, healers, midwives, and prostitutes.

Korean women work as laundresses, seamstresses, vendors, and peasant farmers.

Women servants in Lyons, France, earn food, shelter, and two to five livres a year.

The English silkwomen's guild charges a five-pound apprenticeship fee. Apprentices begin at seven years old and finish their training at fifteen.

In various parts of Europe, women work as blacksmiths, gardeners, goldsmiths, wagoners, grain dealers, tailors, coopers, taffeta weavers, silk carders, embroiderers, watch chain makers, agricultural laborers (making half as much as men), and merchants.

1503 The job of packing wool onto ships in Southampton, England, seems to be done almost universally by women, judging from a statute that provides for elections of two women to be wardens of their company and warns the workers "not to bawl nor scold one another."

1551 The town of Ulm, Germany, which closed its brothels in 1537, reopens them "to avoid worse disorders."

1560 German entrepreneur Barbara Uttman begins a lace-making business; eventually she will employ nearly 900 pieceworkers and run her late husband's mining operation.

1563 England sets women laborers' wages at one-third to one-half of men's.

1565 Venice's *Most Honored Courtesans* is a visitor's guide to the 215 best prostitutes in town. It lists two of Italy's most prominent female poets, Gaspara Stampa (1523–1554) and Veronica Franco (1546–1591). Franco's clients include Henri III of France.

Science and Medicine

Swiss physician Marie Colinet is so skilled that she earns honorary Parisian citizenship. She sets bones, delivers babies, and develops a pioneering technique of removing metal fragments from the eye with a magnet. The magnet technique, which will be used as late as the twentieth century, will later be attributed to her husband, even though his contribution consists merely of describing how she performs it.

Fourteen successful cesarean sections are performed in this century throughout Europe.

1526 The first known woman pathologist dies at the University of Bologna. She was a pioneer in the study of the circulatory system and died of overwork at nineteen.

1540 The new London surgeons' guild excludes women.

1566 French scientist Marie de Coste Blanche publishes *The Nature of the Sun and Earth*.

Education and Scholarship

There are a few schools for girls in most European countries, but they are far outnumbered by schools for boys.

1509 Margaret Beaufort (b. 1443), mother of Henry VII of England, translator, patron of early printing presses, endower of divinity professorships at Oxford and Cambridge, and founder of Christ's College, Cambridge, and St. John's College, dies.

1520–1560 For a brief period, upper-class European girls receive thorough classical educations.

1524 Nun and saint Camilla da Varano dies; she has written twenty-two works since 1479, including prayers, letters, an autobiography, and Latin treatises.

1534 Spanish scholar Beatrix Galindo (b. 1474) dies. She was an author of scholarly works and Latin poetry, a founder of schools and hospitals, a tutor of Queen Isabella I, and a professor of philosophy, rhetoric, and medicine at the University of Salamanca. Her contemporary Francisca de Lebrixa taught at the University of Alcalá.

1536 All children in Geneva, Switzerland, male and female, are ordered to attend elementary schools.

1544 English scholar Margaret Roper (b. 1505) dies. The daughter of Sir Thomas More, she was well versed in philosophy, science, and music and was an accomplished translator of Greek and Latin. After her father's execution, she defied the law to recover and bury his head.

1548 In England, only eight books by women have been printed since 1486, but ninety-five more will be published by 1640.

1556 Venetian scholar Cassandra Fedele (1465–1558) delivers a Latin oration for the visiting Queen of Poland.

1587 About 12–13% of Venetian girls are literate (and about 33% of boys).

1591 Queen Elizabeth I establishes Trinity College in Dublin.

1600 In London, 90% of women are illiterate.

Religion

English prophet Mother Shipton, possibly an apocryphal figure, writes *Mother Shipton's Fortune-Telling Book*. Charged with, but never convicted of, witchcraft, she allegedly utters one prophecy per day.

Witch hunts continue throughout Europe, with thousands of women being burned. Between 1587 and 1593, 22 villages near Trier will burn 368; by 1595, two villages in the area will have only one female inhabitant each.

1505 French queen and saint Joan of Valois (b. 1464) dies. The daughter of King Louis XI, she established a women's religious order and never consummated her own marriage.

1529 Anabaptist leaders, who have previously condoned women's preaching, begin to withdraw their support.

1534 There are about 1,900 nuns in England.

1534 Elizabeth Barton, an English ecstatic known as "The Nun of Kent," is burned at Tyburn for her opposition to Henry VIII's marriage to Anne Boleyn.

1538 German noblewoman Elisabeth of Braunschweig is converted to Protestantism and, upon becoming regent of her husband's lands after his death, changes the religion of the region within five years.

Jan. 27, 1540 Italian saint Angela of Brescia (b. 1474), who established the Ursuline Order to educate young girls, dies. An orphan, she first came to the attention of the church as a skilled catechism teacher. In about 1540 she founded the Company of St. Ursula, dedicated to the education of girls. The first women's teaching order, it will not be formally incorporated into the Catholic church until after her death.

July 16, 1546 English Protestant martyr Anne Askew is tortured and burned at the stake for denying the doctrine of transsubstantiation.

1552 Florence has forty-seven convents. Female

religious, including quasi-religious conversae or convent servants, are 13% of the city's female population.

1554 Renee d'Este, duchess of Ferrara, is imprisoned for heresy by her husband the duke, who resents her tolerance of Protestants.

1559 Dutch Anabaptist Elizabeth Dirks is arrested and tortured with thumbscrews and leg screws but refuses to renounce her faith. Told by her interrogators that she speaks "with a haughty tongue," she replies, "No, my Lords, I speak with a free tongue."

1565 A Jewish lawbook, *Shulchan Aruch*, restates the Levitical rule that a menstruating woman (*niddah*) is impure and may not sleep in her husband's bed, eat with her family, be in the same room with others, light the Sabbath candles, enter the synagogue, touch her husband, or pass any object directly to her husband. In some areas, Jewish women wear special clothing during menstruation to warn others of their uncleanness.

1566 Pope Pius V's bull *Circa Pastoralis* orders nuns to stay inside the convent walls and to limit contact with the outside world.

Apr. 19, 1566 Italian religious leader Giulia Gonzaga dies. For twenty-five years, she led an evangelical sect founded by Juan de Valdés, risking being burned alive for her views. Her death from natural causes takes place just as an ecclesiastical investigation has linked her to the *valdesiani*.

June 1572 French Huguenot leader Jeanne d'Albret, queen of Navarre (b. 1528) dies, only a few months after making peace with Catholic Regent Catherine de Medici.

Jeanne's first, unconsummated marriage to a Catholic duke took place against her will when she was fourteen years old; she was so firmly resolved against the match that she had to be carried to the altar. Later, she resisted pressure to abandon her faith with equal fervor, remaining steadfast despite being imprisoned by her second husband, being excommunicated and threatened by the pope, and having her child taken from her to be raised as a Catholic.

She inherited the kingdom of Navarre in 1555 and immediately devoted herself to religious reform. Within a few years she was one of the most powerful Protestant leaders in France and one of the fiercest opponents of the Catholic Guise party. In 1561 she made Catholicism and Protestantism coequal in her kingdom. In 1571 she made the kingdom officially Protestant but continued to allow Catholics freedom of worship.

Oct. 4, 1582 Spanish mystic St. Teresa of Avila (b. 1515) dies. She founded the order of barefoot Carmelite nuns in 1568 and established eighteen convents—so many that in 1576 she was forbidden to found any more. She was also a respected religious author, writing such works as *The Way of Perfection* (1573) and *The Book of the Foundations* (1572). Her best-known work is *Castillo Interior* (the inner castle or soul), which is both pious and ecstatic, even erotic, in tone. She also defended women, writing, "When thou wert in the world, Lord, thou didst not despise women, but didst find more faith and no less love in them than men...it is not right to repel minds which are virtuous and brave, even though they be the minds of women."

1588 Englishwoman Margaret Ward is executed for helping a priest to escape from jail.

1590 Italian visionary St. Catherine dei Ricci (b. 1522) dies. A Dominican prioress in Tuscany who worked to reform the church, she experienced twelve years of weekly religious ecstasies.

1592 Scottish witch Agnes Sampson is executed. A healer, she was named as chief of some seventy witches and, after torture, confessed to holding black masses and plotting the death of the king and queen. In this era, witchcraft and treason are often closely linked. Most people accused of sorcery are women, who are often elderly, widowed, or otherwise on the fringes of society. Many are "wisewomen"—healers and herbalists.

1601–1625

General Status and Daily Life

Life in the seventeenth century is hazardous for most women. Death rates are high, especially for Native Americans, who succumb to imported diseases. African women, especially those near the western coast, are, like men, often enslaved and shipped to the Americas.

Some women are endangered by their own husbands. During the Jamestown colony's "starving time," in 1609–1610, one man is executed for eating his wife's body. In Russia, an English doctor writes, "The Russians [*sic*] discipline to their wives is very rigid and severe . . . . Yet three or four years ago a merchant beat his wife as long as he was able, with a whip two inches about, and then caused [her] to put on a smock dipt in brandy . . . which he set on fire, and so the poor creature perished miserably in the flames . . . . And yet what is more strange, none prosecuted her death." Russian women who murder their husbands, on the other hand, are "set alive in the ground, standing upright, with the earth fill'd about them, and only their heads left just above the earth, " until they die; one observer says that such a sight is common and that the women's heads can usually be observed for seven or eight days before death occurs.

Of course, not all husbands are so brutal. Quakers, in particular, encourage husbands to treat their wives as partners, not servants; the London Yearly Meeting tells Quaker couples to have "no rule but love between them." But they are decidedly in the minority. More typical is diarist Samuel Pepys, who marries his wife, Elizabeth, when she is only fifteen, complains about her housekeeping, confines her to meager meals while he eats eight-course dinners, and deliberately dirties things to keep her from boredom while he amuses himself in London.

In the English-speaking world, a married woman may be referred to as "Mrs.," but not because she has a husband. Until this century, adult women are called "Mistress" as a sign of respect. In the seventeenth century, the abbreviation "Mrs." takes the place of the full title but still refers to any adult woman, single or married. During this century, also, the term "Miss" comes into vogue, but it does not at first mean an unmarried woman. Instead, it is initially an insult, meaning an immoral woman.

Marriage is a lasting bond in most parts of the world, sometimes virtually inescapable. In the Chesapeake region of North America, unmarried adult women are practically unheard of, and even widows rarely stay single for long. In Europe, wives are less frantically in demand, and the average woman's age at marriage ranges from about twenty-two in parts of France to about twenty-six in England, with the upper classes marrying earlier (to ensure the birth of heirs) and the lower classes marrying later (after they have saved enough money). Englishwomen have an average of five children; American women, despite their high marriage rate, usually have only one to three. Queen Anne of England endures eighteen pregnancies in eighteen years.

Women raise the children in most parts of the world, though in many places upper-class women hire wet nurses and governesses to do most of the work. In England, children of upper-class families are sent for twelve to eighteen months to wet nurses, where infant mortality is twice as high as with the mother; then they are handed over to governesses and tutors. Infant mortality is high (none of Queen Anne's children lives to adulthood), as are deaths during childbirth, and many women compose letters to their unborn children, fearing death during labor. Contraception is used only sporadically and consists largely of *coitus interruptus*—a method that requires considerable cooperation on the part of one's partner.

Europeans differ widely in personal cleanliness, with women being often more fastidious than men. The poor are dirtier than the rich because of the high cost of soap and the lack of available bathing water. Bed sheets are changed about three times a year, and corsets go unwashed for decades, while petticoats are worn unwashed until they fall apart.

Japanese ruler Iyeyasu is petitioned by a woman whose husband was killed by a government official so that the official might gain sexual access to her. Iyeyasu orders the official to commit suicide and then makes the woman his own concubine.

In Iyeyasu's time, a man can kill his wife and her lover if he catches them in adultery; Iyeyasu decrees that if the man kills his wife but not the lover, he himself shall die. Women and the poor in Japan are forbidden to commit the dignified and ritualized form of suicide known as *hara-kiri* or *seppuku*, but upper-class women are trained in *jigaki*, the cutting of the arteries in the throat with a single stroke; they are advised to tie their legs together first so that they will not be found in a compromising position.

Japanese women can be divorced for talking too much, though they are expected to be especially patient with bad-tempered husbands. Daughters cannot inherit property; a man without sons will adopt one.

A samurai's wife cooks, entertains, sews, waits on her husband, and manages the servants. She has wet nurses and governesses to raise her children. The samurai's daughters sweep, prune bushes, make quilts, and weave mosquito nets. The wives of craftsmen often help them at their work, making fans, shoes, furniture, lacquered goods, stoves, and other objects.

In northwestern Europe and America, couples court by "bundling." The young man and woman are permitted to spend the night together in her bed, usually separated by a board. The practice will continue into the next century.

Japanese women play the board games *go* and *shogi*, an incense-identification game, and games in which paintings or lines from poems are matched.

1604 Male adulterers in Geneva, Switzerland, are fined; female adulterers are whipped for the first offense and banished for the second.

1623 The scold's bridle, or brank, begins to be used in England; it has already been in use in Scotland for about fifty years. Any woman found by a court to be too loud and frank in her speech may be confined in this device, a metal cage for the head with a sharp or spiked plate that wounds the tongue if the woman attempts to talk. She is then publicly displayed and humiliated.

Government, the Military, and the Law

The seventeenth century witnesses the rise and fall of several powerful women who use their power with varying degrees of willingness and skill. It also sees the rise of the Mujaji, a women's dynasty of the Lobedu in the northern Transvaal. The Mujaji is reported to possess fearsome magical powers, including weather control, and the dynasty will persist at least through the late nineteenth century. Also during the seventeenth century, Dutch colonizers of Java find that a woman, Cut Nyak Dien, has been the ruler of Aceh for fifty years.

Mar. 24, 1603 Elizabeth I dies. Her forty-five-year reign was marked by peace through diplomacy, expansion of trade, exploration, and patronage of the arts. In her old age, she was told by one of her ministers that she must go to bed. Always imperious, she replied, "Little man, little man, is must a word to use to princes?"

Sept. 20, 1604 The Spanish capture the Dutch town of Ostend, and Spanish archduchess Isabella gets to change her blouse after two years of siege. She had sworn, like knights of old, not to change it until the town had fallen; a faint yellow color is still sometimes called "isabella."

Dec. 29, 1607 John Smith, Jamestown colonist, is threatened with execution by Algonkian chief Powhatan and saved only when the chief's daughter, Pocahontas (also known as Matoaka or Rebecca, b. 1595), pleads for his life and lays her head between his head and the raised clubs of Powhatan's warriors. Over the next three years, she will bring food to the colonists, act as a mediator between the English and the Native Americans, warn Smith of an impending attack, and save the life of colonist Henry Spelman.

1610 Hausa queen Amina dies at about fifty in present-day Nigeria. At sixteen, she began leading her people in an aggressive campaign to extend their territory, building walled camps, capturing many cities, establishing new trade routes, and taking a lover in each conquered town, only to have him beheaded in the morning.

May 14, 1610 King Henri IV of France dies; his wife, Marie de Medici, already the king's wartime regent, becomes regent for their nine-year-old son, Louis XIII. During her regency, she will try to limit the power of the nobility.

1611 Nur Jahan (Light of the World, b. 1571), the beautiful and ambitious daughter of a Persian adventurer, marries Moghul emperor Jahangir. She dominates him and ultimately gains control of India, administering the government, issuing her own coinage, and killing one of Jahangir's sons and manipulating the others. She also increases Persian influence over Indian culture and government.

1613 Pocahontas is captured and held by sea captain Samuel Argall to force the release of Jamestown prisoners by her father Powhatan; she is well treated, especially by those who feel her kidnapping was wrong, and given Bible lessons. In April she is baptized and takes the name Rebecca, later marrying colonist John Rolfe. Pocahontas dies in 1617 after a trip to England,

where she will be much celebrated in society and entertained by the king.

1614 Transylvanian murderess Elisabeth Bathory (b. 1560) dies. Between 1600 and 1610, she tortured and killed about 500 young women in bizarre rites that she believed would extend her youth. Because of her aristocratic birth, she was not executed for her crimes but was instead walled up in a room of her castle and fed through a small slit in the wall.

1618 Cardinal Richelieu is exiled to Avignon for conspiring with Marie de Medici, who was banished to Blois in 1615, against her son Louis XIII. When she rebels again next year, Richelieu will switch sides and work with the king to defeat her. Her army will be defeated at Ponts de Ce on February 10, 1620.

1619 Princess Diane of France (b. 1538), who mediated disputes between Henri III and Henri of Navarre, worked for religious tolerance, and gained for herself the duchy of Angoulême, dies.

1620 Land in Massachusetts is sold to a group of English settlers by an Native American "queen" or squaw sachem. Powerful women are common in many Native American tribes.

1622 Nzinga (b. c. 1582), sister of King Ngola Mbandi (of the Mbundu nation of Ndongo in what is now Angola), goes to Luanda as his envoy to the Portuguese governor. When the governor offers her no chair, she provides one of her own by having a slave kneel on all fours. She wins recognition of Ndongo's independence in exchange for her own conversion to Christianity. When her brother dies in 1624, she will become queen of the Mbundu.

1623 The oldest son of Greek harem slave Kösem becomes Murad IV, making her the Ottoman *valide sultana* (mother of the sultan), an extremely influential position. She will remain powerful throughout the reigns of Murad and his brother, Ibrahim (rules 1640–1648).

1624 Spanish soldier Catalina de Erauzú (1592–1650), using the name Alonso Diaz Ramiros de Guzman, is revealed to be a woman. Since escaping from a convent at fifteen, she has served in Latin America fighting the Dutch and the Native Americans, becoming conspicuous for bravery and belligerence (she even killed her own brother, Miguel, in a duel). After confessing her sex, she is forgiven and awarded a pension by Philip IV. A papal dispensation allows her to continue to dress as a man. She will later start a mule train business, call herself by the masculine titles "Don" and "Señor," and challenge a man to a duel after he objects to her friendship with his wife.

Literature and the Visual Arts

Seventeenth-century poets include India's Kshetrayya, who writes about the god Krishna, and China's Wang Wei, a courtesan and Taoist priestess who travels through Central China in a small boat, writing about nature.

Artists of the era include Chinese sisters Chai Zhenyi and Chai Jingyi. Zhenyi paints flowers, grasses, and insects, while Jingyi paints predominantly plum blossoms and bamboo. Jingyi is perhaps more famous for her poetry. She publishes a collection of her works, *Ningxiang shi shichao* (*Poetic Transcriptions of the Frozen Fragrance Chamber*). Other Chinese women artists of this era include Chen Yi of Jiangsu and Lin Xue (Lin Tiansu), a courtesan and calligrapher who paints landscapes and copies ancient paintings onto fans.

1604 Chinese painter and courtesan Ma Shouzhen (also known as Ma Xianglan, b. 1548) dies. Best known for her outline paintings of orchids, she also wrote one play and was an accomplished poet and calligrapher. Her painted fans were treasured as far away as Thailand.

1611 English poet Emilia Lanier (1569–1645), the probable Dark Lady of Shakespeare's sonnets, publishes the long poem *Salve Deus Rex Judaeorum*.

Aug. 11, 1614 Italian artist Lavinia Fontana (b. 1552) of Bologna dies in Rome. She had a successful career as a painter of portraits and religious scenes, despite bearing eleven children. Her work suffered at times not only from the demands of motherhood but also from enduring, like most seventeenth-century mothers, the deaths of most of her children in infancy. Only three of her children survived her.

1616 Chinese poet, calligrapher, painter, and musician Ye Xiaoluan is born. Her mother is the poet Shen Yixiu, and her sisters Ye Wanwan (1610–1633) and Ye Xiaowan (b. 1613) are also gifted poets. Xiaoluan will die five days before her wedding in 1632, but her works will remain famous, and fourteen of her poems will be included in Qian Qianyi's anthology of Ming dynasty poetry.

1616 Italian artist Artemisia Gentileschi (b. 1593) becomes the first woman admitted to the Accademia del Disegno. She is the creator of the masterful painting *Susanna and the Elders*, a representation of sexual harassment that shows a pair of hulking, conspiratorial men leaning toward the twisted, anguished, protesting Susanna. In about 1625, she paints *Judith and Maidservant with the Head of Holofernes*, a painting that displays particularly skillful use of light.

Performing Arts and Entertainment

1603 In a dry riverbed in Japan, Okuni, a priestess at the Izumo shrine, introduces a new type of theater, which includes dancing and comedy. The audience calls it *kabuki*, a word that refers to its "unusual or shocking nature."

1604 Italian actress Isabella Andreini (b. 1562), the leading lady of the Gelosi Company, dies.

1619 Venetian singer and prolific cantata composer Barbara Strozzi is born.

1619 One of the great tragediennes of the French stage for the past twenty-nine years is Marie Venier.

1623 Italian composer Francesca Caccini (b. 1587), author of the song anthology *Il primo libro delle musiche* (1618) and the opera *La liberazione de Ruggiero* (1625), is the star of the Medici court in Florence, earning more than anyone else in the duke's employ except his secretary. She is supported by a group of female singers whom she has trained.

Athletics and Exploration

1609 The first woman arrives in the Jamestown colony.

Aug. 1619 Virginia's 1,200 new colonists include only 100 children and 90 women. The women, "willing maidens," are "sold with their consent" for the price of their passage—120 pounds of tobacco.

Dec. 1620 The *Mayflower* Pilgrims arrive in Massachusetts; the ship has 102 passengers, 28 of them women. Two women, Elizabeth Hopkins and Susanna White, have given birth aboard ship; a third woman who was in early pregnancy on the voyage, Mary Allerton, dies in the spring of 1621 in childbirth. William Bradford's wife, Dorothy, drowns almost immediately after arrival when she falls overboard. The surviving women, as their first task, are directed to wash out the fetid laundry.

Activism

1611 A major uprising of Mexicans of African descent starts after the death of a maltreated female slave. A plot to kill all the Spaniards in Mexico City during Holy Week 1612 is discovered when two slave traders overhear an Angolan woman speaking of the plot in her native language. Seven women are among the conspirators hanged on May 2, 1612.

1622 French writer Marie de Gournay (b. 1566) publishes *Egalité des Hommes et des Femmes*, attacking hypocritical attitudes toward her sex. Plain, intelligent, stubborn, and assertive, she is one of the first professional women writers.

Business and Industry

Women in the American colonies and Europe can become indentured servants, though such servitude is difficult, requiring six ten- to fourteen-hour days a week, often under severe discipline and fear of possible sale. Female indentured servants are forbidden to marry, since pregnancy reduces work capacity; they are also subject to sexual harassment from male employers. However, they are usually protected to some extent by the law, which guarantees them the right to food, clothing, and shelter.

Many women engage in trade or paid labor, though usually not for the same wages as men. In England, female laborers are paid threepence per day if they are fed by their employer. Male laborers are paid sixpence. However, this imbalance is not present everywhere. In West Africa, particularly in places like Gambia and Benin, women, not men, control trade. When these women are unfortunate enough to fall into the hands of slave traders, they continue to keep control of their economy within the slave community. One South Carolina observer notes, "These women have such a connection with and influence on the country negroes who come to that market, that they generally find means to obtain whatever they choose, in preference to any white person; thus they forestall and engross many articles, which some hours afterward you must buy back from them at 100 or 150 per cent advance."

Furuichi Street in Ise, Japan, is famous for its brothels.

July 1619 The Virginia House of Burgesses debates giving women an equal share in colonial lands, "because in a plantation it is not known whether man or woman be the most necessary." The proposal is rejected.

Science and Medicine

1609 French midwife Louise Bourgeois (1563–1643), also known as Madame Boursier, publishes *Several Observations on Sterility, Miscarriage, Fertility, Childbirth and Illnesses of Women and Newborn Infants*. It quickly becomes a standard work and is translated into both German and Dutch. Bourgeois is her country's foremost midwife; by 1610 she will have delivered six children of King Henri IV, including the Dauphin.

Education and Scholarship

More and more books are being printed in English specifically for a female audience.

In the seventeeth century, about 15% of Japanese women are literate.

1610 Oxford's Wadham College is co-established by Dorothy Wadham.

Religion

One of the most important shrines in Tokugawa Japan (1600–1868) is the one to the sun goddess at Ise. Increasingly in this period, it becomes a goal of every *shinto* adherent to make a pilgrimage to Ise at least once in his or her lifetime.

1601 English widow Anne Line is executed for being a "harborer of priests."

1601 French shepherdess St. Germaine of Pibrac (b. Germaine Cousin c. 1579) dies. A pious, mistreated child, she was known for her charity and patience in the face of abuse. Half-starved and given no bed, she is found dead in her sleeping place, a cupboard beneath the stairs.

1608–1609 French nun Angélique Arnauld (1591–1661), who, due to her family's influence and wealth, became abbess of Port-Royal-les-Champs in 1602 at the age of eleven, is convinced by a Capuchin monk that her worldly ways are wrong. She begins to purify her convent by limiting contact with the outside world and enforcing vows of abstinence, communal property, and silence.

1618 Marie de l'Incarnation (b. 1566), French Carmelite mystic, dies at Pontoise. Known as Barbe Acarie until the death of her husband freed her to take holy orders in 1613, she was responsible for bringing the Carmelites to France in 1603.

1626–1650

General Status and Daily Life

Farm women in Japan are usually responsible for the planting of rice, which they do working backward across the field, singing ancient songs to relieve the monotony. They also strip the grains from the stalks of rice after harvest and care for silkworms. Peasant women wear breeches or bloomers, often covered with an apron, and a girdle about five inches wide. In winter, if there is little work to be done, they may wear full-length kimonos. At dinner, the wife sits at a right angle to her husband and opposite her oldest son (or son-in-law) or a guest.

Mothers sleep in the same bed with their children for several years. A Japanese man may divorce his wife by writing three and a half lines (the *mikudari-han*) that state that she is free to leave him and form another attachment. He must return whatever is left of her dowry and possessions and send her back to her family.

1632 Massachusetts law makes adultery by either sex punishable by death. By December 1641 the penalty has changed to whipping and the public display of the letters "AD" on the adulterer's clothes.

1634 Maryland law requires heiresses to marry within seven years of inheriting or forfeit their lands.

May 17, 1637 Scores of thousands of female captives taken prisoner by the Manchu rulers of China in two invasions of Korea are permitted to be ransomed. Ransoms are high, and those who cannot afford to buy their freedom or have no relatives willing to purchase them are forced to remain in captivity. Those who do return face discrimination because it is assumed they have been raped by their captors.

1641 Massachusetts forbids a man to beat his wife "unless it be in his own defense upon her assault."

c. 1644 In China, flesh from a daughter's body is believed to cure sick parents. At about this time, the practice of women's cutting off their own flesh to effect this cure is outlawed.

Chinese marriages are arranged by the parents. The woman becomes part of her husband's family and is dominated by her mother-in-law, whose approval is perhaps even more important than her husband's. The new bride must produce a male heir as soon as possible, accept the fact that her husband may keep concubines, and be prepared to smother her own daughters if they are unwanted. Her husband can divorce her easily, and she has few property rights in marriage and not much chance of remarrying after the marriage is over.

1649 A Japanese ordinance pertaining to the peasantry states: "The husband must work in the fields, the wife must work at the loom. Both must do night work. However good-looking a wife may be, if she neglects her household duties by drinking tea or sightseeing or rambling on the hill-sides, she must be divorced."

1650 Germany, with its population decimated by the Thirty Years' War, legalizes polygyny and taxes unmarried women to increase the birthrate.

Mid-17th century Life expectancy for mid- to upper-class Englishwomen is thirty-two.

Government, the Military, and the Law

1626 While Moghul emperor Jahangir lies ill, Mahabat Khan stages a rebellion against the de facto ruler of India, Empress Nur Jahan. Nur Jahan, who recruited Mahabat Khan to quell a rebellion by Shah Jahan and then grew jealous of his growing power and popularity, had banished him and accused him of embezzlement.

For a time, Mahabat Khan is successful. He imprisons Jahangir and Nur Jahan, then thinks better of it and allows them to escape. Nur Jahan pardons him and sends him to attack Shah Jahan again. However, Shah Jahan ultimately triumphs. After Jahangir's death on October 29, 1627, Nur Jahan maintains power only until 1628, when she is deposed, given a pension, and exiled to Lahore until her death in 1645.

1626 Anne of Austria, the wife of France's King Louis XIII, and Mme. de Chevreuse plot to kill the powerful Cardinal Richelieu. Failing, Anne will connive unsuccessfully in 1628 with Queen Mother Marie de Medici to get him dismissed. She will be accused of treason in 1637 and pardoned.

1626 The Portuguese oust Angolan queen Nzinga of the Mbundu; driven eastward, Nzinga establishes a government in exile, becoming queen of Matamba in 1630. Over the next year she successfully battles the Portuguese and gives her sister a position of power. By 1641, her war against Portugal will occupy so much of its attention that it will lose Luanda to the Dutch. According to her Dutch bodyguard, Captain Fuller, Nzinga dresses "in man's apparel . . . hanging about her the skins of beasts, . . . with a Sword about her neck, an Axe at her girdle, and a Bow and Arrows in her hand." She keeps about fifty male concubines and dresses some of them in women's clothing.

1628 French Protestant Catherine de Parthenay, Mme. de Rohan, leads the defense of the besieged town of La Rochelle.

1631 Marie de Medici stages a rebellion against her son Louis XIII.

1632 Emperor Shah Jahan of India orders the building of the Taj Mahal (completed in 1653) in memory of his late wife, Mumtaz Mahal (the niece of Nur Jahan), who died in 1631 bearing her fourteenth child in eighteen years.

May 14, 1643 Louis XIII dies, naming a regency council for four-year-old Louis XIV that includes Anne of Austria. Within four days, Louis XIII's will is discarded, and Anne is given sole regency. She is helped in her maneuvering by her lover and chief minister, Cardinal Mazarin, who will help her suppress rebellions from 1648 to 1653.

1643 In England's civil war, Lady Mary Bankes defends Corfe Castle with a force consisting of herself, her daughters, her ladies-in-waiting, and five men.

Jan. 21, 1648 Wealthy Maryland landowner Margaret Brent (c. 1601–1671) unsuccessfully demands two votes in the Maryland Assembly: one for her own wealth and one for her position as Governor Calvert's executor, a post she won in 1647 after quelling an incipient soldiers' rebellion.

Aug. 8, 1648 Ottoman sultan Ibrahim is deposed and strangled with the consent of his mother, Kösem. Utterly insane, he once found the fattest woman in his empire and made her governor general of Damascus. On another occasion, he had every woman in his harem drowned.

Ibrahim is succeeded by his seven-year-old son, Mehmed. Technically, Mehmed's mother, Turhan Sultana is now the *valide sultana* (mother of the sultan, a post equivalent to regent), but Mehmed's powerful grandmother Kösem refuses to retire and turn over her power to Turhan.

In 1651, war breaks out between the two sultanas, each determined to control her own candidate for the throne. Kösem is backed by the Janissaries, or imperial guards; Turhan is supported by the palace eunuchs and the grand vizier. In the end, Turhan triumphs, and Kösem is strangled by the eunuchs.

Literature and the Visual Arts

1630 Italian painter Fede Galizia (b. 1578), an internationally famous artist who helped to originate the genre of still life in Italy, dies.

1631 Japanese painter, calligrapher, poet, and musician Ono Ozu (b. 1559 or 1568) dies. She divorced her husband for drunkenness, became a tutor to upper-class girls, and sold her artwork, even working for the Tokugawa shoguns. Her style of calligraphy will be used as a model for aristocratic women and will be the standard for 150 years.

1631 Dutch genre painter Judith Leyster (July 28, 1609–February 10, 1660) paints *The Proposition*, unique in its time because the woman in the picture is so clearly unhappy about the man's advances. Later male critics will so completely miss the point that they will name it *The Tempting Offer*. In 1663, Leyster becomes one of the very few women ever admitted to the prestigious Guild of St. Luke. She is a former pupil of

Franz Hals and once sued him successfully over his theft of one of her apprentices.

1634 Chinese painter and teacher of painting Wen Shu (b. 1595) dies. Her works were so highly regarded that they were often imitated and forged. Most of her paintings depict the plants and insects of Hanshan. She will inspire many later Chinese women painters, including Yao Yi, Huang Ro, and Wang Yuyan. Gao Qingyu will change her name to Wen Qingyu in honor of Wen Shu, and many women artists will copy Wen Shu's style. Wen Shu's daughter, Zhao Zhao, will also be recognized as a remarkable woman; she will write a biography of her parents, become a painter like her mother, write several works compiled as *Lüyun ju yigao*, and become a Buddhist nun and recluse.

1637 Spanish author Maria de Zayas y Sofomayor publishes a popular collection of novels, *Novelas Amorosas y Exemplares*, which feature strong women, horror, melodrama, and happy endings.

1641 French author Madeleine de Scudéry (1607–1701) publishes her novel *Ibraham, ou L'Illustre Bassa*. It is one of Europe's first examples of the novel, which within a century or two will be considered a "woman's genre." From 1649 to 1653, Scudéry will publish another novel, the mammoth *Artamène, ou le grand Cyrus*.

1646 Portuguese poet and nun Sor Violante do Céu publishes her *Collected Poems*.

1650 *The Tenth Muse Lately Sprung Up in America*, a collection of poems, is published in England, making its author, Anne Bradstreet (1612–1672), America's first published woman writer and its first published poet. In her poem, "In Honour of That High and Mighty Princess Queen Elizabeth of Happy Memory," she writes, "Let such as say our sex is void of reason / Know 'tis a slander now but once was treason."

Performing Arts and Entertainment

Japanese women work as jesters and entertainers.

France has several notable actresses, including Madeleine Béjart, but Englishwomen are not allowed on stage.

1629 The Tokugawa shogunate ousts women from *kabuki* troupes, as their erotic performances have been leading to audience riots.

Athletics and Exploration

1643 Lady Deborah Moody (d. 1659?) founds the first English settlement in Kings County (Brooklyn) on New York's Long Island.

Activism

1626 French feminist writer Marie de Gournay (1566–1645) publishes *Grief des Dames* and a collection of her pamphlets, *L'ombre*. She is a successful professional author who will translate Virgil, Ovid, Sallust, and Tacitus and be ridiculed for her unfashionable clothes.

Aug. 1643 Women present a petition to England's Parliament, complaining about economic conditions. The next day, 2,000–3,000 women attack members of Parliament, shouting, "Peace and our King." While their male companions in the demonstrations are left unharmed, they themselves are attacked by soldiers, and three or four women are killed.

1649 Women in Naples, Italy, seize the local tax collector's house and burn his possessions to protest a tax on salt.

Apr. 1649 Ten thousand women petition Britain's Parliament on behalf of the "multitudes ready to starve and perish for want of work, employment, necessaries and subsistence." They claim that "we are not able to keep in our compass, to be bounded in the custom of our Sex . . . considering that we have an equal share and interest with men in the Commonwealth" and are told "to goe home, and looke after your owne businesse, an meddle with your huswifery."

Business and Industry

Some bakers in Guadalajara, Mexico, are women.

1630 English merchant Edith Doddington sells wheat, butter, and cheese in four counties.

1640 About 10% of London publishers over the past century have been women.

1643 Goody Armitage of Massachusetts becomes the first woman innkeeper in the American colonies; she has a license to serve meals "but not to drawe wine."

Science and Medicine

Early 17th century England's new apothecaries' guild admits women.

1634 London's most prominent midwives, Elizabeth Cellier, Jane Sharp, and Hester Shaw (whose fee for a single delivery can reach £1,000), petition the College of Physicians unsuccessfully for permission to incorporate a midwives' guild.

1638 Spanish noblewoman Ana de Osorio, countess of Chinchona, living in Peru, is treated with quinine; she will introduce this miraculous cure to Europe, and it will be known for centuries as *pulvia comitessa* (the countess's powder) and its source as chinchona or cinchona.

1650 German astronomer Maria Cunitz (1610–1664) publishes a simplification of Kepler's theories.

Education and Scholarship

1632 The first girls' school in Sweden is established.

1638 German scholar Anna Maria van Schurman publishes *De capacitate ingenii muliebris ad scientias (On the Capacity of the Female Mind for Learning)*, a treatise on behalf of women's education. The work will be translated into French and English before 1700.

1640 An English treatise, *The Woman's Sharpe Revenge*, attacks the male monopoly on serious education.

1640 In London, 80% of women are illiterate.

1642 Ursuline nuns start girls' schools in Quebec.

1645 Ann Hopkins, the wife of the governor of Connecticut, goes insane. Massachusetts Governor William Bradford attributes her plight to "giving herself wholly to reading and writing" and says that "such things as are proper for men whose minds are stronger."

Religion

Japanese women are no longer priestesses in the shinto religion, as they were long ago, when they served as mediums between the living and the dead. Now they are only village wisewomen and shrine dancers.

1630 Angélique Arnauld, influential abbess of Port-Royal-les-Champs, is replaced as abbess by her sister Agnes but remains powerful. From 1642 to 1655, she will serve as abbess again, defending the convent's Jansenist beliefs against Pope Innocent X.

1633 English prophet Lady Eleanor Davies (d. 1652) is jailed and fined £3,000 for her religious fanaticism.

1636 Popular Boston midwife Anne Hutchinson (b.

1591) begins holding women's theological meetings. Advocating the covenant of grace, she is largely ignored until men begin attending her meetings as well. In September 1637, a church council denounces her theology. On November 17, she is tried for verbal attacks on the colony's ministers. Claiming that God will punish her persecutors, she is found guilty and sentenced to banishment. One of her judges tells her, "You have stept out of your place, you have rather bine a Husband than a Wife and a preacher than a Hearer; and a Magistrate than a Subject." Since travel and settlement during the winter are impossible, the court orders the pregnant Hutchinson jailed until spring. In March 1638, confused and weakened by her imprisonment, she is formally excommunicated. She leaves the colony with several followers, including future Quaker martyr Mary Dyer. In September 1643, Hutchinson and most of her family will be killed in an Indian attack, an event viewed by many in Massachusetts as proper punishment for her arrogance.

1640 French saint Joan de Lestonnac (b. 1556) dies. She established the teaching Sisters of Notre Dame of Bordeaux and was once briefly ousted by a coup within the order.

1641 French saint Jeanne-Françoise de Chantal (b. 1572) dies. The head of a new women's order, the Order of the Visitation, she expanded it to include over eighty houses by the time of her death.

1645 Ecuadoran saint Mariana Paredes y Flores dies. She taught Indian children, performed charitable work among the poor, and nursed the sick in a Quito epidemic, dying as a result.

1645 English nun Mary Ward (b. 1585) dies. She founded a boarding school for girls and stressed education, especially in Latin, as a means to creating a fine community of "English Virgins." Arrested in England for her Catholicism, she returned to the Continent and founded the Institute of the Blessed Virgin Mary, a teaching order, in 1610. The order was the target of bitter attacks from bishops who did not wish it to be directly responsible to the papacy, and the pope dissolved the order in 1629, excommunicating Ward when she continues her work. It will thrive, however, and in 1703 will again receive papal sanction.

1645–1647 Essex, England, executes 490 women as witches.

1648 Margaret Jones of Charlestown, Massachusetts, judged to have a "malignant touch" that causes pain and vomiting and to have prescribed ineffective or harmful medicine, is the first person in the future United States executed for witchcraft.

1649 Englishwomen submit a petition to the House of Commons on behalf of religious nonconformists; they are told "to spin or knit and not to meddle with State Affairs." "It is fitter," they are instructed, "for you to be washing your dishes, and meddle with the wheel and distaffe."

1651–1675

General Status and Daily Life

The Japanese shogun's women live isolated in women's quarters. They are trained to defend themselves with halberds. Women who serve in this "great interior" are usually selected at about the age of twelve. They usually serve for life, though sometimes concubines are released so that they may marry.

Mid-17th century Marie l'Hermite establishes the prison of Sainte Pélagie as a home for ill-behaved women, who may either commit themselves voluntarily or be placed there by male relatives.

1653 Englishman William Blundell reports the death of his sixth daughter: "My wife has much disappointed my hopes, in bringing forth a daughter, which, finding herself not so welcome in this world as a son, hath made already a discreet choice of a better."

1660s "Miss" becomes the standard title for English-speaking girls, who begin calling themselves "Mrs." at about thirteen.

1660 The first divorce in Delaware is granted to a woman who "receives daily a severe drubbing" from her adulterous husband.

1661 Footbinding is outlawed in China, though the ban is repealed in 1668.

1662 Virginia law dictates that black residents inherit their mothers' slave or free condition.

1663 New Netherland (New York) colonist Laurens Duyts has his ear cut off for selling his wife.

1665 Corseting little girls too tightly results in many injuries, with some toddlers dying after being laced too firmly into whalebone or metal-banded frames. Two-year-old Elizabeth Evelyn dies this year, and her physician finds that "her iron bodice was her pain, and had hindered the lungs to grow." Two of her ribs, another doctor finds, had actually been broken by the device.

1671 Fertility enhancers in England include powdered white ginger; boiling yarn in water, mixing the water with ashes, and sitting over it; and a bath of "ale-hoof, oaten and pease straw . . . then let her dry herself, and presently let her Husband do his best endeavour."

c. 1672 Massachusetts housewives are expected to cook, build and tend the fire, bake bread, tend cows and calves, make cheese and butter, slaughter animals, make sausage, brew cider and beer, prepare pork for bacon, wash clothes, iron with heavy flatirons heated in the fire, sew and mend, raise children, and spin wool.

1673 French law allows a father to imprison his daughter in a convent until she is twenty-five years old.

Government, the Military, and the Law

1652 Two factions struggle for control of France, one led by French queen Anne of Austria (1601–January 20, 1666, regent 1643–1661), the other led by the Duchesse de Chevreuse, Anne's old friend and co-conspirator against Cardinal Richelieu.

June 16, 1654 Queen Christina of Sweden (1626–1689), upset by her restrictions as monarch and troubled by her sympathy for Catholics in her Protestant country, abdicates in favor of her cousin (and former suitor), Charles Gustav. She leaves the country dressed as a man, with her hair cut short, and converts to Catholicism in 1655.

Sept. 22, 1656 In Maryland, the first formal all-female jury acquits Judith Catchpole of infanticide.

Oct. 1656 Peace is established between Portugal and Queen Nzinga of Angola (d. December 1663). Nzinga has waged war against the Portuguese for decades but agrees to the treaty because of the trade benefits for her people and because the Portuguese are holding her sister Mukumbu as a hostage; later she will buy Mukumbu's freedom for more than one hundred slaves.

1667 The princess of Savoy, wife of King Alfonso VI of Portugal, has her husband deposed, imprisoned, and replaced by his brother.

1670 Henrietta Anne, sister-in-law of King Louis XIV of France and sister of King Charles II of England, convinces Charles to sign a secret peace treaty with Louis.

1670 Russian peasant leader Alyona, a former nun, captures the town of Temnikov with 600 followers. Famed for her bravery in battle and in interrogation after capture, she is later burned to death by the government.

1674 The administrator of New Netherland (New York) dies; his widow, Maria van Rensselaer, assumes his duties.

1674 Sainte-Croix, the lover of French noblewoman Marie-Madeleine d'Aubray, marquise de Brinvilliers (1630–1676) dies suddenly, asking that a casket of letters be returned to her. Upon inspection, the letters are found to contain evidence that the marquise and her lover poisoned or tried to poison her father, brothers, sisters, husband, and children. The subsequent scandal, trial, and execution will lead to uproar and accusations throughout the French nobility.

Literature and the Visual Arts

Chinese artists active at about this time include Mao Yuyuan, a painter of landscapes, flowers, and birds, and painter Su Chenjie.

2nd half of 17th century Chinese poet Gu Yurui establishes the Banana Garden Poetry Society, whose famous female members include painter and poet Chai Jingyi, calligrapher and bamboo painter Lin Yining, painter and poet Zhu Rouze, and Xu Can, who paints women, Guanyins (Buddhas), flowers, and plants.

1651 Chinese painter and calligrapher Dong Bai (b. 1625) dies of tuberculosis. A beautiful "singing girl" of Nanjing, she became a private concubine, humbling herself to the other women of her new household and devoting herself to embroidery.

1652? Italian artist Artemisia Gentileschi dies. A rape victim in her early teens, she became famous for her scenes of powerful women from history and mythology, including Susanna, Lucretia, Bathsheba, Cleopatra, and Diana. She was also instrumental in spreading the Caravaggesque style to Florence, Genoa, and Naples.

1653 Spanish sculptor Luisa Roldan (d. 1704) is born. She will be a court artist for Charles II and Philip V, though she will never become rich.

1653 Margaret Cavendish, duchess of Newcastle (1623–1674), publishes *Poems and Fancies*. Letter-writer Dorothy Osborne calls her "a little distracted, she could never have been so ridiculous else as to venture at writing books and in verse too." Cavendish will continue being "ridiculous," however, producing one of the earliest known autobiographies in English (1655), *Nature's Pictures Drawn by Fancie's Pencil* (1656), and several plays.

1654 French author Madeleine de Scudéry (d. 1701), author of *Amalida, ou l'esclave riche* (1660–1663), publishes the ten-volume novel *Clélie*.

c. 1661 Mexican poet Juana Inés de la Cruz (b. c. 1648), the first important author in the Americas, is exhibited at viceroy's court as a prodigy, and holds disputations on physics, music, philosophy, and mathematics.

1662 Chinese artist Jin Yue paints *The Hundred Flowers*, a scroll painting of a variety of blooms that displays great attention to detail. Jin often copies masterworks by different artists, so she does not have a true style of her own.

1663 Catherine Duchemin (1630–1698) submits a still life, *Basket of Flowers on a Table*, to the French Académie Royale and becomes the first woman admitted since the academy's founding in 1648. Louis XIV says of her admission that he wishes "to extend his support to all those who are excellent in the arts of Painting and Sculpture and to include all worthy of judgment without regard to the differeve of sex."

1664 Chinese painter-courtesans Gu (Xu) Mei (b. 1619) and Liu Shi (b. 1618) die. Gu was knowledgeable about literature and history and especially good at painting orchids; many courtesans specialize in this genre. Liu was also a poet; she committed suicide to avoid burdening her daughter and stepson. A specialist in landscapes, she studied with a noted poet and official and became his concubine.

1665 Italian artist Elisabetta Sirani (b. 1638) dies. A professional painter by the age of seventeen, she produced over 90 works by 1662 and over 180 before her death, including a very rare representation of *Porcia Wounding Her Thigh*. After she died (probably of ulcers), an autopsy was performed, and the holes in her stomach lining were attributed variously to poisoning, female temperament, and unrequited love.

1667 Madeleine de Scudéry publishes her last novel, *Mathilde d'Aguilan*.

Dec. 7, 1669 The French Académie Royale admits the painters Geneviève (1645–1708) and Madeleine de Boulogne (1646–1710), who are sisters. It is still extremely rare for a woman to be admitted to the Académie.

1670–1680 German entomological and botanical illustrator Maria Sibylla Merian (April 2, 1647–January 13, 1717) publishes her three-volume catalogue of flower engravings, *Neue Blumenbuch* (*New Flower Book*).

1670 Italian painter Giovanna Garzoni (b. 1600), noted for her studies of plants and animals, dies. One of the few female members of Rome's Accademia di San Luca, she successfully blended still life and scientific drawing.

1671 English dramatist Aphra Behn has two of her plays, *The Forc'd Marriage* and *The Amorous Prince*, performed at the Duke's Theatre.

1671 The marquise de Sévigné (1626–Apr. 17, 1696) begins writing 1,500 famous letters, which describe the court of Louis XIV, to her daughter, Mme. de Grignan.

1672 French miniaturist, enameler, poet, and engraver Sophie Cheron (1648–1711) is unanimously elected to the Académie Royale.

1674 The second collection of novels by outspoken author and women's rights advocate Maria de Zayas y Sofomayor is published posthumously. She also wrote plays and poetry.

Performing Arts and Entertainment

1658 A new theater company, starring Madeleine Béjart (1618–1672), performs Molière's *Le docteur amoureux*; Louis XIV approves of the show, and Molière and Béjart begin a thirteen-year stay at the Palais Royal.

1662 King Charles II of England authorizes the presence of women on stage, more as royal prostitutes than as actresses; for years, they refuse to play old women, are chosen on the basis of beauty rather than talent, and occasionally miss performances to meet their high-ranking lovers. Actresses of the period include Nell Gwyn, Anne Bracegirdle, Susannah Marie Cibber, Hannah Pritchard, and Mrs. Percival, a comedienne, who, due to marriage, becomes at various points in her career Mrs. Mountfort and Mrs. Verbruggen.

Athletics and Exploration

Mid-17th century Chinese courtesan Xue Susu (also known as Xue Wu) dies. She was a "superb archer" who could fire from a crossbow and hit her first shot in midair with her second. She was also known to shoot balls off her maid's head or from the ground "while her body is turned and her arms are crossed backwards," never missing "a single of such shots in a hundred." Xue was also an "amiable and graceful" companion, a gifted calligrapher and painter of bamboo and orchids, and a philanthropist willing to pay large sums to rescue others from trouble.

c. 1652 Eva (c. 1641–1674), member of a South African Khoikhoi tribe, becomes a household servant after the Dutch arrive in South Africa, learning Dutch and Portuguese and becoming an unofficial interpreter. She converts to Christianity in 1664 and marries explorer Pieter van Meerhoff in 1666, becoming the first black South African to marry a white settler in a Christian ceremony. When he dies in 1667, she falls into what the Europeans call a "degenerate" life-style, loses custody of her children, and becomes a symbol for Europeans of the unsuitability of intermarriage.

1666 The colony of South Carolina advertises for female colonists in England, promising, "If any maid or single woman have a desire to go over, they will think themselves in the golden age, when men paid a dowry for their wives; for if they be but civil, and under fifty years of age, some honest man or other, will purchase them for their wives."

Activism

May 1652 A woman whose son has died of starvation begins carrying his body through the streets of Córdoba, Spain. Her actions crystallize the discontent of the masses, and a week of demonstrations and rioting follows.

July 1659 Seven thousand English Quaker women petition Parliament to end the tithe system.

1662 Margaret Cavendish, Duchess of Newcastle, publishes *Orations of Diverse Persons*, in which female speakers attempt to argue for women's equality. Cavendish is a strong supporter of women's education, attacking the old system of "women breeding up women, one fool breeding up another."

Business and Industry

1655 A Maryland indentured servant charges her mistress with "Extream Usage" for beating her "two hours by the clock." The servant is freed but ordered to reimburse her mistress for the loss of her service; a group of local landowners, taking pity on the servant, pay the sum for her.

1659 English thief Mary Frith (b. 1584), known as "Moll Cutpurse," dies. A cobbler's daughter who dressed as a man, she made a comfortable living from picking pockets, telling fortunes, forgery, receiving stolen goods, and selling the stolen property back to the rightful owners from a pawnshop in Fleet Street. She was jailed only once. Women are often pickpockets in this era and are usually acquitted of stealing on the grounds that they must be under a man's influence, being neither strong nor smart enough to steal on their own behalf.

1661 Dutch American colonist Margaret Hardenbrook Philipse, upon her husband's death, takes over his business and becomes a prosperous merchant and shipowner, one of the few women in the colony to conduct extensive trade overseas.

1674 Dutch colonist Maria van Rensselaer inherits her husband's 700,000-acre estate in New Netherland (New York) near Albany. Over nearly two decades, she will direct the operation of the estate, gaining clear title in 1685 after much confusion resulting from three successive conquests of the colony.

Science and Medicine

1651 Physician William Harvey publishes *De Generatione Animalium*, in which he theorizes that the mother's contribution to the fetus is not menstrual blood, as was previously thought, but some kind of egg.

1665 Obstetrical forceps are invented.

1671 British midwife Jane Sharp, who began her career around 1640, publishes *The Midwives' Book; or the Whole Art of Midwifery Discovered*, the first textbook by an English midwife.

Education and Scholarship

1655 Illiteracy among women is about 50% in Massachusetts, 60% in New Netherland (later New York), and 75% in Virginia.

1665 The inventor of the modern intellectual salon, French noblewoman Catherine de Vivonne, Marquise de Rambouillet (b. 1588), dies. She and her female friends, the first salon women, swore themselves to chastity and became known as *précieuses* (precious women).

1673 English educator Basua Makin (1608–1675), head of a school at Tottenham High Cross and tutor to the daughters of Charles I, publishes *Essay to Revive the Antient Education of Gentlewomen*. The essay strongly favors a thorough classical education for women.

Religion

Mid-17th century Venice has 3,000 nuns—about 3% of the city's total population.

1652 English Quaker founder George Fox meets Margaret Fell (1614–1702), wife of Judge Thomas Fell of Swarthmoor Hall. Moved by his words, she cries aloud in church a few days later, "We are all thieves, we are all thieves, we have taken the Scripture in words, and know nothing of them in ourselves." Swarthmoor Hall becomes a center of Quaker activity, and Judge Fell's position protects his wife from persecution. When Fell dies in 1658, however, Margaret is harassed by the government, frequently imprisoned, and threatened with the seizure of her estate. Later she marries George Fox, becoming a principal leader of the Society of Friends and a strong defender of women's right to preach.

1652 Venetian scholar Arcangela Tarabotti (b. 1604) dies. Forced into a convent by her miserly father, who was unwilling to provide her with an adequate dowry to marry, she wrote the pamphlet *Tirannia paterna* (*Parental Tyranny*, published in 1654 as *Simplicity Betrayed*). It calls convents "female prisons" and fathers "pimps and procurers who abused their daughters."

1653 English Quakers Mary Fisher and Elizabeth Williams visit Cambridge to argue theology with students. After calling the university a "Cage of Uncleaned Birds," they are sentenced by the mayor to be whipped until they bleed.

1654 Quakers Elizabeth Fletcher and Elizabeth Leavens go to Cambridge to preach; they are ordered whipped and are so badly beaten that Fletcher never recovers from her injuries. A year later, Fletcher returns and walks naked through the streets "as a sign against the hypocritical profession they made there."

July 11, 1656 The first Quakers to arrive in Boston harbor, Mary Fisher and Ann Austin, are at first refused the right to land; after permission is granted, they are strip-searched for witch-signs, imprisoned for five weeks, and then thrown out of the colony.

1657 Quakers Mary Dyer and Ann Burden arrive in Boston; Dyer, a former follower of Massachusetts religious radical Anne Hutchinson, is jailed, then banished. Dyer returns to Boston in the summer of 1659 and is threatened with execution if she does not leave for good. Undaunted, she returns on October 27, 1659, to "look their bloody laws in the face." She is sentenced to death, led to the gallows, and released after the noose is placed around her throat. She receives another warning not to come back. On June 1, 1660, after returning to Boston again, she is hanged.

1657 Mary Fisher joins a Quaker mission to the Near East, but the mission is turned back at Smyrna by the English consul. Fisher goes on alone, traveling over 600 miles to Turkey, gaining an audience with the sultan, and introducing herself as an ambassador of "the Most High God."

1660 Women now outnumber men in Puritan congregations, though they are still denied positions of leadership.

1660 French saint Louise de Marillac (b. 1591), founder of the Order of the Daughters of Charity, dies. By the time of her death, the order has forty houses, with additional services being provided to the sick from private homes.

1663 Ten witches are hanged in Connecticut, one for saying that "Christ was a Bastard and she could prove it by scripture."

1671 Peruvian recluse St. Rose of Lima (1586–1617) becomes the first person born in the Americas to be canonized. Her life was devoted to prayer, penance, and the care of the sick, the poor, Indians, and slaves.

1672 French missionary to Quebec Marie Guyard (b. 1599) dies.

1672 Japanese imperial court attendant Ryonen Genso (b. 1646) becomes a Zen nun after finding a concubine to take care of her husband and family. Finding the typical training for Buddhist women less demanding than she would like, she endeavors to study at male monasteries, but two refuse to accept her, saying her beauty will disturb the monks. She solves this problem by scarring her face with a hot iron, and the monk Hakuo agrees to accept her as a pupil. She will reach enlightenment in 1682.

1675 French nun St. Marguerite Marie Alcoque (d. 1690), inspired by a religious vision, founds a society for the worship of the Sacred Heart of Jesus.

1676–1700

General Status and Daily Life

A Japanese samurai has one official wife, who is usually chosen for political reasons. He may then also take mistresses and concubines, though his wife is expected to be strictly chaste. Infanticide and abortion are officially discouraged in Japan, but they flourish anyway.

Among the coastal Algonkian Indians in the American colonies, women are in charge of agriculture, producing 90% of tribal food supplies. They prepare food, fish, gather wild plants, and help on hunts by carrying game and performing other basic tasks. They also make such items as baskets and bowls.

Late 17th century In Russia, a husband can effectively divorce his wife by forcing her into a convent, and there is virtually no penalty for a man who kills his wife. Husbands are, however, limited to three wives, so a man who kills or divorces his first two wives is likely to be more careful with the third.

Late 17th century Condoms appear in England, though they are not in common use yet. They are chiefly available in London, where they are used to prevent sexually transmitted diseases, rather than to prevent conception.

1695 In the French Caribbean, a man who "debauches" his slave so that a mixed-race child is born is fined 2,000 pounds of sugar and forced to relinquish ownership of the woman and child.

1700 Unmarried women in Berlin are taxed.

Government, the Military, and the Law

Among the coastal Indians in the American colonies, some women are tribal leaders or "squaw sachems." One of these is Wetamoo, the Wampanoag Squaw Sachem of the Pocasset, who helps to lead her tribe in the conflict with European settlers known as King Philip's War.

1676 Women participate in the American colonial uprising known as Bacon's Rebellion; one, Sarah Grendon, is specifically excluded from a general pardon for her part in the rebellion. Another rebel, Sarah, Mistress Drummond, tells an English governor, "I fear the power of England no more than a broken straw!"

1676 The Russian tsarevna Sophia's brother Fedor II becomes tsar; Sophia (b. 1657) uses the opportunity to become more involved in public affairs, and when he dies in 1682, she manipulates public opinion and a soldiers' rebellion to get her brother, Ivan V, named co-tsar with her half-brother Peter I. She herself, on May 29, 1682, replaces Peter's mother, Natalya, as regent, attacking religious schismatics, carrying on an affair with Prince Vasily Golitsyn, and engaging in successful diplomatic negotiations for possession of the city of Kiev. Sophia will be deposed in 1689 by Peter, and most of her supporters will be tortured and executed. Sophia herself is confined to a convent, though she is not forced to become a nun until 1698, when Peter suspects her of complicity in a soldiers' revolt.

1687 Ottoman empress Turhan Sultana dies, ending the century and a half of powerful sultanas known as the Reign of Women.

Feb. 13, 1689 After the unpopular James II of England's flight from the country in 1688, James's daughter Mary (1662–December 28, 1694) and her husband, William, are offered the Crown. The initial plan, of having Mary rule alone, was rejected by both. Mary insists "that she was the Prince's wife and never meant to be other than in subjection to him."

1699 English royalist adventuress Anne Halkett (b.

1622) dies. During the English civil war, she helped the duke of York to escape his pursuers, nursed royalist troops, and sacrificed her own properties to join Charles II in Scotland. She was never compensated for her lost lands.

Literature and the Visual Arts

Late 17th century Chinese painters Fu Derong, Fan Xueyi, and Zhou Xi (also known as Zhou Shuxi) are active. Zhou paints Buddhist scenes and horses. Her works include sixteen celebrated pictures of Guanyin (Buddha). Her sister Zhou Hu (or Zhou Shuhu) paints flowers, insects, and birds.

Late 17th century Japanese *ukiyo-e* painter San is active. *Ukiyo-e*, the floating world, is the term used to refer to places of worldly pleasure: brothels, theaters, teahouses, and baths.

Late 17th century Indian poet Honnamma writes in the Kannada language.

1677 English playwright Aphra Behn's most successful play, *The Rover*, is produced.

1678 Aphra Behn's play *Sir Patient Fancy*, an adaptation of Molière's *La malade imaginaire*, is produced.

Mar. 1678 French author Marie-Madeleine de Lafayette (1634–1693) anonymously publishes her novel *La Princesse de Clèves*, about a married woman pursued by the passionate Duc de Nemours in the time of Henri II. The book is an immediate success and generates a good deal of scandal and debate, with Lafayette enthusiastically defending the unknown author.

1680 Aphra Behn (1640–1689), the first Englishwoman to support herself entirely by her writing, writes the poem "The Disappointment," about an amorous young man "damned...to the hell of impotence."

1682 Japanese artist Kiyohara Yukinobu (b. 1643) dies. She painted birds, flowers, figures, and Buddhist and Taoist religious scenes.

1682 French artist Catherine Perrot, writer and illustrator of two books, is admitted to the Académie Royale.

1684 Josefa D'Obidos (b. c. 1630), the only recorded female Spanish painter of the seventeenth century, dies. Born in Seville, she lived most of her life in Portugal and did her best work in still life painting.

1685 Anne Killigrew (b. 1660), an English author and

painter who wrote about court life, dies.

1685 Chinese artist Li Yin (b. 1616) dies. She began studying poetry and painting as a child and was famous by the age of fifteen. She became the concubine of a scholar and painter and grew adept at flower paintings, usually in monochrome.

1686 Chinese painter Cai Han (b. 1647) dies. With artists Dong Bai and Jin Yue, she was a concubine of Mao Xiang, who took pride in his household of talented women. Cai painted landscapes, flowers, birds, fish, figures, and pine trees.

1687 English author Aphra Behn publishes *The Luckey Chance*, referring in its preface to "my masculine Part, the Poet in me."

1688 Literature published this year includes the *Memoirs* of the French duchesse de Montpensier and Aphra Behn's *Oroonoko*, an abolitionist novel about a slave rebellion, based on her own experiences in Surinam.

1693 Dutch painter Maria van Oosterwyck (b. 1630) dies. Her flower paintings and still lifes were purchased by such lofty patrons as Louis XIV of France, Emperor Leopold, and the king of Poland.

1693 Portuguese poet and nun Sor Violante do Céu (b. 1602?) dies. Famous for her poems about religion and death, she had poems written about her as well. Her play *Saint Eufemia* was performed for Philip III of Spain.

1693 The first European women's magazine is England's *Ladies Mercury*.

Apr. 17, 1695 Sor Juana Inés de la Cruz, Mexican nun, playwright, critic of the Inquisition, feminist, musician, and collector of a 4,000-volume library (at the time the largest in South and Central America), dies at forty-four in Mexico as a result of nursing the sick.

1696 English author Mary Manley has two plays, *The Lost Lover* and *The Royal Mischief*, produced in London.

1700 English miniaturist Susan Penelope Rosse (b. c. 1652), whose sitters included the actress and royal mistress Nell Gwyn, dies.

Performing Arts and Entertainment

1681 The Paris Opéra features its first professional female dancers.

1682 Francesca Caccini's opera *La liberazione de Ruggiero*, the first Italian opera to be performed outside Italy, is performed in Warsaw.

1687 Nell Gwyn (b. 1651), English actress and mistress of Charles II, dies. She once pacified an angry mob, who mistook her for Charles's Catholic mistress, by saying, "Pray, good people, be civil; I am the *Protestant* whore."

1694 French composer and harpsichordist Elisabeth-Claude Jacquet de la Guerre composes the opera *Cephale et Procris*.

1698 French actress Marie Desmares Champmeslé (b. 1642) dies. She created the roles of Bérénice, Atalida, Iphigénie, and Phèdre in Racine's plays, as well as Corneille's Ariadne.

1700 English dramatist Susanna Centlivre (b. 1667) produces and stars in her first play, *The Perjured Husband*.

Athletics and Exploration

Feb. 20, 1676 American colonist Mary Rowlandson is captured by Narragansett Indians. She will remain a hostage for eleven weeks. Her owner, Quinnapin, gives her to his third wife Wetamoo (sister-in-law of the Narragansett chief Philip and a leader in her own right of the Pocasset), who often beats Rowlandson and threatens her. Rowlandson is eventually ransomed from her captors; Wetamoo drowns trying to escape from the English, and her body is beheaded by them. Rowlandson's account of her captivity is published in 1682.

Activism

1680 English midwife Elizabeth Cellier is accused of conspiring against the king in the "Meal Tub" plot. Arrested and released, she publishes *Malice Defeated; or a Brief Relation of the Accusation and Deliverance of Elizabeth Cellier*, in which she lambastes conditions in Newgate Prison, where she was held. Outraged, the government arrests her again for libel and fines her £1,000.

1695 Quaker Elizabeth Redford is censured by the Men's London Yearly Meeting for suggesting that it is wrong to pay taxes that support violence.

Business and Industry

Late 17th century Geneva watchmakers who teach

their trade to female relatives are fined by their guild.

1670s–1680s Senegalese merchant Biblana Vaz establishes her trade supremacy from the Gambia River to the Sierra Leone.

1684 Prostitutes incarcerated in Paris's Salpetrière prison must pray daily. They wear plain wool clothes, sleep on straw, and live on a diet of bread and soup. Failure to work hard enough results in the loss of the soup or in more stringent punishment.

1685 English highway bandit Joan Bracey (b. 1640) is hanged. For most of her criminal career, she worked with a gang, dressing as a man and using the name John Phillips.

1693 Swiss entrepreneur Elizabeth Baulacre (b. 1613) dies. She built a lucrative business in gold decoration and died with the second largest personal fortune in Geneva.

Science and Medicine

1679 German entomological and botanical illustrator Maria Sibylla Merian begins publishing her three-volume entomological study, *Der Raupen wunderbare Verwandlung und sonderbare Blumennahrung* (*The Wonderful Transformation of Caterpillars and [Their] Singular Plant Nourishment*). Completed in 1717, it catalogues 186 types of European moths, butterflies, and other insects, showing them with the plants they prefer to eat. Her extensive research for the project is, for many species, the first investigation of their habits.

1680 French astronomer Jeanne Dumée publishes *Entretiens sur l'opnion de Copernic touchant la mobilité de la terre*, summarizing the arguments in favor of Copernican theory. The text, praised for its clarity, includes a claim that "between the brain of a woman and that of a man there is no difference."

1686 English author Aphra Behn publishes a translation of Bernard le Bovier de Fontenelle's astronomical treatise *Entretiens sur la pluralité des mondes*.

1687 English midwife Elizabeth Cellier lobbies for licensing of midwives, publishing two tracts in support of her plan.

1690 Polish astronomer Elisabetha Hevelius (b. c. 1647), who helps her husband run the Danzig observatory, edits his *Prodromus astronomiae*, a catalogue of 1,564 stars.

1692 English queen Mary II founds Greenwich Hospital.

Education and Scholarship

There are no schools for Japanese women of the samurai class. They are taught housekeeping and the social graces at home. They learn to dance, sing, play the koto (horizontal harp), write beautifully, read, arrange flowers, and perform the tea ceremony.

1678 German scholar Anna Maria van Schurman (b. 1607) dies. Author of theological works and an Ethiopian grammar, she studied Asian languages at Utrecht University, shielded by a special cubicle so that she would not be seen by the male scholars.

June 1678 Venetian noblewoman Elena Lucrezia Cornaro Piscopia (1645–1684), through the University of Padua, becomes the first woman to earn a Ph.D. Piscopia is a relative of Caterina Cornaro, former queen of Cyprus.

1684 King Louis XIV and his secret wife, Françoise de Maintenon (1635–1719), a former governess, establish a school for impoverished girls of noble birth at the Convent of St. Cyr. Each student is expected to be virtuous, modest, and, like a good wife, obedient: "Learn to obey," advises Mme. de Maintenon, "for you will obey forever."

1684 Greek intellectual Alexandra Mavrokordatu (b. 1605), leader of Greece's first literary salon, dies in prison.

1688 François Fenelon publishes his *Treatise on the Education of Daughters*, which will be reprinted and widely read as late as 1821. It urges women not to be "ridiculously learned" and advises them instead to be "the ornament and comfort of the home."

1690 About 14% of Frenchwomen are literate enough to sign their names on their marriage contracts.

1690 About 2% of all printed books have been written by women.

1694-1697 Englishwoman Mary Astell (1666–1731) publishes *A Serious Proposal to the Ladies for the Advancement of Their Time and Greatest Interest*, in which she suggests forming an academic community of women. The treatise is the first published demand for women's higher education. Her idea is almost implemented but is shouted down at the last moment by public ridicule.

Religion

1680 Since 1591, the Swiss canton of Vaud has burned 3,371 women as witches.

c. 1682 Kongo prophet Kimpa Vita, known as Dona Beatrice, is born in Zaire.

1684 French witch and poisoner La Voison (Catherine Monvoisin) is burned alive. A midwife and fortune-teller, she came to public attention as a result of the notorious Brinvilliers poisoning case of 1674.

1685 The last Englishwoman executed for witchcraft is killed in Exeter.

May 11, 1685 Two Scotswomen, Margaret M'Lachlan and Margaret Wilson, are drowned for claiming that the king's power over the church is limited.

Jan.–Oct. 1692 Salem, Massachusetts, girls, most between twelve and twenty years old, suffer fits and name a slave named Tituba as the source. In preliminary trials, Tituba claims to be the devil's servant. By the time the furor is over, twenty people will be executed as witches.

1693 Japanese Zen nun Ryonen Genso (d. 1711), one of the most famous women in the history of Buddhism, builds a temple in honor of her late teacher, Hakuo. She becomes the temple's head and dedicates herself to teaching local children.

1694 English scholar Damaris Masham publishes *Occasional Thoughts in Reference to a Christian Life*. In 1696, she publishes *Discourse Concerning the Love of God*.

1701–1725

General Status and Daily Life

Tsar Peter the Great of Russia reforms some laws and customs regarding women and brings them out of the seclusion of the *terem*, or women's quarters. Women will not be married "without their own free liking and consent" and will be able to meet their future husbands "at least six weeks before they were married together." The reforms, however, are limited in scope and are hardly ever enforced outside the capital. A typical Russian woman is married at about thirteen years old.

In the American colonies, most of the poor are women, many of them widows and working women making half as much as their male counterparts. Only widows and spinsters have any legal ability to act for themselves; wives are limited by the principle of English common law known as coverture, which means that a wife's legal identity is incorporated into that of her husband. Wives cannot sue, be sued, sign contracts, buy goods, sell property, make wills, control the property that was theirs before marriage, control their wages, or get custody of their children. Divorce is almost entirely inaccessible.

Ninety percent of women live in the country, farming and perhaps selling eggs or cheese for extra money. Rural women wash clothes, clean, sew, cook, bake, mend, garden, harvest, salt and smoke meat, dry apples, brew cider, milk the cows, make butter and cheese, spin, weave, dye cloth, make soap, and carry water. Autumn is spent preserving food after the harvest, and winter is spent making clothing. Girls go to school in the summer, when their workload is lightest.

Most female slaves work outdoors, doing heavy agricultural tasks; to European masters, inclined to think of field work as masculine, the African woman's ability to do manual labor is seen as a sign of her supposed barbarism. Ten to twenty percent of female slaves are trained for specialized "feminine" tasks and become milkmaids, seamstresses, cooks, and midwives.

In Japan's Tokugawa era (1600–1868), townswomen and courtesans are more likely than rural wives to practice abortion, which is chancy at best and often results in serious complications or death. In rural areas, a woman is more likely to wait for the birth. A boy, even if there are too many mouths to feed already, is usually spared, while a girl will often be smothered.

In a woman's fifth month of pregnancy, a cloth called the *Iwata-obi*, often made of an item of the father's clothing, is tied around her waist. Women who can afford the cost and space are moved into separate quarters for the delivery; for a first child, the woman returns to her parents' house to deliver. Babies are weaned late and are carried on the mother's back. Baby boys are presented to the family god at the age of thirty-two days; girls are presented at thirty-three days. At the age of three years, children of both sexes leave babyhood and get new hairstyles. At seven, girls transfer to a new kimono and obi.

1713 In England, infanticide is common. Joseph Addison writes, "There is scarce an assizes where some unhappy wretch is not executed for the murder of a child."

Mar. 1719 Minimum legal age for marriage in New Jersey is set at twenty-one for both sexes.

c. 1720–1730 In England's upper classes, "Miss" comes to mean an unmarried woman of any age. Until now, "Miss" and "Mrs." have been indicators of age, not marital status. Within about twenty or twenty-five years, the change will become universal.

1721 German woman Catharina Margaretha Linck is burned at the stake for marrying another woman; it is not her lesbianism that offends the authorities so much as the fact that Linck dresses as a man to get away with it.

1725 An Englishwoman is burned alive at Tyburn for killing her husband, one of the last times this sentence is actually carried out. Burning is the standard penalty for husband-murderers, while wife-killers are more mercifully hanged.

Government, the Military, and the Law

Ottoman princess Hatice Sultana, daughter of Ahmed III, supports France and opposes Russia. She uses her considerable influence over her father and her husband the grand vizier to further the French cause.

The king of Dahomey organizes a women's army that will last for nearly two centuries.

Mar. 1702 Anne Stuart (February 6, 1665–August 1, 1714), sister of Mary II, inherits the English throne. Anne is homely, bibulous, sick with gout, and overweight; she has to be carried to her coronation on April 23. However, she becomes instantly popular with the common people for her references to her "English heart."

Anne's favorite for most of her life is Sarah Churchill, duchess of Marlborough (1660–1744), Lady of the Queen's Bedchamber. Anne, far more passionately in love with Churchill than with her own husband, Prince George, allows her to wield enormous power. Sarah, a Whig, falls from favor later and is replaced by a more attentive companion, Abigail (Hill) Masham, a Tory.

Nov. 1707 Russian tsar Peter the Great secretly marries Catherine, an illiterate, courageous, energetic Lithuanian peasant who has already borne him several children. He will marry her publicly in February 1712 and crown her tsarina in 1724. Upon Peter's death in 1725, his wife becomes Catherine I, ruling until 1727.

Aug. 25, 1711 French Canadian interpreter Madame Montour (c. 1684–c. 1752) begins working as an intermediary between the English colonies and the Native American nations. Captured by the Iroquois at the age of ten, she married a member of the Seneca tribe and later became the wife of an Oneida chief. She will be paid well for her services at important conferences, respected by both Indians and Europeans, and wooed by the French, who desire her influence for themselves.

1712–1718 Hannah Penn, second wife of colony founder William Penn, runs his business affairs and much of the government of Pennsylvania while he remains incapacitated by a series of strokes.

Feb. 20, 1720 Queen Ulrika Eleonora of Sweden, who came to power in 1718, abdicates in favor of her husband, Frederick.

Literature and the Visual Arts

Japanese calligrapher Sasaki Shogen is active. Gifted in several calligraphic styles, she is widely sought as a teacher of nobles and royalty.

Chinese painter, calligrapher, and poet Jiang Jixi dies. Part of a family that included many women artists, she wrote a volume of poems, *Qingfen ge ji* (*The Pure Fragrance Pavilion Collection*).

1702 Indian princess and poet Zeb-un-Nissa (b. 1638) dies. A patron of authors and scholars as well as a writer of Persian verse, she was jailed by her father, possibly for participating in a rebellion against him.

1705 English literature published this year includes Susanna Centlivre's play *The Gamester* and Mary Manley's novel, *The Secret of Queen Zarah*, which is really an exposé of the private life of Sarah Churchill, duchess of Marlborough.

1706 The French Académie Royale bars women painters from its ranks. However, over the next several years, it will continue to elect them despite its own rules. It will finally determine that there can be no more than four women members at any time and will accord lesser privileges to women members.

1707 Japanese *waka* and *haiku* poet Kaji publishes 120 *waka* verses as *Kaji no ha*. Kaji runs the Matsuya teahouse in Kyoto. One of the most famous female poets of her day, she never marries, but she adopts a daughter, Yuri, to take over the teahouse.

1710 English poet Lady Mary Chudleigh (b. 1656) dies. Her writings encourage women to learn and read; she sometimes remarks bitterly on woman's lot in life, as in "To the Ladies," in which she claims, "Wife and servant are the same, / But only differ in the name." She advises women to "value your selves, and men despise."

1711 Mary Manley succeeds Jonathan Swift as editor of *The Examiner*.

1713 English author Anne Finch, countess of Winchilsea (1661–1720), publishes *Miscellany Poems* under the name "A Lady."

1716–1735 Japanese *ukiyo-e* painters Mu-me and Yamazaki Ryu-jo (b. 1708?) are active. Yamazaki began painting good works at the age of six or seven and was recognized as quite talented from the age of fourteen. She paints mostly courtesans, using bright colors.

1719 Italian painter Rosalba Carriera makes a triumphant trip to Paris and paints the young Louis XV. In October 1720 she is elected to the Académie Royale.

1719 *Songs for the Nursery; or, Mother Goose's Melodies for Children* is first published. However, Mother Goose herself may be as much an invention as her rhymes; there will be considerable debate as to whether or not she was a real person.

1723 English novelist and playwright Eliza Haywood has her first play, *A Wife to Be Left*, produced at Drury Lane.

1723 Chinese artist Ma Quan (b. c. 1690?) paints *Flowers and Insects After Song Masters*, a work in which bright insects contrast with a muted background, with spots of vivid color on butterflies and flowers. Active throughout the first half of this century, Ma trains several students and is assisted by other women artists, including Qian E, who makes copies of her works, and Zhen, her maid, who paints for her in old age after she goes blind.

1723 English playwright Susanna Centlivre (b. 1667), author of seventeen comedies and several tragedies that will remain popular for 200 years, dies. Her plays include *The Busie Body* (1709), *The Wonder! A Woman Keeps a Secret* (1714), and *A Bold Stroke for a Wife* (1718).

Performing Arts and Entertainment

1717 French actress Adrienne Lecouvreur (1692–1730), notable for her natural style and insistence on historically accurate costumes, makes her first appearance at the Comédie Française.

1721 A *Te Deum* for the health of Louis XV, composed by French musician Elisabeth-Claude Jacquet de la Guerre (c. 1666–1729), is played at the chapel in the Louvre. De la Guerre is the composer of several kinds of works, including opera, ballet, harpsichord music, violin music, and choral cantatas.

c. 1722 Kathrin Lise, the world's last female court jester, dies.

Athletics and Exploration

1721 Twenty-five female prisoners and orphans from France are sent to the colony at New Orleans and sold or given away to lonely bachelors in an effort to keep the French settlers from establishing relationships with Native American women.

June 23, 1722 A boxing match between two women is held in London. Another will be held in 1723.

1725 A fencing match with two female competitors, an Englishwoman and an Irishwoman, is held in England.

Activism

1706 English author Mary Astell writes, "If absolute sovereignty be not necessary in a state, how comes it to be so in a family?" and "If all men are born free, how is it that all women are born slaves?"

1709 English author Mary Manley publishes *The New Atlantis*, an attack on Whig corruption that leads to a libel suit.

Business and Industry

A typical servant in Aix-en-Provence, France, earns twenty-one livres per year.

Mar. 11, 1702 English printer Elizabeth Mallet begins publishing *The Daily Courant*, the first daily paper in the world to be published by a woman. She is forced out of control of the paper by a male publisher after only nine days.

1709 Italian poisoner Tofana, who supposedly enabled the murders of about 600 people with her deadly *aqua tofana*, is arrested and possibly killed. She sold her poisons to many clients, most of whom were allegedly women seeking to kill their husbands.

Nov. 25, 1715 American inventor Sybilla Masters (d. August 23, 1720) receives an English patent for a machine to process corn. In 1716 she will invent another device (patented by her husband) for preparing palmetto leaves for the manufacture of hats.

1717 English soldier and pirate Mary Read (b. 1690) is pardoned. She spent her childhood dressed as a boy to fool her grandmother into giving her an inheritance, then worked as a servant at an inn, a footboy, a sailor, a foot soldier, and a tavern keeper before being captured by West Indian pirates and joining their ship. Next year she will become a legitimate sailor in New England; however, she is soon captured by pirates Jack Rackham and Anne Bonney. She joins their ship, taking lovers among the sailors and carrying on an affair with Bonney.

   Rackham's ship is captured near Jamaica in October 1720. Bonney and Read gain a reprieve by pleading pregnancy, but Rackham and his crew are hanged; Bonney, who fought their captors with Read long after the men had given up, taunts Rackham by saying that "if he had fought like a man, he need not have been hang'd like a Dog." Read dies shortly afterward of fever, but Bonney's fate remains unknown.

Sept. 1723 American counterfeiter Mary Peck Butterworth is brought before a grand jury with her brother, Israel Peck, but charges are dropped for lack of physical evidence. From 1716 to 1722, Butterworth made a fortune from counterfeiting, using a technique she devised herself; muslin cloth was used to print the money instead of metal plates, since muslin could be conveniently destroyed.

Sept. 19, 1724 German Jewish merchant Glückel of Hameln (b. 1646) dies. Married at fourteen, she had twelve children and helped her husband in his gem trade. After his death, she preserved and enlarged the family fortune, though her second husband suffered business reversals and lost all her property. She wrote her memoirs, an unusual endeavor for a woman at the time.

Science and Medicine

1705 German entomological and botanical illustrator Maria Sibylla Merian publishes *Metamorphosis insectorum Surinamsium*, an exhaustively researched study of the insects of Surinam. In addition to providing information on the insects' life cycles and dietary habits, she includes stories of local customs, native plant uses, and abortifacients.

1717 English author Lady Mary Wortley Montagu, on a trip to Turkey, discovers the practice of smallpox inoculation, which is practiced by village women. She brings the custom back to England, publishes a paper on the subject, and conducts successful experiments. However, her contribution is largely overlooked, and credit goes to Edward Jenner's much later work on the subject.

1720 German astronomer Maria Kirch (b. 1670) dies. She discovered a comet in 1702, calculated calendars, and published papers on heavenly conjunctions. Her daughter and son also became astronomers.

1725 British midwife Jane Sharp publishes *The Compleat Midwife's Companion; or, the Art of Midwifery Improv'd*.

Education and Scholarship

Japanese women of the merchant class are more often sent to school than women of the samurai or peasant classes. In the eighteenth century, about 15% of Japanese women are literate.

Girls in England and the American colonies rarely receive any formal education and generally learn music,

dancing, and needlework. In 1706, Jonathan Swift expresses the widespread pessimism about female intellect when he says, "A very little wit is valued in a woman, as we are pleased with a few words spoken plain by a parrot."

1705–1715 Forty-one percent of women in New England can write well enough to sign their wills.

1708 English scholar Elizabeth Elstob (1683–1756) publishes a translation of Madeleine de Scudéry's *Essay on Glory*. Her other works include a translation of the *Anglo-Saxon Homily on the Nativity of St. Gregory* (1709) and *Rudiments of Grammar for the English-Saxon Tongue, first given in English, with an Apology for the Study of Northern Antiquities* (1715).

Religion

1705 English writer Mary Astell publishes *The Christian Religion, as professed by a Daughter of the Church of England*.

1714 Prussia abolishes witchcraft trials.

1726–1750

General Status and Daily Life

Slave women are captured, kidnapped, or purchased in Africa and transported on crowded ships to the Americas. As women, they have some privileges; in slave ships, men are kept chained throughout the entire voyage, but women and children are sometimes allowed more freedom of movement. However, they are also more subject to sexual attack and equally susceptible to the disease and malnutrition that ravage slave ships.

At the other end of the socioeconomic spectrum are the wealthy ladies of Philadelphia described by a Scots physician in June 1744: "The ladies, for the most part, keep att home and seldom appear in the streets, never in publick assemblies except att the churches or meetings." These women, like their European counterparts, may have delicate health as a result of their cosmetics. One means of achieving a fashionable pallor is the ingestion of arsenic, which damages the ability of blood to circulate. Upper-class women, unlike poor women, do not nurse their own children. Instead, they hire wet nurses, at a yearly salary of twenty-five to fifty pounds.

White women in the colonies marry in their early twenties, black women in their late teens. A married woman can expect to be pregnant every two or three years and bear five to eight children. If she does not want the child (4–6% of births are illegitimate), she may commit infanticide, but she is more likely to abandon the child somewhere where it is likely to be found and cared for.

Premarital sex in the Western world, though frowned upon by clergy, is actually quite common. In some parts of England, as many as 40% of first children are conceived before marriage. Marriage itself is changing, with greater emotional expectations and a corresponding rise in separations as couples find themselves dissatisfied with their partners. Honeymoon couples are still often accompanied by a chaperone or female relative of the bride; not until the nineteenth century will couples typically take such a journey alone.

Women in northern Africa marry at about twelve or thirteen, usually no later than sixteen.

1733 A Jamaican law prohibits the separation by sale of slave families.

Government, the Military, and the Law

Nov. 13, 1726 Sophia Dorotea, electoral princess of Hanover and wife of George I of England, dies. She has been imprisoned by her husband for thirty-two years on suspicion of adultery (though he publicly consorts with mistresses). Shortly before her death, George offered to take her back, but she responded, "If what I am accused of is true, I am unworthy of his bed; and if it is false, he is unworthy of mine."

1729 Ethiopian ruler Menetewab becomes regent for her son, Iyasu II; she will continue to hold effective power until his death in 1755.

Jan. 29, 1730 Anna Ivanovna, daughter of Ivan V, is offered the throne of Russia if she agrees not to marry, appoint a successor, or limit the vast powers awarded to itself by the Supreme Privy Council. She agrees, wins the military's support, and abolishes the Council.

1733 Creek Indian trader Mary Musgrove (c. 1700–c. 1763) is one of the first to greet Georgia's founder, James Oglethorpe, when he arrives at the colony. Her skills as interpreter and negotiator secure peace between the settlers and the Creeks, a peace that secures the safety of the colony during various imperial wars. Musgrove manages to secure good rewards for her services, including £200 and a diamond ring from Oglethorpe, three coastal islands from the Creeks, and £2,100 and clear title to St. Catherines Island from the English government.

1736? American colonist Hannah Duston (b. December 23, 1657) dies. Captured by twelve Indians, she managed, with the help of a boy, to kill ten of them;

one woman and one of the seven children escaped. Duston scalped the dead Indians to earn a reward of £25.

1737 Queen Caroline of England, wife of George II, dies. Popular doggerel has ascribed the achievements of George's reign to his wife, who has always taken more of an interest in politics than he has: "You may strut, dapper George, but 'twill all be in vain; / We know 'tis Queen Caroline, not you that reign."

1739 Jamaican leader Nanny of the Maroons is an influential woman and an obeah (spiritual leader), although the British refuse to recognize her authority directly. She leads guerrilla troops and helps to establish Jamaican independence.

1739 Irish soldier Kit Cavanagh (b. 1667), known also as "Mother Ross" and Christian Davies, dies and is buried with military honors. She fought with distinction in the British army for about ten years before her sex was discovered. She was then allowed to remain with the army until 1712, but only as a cook. After finishing her military career, she used her pensions to start a profitable brewing business.

1740 British sailor Ann Mills serves in war aboard the frigate *Maidstone*.

Oct. 17, 1740 Russian empress Anna Ivanovna dies. She is succeeded by Ivan VI, whose mother, Anna Leopoldovna, serves as regent. On November 26, 1741, the fifteen-month-old Ivan will be deposed and replaced by Peter the Great's daughter Elizabeth (b. 1709).

Oct. 19, 1740 Maria Theresa (b. 1717), pregnant with the fourth of sixteen children, becomes empress of Austria; she will add Hungary to her territories in 1741. She immediately begins to limit the powers of the nobles and the church and to reform the civil service, treasury, and universities. Soon after Maria Theresa's accession, Austria is attacked by various European powers, including Prussia and Bavaria, in the belief that as a woman she will be too weak to defend her inheritance.

c. 1743 English soldier Hannah Snell (1723–1792), having been deserted by her sailor husband, dresses as a man and enlists to find him. She deserts after being flogged for defending a woman from her sergeant, reenlists, fights the French, and learns of her husband's execution. She is wounded in 1748 at the Battle of Pondicherry and removes a bullet from her groin rather than be discovered as a woman. In 1750, she reveals her sex and leaves the military, publishing *The Female Soldier: or the Surprising Adventures of Hannah Snell*. Thereafter, she will make her living running an inn called the Female Soldier and appearing on stage in her uniform.

Sept. 1745 Louis XV of France formally presents his new mistress Mme. de Pompadour to his wife the Queen. Loyal to her family, intelligent, charming, and a patron of the arts, Pompadour is nonetheless extravagant and quickly grows unpopular with the French people. Between September 9, 1745, and April 15, 1764, she will spend 36,827,268 livres of the treasury's money, or approximately $73,000,000 (1953) dollars.

1746 Scottish heroine Flora Macdonald (1722–1790) helps Bonnie Prince Charlie to escape from his British pursuers, disguising him as "an Irish spinning maid." He gets away safely, but she is captured, jailed, and freed in 1747.

c. 1750 Ibo tribeswomen in West Africa often fight in wars.

Literature and the Visual Arts

1726 Chinese artist Ma Quan paints *Chrysanthemums*, a colorful work that depicts a profusion of blooms growing from a low rock. Ma is an adept painter of flowers, but she is best known for her pictures of butterflies. In Chinese art, butterflies are often associated with women, in order to indicate that women are as lovely and fragrant as flowers.

1727 Japanese poet Yuri (1694–1764) publishes 159 poems as *Sayuri ba* (*Leaves from a Small Lily*). Her daughter Ike Gyokuran, born at about this time, will also be a poet.

1736 Chinese artist Chen Shu (b. 1660) dies. She learned to read in bits and pieces from boys of her clan who attended school. Her mother wanted her to stop painting and devote herself to needlework, until a god spoke to the mother in a dream, saying, "I have given your daughter a brush. Some day she will be famous. How can you forbid it?" Chen worked in most of the popular genres of the day: religious figures, landscapes, birds, and flowers, with special attention to the last two. Twenty-three of her works were included in the imperial palace collection.

1738 English author Elizabeth Carter publishes *Poems Upon Particular Occasions*.

Apr. 1744–May 1746 British author Eliza Haywood publishes the monthly *Female Spectator*, one of the world's first periodicals for women. Each issue is filled with about fifty pages of essays and romantic fiction.

1747 Chinese artist Yun Bing, a distant descendant of the famous male artist Yun Shouping, paints *Ducks Under Bamboo and Peach Blossoms*. She specializes in paintings of flowers, insects, and plants.

1749 The marquise de Tencin, author of *Les malheurs de l'amour* (1747,) *Les memoires du Comte de Comminges* (1735), and the historical romance *Le siège de Calais* (1739), dies. Tencin, who inherited her literary salon and its prestigious guest list from the marquise de Lambert in 1733, passes it to her protegée Mme. Geoffrin.

1750 Dutch fruit and flower painter Rachel Ruysch (b. 1664) dies. She completed about one hundred paintings during her lifetime, despite the rigors of bearing ten children.

Performing Arts and Entertainment

1726 French ballerina Marie Camargo makes her Paris Opéra debut and becomes immediately popular.

1734 French ballerina Marie Sallé (1707–1756) causes a sensation at London's Drury Lane with her revolutionary, simple costume in *Pygmalion*. A popular performer, she retires in 1740.

1736 English singer and actress Susannah Cibber (1714–1766), later the leading tragedienne of the Drury Lane Theatre, gives a celebrated performance in Voltaire's *Zaire*.

1748 English actress Anne Bracegirdle (b. 1663), noted for her performances as Portia, Desdemona, Cordelia, and Ophelia, dies and is buried in Westminster Abbey.

Mid-18th century Women in Senegal can be *griots*, members of a special caste who serve as hairdressers, troubadours, dancers, and praise-singers/genealogists to great families. They traditionally have the right to unlimited verbal license, so most people try to please the *griots* rather than be subject to their abuse. *Griots* are found not only in Senegal but in other parts of coastal and interior Africa.

Athletics and Exploration

English peasant women compete in "smock races," footraces with some item of clothing as the prize. The women are "lightly clad," probably less for ease of movement than for the voyeuristic pleasure of the audience.

1728 Boxing matches between women are fairly common in England; the self-proclaimed champion of them all is Elisabeth Stokes.

July 26, 1745 The first recorded cricket match between two women's teams takes place near Guilford,

Surrey, England. A newspaper account claims, "The girls bowled, batted, ran and catched as well as most men could do in that game." Cricket is quite popular with women at this time.

Activism

1730 Eight female and three male escaped slaves, part of the group known as the Seramica rebels, are executed by the colonial government of Surinam. Two of the youngest women are decapitated; the others are broken on the rack, but they make no outcry.

1736 A planned slave uprising in Antigua is betrayed, probably under torture, by Phillida, a female slave.

Business and Industry

In the American colonies, some women are merchants. Most women work on farms with their families, but widows often move to the cities, working as nurses, governesses, teachers, seamstresses, servants, laundresses, or prostitutes; those in better financial condition run boardinghouses, inns, and shops.

1738 South Carolina printer Lewis Timothy dies. His widow, Elizabeth (d. 1757), continues to print his *South Carolina Gazette* without missing a single issue, turning the business over to their son Peter when he comes of age. She is the first American woman to publish a newspaper; Benjamin Franklin will praise her "Regularity and Exactitude." Later, Peter's widow, Ann Timothy (c. 1727–September 11, 1792), will also run the paper, becoming printer to the state of South Carolina in 1785.

1738–mid 1740s American planter Eliza Pinckney (December 28, 1722?–May 26, 1793) experiments with ginger, alfalfa, and cotton on her father's South Carolina plantation, finally introducing indigo to the colonies and setting policy on its cultivation for the entire colony. Later she will work with hemp, flax, and silk production on her husband's lands.

July 11, 1748 American tobacconist Mary Copley Pelham advertises a change of address for her shop, reminding her customers that "she continues to sell the best Virginia Tobacco, Cut, Pigtail and spun, of all Sorts, by Wholesale, or Retail, at the cheapest Rates."

1750 American confidence artist Sarah Wilson is born. Her colorful career will begin with her appointment as servant to one of English queen Charlotte's ladies-in-waiting; she will use this position to steal a gown, a diamond necklace, and a miniature of the queen. Arrested and deported to the American colonies, she will then use these items to convince rich southerners that she is the

sister of the queen, securing an introduction to the governor of North Carolina and collecting sizable fees for supposed political favors. Discovered, she will escape to the northern colonies and disappear from sight.

Mid-18th century Senegal has many wealthy women traders, known by the honorary title *signare*. Some own as many as thirty to forty slaves and do a great deal of business with European men, despite regulations against such men's cohabiting or trading with African women. These female traders often throw immense celebrations, at which copious amounts of local beer are served and sometimes French wine as well.

Science and Medicine

1738 Italian mathematician Maria Agnesi (May 16, 1718–January 9, 1799) defends 190 theses before a crowd of spectators and publishes *Propositiones philosophicae*, a collection of essays on science and philosophy. She then tries to retire to a convent and is stopped only by the vociferous protests of her teachers.

1746 French astronomer Louise du Pierry is born. She will teach astronomy to women, predict eclipses, compute lengths of day and night, and assemble refraction tables.

1748 Maria Agnesi publishes a treatise on calculus, *Istituzioni analitiche*, dedicating it to Austrian empress Maria Theresa. Her knowledge of several languages, including French, Latin, Greek, Italian, and Hebrew, enables her to compile the discoveries of Newton, Liebniz, and others. The book, one of the most significant works of its time and one of the first works on finite and infinitesimal analysis, discusses finite quantities, conic sections, tangents, inflections, maxima and minima, infinitesimals, integral calculus, differential equations, and a versed sine curve, or *versiera*, studied earlier by Fermat and Guido Grandia. This *versiera* is subsequently attributed to Agnesi, and a later mistranslation of the word *versiera* as "wife of the devil" will cause generations of English mathematicians to refer to her as "the witch of Agnesi."

Istituzioni analitiche is widely admired and translated and brings Agnesi several awards, including a gold medal from Pope Benedict XIV and, from Empress Maria Theresa, a diamond ring and a letter sealed in a diamond and crystal case. (Years later, Agnesi will sell Maria Theresa's gifts in order to raise money for the poor.) In 1750, Agnesi is appointed to a chair at the University of Bologna, which she holds until about 1796, though she gradually turns from mathematics to religion and refuses to engage in mathematical discussions by 1762.

Sept. 10, 1749 Emilie de Breteuil, the marquise du Châtelet (b. December 17, 1706), dies. She composed works on science and mathematics, translated the works of Newton into French for the first time, and had a profound influence on the work of Voltaire. In 1738, she entered an Académie des Sciences competition on the nature of fire after disagreeing with her friend Voltaire's conclusions on the subject. She did not tell him she was entering the contest and wrote furiously at night, "keeping herself awake by plunging her hands into iced water." Her essay did not win but was considered good enough to be published with the winning entries. In 1740 she anonymously published *Institutions de physique*, proposing a compromise of Newtonian and Liebnitzian theories of physics; a former tutor accused her unsuccessfully of stealing her information from his lessons and using it in her treatise.

Education and Scholarship

May 4, 1746 The Moravian's Women's Seminary, the first girls' boarding school in the American colonies, is founded.

1748 American Sophia Hume publishes an attack on luxury, *An Exhortation to the Inhabitants of the Province of South Carolina*.

1749 German doctor Dorothea Erxleben publishes *Rational Thoughts on Education of the Fair Sex*.

1750 Forty percent of Englishwomen and 27% of Frenchwomen are literate enough to sign their names.

Religion

In West Africa and in American communities of African slaves, obeah is a powerful religion. Obeah practitioners are often female, and they sometimes use their influence as spiritual leaders to encourage rebellion against slave owners. Obeah is actually composed of two separate components; obeah itself is private and often involves knowledge of poisons, magic, and herbal medicines, while myalism is the public form of worship and involves group dances.

Aug. 6, 1727 Ursuline nuns land in Louisiana to found an orphanage, a girls' school, and a hospital—the first charitable institutions in what will later be the United States.

Mar. 15, 1729 Sister St. Stanislaus Hachard of New Orleans becomes the first nun to take her vows in the American colonies.

1737 China's emperor declares Tian Hu (Ma Zu) Empress of Heaven. Originally a minor deity, this patroness of mariners has become quite important in Chinese religion, with many temples built to her by shipping merchants.

Mid-18th century Japanese Buddhist Ohashi is sold to a brothel when her samurai father falls on hard times. It is fairly common for daughters to be sold as courtesans or entertainers to pay their family's debts. She is unhappy until she achieves Zen enlightenment during a thunderstorm, and eventually she leaves the brothel to marry, afterward leaving her husband to study Zen.

1751–1775

General Status and Daily Life

Women in the Ottoman Empire are restricted to the women's quarters, or harem, within the home. Outdoors they must be veiled; no man but a close relative or husband may enter their rooms. Women bathe frequently at public baths.

On Jamaica's sugar plantations, male slaves are trained for a wider variety of tasks than female slaves, with the result that most field work is done by women.

In Europe, contraception is being used more widely, with the chief methods being condoms, vaginal sponges, and coitus interruptus ("pullbacks"). Condoms are advertised as "preservatives from claps and impediments to procreation."

European girls are laced into corsets at an early age and sometimes put in restraints to "improve" their posture and prevent stooping. One woman describes wearing, all day from the ages of six to thirteen, an iron collar "with a back-board strapped over the shoulders."

Jan. 1755 In an effort to limit the excesses of fashion, Korean women are forbidden by the government to wear wigs and encouraged to wear small hats instead. Like most sumptuary laws, this decree is largely ineffective.

1761 Mrs. E. Smith publishes one of the first cookbooks in the American colonies, *The Complete Housewife*. The American housewife in this period usually makes her own candles, soap, clothes, and cheese. Cooking is tricky, as it is done not on a stove but on an open fireplace full of racks and hooks for iron pots. Women socialize at quilting bees, barn raisings, harvest festivals, and other communal work-centered celebrations.

1765 According to English law, "By marriage, the husband and wife are one person in law; that is, the very being of legal existence of the woman is suspended during the marriage, or at least it is incorporated and consolidated into that of the husband: under whose wing, protection, and cover, she performs everything." The "covered" or married woman is known as a *feme* (or *femme*) *covert*, and the single woman, still a legal entity in her own right, is a *feme sole*.

c. 1768–1774 The female cook of French royal mistress Mme. du Barry is the first chef ever to receive the *cordon bleu* for fine cooking.

1770 English cook Hannah Glasse (b. 1708) dies. She was the author of the immensely popular *The Art of Cooking Made Plain and Simple* (probably the first English guide to meal planning), *The Compleat Confectioner*, and *The Servant's Directory or Housekeeper's Companion*.

1770 Englishwomen begin using visiting cards—cards printed with a person's name, intended to be left at friends' houses when social calls are made.

1775 Connecticut housewife Abigail Foote records her day's activities: "Fixed gown for Prude, mended her mother's riding hood, spun short bread, carded tow, spun linen, worked on cheese basket, hatchel'd flax, pleated and ironed, read a sermon of Doddridge's, spooled a piece, milked the cows, made a broom of Guinea wheat straw, set a red dye, had two scholars from Mr. Taylor's, carded two pounds of wool, spun harness twine, and scoured the pewter." Constant work is also the norm for the Long Island housewife who wrote in 1768, "It has been a tiresome day it is now Bed time and I have not had won minutts rest."

Government, the Military, and the Law

1761 George III marries Princess Charlotte of Mecklenberg-Strelitz. The common people, seeing her uptilted nose, yell, "Pug! Pug!" Charlotte asks for a translation of the word and is told it means, "God bless Your Royal Highness."

1762 Fifty English ships with 12,000 men aboard attempt to invade Nicaragua. The commander of the defending fortress dies, and his nineteen-year-old daughter, Rafaela Herrera, assumes command. She keeps the English at bay for five days, killing their commander, then finds them at night and frightens them away by setting blazing cloth adrift on the water.

1762 Seneca Indian women expect to be included in high-level meetings with other powers. As one Seneca man puts it, they have the right to be involved in important conferences, since they are "of Much Estimation Amongst Us, in that we proceed from them and they provide our Warriors with Provisions when they go abroad."

Jan. 5, 1762 Russian empress Elizabeth, daughter of Peter the Great, dies. During her reign, she established the University of Moscow, encouraged economic growth, reformed the banking system, founded the Academy of Arts, waged successful wars with her neighbors, and attempted to develop eastern Russia. She is succeeded by her nephew Peter III, whose behavior offends almost everyone. On June 29, Catherine II, Peter III's wife, is warned by her friend Ekaterina Dashkova of plots on her life. She organizes rebel troops, dons a man's uniform, and deposes Peter, who is assassinated shortly thereafter.

Apr. 15, 1764 Mme. de Pompadour (b. December 29, 1721), mistress of Louis XV, dies. After she ceased to be his mistress, Pompadour became Louis's confidante and adviser, acquiring even greater political power. She used her influence to establish closer ties between Austria and France, establish the royal porcelain factory at Sevres, and further the careers of her favorite courtiers. She also reconciled the king and the Parlement after a religious controversy over the doctrine of Jansenism and founded, on January 22, 1751, the École Militaire for sons of impoverished nobles or officers killed in action. Its pupils will include several distinguished military men, including Napoleon Bonaparte.

1765 Austrian empress Maria Theresa (d. November 29, 1780) begins reforming the penal code, legal system, and educational system of the Holy Roman Empire. On August 15, her husband dies, and Maria Theresa abdicates in favor of her son, Josef II. However, she soon comes out of retirement and becomes his co-ruler.

1767 Catherine II selects 564 commissioners to reform Russia's legal code; special attention is to be given to the rights of serfs and to educational reform. In 1772, she will end the privileges of the Cossacks, and in 1775, she will reform the bureaucracy.

1769 Ethiopian ruler Menetewab (d. 1770) is removed from power, largely due to her alienation of the nobility.

Apr. 1769 Former governess and seamstress Mme. du Barry (1743–December 8, 1793) comes to the attention of Louis XV of France, who will be her lover, her benefactor, and, ultimately (when hatred of aristocrats and royal favorites erupts during the French Revolution), the cause of her death. Du Barry meddles in politics, influencing Choiseul's fall from power.

1775 Cherokee leader Nancy Ward takes her husband's place in battle when he is killed in a fight against the Creeks; leading the Cherokee to victory, she is dubbed Agi-ga-u-e (Beloved Woman) and becomes head of the Woman's Council and a member of the Council of Chiefs.

1775 Empress Maria Theresa forces the Ottoman Empire to surrender the province of Bukovina, north of Transylvania. She also abolishes forced labor by tenant farmers in Bohemia and the Austrian states.

Literature and the Visual Arts

1751–1763 Japan has many female *waka* poets. The *waka* is a poem of five lines, with five syllables in the first and third lines and seven syllables in each other line. It is a genre thought to be especially suitable for women.

1751 English novelist and playwright Eliza Haywood (1693–1756), satirized in Pope's *Dunciad* and called a "stupid, infamous, scribbling woman" by Jonathan Swift, publishes *The History of Miss Betsy Thoughtless*, a novel about a young woman who enjoys admiration but has no desire to love or to marry.

1752 Charlotte Lennox publishes the novel *The Female Quixote*, which satirizes women who read too many novels. Novel reading is beginning to be denounced by the arbiters of etiquette, who feel that it is a waste of time and detrimental to the morals.

1757 Miniaturist Marie Thérèse Reboul (1729–1805) is elected to the Académie Royale, the first Frenchwoman to become a member in seventy-five years.

Apr. 15, 1757 Italian painter Rosalba Carriera (b. October 7, 1675), one of the first rococo artists, dies after years of increasing blindness. She began her career as a miniaturist but became known for her portraits, influential pastel technique, and allegorical paintings. Her patrons included Augustus of Poland, Maximilian II of Bavaria, and the kings of Norway and Denmark.

1759 The French *Journal des Dames* (*Ladies' Journal*) begins publication. It will run until 1778 and will be edited by women after 1764.

1762 English traveler, author, and feminist Lady Mary Wortley Montagu (b. 1689) dies. The first American edition of her letters (1766) will be printed by a female publisher, Sarah Goddard.

1764 In St. Petersburg, construction begins on Catherine II's art museum, Gostiny Dvor.

1768 England's Royal Academy of Art is founded, with only two female members, British painter Mary Moser (1744-1819) and Swiss painter Angelica Kauffmann. They will be the only two female members of the academy until the twentieth century.

1770 Still-life artist Anne Vallayer-Coster (1744-1818) and pastel portraitist Marie Suzanne Giroust (d. 1772) are elected to the Académie Royale. In 1771, Vallayer-Coster paints one of her most famous works, *The White Soup Bowl*, notable for its skillful rendering of the various textures of several white surfaces.

1773 American playwright Mercy Otis Warren publishes *The Adulateur*, a satire on prominent Massachusetts leaders.

1773 English essayist Hester Chapone (b. 1727) publishes her immensely popular *Letters on the Improvement of the Mind*, which will serve as a guide for female conduct well into the nineteenth century.

Sept. 1, 1773 Phillis Wheatley (c. 1752–December 5, 1784) becomes the first published black American author with the appearance of her book, *Poems on Various Subjects, Religious and Moral*. The twenty-year-old slave had to find a London publisher, as no American press would accept the book. She began writing at the age of twelve and met with her first public success in 1771, after writing an elegy for a British evangelist; her work will be popular with many of the Founding Fathers and features heroic couplets, mythological and biblical references, and attacks on racism. Almost half her poems are elegies.

1775 Japanese poet Chiyo (b. 1703), the chief *haiku* poet of the classical period, dies. In 1754, she became a Buddhist nun, a move that gave her the freedom to travel and to mingle with men. Free access to the outside world was denied to most upper-class women by the Confucian code of conduct popular at this time. She occasionally collaborated with Shisen, another woman poet, and taught and traveled with the female *haiku* poet Suye. Her fame was demonstrated by the publication of her poems in her lifetime, a rare accomplishment for a Japanese poet of either sex, and by the Tokugawa government's gift of her poems to Korean envoys in 1763.

1775 Chinese poet Zhong Lingjia (b. 1706) dies.

Performing Arts and Entertainment

Egyptian professional musicians are often women. Women, especially prostitutes, also perform erotic dances.

1754 German princess, art patron, composer, singer, painter, and author Maria Antonia Walpurgis, electress of Saxony (1724–1780), writes, composes, and stars in the première of her first opera, *Il trionfo della fedeltà*.

1760   Several prominent actresses die this year, including the British duchess of Bolton, otherwise known as Lavinia Fenton (b. 1708), who was England's most popular actress for a few years around 1727; Friederike Caroline Neuber (b. 1697) of Germany; and Irish comedienne Peg Woffington (b. c. 1714).

1760   Maria Antonia Walpurgis writes, composes, and stars in the première of her second opera, *Talestri, regina delle amazoni*.

1762   French actress and opera singer Sophie Arnould creates the role of Eurydice in Gluck's *Orpheus and Eurydice*. The Paris Opéra's reigning soprano for more than twenty years, Arnould once, after growing bored with an aristocratic lover, sent his wife all the gifts he had ever given her, including her children by him.

1770   French ballerina Marie de Camargo (b. 1710) dies. She was famous for her complicated footwork, her short skirts, and her affair with the comte de Clermont, which kept her off the stage for five years. Her admirers included Voltaire and Casanova.

1774   Sophie Arnould creates the role of Iphigénie in Gluck's *Iphigénie en Aulide*. The role is the greatest success of her illustrious career.

Athletics and Exploration

1764   Catherine II of Russia encourages exploration of Alaska.

1765   In Upham, England, a cricket match is held with "eleven married against eleven maiden women, for a large plum-cake, a barrel of ale and a regale of tea, which was won by the latter."

1766   Jeanne Baret becomes the first woman to circumnavigate the globe by posing as her botanist husband's manservant on the ship of French navigator Louis Antoine de Bougainville.

Activism

During this era, American women participate in political boycotts; the Daughters of Liberty hold public spinnings to encourage the use of homemade rather than British-imported cloth. Others boycott British food and drink; Wilmington, North Carolina, women parade through town and then burn their tea. Throughout the colonies, women exchange recipes for tea substitutes; some opt to drink coffee. Edenton, North Carolina, women sign an anti-British petition and are satirized in a British cartoon of 1775.

1760   During a Jamaican slave rebellion, a woman named Cubah is named queen of the rebels and given a robe, a crown, and a canopy as emblems of state. She is captured, sentenced to transportation, released, recaptured, and finally executed.

1768   A planned slave rebellion in Montserrat is betrayed by a female slave.

c. Oct. 1775   American women strip a Tory to the waist and tar and feather him with molasses and weeds.

Business and Industry

Many women flourish as printers and publishers in the American colonies. Anne Catherine Green (d. 1775) takes over her husband's *Maryland Gazette* when he dies in 1767 and continues printing the paper and carrying out government contracts for the Maryland General Assembly at a yearly salary of 36,109 to 48,000 pounds of tobacco. She refuses to publish anonymous attacks in her paper, saying, "Pieces . . . free from personal abuse, and otherwise instructive or entertaining, are gratefully acknowledged; but whenever they shall exceed the Boundaries of Delicacy, or be replete with personal invective, the Author must expect to offer his Name." Later, during the turmoil leading to the Revolutionary War, she will report on the First Continental Congress and the Boston Tea Party.

Most women publishers, like Green, take over for a deceased or absent male relative. Clementina Rind (c. 1740–September 25, 1774), takes over the *Virginia Gazette* upon the death of her husband in August 1773, maintaining high standards and good literary judgment. The House of Burgesses continues to use her business as the official public press and names her a public printer in her own right in May 1774. Mary Katherine Goddard (b. 1738), daughter of printer Sarah Goddard (c. 1700–January 5, 1770), takes over her brother's newspaper, the *Maryland Journal*, so that he can concentrate on other aspects of his business.

Apr. 18, 1760   American colonial businesswoman Mary Provoost Alexander (b. April 17, 1693), who nurtured a thriving mercantile enterprise while giving birth to ten children, dies.

1767   Caty Louette is the richest woman in the West African community of Gorée. She owns sixty-eight slaves, about two-thirds of whom are female. Many of Gorée's private estates are owned by African or Eurafrican women, who build large brick or stone houses for themselves.

May 1767   American Abigail Stoneman, one of the few licensed women tavern keepers of the time, opens the Merchant's Coffee House. Between 1768 and 1774, she will open a teahouse, boardinghouse, and ballroom in Newport, Rhode Island, and a coffeehouse called the

Royal Exchange on the site of the Boston Massacre.

Science and Medicine

June 12, 1754   Dorothea Erxleben (1715–1762) becomes the first woman to earn a full medical degree from a German university, graduating from the University of Halle with King Frederick's authorization. She began her medical education in 1741, but her studies were delayed by family obligations.

1757   American Catherine Schuyler nurses wounded British soldiers from the battle at Ticonderoga.

1759   French midwife Angélique du Coudray publishes *Abrégé de l'art des accouchements avec plusiers observations sur des cas singuliers*, a revision of a midwifery textbook from 1667.

1759   French astronomer Nicole-Reine Lepaute (1723–1788) begins work at the Paris Observatory, where she will do important work on the movements of the sun, moon, and planets, including a monograph about Venus and calculations for a solar eclipse.

1760   Italian anatomist Anna Manzolini becomes a professor of anatomy at the University of Bologna, a position she will hold until her death in 1774. She makes splendid anatomical models in wax despite her obsessive fear of dead things, becoming so renowned that her clients include Emperor Josef II and Empress Catherine II. She is a member of the Russian Royal Scientific Society.

Mar. 10, 1766   American botanist Jane Colden Farquhar (b. March 27, 1724), who collected and classified many of the native plants of New York, dies. She catalogued more than 300 plants and discovered and named the gardenia, though at least one fellow-scientist was less concerned with whether she could identify plants than with whether she could make good cheese.

1771   The Pio Instituto Trivulzio, an Italian charity hospital, opens; Italian mathematician Maria Agnesi, who has already been tending the sick for some time, often in her own home, is placed in charge.

1771 Japan's first scientific dissection of a human body takes place. The body is that of "a notorious woman criminal, 'Old Mother Green Tea.'"

1775   Nicole-Reine Lepaute coauthors the *Traité de horlogerie*, a work on pendulum motion.

Education and Scholarship

1753   English author Lady Mary Wortley Montagu

expresses the hope that her granddaughter will be well educated but will "conceal whatever Learning she attains, with as much solicitude as she would hide crookedness or lameness."

1755   About 35% of Englishwomen can write well enough to sign their own names.

1760   Charlotte Lennox, editor of the English magazine *Lady's Museum*, advises her readers "to avoid all abstract learning, all thorny researches." She does not "wish to see assemblies made up of doctors in petticoats, who will regale us with Greek and the system of Liebniz."

1763   English historian Catharine Graham Macaulay (1731–1791) begins publishing her eight-volume *History of England*.

1765   A mixed-sex intellectual society, Almack's Club, is established in England. Male members are elected by the women, and female members by the men.

Religion

In Islam, women and men are believed to go to separate paradises after death; in the men's, the virtuous are entertained eternally by houris, beautiful maidens who become virgins again no matter how many times they are defiled.

Jan. 31, 1752   Ursuline Sister St. Martha Turpin of Louisiana becomes the first American-born nun.

1753   American Quaker Susanna Morris is told that female Quakers are not allowed at the London Yearly Meeting, nor are they allowed to hold a meeting of their own, for "there could not be two heads to one body."

1760s   Catholic schools are banned in Maryland; Catholic parents hire French seamstresses who teach religion under the pretense of teaching their daughters to sew and weave.

1763   Quakers hold the first yearly women's meetings in Virginia and North Carolina. New England establishes a women's meeting in 1764.

1768   English countess Selina Huntingdon founds Trevecca College, a Methodist seminary.

1774   Empress Maria Theresa grants religious tolerance to Hungarian Protestants.

1775   Anna Maria Swaegel is the last witch executed in Germany.

1776–1800

General Status and Daily Life

Divorce among African peoples is usually fairly simple and straightforward. In one ritual, carried to Jamaica by African slaves, the *cotta*, or dried-leaf pad a woman uses to cushion loads carried on her head, is cut in two to symbolize the end of the marriage.

Life expectancy for a mid- to upper-class Englishwoman is fifty. More upper-class women are breast-feeding than before.

In Europe, to achieve a fashionable pallor, thinness, and languor, schoolgirls are often deprived of fresh air, adequate food, and exercise. In the 1770s and 1780s, hair is piled high on the head in a pompadour, supplemented with wigs and pads. It is greased, then powdered, and often not washed for weeks at a time. The most extreme proponents of this style have bizarre objects woven into the hair, like fruit or even model ships. Tight corseting is still popular, with girls being squeezed into their first stays almost as soon as they can walk. During the French Revolution, wide hoops and tight corsets are discarded, and fashionable young ladies wear flesh-colored stockings and Greek-style gowns with high slits, to convey the idea of nudity or near-nudity.

During the American Revolution, many women run farms and businesses while men are at war. Divorce becomes more common during this period. Most Massachusetts divorces are initiated by wives, usually for desertion.

1776   New York tavern keeper Elizabeth "Betsy" Flanagan mixes rum and fruit juice, inventing the cocktail. The drink gets its name from the rooster feathers she uses to adorn the glasses.

1780   The raja of Marwar, India, dies; his sixty-four wives commit sati—that is, they burn themselves on his funeral pyre so as not to outlive him. Sati is considered highly commendable behavior for a widow; 378 Bengali women will immolate themselves in this fashion in 1785 alone.

1783   Austria introduces civil marriage and divorce.

c. 1788   In New Orleans, light-skinned "quadroons" (women with one black grandparent, who are required to wear scarves or chignons to identify themselves as nonwhite) are trained as courtesans and carefully dressed and watched by their mothers, who escort them to "quadroon balls," where rich white men hunt for mistresses. The mothers negotiate the settlement, which usually includes cash and a house.

1789   In Barbados, slaves cannot marry legally, but informal marriages are common. Some slaves form polygynous unions based on tribal marriages in West Africa; as in Africa, the first or chief wife has many privileges not accorded to her cowives.

1790   Virgin slave girls in the Ottoman Empire are considerably cheaper than horses.

1790   In Surinam, black women slaves are often sexually exploited by their white masters; white women, in turn, take out their jealousy and anger on the slave women. In the same year, a Jamaican plantation owner nails one of his female slaves by her ear to a tree for breaking a plate.

1790   An anonymous female "Matrimonial Republican" in France says that "marriage ought never to be considered as a contract between a superior and an inferior, but a reciprocal union of interest . . . . The obedience between man and wife is, or ought to be mutual."

July 4, 1790   A woman identified by initials only in *Le Moniteur* suggests a joined surname for both spouses.

1791   English law forbids the whipping of female vagrants.

Sept. 20, 1792   Marriages in France move from religious to civil control. Seven grounds are allowed for immediate divorce: insanity, conviction for certain crimes, physical cruelty, immorality, desertion for two years, disappearance for five years, and political emigration. Divorce by mutual consent and for incompatibility can be obtained with a few months' delay. Parties must wait one year before remarrying. Divorce becomes more difficult in September 1797, when women will be filing two-thirds of divorce petitions.

June 28, 1793   The French Assembly orders each district to set up a home for poor pregnant women, who can be housed there until their deliveries.

1794   The Prussian Civil Code grants women equal rights in divorce and child custody, but when a woman gives birth, her husband has the right to decide "how long the child is nourished at the breast."

1794   Thisbe, a slave nurse on a Trinidad plantation, confesses under torture to a mass poisoning. Women are especially likely to be blamed by whites for poisonings.

1795   The British try to legislate against female infanticide in India, with little success.

1796   Eight percent of Baltimore, Maryland,

households are headed by women, two-thirds of them widows.

1798 In the Leeward Islands, female slaves are not legally required to perform heavy work if they are five months pregnant or have six living children. Owners are to be fined one hundred pounds if convicted of sexual intercourse with married female slaves. However, these laws are not strictly enforced.

1800 The U.S. birthrate is 7.04 per woman, the highest in the world.

Government, the Military, and the Law

Revolutions around the world call for increased military activity on the part of women. Some women support the rebellious armies, like the members of the Republican Women's Society of Besançon, France, honored on April 15, 1793, for making clothes for troops all week and staging plays on Sundays to raise money for the military. U.S. patriots Esther Reed and Sarah Bache raise $300,000 to buy soldiers' shirts. Boston entrepreneur Elizabeth Perkins helps more directly, donating $1,000 to the Continental army. Other women actually participate in the fighting, like Vietnamese peasant general Bui Thi Xuan, killed in a rebellion.

In France, many women, armed with swords or pikes, are among the sans-culottes, the most radical republican soldiers. During 1792 and 1793, many enlist openly in the French army. Among them are Reine Chapuy, Rose Bouillon, and Catherine Pochetat, all lauded for their courage; Pochetat, a gunner, is promoted to sublieutenant. Two sisters, Félicité and Théophile Fernig, sixteen and eighteen years old respectively, exhibit heroism in a victory over the Prussians at Valmy on September 20, 1792. On November 6, they lead a cavalry unit, defeating a Hungarian battalion and capturing its commander. However, women are banned from the military on April 30, 1793. All are sent home, compensated by a mere five sous for every league they must travel to get home.

However, some Frenchwomen still fight. In 1793, Madeleine Petit Jean joins her husband in the 4th Sorbonne Gunners' Company. She is later wounded and given a pension. On September 13, 1795, Jeanne Robin reveals herself to General Lescure as a woman, saying, "Once you have seen how I fight, I'm sure you won't send me away." The next day, after distinguishing herself at Thouars, she is killed in battle. At least two soldiers, Angélique Duchemin and Thérèse Figueur, are allowed to remain despite their sex. Duchemin, a soldier for seven years, retires in 1798 after being badly wounded at Calvi. Figueur, known as "Madame Easy-Going," enlists in 1793, fights in Italy, and is captured in 1799 while accompanying a wounded comrade to the hospital.

Fewer women fight in the U.S. army, and those who do are usually disguised as men, but a significant number of female camp followers, usually the wives or widows of soldiers, perform tasks such as washing, cooking, and nursing in exchange for food and wages. Sarah McCalla nurses wounded at Brandywine, follows her husband until his capture, runs their farm while negotiating for his release, and visits him in prison, meanwhile gathering intelligence for the U.S. army. Margaret Sharpe Gaston (b. 1755) is widowed when the British shoot her husband as he flees across a river. Despite the danger, she returns in their boat and retrieves his body. Margaret Corbin is severely wounded defending Fort Washington on November 16, 1776, defending the post of her fallen husband; in 1777, Catherine Schuyler returns to her house despite danger and burns her wheat fields to prevent their use by British forces. On April 26, 1777, sixteen-year-old Sybil Ludington, daughter of a militia colonel, rides to summon her father's unit, braving British patrols, spies, and the ordinary perils of the road.

Of course, not all of the women fighting in the Revolutionary War are sympathetic to the colonists. In the summer of 1777, a Tory, Lady Harriet Acland, sails along the Hudson River, past snipers and American defenses, up to the guns of a fort. There she demands her husband, wounded prisoner John Dyke Acland, and nurses him until he recovers from wounds in his stomach and both legs.

c. 1776 Iroquois leader Molly Brant (1736-Apr. 16, 1796), with her brother Joseph, encourages the Six Nations to support the British in the Revolutionary War, hoping to stop Americans from taking their land. A contemporary says of Molly, "One word from her goes farther with them than a thousand from any white man without exception." She convinces the Seneca, Cayuga, and Mohawk to join the British.

July 1776 Cherokee leader Nancy Ward (c. 1738–1822) notifies American rebels of a British-backed Cherokee attack; in exchange, her village is spared in a retaliatory raid in October. In this year, she also saves a white prisoner, Mrs. William Bean, from death; Bean, in return, teaches her the skills of dairy cultivation, which Ward then teaches to her people, buying the first Cherokee-owned cattle.

July 2, 1776 New Jersey's state constitution gives holders of property worth more than fifty pounds the right to vote—which accidentally includes some women. The right will be withdrawn in 1807.

Feb. 24, 1777 Maria I (d. March 1816), who is at least partially controlled by her mother, Marianna Victoria, becomes queen of Portugal.

1778 Ecuadoran soldier Baltazara Chiza leads a revolt

against the Spanish.

June 28, 1778 Mary "Molly Pitcher" Hays (October 13, 1754?–January 22, 1832), wife of an American gunner, brings water to troops during the battle of Monmouth; when her husband is wounded, she takes his position, fighting coolly throughout the battle. At one point, a cannonball passes through her skirts, and she calmly remarks that she is glad it did not hit any higher.

1779 Peruvian rebel Micaela Bastidas Puyucahua helps her husband, José Gabriel Túpac Amaru, wage a war against Spanish rule. She is an able strategist and adviser who fights, locates supplies, and recruits soldiers, but she and Túpac Amaru are captured in 1781 and executed.

1780 Colombian Manuela Beltran organizes a tax revolt.

May 20, 1782 American soldier Deborah Sampson (December 17, 1760–April 29, 1827) enlists in the 4th Massachusetts regiment of the Continental army as Robert Shirtliffe. On October 25, 1783, she is honorably discharged after her sex is discovered during a hospitalization for fever. In recognition of her battle wounds, she is given money by George Washington to "bear her expenses to some place where she might find a home." In 1792 she will be awarded an official pension by the state of Massachusetts.

Sept. 1782 Fort Henry in Wheeling, (West) Virginia, is besieged by Indians, with so little warning that most of the available gunpowder is not in the fort but nearby at the house of Colonel Zane. According to tradition, Zane's daughter Betty (1766?-1831?) dashes from the fort in an attempt to retrieve the stranded and desperately needed powder. The powder she brings, wrapped in a tablecloth and tied around her waist, is sufficient to hold off the attackers until help arrives.

1783 Russian cavalry officer Nadezhda Durova is born.

1783 Russian empress Catherine II annexes the Crimea from Turkey and introduces serfdom in the Ukraine. The latter move shocks many in Europe, who have perceived her as an enlightened ruler.

1789 Mary Katherine Goddard, the first female postmaster in the United States, loses her job to a man when the post becomes more desirable and highly paid.

1789 Ottoman sultan Abdulhamid I dies. According to custom, his wives and concubines retire to the House of Tears. However, his favorite, Nakshedil (Aimée DeBucq de Rivery, b. 1763, a cousin of Joséphine Bonaparte), is invited to remain by Abdulhamid's son and successor, Selim III. Nakshedil teaches Selim French, becomes his adviser, and helps him open diplomatic channels with

France. When Selim is assassinated in 1807, Nakshedil will save her own son, Mahmud, by hiding him in a furnace, and Mahmud will become the next sultan, guided in his widespread reforms by his mother.

July 14, 1789 In what is generally considered the opening of the French Revolution, the Bastille, a Parisian fortress, is attacked by a mob led by a woman dressed as an Amazon.

June 29, 1790 Mme. de Vuignerais petitions the French National Assembly for women's right to bear arms. On March 6, 1792, Pauline Léon (b. 1758) presents a similar petition signed by 315 women. It asks for women's right to carry pistols, sabers, and rifles, not because "we want to stop looking after our families and our homes. No, gentlemen! We simply wish to be able to defend ourselves in case our enemies are victorious because our side has betrayed us, or due to a clever ploy by the other side." Permission is denied.

July 25, 1792 French actress Claire "Red Rosa" Lacombe (b. March 4, 1765) appears before the Assembly, offering to fight in her country's defense. She is warmly received, mostly because she is attractive, but her offer is refused; one suggests after her departure that she would "be better at softening up tyrants than at fighting against them."

Dec. 15, 1792 French feminist and revolutionary Olympe de Gouges (b. May 7, 1748) offers to act as Louis XVI's lawyer: "He was weak, he was duped, he duped us and he duped himself. That is the trial in a nutshell." She suggests exile rather than death, as more humiliating for the king and more honorable for France, but her offer is met with anger and contempt by the radicals.

1793 In France, women's political activity continues to increase. On February 24, a Girondin (moderate revolutionary) organization, the Society of Women Favoring Freedom and Equality, congratulates the Convention (the Republican legislature) on King Louis XVI's execution. On May 18, radical Jacobin women, who by now consider themselves monitors of the Convention, cause several disturbances by trying to eject or bar those they consider unsuitable.

Oct. 16, 1793 French queen Marie Antoinette (b. November 2, 1755), wife of Louis XVI, is guillotined. She became unpopular in the 1780s, when rumors of supposed affairs and extravagant expenditures led to nicknames like "Madame Deficit." She refused to flee without Louis after the revolution, saying, "My duty is to die at the King's feet," and spent her days pleading with foreign powers to intervene on behalf of the monarchy.

Nov. 8, 1793 French political salon hostess Manon

Roland (b. March 17, 1754), who in 1791 advocated an end to the monarchy, is guillotined. A disciple of Rousseau, she is known for her simple tastes, beauty, and intelligence. Calm and smiling, she refuses to have her hands tied before the execution, saying, "Excuse me, I am not used to that sort of thing." Her last words are, "O Liberty, what crimes are committed in your name!"

Dec. 26, 1793 Women are granted permission to attend (and knit at) meetings of the Paris Commune.

Nov. 7, 1796 Catherine II of Russia, born Princess Sophia Augusta Frederika of Anhalt-Zerbst and known as Catherine the Great, dies. She was also known for her active love life and said, "Nothing in my opinion is more difficult to resist than what gives us pleasure. All arguments to the contrary are prudery."

Literature and the Visual Arts

Late 18th century Vietnamese poet Huo Xuan Huong flourishes.

Late 18th century Japanese *bunjin* (Chinese-style) painter, poet, and calligrapher Ko Raikin is active. She specializes in bird-and-flower paintings; her work is distinctive for its small dots and delicate lines. Another Japanese painter active at this time is Inagaki Tsuru-jo, who specializes in pictures of courtesans.

Late 18th century Korean *kisaeng* (entertainer) Myong-ok writes poetry in the city of Suwon.

Jan. 1778 English novelist Frances Burney (June 13, 1752–January 6, 1840) anonymously publishes *Evelina, or the History of a Young Lady's Entrance into the World*, an immediate critical and popular success. Burney, whose specialty is fiction about young women learning the rules of genteel society, will also publish *Cecilia* (1782) and *Camilla: or, a Picture of Youth* (1796), and *The Wanderer; or, Female Difficulties* (1814).

1779 Chinese poet, calligrapher, and painter Fang Wangyi (b. 1732) dies. A devout Buddhist who called herself the "White-lotus Recluse," she had a husband who admired and encouraged her work. She wrote two volumes of verse and painted plum blossoms, orchids, bamboo, and rocks.

1779 Literature published this year includes *Théâtre à l'usage des jeunes personnes*, a guide to drama for young people by French writer and educator Mme. de Genlis (Félicité du Crest de Saint Aubin, 1746–December 31, 1830), and U.S. playwright Mercy Otis Warren's *The Motley Assembly*, which satirizes Boston Tories.

1779 Elisabeth Vigée-Lebrun (b. April 16, 1755) is established as Marie Antoinette's court painter; in all, she will paint about twenty portraits of the queen. After the French Revolution, she will flee with her daughter to Rome, where she will become quite popular.

1782 German portraitist Anna Dorothea Lisiewska-Therbusch (b. July 23, 1721) dies. Her sitters included Frederick the Great and Diderot, and she was admitted to the French Académie Royale, but she did not achieve great popular success because of her blunt, unfeminine manner.

May 31, 1783 French artists Elisabeth Vigée-Lebrun and Adélaïde Labille-Guiard (1749–1803) are elected to the Académie Royale. Labille-Guiard, who has been working primarily in pastels, now switches to oil as her preferred medium. Pastels, however, have served their purpose for her; her admission to the Académie is in part the result of her series of pastel portraits of Académie members. Traditionally, Académie members are entitled to apartments in the Louvre, but Labille-Guiard will not receive this privilege for another twelve years.

1784 Renowned Japanese *waka* poet and painter Ike Gyokuran dies. She painted landscapes, plum blossoms, bamboo, orchids, and chrysanthemums. Her husband, also an artist, encouraged her work, and together they lived an unconventional life, ignoring housework in favor of playing music in the nude and wearing each other's clothes. Gyokuran did not shave her eyebrows or wear makeup, customs that were fashionable.

May 1784 The first U.S. journal for women as well as men—the *Gentlemen and Ladies' Country Magazine*—appears. Its first issue features advice for girls on marriage and encourages female readers to contribute their thoughts to its pages.

1785 English actress Elizabeth Inchbald (1735–1821) writes the comic play *I'll Tell You What*.

1785 The king of France orders that no female art students are to be given lessons in the Louvre.

Dec. 28, 1789 French playwright and feminist Olympe de Gouges's abolitionist play, *L'Esclavage des Nègres*, is performed by the Théâtre de la Nation, as the Comédie Française is now known. The play causes controversy, with half the audience cheering and half booing throughout the performance.

1790 English novelist Ann Radcliffe (July 9, 1764–February 7, 1823), one of the principal creators of the Gothic genre, publishes her first novel, *A Sicilian Romance*. Radcliffe's novels feature picturesque and crumbling castles, dark and sensual villains, and a hint of the supernatural, which is always rationally explained by the story's end. Her other novels include *The Italian* (1797) and *The Mysteries of Udolpho*, in which the heroine, Emily, is wooed by the honorable Valancourt and menaced by the sinister Count Montoni.

1790 Scottish poet Joanna Baillie (1762–1851) publishes *Fugitive Verses*, a collection admired by such notable literary figures as Robert Burns.

Sept. 8, 1791 The Paris Salon, the formal yearly exhibit of French art, opens at the Louvre; of the 247 artists exhibiting, 19 are women. This is the first year that women have been allowed to show their work at the Salon.

1793 Adélaïde Labille-Guiard, hoping to break into the prestigious, male-dominated field of history painting, has spent two and a half years on what she considers her masterpiece but is forced by the revolutionary government to destroy it because it seems too sympathetic to the monarchy. She will never again attempt such an ambitious project.

1794 Actress, novelist, and playwright Susanna Rowson publishes the first U.S. best-seller: *Charlotte Temple*, a tragic, sentimental novel about the fate of a girl seduced and abandoned.

1795 Chinese poet Luo Qilan publishes *Tingqiuxuan shiji* (*Poems from the Listening-to-Autumn Studio*), a collection of her works. Her poems speak of travel and the contrast between her dreams of leading "a troop of wolfish and tigerish men" and the reality of her bound and crippled feet. She addresses one poem to the renowned ink bamboo painter of the thirteenth and fourteenth centuries, Guan Daosheng.

1795 After harsh critical attacks, French painter Marie Guillemine Benoist gives up history painting and returns to less prestigious, more "feminine" genres. In 1800 she will paint her most famous work, *Portrait of a Negress*.

1796 A collection of Chinese women's poetry, *Sui-yüan nü-ti-tzu hsüan* (*Selections from Sui-yüan's Women Pupils*) is published. Later published in Japan, it does much to improve the image of educated women and to open opportunities for women to study poetry.

1796 Chinese painter Liang Ruozhu is active. She specializes in butterflies, which she captures and presses in order to study them and paint them more accurately, but she also paints insects, shellfish, and birds.

1797 English author Mary Wollstonecraft gives birth to a daughter, Mary Wollstonecraft Shelley, author of *Frankenstein*. Complications after the birth result in Wollstonecraft's death.

1798 Joanna Baillie begins publishing, anonymously, three volumes of blank-verse *Plays on the Passions*. At

first the works are attributed to Sir Walter Scott, but Baillie soon takes credit for them.

1799 Japanese *bunjin* artist Tani Kankan (b. 1770) dies. A devoted Buddhist, she painted over 1,000 pictures of the bodhisattva Kannon, as well as numerous images of landscapes, figures, birds, and flowers.

c. 1800 Chinese courtesan, poet, painter, and calligrapher Yuexiang is active. She specializes in painting ink orchids and sometimes collaborates with another courtesan-painter, Moxiang.

1800 About 75% of English readers of novels are women.

1800 Anglo-Irish author Maria Edgeworth (1767–1849) publishes *Castle Rackrent*, a novel condemning the rapacious absentee landlords who keep the Irish peasantry in poverty.

Performing Arts and Entertainment

1776 Italian soprano Brigitta Banti makes her debut between acts at the Paris Opéra.

1778 French musician Marguerite Antoinette Couperin (b. 1705), royal chamber harpsichordist to the French court, dies.

1785 English actress, salon hostess, and playwright Kitty Clive (b. 1711), admired by Samuel Johnson, Oliver Goldsmith, and Horace Walpole, dies.

1785 English actress Sarah Siddons (1755–1831), one of the greatest tragedians of her day, plays Lady Macbeth for the first time. In 1788, she plays Volumnia in Shakespeare's *Coriolanus*, and in 1796 she plays Queen Gertrude in *Hamlet*.

1790 French musician Angélique-Dorothée-Lucie Grétry (b. 1772), patronized by Marie Antoinette, dies.

Feb. 20, 1792 French singer Rosalie Dugazon, during a performance of *Evénements Imprévus*, turns to the royal box and pointedly sings the line, "Oh, how I love my mistress," to Marie Antoinette; a riot ensues, and Jacobins try to murder Dugazon. Within a few months, Dugazon's royalist sympathies will force her retirement. However, she will return to the stage on December 4, 1794.

Nov. 14, 1793 French theater manager Marguerite Montansier (d. July 13, 1820), director of the Théâtre National, is denounced to the Paris Commune, despite her past donations of theater proceeds to the state. The next day, she is arrested on charges that she has run her theater with money from Marie Antoinette. However, she will survive the purges of the revolution and will be placed in charge of Italian opera by Napoleon in 1799.

June 30, 1794 U.S. playwright Susanna Rowson appears in her own operetta, *Slaves in Algiers*, in Philadelphia.

Athletics and Exploration

1777 The first cricket game between upper-class women is held in Surrey, England.

1780 A horse race for women riders is held in Long Island, New York.

1781 Britain's Toxophilite Society, a dual-sex archery group, is founded.

May 20, 1784 The French marchioness de Montalembert becomes the first woman to ascend in a tethered hot-air balloon. In June, Mme. Thible becomes the first woman to make a free flight in a balloon.

1787 Women are admitted to the Royal British Bowmen archery club. On October 17, 1788, Harriet Boycott wins the Bowmen's first prize.

1788 The First Fleet arrives in Australia with 192 female and 586 male convicts. Women, regardless of the crime for which they have been transported, are given away at landing to any man who wants them. Wealthy men soon make a practice of collecting such women and then discarding them when the next boat comes in.

1788 The first European-Australian baby, Rebekah Small, is born. She will later marry a missionary and have fourteen children.

July 11, 1788 Miss S. Norcross of England scores cricket's first "century"—one hundred runs in one match.

1793 The marchioness of Salisbury becomes Master of the Hatfield Hunt, an unusual post for a woman. She will hunt actively until the age of seventy and will be praised for her bravery, elegance, and "ardor in the chase."

Activism

Mar. 31, 1776 U.S. First Lady Abigail Adams (November 11, 1744–October 28, 1818) writes to her congressman husband John, "In the new Code of Laws which I suppose it will be necessary for you to make I desire you would Remember the Ladies. Remember all Men would be tyrants if they could. If perticuliar care

and attention is not paid to the Ladies we are determined to foment a Rebelion, and will not hold ourselves bound by any Laws in which we have no Voice, or Representation." She says the new laws should "put it out of the power of the vicious and the Lawless to use us with cruelty and indignity." John, amused, replies, "As to your extraordinary Code of Laws, I cannot but Laugh" and refuses to endorse "the Despotism of the Petticoat."

May 1, 1788 French reformer Mme. Fougeret, with the backing of Marie Antoinette, establishes the Society for Motherly Charity to help poor mothers by giving them money to help raise their children.

Aug. 13, 1789 French translator, journalist, biographer, and author Louise Félicité de Kéralio (August 25, 1758–1821) founds the first political newspaper run by a woman, the *Journal d'Etat et du Citoyen*. Her professed hope is to "spread the sacred principles of liberty, the eternal and sublime law of equality, the hatred of tyrants and the horror of prejudice."

Oct. 5, 1789 Women from Paris and surrounding regions, led by revolutionary Théroigne de Méricourt (1762–May 9, 1817), and allegedly by some men dressed as women, demand bread and arms. Grabbing pitchforks, sticks, and pikes, they march on Versailles, followed by 15,000 citizens and National Guardsmen. Fifteen of the women visit the National Assembly, pleading for action against food hoarders. Some of the women get an audience with the King, but one faints in fear. The demonstration results in the forcible return of the royal family to Paris.

Dec. 1789 An anonymous woman asks the French National Assembly for reforms in dowry customs and access for women to high-paying jobs.

1791 Dutch feminist Etta Palm (b. 1743) appears before the French Assembly, asking for attention to "women's rights in education, politics, law, and employment." On March 23, she organizes a union of women's clubs, the Confederation of Friends of Truth, to provide charitable services to the poor, sick, handicapped, and undereducated.

1791 Haitian rebels Marie Jeanne à-la-Crete-a-Pierrot, Victoria "Toya," and Henriette St. Marc are active in Toussaint L'Ouverture's slave revolt.

Sept. 1791 French feminist Olympe de Gouges, founder in 1790 of a famous radical political group, the Club des Tricoteuses, writes her *Declaration of the Rights of Woman and Citizeness*, in which she says, "Woman is born free and her rights are the same as those of a man . . . All citizens, be they men or women, must be equally eligible for all public offices, positions, and jobs, according to their capacity and without any other criteria." Equal rights, she says, are called for by both "nature and reason." De Gouges will be guillotined on November 3, 1793.

1792 English author Mary Wollstonecraft (b. 1759) publishes *A Vindication of the Rights of Woman*, one of the first extensive feminist arguments. She is no idle theorist when it comes to women's rights. In 1784, she helped her sister Eliza, cruelly abused by her husband, to run away. Eliza was forced to hide, since the law allowed her to be forcibly returned to her abuser. Her infant daughter, in accordance with the law, was automatically placed in the father's custody.

Feb. 26, 1793 Women, outraged by high prices for soap, sugar, and candles, loot groceries in Paris. The incident comes only two days after Parisian women seized two boatloads of soap and sold it at low prices to the community and one day after women petitioned the National Convention for a reduction in bread and soap prices. The Convention adjourned without a decision, and the women complained, "When our children ask us for milk, we don't adjourn them until the day after tomorrow."

July 13, 1793 French assassin Charlotte Corday (b. July 28, 1768) goes to the home of revolutionary leader Jean-Paul Marat. Pretending to reveal a Girondin plot, she pulls a kitchen knife from her dress and stabs Marat to death in his bath, then calmly waits to be arrested. She is guillotined four days later.

Oct. 20, 1793 French revolutionary and feminist Claire Lacombe's Society of Revolutionary Republican Women, established earlier this year with Pauline Léon as its president, is among several organizations dissolved, including all women's political clubs, banned by the government. Lacombe continues to hold meetings anyway and will be arrested in March 1794 and released on August 20, 1795. Afterward, she is less revolutionary than before her imprisonment. She ceases political activity and dies probably c. 1820.

May 24, 1794 Cecile Renault, twenty-five, tries unsuccessfully to kill French leader Robespierre.

1795 Ann Parrish founds the first charity organization in the United States run by and for women, the Friendly Circle, later known as the Female Society of Philadelphia for the Relief and Employment of the Poor.

Apr. 1, 1795 Women begin bread riots in Paris, when told they will be given only four ounces of bread each for their children. The women attack the guardhouse, seize a drum, and march on the Convention. Further female-led bread riots in May will lead to the declaration of martial law.

Jan. 24, 1796 Women in Ligueil, France, refuse to knit for soldiers as a protest against the government and publicly twiddle their thumbs. One is fined the price of a pair of men's stockings.

1798 English feminist Mary Hays coauthors *Appeal to the Men of Great Britain on Behalf of the Women*, demanding marriage, property, and sexual rights for women.

1800 Danner House, a shelter for homeless women, is opened in Copenhagen, Denmark.

Business and Industry

Most free black women in the U.S. work as domestic servants.

In France, women can be found in the streets selling everything from oranges to their own bodies. Some mend clothes while sitting on stools. At the time of the revolution, the average woman earns fourteen to fifteen sous a day.

Chinese courtesans are expected to be well educated and skilled in the arts as well as beautiful. The most successful courtesans are talented painters, poets, musicians, and calligraphers.

1777 French wine maker Nicole-Barbe Cliquot is born. Until she takes over her late husband's champagne cellars in the 1790s, champagne is cloudy and gritty; the yeast-sugar sediment used to create the bubbles cannot be removed without the loss of carbonation. Cliquot devises the *sur pointe* method of bottle storage: the bottles are stored upside down, so that the sediment gradually gathers at the cork, allowing easier removal. Cliquot also, by pressing her grapes immediately, creates pink champagne, but her storage innovation is of greater significance, since it saves the champagne industry from almost certain disappearance.

Jan. 18, 1777 The U.S. Congress orders its Declaration of Independence printed and distributed; the contract goes to a female printer, Mary Katherine Goddard, editor of the *Maryland Journal.*

1788 British-U.S. businesswoman Sarah Gould Troutbeck, whose Tory husband lost many of their holdings during the Revolutionary War, works to collect money owed her. She is one of the few Tory sympathizers to return to the United States to try to reclaim her property, and she eventually recovers most of her wealth.

1789 French seamstresses and embroiderers petition the government to prevent men from entering their traditional employments.

1790 U.S. blockade runner Keziah Coffin (b. 1723) dies. During the Revolutionary War she posed as a Tory to get British permission to take goods to Nantucket Island; then she used her monopoly to gouge the residents and acquire liens on their property. She lost her entire fortune after the war.

1790 British-Australian businesswoman Mary Reibey (d. 1855) is transported to Australia for horse theft; she will become Australia's most successful businesswoman, building an empire based on hotels, grain, shipping, and real estate.

1791 Women spinners in Troyes, France, riot successfully to prevent the installation of spinning machines.

1792 Catherine Greene (February 17, 1755–September 2, 1814), widow of U.S. Revolutionary War general Nathanael Greene, suggests the idea for the cotton gin to Eli Whitney, gives him her basement as a laboratory, and, according to some sources, suggests design improvements that make the machine possible. She will also expend her entire fortune in a long legal battle to secure Whitney's patent rights.

1793 Mrs. Samuel Slater becomes the first U.S. woman to be granted a patent. Her invention, a type of cotton sewing thread, will enable her husband to build a textile empire.

1794 English silversmith Hester Bateman (b. 1709) dies. One of the greatest silversmiths of the eighteenth century, especially well known for her coffeepots, teapots, and spoons, she took over the business from her late husband and registered her own hallmark.

Science and Medicine

1776 "Doctoress and apothecary" Mary Waters emigrates from Ireland to the United States; she will nurse the wounded in military hospitals during the Revolutionary War.

1778 Frenchwoman Mme. Necker establishes a hospital.

1778 Italian physicist Laura Bassi (b. 1711) dies. Bassi was the mother of twelve and the author of two noted texts, *De problemate quodam mechanico* and *De problemate quodam hydrometrico*; she was also the first woman professor of physics at any university. She held the chair of anatomy at the University of Bologna and gave lectures on experimental physics.

c. 1780 Italian anatomist and physician Maria Pettracini teaches at the University of Ferrara; her daughter, Zaffira Peretti, will also teach there.

1783 German astronomer Caroline Herschel discovers three nebulae. Between 1786 and 1797, she will also discover eight comets.

1786 French anatomist Marie Catherine Bicheron (b. 1719) dies. She was noted for the accuracy of her anatomical models, which were said to lack only the odor of an actual body.

1789 French midwife Angélique du Coudray (b. 1712) dies. Allowed by the church to baptize babies and paid by Louis XV to educate other midwives, she trained over 4,000 pupils and used innovative teaching methods, encouraging her students to experiment with a model of a female torso.

1794 British chemist Elizabeth Fulhame publishes *Essay on Combustion*.

1797 British natural philosophy teacher Margaret Bryan publishes *A Compendious System of Astronomy*.

1797 The first anatomy book with a diagram of the female skeleton is published; until now, the "standard," "normal" skeleton has always been male, with no indication of the differences between male and female bone structure.

1797 Chinese astronomer Wang Zhenyi (b. 1768), who studied lunar eclipses, dies.

Education and Scholarship

A few Chinese educators encourage women to study and write, and some artists and poets accept female students, but most male authors feel that scholarly pursuits distract women from their true role in the home.

In England, female literacy is improving somewhat, and women are beginning to subscribe in great numbers to circulating libraries.

Judith Sargent Murray (May 1, 1751–July 6, 1820), possibly the first U.S. feminist theorist, writes essays contending that girls should be taught better and enabled to be financially independent. "We can only reason from what we know, and if an opportunity of acquiring knowledge hath been denied us, the inferiority of our sex cannot fairly be deduced from thence."

1776 French intellectual Julie Lespinasse dies. She, Marie-Thérèse de Geoffrin, and Marie de Vichy-Chamrond, marquise du Deffand (1697–1780), were the principal salon hostesses of the past quarter-century. Mme. Geoffrin (1699–1777) provided financial and social assistance to the production of Diderot's great *Encyclopédie* when no support was found for the project at court. She forbade any talk of religion or politics in her salon, which included such visitors as Boucher, Walpole, La Tour, and Fontenelle; her Monday and Wednesday evening salons were so influential that Catherine the Great had a salaried official to attend them.

1783 Russian empress Catherine II makes her friend Ekaterina Dashkova (1743–1806) head of the new Academy of Arts and Sciences. Dashkova also becomes the first president of the Russian Academy, which she proposes to Catherine as an agency for guarding the national language. Later she will publish works on linguistics and science, organize public lectures, compile an atlas, and found a theater magazine, only to be forcibly retired when Catherine concludes she has become too radical. In 1789, on the recommendation of her correspondent Benjamin Franklin, she will become the first woman member of the American Philosophical Society.

1788 U.S. author Hannah More (d. 1833), whose untidy dress makes her an object lesson to Boston's young girls in the dangers of becoming too learned, anonymously publishes *Thoughts on the Importance of the Manners of the Great*; it is immediately attributed to the great male thinkers of the time, and there is much discussion about who could have penned such a fine work. Poet William Cowper, discovering the true authorship, is livid. "How comes it to pass that she, being a woman, writes with a force and energy and a correctness hitherto arrogated by the man?"

Oct. 1789 French novelist, literary critic, and political theorist Germaine de Staël (April 22, 1766– July 14, 1817), a mesmerizing speaker, turns her home at the Rue de Bac into an influential political salon.

1790 About 40% of Englishwomen can write well enough to sign their own names, and 63% of wives in Turin, Italy, are able to sign their marriage contracts.

1793 Anglo-Irish author Maria Edgeworth defends education for women in *Letters to Literary Ladies*. In 1798, she coauthors an adaptation of Rousseau's theories, *Practical Education*.

1795 English feminist Mary Wollstonecraft, who studied the relevant events firsthand in 1792 and 1793, publishes *A Historical and Moral View of the Origin and Progress of the French Revolution*.

1799 The Visitation nuns establish the first Catholic girls' school in the original American colonies.

1799 Hannah More publishes *A Summary History of New England*, one of the first histories of the whole region rather than just Massachusetts.

1800 English intellectual Elizabeth Montagu (b. 1720) dies. Her literary salons were casual, not requiring

women to wear formal black silk stockings, and intellectual women soon became known as "bluestockings" as a result.

Religion

Caribbean slave women are often practitioners of obeah and myalism, spiritual practices derived from African religions. They are described by a European observer as "Sybils, who deal in oracles; these sage matrons [are found] dancing and whirling round in the middle of an assembly with amazing rapidity until they foam at the mouth and drop down convulsed. Whatever the prophetess orders to be done, during this paroxysm is most sacredly performed by the surrounding multitude which renders these meetings extremely dangerous, as she frequently enjoins them to murder their masters, or desert to the woods."

1781 The last female mystic executed by a Mediterranean Inquisition, María de las Dolores Lopez, is hanged and burned in Seville, Spain.

1781 English poet, essayist, critic, and textbook author Anna Letitia Barbauld publishes *Hymns in Prose*.

1782 Anna Goddi of Switzerland is the last person in Europe to be legally executed as a witch.

1784 French educator Mme. de Genlis publishes an attack on atheism, *Deux réputations*.

1784 U.S. author Hannah More publishes *An Alphabetical Compendium of the Various Sects*, a guide to world religions.

1784 The London Yearly Meeting of Friends, which has never before admitted women, is attended by four U.S. Quaker women: Rebecca Wright, Patience Brayton, Mehetabel Jenkins, and Rebecca Jones. They secure permission for a Yearly Women's Meeting.

Sept. 8, 1784 U.S. Shaker founder "Mother" Ann Lee (b. 1736) dies. Her 1781 tour of New England aroused controversy over her followers' claim that she was the Second Coming of Christ. Her sect has bans against marriage, sex, warfare, and the swearing of oaths.

1787 U.S. religious leader Lucy Wright (February 5, 1760–February 7, 1821) becomes head of the female segment of the Shaker sect.

1788 Philadelphia Quaker minister Sarah Harrison travels among southern Quakers, urging them to free their slaves and succeeding in arranging the emancipation of about 200.

1790 Four nuns, including Ann Mathews (1732–June

12, 1800) and Frances Dickinson (July 12, 1755–March 27, 1830) open the first convent in the United States. One week after opening, the convent accepts its first postulant, Elizabeth Carberry (1745–1814), forty-nine years old, whose father forbade her twenty years ago to leave the colonies to become a nun.

c. 1790–1800 The United States begins the Second Great Awakening, with more women than men undergoing a profound religious revival. It will last until about the 1840s.

Feb. 13, 1790 The French National Assembly bans monasteries and dissolves many; convents are often spared because the sale of their meager holdings would raise so little money for the state. Nuns are, however, sometimes guillotined or attacked during the revolution.

1792 English religious leader Joanna Southcott claims to be the prophet of the Second Coming of Christ; she issues 14,000 sealed documents, which are distributed to her followers.

1793 The last execution for witchcraft in Europe takes place in Poland, although witch trials were officially outlawed six years ago.

Mar. 4, 1794 Demolition of church bell towers in Aveyron, France, is canceled when a group of local women show up and make "the direst possible threats" against the workers.

May 17, 1794 Police arrest French spiritualist Catherine Théot. She promises immortality if paid and calls herself the "mother of God." She dies in prison on August 31.

1796 Blacks are admitted to a prominent U.S. Quaker Yearly Meeting, largely due to the arguments of women.

1799 French saint Joan Thouret (1765–1826), whose convent was dispersed during the French Revolution, opens a school in Besançon that becomes the center of the Sisters of Charity under St. Vincent's Protection.

1801–1805

General Status and Daily Life

At the beginning of the nineteenth century, there are still many places where women keep their birth names after marriage; the practice is known in England, Spain, and America and is more common in Scotland, Ireland, Wales, Iceland, Sweden, Norway, the Netherlands, Persia, Ethiopia, South Africa, and Hawaii.

In the early years of the century, hand-cranked washing and drying machines are invented. A cast-iron cooking range and the first gas-powered stove are invented in 1802.

1803 Abortion is criminalized in England. The rich find means to circumvent the law, while the poor resort to dangerous chemicals or knitting needles to induce abortions.

Mar. 21, 1804 France's Napoleonic Code reverses many of the legal gains made by women during the revolution, classifying them as legal minors with children, criminals, and the insane. A husband can dictate where his wife lives and controls all her property; he gets the children automatically in case of divorce.

Divorce is harder to obtain; the code recognizes only three grounds: conviction for certain crimes, cruelty, and adultery. A husband can get a divorce for simple adultery, but the wife can divorce for adultery only if the husband keeps his mistress in the family home. A husband's adultery is not punishable by law; a wife's is subject to two years' imprisonment. Divorce by mutual consent is still legal, but there are new restrictions on the age of the partners, the duration of the marriage, and the involvement of the couple's parents in obtaining permission for the divorce. Divorce rates drop sharply after the institution of this legislation.

Government, the Military, and the Law

1802 Haitian rebel Henriette St. Marc is executed by the French government.

May 22, 1802 The first U.S. First Lady, Martha Washington (b. June 2, 1731), dies. As First Lady, she wrote, "I live a very dull life . . . I am more like a state prisoner than anything else." It was a difficult position for a spirited woman, who, in her youth, once rode her horse up and down her uncle William's staircase. The women of the family protested, but Martha's father said, "She's not harmed William's staircase. And, by heavens, how she can ride!"

1803 Ecuadoran Indian Lorenza Avemanay leads a rebellion against the Spanish in Guamote.

1803 Greek guerrilla fighter Captain Moscho Travella (b. 1760) dies. She became famous when she drove the forces of Ali Pasha out of the town of Souli, leading a band of women armed with sticks and stones.

Nov. 3, 1805 Largely due to the influence of his wife, Queen Louise, King Frederick William of Prussia allies with Russia against Napoleon's France. To those who worry about Napoleon's armies, Louise says, "There is only one thing to be done, let us fight the Monster, let us beat the Monster down, and then we can talk of worries!"

Literature and the Visual Arts

1802 French salon hostess, literary critic, and political theorist Germaine de Staël publishes the novel *Delphine*. An opponent of Napoleon, she is banished by him in 1803 and re-establishes her salon in Switzerland.

1804 British author Amelia Opie publishes *Adeline Mowbray*, a novel that defends free love through the trials of its heroine, a young woman raised on rational principles.

1804 At the Paris Salon, Angélique Mongez (d. 1855) exhibits her *Ulysses Finding Young Astyanax at Hector's Grave* and *Alexander Weeping at the Death of the Wife of Darius*, winning a first-class gold medal. Only a year later, however, one critic will say of her that she failed to create good history paintings and that women "must abandon these great subjects to our sex, or content yourselves with sweet, tender subjects."

Performing Arts and Entertainment

1801 Frenchwoman Marguerite Montansier manages the Olympique theater, moving to the Favart in 1803.

1802 French actress and opera singer Sophie Arnould (b. 1740) dies. Of a dancer whose reputation was based chiefly on her love life and her graceful poses and whose arm had been broken, Arnould once said, "What a pity it wasn't her leg; then it wouldn't have interfered with her dancing." Of another woman whose too-long diamond necklace (the gift of a lover) was falling into her cleavage, Arnould said, "It's simply returning to its source."

1803 French actress Marie-Françoise Dumesnil (b. 1713), a star of the Comédie Française in the mid-eighteenth century, known especially for her work in the plays of Voltaire, dies.

Athletics and Exploration

Dec. 23, 1804 Frances "Fanny" Calderón de la Barca, author of *Life in Mexico*, one of the best nineteenth-century travel books on Latin America, is born.

1805 The first recorded women's ice-skating race is

held in Leeuwarden, in the Netherlands.

Nov. 7, 1805 Lewis and Clark's expedition reaches the Pacific. It includes a Shoshone woman, Sacagawea (c. 1786–December 20, 1812), wife of Toussaint Charbonneau, the team's interpreter. Carrying her infant son, Baptiste, with her, she has served as a guide (though not the chief guide), interpreter, plant gatherer, cook, and liaison with Native American tribes. At one point she obtained thirty horses for the explorers; at another point she saved Lewis's life when he was in danger of being killed by a Native American chief. She also rescued the expedition's equipment during a violent storm.

Business and Industry

Female Japanese agricultural laborers make about two-thirds as much as their male counterparts. Even when they are most in demand, at rice-transplanting time, their wages are not quite as high as men's.

Science and Medicine

1803 Italian physician Maria Dalle Donne (1778–1842) becomes director of midwives at the University of Bologna, giving lectures not at the university but at her home. She takes students even if they cannot pay and works to get midwives installed in rural villages.

1805 French medical writer Geneviève d'Aronville (b. 1720), who wrote and illustrated biographies, translations, and books on anatomy, chemistry, medicine, natural history, and philosophy, dies.

1805 The wife of Japanese surgeon Hanaoka Seishu becomes the world's first anesthetized patient. She survives the operation for breast cancer.

Education and Scholarship

1803 English feminist Mary Hays publishes the six-volume *Dictionary of Female Biography*.

1803 Too much learning is perceived as unfeminine. Novelist Sydney Owenson, author of *The Wild Irish Girl*, writes to a friend that she has stopped learning chemistry "lest I should be less the *woman*. Seduced by taste . . . to Greek and Latin, I resisted, lest I should not be a *very woman*."

1804 English writer Anna Letitia Barbauld (1743–1825) edits *Selections from the Spectator, Tatler, Guardian and Freeholder*.

1805 Mercy Otis Warren publishes her history of the *Rise, Progress, and Termination of the American Revolution*. Her anecdotes about the leading figures of the war, based on her personal knowledge of them and correspondence with them, will influence many future histories and biographies.

Religion

1801 French saint Madeleine Sophie (1779–1865) founds the Society of the Sacred Heart, dedicated to teaching girls. She will lead it for sixty-three years and oversee its spread to twelve countries.

1801 Korean Catholic Kang Wan-suk is martyred. In the late eighteenth century, she organized a group of Christian Korean women, converted several people to Christianity (including members of the court), and hid the missionary Father Chu Mun-mo from government officials.

Jan. 1802 U.S. Quaker minister Hannah Barnard (1754?–1825) is removed from her ministry after espousing the heretical idea that not all Scripture must be believed. She feels that a compassionate God would neither endorse the wars described in the Old Testament nor command Abraham to kill his own son.

1806–1810

Government, the Military, and the Law

1808 The Spanish city of Saragossa is attacked by the French, and a young woman named Agostina and known as "La Saragossa" (1786–1857) distinguishes herself by rescuing wounded defenders under heavy fire and nursing them. Her heroism is widely celebrated, and she is given the military rank of engineer and the right to bear the arms of the city.

1809 Colombian rebels Camila Torres and Josefa Palacios help to start the national independence movement. Several women, sometimes dressed as men, will fight in the Colombian wars of independence (1810–1822).

Dec. 16, 1809 French Emperor Napoleon Bonaparte divorces his wife Joséphine (June 26, 1763–May 29, 1814) for barrenness, granting her a large pension and the right to keep calling herself empress.

1810–1821 Argentina's independence movement is nurtured in the salon of Mariquita Sánchez de Thompson and fought in part by General Juana Azurday de Padilla, who fights alongside her husband.

July 1810 Queen Louise of Prussia, a longtime enemy of Napoleon defeated by him in 1806, dies. She inspired two Prussian decorations: the Iron Cross (instituted on her birthday in 1813) and the Luisenorde, a medal for women.

Literature and the Visual Arts

1806 British author Charlotte Smith (b. 1749) dies. Admired by Sir Walter Scott, she wrote novels, poems, letters, children's books, and translations to support her ten children.

1807 Swiss painter Angelica Kauffmann (b. 1741) dies. Known for her history paintings when that prestigious genre was almost exclusively reserved for men, she had clients among the English, Polish, Russian, and Austrian nobility.

1807 French author Germaine de Staël publishes the novel *Corinne ou l'Italie*, a landmark for the romantic movement.

1808 U.S. author Hannah More publishes her most popular work, the religious novel *Coelebs in Search of a Wife*, in which the hero chooses modest, devout, charitable housewife Lucilla Stanley rather than glittering salon hostess Lady Bab Lawless. The novel will go into twelve editions by 1834 and will make it fashionable for well-to-do young ladies to visit the poor two evenings a week, just as Lucilla does.

1810 Germaine de Staël writes *De l'Allemagne*; the book is banned by Napoleon and will not be printed until 1813. Staël is placed under house arrest.

Performing Arts and Entertainment

1806 Italian soprano Brigitta Banti dies, leaving her larynx to the city of Bologna.

1808 German glass harmonica player Marianne Kirchgessner (b. 1769) dies.

1808 Blind Austrian composer, pianist, organist, and singer Maria Theresia von Paradis establishes a music school, the Paradis Institute, in Vienna.

Athletics and Exploration

Mar. 1807 Englishwomen Betty Dyson and Mary Mahoney box for forty minutes.

Activism

1806 Alice Jackson Lewis becomes the first U.S. Quaker to advocate a boycott of slave-produced products.

Business and Industry

1807 Chinese pirate Zheng Yi dies. His wife, Zheng Yi Sao, a former prostitute, takes over his ships and men, supported by her lover and adopted son Zheng Bao. Armed with 1800 junks and 70,000 men, supreme tactical skills, and clever negotiations, she is formidable. She finally surrenders in 1810 in exchange for amnesty for all her pirates and high-ranking military posts for herself and her senior officers.

1808 Printer Jane Aitken (1764–1832), owner of her late father's publishing business from 1802 to 1813, becomes the first woman in the United States to publish an edition of the Bible. Her Bible, one of sixty books issued by her press, is the first English translation of the Septuagint (the Greek version of the Old Testament).

Science and Medicine

1806 British natural philosophy teacher Margaret Bryan publishes *Lectures on Natural Philosophy*, discussing optics, acoustics, pneumatics, and hydrostatics.

1806 British natural philosophy writer Jane Marcet publishes the popular *Conversations on Chemistry*, which will profoundly influence Michael Faraday.

Education and Scholarship

1806 English writer and intellectual Elizabeth Carter (b. 1717) dies. She was a frequent contributor to *The Gentleman's Magazine* and *The Rambler*. She made the first translation of the Greek philosopher Epictetus into English and was rescued from working as a seamstress by salon hostess Elizabeth Montagu, who enabled her to pursue her studies; she never relied on a husband, calling marriage "a very right scheme for everybody but myself."

Dec. 15, 1810 Englishwoman Sarah Trimmer, friend of Samuel Johnson, pioneer in the education of the poor,

writer on education, and publisher of the magazines *The Family Magazine* and *Guardian of Education*, dies.

Religion

June 1809 U.S. Catholic St. Elizabeth Seton founds the Sisters of Charity of St. Joseph.

1811–1815

Government, the Military, and the Law

1812 French dragoon Thérèse Figueur leaves the cavalry after serving for fourteen years and having four horses shot from under her.

Aug. 19, 1812 Sailor Lucy Brewer, who will serve undetected aboard the U.S. ship *Constitution* for three years disguised as a man named Nicholas Baker, fights in the battle against the British ship *Guerrière*.

Aug. 25, 1814 During the War of 1812, British troops set fire to the White House. First Lady Dolley Madison (May 20, 1768–July 12, 1849), rescues many items from the building, including a portrait of George Washington and the Declaration of Independence.

Literature and the Visual Arts

1811 English author Anna Letitia Barbauld edits *The Female Speaker*, a prose anthology for girls.

Nov. 1811 English novelist Jane Austen (December 16, 1775–July 18, 1817) anonymously publishes *Sense and Sensibility*, which makes her a profit of £150. The book, the first of her works to be published, is typical of all her novels. A middle-class woman navigates through the delicate etiquette of dances, dinners, and other social occasions in a witty, perilous search for the proper husband. In 1813, she publishes *Pride and Prejudice*, in which acid-tongued Elizabeth Bennett spars with the supercilious Mr. Darcy, who finds her family vulgar.

1814 Chinese poet Sun Yün-feng (b. 1764), a favorite student of the Ch'ing poet Yüan Mei, dies.

Oct. 1, 1814 French painter Marie Guillemine Benoist (b. 1768), forced to retire after her husband gets a government job, writes to him: "So much study, so many efforts, a life of hard work, and after that long time of testing—successes; and then to see them almost an object of humiliation . . . . Let's not talk about it any more or the wound will open up once more."

Oct. 19, 1814 U.S. poet, patriot, opponent of the federal Constitution, and historian Mercy Otis Warren (b. September 14, 1728) dies. Her plays, thick with political satire, supported the revolutionary cause as early as 1772; after independence, she published a volume of poetry that included two verse dramas.

1815 Korean Queen Mother Lady Hong (b. 1735), author of the autobiography *Hanjung-nok*, dies.

Performing Arts and Entertainment

1812 Italian soprano Angelica Catalani plays Susanna in the first London performance of *Le nozze di Figaro*.

Athletics and Exploration

1813 English traveler Lady Hester Stanhope journeys with a Bedouin tribe through the desert to Palmyra.

1814 Jane Barnes, reaching Fort George in Oregon Territory, becomes the first white woman to enter the Pacific Northwest.

Activism

1811 A Cuban women's magazine, *El Correo de las Damas* (*The Women's Post*), begins publication. It is soon attacked by the church for its references to women's sexuality.

1813 English prison reformer Elizabeth Fry (1780–1845) begins working to improve conditions in Newgate Prison, where 300 women and their children are confined without adequate clothes or bedding. She starts a school, teaches needlework, institutes religious services, and arranges for the hiring of prison matrons.

Science and Medicine

1811 British paleontologist Mary Anning (1799–1847) discovers the first complete ichthyosaur skeleton.

1812 Scottish mathematician Mary Somerville wins a prize for a paper on Diophantine algebra.

1814 French midwife Marie Boivin, author of *Memorial de l'art des accouchements* (1812), becomes codirector of the General Hospital for Seine and Oise and

receives an order of merit from the king of Prussia.

1815 German physician Josepha Siebold becomes the first woman in Germany to earn a doctorate in obstetrics.

Education and Scholarship

1812 French writer and educator Mme. de Genlis becomes Napoleon's inspector of primary schools in Paris.

1812 U.S. author Hannah Adams, ridiculed by other women because of the holes in her stockings, publishes her *History of the Jews*.

Religion

1812 U.S. nuns Mary Rhodes (1782?–1853), Christina Stuart, and Anne Haven establish the Sisters of Loretto at the Foot of the Cross, a teaching order of nuns and the first American sisterhood without a European affiliation.

June 1813 U.S. nun Catherine Spalding (1793–1858) becomes the first mother superior of the Sisters of Charity of Nazareth, a teaching order near Bardstown, Kentucky.

Oct. 19, 1814 English mystic and prophet Joanna Southcott declares, at age sixty-four, that she will give birth to the Second Coming of Christ. She dies shortly thereafter, and her approximately 100,000 followers quickly abandon her faith.

1816–1820

General Status and Daily Life

c. 1816 Some Japanese women who want divorces appeal to the government; some have their families offer bribes to their husbands; some pay for the services of Buddhist temple officials, who, for a fee, will negotiate a settlement. Women willing to invest more time can spend three years in a special temple called an *enkiridera*, after which service they are free. Some poor women simply leave their husbands. Children usually remain in the husband's custody, though this practice is not universal.

1816 Divorce is outlawed in France.

1818 In Bengal, India, 839 women commit sati.

1820 A good wife is expected to be nonchalant about her husband's adultery. In this year, Caroline, Italian-French duchesse de Berri, receives about twenty women claiming to have been impregnated by her husband during his visit to Nantes. Like most wellborn women, she expects her husband to philander, and she calmly asks how long the duc was in Nantes. When she is told he was there for only a week, she replies, "Ah, then in that case, it's quite possible."

Government, the Military, and the Law

1816 Barbados slave Nanny Grigg incites local blacks to riot in the island's only major slave rebellion.

1817 Mexican rebel Gertrudis Bocanegra (b. 1765), who organized a women's army in 1810, is tortured and executed by the government.

1817 Southern African warrior queen Mmanthatisi (b. 1780) becomes the leader of the Tlokwa nation when her thirteen-year-old son inherits the chieftainship. She leads her people during the time known as the *mfecane*, or crushing, when many tribes are displaced by European and Zulu encroachments. Mmanthatisi plans military strategy, although she does not actually fight, and guides her people to a new homeland in Lesotho.

Nov. 1817 Colombian spy Policarpa "La Pola" Salavarrieta (b. 1795) becomes one of the approximately fifty female agents executed in the rebellion against Spain. A seamstress, she passed information from the homes of her royalist clients to the rebels. Her death by firing squad in Bogotá Square leads to a successful uprising against the man who ordered her death.

1819 Hawaiian ruler Kaahumanu becomes *kuhina nui* (co-ruler) during the reign of Kamehameha II. From 1823 to 1832, she will be regent for Kamehameha III.

1819 Colombian captain Evangelista Tamoya fights in the battle of Boyaco under Simón Bolívar during Colombia's revolution.

1820 Guatemalan Indians, led in part by Felipa Soc, rebel against Spain.

1820 George IV inherits the British throne, determined that his unloved wife, Caroline of Brunswick, not be crowned queen. The angry Caroline arrives in England to claim her due and is greeted with divorce proceedings that will occupy scandalmongers for months. A popular verse of the time asks her, "Most gracious queen, we thee implore / To go away and sin no more; / Or if that effort be too great, / To go away at any rate." Caroline's popularity, however, soon soars as people begin to sympathize with her plight.

Literature and the Visual Arts

1816 Jane Austen publishes *Emma*, a novel whose heroine is a young woman addicted to matchmaking.

1816 English writer Lady Caroline Lamb, wife of Prime Minister Lord Melbourne, publishes *Glenarvon*, a novelization of her affair with poet Lord Byron.

1816 While stranded by bad weather at Lake Geneva in Switzerland, English authors Lord Byron, Percy Bysshe Shelley, and Mary Wollstonecraft Shelley (d. 1851) hold a ghost-story writing contest. Byron and Percy Shelley produce nothing worthwhile as a result, but Mary Shelley's entry develops into one of the world's most famous novels, *Frankenstein*, published in 1818. Associated in most twentieth-century minds with the image of Boris Karloff clumping through shadows, the novel is really a powerful analysis of human ambition, love, rejection, revenge, and men's envy of the power of God (and women) to create life. It will make Shelley so famous in her time that her poet husband, Percy, is considered a minor artist by comparison.

1817 French painter Gabrielle Capet (b. September 6, 1761) dies. She was the close friend and pupil of famed portraitist Adélaïde Labille-Guiard, whom she nursed through her final illness.

1818 Jane Austen's last two novels are published posthumously by her brother Henry, who reveals her identity; all of her works so far have been printed anonymously. *Northanger Abbey* (the first complete novel Austen wrote but the last published) is a parody of the eighteenth-century Gothic novels Austen read as a young woman. *Persuasion* is the bittersweet story of an older woman who has very nearly resigned herself to being an old maid.

1819 French artist Antoinette Cecile Hortense Haudebort-Lescot (1784–1845) paints a large *François Premier et Diane de Poitiers*. Critics object, not to the quality of the painting, but to its unfeminine size, and advise her to stick to "small easel paintings, to charming but popular subjects."

1819 French artist Constance Charpentier (1767–1849) wins the Musée Royale gold medal.

1820 French artist Marie Victoire Lemoine (b. 1754), noted for her portraits, miniatures, and genre scenes of children, dies.

Performing Arts and Entertainment

1816 English theater manager Sarah Baker (b. 1736),

who ran theatrical companies and had ten theaters built for her, dies.

1819 Russian ballerina Anastasia Novitskaya dances in a mildly feminist ballet written especially for her. In 1820, she is replaced in a ballet by the mistress of a local nobleman. When she objects, she is threatened with imprisonment in an insane asylum; fear and confusion cause her to run barefoot in the snowy streets until she is found and restrained by policemen, who carry her home to die.

Athletics and Exploration

1819 French balloonist Madeleine Sophie Blanchard is the first woman killed in an air crash when her balloon, aloft during a fireworks display, catches fire.

Activism

1817 Japanese scholar Tadano Makuzu (1763–1825), an expert in Chinese and Japanese literature, publishes the feminist essay *Hitori kangae*.

1818 English prison reformer Elizabeth Fry becomes the first woman to speak to a parliamentary committee.

Business and Industry

Aug. 12, 1816 U.S. printer Mary Katherine Goddard dies. Her career was intertwined with that of her brother William. He gave her opportunities usually unavailable to women, but it was she who kept his businesses afloat. They often fought; he forced her out of her editorship at the *Maryland Journal*, and she once brought five lawsuits against him in a single day.

1818 U.S. businesswoman Sarah King (d. c. 1880), guitar teacher, real estate speculator, and tea merchant, is born.

1818 Laundresses in Valencia hold the first known labor strike in Venezuelan history.

Science and Medicine

1816 French mathematician Sophie Germain (b. April 1, 1776) submits a paper, *Memoir on the Vibrations of Elastic Plates*, to the Académie des Sciences, winning the prize offered for a paper on mathematical models of elastic surface vibration. Although her paper has some flaws for which she is widely criticized, it makes her famous and brings her respect in the mathematical community.

1818 French obstetrician Marie Boivin (b. 1773) publishes *Nouveau traité des hemorrhages de l'uterus*.

May 24, 1819 German obstetrician Charlotte Siebold, daughter of doctor Josepha Siebold, assists at the birth of Britain's Queen Victoria.

1820 Cuban doctor Henrietta Faber, who has practiced medicine for years disguised as a man, reveals herself as a woman and is sentenced to ten years in jail for working as a physician.

Education and Scholarship

1817 Germaine de Staël's *Considerations sur la Révolution Française* is published posthumously.

1820 English educator and feminist Anne Jemima Clough (d. 1892), founder and first president of Newnham College, Cambridge, is born.

1820 The first girls' school in India opens in Calcutta.

Religion

Apr. 15, 1818 U.S. Quaker minister Rebecca Jones (b. July 8, 1739) dies. She taught, preached, and collected alms for the poor.

1821–1825

General Status and Daily Life

1823 London handbills popularize the contraceptive sponge.

1823 An English case, *The King* v. *The Inhabitants of St. Faith's*, determines that a married woman may legally retain her birth name.

Government, the Military, and the Law

Aug. 7, 1821 Queen Caroline of England dies. Her husband, George IV, called for a drink after first laying eyes on her, tried to prevent her from seeing their only child, and ordered the prayer for "our gracious Queen" to be removed from the Anglican service. Only a few months ago, George was told of Napoleon's death by a courtier, who said, "Your greatest enemy is dead."

George, knowing Caroline to be ill, replied, "Is she, by God?"

1824 Hawaiian Dowager Queen Kaahumanu (d. June 5, 1832), a patron of Christianity, becomes regent for her brother Kauikeaouli.

1825 Greek rebel Laskarina Bouboulina (b. 1771), who began leading armed forces against the Turks at the age of fifty and won many sea battles against them, dies. A fierce fighter and a defender of Turkish female prisoners, her heroism was extolled in many songs and poems.

Literature and the Visual Arts

1822 Ten cultural leaders in Ogaki, Japan, form the Hakuosha (White Sea Gull) Poetry Society. Two of the founding members are women: artist, poet, musician, and girls' school founder Cho Koran (1804–1879), wife of the principal founder, Yanagawa Seigan; and Ema Saiko, a painter, poet, and Chinese classical scholar.

1822 Chinese painter, calligrapher, and poet Xiang Jianzhang is active. The second wife of a high-ranking Hangzhou official, she paints flowers and birds and even produces four paintings for the emperor. She is the author of a volume of poems, *Hanmo heming guan ji* (*Collected Works from the Brush-and-Ink Harmony Hall*).

1823 English novelist Mary Wollstonecraft Shelley publishes *Valperga*, a historical romance set in medieval Sicily.

1824 U.S. miniaturist Anna Peale (March 6, 1791– December 25, 1878) and her sister, portraitist Sarah Peale, become the only two women members of the Pennsylvania Academy of Fine Arts.

1825 Portraitists Marie Geneviève Bouliar (b. 1762) of France and Barbara Krafft, a member of the Vienna Academy, die.

1825 Sarah Peale paints a portrait of General Lafayette.

Performing Arts and Entertainment

1821 Austrian contralto Karoline Unger (1803–1877), who will have operas written for her by Donizetti, Pacini, Bellini, and Mercadante, makes her debut as Dorabella in *Cosi fan tutte*.

1823 U.S. tragedienne Charlotte Melmoth (b. 1749) dies.

1823 German soprano Henriette Sontag gives the first performance of Weber's *Euryanthe*. In 1825, she will make such a successful Berlin debut that the populace will be said to have caught "Sontag fever."

1824 Soprano Henriette Sontag and contralto Karoline Unger appear in the première of Beethoven's *Missa solemnis* and Ninth Symphony. Beethoven is deaf, but after the performance, Unger turns him around so that he can see the applause.

Athletics and Exploration

1821 Scottish writer and reformer Frances Wright publishes *Views of Society and Manners in America*, one of the most celebrated travel books of its time. It meets with enthusiastic praise from liberals and leads to a friendship with the marquis de Lafayette. Quite complimentary of American habits, this popular book is soon translated into three languages.

1822 A boxing match is held between two working-class women, Englishwoman Peg Carye and Irishwoman Martha Flaharty. Flaharty wins, after downing half a pint of gin.

Activism

1823 Mary Waln Wistar, inspired by British prison reformer Elizabeth Fry, organizes the Female Prison Association of Friends in Philadelphia and visits Arch Street Prison to read Scripture with a group of female convicts. Wistar's organization visits convicts, teaches sewing and writing, finds homes for the discharged, and works for better conditions for those still incarcerated.

1824 British Quaker Elizabeth Heydrick publishes *Immediate, Not Gradual Emancipation*, an influential work that sways British opinion toward the freeing of slaves.

1825 Scottish reformer Frances Wright (September 6, 1795–December 13, 1852) publishes the pamphlet *A Plan for the Gradual Abolition of Slavery in the United States Without Danger of Loss to the Citizens of the South*. In December, she puts her plan into action, buying 640 acres in Tennessee and naming the plantation Nashoba. Extremely unsuccessful, the project puts slaves to work with a promise of future emancipation and gains notoriety for the "free love" views of some of its members. By 1828 the plan will be abandoned as a failure, though Wright's enthusiasm for emancipation will remain undiminished, and she will keep her promise by freeing the Nashoba slaves.

Business and Industry

1822 Japanese shogun Iyenari denounces *geisha* as mere prostitutes and tries unsuccessfully to discourage their popularity.

1824 In the first U.S. strike that includes women workers, female weavers in Pawtucket, Rhode Island, refuse to work.

1825 The United States witnesses its first labor strike by women only, as New York tailors strike for better wages.

Science and Medicine

1821 .... e Lachapelle (b. 1769) ...s. .ne .as . .ad . ma. .rnity at the Hôtel Dieu, .ce .ing .r .th .r .. . post. She worked to .... ical instruments, train .midv ... .w procedures for the ... ...s such as torn perineum and ....massive three-volume *Pratique des* ....ring 40,000 cases, is published

and Scholarship

.ter Hester Thrale (b. 1741), who intellectual career despite twelve

n get the right to attend

.itor Emma Willard (February .870) opens the Troy Female .. The first endowed girls' school .t features a rigorous curriculum; .ne pupils, the average student is .ding, writing, spelling, arithmetic, ..., history, maps, the globe, algebra, geometry, trigonometry, astronomy, natural philosophy, chemistry, botany, physiology, mineralogy, geology, and zoology in the morning; and dancing, drawing, painting, French, Italian, Spanish, and German in the afternoon. Greek and the higher branches of mathematics were only studied by the *tall* [older] girls." Willard will run the school until 1838, when she will turn it over to her daughter-in-law, Sarah Lucretia Hudson.

Religion

Jan. 4, 1821 U.S. founder and saint Elizabeth Ann Bayley Seton (b. August 28, 1774) dies. A convert to Catholicism, she established parochial schools, translated and composed religious texts, performed acts of charity, and led an order of teaching sisters. She once compared herself in her battles with church authorities to "a fiery horse I had when a girl which they tried to break by making him drag a heavy cart, and the poor beast was so humbled that he could never more be inspired by whips or caresses and wasted a skeleton until he died."

1824 U.S. author Hannah Adams (October 2, 1755–December 15, 1831) publishes *Letters on the Gospels.*

c. Dec. 22, 1824 High chief and Christian convert Kapiolani of Hawaii contributes substantially to the acceptance of Christianity by publicly defying the volcano goddess Pele. She leads a group into the crater of Kilauea without making the tradtional ohelo-berry sacrifice and there announces her devotion to the Christian God.

1826–1830

General Status and Daily Life

1826 Noted German author Countess Ida von Hahn marries her cousin Count F. W. Adolph von Hahn, changes her last name to Hahn-Hahn, and starts a fashion among German literati for hyphenated married names.

1826 A Jamaican law provides the death penalty for any owner who rapes a female slave.

1829 Sati, the burning of widows on their husbands' funeral pyres, is banned in British India. In some parts of India, the custom is lauded by women, who undergo it voluntarily; in other parts, such as Bengal, the women are often "dragged screaming to pyres by sons anxious to avoid supporting aged relatives."

1829 Lydia Maria Child publishes *The Frugal Housewife*, one of the first U.S. housekeeping manuals. It will go through thirty-three printings by 1870.

Government, the Military, and the Law

1826 Empress Leopoldina (b. 1797) of Portugal, one of the leaders of the Brazilian independence movement, dies of puerperal fever.

May 2, 1826 Maria II (b. 1819) becomes queen of

Portugal. She marries her uncle Dom Miguel, who deposes her in 1828.

1827 Zulu queen Nandi (b. c. 1760), mother of King Shaka, dies. Known as Ndlorukazi ("Great She-Elephant"), she is so beloved by her brutal son that, in mourning, he executes 7,000 people, assigns 12,000 soldiers to guard her tomb for a year, orders the deaths of all pregnant women, destroys all milk, and forbids the planting of crops. Within three months, he is deposed in a coup arranged by Mnkabayi, his aunt.

1827 Thai warrior Khun Ying Mo, held prisoner by Laotian invaders, organizes an army of women prisoners to fight the Laotians.

1828 Ranavalona I becomes queen of Madagascar upon the death of her husband, King Radama. She will rule until 1861.

1829 The Washington, D.C., scandal known as the Petticoat War erupts. It is sparked by the marriage of Secretary of War Eaton to Peggy O'Neal Timberlake. Both for her low birth and for her supposedly loose morals, Mrs. Eaton is despised by the cabinet wives, who, led by the vice president's wife, Floride Calhoun, refuse to socialize with her. President Andrew Jackson, sympathizing with her plight, defends her virtue. The affair precipitates a break between Calhoun and Jackson and contributes indirectly to growing tensions between the North and South.

Mar. 11, 1830 Future British monarch Victoria, examining a book about the English succession, discovers how close she is to the throne and weeps in anxiety and despair. She vows to her nurse that she will be better about her lessons, particularly her Latin, and promises, "I will be good."

Literature and the Visual Arts

Chinese painter Yu Ling is active. An artist's concubine, she specializes in detailed figure paintings and also creates several large works.

1826 French artist Marie Guillemine Benoist dies. A pupil of David's, she painted historical scenes, genre scenes, and portraits, including Napoleon's. She also founded a studio for women.

1826 English novelist Mary Shelley publishes *The Last Man*, a tale about the final survivor of a great plague that destroys the population of the Earth.

1826 Japanese artist Tokai Okon (1816–1888) is honored by the Emperor for her calligraphy.

1826 U.S. author Lydia Maria Child begins publishing

a magazine, *Juvenile Monthly*, which she will produce until 1834.

1827 New books include British botanist Jane Webb London's science-fiction romance *The Mummy, a Tale of the Twenty-Second Century* and U.S. editor Sarah Josepha Hale's *Northwood*, the first U.S. antislavery novel.

1828 English sculptor Anne Seymour Damer (b. 1749) dies. The subjects of her portrait busts included Napoleon, Lord Nelson, and King George III.

1828 German poet Annette Dröste-Hulshoff publishes the epic *Das Hospiz am Grossen Sant Bernard*.

Jan. 1828 Sarah Josepha Hale (b. 1788) publishes the first issue of her Boston-based *Ladies Magazine*. Most women's magazines of this period are short-lived, edited by men, and filled with material previously printed elsewhere, but the *Ladies Magazine* is successful (the first of its kind to run longer than five years), edited by a woman, and composed of original articles, most of them written by Hale herself. Hale is an enthusiastic supporter of education for women, but she also feels that woman's proper place is in the home.

Performing Arts and Entertainment

1826 German soprano Henriette Sontag (1806–1854) makes her Paris debut. She will debut in London in 1828.

1827 Italian ballerina Marie Taglioni (1804–1884) begins dancing at the Paris Opéra.

Feb. 7, 1827 The leg-showing New York City performance by a ballerina billed as "une jeune and jolie personne of distinguished reputation" causes many ladies to walk out in protest.

1829 English actress Fanny Kemble (b. 1819) stars as Juliet at Covent Garden.

1829 Italian ballerina Carlotta Grisi (d. 1899) makes her debut at La Scala in Milan.

1830 At the premiere of *I Capuleti e i Montecchi*, Italian soprano Giulia Grisi (1811–1869, cousin of Carlotta Grisi) sings the part of Juliet, while her sister, mezzo-soprano Giuditta (1805–1840), sings the part of Romeo.

1830 Actress and director Lucia Vestris takes over the management of Britain's Olympic theater; later she will run Covent Garden and the Lyceum as well, introducing innovative sets and costumes.

Athletics and Exploration

c. 1829 Rosa Baglioni, a noted Italian fencer, displays her talent in Germany.

Activism

1826 Delaware Quaker Elizabeth Margaret Chandler writes articles urging women to boycott products made by slaves.

1828 Scottish writer and reformer Frances Wright begins a controversial series of lectures on abolition, becoming the first woman in the United States to lecture to mixed-sex or "promiscuous" audiences. She is met with curiosity, then hostility as she attacks organized religion. One newspaper cartoon, labeled "A Downwright Gabbler," depicts her as a goose. Newspapers attack her as "a bold blasphemer and a voluptuous preacher of licentiousness" and accuse her of wanting to "turn the world into a universal brothel."

However, she stirs the imagination of many, including ten-year-old Walt Whitman, who describes her later as "one of the few characters to excite in me a wholesale respect and love." In 1829 she becomes co-owner and editor of the *Free Enquirer*, in which she supports equal education for women, more equitable divorce and marriage laws, birth control, and the abolition of capital punishment.

1830 A report on prostitution in New York City stirs middle-class women, especially those in the Female Moral Reform Society, to begin rescuing the "fallen women."

1830 Argentina's first women's newspaper, *La Argentina*, begins publication.

Business and Industry

1826 U.S. inventor Martha Coston, developer of the maritime signal flare, is born.

1830 Women are 60% of the United States' 67,000 textile workers.

1830 A survey of Paris prostitutes reveals that 28% were formerly domestic servants.

Science and Medicine

1826 Scottish scientific writer Mary Somerville's husband presents her paper on solar rays to the Royal Society. Somerville has taught herself about algebra, geometry, astronomy, conic sections, plane and spherical trigonometry, and Newton's theories.

1827 The mammalian ovum is discovered. Most scientists believe it provides the fetus with nourishment only and maintain that the genetic material comes solely from the sperm.

1828 British paleontologist Many Anning discovers a pterodactyl skeleton.

1829 U.S. educator Almira Lincoln Phelps publishes *Familiar Lectures on Botany*, which will sell 275,000 copies by 1872 and become a standard college text.

Education and Scholarship

1826 The first U.S. public high schools for girls are opened in New York and Boston.

1827 Educator Joanne Bethune (1770–July 28, 1860) becomes the first director of a nursery school in the United States.

Religion

One form of worship of the destructive Indian mother goddess Kali is called *thugi*; it entails robbing and strangling travelers.

1826 Japanese Buddhist nun and *haiku* poet Kikusha (Tagami Michi, b. 1753) dies.

1829 The Oblate Sisters of Providence, the first black Catholic religious order in the United States, is founded in Baltimore. The order faces prejudice from outsiders and other clergy, including Archbishop Samuel Eccleston, who feels the sisters would be more useful as domestics.

1830 A Dominican sisterhood in Kentucky is ordered to disband by Father Raphael Muños because it participated in the "foolish experiment" of running a girls' school. The order refuses and resists, despite the sale of some of its lands and the withholding of the Sacrament as punishment for "feminine insubordination."

1831–1835

General Status and Daily Life

At about this time, a local chief in Tierra del Fuego says

that "to survive in a famine they would kill and eat their old women, but never their dogs."

In the United States, the principal birth control methods are abstinence, douching, the rhythm method, and *coitus interruptus*. Surgical abortions are fairly common among the middle and upper classes, but states and territories are beginning to legislate against the procedure; by 1860, abortion will be illegal in twenty states. However, only three of those twenty provide any penalty for the mother, and the laws are only loosely enforced.

Japanese girls are expected to be industrious, polite, and neat. They work at home during the day and at night go to the *musume yado* (girls' rooms) to socialize and learn needle crafts with girls and women.

1834 U.S. wives have few legal rights. They cannot sue in their own names or continue contracts made before marriage. Their property becomes their husbands' upon marriage.

Aug. 14, 1834 An amendment to England's Poor Law bars unwed mothers from suing their children's fathers for support or marriage and sets up workhouses for the poor. Women who want government assistance must be able-bodied and willing to live in the workhouses, designed to be "uninviting places of wholesome restraint." They are separated from their husbands and children and required to be silent during meals.

Government, the Military, and the Law

Argentina's Doña Encarnación de Rosas masterminds her husband's coup d'état, directing a group of thugs and spies.

1831 Lithuanian soldier Emilija Plater (b. 1806) dies. An opponent of the Russians, she organized hundreds of soldiers and fought with mixed success, eventually earning the rank of captain.

1833 Isabella II (b. 1830) becomes queen of Spain with her mother, María Cristina, as her regent. On September 29, war erupts between the Carlists (supporters of Don Carlos, the pretender to the throne) and Isabella's supporters. Russia, Prussia, and Austria side with Don Carlos; France and Britain agree to support Isabella. She will weather these storms and rule until 1868.

1834 Persian ruler Fath Ali-Shah dies. He involved his daughters in government, making Khazin-o-doleh treasurer in charge of the royal jewels, Anis-o-doleh head of the court secretariat, and Zia o-Saltaneh a political adviser.

1834 Maria III becomes queen of Portugal, ruling until 1853 and building schools, roads, and Portugal's first railroad.

Literature and the Visual Arts

1831 Amandine Aurore Lucie Dupin Dudevant (July 1, 1804–June 8, 1876) leaves her husband, moves to Paris, and begins wearing men's clothes and writing books under the name George Sand. Her novel *Indiana*, published in 1832, champions love over convention and deplores the absolute legal power of the husband.

1832 Brazilian author Nisia Floresta Brasileira Augusta (b. 1810) translates Mary Wollstonecraft's *Vindication of the Rights of Woman* into Portuguese.

1833 Chinese poet and embroiderer Yun Zhu (b. 1771), niece of the woman artist Yun Bing, dies.

1833 The translation of Shakespeare into German is completed. Begun in 1794, the work was accomplished by four translators, one of whom was a woman, Dorothea Tieck.

Jan. 1833 The first U.S. mother's periodical, the *Mother's Magazine*, prints its first issue; Abigail Whittelsey will serve as editor until, in 1850, she founds her own journal, *Mrs. Whittelsey's Magazine for Mothers*.

June 1833 George Sand publishes the novel *Lélia*.

1834 Swiss wax sculptor and entrepreneur Marie Tussaud (1761–1850) founds a museum in London for her traveling exhibition. During the French Revolution, she waited by the guillotine to take death masks of the executed until she herself was briefly imprisoned; after release, she emigrated to England with her two children.

1834 English novelist Caroline Norton (1808–1877) becomes editor of the *English Annual*.

1835 French painter Pauline Auzou (b. 1775) dies. Noted for her portraits, genre scenes, and history paintings, she used her talents to glorify Napoleon and was rewarded with annual stipends ranging from 2,000 to 4,000 francs.

1835 At the Paris Salon, the annual official exhibition of French art, 178 of the 801 exhibitors are women.

1835 New books include French portraitist Elisabeth Vigée-Lebrun's *Souvenirs*, Englishwoman Grace Aguilar's first collection of poems, *Magic Wreath*, and

American Catherine Sedgwick's novel *The Linwoods*.

Performing Arts and Entertainment

1832 Italian ballerina and choreographer Fanny Cerrito (1817–1909) makes her debut in Naples.

1832 Italian soprano Giulia Grisi makes her Paris debut in *Semiramide*. In 1834 she makes her London debut as Ninetta in *La gazza ladra*, and in 1835 the role of Elvira in *Il puritani* is written especially for her.

1833 German violinist and soprano Gertrud Mara (b. 1749), court musician to Frederick II of Prussia, dies.

1835 U.S. actress Charlotte Cushman (July 23, 1816–February 18, 1876) makes her operatic debut in *Le nozze di Figaro*, but she soon abandons opera for drama, where she plays not only classic women's roles but also Hamlet and Romeo.

Athletics and Exploration

Mar. 19, 1832 English traveler Frances Trollope (1780–1863) publishes *Domestic Manners of the Americans*. Her account of a Cincinnati theater audience indicates that "the spitting was incessant" and describes "the mixed smell of onions and whiskey . . . . The noises, too, were perpetual, and of the most unpleasant kind."

1835 In cricket, fast, "roundarm" bowling, invented by British bowler Christina Willes, is legalized. Willes often bowled to her brother but found that the wide skirts popular in the late eighteenth century prevented her from doing so in the typical fashion.

Activism

1833 U.S. abolitionist Maria Chapman (July 25, 1806–July 12, 1885) cofounds the Boston Female Anti-Slavery Society. Her membership in the organization will earn her physical, social, and verbal harassment.

1833 U.S. author and editor Sarah Josepha Hale founds the Seaman's Aid Society, an organization for the relief of families of disappeared or deceased sailors.

1833 U.S. author and abolitionist Lydia Maria Child (February 11, 1802–October 20, 1880) publishes a pioneering abolitionist tract, *An Appeal in Favor of the Class of Americans Called Africans*.

Dec. 1833 After being banned from the American Anti-Slavery Society because of her sex, U.S. reformer and feminist Lucretia Mott (January 3, 1793–November 11, 1880) founds the Philadelphia Female Anti-Slavery Society. In 1835, it is joined by two sisters, Angelina (February 20, 1805–October 26, 1879) and Sarah Grimké (November 26, 1792–December 23, 1873), who have already been rebuked for sitting on the "black" bench of their Quaker meeting house.

Business and Industry

Cloth making, originally done at home by women for their own families, is moving to the factories as the Western world industrializes. Some women, especially the young and unmarried, go to work in the new textile mills; others work at home, taking in thread and returning finished cloth on a piecework basis. The most common employment for women, however, is still domestic service.

1831 In Maryland textile mills, men make an average of $3.87 per week, while women make $1.81. In Virginia, men make $2.73, women $1.58.

1834 About 1,000 female shoe binders in the United States form a union. They go on strike for two months, supported in their efforts by the men's union, and return to work after convincing their employers to raise their wages.

1834 Women workers in the Lowell, Massachusetts, textile mills have their pay cut by 25%; they engage in a successful strike against the company.

1834 Ten thousand women work as weavers in Lancashire cotton mills. Mill women make a maximum of 9 shillings, 8 1/2 pence per week; men make a maximum of 22 shillings, 8 1/2 pence. Women work from 6 A.M. to 7 P.M., sometimes from 5 A.M. to 9 P.M., with their only break being forty minutes for lunch. They are sometimes beaten or fined if their work falls short of the manager's expectations.

Science and Medicine

1831 Scottish mathematician Mary Somerville publishes *The Mechanism of the Heavens*, a translation of, and commentary on, Laplace's *Mécanique celeste*. It makes her the principal scientific writer in Britain and earns praise from Laplace himself. The British Royal Society places a bust of her in its hall, and her book becomes a standard part of the honors curriculum at Cambridge. It will go through ten editions by 1877 and will be a standard textbook for nearly a century.

June 26, 1831 French mathematician Sophie Germain, whose examination of the laws governing elasticity allowed, in part, the construction of the Eiffel Tower, dies. As a child, she wanted so desperately to be a mathematician that she disobeyed her parents and stayed up late at night solving problems by the light of hidden candles. An associate of the greatest mathematicians of the time, she worked on problems related to elastic surfaces and on number theory, narrowing the possible solutions of Fermat's last theorem.

1833 British mathematician Ada Byron (1815–1852), countess of Lovelace, becomes interested in Charles Babbage's "difference engine." Her interest in such devices will lead her to become, arguably, the world's first computer programmer.

1834 French-Brazilian obstetrician Marie Durocher is the first diploma recipient of the Medical School in Rio de Janeiro. She is also one of Brazil's first female doctors, encouraging midwives to learn the latest methods from Europe and advocating a noninterventionist policy during delivery.

1834 Mary Somerville publishes *On the Connexion of the Physical Sciences*, which gives John Couch Adams the idea to look for an eighth planet and leads to the discovery of Neptune. In the same year, Somerville is residing in Italy when a celebrated comet passes overhead; she longs to view it, but the only suitable instruments are located in a Jesuit observatory that does not admit women.

1835 U.S. physician Harriot Kezia Hunt (Nov. 9, 1805-Jan. 2, 1875) begins practicing, though she has been unable to enter medical school. Her repeated petitions to Oliver Wendell Holmes, dean of Harvard's medical school, will be granted at last, but a student riot will force her withdrawal. In 1853, she will finally be granted an honorary M.D. by the Female Medical College of Pennsylvania.

1835 Mary Somerville and German astronomer Caroline Herschel become the first female honorary members of Britain's Royal Astronomical Society.

Education and Scholarship

Girls in Japan generally go to school for two to five years, usually only in lower-middle-class families and above.

1831 English historian Mary Berry completes her *Social Life of England and France, from Charles II to 1830.*

1833 German salon hostess Rahel Levin (b. 1771) dies. Her guests included Austrian playwright Franz Grillparzer and German philosopher G.W.F. Hegel.

1833 Connecticut schoolteacher Prudence Crandall (September 3, 1803–January 28, 1890) admits black students to her school. The move will start a furious controversy, which will result in the closing of the school in 1834.

May 1833 Oberlin College is the first U.S. institution of higher learning chartered as coeducational. The programs for men and women are not exactly equal; for example, women are required to attend classes in rhetoric but not allowed to speak in these classes.

1833–1834 British writer Harriet Martineau publishes *Poor Laws and Paupers Illustrated*, a collection of stories designed to teach aspects of the poor laws.

1834 The first girls' school in the Ottoman Empire is founded by missionaries in Beirut, Lebanon.

Religion

There are about 1,500 female shamans in Korea, constituting about two-thirds of all shamans.

1833 Italian saint Bartholomea Capitanio (b. 1807), cofounder of the Sisters of Charity of Lovere, a teaching and nursing order, dies.

1836–1840

General Status and Daily Life

1836 Russian law states that "the woman must obey her husband, reside with him in love, respect, and unlimited obedience, and offer him every pleasantness and affection as the ruler of the household."

1837 British law ceases to regard performing an abortion as a capital offense.

Sept. 1838 The steamboat *Forfarshire* sinks, leaving five survivors stranded on the rocks. Grace Darling (1815–1842) and her father, a lighthouse keeper, brave fierce winds and waves to rescue them, and Grace becomes famous throughout Britain.

1839 Mississippi becomes the first state to grant property rights to married women. The law is not meant as a reform, but as a way of saving the men's property from seizure during economic hard times.

1839 Britain's Infant Custody Act, passed by Parliament largely due to the activism of novelist

Caroline Norton, grants divorced and separated women visitation rights and a chance for custody of children under the age of seven. Until now, a separated wife, even if she has been abandoned, has had no legal claim on her children.

1839 Sarah Stickney Ellis publishes *Women of England*, a very popular conduct guide that espouses supportive, submissive behavior.

1840 The world's first postage stamp, the "penny black," is issued, with Queen Victoria's picture on it.

1840 An English court confirms the right of a man to keep his wife a prisoner in her own home, citing the legal dictum, "The husband hath by law power and dominion over his wife and may keep her by force, within the bounds of duty, and may beat her, but not in a violent or cruel manner."

Government, the Military, and the Law

1836 African warrior queen Nyamazana of Mozambique defeats the Rozvi kingdom of Zimbabwe and has its ruler skinned alive.

1836 Women are involved in various aspects of the Mexican-American War. In February, the town of St. Augustine, Texas, raises money to form a "ladies battalion" for defense; in March, only the women of the Alamo are spared, and Susanna Dickinson, a blacksmith's wife, tells the story of the battle. In April, a Texas slave named Emily, "the Yellow Rose of Texas," keeps Mexican general Santa Anna so well entertained that he loses the Battle of San Jacinto.

June 20, 1837 Eighteen-year-old Victoria becomes queen of Great Britain. In her diary, she writes, "I am very young and perhaps in many, though not all things, inexperienced, but I am sure that very few have more real good will and more real desire to do what is right than I have." Raised in almost complete isolation by people hoping to control her, Victoria still sleeps in the same room as her mother. She immediately begins to show signs of independence, changing her name from Alexandrina Victoria to simply Victoria and dismissing several of her domineering advisers and relatives, including her mother. In 1839, she gives further evidence of her determination in a battle with the new Tory Parliament over her household staff. She wants to maintain it as it is, with her Whig ladies; they want the top positions to go to their own female relatives. In the end, a compromise is reached, with only one lady being replaced at each change of power.

Literature and the Visual Arts

1837 Marguerite Gérard (b. 1761), the first Frenchwoman to be successful as a genre painter, dies.

1837 U.S. author and editor Sarah Josepha Hale becomes editor of *Godey's Lady's Book*. It currently has 10,000 subscribers but by 1860 will have 160,000, making it one of the best-selling periodicals in the country.

1837 Swedish novelist Fredrika Bremer publishes *The Neighbors*.

1837 French novelist George Sand publishes *Mauprat*, writes *Les Maîtres Mosaïstes* and *La Dernière Aldini*, and rescues her daughter Solange after she is kidnapped by Sand's ex-husband, Casimir. In 1840, she will receive the dubious distinction of having all her love stories placed on the Catholic Index of Forbidden Books.

1838 New literature includes English poet Elizabeth Barrett Browning's *The Seraphim*, English feminist Caroline Norton's novel *The Wife and Woman's Reward*, and French socialist Flora Tristan's (1803–1844) novel *Mephis*.

1839 Chinese author Wang Duan (b. 1793) dies. She wrote poems and edited *Ming sanshijia shixuan*, an anthology of Ming dynasty poets.

1839 German countess Ida von Hahn-Hahn publishes the novel *Der Rechte*, in which the heroine denounces the wife's taking of her husband's name as "barbarous."

Performing Arts and Entertainment

1836 French-Spanish mezzo-soprano Maria Malibran (b. 1808) dies in a riding accident. Internationally celebrated, she had a personal life overshadowed by a controlling father and an unsuccessful marriage.

1836 Austrian dancer Fanny Elssler (1810–1884) stars in Coralli's *Le diable boiteux*, and Danish ballerina Lucile Grahn (1819–1907) creates the title role in *La Sylphide*.

1836 German pianist and composer Clara Wieck Schumann (1819–1896), the first performer to play the works of Chopin in Germany, composes a piano concerto. In 1838, she is made *Kammervirtuosin* to the Austrian court, elected to the Gesellschaft der Musikfreunde, and ranked third among all living piano players.

1837 U.S. actress Charlotte Cushman plays Meg

Merrilees in *Guy Mannering*. In 1839, she plays Nancy Sykes in *Oliver Twist*.

1838 Swedish soprano Jenny Lind (1820–1887) debuts in Stockholm in Weber's *Der Freischütz*.

1838 French tragedienne Rachel (pseudonym of Elisa Felix, 1821–1858) joins the Comédie Française.

1839 Italian soprano Giulia Grisi sings at the London première of *Lucrezia Borgia*.

1840 Fanny Elssler stars in Coralli's *La tarentule* and becomes the first major ballerina to tour the United States. Extremely popular, she is so much admired in Washington, D.C., that during her performances Congress adjourns for lack of a quorum.

Athletics and Exploration

Sept. 1, 1836 U.S. missionaries Narcissa Whitman and Eliza Spalding become the first white women to travel overland to Oregon. Eliza was run over by a mule team and thrown and dragged by her horse on the way. Their determination and stamina are typical of pioneer women, who must be prepared to milk cows, prepare meat, nurse the sick, fix roofs and chimneys, and make carpets, candles, cheese, butter, and clothing.

1839 English traveler Lady Hester Stanhope (b. March 12, 1776), whose exploratory and romantic adventures took her to Gibraltar, Malta, Greece, Constantinople, Egypt, and Syria, dies.

Activism

The United States is a hotbed of female activism as women's involvement with the church expands into work for temperance and abolition. This activism on behalf of others will in turn feed women's attempts to gain rights for themselves.

1836 Blacks are banned from the New York Women's Anti-Slavery Society.

1836 Three notable abolitionist works by U.S. women are published: Lydia Maria Child's pamphlet *Anti-Slavery Catechism*, Sarah Grimké's *Epistle to the Clergy of the Southern States*, and Angelina Grimké's *Appeal to the Christian Women of the South*.

1837 U.S. abolitionist and feminist Angelina Grimké publishes an *Appeal to the Women of the Nominally Free States* and begins lecturing with her sister. The Council of Congregational Ministers of Massachusetts issues a warning against her and other "females who itinerate," and U.S. educator Catharine Beecher addresses

her *Essay on Slavery and Abolitionism, with Reference to the Duty of American Females* to Angelina, criticizing work that "throws woman into the attitude of a combatant, whether for herself or for others."

The Grimkés plunge gleefully into the controversy. In 1838, Angelina responds with *Letters to Catharine Beecher*, and Sarah publishes *Letters on the Condition of Women and the Equality of the Sexes*, in which she states, "I ask no favors for my sex. I surrender not our claim to equality. All I ask of our brethren is that they will take their feet from off our necks, and permit us to stand upright on the ground which God has designed for us to occupy."

1837 The first Anti-Slavery Convention of American Women is held in New York City; delegates include Abba Alcott, mother of novelist Louisa May Alcott.

May 14, 1838 The Anti-Slavery Convention of American Women, which includes black delegates, meets in Philadelphia. An outraged mob gathers, and on the night of the sixteenth, it throws stones and bricks and interrupts the speakers; Angelina Grimké delivers her last public oration. Young Abby Kelley Foster makes such a good speech that Grimké's husband, Theodore Weld, tells her that she must devote her talents to abolition or "God will smite you."

On the seventeenth, the mob burns the hall and tries to burn abolitionist Lucretia Mott's house but cannot get there. Frustrated, it burns several homes belonging to blacks. On the eighteenth, the convention meets in abolitionist Sarah Pugh's schoolhouse rather than admit defeat. During the worst of the rioting, Mott led a group of women to safety, two by two, out of the hall and through the angry crowd.

1839 English author Sarah Lewis publishes *Woman's Mission*, urging women to use their influence over their husbands, fathers, brothers, and sons, rather than demanding power for themselves. The book will go into thirteen editions by 1849.

1840 At the World's Anti-Slavery Convention in London, female delegates are rejected, including the American Anti-Slavery Society's national representative, Lucretia Mott. Women are told they can be only onlookers in the gallery. Outraged, Mott and fellow American Elizabeth Cady Stanton meet and vow to do something about the position of women. Stanton writes later that "Mrs. Mott was to me an entirely new revelation of womanhood."

Business and Industry

Jan. 30, 1836 U.S. seamstress Betsy Ross (b. January 1, 1752), purportedly the sewer of the first stars-and-stripes American flag, dies.

1837 In New England, 15,000 women are employed in shoe and boot manufacture.

1839 Englishwoman Maria Ann Smith goes to Australia, where her experiments with apples result in the world-famous Granny Smith.

Science and Medicine

1837 U.S. water-cure physician Mary Gove Nichols (1810–1884) begins lecturing to women on anatomy and physiology.

1837 U.S. phrenologist Charlotte Fowler Wells (August 14, 1814–June 4, 1901) joins her brothers' phrenological institute; for the next sixty years she will be associated with the later-discredited "science" of determining personality through skull shape.

c. 1840 In Germany, wealthy women are increasingly insisting on having "male midwives" attend them in childbirth. Poor women still rely on the local "handywoman" or *Wickelfrau*.

Education and Scholarship

1836 The University of London opens, granting women equal access to degree programs.

1837 New England's Transcendentalist Club is formed, with philosopher Margaret Fuller (May 23, 1810–July 19, 1850) and educator Elizabeth Peabody as its only female members. In 1840, Fuller becomes editor of the transcendentalist journal *The Dial*.

Nov. 8, 1837 U.S. educator Mary Lyon (February 28, 1797–March 5, 1849) opens Mount Holyoke Female Seminary with eighty pupils.

1838 In Mexico City, 3,280 girls are registered in 82 schools.

Oct. 30, 1838 Oberlin College becomes the first in the United States to admit men and women on an equal basis.

1840 French socialist Flora Tristan publishes a study of Chartism, *Promenades des Londres*.

Religion

1837 Italian saint Josepha Rossello (1811–December 7, 1880) founds a women's religious order, the Daughters of Our Lady of Mercy.

1838 French saint Elizabeth Bichier des Ages (b. 1773) dies. She organized secret religious services during the French Revolution and later cofounded the Daughters of the Cross (also known as the Sisters of St. Andrew the Apostle), a community devoted to nursing and to the education of girls. Between 1811 and 1830 she presided over the founding of more than sixty branches of the order.

1840 Italian saint Mary di Rosa (1813–1855) founds the Handmaids of Charity at Brescia.

1841–1845

General Status and Daily Life

1841 U.S. author and educator Catharine Beecher publishes her popular *Treatise on Domestic Economy*, which offers advice on "domestic science" to housewives curious about child-rearing, cooking, and the management of servants.

1843 Sarah Stickney Ellis publishes *The Wives of England*, in which she recommends a slavish devotion to one's husband, despite his faults.

1843 The vulcanization of rubber makes condoms more widely available, though they are still chiefly used by the middle and upper classes.

1845 English cookery writer Elizabeth Acton (1799–1859) publishes *Modern Cookery*. Immensely popular, it will remain in print until 1914.

1845 Women in Sweden get equal inheritance rights.

Government, the Military, and the Law

May 5, 1841 High chief and Christian convert Kapiolani of Hawaii (b. c. 1781) dies. One of the greeters of Hawaii's first missionaries, she discarded all her husbands but one when she converted.

1844 Eliza Farnham (November 17, 1815–December 15, 1864) becomes women's matron at Sing Sing prison; the governing board allows prisoners to work and eat together but mandates strict silence, allowing the prisoners to have no verbal contact, a policy that led to riots. Farnham ignores the rule, bringing in flowers, books, curtains, dolls, and a piano for sing-alongs.

Literature and the Visual Arts

1841 German poet Annette Dröste-Hulshoff (1797–1848) publishes the novella *Die Judenbuche*.

1841 English writer Harriet Martineau publishes *Playfellow*, a collection of children's stories, and a novel about Toussaint l'Ouverture, *The Hour and the Man*.

1842 Upon his death, U.S. journalist Cornelia Walker replaces her brother as editor of the *Boston Transcript*, a newspaper he founded. During her five years as editor, she will favor higher education for women and oppose women's suffrage. She will also oppose the ideas of theologian Theodore Parker and authors Ralph Waldo Emerson and Edgar Allan Poe.

Mar. 30, 1842 French court portraitist Marie Elisabeth Vigée-Lebrun dies. A close friend of Marie Antoinette's, she produced over 800 paintings and was a favorite with aristocrats by the age of twenty, but her sizable fees for portraits were squandered by her husband, a compulsive gambler.

1843 English landscape architect Gertrude Jekyll (d. 1932) is born. Originally a painter, she will turn to gardening when her eyesight begins to fail. Her impressionistic mixes of hollyhocks and other humble native flowers will replace the regimented, uniform-height formal gardens of her childhood.

1843 New novels include George Sand's sequel to *Consuelo* (1842), *La Comtesse de Ruolstadt*, and Swedish novelist Fredrika Bremer's (1801–1865) *The House*.

1844 English author Elizabeth Barrett Browning (b. 1806) publishes her *Poems*.

Performing Arts and Entertainment

1842 U.S. actress Charlotte Cushman becomes the manager of Philadelphia's Walnut Street Theatre.

1842 Italian contralto Marietta Alboni (1823–1894) makes her debut in Bologna in *Saffo*. Later this year she makes her first appearance at Milan's La Scala in *La siége de Corinthe*, composed for her by Rossini.

1842 German composer Felix Mendelssohn performs for Queen Victoria, who particularly admires one of his songs; he confesses that the real composer is his sister Fanny (b. 1805), who has published many compositions under his name for fear of unfeminine publicity.

1842 German pianist Clara Wieck Schumann performs in Copenhagen and receives an invitation to play at the imperial court. Her envious husband, Robert, receives no such invitation and writes, "The thought of my undignified position in such cases, prevented me from feeling any pleasure."

1843 Austrian dancer Fanny Elssler and Italian ballerina and choreographer Fanny Cerrito perform a *pas de deux* at a Royal Command Performance for Queen Victoria.

1843 Italian soprano Giulia Grisi creates the role of Norina in *Don Pasquale*.

1843 Italian ballerina Carlotta Grisi creates the role of *La Péri*, becoming famous for her dangerous leap from a high platform. In 1844, she, Fanny Cerrito, Marie Taglioni, and Lucille Grahn will dance a *pas de quatre*.

1843–1844 Charlotte Cushman performs in *Macbeth* on alternate nights in New York and Philadelphia.

Athletics and Exploration

1844 Eleven women compete at England's second Grand National Archery Meeting.

Activism

1841 U.S. abolitionist Lydia Maria Child is made editor of the *National Anti-Slavery Standard*, protesting modestly that *Mr.* Child would have been a much better choice. In 1844, Maria Chapman becomes co-editor of the same periodical.

1841 Australian philanthropist Caroline Chisholm (1808–1877) establishes a Female Immigrants' Home in Sydney to help find poor women work and shelter. In the first year of the home's free employment registry, jobs are found for 1,400 women and 600 men.

1841 U.S. reformer Dorothea Dix begins teaching Sunday school at a Massachusetts prison and is horrified to find insane women confined with criminals, kept in chains, and confined in cages, closets, and cellars. She finds that there are only eight insane asylums in the nation, all of them wretched. The experience leads her to survey asylums throughout the state, and her report to the Massachusetts legislature in 1843 leads to extensive reform in the treatment of the mentally ill.

Jan. 1841 Sophia Ripley, U.S. transcendentalist and cofounder of the utopian community Brook Farm, publishes the feminist article "Woman" in *The Dial*.

1843 English reformer and traveler Jane Franklin establishes the Tasmanian Society for the Reformation of Female Prisoners.

1844 English writer Ann Richelieu Lamb attacks the popular notion that women should strive for influence over men rather than direct power for themselves. She says women should rebel against dependency and criticizes prejudice against women who choose not to marry.

1845 Quaker Abby Kelley Foster speaks on antislavery at the Orthodox Ohio Yearly Meeting and is carried bodily from the room.

Business and Industry

In England, about 150,000 women over the age of twenty sew for a living, mostly in their homes, doing piecework in isolation.

Department stores begin hiring female clerks.

Women in domestic service often leave home for good at the age of twelve or thirteen and work their whole lives with only brief respites for childbirth and childrearing.

1841 There are 22 female coopers and 3,717 female shoe makers and boot makers in England; 66,329 women above the age of twenty work as agricultural laborers.

June 7, 1842 Parliament bars women and children from underground labor after hearing a report on women's work in mines. Among other jobs, women pull loaded carts of ore weighing 224-560 pounds. About 6,000 women are employed in British mines, making two shillings per day (as opposed to the man's wage of three shillings, sixpence) for twelve- to sixteen-hour days.

1843 French fortune-teller Marie Lenormand, whose clients included Danton, Desmoulins, Marat, Saint-Just, Robespierre, David, Mme. de Staël, and Joséphine Bonaparte, dies.

1843 Italian revolutionary Cristina Trivulzio establishes the *Gazetta Italiana*.

1844 The English Factory Act limits female industrial workers to a twelve-hour workday.

1845 The first Female Labor Reform Association is organized in Lowell, Massachusetts, with Sarah G. Bagley as its president. Membership quickly increases from 12 to 500.

Science and Medicine

Ether is first used as an anaesthetic during childbirth.

1841 French obstetrician Marie Boivin dies. She translated medical works, invented obstetrical instruments, and was one of the earliest users of the stethoscope to listen to the fetal heartbeat.

1841 British botanist Jane Marcet (1769–1858) publishes *The Ladies' Companion to the Flower Garden*.

1842 Egyptian pasha Mohammed Ali establishes a school for midwives.

1844 English writer Harriet Martineau publishes *Life in the Sickroom*, a work on hypnotism.

Education and Scholarship

1841 Three Oberlin students become the first women in the United States to receive university degrees.

1842 Brazilian author Nisia Floresta Brasileira Augusta publishes "Advice to My Daughter," an article on the education of women.

1843 Englishwoman Marion Reid publishes *A Plea for Women*, arguing for better education for women, as current girls' schools "produce a mere automaton—a subdued, passive tool, which the elements of society fashion outwardly, but which has no inward power to seize upon those elements and convert them into means of growth, both moral and intellectual."

1843 In England, the Governesses' Benevolent Institution is established to help private teachers find jobs in youth and receive pensions in old age.

1844 U.S. writer and feminist Margaret Fuller becomes a literary critic at the *New York Tribune* and publishes *Woman in the Nineteenth Century*, an important work of feminist theory in which Fuller defends a woman's right "as a soul to live free and unimpeded."

Religion

Iranian poet and warrior Qurrat Ul Ayn appears unveiled in public to protest Islamic dress codes for women.

1842 English author Grace Aguilar publishes *The Spirit of Judaism*. In 1845, she publishes *The Jewish Faith*.

1842 Italian revolutionary Cristina Trivulzio begins publishing her four-volume *Essai sur la formation du dogme Catholique* (completed 1846).

Sept. 13, 1844 Ann Eliza Young, twenty-seventh wife of Brigham Young, and a passionate opponent of Mormon polygamy, is born.

1845 U.S. evangelist Phoebe Palmer publishes *The Way of Holiness*.

1846–1850

General Status and Daily Life

1847 U.S. feminist Elizabeth Cady Stanton (November 12, 1815–October 26, 1902) writes to a friend, "There is a great deal in a name. . . . Ask our colored brethren if there is nothing in a name. . . . The custom of calling women Mrs. John This and Mrs. Tom That, and colored men Sambo and Zip Coon, is founded on the principle that white men are lords of all. I cannot acknowledge the principle as just; therefore, I cannot wear the name of another."

1850 The average U.S. woman has 5.92 children.

Government, the Military, and the Law

1848 Greek rebel Manto Mavrogenous, who led a band of guerrillas against the Turks and earned the rank of lieutenant-general, dies.

1849 French socialist Jeanne Déroin (c. 1810–1894) becomes the first woman to run for the National Assembly.

Literature and the Visual Arts

1846 Irish writer and salon hostess Marguerite Blessington becomes a gossip columnist and publishes a novel, *Memoirs of a Femme de Chambre*. Other new novels include *Azeth the Egyptian*, by English antifeminist Eliza Lynn Linton; *Nélida*, by the French comtesse d'Agoult; and *La Mare au diable*, by French novelist George Sand.

1847 Japanese artist Katsushika Oi illustrates the *E-iri nichiyo onna choho-ki*, an encyclopedia for women that gives advice on behavior, traditional values, health, pregnancy, cooking, cosmetics, sewing, weaving, poetry, calligraphy, music, and games.

1847 England's Brontë sisters publish their first

novels, under male pseudonyms. Emily (July 30, 1818–December 1848, pseudonym Ellis Bell) publishes *Wuthering Heights*, an immediate and rather infamous sensation. Anne (1820–1849, pseudonym Acton Bell) publishes *Agnes Grey*, a novel based on her own experiences as a governess.

Charlotte (pseudonym Currer Bell) publishes the best-seller *Jane Eyre* after her first attempt, *The Professor*, is rejected. In it, she defends the ambitions of women: "Women are supposed to be very calm generally: but women feel just as men feel; they need exercise for their faculties, and a field for their efforts as much as their brothers do; they suffer from too rigid a constraint, too absolute a stagnation, precisely as men would suffer; and it is narrowed-minded in their more privileged fellow-creatures to say that they ought to confine themselves to making puddings and knitting stockings, to playing on the piano and embroidering bags."

1848 Anne Brontë publishes *The Tenant of Wildfell Hall*, in which she protests against the social and legal confinement of women. The novel treats sympathetically a woman who leaves her husband, takes custody of her son, and tries to make a living on her own. Other new British novels include Eliza Lynn Linton's *Amynone* and Elizabeth Gaskell's *Mary Barton*.

July 22, 1848 Anne Brontë defends her work against those who suspect it is written by a woman: "I am satisfied that if a book is a good one, it is so whatever the sex of the author . . . All novels are, or should be, written for both men and women to read, and I am at a loss to conceive how a man should permit himself to write anything that would be really disgraceful to a woman, or why a woman should be censured for writing anything that would be proper and becoming for a man."

1849 Charlotte Brontë publishes the novel *Shirley*, which features two heroines: feminine, passive Caroline Helstone and tomboyish, independent Shirley Keeldar. It is the first time the name "Shirley" is used as a woman's name in fiction.

1849 Japanese artist Katsushika Oi illustrates a tea dictionary.

1849 French painter Rosa Bonheur becomes director of the women's Ecole de Dessin and paints *Plowing in Nivernais*.

1849 U.S. popular novelist E.D.E.N. (Emma Dorothy Eliza Nevitte, b. December 26, 1819) Southworth publishes her first novel, the best-selling *Retribution*.

1850 Elizabeth Barrett Browning publishes *Sonnets from the Portuguese*, which includes the famous line "How do I love thee? Let me count the ways."

Performing Arts and Entertainment

1847   German composer Fanny Mendelssohn, considered by many to have been as talented as her brother Felix, dies. Her father told her that to remain feminine she must make music "only . . . an ornament, never the root of your being and doing." She herself lamented, "My songs lie unheeded and unknown."

1848 Austrian ballerina Fanny Elssler performs at La Scala in Milan, where audiences hiss her because of her nationality. She then travels to Russia, performing for two years in St. Petersburg.

1849 Italian soprano Angelica Catalani (b. 1780) dies. At the height of her career, she was paid ten times the fees commanded by other singers.

1849 French tragedienne Rachel stars in *Adrienne Lecouvreur*.

1850 German soprano Henriette Sontag appears in the première of Halévy's *La tempesta*.

Sept. 1850 Jenny Lind begins a tour of the United States under the management of P. T. Barnum. Forty thousand people meet her boat when it docks in New York; 20,000 line the streets near her hotel trying to see her. Her deal with Barnum includes 150 concerts at a fee of $1,000 each.

Athletics and Exploration

Mar. 9, 1847 U.S. pioneer Frances Slocum (b. March 4, 1773), taken captive by the Delaware Indians at the age of five, dies. She became so attached to the Delawares that she refused to go back to white society when she had the chance, saying that she wished to die where "the Great Spirit will know where to find me."

Spring 1849 There are only fifteen women residing in San Francisco; in 1850 the population will still be less than 8% female.

1850 English reformer and traveler Jane Franklin (d. 1875) sends the first of five expeditions in search of her husband, John, lost at sea while exploring the Arctic. Her husband will never be found, but the expeditions she funds will help to map the Arctic regions.

Activism

1846 The world's first halfway house for freed women inmates, the Home for Discharged Female Convicts, opens in New York. The residents face strict discipline; they rise at 5:30, retire at 9:00, and engage in a full day of Scripture and education, with sewing in between. The home, a strictly voluntary enterprise, has a good rehabilitation rate and ejects any woman suffering from drunkenness.

1846 English philanthropist Angela Burdett-Coutts establishes a home for wayward women, supervised at one point by Charles Dickens. Visits to the residents are limited. The inmates must apply for permission to write letters, even to relatives, and then they are restricted to one letter per month. All letters, whether sent or received, are read by the superintendent. Inmates are paid for good behavior and fined for bad; they are expected to exhibit "Truthfulness, Industry, Temper, Propriety of Conduct and Conversation, Temperance, Order, Punctuality, Economy, [and] Cleanliness."

1846 U.S. feminist Lucy Stone's sister writes to her, "I don't believe woman is groaning under half so heavy a yoke of bondage as you imagine. I am sure I do not feel burdened by anything man has laid upon me, to be sure I can't vote, but what care I for that, I would not if I could."

1847 Australian philanthropist Caroline Chisholm suggests that an influx of "good and virtuous women" will tame Australia. In 1849, she founds a Family Colonization Loan Society, backed by Angela Burdett-Coutts, to bring families to Australia.

1848 Dutch feminist Mina Drucker is born. Her nickname, Dolle Mina (Mad Mina), will become the name of a feminist group formed in 1970 and will eventually be synonymous in Dutch life with anything feminist.

1848 New York passes the Married Women's Property Act, largely due to the efforts of U.S. feminist Elizabeth Cady Stanton.

1848 French feminist Jeanne Déroin publishes a vitriolic pamphlet, *Cours de droit social pour les femmes*.

1848 U.S. journalist Jane Swisshelm begins publishing the *Saturday Visiter*, an abolitionist newspaper.

1848 Many working-class women's organizations are formed in France during the Second Republic. Novelist George Sand establishes a republican newspaper, *La Cause du Peuple*.

July 19–21, 1848 U.S. feminists Elizabeth Cady Stanton and Lucretia Mott, with help from Jane Hunt, Mary McClintock, and Martha C. Wright, hold the country's first women's rights convention in Seneca Falls, New York. Some of the delegates compose a

Declaration of Sentiments which lists the grievances of U.S. women. This document is read to a crowd of about 300 women and 40 men. Sixty-eight women sign it, using their own first names (rather than signing, according to custom, as Mrs. John This or Mrs. Frank That), and using no titles such as Mrs. or Miss.

The resolutions of the Declaration include one that states "that woman is man's equal, was intended to be so by the Creator, and the highest good of the race demands that she should be recognized as such." The list of the crimes of man against woman is long and includes woman's inability to vote, lack of property rights in marriage (even over her own wages), subordination to her husband's will, vulnerability to violence, lack of access to profitable and prestigious occupations, inferior educational opportunities, and exclusion from the clergy. The declaration also complains of the double standard "by which moral delinquencies which exclude women from society are not only tolerated but deemed of little account in man." Stanton introduces a demand for women's suffrage, much to the dismay of Mott and her own husband, but after a stirring defense of the idea by Frederick Douglass, the resolution passes and soon becomes the backbone of the nineteenth-century feminist movement.

Jan. 1849 U.S. feminist Amelia Bloomer begins publishing *The Lily*, in which she advocates dress reform, temperance, and women's rights.

July 1849 U.S. abolitionist Harriet Tubman, currently a slave in Maryland, escapes to Philadelphia and freedom after her master's death and rumors that she is to be sold south. She returns in December 1850 to rescue her sister and two children.

1850 Italian revolutionary Cristina Trivulzio establishes the Turin newspaper *Italia* and publishes her autobiography, *Souvenirs d'exil*.

Business and Industry

English prostitutes usually work at the trade part-time to supplement their earnings from their "legitimate" work. They make about a shilling per customer after fees to pimps are deducted. Prostitutes, on the whole, are healthier than other poor women, because their additional income allows them to eat better.

1846 U.S. labor organizer Sarah Bagley becomes the first female telegraph operator.

1847 Marie Duplessis, former corset maker and milliner, then courtesan and the inspiration for Alexandre Dumas fils' Camille, dies of tuberculosis.

June 8, 1847 Women's workday is reduced to ten hours by the British Factory Act.

1848 A survey of workers in a poorer London neighborhood finds that the men earn an average of twenty shillings, twopence per week, while the women earn only six shillings, tenpence.

1849 U.S. businesswoman Mary Ellen Pleasant moves to San Francisco. There she establishes a successful boardinghouse; some claim she also deals in brothels and moneylending. An ex-slave, she will fight courageously for the rights of blacks to testify in court and to ride on streetcars, rescue black workers being held illegally as slaves, and allegedly offer financial support to abolitionist rebel John Brown.

May 1849 U.S. educator, transcendentalist, and bookstore owner Elizabeth Peabody publishes Thoreau's influential essay *Civil Disobedience*.

Late 1849 During the gold rush, women in San Francisco take in wash, which few men are willing to do, charging the astronomical price of twenty dollars for twelve items.

1850 Rural girls flock to the new textile factories of New England, often with friends or relatives. They find complete mill towns, in which housekeepers enforce curfews and ensure that the workers adhere to strict rules of womanly conduct. Most find the wages, which are higher than for sewing or domestic work, adequate compensation for the lack of freedom. The average new worker is sixteen and a half years old and stays at the mills for about five years before leaving for marriage.

1850 Irish courtesan Laura Bell (b. 1829), acknowledged as the "Queen of London Whoredom," charges the prime minister of Nepal £250,000 for one night of pleasure.

1850 Australian pioneer and wool merchant Elizabeth Macarthur (b. 1767), who amassed huge merino flocks and established the wool trade in New South Wales, dies.

Science and Medicine

c. 1847 Sterilizing of hands becomes a more common practice among doctors, reducing the incidence of puerperal or childbed fever; ether gains popularity as an anesthetic for use during surgery and childbirth.

Oct. 1, 1847 U.S. astronomer Maria Mitchell, who claimed, "Nature made woman an observer," discovers a comet, an achievement that wins her fame and a gold medal from the king of Denmark. Later, she becomes the first female member of the American Academy of Arts and Sciences (1848) and the American Association for the Advancement of Science (1850).

1848 Lydia Fowler (1822-1879), the first U.S.-born

woman to earn an M.D. (1850), publishes *Familiar Lectures on Astronomy* and *Familiar Lectures on Physiology*.

1848   Scottish science writer Mary Somerville publishes her most popular book, *Physical Geography*.

Jan. 1848   German astronomer Caroline Herschel (b. March 16, 1750), who had two books published by the Royal Society, dies after a lifetime of what she called "minding the heavens." After a brief singing career, she became involved in astronomy to please and support her brother William. In addition to her contributions to his work, she discovered fourteen nebulae, eight comets, and star clusters; she also catalogued 2,500 nebulae and reorganized the 3,000 stars in Flamsteed's *British Catalogue*.

Jan. 23, 1849   English-American physician Elizabeth Blackwell (February 3, 1821), the first woman doctor in the United States, receives her medical degree from New York's Geneva College before a crowd of 20,000.

1850   William Mullen founds the Female Medical College of Pennsylvania; classes open in October for eight full-time students and thirty-two "listeners." The board and faculty are entirely male.

Education and Scholarship

In Russia, a country of 60 million, there are only 148 girls' secondary schools.

1849   Brazilian author Anna Eugenia Lopes de Cadaval publishes the article "The Education of Girls."

1849   British educator Joan Bethune establishes the first women's college in India.

1849   Queen's College opens in London to provide girls with a university education in "mathematics, classics, and sport." Two noteworthy pupils at Queen's are destined to be the great pioneers of English women's education: Frances Buss and Dorothea Beale.

1850   There are about 21,000 governesses in England, making £20–300 per year. Most make £20–30 plus room and board.

Religion

1846   French saint Mary-Magdalene Postel (b. Julie Postel in 1765) dies. She established a girls' school in Normandy and held services there during the religious suppressions of the French Revolution. She also established the Sisters of the Christian Schools of Mercy, though she herself did not take vows until the

age of fifty-one.

1847   Italian saint Vincentia Gerosa (b. 1784), cofounder of the Sisters of Charity of Lovere, a nursing and teaching order, dies.

Nov. 29, 1847   U.S. missionary Narcissa Whitman (b. March 14, 1808) dies with thirteen other whites in an Indian uprising in Oregon. Whitman, who lost her only child in a drowning accident, opened her home to eleven foster children. She was dedicated to her work as a missionary and tried her best to nurse the Indians in the area during times of illness, but she was disliked by them because of her open contempt for their "uncivilized" ways. Her fellow missionary Eliza Spalding is saved from death by some of the Nez Percés with whom she has worked.

1851–1855

General Status and Daily Life

1851   The Guatemalan Constitution grants citizenship to financially independent women.

1851   Dress reformers try unsuccessfully to popularize a pair of baggy pants beneath a knee-length tunic designed by U.S. dress reformer Elizabeth Miller (September 20, 1822–May 22, 1911). U.S. journalist Amelia Bloomer defends the costume as safer and more sensible than voluminous hoopskirts, but she is widely ridiculed and succeeds only in having her name inextricably linked with the "bloomers."

1854   English feminist Barbara Bodichon's (1827–1891) *A Brief Summary in Plain Language of the Most Important Laws Concerning Woman* explains that married women have no legal or financial rights. The husband has physical custody of his wife and children; the wife cannot make contracts on her own or be found guilty of conspiracy with her husband, "as that offense cannot be committed unless there are two persons."

1855   Eighteen percent of Irish-American households are headed by women.

Government, the Military, and the Law

1851   Women in France and Germany are banned from political action. Women are also forbidden to edit newspapers, so German publisher Louise Otto-Peters's two-year-old *Women's Newspaper* is closed down.

Literature and the Visual Arts

1851　The religious novel *The Sunny Side*, by U.S. author Elizabeth Stuart Phelps (August 13, 1815–November 30, 1852), sells 100,000 copies and is translated into several languages.

1851　English novelist George Eliot (pseudonym of Mary Ann Evans, November 29, 1819–December 22, 1880) becomes an assistant editor of the radical *Westminster Review*. In 1854, she begins living openly with her married lover George Henry Lewes, a move that shocks Victorian society.

1851　English popular novelist Charlotte Yonge (1823–1901), author of more than 150 books, becomes editor of the children's magazine *The Monthly Packet*, a position she will hold until 1890.

1852　Japanese artist Ema Saiko (b. 1787) paints *Bamboo and Rock*, a delicate, sparse ink painting on a satin scroll.

1852　German-Spanish novelist Fernán Caballero (pseudonym of Cecilia Boehl von Faber, 1796–1877) publishes the novel *Clemencia*, the story of a woman trapped in an unhappy marriage.

1852　U.S. novelist Harriet Beecher Stowe (June 14, 1811–July 1, 1896) publishes *Uncle Tom's Cabin: or Life Among the Lowly*. It will sell 300,000 copies by the end of the year and 1 million by the middle of 1853, breaking all previous American records for a single book. It inspires numerous pastiches and arouses widespread anger against slavery. Pro-slavery forces, in panic and outrage, issue a reply, *In Defense of Slavery*, and several "anti-Uncle Tom" novels are published, including Virginia author Mary Eastman's *Aunt Phillis's Cabin: or, Southern Life as It Is*. Poet Henry Wadsworth Longfellow writes of Stowe, "How she is shaking the world with her Uncle Tom's Cabin! At one step she has reached the top of the stair-case up which the rest of us climb on our knees year after year."

1853　Elizabeth Gaskell (b. 1810) publishes the controversial novel *Ruth*, which sympathetically portrays an unwed mother. Gaskell's close friend Charlotte Brontë publishes *Villette*, a novel about a repressed Englishwoman living in Belgium.

1853　At the Paris Salon, French painter Rosa Bonheur shows her masterpiece *The Horse Fair*, a work so popular that even Britain's Queen Victoria requests a private viewing.

1854　Australian feminist, reformer, and novelist Catherine Spence (1825–1910) publishes *Clara Morison: A Tale of South Australia During the Gold Fever*.

1854　Chinese artist and poet Wu Shangxi is active. She is skilled in both the double-outline and no-outline (or "boneless") styles of painting. She is unusually well traveled for a woman of her time, traveling 10,000 miles with her father and husband. Her poems will be collected in *Xieyunlou ci* (*Poetry from the Pavilion of Rhyme Writing*).

1855　Japanese *bunjin* artist Tachihara Shunsa (b. 1814), a specialist in bird-and-flower paintings, dies.

1855　New literature includes Elizabeth Gaskell's novel *North and South*, George Eliot's attack on popular literature, *Silly Novels by Lady Novelists*, and George Sand's *Histoire De Ma Vie*.

Mar. 31, 1855　Charlotte Brontë (b. April 21, 1816), best known for her novel *Jane Eyre*, dies. Her husband, Rev. Arthur Nicholls, develops an aversion to being known and remembered as the husband of a famous woman and resists any mention or remembrance of her.

Performing Arts and Entertainment

1851　Composer Robert Schumann is appointed conductor of the Düsseldorf Orchestra; his wife, pianist Clara Wieck Schumann, gives his opening performance, a piano concerto played from memory; she steals the show, and Robert is furious.

1851　Irish dancer Lola Montez (stage name of Marie Dolores Eliza Rosanna Gilbert, 1818–January 17, 1861) makes her New York debut. In 1853, she goes to San Francisco, becoming famous for her somewhat revealing Spider Dance. Shortly afterward, English actress Caroline "Merry Carrie" Chapman (1818?–May 8, 1876) tours the United States lampooning the Spider Dance.

Nov. 22, 1851　Italian-American soprano Adelina Patti (February 10, 1843–September 27, 1919) gives her first public performance. She will be closely identified with the simple song "Home, Sweet Home" as well as with arias and will be admired by Giuseppi Verdi, Jenny Lind, and Queen Victoria.

1852　Italian ballerina and choreographer Fanny Cerrito stars in *Orfa* at the Paris Opéra. In 1854, she stars in the self-choreographed *Gemma*.

1852　Swedish soprano Jenny Lind marries her accompanist, Otto Goldschmidt; like a good, submissive Victorian wife, she tries unsuccessfully to become famous again as Jenny Goldschmidt. In frustration, she asks a friend, "Why do people persist in saying 'Jenny

Lind was there with her husband?' They ought to say, 'Herr Goldschmidt was there with his wife.'"

1853 English actress Laura Keene (1820?–November 4, 1873) becomes the first actress in the United States to manage a theater.

Athletics and Exploration

1851 Princess Amalie of Saxony wins a prize for accuracy with a crossbow.

1851 German Maria Weigel is pelted with stones after appearing in public on ice skates.

Activism

1851 U.S. abolitionist Harriet Tubman (b. 1821), an escaped slave, returns to Maryland twice, guiding two of her brothers and their families to freedom. Over the next ten years she will make nearly twenty trips back to the slave state of Maryland, rescuing 60 to 300 slaves from bondage and employing a variety of clever tactics to evade her pursuers. At one point, rewards totaling $40,000 will be offered for her capture.

1851 Greek-Italian writer Angeliki Palli publishes a feminist essay addressed to mothers, *Discorso di una donna alle giovani maritote del suo paese.*

1851 English philosopher Harriet Taylor Mill (1808–1858) publishes "The Enfranchisement of Women," in which she proposes, "Let every occupation be open to all, without favor or discouragement to any, and employments will fall into the hands of those . . . who are found by experience to be most capable of worthily exercising them. There need be no fear that women will take out of the hands of men any occupation which men perform better than they." Mill points out that woman is educated chiefly as a companion to man: "Very agreeable to him, no doubt, but unfortunately the reverse of improving. . . . The most eminent men cease to improve, if they associate only with disciples."

May 29, 1851 At the second Women's Rights Convention, in Akron, Ohio, abolitionist and feminist Sojourner Truth (c. 1797–November 26, 1883) delivers her famous "Ain't I a Woman?" speech, in which she contrasts her experiences as a former slave with the image of fragile middle-class femininity: "Nobody helps me into carriages or over puddles, or gives me the best place—and ain't I a woman? I have ploughed and planted and gathered into barns, and no man could head me—and ain't I a woman? . . . I have borne thirteen children, and seen most of 'em sold into slavery, and when I cried out with my mother's grief, none but Jesus heard me—and ain't I a woman?"

1852 English nurse Florence Nightingale (May 12, 1820–August 13, 1910) publishes *Cassandra*, "a meditation on the spiritual and intellectual costs of women's domestic confinement," in which she says, "Women never have an half-hour in all their lives...that they can call their own, without fear of offending or of hurting someone."

1852 Argentinian-Brazilian feminist Joana Paula Manso de Noronha establishes the feminist newspaper *O jornal das senhoras*, which founds the Brazilian feminist movement.

1853 U.S. abolitionist Sarah Remond is ejected from a Boston theatre because she is black; she takes the case to court and wins.

1853 U.S. reformer Amelia Bloomer (May 27, 1818–December 30, 1894) moves to Ohio and begins publishing her temperance journal *The Lily* from a new headquarters, employing female typesetters despite strong resistance from male printers. On July 4, she makes an Independence Day address dressed in the "bloomer" costume.

Feb. 1853 U.S. reformer Paulina Wright Davis founds the feminist magazine *Una.*

Sept. 1853 Women are barred from the Whole World's Temperance Convention in New York. Rev. Antoinette Brown Blackwell, an appointed delegate, tries to speak at the meeting but is shouted down after trying for an hour and a half to make herself heard.

1854 Elizabeth Cady Stanton founds the New York Suffrage Society and becomes the first woman to speak in the New York State Senate.

1854 Swedish novelist Fredrika Bremer appeals to women to start an international peace movement.

May 1, 1855 U.S. feminist Lucy Stone (August 13, 1818–October 18, 1893) marries, taking her husband's name at first but soon reverting to her birth name. Eventually, her gesture will become so famous that women who do not change their names at marriage will be known as "Lucy Stoners." Banks and hotels often refuse to accept her decision, forcing her to sign as "Lucy Stone, wife of Henry Blackwell," to which her husband responds by signing, "Henry Blackwell, husband of Lucy Stone." The government, however, makes no objection to her paying her taxes as Lucy Stone.

Business and Industry

1851 Half of England's women work for a living. About 385,000 women are employed in the textile industry. Another 388,302 over the age of twenty sew for a living, mostly in their homes, doing piecework in isolation.

1852 Near Manchester and Salford, England, 76% of fourteen-year-old girls work in factories.

Oct. 31, 1854 The 128 women who work for the U.S. Post Office are the only female employees officially earning equal pay for equal work in the United States.

Dec. 10, 1854 U.S. businesswoman Rebecca Lukens (b. January 6, 1794) dies. When her husband died in 1825, she took over his iron mill, which was behind schedule on a military contract for the first American metal-hulled ship. She completed the contract, paid off her husband's debts, and expanded into boiler plates for railroads and steamboats, amassing an estate of $100,000. In 1974 her firm, Lukens Steel Company, will gross $283 million.

1855 There are about 2,000 prostitutes in New York City; 40% were previously seamstresses or domestics, but turned to prostitution because other work paid so poorly.

Science and Medicine

"Female physician" at this time in New York is considered a euphemism for "abortionist."

Sept. 1851 Hannah Longshore, a student at the Female Medical College of Pennsylvania, becomes the college's first female faculty member. She later becomes the first woman doctor in Pennsylvania.

1852 A Chinese medical journal advises the pregnant woman to avoid pepper and garlic, dress warmly, and keep calm. "She should eat chicken, pigeon, and duck broth in preference to anything else. She should not frequent gossips who by their presence may disturb her repose."

1853 Queen Victoria delivers her seventh child, Prince Leopold, under chloroform, thus making her the first monarch to be anesthetized and greatly popularizing the use of painkillers during labor. Many doctors resist the practice, believing that pain is woman's rightful inheritance from Eve. Victoria disagrees and describes the chloroform as "soothing, quieting and delightful beyond measure."

1854 During the Crimean war, English nurse Florence Nightingale reads an account of the conditions at Scutari in the Crimea and collects thirty-eight nurses and £30,000 to improve medical treatment in the war zone. Doctors resent her presence and obstruct her until

November 7, 1854, when they are flooded with casualties from the Battle of Inkermann. Nightingale nurses, improves sanitation, and walks the Scutari hospital corridors at night, becoming known as "the Lady with the Lamp." She reduces the death rate from 42% to 2.2% and improves the reputation of nurses, who are generally perceived incompetent, drunken, and immoral.

Education and Scholarship

1851 Comtesse Marie D'Agoult publishes her much-lauded *Histoire de la Révolution de 1848*.

1852 The first building of Rockford Female Seminary (later Rockford College), founded by U.S. educator Anna Sill, is constructed in Illinois. Sill, like many educators of the day, is firmly in favor of women's higher education but disapproves of women who enter public life.

Aug. 3, 1853 U.S. feminist Susan B. Anthony (b. February 15, 1820) becomes the first woman to speak to the New York State Teachers' Convention. Her speech asks why teachers get so little respect and answers, "So long as society says that woman has not brains enough to be a doctor, lawyer, or minister, but has plenty to be a teacher, every man of you who condescends to teach tacitly admits . . . that he has no more brains than a woman." Afterward, many women in the audience remark audibly, "Did you ever see such a disgraceful performance?" and "I was never so ashamed of my sex."

1855–1858 Indian educational reformer Iswar Chandra Vidyasagar founds forty girls' schools in Bengal.

Religion

1851 German poet Annette Dröste-Hulshoff publishes *Geistliche Jahre*, a collection of devotional poems.

1852 Mormons make polygamy a formal part of their religion.

1852 American Anne Ayres (January 3, 1816–February 9, 1896) founds the first U.S. Episcopal sisterhood. The sisters are required to take short-term (three-year) vows against marriage.

1852 The United States now has over one hundred schools for girls run by women's religious communities.

1852-1853 German-American nun Mother Benedicta Riepp establishes the first community of Benedictine nuns in the United States; she will play a part in founding six others.

Sept. 15, 1853 U.S. author and lecturer Antoinette Brown Blackwell (b. May 20, 1825) becomes the first U.S. woman ordained in a recognized denomination when she is given charge of a Congregational church in New York.

1854 Spanish saint Joaquina de Vedruna (b. 1783) dies. A bride at sixteen, mother of eight, and an early widow, she founded the Carmelites of Charity, a nursing and teaching community in Catalonia.

Dec. 8, 1854 Pope Pius IX declares that "from the first moment of her conception . . . , by the singular grace and privilege of Almighty God, and in view of the merits of Jesus Christ, Saviour of mankind," the Virgin Mary was free of all sin. For the first time, the Immaculate Conception is a tenet of the Catholic faith.

1856–1860

General Status and Daily Life

1856 The Hindu Widow Remarriage Act allows widows in British India to remarry. It is not followed by most widows, partly because it remains unknown to them, and partly because tradition militates so strongly against remarriage.

1856 A South Carolina court rules that a woman can change her name against the wishes of her husband.

1857 Britain's Matrimonial Causes Act allows men to divorce their wives for adultery; women must prove both adultery and some other cause, such as desertion, cruelty, rape, sodomy, bestiality, or incest. Divorced, separated, and abandoned wives have some property rights.

c. 1858 Newport lighthouse keeper Ida Lewis (February 25, 1842–October 24, 1911) begins rescuing drowning sailors. She will save at least seven people and one sheep from drowning, and become a national heroine.

1860 The average U.S. woman bears five children; the average southern woman bears eight.

Government, the Military, and the Law

1857 In India, the Sepoy Rebellion against British rule involves women on both sides. Englishwoman Mrs. Beresford, wife of the manager of the Bank of Delhi,

defends her family with a spear, killing one rebel before being cut into pieces. In Cawnpore, rebels seize the bibighar (women's house) that British troops used for their concubines. The slaughter there of more than 200 British prisoners, many of them women, fuels outrage at the rebellion.

On the Indian side, warrior queen Lakshmi Bai (b. 1835), rani of Jhansi, becomes famed for her bravery. From March 20 to April 3, 1858, the British besiege Jhansi; Lakshmi Bai defends her home with both male and female troops. In the final assault, thousands are slain, but Lakshmi Bai manages to escape. She goes to Kalpi to join other Indian rebels, later helping to capture the fortress of Gwalior. On June 17, 1858, she is commanding the Indian east flank at Gwalior when she and two of her maids, Mandar and Kashi, are killed in hand-to-hand combat. Her motto was, "If killed in battle we enter the heaven and if victorious, we rule the earth."

Jan. 14, 1858 A would-be assassin hurls a bomb at the carriage of French emperor Napoleon III and Empress Eugénie. The empress, spattered with blood, says, "Don't bother about us, such things are our profession. Look after the wounded."

Nov. 1, 1858 Queen Victoria transfers rule of India from the East India Company to herself.

Literature and the Visual Arts

1856 German-Spanish novelist Fernán Caballero publishes the novels *La gaviota* and *La familia de Alvareda*. Swedish novelist Fredrika Bremer publishes a controversial feminist tale, *Hertha*.

1856 Poetry published this year includes Scottish feminist author Isa Craig's (1831–1903) *Poems by Isa* and French poet Louise Colet's *La poème de la femme*.

1857 English poet Elizabeth Barrett Browning, whose works champion such causes as child labor reform and Italian nationalism, publishes the best-selling long poem *Aurora Leigh*.

1857 Notable artworks this year include U.S. sculptor Harriet Hosmer's (October 9, 1830–February 21, 1908) famous and much-reproduced statue of *Puck* and British artist Emily Osborn's (b. 1834) painting *Nameless and Friendless*, a sympathetic portrait of the problems faced by women artists.

1858 Chinese painter and poet Ju Qing is active. Her poetry will be included in the anthology *Yichunge yincao (The Songs of Grass from a Mild Spring Chamber)*.

1858 George Eliot publishes *Scenes of Clerical Life*, an expanded version of her 1857 story "The Sad Fortunes of the Reverend Amos Barton."

1859 French author Marceline Desbordes-Valmore (b. 1786) dies. A writer of sentimental romantic poems, she was also an actress for twenty years.

1859 American E.D.E.N. Southworth publishes her most popular novel, *The Hidden Hand*, in which the heroine, Capitola, is subjected to almost every indignity known to women at the time. However, Capitola, a courageous woman, manages to save herself from her plight without waiting passively for a male rescuer. Other novels published this year include George Eliot's *Adam Bede* and George Sand's *Elle et lui*, *Jean de la Roche*, and *L'Homme de Neige*.

1859 The first Russian magazine for women begins publication.

1860 Emily Osborn's (b. 1834) *The Governess* wins great acclaim at the Royal Academy show.

1860 George Eliot publishes *The Mill on the Floss*, whose heroine refuses to allow her independent spirit to be bowed by society.

1860 U.S. author Ann Sophia Stevens publishes the dime novel *Maleska: The Indian Wife of the White Hunter*, which sells 300,000 copies.

June 9, 1860 U.S. poet Elizabeth Akers Allen (October 9, 1832–August 7, 1911), a skillful writer of light, sentimental verse, publishes her only well-known work, "Rock Me to Sleep," which begins with the famous couplet, "Backward, turn backward, O Time, in your flight, / Make me a child again, just for to-night!"

Performing Arts and Entertainment

1858 Italian ballerina Marie Taglioni becomes the principal dance teacher of the Paris Opéra; Danish ballerina Lucile Grahn becomes ballet mistress at Leipzig.

Nov. 24, 1859 Italian soprano Adelina Patti makes her operatic debut as *Lucia di Lammermoor* in New York.

Athletics and Exploration

1858 Austrian traveler Ida Pfeiffer, who logged hundreds of thousands of miles in search of specimens for museums, dies. She was an honorary member of the Geographical Society of Berlin and the recipient of a gold medal from the king of Prussia.

1860 Sixteen women make a pilgrimage up Mt. Fuji, even though the mountain is supposedly forbidden to women.

1860 English reformer and traveler Jane Franklin receives the Royal Geographical Society's Founder's Medal.

Activism

1856 English feminist Barbara Bodichon publishes *Women and Work*, in which she argues, "Love is not the end of life. It is nothing to be sought for; it should come. If we work, love may meet us in life; if not, we have something still, beyond all price." She says, "WORK—not drudgery, but WORK—is the great beautifier. Activity of brain, heart, and limb, gives health and beauty, and makes women fit to be the mothers of children."

1858 U.S. feminist Lucy Stone, like all U.S. women unable to vote, refuses to pay taxes on the grounds that the government is not entitled to taxation without representation; her belongings are forcibly auctioned to pay the taxes, purchased by a neighbor, and returned to her.

1858 Julia Branch, a U.S. advocate of free love, submits a resolution to the annual National Woman's Rights Convention "that the slavery and degradation of woman proceeds from the institution of marriage; that by the marriage contract she loses the control of her name, her person, her property, her labor, her affections, her children and her freedom." Her views are greeted with general horror even by the most ardent suffragists.

1859 The first Russian women's club is formed.

Nov. 1859 U.S. abolitionist Sarah Remond is denied a visa by the State Department on the grounds that she is a "negress" and therefore not entitled to the rights of citizenship.

1860 U.S. author Lydia Maria Child publishes the abolitionist tract *Correspondence Between Lydia Maria Child and Governor Wise and Mrs. Mason of Virginia*, which sells more than 300,000 copies.

Business and Industry

1857 English feminist Emily Faithfull (1835–1895) establishes a printing house in Edinburgh. The press will issue the *English Woman's Journal* and the *Victoria Magazine*. She uses female compositors and allows men to do the actual printing.

1859 French inventor Madame Lefebre patents the first

process for turning nitrogen gas into nitrates for fertilizer.

1859 England has 400,000 "maids of all work," composing half of all female domestic servants. Such maids do a variety of tasks and are not as well trained or paid as ladies's maids. Maids of all work are generally paid five or six pounds a year at first, with their earnings rising to a maximum yearly salary of about ten pounds.

1859 The manager of an English pottery works that employs women describes their duties: "They turn the wheel, serve the molder with clay, put the patterns on dishes, polish the gilding, and do the inferior painting: but they *haven't skill* of hand or mind *for the higher artistic work*. Some few have, but we daren't employ them, the *men wouldn't stand it*." The male employees, but not the female ones, are allowed to use arm rests for the tiring work.

1859 British feminists Jessie Boucherett, Barbara Bodichon, and Adelaide Anne Proctor establish the Society for Promoting the Employment of Women, which offers women training, loans, and job referrals for clerical work.

1860 About 5,000 female slaves in the United States have been hired out to work in textile mills, sugar refineries, tobacco plants, and other factories.

1860 Female shoemakers in Lynn, Massachusetts, make one dollar per week for days as long as sixteen hours. Male shoemakers earn three dollars per week for the same work.

Science and Medicine

Sept. 21, 1856 Queen Victoria receives Florence Nightingale, of whom she once wrote: "I envy her being able to do so much good & look after the noble brave heroes" of the Crimean War. Nightingale, successful in her attempts to reduce death rates in the Crimea, has returned to England to popular acclaim and a gift of £44,000, which she uses to endow a school of nursing.

May 1, 1857 Elizabeth Blackwell, Emily Blackwell (October 8, 1826–September 7, 1910), and Marie Zakrzewska (September 6, 1829–May 12, 1902) establish the New York Infirmary for Indigent Women and Children, the first U.S. hospital staffed by female physicians. Elizabeth is famous as America's first woman doctor, but Emily will largely run the Infirmary for the next forty years.

1859 An estimated 300 women have earned medical degrees in the United States.

1859 On a trip to England, Elizabeth Blackwell meets Elizabeth Garrett Anderson, who is destined to become England's first licensed woman doctor. Inspired by Blackwell, Anderson informs her parents that she wishes to study medicine. Her parents, unimpressed, refer to her plan as "disgusting" and "a disgrace."

1859 U.S. science educator and writer Almira Phelps becomes the second female member of the American Association for the Advancement of Science.

Education and Scholarship

Strong-minded, once a term of praise for men, comes into wide use as an insult for assertive or intelligent women.

1856 U.S. literary critic Delia Salter Bacon (February 2, 1811–September 2, 1859) becomes the first person to propose that Francis Bacon wrote the plays attributed to Shakespeare. Her theory, which she will elucidate in 1857 in a book, *The Philosophy of the Plays of Shakespeare Unfolded*, is widely ridiculed.

1858 English feminist and educator Dorothea Beale (1831–1906), founder of St. Hilda's Hall, Oxford, becomes principal of Cheltenham Ladies' College, which she guides to fame and success.

1859 Italy's Casati Law authorizes the training of women as public school teachers.

1860 U.S. educator Elizabeth Peabody opens the first official kindergarten in the United States.

Religion

1856 French saint Emily de Vialar (b. 1797) dies. She founded charitable houses in Algeria, Jerusalem, Australia, and Gaillac, France.

Oct. 1856 Driven to desperation by the British, the Xhosa of South Africa follow the prophecy of Nongquause, the teenage niece of the country's chief diviner. She dreams that the Europeans will disappear if the tribe destroys all its goods, grain, and cattle by February 18, 1857. The tribe complies, and 25,000 die in the subsequent famine.

Feb. 11, 1858 Fourteen-year-old French peasant Bernadette Soubirous (1844–1879) begins seeing visions of the Virgin Mary in a cave near Lourdes. The Virgin orders Bernadette to build a chapel, at which miracles are reported, leading to much notoriety for Soubirous.

1859 English Salvation Army cofounder Catherine Booth (1829–1890) publishes *Female Ministry*, a defense of women's right to preach.

1860 U.S. minister Olympia Brown (January 5, 1835–October 23, 1926) becomes the first woman to study theology formally with men.

1861–1865

General Status and Daily Life

In the United States, canned goods are more common. Gas stoves begin to replace coal stoves as the principal cooking devices.

1861 Isabella Beeton (1837–1865) publishes *Beeton's Book of Household Management*, the Victorian middle-class housewife's Bible, in which she explains that the woman of the house must care for and teach the children, supervise the servants, sew the clothes, nurse the sick, dabble in fine needlework, make and receive visits after lunch, and devote any spare time to "the pleasures of literature, the innocent delights of the garden, and . . . music, painting, and other elegant arts." She must not discuss "small disappointments, petty annoyances," or "her husband's failings."

1861 Britain's Parliament makes it punishable by life in jail to seek or perform an abortion.

July 8, 1862 U.S. law bans polygamy.

1864 Britain's Contagious Diseases Acts attempt to control prostitution in eighteen towns frequented by soldiers and sailors. Any suspected woman can be detained and medically examined for sexually transmitted diseases. Unless she can demonstrate her virtue, she is registered as a prostitute and forced to submit to periodic examination and possible detention.

Government, the Military, and the Law

In China's Taiping era (1851–1864), women sometimes serve in the army or replace eunuchs in running imperial palaces.

During the American Civil War, Bridget Drivers (known as "the Irish Biddy") follows her husband's First Michigan Cavalry, serving as chaplain, nurse, soldier, scout, raider, and quartermaster. Two horses are killed under her, and twice she rallies fleeing troops. Mary Dennis and Anne Lillybridge also serve in the Union

army, and Anna Carroll serves Lincoln as a propagandist.

A leading Confederate spy is Rose O'Neal Greenhow (c. 1815–October 1, 1864), the widowed aunt of Stephen Douglas. Union general George McClellan says, "She knows my plans better than Lincoln or the Cabinet and has four times compelled me to drop them." Greenhow is arrested and finally released on the condition that she not come back to the North during the war; she goes to Europe as a Confederate diplomat and drowns on the return voyage.

1861 Emperor Wenzong (Hs'en Feng) of China dies, one day after naming as his heir the son of one of his concubines, Tz'u-Hsi (Cixi, b. Yehe Nala in 1835). Decisions of the board of regency must be approved by Tz'u-Hsi and Wenzong's senior wife, Tz'uan (d. 1881), who are both granted the title of dowager empress. Two months later, the regents are deposed, and the two Dowager Empresses become the rulers of China, crushing rebellions, beginning Westernization, and reforming the bureaucracy and the military. By 1865, Tz'u-Hsi will have accumulated enough power to oust her nearest male rival, Prince Gong. She plays conservatives and progressives against each other with a resulting stability and stagnation in the government.

1861 Two Muslim women, the Begum of Bhopal and the Begum of Oudh, Hazrat Mahal, rule portions of India.

July 1861 Spanish-American soldier Loreta Velasquez (1842–1897), under the name "Lt. Harry Burford," fights in the Battle of Bull Run. Later she will act as a spy and defend Fort Donelson.

1862 A woman with the last name Hodges enlists and serves in the Union army under the name Albert D. J. Cashier. She will not be revealed as a woman until a 1911 auto accident.

1862 Single taxpaying women in Sweden get the right to vote in municipal elections.

May 23, 1862 Confederate spy Belle Boyd (May 9, 1844–June 11, 1900) races through Union lines at Front Royal, Virginia, to deliver information that helps General Jackson proceed quickly through the town and on to Harper's Ferry. Often captured by the Union, Boyd always manages to charm her way to freedom; she will eventually marry an English-born Union officer and become a popular actress and lecturer.

1863 Rasoherina becomes queen of Madagascar.

1863 The Dahomey women's army has about 2,500 members, all technically wives of the king, with about 1,700 active warriors. They launch surprise attacks with bows, guns, and knives, killing only when necessary.

Their goal is to capture prisoners to be used as slaves and human sacrifices.

1864 The U.S. Congress sets a maximum salary of $600 per year for female government clerks, while the top male clerical salaries are $1,200 to $1,800. By 1865, 445 women will be federal clerks.

1865 U.S. soldier Sarah Edmonds (December 1841–September 5, 1898) publishes her popular autobiography, *Nurse and Spy in the Union Army*. She served for two years, pretending to be a male soldier named Frank Thompson. She participated in the Battle of Blackburn's Ford, the first Battle of Bull Run, and the first peninsular campaign of 1862, occasionally doing some spying behind Confederate lines (on at least one occasion, "disguised" as a woman).

Apr. 2, 1865 Union sympathizer and spy Elizabeth Van Lew (1818–1900) raises over her Richmond, Virginia, home the first U.S. flag flown in that city since 1861. During the war, Van Lew supplied Union prisoners with food and clothing and helped them to escape. She also gathered information, placing an agent in Jefferson Davis's own home, smuggling information in the soles of her servants' shoes, and convincing her friends and neighbors that she was insane so as to lull their suspicions.

Literature and the Visual Arts

1861 English poet Elizabeth Barrett Browning dies. She read Greek at eight, published her first work at twelve, and was considered for poet laureate.

1861 Japanese painter, calligrapher, poet, and *bunjin* (scholar of Chinese culture) Ema Saiko dies. She was one of the first famous female *bunjin*. Half of her paintings were of bamboo, and her second favorite subject was the chrysanthemum.

1861 Novels published this year include Mrs. Henry Wood's sensational best-seller *East Lynne* and English author George Eliot's *Silas Marner*, the story of a miser who is redeemed by the love of an abandoned child.

1861 Chinese painter and poet Qian Juying is active.

c. 1861–1864 Japanese ukiyo-e painter Kakuju-jo is active. A print designer who reproduced scenes from kabuki plays, she was trained by another woman artist, Sadaka-me.

1862 Novels published this year include English author Mary Elizabeth Braddon's best-selling *Lady Audley's Secret* and U.S. novelist Harriet Beecher Stowe's *The Pearl of Orr's Island*, a work which inspires and influences local-color writer Sarah Orne Jewett.

1862 Julia Ward Howe (May 27, 1819–October 17, 1910) sells the rights to "The Battle Hymn of the Republic" for five dollars.

1862 English poet Christina Rossetti (1830–1894) publishes *Goblin Market and Other Poems*. Heavily influenced by the Pre-Raphaelite aesthetic, the collection is praised by many, including author Virginia Woolf.

1862 Five women art students are admitted to the Royal Academy's Antique School after a woman, Laura Herford, submits her work under her initials and is accidentally accepted.

1862 Adelaide Anne Proctor (b. 1825), as popular in her day as Tennyson, publishes the poetry collection *A Chaplet of Verse* and donates the profits to a homeless women's shelter. Her 1861 anthology, *Victoria regia*, was published by Emily Faithfull's Victoria Press.

1863 Spanish poet Rosalía de Castro publishes the poem collection *Cantares gallegos*.

1863 George Eliot publishes *Romola*, whose main character is reportedly based on the forceful English feminist Barbara Bodichon. Other new English novels include Elizabeth Gaskell's *Sylvia's Lovers* and Ouida's *Held in Bondage*; French novels include Maria Deraismes's *Le théâtre chez soi* and George Sand's anticlerical *Mademoiselle La Quintinie*.

June 1863 Royal Academy art examinations, once open to women, are now closed to them. Women immediately begin petitioning for restoration of their right to compete.

1864 Notable U.S. sculptures include Anne Whitney's *Lady Godiva* and a bust of Lincoln by Vinnie Ream (Sept. 25, 1847-Nov. 20, 1914), completed shortly before his assassination. During her career, Ream will also sculpt Thaddeus Stevens, General Custer, and Horace Greeley.

1864 U.S. novelist Elizabeth Stuart Phelps publishes *The Gates Ajar*, a fictionalized theological argument about the nature of heaven; it becomes a best-seller in the United States and Britain and makes her famous and financially independent.

1865 Elizabeth Gaskell dies, leaving her last novel, *Wives and Daughters*, unfinished.

1865 U.S. author Mary Mapes Dodge publishes the children's book *Hans Brinker, or the Silver Skates*, which will go through over one hundred editions by 1905.

1865 Anne Whitney (September 2, 1821–January 23, 1915) sculpts the abolitionist statue *Africa*. Her other subjects during her career will include Wellesley president Alice Freeman Palmer, abolitionist William Lloyd Garrison, feminist Lucy Stone, authors Harriet Beecher Stowe and Harriet Martineau (1802–1876), and temperance activist Frances Willard.

Performing Arts and Entertainment

1861 U.S. actress and poet Adah Isaacs Menken stars, apparently nude but actually wearing a flesh-colored body stocking, in the popular *Mazeppa*.

1862 French actress Sarah Bernhardt makes her Comédie Française debut as Iphigénie.

1863 Venezuelan pianist Teresa Carreño (December 22, 1853–June 12, 1917) plays at the Lincoln White House.

1863 Violinist Camilla Urso (June 13, 1842–January 20, 1902) plays with the New York Philharmonic.

Oct. 8, 1863 U.S. actress and theater manager Matilda Vining Wood takes over New York's Olympic Theatre, previously owned by English actress Laura Keene. In 1865, Keene stars in the play Lincoln is watching when he is assassinated.

Athletics and Exploration

1862 English mountaineer Lucy Walker (1836–1916), who between the ages of twenty-two and forty-four will make ninety-eight ascents with guide Melchior Anderegg, climbs Finsterarhorn. In 1864, she makes the first ascent of Balmhorn.

1865 British traveler Lady Lucie Duff-Gordon publishes *Letters from Egypt*; ill health forced her to move to a warm climate, and she settled in Luxor in 1863, becoming popular with the local people for her skill in healing.

1865 The St. Petersburg, Russia, Yacht Club holds an all-female regatta.

Activism

1861 Maria Turbnikova, Nadezhda Stasova, and Anna Filosofova establish a union of women's charities, helping women in Russia to find work, shelter, trade unions, higher wages, and higher education.

Oct. 1862 U.S. abolitionist and feminist Sojourner Truth meets Abraham Lincoln at the White House.

1863 Mary Livermore and Jane Hoge of the U.S. Sanitary Commission auction items like the original Emancipation Proclamation to raise $72,000 for the Union cause.

1863 Catherine Breshkovskaya (1844–1934), "the little grandmother of the Russian revolution," joins the revolutionary forces. Later, she opens a school for girls, works for the welfare of the serfs, and spends twenty-three years in Siberian exile, the first woman in Russia to be imprisoned for political crimes.

1864 Octavia Hill (1838–1912) begins her reforms of London tenements.

1865 The German Women's Association is formed to liberalize the Civil Code and improve women's rights in the family and in education.

July 7, 1865 U.S. boardinghouse keeper Mary Surratt is hanged for allegedly assisting the assassination of President Lincoln.

Dec. 1865 U.S. journalist Jane Swisshelm begins publishing the *Reconstructionist*, a radical Republican newspaper.

Business and Industry

Women in England make sacks and scrape the feet of sheep, horse, and cattle carcasses. Some haul clay, as much as twelve tons a day, for a wage of one shilling per day. Others work in paper mills. Some work in trousers at the mouths of mines and are known as "pit-brow girls." Women in Yorkshire wash fish and collect limpets from rocks with knives. In the herring season, they mend nets and bait lines. In London, women deliver milk, carrying forty to fifty quarts of it at a time in buckets suspended from a shoulder yoke.

Some Belgian mine workers are women.

Katharine Prescott Wormeley of Newport, Rhode Island, starts a factory to produce shirts for the Union soldiers. Employing the female relatives of soldiers, she makes fifty thousand shirts before the war's end.

A housemaid in England earns £9–£14 per year. A lady's maid earns £16–£20, but her skills are more specialized; she must remove mud from clothes, brush wool and velvet clothes, beat clothing for dust, iron, care for silk and muslin, care for her mistress's boots and shoes, dress her mistress and arrange her hair, light fires, make cosmetics, clean the boudoir, make the bed, polish the furniture, dust, sweep, and mend clothes. She must speak only when spoken to, never sit or wear a hat in the mistress's presence, and be polite at all times, regardless of her own fatigue or temper.

1861 In England and Wales, 26% of women over fifteen are employed—a total of 2,700,000. Only 279 are clerical workers. England has 419 female printers and 87,000 women working as retail clerks.

1862 English feminist printer Emily Faithfull becomes Printer and Publisher in Ordinary to the Queen. Next year she begins publishing the *Victoria Magazine*, which will run until 1870.

1863 English seamstress Mary Ann Walkley, twenty, dies of strain and suffocation after working 26.5 hours without interuption. During the social season, from March to July, seamstresses work 14 to 20 hours a day. A silk dress takes about 8 or 9 hours to make.

1864 Female glove makers in England earn 2.5 to 3 shillings for making a dozen pairs of gloves; if a glover spoils a pair, she is fined the retail price, 3 shillings, sixpence.

1864 Russian women can now enter government telegraph service, but, unlike male employees, they cannot receive pensions.

Science and Medicine

1861 Ann Preston founds a women's hospital in Pennsylvania so that students at the state's Female Medical College can obtain bedside instruction; the local male medical society has forbidden women to attend its clinics.

1861 The female ovum is discovered to be an actual generative cell, not just a sac of nutrients that nurtures the sperm.

Apr. 19, 1861 Union troops are wounded by a pro-southern mob in Baltimore; local Episcopal deaconess Adeline Tyler springs into action, treating their wounds at her Deaconess House despite the protests of local police. In September she is named superintendent of a federal military hospital, losing the post when she feeds and cares equally for southern and northern prisoners.

June 9, 1861 U.S. Civil War hospital worker Mary Ann "Mother" Bickerdyke (July 19, 1817–November 8, 1901) begins working in Union hospitals, dealing with laundry, food, and supplies, and nursing the wounded. Always impatient with bureaucracy, she replies to an army surgeon who asks her on whose authority she is acting, "On the authority of Lord God Almighty; have you anything that outranks that?" General Sherman admits, "She outranks me." This is technically the truth; she has a pass from General Grant that allows her to travel anywhere and commandeer any needed transportation.

June 10, 1861 Dorothea Dix is made superintendent of women nurses for the Union. Her recruits, who receive twelve dollars a month, must be reputable and recommended by a minister: "No woman under 30 years need apply to serve in government hospitals. All nurses are required to be very plain-looking women. Their dresses must be brown or black, with no bows, no curls, no jewelry, and no hoopskirts." Some of the most famous U.S. women of the century will work as nurses and relief workers during the Civil War, including lawyer Myra Bradwell and children's author Louisa May Alcott.

Aug. 1, 1861 Confederate hospital volunteer Sally Tompkins sets up the Robertson Hospital in Richmond, Virginia. The hospital, which closes on June 13, 1865, quickly becomes noted for its high standards and success rate; in its four years of operation, it will lose only 73 of 1,333 patients. On September 9, 1861, after a surgeon general's edict abolishing private hospitals in Richmond, Jefferson Davis makes Tompkins a cavalry captain so that she can continue her work. She is the only commissioned woman in the Confederate army.

1862 U.S. physician Mary Edwards Walker (November 26, 1832–February 21, 1919) goes to the front to treat the wounded. In September 1863, she becomes a surgeon for the Union army, wearing an officer's trousered uniform. She often works behind enemy lines and is captured on one of these missions in 1864. Released in August of that year, she will be awarded the Congressional Medal of Honor in 1865, only to have it revoked shortly before her death and reawarded posthumously.

July 1, 1862 Polish-German-American doctor Marie Zakrzewska opens the New England Hospital for Women and Children to provide women access to female physicians and to train women as doctors and nurses. In 1863, she becomes the first woman to establish a medical society.

Nov. 1862 Confederate administrator Phoebe Pember becomes matron of Chimborazo Hospital (eventually the world's largest military hospital to that date), supervising the care of some 15,200 soldiers during her tenure. The first woman administrator there, she has control of the whiskey and keeps a pistol handy to deal with resentful men.

1863 U.S. botanist Julia Snow, an expert on freshwater algae and conductive tissues in plants, is born.

Feb. 1863 U.S. nurse Emily Parsons becomes head of the 2,500-bed Benton Barracks Hospital near St. Louis, the West's largest miltary hospital.

1865 U.S. astronomer Maria Mitchell (b. August 1,

1818) becomes the first female professor at the new women's college of Vassar. She has a brand new observatory with the largest telescope (twelve inches) in the nation.

1865 After the Civil War, battlefield nurse Clara Barton begins four years of locating missing men. She manages to find out the fate of 22,000 men, as well as identifying and marking the graves of 14,000 who died in the Confederate prison camp at Andersonville, Georgia.

1865 U.S. scientist and educator Elizabeth Agassiz travels to Brazil with her husband, naturalist Louis Agassiz. On the trip, she documents the data gathered and is the only member of the team to publish any findings.

May 8, 1865 The Chicago Hospital for Women and Children (later the Mary Thompson Hospital of Chicago), the brainchild of Dr. Mary Thompson, opens with Dr. Thompson as its head of medicine and surgery.

July 1865 Distinguished British medical inspector general Dr. James Barry (b. 1795), who served as an army doctor around the world and rose rapidly through the ranks, is discovered at his death to have been a woman all along. Probably originally named Miranda Stuart, Barry served with distinction in South Africa, the West Indies, the Crimea, and Canada; she is deprived of a military funeral when her sex is revealed.

Education and Scholarship

1861 Julie Daubié becomes the first Frenchwoman to pass the baccalaureate exam, but she is denied her degree until pressure from Empress Eugénie is brought to bear.

1861 Spanish social scientist and philanthropist Concepción Arenal publishes *La beneficencia, la filantropía y la caridad*, which wins first prize from the Madrid Academy of Moral and Political Science. In 1865, she publishes *Cortas a los delincuentes*.

Sept. 1862 U.S. educator Laura Towne founds one of the first and most successful schools for freedmen.

1863 English feminist and educational reformer Emily Davies (1830–1921) gets women admitted to the Cambridge Local Examinations, a series of secondary school tests.

1865 The University of Zurich becomes the first European university to admit women. Most universities begin their experiments in coeducation by allowing women to audit classes informally. Later, women are admitted to the schools, but with unequal privileges or without the right to earn degrees. Few nineteenth-

century universities will admit women on an equal basis without such an "experiment."

Religion

1862 U.S. evangelist Phoebe Palmer becomes editor in chief of the *Guide to Holiness*, the most prominent periodical in the perfectionist movement. She quickly increases circulation by more than 100% and will remain editor until her death in 1874.

1866–1870

General Status and Daily Life

1866 In Japan, if a woman reports a pregnancy within three months of being divorced, the child is considered her ex-husband's, and he must provide child support.

1866 The Italian Civil Code bars women from filing paternity suits except in cases of rape or abduction.

1869 Britain legalizes individual ownership of property by married women.

1869 Illinois passes a law written by Myra Bradwell giving married women control over their own property.

1869 Christian men in India may divorce on the grounds of adultery, but wives must prove not only adultery but also cruelty, incest, or bigamy.

1869 U.S. physician Mary Edwards Walker gives a lecture on the subject of women's changing names upon marriage. She objects to "Mrs.," wondering why anyone needs to know a woman's marital status, and suggests, to be consistent, that married men be called "Misterer."

1870 Western women wear corsets stiffened with whalebone to achieve a fashionable seventeen or eighteen-inch waist. Corsets cause ulcers, gallstones, rib dislocation, headaches, dizziness, spinal curvature, lung disease, and a host of other ailments.

Government, the Military, and the Law

1866 A woman of obscure family is married to Korean king Kojong and becomes Queen Min. Destined to be the most powerful queen of the Yi dynasty, she is faced at first with a weak, unaffectionate husband and an influential rival, her husband's mistress, Lady Yi.

Feb. 6, 1866 Queen Victoria opens Parliament for the first time since the death of her husband, Prince Albert, in 1861.

Summer 1866 Prussian sculptor Elisabet Ney (Jan. 26, 1833-June 29, 1907) and her secret husband, Dr. Edmund Montgomery, work as spies for Garibaldi.

Aug. 1866 U.S. feminist Elizabeth Cady Stanton runs for Congress to protest the inclusion of the word *male* in the Fourteenth Amendment, a word not used in the rest of the Constitution. She receives twenty-four votes.

1868 U.S. stenographer Isabel Hayes Barrows (1845–1913) becomes the first female employee of the U.S. State Department.

1868 Ranavalona II succeeds Rasoherina as queen of Madagascar; she will rule until 1883.

1868 During the Paraguayan War of 1864–1870, 600 women make a futile stand at Piribebuy, resorting at last to throwing stones, sand, and bottles; all are killed.

Sept. 28, 1868 Rebellion and reform drive Queen Isabella II of Spain to refuge in France. She abdicates in 1870.

1869 Iowa lawyer Arabella "Belle" Mansfield (August 23, 1846–August 1, 1911) becomes the first woman admitted to the bar in the United States. Despite her high score on the bar exam, she is not admitted automatically, as Iowa law states that "any white male person" may become a lawyer. However, a liberal judge asserts that "the affirmative declaration [for men] is not a denial of the right of females." Cheifly a legal scholar, Mansfield will never practice law, and she will not be the first woman in the U.S. to earn a formal law degree. That honor will fall to Ada Kepley in 1870.

Dec. 10, 1869 Wyoming is the first U.S. state to give women the vote. Louisa Swain becomes the first Wyoming woman to vote on September 6, 1870.

1870 Congress grants equal pay and grade to female federal employees. Most are simply reclassified to avoid compliance with the new law.

Literature and the Visual Arts

1866 Japanese artist and musician Yoshida Shuran (b. 1797) dies. She specialized in painting orchids and sometimes collaborated with the *bunjin* Cho Koran.

1866 English feminist Jessie Boucherett founds *The*

Englishwoman's Review, the principal feminist magazine in England until 1910.

1866 English novelist Mary Elizabeth Braddon becomes the editor of the London magazine *Belgravia*.

1866 English novels this year include George Eliot's *Felix Holt* and Ouida's (pseudonym of Marie Louise de la Ramée, 1839–1908) *Under Two Flags*.

1866 U.S. sculptor Vinnie Ream, eighteen years old, receives a $10,000 congressional commission for a statue of Abraham Lincoln for the Capitol rotunda.

1867 U.S. journalist Mary Booth becomes the first editor of *Harper's Bazaar*.

1868 In what is probably the earliest formal opportunity for women artists to draw from the nude, the Pennsylvania Academy establishes a Ladies' Life Class. Only female models are used at first, though later male models are allowed to pose with their genitals discreetly draped.

1868 Japanese poet, musician, painter, calligrapher, and sculptor Takabatake Shikibu (1785–1881) and poet-potter Otagaki Rengetsu (b. 1791) publish the poetry collection *Rengetsu Shikibu nijo waka shu*. The two women also collaborate at times on works of art. In 1870, Otagaki publishes 300 of her *waka* verses as *Ama no karumo*.

1868–1869 U.S. children's author Louisa May Alcott (November 29, 1832–March 6, 1888) publishes *Little Women*. This sentimental novel is an immediate success, setting sales records in many parts of the country.

1869 U.S. painter Lilly Martin Spencer (b. November 26, 1822) creates her greatest work, *Truth Unveiling Falsehood*, for which she refuses an offer of $20,000.

1869 U.S. sculptor Anne Whitney creates the controversial *Roma*, a sculpture of a beggar woman.

1870 U.S. popular poet Rose Hartwick Thorpe publishes the sentimental poem "Curfew Must Not Ring Tonight."

Performing Arts and Entertainment

1866 Popular songs include Mrs. E. G. Pankhurst's "Father's a Drunkard and Mother Is Dead."

Aug. 10, 1868 U.S. actress Adah Isaacs Menken (b. June 15, 1835?) dies. A poet who advised women to "marry early and often," she was once given $2,000 in bullion by the residents of Virginia City, Nevada, in exchange for a promise to perform there again. Her admirers and friends included Charles Dickens, Dante Gabriel Rossetti, and George Sand.

1869 U.S. actress and theatre manager Matilda Vining Wood (Nov. 6, 1831-Jan. 11, 1915) begins ten years as manager of London's St. James Theatre.

1869 English actress Laura Keene begins publishing a monthly magazine, *Fine Arts*.

1869 Danish ballerina Lucile Grahn becomes ballet mistress at Munich.

1870 George Sand's play *L'Autre* is produced at the Theatre Francais, with Sarah Bernhardt.

Athletics and Exploration

In the United States, several sports, including croquet and ice skating, have become popular for both men and women, mostly because they allow social contact between the sexes.

1866 Two women's baseball clubs are formed at Vassar College.

1868 Apache and Navajo girls participate in footraces.

1868 France has several female wrestlers.

1869 Four Frenchwomen compete with men in a bicycle race from Paris to Rouen.

1869 The All-England Croquet Club, which admits both men and women, is formed.

Activism

1866 In Great Britain, 1,498 women, including reformer Josephine Butler, educator Emily Davies, and physician Elizabeth Garrett Anderson, establish a committee to legalize women's suffrage. Through John Stuart Mill, it presents Britain's first women's suffrage petition to Parliament.

1866, 1869 The second and third Contagious Diseases Acts are passed. The laws allow any woman suspected of prostitution in certain towns to be detained and inspected for disease. Women found to be infected can be kept against their will for treatment in so-called lock hospitals. Josephine Butler (1828–1906) leads the fight against the Contagious Diseases Acts, publishing powerful articles detailing the horrors awaiting those detained. On March 14, 1870, 251 women protest the Contagious Diseases Acts in print, including Butler,

Harriet Martineau, and Florence Nightingale. The acts will be repealed in 1886.

1866 Civil War doctor Mary Edwards Walker becomes president of the National Dress Reform Association. Later, she will adopt full male dress, complete with top hat and bow tie, and she will be abandoned as an eccentric by even the most radical proponents of dress reform.

1866 France's first Society for Women's Rights, the Société pour la Revendication des Droits de la Femme, is established by moderate feminist and author Maria Deraismes (1828–1894), who also founds the Association pour le Droit des Femmes in 1870.

May 10, 1866 The National Women's Rights Convention establishes the American Equal Rights Association to fight for the rights of both blacks and women.

1867 At the Constitutional Convention in Albany, New York, newspaper editor Horace Greeley presents a report against women's suffrage, while Elizabeth Cady Stanton presents a petition for it. Stanton speaks immediately before Greeley, and the first signatory whose name she reads is "Mrs. Horace Greeley." The audience and reporters revel in his embarrassment, and Greeley retaliates by afterward printing Stanton's name as "Mrs. Henry Stanton," which she loathes.

Jan. 1867 Susan B. Anthony and Elizabeth Cady Stanton accept support from George Francis Train, a racist who is willing to provide support for women's suffrage in Kansas at the expense of blacks. Abolitionists desert the cause in indignation. Even Lucretia Mott, a peacekeeper within the suffrage movement, is angry.

1868 When female reporters are banned from a New York Press Club luncheon for Charles Dickens, they form their own group, Sorosis, in protest; Alice Cary becomes the first president. Fashion journalist Jane Croly (December 19, 1829–December 23, 1901, pseudonym "Jennie June"), who opposes long skirts, hoops, and crinolines, becomes the second president in 1870. The women's club movement will be a major force in women's lives for the rest of the century and much of the next. Some of the clubs formed will concern themselves with literature and culture, others with feminism and reform, and still others with charitable works.

1868 Italian feminist Gualberta Beccari, eighteen, founds the journal *Donna* and starts a national interest in women's issues.

1868 Amdang Munan, a Thai woman who refuses to marry the husband of her parents' choice, convinces the king to decree that women may select their own husbands.

1868 Black and white women in Vineland, New Jersey, attempt to vote with the men and then, when that fails, hold a mimicking "mock vote" in protest.

1868 English feminist and reformer Maria Rye opens a home in London for poor children.

Jan. 1, 1868 In New York City, Susan B. Anthony begins publishing *The Revolution*, a weekly suffragist paper. The first issue deals with everything from suffrage to calming a crying baby. Ultimately the paper, edited by Anthony for its first two years, will discuss divorce, church attitudes toward women, unions, and equal pay. Its motto is, "Men their rights and nothing more; women their rights and nothing less."

Mar. 14, 1868 Eliza Lynn Linton (1882–1898), England's first salaried woman journalist and an opponent of women's rights who refers to feminists as the "Shrieking Sisterhood," attacks women's emancipation in the essay "The Girl of the Period."

1869 New Zealand writer Mary Muller, who had to work in secret lest her disapproving husband discover her activities, publishes the women's rights tract *An Appeal to the Men of New Zealand*.

1869 At Cuba's Revolutionary Assembly, feminist Ana Betancourt pleads unsuccessfully for equal rights for women, based on women's participation in the Cuban war of independence.

May 1869 Susan B. Anthony and Elizabeth Cady Stanton feel betrayed by the American Equal Rights Association, which is willing to work for black suffrage first at the expense of women's suffrage. They establish the National Woman Suffrage Association (NWSA), with Stanton as its president.

This summer, Lucretia Mott visits Anthony and Stanton and the more conservative suffragist Lucy Stone, vainly trying to heal the breach that has occurred between them. In November, Stone, Julia Ward Howe, and other conservative feminists establish the American Woman Suffrage Association (AWSA). Their organization, unlike NWSA, allows male members and adopts a state-by-state strategy rather than a national campaign. It is a predominantly middle-class group, while NWSA has many working women and comparative radicals in its ranks. Many suffragists, unable to choose between the two organizations, belong to both.

1870 U.S. sisters Victoria Woodhull (September 28, 1839–June 10, 1927) and Tennessee Claflin (October 26, 1845–January 18, 1923) start a newspaper, *Woodhull & Claflin's Weekly*, which for six years will support such

causes as dress reform, free love, legalized prostitution, and dietary reform. The *Weekly* will also publish the first U.S. English translation of Marx's *Communist Manifesto*.

1870 Mexican educator and poet Rita Cetina Gutiérrez founds La Siempreviva, a feminist group that publishes its own newspaper.

Business and Industry

Women work as brickworkers in England, each making about 2,000 bricks a day.

1867 Baltimore ex-slave Mary Prout founds the Grand United Order of St. Luke to provide medical and burial insurance for blacks.

1867 The Cigar Makers' International Union becomes the first national male union in the United States to admit women.

Sept. 16, 1867 In Helena, Montana, Asian businesswoman "Chinese Mary" is burned to death by whites for her gold.

1868 The National Labor Union is the first in the United States to support equal pay for women. The union is praised for this by Susan B. Anthony in *The Revolution*, but the union criticizes her as a strikebreaker and treats her efforts at cooperation coolly.

1868 Many women get the opportunity to train as hairdressers when male hairdressers go on strike.

1868 Victoria Woodhull and Tennessee Claflin, both of whom spent their childhood in a traveling medicine and fortune-telling show, convince Cornelius Vanderbilt that they can put him in spiritual contact with his late wife. In exchange, he backs them financially, and they become the first female stockbrokers in the United States.

1869 English crusader against prostitution Josephine Butler reports that of 9,000 prostitutes in one of England's ports, 1,500 are under fifteen, and 500 of these are under thirteen.

c. 1870 Some fashionable English prostitutes solicit customers (discreetly and sedately) at dancing rooms, the Argyll Rooms and the Holborn in particular. Prostitutes in army towns rent lodgings for about three shillings, sixpence a week. They make about one shilling per customer.

1870 Augusta Lewis (1848–1920), founder and first president of the Women's Typographical Union No. 1 in 1868, becomes the first woman national officer of the

International Typographical Union when she is elected corresponding secretary.

1870 In the United States, 9.7% of women are in the work force, constituting 14.8% of the total labor force. Married women are 15% of the total female work force; 88% of female workers are concentrated in ten types of work: domestic service, agricultural labor, sewing, millinery and dressmaking, teaching, cotton cloth production, laundering, wool cloth production, farming, and nursing.

Science and Medicine

Most women's ailments are attributed to uterine trouble, including exhaustion, weeping, lack of appetite, and insomnia. Treatments include bleeding the vulva with leeches and cauterizing the uterus. British gynecologist Isaac Baker Brown recommends clitoridectomy for curing antisocial behavior, hysteria, monomania, and menstrual irregularity, going so far as to suggest it in cases of marital separation, to encourage the wife to return to her husband. Many British doctors perform the procedure, which involves the partial or total removal of the clitoris, but Brown is so extreme that he discredits the operation quite effectively.

1866 The panic of a cholera epidemic allows Elizabeth Garrett Anderson (1836–December 17, 1917) to begin practicing medicine successfully in England, even though she has not been able to enter a British medical school. She establishes St. Mary's Dispensary for Women and Children, which will later be renamed in her honor. She will get her M.D. from the University of Paris in 1870.

1866 U.S. physician Ann Preston (1813–1872), an opponent of bloodletting, an advocate of medical ethics classes for physicians, and an expert on psychosomatic illness, becomes the first woman dean of a medical college with her appointment to that post at the Female Medical College of Pennsylvania.

Feb. 21, 1866 Lucy Hobbs (March 13, 1833–October 3, 1910), the first U.S. woman dentist, graduates at the top of her class from Ohio Dental College.

1868 Women are admitted to medical degree programs in France.

1868 Emily Stowe (1831–1903) becomes Canada's first woman doctor.

1868 Elizabeth Blackwell opens a women's medical college at her New York Infirmary for Women and Children. Her sister Emily becomes the college's dean and professor of obstetrics and diseases of women.

1869 Scottish mathematician Mary Somerville (b. December 26, 1780) publishes *Molecular and Microscopic Science*, a summary of the latest chemical and physical research; in the same year, she receives a gold medal from the Royal Geographical Society.

1869 Despite the predominance of men in the medical profession, about 70% of births in England are still attended by female practitioners only.

1869 After obtaining her degree in the United States, Henriette Pagelson returns to become the first woman dentist in Germany.

Oct. 1869 English medical students Sophia Jex-Blake (1840-1910), Edith Pechey-Phipson, and three other women enter the University of Edinburgh, only to be harassed by the male students. Pechey-Phipson wins the Chemistry Prize and the Hope Scholarship but is not awarded them because of her sex. The tension eventually leads to a riot.

Mar. 1870 U.S. medical missionary Clara Swain (July 18, 1834–December 25, 1910) begins training women in medicine in Bareilly, India.

May 6, 1870 Queen Victoria tells Prime Minister William Gladstone not to let women become doctors, saying, "What an *awful* idea this is—of allowing *young girls* & young men to enter the dissecting room together."

Education and Scholarship

1866 Comtesse Marie d'Agoult publishes the critical essay *Dante et Goethe*.

1867 American Lucy McKim Garrison (October 30, 1842–May 11, 1877) publishes one of the most important folk song collections of the nineteenth century, *Slave Songs of the United States*.

1867 English feminist Emily Davies establishes the forerunner of Girton College, Cambridge, with five pupils.

1867 Russian women petition unsuccessfully for permission to enter universities.

1868 About 10% of Japanese girls (as opposed to 40% of boys) are attending schools.

1868 English antifeminist Sarah Sewell publishes *Women and the Times We Live In*, arguing against women's higher education. Girls, she says, need learn only "history, geography, figures, the poets, and general literature, with a sure groundwork of religion and obedience. The profoundly educated women rarely make good wives or mothers. . . . and those women, poor things, who have lost their most attractive charm of womanliness, and are seen on the public platforms, usurping the exclusive duties of men, are seldom seen in their nurseries."

1870   U.S. chemist and home economist Ellen Swallow Richards (December 3, 1842–March 30, 1911) is the first woman accepted at the Massachusetts Institute of Technology (M. I. T.). She is given the status of "special student" with no fees, so that she can be disowned by the president if anyone makes a fuss.

1870 India's first institution to train women as teachers opens.

1870   There are 5,553 women working in higher education faculties in the United States; women are 12% of all higher education teachers.

1870   English doctor Elizabeth Garrett Anderson runs successfully for the London School Board, a rare feat for a woman at the time.

June 12, 1870 U.S. philanthropist Sophia Smith (b. Aug. 27, 1796) dies, leaving nearly $400,000 for the founding of Smith College.

Religion

Feb. 4, 1866 U.S. religious leader Mary Baker Eddy (July 16, 1821–1910) heals herself after a fall. Soon she is charging $300 a person for her healing classes. Many women sign up for her lectures and become Christian Science practitioners.

1867 Japanese nun and poet Nomura Boto (b. 1806) dies.

1868 French saint Euphrasia Pelletier (b. 1796) dies. A nun, she established the Institute of the Good Shepherd in 1835, directed it for thirty-three years, and helped it expand to include 110 convents by her death.

Mar. 6, 1869 Margaret Van Cott becomes the first licensed woman Methodist Episcopal preacher in the United States.

1871–1875

General Status and Daily Life

1871 Massachusetts and Alabama become the first

U.S. states to outlaw wife-beating.

1871   The average English wife has six children; almost 20% of wives have ten or more.

1874 Civil marriage becomes mandatory in Germany.

1875 Britain's Parliament raises the age of consent for girls from twelve to thirteen.

Government, the Military, and the Law

1871   In the wake of the Great Chicago Fire, lawyer Myra Bradwell gets a law passed to protect real estate titles lost in the blaze. She loses her home and law library in the fire, but manages to print the next issue of her weekly *Chicago Legal News* on time, thanks to her thirteen-year-old daughter Bessie (later her mother's successor as editor), who saves the subscription list.

1871 Women fight for the Paris Commune, thousands of them dying at the barricades and more than a thousand living to be arraigned after the commune's fall.

Mar. 1872   Charlotte E. Ray (January 13, 1850–January 4, 1911) becomes the first black woman lawyer in the United States and the first woman admitted to the District of Columbia bar.

May 10, 1872 U.S. reformer, feminist, stockbroker, and publisher Victoria Woodhull is nominated for president by the Equal Rights party; her running mate is Frederick Douglass, who is not interested in the position and supports Grant instead.

Woodhull spends election day in jail for publishing an account of the affair between minister Henry Ward Beecher (brother of novelist Harriet Beecher Stowe and educator Catharine Beecher) and one of his parishioners, Elizabeth Tilton. Woodhull was sent to jail under the Comstock law regarding the mailing of obscene materials; she will eventually be acquitted.

Dec. 1872   The U.S. Supreme Court rules that the state of Illinois can bar Myra Bradwell from the practice of law on the grounds that she is a married woman; Justice Bradley says, "The paramount destiny and mission of woman are to fulfill the noble and benign office of wife and mother."

1873   Chinese dowager empress Tz'u-Hsi's regency ends, but she still continues to rule for her son. He later dies of smallpox, and she overrides tradition by choosing his three-year-old cousin as his heir.

Nov. 1873 Korean queen Min drives her husband's influential father out of the capital by judicious manipulation of his enemies, leaving her in sole control of her weak husband, King Kojong.

Feb. 12, 1874 Hawaiian queen Emma (January 2, 1836–April 25, 1885), widow of King Kamehameha IV, makes an unsuccessful bid for the throne.

Literature and the Visual Arts

1871 New novels include Louisa May Alcott's *Little Men*, a sequel to her immensely popular children's book *Little Women*; and George Eliot's *Middlemarch*, generally considered one of her finest works.

1873 Cuban author Gertrudis Gómez de Avellaneda (b. 1814), known as "La Avellaneda," dies. She was best known for her abolitionist novel *El Mulato Sab*.

1873 French poet Louise Colet (1810–1876) publishes *Les dévotés du grande monde*.

1873 U.S. sculptor Edmondia Lewis, whose work often depicts the struggles of blacks, Native Americans, and women, exhibits her work in San Francisco.

1874 Japanese artist Okuhara Seiko (b. 1837) coestablishes an art society, Hankansha.

1874 French painter Berthe Morisot (1841–1894), who has shown at the official salons since 1864, joins the first Impressionist exhibition and vows never to exhibit through formal channels again.

1874 British military painter Lady Elizabeth Butler (1850–1933) shows *Calling of the Roll After an Engagement, Crimea* at the Royal Academy. It is so popular that it has to be guarded from crowds by the police, and it is quickly obtained from its original purchaser by Queen Victoria.

1875 Japanese *waka* poet, calligrapher, painter, and potter Otagaki Rengetsu dies. Her poems, well received commercially as well as artistically, were often inscribed on her pottery. Otagaki was also a Buddhist nun and a student of swordfighting and *jujutsu*.

1875 Lady Elizabeth Butler paints *Quatre Bras*. To ensure the authenticity of this military scene, she purchases a field of rye and tramples it, has herself charged on horseback, recreates Crimean uniforms, fires cannons, and enlists the aid of 300 British soldiers. Art critic John Ruskin calls it "amazon's work . . . the first fine Pre-Raphaelite picture of battle we have had."

1875 English poet and essayist Alice Meynell (1847–1922), sister of painter Elizabeth Butler, publishes a much-praised volume of poems, *Preludes*. She will later be considered, but not chosen, for the post of poet laureate.

1875 U.S. sculptor Anne Whitney wins a commission for a memorial to Boston's Charles Sumner, only to have the job taken away from her when it is discovered that she is a woman.

Performing Arts and Entertainment

1872 French actress Sarah Bernhardt (October 23, 1844–March 26, 1923), most famous for her roles in *Phèdre* and *La dame aux caméllias*, stars in *Ruy Blas* at the Comédie Française; in Verona, fourteen-year-old Italian tragedian Eleonora Duse, soon to be Bernhardt's greatest rival, makes her stage debut as Juliet.

1875 French actress Pauline Virginie Déjazet (b. 1798), who made a name for herself in the 1820s playing male roles, dies.

Athletics and Exploration

English traveler Amelia Edwards (b. 1831) travels in Egypt for three months, expressing contempt for careless tourists while herself participating in illegal antiquities purchases. She publishes an account of her adventures, *A Thousand Miles up the Nile*, and becomes determined to halt the depredation of Egypt by treasure hunters.

1871 French mountaineer Henriette d'Angeville (b. 1795) dies. She made twenty-one ascents in twenty-five years and, at the age of sixty-nine, climbed Oldenhorn in the Alps wearing a hoopskirt. In 1838, she became the first woman to organize an ascent of Mont Blanc.

July 20, 1871 English mountaineer Lucy Walker becomes the first woman to climb the Matterhorn.

1872 The Ladies' Golf Club is founded at St. Andrews.

1872 British boxer Lydia Harris flees to France after injuring an opponent in a match.

1873 English traveler Isabella Bird Bishop (1831–1904) climbs Long's Peak in the Rocky Mountains.

1874 American Mary Outerbridge introduces tennis to the United States after watching a game played by English officers in Bermuda.

1875 Isabella Bird Bishop publishes *The Hawaiian Archipelago*.

1875 U.S. adventurer Martha "Calamity Jane" Cannary (b. May 1, 1852) joins General George Crook's expedition against the Sioux. When she is discovered to be a woman, she is expelled from the group and sent home.

Activism

1871 Italian revolutionary Cristina Trivulzio (b. 1808), who participated in the rebellions of 1831 and 1848, dies.

1871 The Danish Women's Society is formed to work for women's educational and economic rights.

1871 French socialist feminist Paule Mink (1839–1900) supports the Paris Commune.

1871 Danish feminist Mathilde Bajer (1840–1934) founds a feminist library and discussion group. In 1872, she cofounds a women's trade school.

1871 Abigail Scott Duniway (October 22, 1834–October 11, 1915), U.S. milliner, schoolteacher, and feminist, establishes a woman's newspaper called the *New Northwest*, in Portland, Oregon.

Jan. 11, 1871 U.S. feminist Victoria Woodhull presents a petition for women's suffrage to the House Judiciary Committee, becoming the first woman to address the committee directly. Later in the year she alienates Susan B. Anthony with a speech at the national NWSA convention that declares, "We mean treason; we mean secession . . . . We are plotting revolution; we will [overthrow] this bogus Republic and plant a government of righteousness in its stead."

May 1871 French socialist and revolutionary Louise Michel (May 29, 1830–1905), a devoted supporter of the Paris Commune, is one of the last defenders of the Montmartre cemetery to surrender. In December, she will be tried and sentenced to life imprisonment in New Caledonia, remaining there until an amnesty in 1881.

Fall 1872 Sixteen women in Rochester, New York, vote, led by Susan B. Anthony. Anthony is arrested. At the trial, she is ruled incompetent to testify, and the jury is instructed by the judge to find her guilty. The judge then asks if Anthony wishes to make a statement. She replies, "Yes, your Honor, I have many things to say, for in your ordered verdict of guilt, you have trampled under foot every vital principle of our government. My natural rights, my civil rights, my political rights are all alike ignored. Robbed of the fundamental privilege of citizenship, I am degraded from the status of citizen to that of a subject, and not only myself individually but all of my sex are, by your Honor's verdict, doomed to political subjection under this so-called Republican government." She is fined one hundred dollars, which she refuses to pay; she is never jailed, for fear she will appeal.

1873 Brazil's feminist journal *O Sexo Feminino*, dedicated to women's education and the abolition of slavery, begins publication; it will run sporadically until 1889. It is edited by Dona Francisca Senhorinha da Motta Diniz.

1873 U.S. suffragists Abby Kelley Foster (1810–January 14, 1887) and Stephen Foster refuse to pay taxes on the grounds that women cannot be taxed without representation; the government sells their property to a neighbor, who eventually gives them back their land. The Fosters continue to refuse to pay taxes till 1880.

Summer 1873 Ninety-six of the 110 women at the University of Zurich are Russian. The female university student, or *kursistka*, is one of the acknowledged subtypes of Russian radicals.

1874 The U.S. Supreme Court rules that Missouri suffragist Virginia Minor (March 27, 1824–August 14, 1894) has no legal right to vote, as some citizens—felons, the insane, and women—can be prevented from voting.

1874 Irish suffragist Helen Blackburn (1842–1903) becomes secretary of the Society for Women's Suffrage, a position she will hold until 1895.

1874 U.S. feminist Abba Woolson edits *Dress-Reform*, containing five essays recommending more sensible clothing for women.

Nov. 18, 1874 In the United States, the Women's Christian Temperance Union (WCTU) is established. Annie Wittenmyer, a former Civil War relief worker, is the organization's first president, and Frances Willard (September 28, 1839–February 17, 1898) becomes corresponding secretary.

1875 Austrian feminist Marianne Hainisch publishes *Brötfrage der Frau*.

Business and Industry

Women in England begin entering clerical and sales jobs.

1871 There are 741 female printers in England.

1871 Women begin to be employed as telegraph clerks in Great Britain because "in the first place, they have in eminent degree the quickness of eye and ear, and the delicacy of touch, which are essential qualifications of a good operator. In the second place, they take more kindly than men or boys do to sedentary employment. . . . In the third place, the wages, which draw male operators from but an inferior class of the community, will draw female operators from a superior class. . . .

They are also less disposed than men to combine for the purpose of extorting higher wages."

1874 The British Women's Trade Union League (WTUL) is established.

1875 U.S. pharmaceutical entrepreneur Lydia Pinkham begins combating her family's poverty by advertising her homemade "Vegetable Compound," a mixture of herbs, roots, and 18% alcohol, as a cure-all.

1875 U.S. newspaper publisher Eliza Nicholson (March 11, 1849–February 15, 1896) inherits the New Orleans *Picayune* and $80,000 in debt from her husband. She establishes new departments, hires more women, introduces a society column and children's features, and sets up news bureaus in other cities. In her twenty years of managing the paper, she opposes organized crime and champions animal rights, temperance, and the interests of working women.

Science and Medicine

1871 French-Brazilian obstetrician Marie Durocher is elected to the National Academy of Medicine.

1872 U.S. physiologist Anne Moore, who will study the effects of electrolyte solutions on muscle tissue, is born.

1872 Due to a desperate need for doctors, Russia's medical schools begin admitting women.

1872 U.S. physician Mary Putnam Jacobi (b. August 31, 1842) establishes the Association for Advancement of the Medical Education of Women.

Jan. 8, 1872 British medical student Sophia Jex-Blake, after long harassment at the University of Edinburgh, is refused her degree, even though she has completed the program. Earlier in her medical school career, she and her fellow female students found a sheep in the anatomy hall; the male students explained that "inferior animals" were now apparently allowed to study medicine. In 1873, she sues unsuccessfully to receive her degree and turns to Parliament for reform. She will receive her license to practice medicine in 1877.

1873 British geologist and conchologist Mary Lyell (b. 1808) dies.

1873 Elizabeth Garrett Anderson becomes the first female member of the British Medical Association. She will be its only female member until 1892.

1873 U.S. astronomer Maria Mitchell co-founds a moderate feminist group, the Association for the Advancement of Women.

1874 Sophia Jex-Blake establishes the London School of Medicine for Women; Elizabeth Blackwell is awarded the chair of gynecology.

Jan. 1, 1874 U.S. medical missionary Clara Swain opens the first women's hospital in India.

1875 British reformers Annie Besant and Charles Bradlaugh distribute a birth control tract, *The Fruits of Philosophy*. They are arrested, tried, and convicted. Besant wins acquittal on appeal but loses custody of her daughter anyway.

1875 U.S. doctors Charlotte Brown (December 22, 1846–April 19, 1904) and Martha Bucknell, along with other women, establish the forerunner of the San Francisco Children's Hospital.

1875 Russian mathematician Sonya Kovalevskaya (b. January 15, 1850) works on partial differential equations and adds to an earlier theorem devised by Augustin Louis Cauchy; thereafter the theorem is known as the Cauchy-Kovalevsky theorem.

Education and Scholarship

1871 U.S. missionaries Cyrus and Susan Mills establish Mills Seminary, one of the forerunners of Mills College for women, near Oakland, California.

1871 English sisters Maria Grey and Emily Shirreff form the National Union for the Education of Girls, which will found more than thirty challenging secondary schools.

1871 Newnham women's college becomes a part of Cambridge University, although the female students are to take different exams, which do not include Greek and Latin.

1872 Greek educator and feminist Kalliopi Kehajia establishes the Society for Promoting Women's Education.

1872 Japan mandates primary education for all boys and girls starting at age six, but the program is not fully in place for several decades.

1872 Russia's first women's universities are founded.

1873 Dr. Edward Clarke, in *Sex and Education*, claims that studying interferes with a girl's reproductive development by taking menstrual blood away from the uterus and up to the brain.

1873 In Japan, U.S. missionaries Eliza Talcott and Julia Dudley establish the forerunner of Kobe College.

1873 Most Swedish university programs are opened to women.

1873 Egypt's first girls' elementary school opens.

Apr. 1874 Some "experts" are beginning to abandon the untenable position that women are incapable of learning and to replace it with the theory that women *can* learn, but should not. Britain's Dr. Henry Maudsley argues that study hampers women's health and reproductive capacity: "It would be an ill thing . . . [to get] the advantages of a quantity of female intellectual work at the price of a puny, enfeebled, sickly race."

In May, Dr. Elizabeth Garrett Anderson responds to Dr. Maudsley: "When we are told that . . . women cannot disregard their special physiological functions without danger to health, it is difficult to understand what is meant, considering that in adult life healthy women do as a rule disregard them almost completely." She points out that poor women work extremely hard without being told to stop. Furthermore, she says, if Dr. Maudsley wishes to lighten women's load, he might consider reducing prejudice rather than female ambition.

1875 In the United States, Smith and Wellesley women's colleges are founded.

Religion

1871 U.S. suffragist Anna Howard Shaw (February 14, 1847–July 2, 1919) is licensed as a Methodist preacher.

1873 The Sisters of Charity of New York open a day-care center for the children of working women.

1874 English socialist and spiritual leader Annie Besant announces her atheism and becomes president of the National Secular Society.

Oct. 30, 1875 U.S. Christian Science founder and leader Mary Baker Eddy publishes *Science and Health*.

Nov. 17, 1875 Russian spiritualist Helena Blavatsky (July 31, 1831-May 8, 1891), author of *Isis Unveiled* (1871), founds the Theosophical Society, which espouses belief in reincarnation and a sense of world community. By the time of her death, Blavatsky will have about 100,000 followers.

1876–1880

General Status and Daily Life

Most U.S. women still live in small towns, making their own soap and sweets, as those luxuries are still quite expensive. Most have no indoor plumbing or electricity. Household trash is burned or fed to animals. Rural women see each other rarely, meeting at church or at occasional social gatherings.

Among the western Indians of the United States, there is great variety of social structure. In some tribes, the sexual division of labor gives men the most powerful positions, but many groups such as the Zuñi, Navajo, and Mandan are matrilocal or matrilineal. In these groups, women often control the bulk of the property, the most prestigious religious rites, or the most valued crafts and skills.

1876 Carpet sweepers are invented and by 1890 will mostly replace brooms.

Nov. 1876 Juliet Corson (January 14, 1841–June 18, 1897) starts the first culinary school in the United States.

1878 Women in eastern Finland get the right to inherit property from their fathers.

1879 Guatemala's constitution refuses citizenship to women.

1880 In the United States, there are ninety-seven women for every hundred men; in Colorado, Nevada, and Arizona, the ratio is more like fifty to one hundred.

Government, the Military, and the Law

1877 Queen Victoria is proclaimed empress of India.

1877 Eudora Clark Atkinson becomes the first woman superintendent of the first women's state reformatory in the United States.

1878 Sierra Leone leader Madam Yoko (c. 1849-1906) becomes chief upon the death of her husband; she promptly uses British support to defeat her rivals, later becoming queen of Seneghun.

1878 Some civil service jobs are opened to women in Germany.

Feb. 15, 1879 Federal law permits women lawyers to practice before the U.S. Supreme Court if they have practiced at the state supreme court level at least three years.

Literature and the Visual Arts

1876 French author Comtesse Marie d'Agoult (b. 1805) dies. A noted salon hostess, the lover of Franz Liszt, and the mother of Cosima Wagner, she wrote novels and nonfiction works under the pseudonym Daniel Stern.

1876 U.S. author Helen Hunt Jackson (b. October 15, 1830) publishes *Mercy Philbrick's Choice*, a novel based on the life of her friend and neighbor, poet Emily Dickinson.

1876 U.S. sculptor Edmondia Lewis, whose subjects have included John Brown and Colonel Robert Gould Shaw, exhibits her work at Philadelphia's Centennial Exposition.

1876 British military artist Lady Elizabeth Butler paints *Balaclava*. In 1877, she paints another Crimean battle, *Inkermann*.

1876 Sophie Anderson shows a painting of torture, an atypical subject for a female artist, at the Royal Academy.

1876 George Eliot publishes the novel *Daniel Deronda*.

Aug. 20, 1876 English-American lithographer Fanny Palmer (b. June 26, 1812), prolific artist for Currier & Ives, dies. Many of her 200 lithographs will remain popular as illustrations well into the twentieth century.

1877 Elizabeth Stuart Phelps publishes *The Story of Avis*, a melodramatic, tragic tale of a woman torn between her "natural destiny" as a wife and mother and her ambitions as an artist. Also published this year are Louisa May Alcott's dark Faustian novella *A Modern Mephistopheles* and English author Harriet Martineau's posthumous *Autobiography*.

1877 U.S. Impressionist Mary Cassatt's (b. May 22, 1844) work is rejected by the Académie Royale Salon. She accepts Degas's invitation to join a group of "Indépendants."

1878 The international detective best-seller *The Leavenworth Case* is published by U.S. author Anna Katharine Green (November 11, 1846–April 11, 1935). Her other detective novels include *Hand and Ring* (1883), *Lost Man's Lane* (1898), *The Filigree Ball* (1903), *The House of the Whispering Pines* (1910), and *The Step on the Stair* (1923).

1879 English portrait photographer Julia Margaret Cameron (b. 1815) dies. She took portraits of Darwin, Sir John Herschel, Robert Browning, Tennyson, Trollope, and Carlyle.

1879 Spanish novelist Emilia Pardo Bazán (1851–1920) publishes her first novel, *Pascual López*.

Apr. 30, 1879 U.S. journalist Sarah Josepha Hale, author of "Mary Had a Little Lamb," dies. For forty years, she was one of the nation's most influential proponents of Victorian femininity. She established the *Ladies Magazine*, which publisher Louis Godey bought just to secure her talents. She then made his *Godey's Lady's Book* America's arbiter of fashion and etiquette. She opposed female lecturers and tight lacing of corsets; she favored playgrounds, preservation of national landmarks, Thanksgiving (she got Lincoln to make it a national holiday), female teachers and school board members, and a "lady principal" for Vassar College (she got that, too).

1880 New children's books this year include Swiss author Johanna Spyri's *Heidi* and U.S. author Margaret Sidney's *Five Little Peppers and How They Grew*.

1880 New literature includes Spanish poet Rosalía de Castro's verse collection *Follas novas* and Austrian writer Marie Ebner-Eschenbach's (1830–1916) *Aphorismen*, a collection of epigrams.

Performing Arts and Entertainment

1876 Italian-American soprano Adelina Patti stars in the first London performance of *Aida*.

1878 Emma Abbott (1850–1891) becomes the first U.S. woman to form an opera company.

Oct. 13, 1878 Bohemian-American opera singer Ernestine Schumann-Heink (June 15, 1861-Nov. 17, 1936)) makes her debut with the Dresden Royal Opera.

Nov. 1878 Spanish-American acrobat Leona Dare performs in London, hanging from a trapeze and holding a man by his waistband with her teeth.

1879 French actress Sarah Bernhardt makes her London debut and leaves the Comédie Française. In 1880, she makes her U.S. debut in *Adrienne Lecouvreur*.

Jan. 1879 U.S. actress Blanche Whiffen plays Buttercup in the first American performance of Gilbert and Sullivan's *H.M.S. Pinafore*.

1880 German soprano Lilli Lehmann (1848–1929) makes her London debut as Violetta in *La traviata*. Best known for her Wagnerian heroines, Lehmann will play about 170 roles in about 120 different operas.

Athletics and Exploration

1877 Swiss adventurer Isabelle Eberhardt is born. During her short life, she will travel through Algeria's mountains and deserts dressed as a man, convert to Islam, author several books, and marry an Arab.

1878 English traveler and writer Isabella Bird Bishop visits Japan, Indonesia, and the Middle East. In 1879, she publishes *A Lady's Life in the Rockies*.

1878 English traveler and author Lady Anne Blunt publishes *The Bedouin Tribes of the Euphrates*.

1880 Britain's Grand National Archery Society begins holding a women's championship.

Activism

1876 The Centennial Exposition is held in Philadelphia; Elizabeth Cady Stanton and Susan B. Anthony suggest to the organizers that Lucretia Mott be allowed to sit on the platform and "present the vice-president with a copy of the women's declaration of independence." Permission is denied, and five seats in the hall are offered instead; Anthony, Matilda Joslyn Gage, and three others take the proffered seats. When Richard Henry Lee finishes reading the original Declaration of Independence, the five women stand. Anthony presents a copy of the women's declaration to the acting vice president, and the others pass out copies to the audience.

1877 The political "Trial of the Fifty" takes place in Russia. Almost half the activists tried are women known as the "Moscow Amazons." Revolutionary Vera Liubatovich is sentenced to nine years at hard labor, then banished instead to Siberia. In 1878, Liubatovich escapes from Siberia by faking her own suicide. After joining Narodnaya Volya (People's Will) in St. Petersburg, she flees to Switzerland.

1878 The "Susan B. Anthony" Amendment is first proposed in Congress by a sympathetic senator, A. A. Sargent of California: "The right of citizens of the United States to vote shall not be denied or abridged by the United States or any state on account of sex." The bill is killed in committee but will be resubmitted to Congress almost every year thereafter, with western representatives tending to favor it and the South and East resisting.

1878 American Indian rights activist Sarah Winnemucca convinces her Paiute tribe not to fight against the army in the Bannock wars. In 1880, she travels to Washington, D.C., to protest conditions on reservations.

1878 Russian revolutionary Vera Zasulich shoots General Trepov, the governor of St. Petersburg, in front of a room full of witnesses. The governor is so detested that Zasulich is acquitted. However, she flees to Switzerland when the tsar orders her rearrest.

1878 Elizabeth Flynn Rodgers (b. 1847) founds Chicago's first women's union.

1878 U.S. novelist Madeline Vinton Dahlgren appeals to the Senate Elections Committee to save the country from the dangers of female suffrage. She feels that women should gently influence current voters (their husbands) and future voters (their sons).

1878 French feminist and socialist Hubertine Auclert establishes the Droit de la Femme, later the Société de Suffrage des Femmes.

Apr. 1878 Frances Power Cobbe publishes the article "Wife Torture in England," denouncing the popular acceptance of violence against women.

1879 U.S. public speaker and civil rights advocate Maria Stewart (b. 1803), one of the first female lecturers in the United States, dies.

1879 U.S. temperance activist Frances Willard, creator of the temperance slogan "For God and Home and Native Land," becomes president of the national WCTU, a position she will hold for the rest of her life. She expands the scope of the organization's activism to include not only temperance but women's suffrage and general philanthropy as well.

1879 The Union of Greek Women is established.

1880 U.S. feminist Matilda Joslyn Gage campaigns for women's suffrage at the national Democratic, Republican, and Greenback-Labor party conventions.

1880 U.S. reformers Mary Lucinda Bonney (June 8, 1816–July 24, 1900) and Amelia Stone Quinton, who will push for passage of the Dawes land reform act of 1887, establish the Women's National Indian Association.

1880 The NWSA convention resolves "that since man has everywhere committed to woman the custody and ownership of the child born out of wedlock, and has required it to bear its mother's name, he should recognize woman's right as a mother to the custody of the child born in marriage, and permit it to bear her name."

1880 French feminists Eugénie Potonie-Pierre (b. 1844) and Léonie Rouzade establish the Union des Femmes.

1880 British housing reformer Octavia Hill uses most of her inheritance to renovate three New York City tenements, renting them at low (but still profitable) rates to the poor.

Nov. 2, 1880 Susan B. Anthony and Elizabeth Cady Stanton attempt to vote; when Stanton is refused the right, she throws a ballot box at the polling official.

Business and Industry

1877 U.S. labor leader Mary Harris "Mother" Jones (May 1, 1830–November 30, 1930) helps lead the Pittsburgh railroad strike.

1878 Germany's Society for the Protection of Motherhood and Sexual Reform agitates successfully for three-week unpaid maternity leave for working women.

c. 1880 Shop assistants in England work more than seventy-five hours per week, all of it on their feet, with a total of forty-five minutes a day in breaks. Seats are sometimes provided for show, but the women are penalized for sitting down. They are paid about ten shillings a week.

1880 In the United States, 2.6 million women are employed, forming 15.2% of the total work force. Only 4% of all U.S. clerical workers are female.

Jan. 25, 1880 U.S. department store executive Margaret Getchell La Forge (b. July 16, 1841) dies. A cousin of R. H. Macy, she joined his firm two years after the opening of Macy's in New York. She rose from bookkeeper to sales clerk to manager of the entire store at twenty-five. A marketing genius, she attracted new customers by choosing to stock new items, such as food, picnic supplies, jewelry, housewares, clocks, and silver. She once said she would sell anything but coffins.

Science and Medicine

During this period, the human ovum is discovered to have an equal role with the sperm in procreation. Until now, woman's role has been overlooked in discussions of heredity; similarities between mother and child have been attributed to environment.

1876 U.S. physician Sarah Stevenson becomes the first woman member of the American Medical Association (AMA).

1876 Parliament permits English universities to grant medical degrees to women.

1876 U.S. physician Mary Putnam Jacobi wins

Harvard's Boyleston Prize for a paper arguing that menstruation is no more taxing than digestion and need not prevent physical or intellectual labor.

1877 English entomologist Eleanor Ormerod (1828–1901) begins publishing her *Annual Report of Observations of Injurious Insects*, which will at its height sell 170,000 copies per year. Her simple, straightforward remedies will save crops and livestock from untold depredation; one of her suggestions alone will save approximately half the cattle in England during a plague of maggots.

1878 U.S. physicist and astronomer Sarah Whiting (1847–1927) opens, at Wellesley, the second undergraduate physics laboratory in the United States. In 1880 she will supplement the physics programs with a course in astronomy, which will be taught for two decades with only a celestial globe and a four-inch telescope as equipment.

Aug. 17, 1878 The British medical journal *Lancet* advises keeping women as nurses rather than training them to be doctors. The author claims that men cannot be nurses because "man's nature rebels against the complete surrender of his own judgment and that implicit obedience in spirit, as well as letter, which are the first essentials of a good nurse."

1879 Mary Eliza Mahoney (April 16, 1845–January 4, 1926) becomes the first professionally trained black nurse in the United States.

Feb. 1879 Hungarian doctor Vilma Hugonnai-Wartha passes the exams for her medical degree, but, since she is a woman, she is given only a midwife's certificate. Her degree will not be recognized by the government until 1897.

1880 British-American mathematician Charlotte Scott (June 8, 1858–November 8, 1931) studies at Girton College, Cambridge, taking the mathematics examination and earning eighth place. If she were a man, this would give her the title "eighth wrangler," but since women are not yet allowed to earn official Cambridge degrees, she is deprived of the title. However, when the name of the official, male eighth wrangler is read, the crowd chants, "Scott of Girton! Scott of Girton!"

1880 U.S. anatomist Alice Bennett (1851–1925) becomes the first woman to earn a Ph.D. from the University of Pennsylvania and becomes probably the first female superintendent of a state mental hospital. She soon abolishes the use of mechanical restraints such as straitjackets and encourages occupational therapy, with good results. Her methods are soon imitated by other institutions.

Education and Scholarship

1876 Tokyo Women's Normal School begins training women as elementary teachers.

1876 Women are allowed to enter Russian universities, a privilege that will be revoked in 1881.

1877 Chile's universities are opened to women, and the first public girls' high school is founded at Copiapó.

1877 Helen Magill White becomes the first woman in the United States to earn a doctoral degree.

1878 Women are accepted on an equal basis with men at M. I. T.

May 12, 1878 U.S. author and educator Catharine Beecher (b. September 6, 1800) dies. She dedicated her entire life to the improvement of women's lot through acceptably feminine means. She cofounded a girls' school, wrote several books on "domestic science" to increase the respect commanded by housework, and almost single-handedly changed primary education from a male to a female profession in two generations.

1879 U.S. businesswoman Mary Seymour (1846–1893) opens the first typewriting school for women. Over the next few decades, many women will learn to operate the new typewriting machines in order to enter the desirable, male-dominated field of clerical work.

1879 Coeducation above the primary level is banned in Japan.

1879 New Zealand educator, feminist, and temperance advocate Learmonth White Dalrymple publishes *The Kindergarten*.

1879 U.S. scientist Elizabeth Agassiz (December 5, 1822–June 27, 1907), an opponent of coeducation, cofounds Radcliffe College, remaining its president until 1903. In England, Oxford's Somerville College (named for scientific writer Mary Somerville, d. 1872) and Lady Margaret Hall are founded.

1880 Spanish social scientist and philanthropist Concepción Arenal publishes the two-volume *La cuestión social*.

Religion

1876 In France, 113,750 women and 22,843 men are members of Catholic religious orders.

1877 English novelist and antisuffragist Mrs. Humphry Ward (b. 1851) publishes the *Dictionary of Christian Biography*.

1877 U.S. Mormon leader Emmeline Wells becomes editor of the *Women's Exponent*, the official Mormon Relief Society's bimonthly journal; she will hold this influential editorship until 1914, using her position to generate support for women's suffrage and women's rights.

Apr. 12, 1879 The Church of Christ, Scientist, is officially chartered, with Mary Baker Eddy as its head.

Apr. 30, 1879 U.S. Mormon Emma Smith (b. July 10, 1804), wife of the prophet Joseph Smith, dies. On one of the Mormons' many flights from their enemies, she crossed the icy Mississippi River on foot with her husband's writings sewn into her petticoats.

1880 The National Catholic Total Abstinence Union lets women's organizations join, but they have to send the local priest as a delegate, not a woman.

1880 Spiritual works this year include Mary Baker Eddy's *Christian Healing* and Annie Besant's *The Gospel of Atheism*.

Oct. 1880 U.S. minister and suffragist Anna Howard Shaw is ordained as the first woman minister in the Methodist Protestant church.

1881–1885

General Status and Daily Life

1880s Chinese foot-binding has about a 10% mortality rate.

July 6, 1881 Iowa teenager Kate Shelby hears a bridge near her house give way to flooding and a train crash on the damaged bridge. Through rain and wind, she crawls across the fifty-foot-high, damaged bridge, then walks a mile and a half to the telegraph office and stops the next train just in time.

June 6, 1882 The first electric iron is patented, though few households have electricity, and electric irons will not become popular for about twenty-five more years. Most households still use the flat irons popular since the fifteenth century, with some models weighing as much as fifteen pounds.

1884 Divorce, banned in France since 1816, is reauthorized for cruelty or injury; male or female, the successful petitioner gets financial support and custody of any children. It is the first time that Frenchwomen can get custody of their own children in case of divorce.

1884 Swedish single women over twenty-one are now considered legal adults and will no longer remain under the perpetual guardianship of their male relatives.

1885 Britain raises the age of consent for girls from thirteen to sixteen.

Government, the Military, and the Law

1882 A soldiers' revolt drives Korean queen Min from the capital. Her husband, King Kojong, recalls her worst enemy, his father, who declares the fugitive Min dead. Funeral preparations are made. However, the king's father is soon taken as a hostage by the Chinese, and Min returns to the capital in triumph. A few years later, when her pro-Russian sympathies threaten Japanese interests in Korea. She is stabbed by soldiers and her body burned.

1882 U.S. lawyer Marion Todd is elected to the platform committee of the Greenback Labor party and runs unsuccessfully for attorney general of California.

Mar. 2, 1882 An assassination attempt is made on Queen Victoria. It is the seventh such incident of her reign.

July 1883 Queen Ranavalona II of Madagascar dies. She is succeeded by her cousin, Queen Ranavalona III, who marries the prime minister.

1884 U.S. lawyer Belva Lockwood (October 24, 1830– May 19, 1917) runs for president of the United States.

Literature and the Visual Arts

1881 French feminist and socialist Hubertine Auclert becomes editor of the journal *La citoyenne*, a position she will hold until 1892.

1881 Irish suffragist Helen Blackburn becomes editor of *The Englishwoman's Review*, a position she will hold until 1890.

1881 French moderate feminist and author Maria Deraismes founds the newspaper *Le Républicain de Seine et Oise*.

1882 Spanish novelist Emilia Pardo Bazán publishes the novel *La tribuna*, about a rebellious female tobacco worker.

1883 Novels published this year include *The Story of an African Farm*, by South African Olive Schreiner (1855–1920), and *La cuestión palpitante*, by Emilia

Pardo Bazán. Schreiner's novel, initially published under a male pseudonym, becomes controversial because of its attacks on sexism and organized religion.

1883 U.S. poet Emma Lazarus (July 22, 1849– November 19, 1887) composes the sonnet "The New Colossus," which begins, "Give me your tired, your poor, / Your huddled masses yearning to breathe free." It will be engraved on the Statue of Liberty in 1903.

1883 British painter Edith Hayllar (b. 1860) shows *A Summer Shower* at the Royal Academy. Depicting a tennis party interrupted by rain, it will be called "one of the most charming genre scenes of the nineteenth century."

1883 Artist's model Suzanne Valadon (1865–1938) gives birth to an illegitimate son, the painter Maurice Utrillo, and becomes inspired by her work for artists (including Toulouse-Lautrec and Renoir) to become an artist herself. She begins producing drawings and pastels, winning praise from Degas and others. Later, she will teach her son to paint as therapy for his alcoholism.

1884 Filipina poet Leona Florentino (b. 1849) dies.

1884 U.S. author Helen Hunt Jackson (d. August 12, 1885) publishes *Ramona*, a novel about mistreatment of American Indians.

1884 Russian artist Marie Bashkirtseff exhibits her best-known work, a study of street urchins entitled *A Meeting*, in the Paris Salon. Later this year, she dies of tuberculosis.

1884 Spanish poet Rosalía de Castro (1837–1885) publishes the poem collection *En las orillas del Sar*.

1884 Japan's first women's magazine, *Jogaku shinshi*, begins publication. It is replaced next year by *Jogaku zasshi*.

1884 U.S. author Sarah Orne Jewett (September 3, 1849–June 24, 1909) publishes the novel *A Country Doctor*, based on her relationship with her physician father.

1885 Norwegian-Danish novelist Bertha Skram (1847–1905) publishes *Constance Ring*.

1885 In Austria, the Women Writers and Artists Organization is founded.

Feb. 4, 1885 U.S. portraitist Sarah Miriam Peale (b. May 19, 1800), the first professional woman artist in the United States, dies. Noted for her portraits and still lives, she was encouraged by her uncle, artist Charles Willson Peale, who favored full educational opportunities for women. Her subjects included Thomas Hart Benton, Daniel Webster, and Lafayette.

Oct. 31, 1885 French portraitist Marie Laurencin, painter of W. Somerset Maugham and Jean Cocteau, designer of fashions, illustrator of the works of Sappho, and designer of sets for the Comédie Française and the Ballets Russes, is born.

Performing Arts and Entertainment

1881 Sarah Bernhardt makes her first appearance as Marguerite in *La dame aux caméllias*, the role with which she will be most strongly identified.

Dec. 1881 English actress Lillie Langtry makes her debut at the Haymarket as Kate Hardcastle in *She Stoops to Conquer*.

1882 Bohemian-American opera singer Ernestine Schumann-Heink is fired from the Dresden Royal Opera for marrying without permission.

1883 Swedish soprano Jenny Lind becomes a professor at London's Royal College of Music.

1884 German soprano Lilli Lehmann sings Isolde at Covent Garden. In 1885, she makes her Metropolitan Opera debut as Brünnhilde in *Die Walküre*.

1885 U.S. sharpshooter Annie Oakley (Phoebe Anne Moses, b. August 13, 1860) joins "Buffalo Bill" Cody's Wild West Show, becoming famous for shooting over her shoulder using only a Bowie knife as a mirror and shooting from horseback. In her seventeen years with the show (at an approximate salary of $1,000 per week), "Little Sure Shot" will miss only five performances.

Athletics and Exploration

1881 English archer Alice Blanche Legh (b. 1855) wins her first British championship; she will win it twenty-two more times. From 1882 to 1885 the title will be won by her mother, Mrs. Piers Legh.

Aug. 1881 English adventuress Jane Digby (b. 1807), who had affairs with King Louis I of Bavaria, King Otto of Greece, and Honoré de Balzac, dies. Her husbands included a lord, a baron, a count, and a Bedouin chieftain named Medjuel.

1882 British mountaineer Elizabeth Le Blond (1861–1934) climbs Mont Blanc.

1884 English athlete Maud Watson wins the first Wimbledon women's singles title, defeating her older sister Lilian. She will repeat her victory next year.

1885 A Hamburg, Germany, ice-skating club holds a race for women.

Activism

1881 Russian nihilist Elizaveta Kovalskaya, guilty of terrorist attacks on landlords, officials, and factory managers, is arrested and sent to Siberia. She escapes but is recaptured and remains in Siberia for twenty years.

1881 Russian revolutionary Vera Figner becomes the head of the radical group Narodnaya Volya (People's Will). Arrested in 1883, she is condemned to death but will instead spend a year in a St. Petersburg jail and twenty years in a notorious island prison on the River Neva.

Feb. 1881 Russian revolutionary Sofya Perovskaya (1853–April 3, 1881) organizes the assassination of Tsar Alexander II. In March, she is arrested, tried, and found guilty. She calmly accepts the verdict and asks for the death penalty, wishing to be treated no differently from the male conspirators. Before the hanging, she asks her mother for "a collar and cuffs with buttons, for I should like to tidy my dress for the proceedings."

1882 Indian feminist, legal scholar, and author Pandita Ramabai (1858-1922), founder of a school and orphanages and a delegate to the Indian National Congress, founds a home for widows.

Nov. 1882 Russian revolutionary Vera Liubatovich is arrested and sentenced to twenty years of Siberian banishment. Wanted by the government, she returned to Russia from Switzerland to search for her husband, who had been arrested.

1883 The Woman's Relief Corps is formed in the United States as an auxiliary to the Grand Army of the Republic; it concerns itself with patriotic activities and support for Union veterans and will have 100,000 members by the turn of the century.

1883 U.S. Indian leader Sarah Winnemucca (c. 1844–October 16, 1891), who made a lecture tour in 1882–1883 about injustices on Indian reservations, publishes *Life Among the Piutes*, a popular work that helps to gain sympathy for the injustices suffered by Native Americans. Her work will lead to land grants for her people in 1884.

1883 Caroline Earle White founds the American Anti-Vivisection Society.

1883 Dutch doctor and birth control advocate Aletta

Jacobs (b. 1851) tries to vote; the government responds by specifying that all voters must be male.

1884 Iranian feminist Taj al-Saltaneh is born. She will write, "Women in Iran are separated from humanity and classified as wild animals, incarcerated throughout their lives behind high walls, shrouded in black garments that they can remove only when their corpse is wrapped in white for burial."

1884 Dutch feminists establish De Vereniging voor Vrouwenkiesrecht (Association for Women's Suffrage).

1884 The Norwegian Association for the Rights of Women is founded. It works for improvements in women's education and married women's legal status.

1885 The first national women's association in Sweden is founded and named in honor of novelist Fredrika Bremer.

Business and Industry

1881 In Italy, 43% of the work force is female.

1881 U.S. author, suffragist, and clubwoman Eliza Sproat Turner founds the New Century Guild of Working Women to provide vocational classes and recreational facilities for working women.

1881 U.S. labor organizer Elizabeth Flynn Rodgers becomes the first female master workman of a district assembly in the Knights of Labor.

1881 One-third of English girls age fifteen to twenty are in domestic service, rising early, going to bed late, and living a life with very little personal liberty. Servants are expected to have virtually no sex life, with other servants in the house or with anyone outside it, but they are often sexually exploited by their male employers.

Sept. 1881 The first all-female local of the Knights of Labor is formed.

1882 Women are 37% of the German work force.

1882 The year-old American Federation of Labor (AFL) invites women to join "upon an equal footing with trade organizations of men."

1882 England's nut and bolt makers agitate to bar women from their line of work.

Feb. 9, 1882 U.S. entrepreneur Margaret Haughery (b. 1813) dies. A former servant, she sold milk from a hand truck in New Orleans, took over a bakery that owed her money for milk, and began delivering bread as well as dairy products. After the Civil War, she sold packaged crackers. A philanthropist as well as a businesswoman, she founded eleven orphanages and several homes for the elderly, nursed yellow fever victims and Civil War soldiers, and gave over $600,000 to charity.

1883 U.S. textile designer and interior decorator Candace Wheeler leaves the design firm founded by Louis Tiffany, where she has created textiles and embroideries for clients such as Mark Twain and President Chester A. Arthur. She founds her own firm, staffing it entirely with women. She continues to boast a prestigious client list, including Andrew Carnegie.

May 17, 1883 U.S. patent medicine entrepreneur Lydia Estes Pinkham (b. February 9, 1819) dies. Her company, which is selling $300,000 of "Vegetable Compound" per year at the time of her death, will gross $3,800,000 in 1925, selling "a Positive Cure for all those Painful Complaints and Weaknesses so common to our best female population."

1884 Women strike in Massachusetts textile mills, Connecticut hat factories, and North Carolina tobacco plants.

Science and Medicine

1881 Pioneering Spanish medical student Pilar Tauregui is pelted with rocks in class. In 1882, she and three other female medical students are denied degrees, even though they have passed the appropriate examinations.

1881 Eight women doctors, including Lucy Sewall, Emily Blackwell, Mary Putnam Jacobi, and Marie Zakrzewska, offer Harvard $50,000 to open its medical school to women; Harvard declines.

1882 U.S. botanist Sarah Plummer Lemmon discovers a new plant genus, named *Plummera floribunda* for her.

1882 Aletta Jacobs, Holland's first woman physician, opens the world's first birth control clinic in Amsterdam.

Mar. 1, 1882 President Arthur, after considerable lobbying by Civil war nurse Clara Barton, signs the Geneva Treaty recognizing the International Red Cross, with an additional clause granting the Red Cross powers to react to peacetime disasters such as floods, fires, and epidemics. Barton will remain the tyrannical leader of the American Red Cross until 1904.

Mar. 27, 1882 English traveler Amelia Edwards founds the Egypt Exploration Fund to excavate historic sites.

1883 Mary Anna Palmer Draper (September 11, 1839–December 8, 1914), endows the Henry Draper Medal of the National Academy of Sciences, to be awarded for "original investigation in Astronomical Physics." In 1886 she establishes a fund in his name at Harvard to photograph and classify stellar spectra. The resulting project will provide work for some of America's leading women astronomers.

1883 U.S. ethnologist Erminnie Smith (April 26, 1836–June 9, 1886), director of science programs for Sorosis and the first woman field ethnographer, publishes *Myths of the Iroquois*.

1883 Russian mathematician Sonya Kovalevskaya becomes a lecturer at the University of Stockholm and publishes a paper on the shape of Saturn's rings. In September she delivers a paper on refraction of light in a crystalline medium at an Odessa scientific conference, and next year she will attain the rank of professor and publish a paper on Abelian integrals.

1883 English physician Elizabeth Garrett Anderson becomes dean of the new London School of Medicine for Women.

1884 British physicist Hertha Ayrton (1854–1923) invents and patents a device "for dividing a line into any number of equal parts."

1884 Paulina Starr becomes the first woman dentist in Chile.

1885 U.S. ethnologist Matilda Stevenson founds and becomes the first president of the Women's Anthropological Society of America.

1885 U.S. ornithologist Florence Merriam Bailey (b. August 8, 1863) becomes the first female associate member of the American Ornithologists' Union.

1885 New publications include Irish writer Agnes Clerke's (1842–1907) first book, *A Popular History of Astronomy During the Nineteenth Century*; and U.S. botanist Clara Cummings' work on mosses and liverworts, *Catalogue of Musci and Hepaticae of North America, North of Mexico*.

1885 British doctor Sophia Jex-Blake establishes the Women's Hospital of Edinburgh.

Education and Scholarship

1881 Primary education becomes compulsory for girls in France; it has been mandatory for boys since 1833.

1881 Women are formally admitted to the Cambridge Tripos exams, though they may not yet receive degrees.

1881 Ada L. Howard, first president of Wellesley College, resigns. She is replaced by Alice Freeman Palmer, who retires to marry in 1887.

1881 U.S. reformer and writer Helen Hunt Jackson publishes *A Century of Dishonor*, a stirring indictment of European settlers' treatment of the Indians.

Apr. 11, 1881 U.S. educators Sophia Packard (January 3, 1824–June 21, 1891) and Harriet Giles open Spelman College for black women in Atlanta, Georgia.

1882 India has 2,700 girls' schools serving 127,000 students.

1882 Marion Talbot, Alice Freeman Palmer, Ellen Swallow Richards, and others establish the Association of Collegiate Alumnae, the forerunner of the American Association of University Women (AAUW).

1882 Since 1866, 109 women have received degrees from French universities.

1883 Italian technical and preparatory schools begin admitting women.

1883 American Charlotte Endymion Porter becomes editor of *Shakespeariana* magazine.

1884 Russian-German intellectual Lou Andreas-Salomé (1861–1937) publishes *Im Kampf um Gott*, drawing on her own personal relationship with philosopher Friedrich Nietzsche.

Oct. 16, 1884 Hawaiian chief, philanthropist, and founder of the Kamehameha Schools Bernice Pauahi Bishop (b. December 19, 1831) dies.

1885 Bryn Mawr, a U.S. women's college, is established. The only woman among the six faculty members is British-American mathematician Charlotte Scott. American educator and feminist Martha Carey Thomas (January 2, 1857–December 2, 1935), the first foreigner and the first woman to graduate *summa cum laude* from the University of Zurich, is the dean and later president.

Nov. 1885 Leland and Jane Stanford (August 25, 1828–February 28, 1905) begin the founding of Stanford University with a grant of 7,000 acres of land.

Religion

1882 A Korean shaman named Chillyonggun rises at court, obtaining political influence, a good government job for her son, and a shrine built in her honor.

1884 Mary Francis Warde (b. 1810), founder of the

Sisters of Mercy in the United States, dies. Much of her career was spent fighting a series of bishops who sought control over the sisterhood.

1884 U.S. temperance reformer Josephine Nateham becomes head of WCTU's Department for the Suppression of Sabbath Desecration, a position she will hold until 1896.

June 20, 1885 Protestant missionary Mary Fitch Scranton arrives in Korea. She achieves much by respecting the Korean segregation of men and women; she does not go out in the daylight and hangs a curtain between women parishioners and their male preacher.

1886-1890

General Status and Daily Life

1886 Nigeria's Guardianship of Infants Act affirms a mother's equal right to custody of her children.

1886 The first commercial cleanser, Bon Ami, is introduced.

1888 The first beauty contest is held in Spa, Belgium.

1890 Female life expectancy in Great Britain is forty-four years.

1890 The first electric stoves appear, but they are not immediately popular, as they are difficult to control and expensive to run.

Government, the Military, and the Law

At about this time, the Igbo tribes of Nigeria have dual-sex political hierarchies; the men and, to a large extent, the general community, are ruled by a male leader, the *obi*. The women are ruled by a separate female leader, the *omu* (mother). The *omu* has an *ilogo*, or cabinet, with titles and duties corresponding to the male council's.
    The *omu* oversees the market held every four days, regulating prices and observance of taboos through a police officer (*awo*) who belongs to the *ilogo*. The *omu* also performs rituals to ensure the safety of the community, informs women of important developments, arbitrates cases involving women, and intercedes with

the *obi* for the women if necessary.
    As British colonial control of Nigeria increases at the beginning of the twentieth century, the *omu* will be shut out of the political hierarchy. The British will recognize only male leaders and provide only male leaders with salaries. The *omu*'s religious functions are usurped by Christianity.

Nov. 1886 U.S. lawyer Catharine Waite founds the *Chicago Law Times*, a quarterly journal that addresses many legal issues important to women, including divorce and abortion. In 1888, she becomes president of the International Woman's Bar Association.

1887 Queen Victoria's Golden Jubilee is celebrated; some in the crowds boo her, but Victoria is so unaccustomed to the sound that she has to ask what the "horrid noise" is.

1887 Emilie Kempin-Spyri (1853–1901) becomes the first woman in Switzerland to qualify as a lawyer.

1887 U.S. ethnologist Alice Cunningham Fletcher (March 15, 1838–April 6, 1923) becomes an agent for the Department of the Interior and helps to implement the Dawes Act, which grants land and citizenship to Indians. Supported by activist Susette La Flèsche Tibbles (1854–May 26, 1903), the act creates unforeseen problems and is generally perceived as a failure.

1887 Utah women, who have had the vote since 1870, are deprived of it by the Edmunds-Tucker Act, which also outlaws polygamy.

1888 Marie Popelin, the first woman law graduate in Belgium, is refused admission to the bar on the grounds of sex.

1888 Chile's Radical party is the first political party in the nation to admit women as members.

1888 Jeanne Chauvin (1862–1926) is the first Frenchwoman to graduate with a law degree.

1888 Isabel, regent for her father Pedro II of Brazil, abolishes slavery.

1889 The young emperor of China comes of age; the powerful dowager empress Tz'u-Hsi, his regent, steps down from power after marrying him to her niece. She retires to her summer palace, which she is refurbishing with the funds for China's badly needed new navy.

1890 Rosa Ginossar, the first woman to practice law in Israel, is born.

1890 U.S. lawyer Myra Bradwell is admitted to the Illinois bar without requesting the honor. She tried to be admitted in 1869 but was denied on the grounds of sex; after she took her case to the U.S. Supreme Court, Illinois decided to permit women to practice law.

Literature and the Visual Arts

1886 Fiction published this year includes U.S. author Sarah Orne Jewett's *A White Heron*, Spanish novelist Emilia Pardo Bazán's *Los pazos de Ulloa* (*The Son of the Bondswoman*), English novelist Frances Hodgson Burnett's best-seller *Little Lord Fauntleroy*, U.S. children's author Louisa May Alcott's last novel, *Jo's Boys*, and English author Marie Corelli's first novel, *A Romance of Two Worlds*.

May 15, 1886 U.S. recluse Emily Dickinson (b. December 10, 1830) dies at the age of fifty-six, leaving a collection of over 1,700 poems, which she asks her sister Lavinia to burn. Lavinia agrees but after Emily's death finds herself unable to complete the task.

Nov. 22, 1886 Civil War diarist Mary Boykin Chesnut (b. March 31, 1823) dies.

1887 Native American potter María Montoya Martínez, famous for her black-on-black wares, and layer of the cornerstone of New York's Rockefeller Center, is born.

1887 New literature includes the chivalric romance *Thelma*, by Marie Corelli (pseudonym of Mary Mackay, 1855–1924), author of twenty-eight best-sellers; Austrian Marie Ebner-Eschenbach's novella *Das Gemeindekind*; Emilia Pardo Bazán's *La madre naturaleza*; and U.S. children's author Kate Douglas Wiggin's *The Birds' Christmas Carol*, a tearjerker about a brave little girl who dies at Christmastime.

1887 U.S. journalist Nelly Bly (pseudonym of Elizabeth Cochrane Seaman, 1867–1922) masquerades as a victim of mental illness in order to expose mistreatment of asylum residents. Bly often goes undercover, eschewing sentimental, "feminine" stories and reporting on factory conditions, slums, divorce, women's prison conditions, and sexual harassment. She is best remembered, however, for her trip around the world in fewer than eighty days, which she completes on January 25, 1890.

1888 *The Women's Newspaper*, the first periodical in Greece run by women for women, is founded by Greek journalist Kalliroe Parren.

1889 U.S. architect Louise Bethune (July 21, 1856–December 18, 1913), a specialist in school design, becomes the first female fellow of the American Institute of Architects.

1889 U.S. potter Maria Storer wins a gold medal at the Paris Exposition for her Rookwood Pottery.

1889 Peruvian novelist Clorinda Matto de Turner (1854–1908) becomes famous with the publication of *Aves sin nido* (*Birds Without a Nest*), a story of the exploitation of Indians by the church and the wealthy. Other novels published this year include *An Irish Cousin*, published by Irish novelist Edith Somerville (b. May 2, 1858) and her cousin Violet Martin under the names "Somerville and Ross," and Austrian Bertha von Suttner's controversial pacifist work *Die Waffen nieder* (*Lay Down Your Arms!*), which inspires her former employer Alfred Nobel to found his peace prize.

Jan. 1889 Americans Charlotte Endymion Porter and Helen Archibald Clarke establish *Poet Lore* magazine.

1890 Emily Dickinson's *Poems* are published posthumously; their unusual use of rhyme and punctuation has been "corrected" by editors Mabel Loomis Todd (November 10, 1856–October 14, 1932) and Thomas Wentworth Higginson.

1890 Anna Sewell publishes the children's novel *Black Beauty*.

Performing Arts and Entertainment

1887 Sarah Bernhardt plays the famous Byzantine courtesan and empress *Theodora*.

1887 Australian soprano Nellie Melba (1861–1931), best known for her performances as Gilda, Mimi, Violetta, and Marguerite, makes her operatic debut.

June 20, 1887 Queen Victoria meets U.S. sharpshooter Annie Oakley, who is touring Europe with Buffalo Bill Cody's Wild West Show, and proclaims her "a wonderful little girl." At thirty paces, Oakley can hit a playing card edge-on; in one contest, she shot at 5,000 targets in nine hours and hit 4,772. On this European tour, she becomes the first woman to shoot at the prestigious London Gun Club. On her second European tour in 1889, she shoots a cigar from Kaiser Wilhelm II's mouth, and the king of Senegal reportedly tries to buy her for 100,000 francs.

1888 Venezuelan pianist Teresa Carreño performs the premiere of MacDowell's D minor Piano Concerto.

1889 German soprano Lilli Lehmann sings the United States's first complete *Ring* cycle.

May 1890 U.S. actress Lillian "Diamond Lil" Russell, now making $35,000 a year and starring in *The Grand Duchess*, is the first person to make a long-distance phone call. From New York, she sings a song for President Benjamin Harrison in Washington, D.C.

Athletics and Exploration

1887 British tennis player Charlotte "Lottie" Dod (1871–1960), also skilled at golf, hockey, skating, and tobogganing, becomes the youngest woman to win a singles title at Wimbledon. In 1888, she repeats her victory.

1887 Etta Hattan, who performs under the stage name Jaguarina, defeats San Francisco soldier Sergeant Owen Davis is a broadsword match. Davis is so outraged at being defeated by a woman that he attacks the referee.

1888 U.S. mountain climber Annie Smith Peck (October 19, 1850–July 18, 1935), who will make her last ascent at age eighty-two, climbs California's 14,380-foot Mount Shasta.

1888 U.S. women participate in a six-day bicycle race.

1890 In Denmark, twenty-seven women form a rowing club.

Activism

1886 Danish activist Mathilde Bajer becomes the first president of the Women's Union for Progress. The organization publishes a paper, *What We Want*, which focuses on various social and political goals, including reductions in military spending.

1886 Women in Palestine agitate unsuccessfully for the right to vote.

1886 Indian feminist and novelist Swarnakumari Devi, editor of the liberal magazine *Bharati*, founds Sakhi Samiti, a women's organization.

1886 French moderate feminist and author Maria Deraismes publishes *Les droits des enfants*.

1886 New U.S. feminist works include temperance advocate Frances Willard's assertiveness handbook *How to Win* and *The History of Woman Suffrage*, by Susan B. Anthony, Elizabeth Cady Stanton, and Matilda Joslyn Gage.

1887 The National Catholic Total Abstinence Union finally allows women's organizations to send their own delegates to the annual meetings, instead of their local priest or other male representative. Catholics are beginning to look at women's suffrage as a way of legislating temperance.

Apr. 1887 The Tennessee Supreme Court overturns a circuit court decision in favor of U.S. journalist and antilynching activist Ida Wells-Barnett, who sued the Chesapeake & Ohio Railroad after she was forcibly moved to a car for blacks only.

July 18, 1887 U.S. nurse and social reformer Dorothea Dix (b. April 4, 1802) dies. She was chiefly responsible for drastic improvements in the care of the mentally ill in mid-nineteenth-century America, who were often housed with criminals and restrained with ropes and chains. She also helped to found at least thirty-two new mental institutions and reformed prisons and hospitals in Scotland, France, Turkey, Russia, and the Channel Islands. She was best known, however, as chief of nurses for the Union army during the Civil War.

1888 Josephina Alvares de Azavedo founds the radical feminist journal *A familia*.

1889 French feminist Eugénie Potonie-Pierre founds La Ligue Socialiste des Femmes.

1889 Australian feminist Louisa Lawson begins seventeen years as editor of *The Dawn*, a periodical produced solely by women.

1889 Dutch feminist Mina Drucker founds De Vrije Vrouwenbeweging (Association of Free Women), later editing its journal, *Evolution*.

Sept. 1889 Jane Addams (September 6, 1860–May 21, 1935) and Ellen Starr (March 19, 1859–February 10, 1940) establish Hull House, the first settlement house in the United States, in Chicago's crowded nineteenth ward.

1890 U.S. social reformer Josephine Shaw Lowell (December 16, 1843–October 12, 1905) becomes the first president of the Consumer Council.

1890 Italian socialist Anna Kulisciov organizes a feminist conference to discuss women's social and economic rights.

1890 U.S. feminist Matilda Joslyn Gage, impatient with the increasing conservatism of the women's movement, forms her own, more progressive organization, the Woman's National Liberal Union.

1890 Women in Persia's royal harem organize a successful anti-British tobacco strike.

Feb. 18, 1890 The NWSA and AWSA reconcile their differences and merge to form the National American Woman Suffrage Association (NAWSA). Elizabeth Cady Stanton is elected president.

Aug. 1890 The first meeting of the Daughters of the American Revolution (DAR) is held in the Washington, D.C., home of one of its three founders, Ellen Hardin

Walworth. The group is formally organized in October.

Business and Industry

c. 1886 U.S. saleswoman P.F.E. Albee becomes the first of about half a million "Avon ladies."

1886 U.S. educator Carrie Everson invents the oil-separation method of ore extraction that becomes the basis of modern mining.

1886 Two hundred female weavers strike successfully in Denmark for higher pay.

1886 Women are about 8–9% of the members of the Knights of Labor.

1886 U.S. entrepreneur Harriet Hubbard Ayer, a successful furniture saleswoman, gets the financial backing to start her own cosmetics firm. She develops the technique of celebrity endorsements, getting actress Lillie Langtry, among others, to describe their successful use of her face cream.

Dec. 1886 U.S. housewife Josephine Cochrane patents the first dishwashing machine, which she designed in a woodshed near her house. In 1893, her dishwasher will win first prize at the Chicago World's Fair.

Dec. 10, 1886 Knights of Labor investigator Leonora Barry, on an inspection of a corset factory in Newark, New Jersey, finds that the workers are fined a dime every time they eat, talk, laugh, or sing.

1888 English women match makers work from 6:30 A.M. to 6:00 P.M. in the summer and from 8:00 A.M. to 6:00 P.M. in the winter. They stand most of the day and have two half-hour meal breaks. Their average salary is four shillings a week. They are fined for various offenses, including threepence for dirty feet, threepence for talking, and fivepence for tardiness. Sexual harassment is common. In this year, English socialist and spiritual leader Annie Besant helps to organize the ambitious Match Girls' Strike in London's East End.

1888 U.S. entrepreneur Anna Bissell (d. 1934), cofounder of the Bissell carpet sweeper company, becomes its head after the death of her husband.

1888 U.S. textile manufacturer Elizabeth Boit (July 9, 1849–November 14, 1932), having risen through the managerial ranks at various textile mills, cofounds the firm of Winship, Boit, and Company. By 1896 it will employ 360 people and produce 300 dozen garments a day. Increasingly successful, Boit will be a considerate employer, sending a streetcar for her workers on rainy days and instituting a profit-sharing plan.

June 1888 Elizabeth Chambers Morgan organizes the first women's federal union in the AFL.

1889 Harriet Morison founds New Zealand's first all-female labor union.

Jan. 1889 U.S. businesswoman and journalist Mary Seymour begins printing the bimonthly *Business Woman's Journal* with an all-female board of officers that includes May Sewall and Frances Willard. The *Journal* sells for a dollar a year and eventually grows to a circulation of 5,000. It features ads for office supplies, articles for working women, recipes, and fashion advice.

Feb. 3, 1889 U.S. outlaw Belle Starr (b. February 5, 1848) is shot and killed, possibly by her own son Edward Reed. A friend and shelterer of bank and train robbers, horse and cattle thieves, and bootleggers, she herself dealt in stolen horses and spent much of her life in saloons, casinos, and dance halls.

1890 In the United States, 13.1% of women are in the work force, constituting 17.2% of the total labor force.

1890 U.S. entrepreneur Rose Markward Knox (1857–1950) cofounds the first company to market gelatin as a dessert.

1890 U.S. inventor Amanda Jones (1835-1914) founds the U.S. Women's Pure Food Vacuum Preserving Company to take advantage of her revolutionary invention, vacuum canning. Jones herself will be forced out of the company in 1893, but it will stay in business for another thirty years.

1890 French socialist and revolutionary Louise Michel leads strikes in the Vienne district.

Science and Medicine

1886 Anandibai Joshee becomes the first Hindu woman and the first Indian woman to earn a medical degree.

1886 U.S. botanist Emily Gregory becomes the first female member of the American Society of Naturalists.

1886 Scottish-American astronomer Williamina Fleming becomes head of the Harvard College Observatory's spectral photograph classification project.

1886 British physician Sophia Jex-Blake establishes the Edinburgh School of Medicine for Women.

1887 Methodist missionary Meta Howard opens Korea's first women's hospital.

1887 Ernestina Pérez and Eloisa Díaz become the first female doctors in Chile.

1888 U.S. astronomer Antonia Maury (March 21, 1866–January 8, 1952) begins working at the Harvard College Observatory for twenty-five cents an hour, classifying the spectra of bright northern stars. She irritates the director, Edward Pickering, by pointing out flaws in his classification structure and developing a better one. In 1889, she discovers the second known spectroscopic binary star (a double star unobservable with the human eye but visible to spectral photographs), and later she will become the first person to calculate the periods of revolution for spectroscopic binaries.

June 15, 1888 U.S. chemist and botanist Rachel Bodley (b. December 7, 1831), a specialist in plant classification and the dean of the Women's Medical College of Pennsylvania from January 1874, dies.

Dec. 24, 1888 Russian mathematician Sonya Kovalevskaya wins the French Académie des Sciences's Prix Bordin for her paper *On the Problem of the Rotation of a Solid Body About a Fixed Point*. Her work in this area will also win her a prize from the Swedish Academy of Sciences. In 1889, she becomes the first woman corresponding member of the Russian Academy of Sciences.

1889 U.S. conchologist Annie Law dies; she discovered eleven new species and one new genus of mollusks.

Jan. 23, 1889 The first nursing school for black women is established in Chicago.

June 28, 1889 U.S. astronomer Maria Mitchell dies. A dedicated teacher and advocate of higher education for women, she studied sunspots, nebulae, and the composition of Jupiter and Saturn. She had profound contempt for all astronomy not based on mathematics and felt that women had a better grasp of detail than men and so made better astronomical observers. A lunar crater was named for her.

1890 U.S. nurse and settlement house worker Lavinia Dock (February 26, 1858–April 17, 1956) publishes *Materia Medica for Nurses*, the first nurses' manual of drugs.

1890 Constance Stone becomes Australia's first woman doctor.

Education and Scholarship

1886 U.S. missionary Mary Fitch Scranton founds the first girls' school in Korea, Ewha Haktang. Food, clothing, and housing are provided free of charge by the

school, but Scranton finds it almost impossible to find girls who will betray Confucian ethics by venturing out of doors in daylight.

1887 English socialist and spiritual leader Annie Besant (1847–1933) is elected to the London School Board. In the latter half of her life, she will become fascinated by India, learning Sanskrit, editing the Madras newspaper *New India*, and translating the Bhagavad Gita.

1888 English author Gertrude Bell (1868–1926) becomes the first woman to earn first-class honors at Oxford. She will later serve as a Red Cross worker during World War I and become a traveler and archaeologist in Israel, Syria, Asia Minor, Iraq, Turkey, and central Arabia.

1889 German conservative feminist Helene Lange (1848–1930) establishes the German Women Teachers' Association.

1889 Barnard College, a women's college affiliated with Columbia University, opens. One of its first trustees is Ella Weed, who supports high academic standards and rejects the finishing-school approach to women's higher education.

1889 St. Hugh's College for women is established at Oxford University.

May 24, 1889 Laura Dewey Bridgman (b. December 21, 1829), the first deaf-blind-mute to be educated, dies.

Mar. 26, 1890 U.S. deaf and blind advocate for the handicapped Helen Keller (June 27, 1880–June 1, 1968) begins to learn to speak. Her teacher is Anne Sullivan (April 14, 1866–October 20, 1936).

Religion

Jan. 21, 1886 U.S. missionary Laura Wright (b. July 10, 1809) dies. In her fifty years among the Seneca Indians of New York, she helped to organize the written version of the Seneca language, wrote bilingual textbooks for schoolchildren, helped to save some of the Seneca lands from confiscation, adopted or otherwise sheltered dozens of orphaned children, and founded the Iroquois Temperance League.

1887 Five women, including U.S. temperance activist Frances Willard, are the first female delegates to the Methodist General Conference, but they are denied their seats.

Dec. 5, 1887 U.S. religious leader Eliza Smith (b. January 21, 1804), known as the "mother of Mormonism," dies. She wrote about a dozen Mormon hymns and led several Mormon women's groups.

1888 U.S. religious leader Mary Baker Eddy opens the first Christian Science reading room.

1889 Italian-American saint and founder Frances Xavier Cabrini expresses a wish to go to China as a missionary, but Pope Leo XIII instead orders her to the United States, where she works with Italian immigrants. With six others, she founds the first U.S. branch of her religious order, the Missionary Sisters of the Sacred Heart. The order eventually founds schools, charitable institutions, and four hospitals.

1889 Annie Besant, an avowed atheist, converts to Theosophy and travels to India to pursue spiritual enlightenment.

1890 In preparation for the World's Columbian Exposition in 1893, American Hannah Solomon organizes a national Jewish Women's Congress. This group later becomes a permanent club, the National Council of Jewish Women, which tries to serve Judaism and the community at large.

1891–1895

General Status and Daily Life

In Nigeria's patrilocal Igbo tribes, a woman belongs to two family groups. Until she is married (and after she is divorced or widowed), she lives in the village of her birth and belongs to the *otu umuada*. The *otu umuada*, led by the oldest woman of the lineage, lobbies for the rights of the lineage and performs certain ceremonial functions, such as the preparation of new brides.

When the woman marries, she moves to her husband's village and becomes part of another group, the *otu inyemedi*, a network of women who have married into a particular village or lineage. This group is led by the *anasi*, the woman who has been married into the group for the longest period of time. She holds meetings, offers advice, and provides support in times of trouble. Women's networks punish lazy husbands and adulterous spouses, make decisions (east of the Niger River, where farming is women's business) about agriculture, and superintend market spaces and women's property.

Among the Luo of western Kenya, women are in charge of agriculture, child care, food storage and preparation, and the repair of houses and granaries. Women are not permitted to eat many kinds of meat and animal-derived foods, including chicken, eggs, milk, rabbit, elephant, and hippo. They also do not own the land they farm; it belongs to the men, who can assign or reassign it to

their wives as they see fit. A woman's land is inherited by her sons, not her daughters.

1891 The age of consent for sexual intercourse is raised from ten to twelve for women in India.

1891 English husbands can no longer enforce their "conjugal rights." Marital rape, however, is still legal in many parts of the world.

Aug. 4, 1892 In Fall River, Massachusetts, Lizzie Borden (1860–1926) reports that her father and stepmother have been murdered. She will be tried for the crime and acquitted on June 21, 1893.

1894 In Korea, child marriage is abolished, and remarriage of widows is legalized.

c. 1895 Gas replaces coal and wood as the principal cooking fuel in industrialized countries.

Government, the Military, and the Law

Jan. 29, 1891 Hawaiian princess Liliuokalani (September 2, 1838–November 11, 1917) becomes queen. The late king's regent while he was ill, she opposed giving the United States a naval base at Pearl Harbor. Her motto is "Hawaii for the Hawaiians." She is deposed in January 1893, and Hawaii is declared an independent republic. In 1895, she is jailed on suspicion of treason after trying to recover her throne.

1892 Mary E. Lease, one of the founders of America's Populist party, gives the party's seconding speech for presidential candidate James B. Weaver.

1892 The women's army of Dahomey, organized in the early eighteenth century, is destroyed by the French.

1893 Polish-German socialist, feminist, and pacifist Rosa Luxemburg (b. March 5, 1870) cofounds Poland's Social Democratic Party.

1893 The French activist group La Solidarité supports five female candidates for National Assembly, including socialist feminist Paule Mink and the group's founder, feminist Eugénie Potonie-Pierre.

1893 Queen Isabella I of Spain is the first woman to appear on a U.S. postage stamp.

Sept. 19, 1893 New Zealand becomes the first nation to grant women the vote.

1894 Cornelia Sorabji (1866–1954) becomes India's first woman law graduate, though she is not allowed to practice until 1923. The second woman law student in

India will not graduate until 1916.

Feb. 14, 1894 U.S. lawyer Myra Bradwell (b. February 12, 1831) dies. She published the *Chicago Legal News*, designed and printed legal forms, practiced before the U.S. Supreme Court, and successfully supported laws favorable to women (including one opening notary public positions to women).

1895 Filipina freedom fighter Trinidad Tescon (1848–1928) joins the rebel forces and begins fighting against Spain, participating in all major battles thereafter. She will be wounded in the Battle of Zaragoza and become a Red Cross organizer.

1895 Ecuadoran colonel Joaquina Galalzo de Larrea fights in the Liberal Revolution, participating in the battles of April 9 and August 6.

Oct. 1895 Queen Ranavalona III offers Madagascar to France as a protectorate provided she can remain queen; the offer is rejected.

Literature and the Visual Arts

The first women's weekly in Turkey begins publication.

1891 New novels include Swedish novelist Selma Lagerlöf's (1858–1940) *Gösta Berling*, South African Olive Schreiner's *Dreams*, Norwegian-Danish novelist Bertha Skram's *Fru Ines*, and Peruvian Clorinda Matto de Turner's *Indole*.

1891 German novelist and historian Ricarda Huch (b. 1864) publishes the poetry collection *Gedichte*.

1891 U.S. author Mary E. Wilkins Freeman (October 31, 1852–March 13, 1930), whose works focus on small-town life in New England, publishes "The Revolt of 'Mother,'" one of her most famous short stories.

1892 U.S. diarist Alice James (August 7, 1848–March 6) and Greek poet Aganice Ainianos (b. 1838) die.

1892 U.S. journalist Winifred Sweet Black, who writes under the pen name "Annie Laurie," gains an exclusive interview with President Benjamin Harrison by hiding under a table in his private railroad car. It is not her first stunt to get a story. She has already exposed the inefficiency of San Francisco's emergency medical system by pretending to faint on a downtown street; the resulting story leads to the purchase of a city ambulance.

1892 The quasi-Renaissance style New Century Club in Philadelphia, designed by U.S. architect Minerva Nichols (May 14, 1861–November 17, 1949), opens.

1892 U.S. economist, author, feminist, and magazine publisher Charlotte Perkins Gilman (July 3, 1860–August 17, 1935) publishes an autobiographical short story, "The Yellow Wallpaper," about the dangers of the "rest cure," in which women (often intelligent professional women) are forced into idleness, gorging, and complete mental inactivity in a misguided attempt to return them to socially acceptable behavior.

Oct. 1892 The Woman's Building for the World's Columbian Exposition is dedicated. The first of the buildings to be started and the first to be finished, it is the creation of architect Sophia Gregoria Hayden (1868–1953) and features two murals by Mary Cassatt. Hayden was paid only $1,500 for her work, one-third to one-tenth as much as the male designers received.

Nov. 20, 1892 Syrian publisher Hind Nawfal founds the women's magazine *al-Fatat* (*Young Girl*) in Alexandria, Egypt.

1893 Author Charlotte Maria Tucker, who published about 150 books under the initials A.L.O.E. (A Lady of England), dies.

1893 New novels include Marie Corelli's *Barabbas*, Ricarda Huch's autobiographical *Erinnerungen von Ludolf Ursleu dem Jüngeren*, and Clorinda Matto de Turner's *Herencia*.

1893 Chinese artist Lady Ailian paints *Nymph of the Luo River* on a fan. The nymph is a beautiful, delicate woman with windblown robes and a peacock feather; she is a character from a poem who is often used as a symbol of love.

1893 A seventeenth-century painting purchased by the Louvre, thought to be by Franz Hals, is discovered to be a Judith Leyster instead. The revelation leads to a rediscovery of Leyster's works.

1893 Women artists exhibiting this year include U.S. Impressionist painter Mary Cassatt and German artist Käthe Kollwitz, both holding their first shows—Cassatt in Paris and Kollwitz in Berlin. U.S. sculptor Adelaide Johnson exhibits busts of Lucretia Mott, Elizabeth Cady Stanton, and Susan B. Anthony at the World's Columbian Exposition in Chicago.

1894 U.S. sculptor Harriet Hosmer completes a statue of Spain's Queen Isabella I for the city of San Francisco.

1894 U.S. author Kate Chopin publishes the short story collection *Bayou Folk*.

May 20, 1894 U.S. journalist Adela Rogers St. Johns is born. She will cover the Lindbergh kidnapping trial, the abdication of Edward VIII, the plight of the Los Angeles poor, and the conspiracy and bank robbery trial of heiress Patricia Hearst.

1895 German artist Käthe Kollwitz begins her series of prints entitled *Revolt of the Weavers*.

Performing Arts and Entertainment

1891 U.S. dancer Loie Fuller (January 15, 1862–January 1, 1928) becomes famous for her skirt dances, in which she exploits the effect of light on voluminous quantities of silk.

1892 English music hall singer Lottie Collins performs "Ta-ra-ra-boom-de-ay."

1892 U.S. composer Amy Marcy Beach's (1867–December 27, 1944) concert aria *Eilende Wolken* is the first work by a woman performed by the New York Philharmonic.

1893 Sarah Bernhardt takes over the Théâtre de la Renaissance, naming it after herself.

1893 Venezuelan pianist Teresa Carreño makes her Berlin debut.

1893 British composer Ethel Smyth's Mass in D is performed at the Albert Hall.

1893 Calamity Jane tours England with Buffalo Bill's Wild West Show.

Jan. 15, 1893 English actress Fanny Kemble (b. November 27, 1809) dies. She played Juliet, Lady Macbeth, Portia, Beatrice, and other roles so well that she single-handedly saved her father's troupe from bankruptcy. Her private life was less successful, and she divorced her American husband, whose slaveholding she abhorred, in 1848.

1895 Brazilian piano prodigy Guiomar Novaës is born.

1895 Russian ballerina and teacher Mathilde Kschessinskaya (1872–1971) earns the title *prima ballerina assoluta*.

1895 Italian tragedian Eleonora Duse (October 3, 1858–April 21, 1924) and French actress Sarah Bernhardt, long rivals, reach the height of their competition when both women play Magda in *Heimat* in London.

July 4, 1895 U.S. professor Katharine Lee Bates (August 12, 1859–March 28, 1929) publishes the song "America the Beautiful," which she wrote after being inspired by the view from Pikes Peak during an 1893 trip to Colorado.

Athletics and Exploration

College women become more interested in sports, taking up rowing, track, and swimming. The bicycle becomes more popular. Some women wear divided skirts in order to pedal more comfortably, and hemlines rise above the ankle to keep from getting entangled. Skirt hems are weighted with lead so they will not fly up while riding.

1891 A proposed tour of a women's rugby team in New Zealand is canceled after an indignant outcry at such unfeminine behavior.

1891 British tennis player Lottie Dod wins the singles title at Wimbledon. She will repeat the feat in 1892 and 1893.

1891 American May Sheldon travels extensively in Africa, negotiating with local tribes and exploring Lake Chala. In 1892 she publishes *Sultan to Sultan* and becomes a fellow of the Royal Geographical Society.

1892 Women from Cambridge's Girton and Newnham Colleges play each other in field hockey. The game is considered most unladylike by many, including Cheltenham Ladies' College principal Dorothea Beale. Upon seeing some of her students playing the game, she once said, "The children will hurt themselves if they all run about after one ball. Get some more balls at once."

1892 The first women's basketball game takes place at Smith College in Massachusetts, introduced to the college by physical education director Senda Berenson.

1893 British traveler Freya Stark, mountain climber, World War I nurse, and author of books about Iraq, Iran, southern Arabia, and other areas of the East, is born.

1893 The Ladies' Golf Union is formed in Britain; English golfer Lady Margaret Scott wins the first British Women's Championship. She will win again in 1894 and 1895.

1893 In the past eleven years, British mountaineer Katy Richardson (1864–1927) has made 116 major ascents, 6 of them first ascents and 14 of them the first ascents by a woman.

1893 British explorer Mary Kingsley travels to the Congo. She spends much of the rest of her life in Africa, garbed in full black dresses and wielding an umbrella. She pilots a 2,000-ton ship and falls into a spiked animal trap, saved from serious injury only by the voluminous layers of her fashionable skirt. In 1895 she will explore the Congo's Ogowe River.

1894 Australian women hold a golf tournament for

themselves, one year before the first national tournament for men.

1894 The U.S. Golf Association, which admits both men and women, is founded.

1894 English explorer Isabella Bird Bishop begins a three-year trip alone that will take her 8,000 miles across China, Canada, Japan, and Korea. En route she will establish three hospitals.

1895 In Germany, a canoe race for women is held by a Berlin rowing club.

1895 The All-England Women's Field Hockey Association is founded.

1895 U.S. mountain climber Annie Smith Peck ascends the Matterhorn, becoming famous for the feat and infamous for her unfeminine climbing attire.

1895 French bicyclist Hélène Dutrieu sets a distance record of 39.19 kilometers in one hour.

Activism

1891 French moderate feminist and author Maria Deraismes publishes *Eve dans l'humanité*.

1891 French feminists Eugénie Potonie-Pierre and Maria Martin establish Le Groupe de la Solidarité des Femmes.

1891 The first convention of the World's WCTU is held in Boston; U.S. temperance activist and feminist Frances Willard is elected the organization's first president.

1891 Australian feminist Rose Scott founds the Womanhood Suffrage League; Mary Windeyer becomes its first president.

1892 Marie Popelin cofounds Belgium's first feminist organization, the Belgian League of Women's Rights.

1892 Eugénie Potonie-Pierre unites eight feminist organizations as the Federation Française des Sociétés Feministes. Founding members include French socialist Aline Valette.

1892 German communist and feminist Clara Zetkin (1857–1933) becomes editor of the journal *Gleichheit* (*Equality*), a position she will hold until 1916.

Jan. 18, 1892 Elizabeth Cady Stanton retires as president of NAWSA and is replaced by Susan B. Anthony.

Mar. 9, 1892 Journalist Ida Wells-Barnett (July 16, 1862–March 25, 1931), half owner of the *Memphis Free Speech*, denounces the recent lynching of three black men and begins to publicize the motives behind other lynchings. On May 27, her newspaper offices are burned by a mob, and Wells-Barnett is driven from Memphis.

Aug. 4, 1892 Polish-American feminist and reformer Ernestine Rose (b. January 13, 1810), an influential figure in the American Equal Rights Association and NWSA, dies.

1893 Antisuffragist Katherine E. Conway presents a paper at the World's Columbian Congress entitled "Woman Has No Vocation to Public Life." Feminist Carrie Chapman Catt (January 9, 1859–March 9, 1947) replies with a speech on the "Evolution of Woman Suffrage."

1894 Irish courtesan Laura Bell dies. She became a prostitute in Dublin and London, married, and then began a life of missionary work among prostitutes.

1894 Dutch doctor, feminist, and birth control advocate Aletta Jacobs establishes the Association for Women's Suffrage.

1894 German feminist and educator Auguste Schmidt becomes the first president of the Bund Deutscher Frauenverein (Federation of German Women's Associations), which unites thirty-four groups.

1894 U.S. clubwoman Josephine St. Pierre Ruffin (August 31, 1842–March 13, 1924), with her daughter, founds the Woman's Era Club, one of the first civic organizations for black women. She becomes its first president, a post she will hold until 1903.

1894 U.S. reformer Ellen M. Henrotin (July 6, 1847–June 29, 1922) becomes president of the General Federation of Women's Clubs (founded 1889), a post she will hold until 1898.

1895 Josephine St. Pierre Ruffin cofounds the National Federation of Afro-American Women, later the National Association of Colored Women (NACW).

1895 German feminist Minna Cauer (1841–1922) establishes a progressive magazine, *The Women's Movement*.

Business and Industry

About 25% of Russian factory workers are female; 37,500 Russian women work at home winding cotton for about five cents a day. Women textile workers earn about thirty cents a day.

1891   Britain's new National Union for Shop Assistants begins admitting women.

1891   German law limits women's work hours so that they will have time for housework.

1891   Kansas farm labor organizer Mary Lease, who tells farmers to "raise less corn and more hell," is elected master workman of a Knights of Labor district assembly.

1892   U.S. labor leader Mary Kenney O'Sullivan becomes the AFL's first woman general organizer.

1893   Grace Neill becomes New Zealand's first female factory inspector.

1893   Austrian activist Louise Kautsky delivers a paper on women workers to the International Socialist Workers Congress.

1893   Six hundred workers stage Austria's first women's strike.

1893   U.S. cosmetics entrepreneur Harriet Hubbard Ayer wages a fierce battle against one of her backers that ends with the loss of her business and her own institutionalization for fourteen months.

1894   English unionist Clementina Black (1854–1922) cofounds the Women's Industrial Council.

c. 1895   U.S. female store clerks make about two dollars for a seventy-hour week; factory work pays more but is considered lower-class and degrading.

Science and Medicine

1891   German naturalist Amalie Dietrich (b. 1821), collector of birds, mammals, and Papuan aborigine skeletons, dies.

1891   Amelia Cardia becomes Portugal's first female physician.

1891   U.S. astronomer Dorothea Klumpke Roberts (1861–1942), a measurer of nebulae and cataloguer of stars, becomes director of the Paris Bureau of Measurements, a post she will hold for ten years. In 1893, she will win a prize from the Académie des Sciences.

1891   There are 101 female doctors in Great Britain.

1891   U.S. botanist Elizabeth Britton (January 9, 1858–February 25, 1934), who will have fifteen species of plants named for her, inspires the establishment of the New York Botanical Garden.

1891   At Wellesley, U.S. psychologist and philosopher Mary Calkins establishes the first psychology lab at a women's college.

Feb. 10, 1891   Russian mathematician Sonya Kovalevskaya, a professor at the University of Stockholm, dies. Her childhood tutor considered her bad at arithmetic, but she became well respected in her field, cowrote a play, and published several autobiographical novels. She had to arrange a marriage of convenience to study at a university, since Russian law at the time forbade women's travel outside the country without the permission of a husband or father.

1892   Isabella Bird Bishop becomes the first female member of the Royal Geographical Society.

1893   French-Brazilian obstetrician Marie Durocher (b. 1809) dies. A practicing physician for sixty years, she wore men's clothing and was influenced by French obstetrician Marie Bovin.

1893   Scientific publications in the United States include ethnologist Alice Cunningham Fletcher's *A Study of Omaha Music* and astronomer Williamina Fleming's article "A Field for Women's Work in Astronomy."

1893   Johns Hopkins Medical School opens, financed by a group of women on the condition that women be admitted equally.

1894   U.S. geologist Florence Bascom (July 14, 1862–June 18, 1945) becomes the first woman fellow of the Geological Society of America.

1894   U.S. physician and bacteriologist Anna Williams discovers Park-Williams #8, a type of diphtheria bacillus. Within months an antitoxin is available for use in fighting the disease, with free medication offered to those who cannot afford to buy it. The result of her work is a sharp decrease in diphtheria deaths throughout the United States and in other countries as well.

1894   Canadian-American botanist Alice Eastwood (b. January 19, 1859), who joined the California Academy of Sciences in 1892 and will remain associated with it for fifty-five more years, replaces Katharine Brandegee as the curator of its herbarium.

1894   The Edinburgh Medical School begins admitting women, largely due to the agitation of British doctor Sophia Jex-Blake.

1895   Lilian Murray becomes the first woman dentist in Britain.

1895   Australian feminist Mary Windeyer helps to found the Women's Hospital in Sydney and becomes its first president.

May 21, 1895 Dr. Mary Thompson (b. April 15, 1829), the most prominent woman physician of her time in the American Midwest, noted for her skill in abdominal and pelvic surgery and for her invention of a type of surgical needle, dies.

Education and Scholarship

1891 Married women are not allowed to work as teachers in Washington, D.C., schools.

1891 Pandita Ramabai introduces the kindergarten to India.

1891 Mary Emma Woolley becomes the first female student at Brown University.

1891 The University of Heidelberg allows women to audit classes.

1892 Current works of literary criticism include Russian-German intellectual Lou Andreas-Salomé's study of Ibsen, *Henrik Ibsens Frauengestalten*, and German socialist and feminist Lily Braun's (1865–1916) *Aus Goethes Freudenkreis*.

1893 U.S. scientist Elizabeth Agassiz becomes the first president of Radcliffe College.

1893 U.S. pacifist, economist, and reformer Emily Greene Balch (January 8, 1867–January 9, 1961) publishes *Public Assistance of the Poor in France*.

1893 U.S. physical education specialist Jessie Bancroft becomes the director of physical training for the Brooklyn public schools, making her the first woman to head a large public school system's physical education program.

1893 Mount Holyoke College is established; St. Hilda's College for women is established at Oxford University by English educator and feminist Dorothea Beale.

1894 English educator Frances Buss (b. 1827), a lifelong proponent of higher education for women and the first president of the Association of Headmistresses, dies.

1894 French socialist feminist Paule Mink becomes editorial secretary of the journal *La question sociale*.

1894 Italian educator Maria Montessori (August 31, 1870–May 6, 1952) becomes the first woman in Italy to earn an M.D.

Jan. 3, 1894 U.S. educator, transcendentalist, author, and publisher Elizabeth Palmer Peabody (b. May 16, 1804) dies. She shaped the careers of such noted transcendentalists as William Ellery Channing, Bronson Alcott, Nathaniel Hawthorne, Ralph Waldo Emerson, and Henry David Thoreau. Her influential Boston bookstore served as transcendentalist headquarters and made her one of the first female publishers in the United States. Peabody was also instrumental in spreading the kindergarten movement in the United States, though her devotion to Christian education set her apart from both the kindergarten advocates and the transcendentalists.

1895 English socialist Beatrice Webb helps to found the London School of Economics.

1895 U.S. reformer and suffragist Mary Church Terrell (September 23, 1863–July 24, 1954) becomes the first black woman on the District of Columbia Board of Education.

1895 Muslim Indian feminist Amina Tyabaji founds a girls' school.

1895 Spanish social scientist Concepción Arenal's (1820–1893) studies *La mujer del pervenir* and *La mujer de su casa* are published posthumously. Other new works include Swedish feminist Ellen Key's *Individualism och Socialism*, U.S. journalist Ida Tarbell's *A Short Life of Napoleon*, which sells 100,000 copies, and Lou Andreas-Salomé's *Jesus der Jude*.

Religion

1892 Mary Baker Eddy's Church of Christ, Scientist is officially recognized as a religion.

1893 U.S. feminist Matilda Joslyn Gage publishes *Woman, Church, and State*, a controversial book blaming Christianity for increasing sexism.

1895 U.S. feminist Elizabeth Cady Stanton publishes the first volume of *The Woman's Bible*, which reinterprets scriptural passages in a feminist, rather than misogynist, light.

1895 Mrs. Chon Samdok is the first baptized Protestant woman in the P'yongyang area of Korea.

1896–1900

General Status and Daily Life

Among the Luo of western Kenya, a bride is captured in

a ritual kidnapping (*yuayo*) that sometimes truly takes place against her will. Whether she is a willing party or not, she is expected to resist the groom's accomplices physically and verbally as they carry her off to her new home. Some brides run away from their new husbands, but usually they are returned by their parents. Polygyny is common.

A new bride lives for a few years in the home of her parents-in-law before establishing her own household, after which she is still expected to please and assist her mother-in-law. The wife cultivates her husband's fields, producing enough grain, yams, beans, and vegetables to feed her family and selling any surplus to accumulate wealth and cattle for herself. She will often use this wealth to help her sons purchase good brides, who in turn help her with her agricultural tasks in old age.

When a woman's husband dies, she is traditionally taken in marriage by one of his relatives. A wife wears a sisal-fiber tassel called a *chieno* around her waist to symbolize her married status.

1896 U.S. cookery author Fannie Farmer publishes the *Boston Cooking School Cookbook*.

1898 Japan's Meiji Civil Code denies women custody of their children in divorce, the right to sign contracts without their husbands' consent, the right to marry under the age of twenty-five without their fathers' permission, and redress for their husbands' adultery (though the husbands may divorce and prosecute them for the same offense). Divorce by mutual consent is, however, legalized.

1899 Yun Ko-ra is the first prominent Korean woman to wear Western clothes.

1900 Life expectancy at birth in the United States is 48.3 for women (64 for white women) and 46.3 for men. The average U.S. woman has 3.56 children.

1900 Ice, which has been producible in factories since the 1870s, is now made in over 2,000 ice plants and delivered for home iceboxes, which are now a common feature of middle-class U.S. houses.

Government, the Military, and the Law

1896 Warrior Ambuya Nehanda of Zimbabwe begins a revolt against the British that will lead to her execution.

Jan. 11, 1897 Utah's M. H. Cannon becomes the first woman state senator.

June 22, 1897 Queen Victoria celebrates her Diamond Jubilee.

1898 Sierra Leone leader Madam Yoko, queen of Seneghun, expands her lands by judiciously supporting the British during a local rebellion.

Sept. 22, 1898 The emperor of China is imprisoned by his former regent, Dowager Empress Tz'u-Hsi. Tz'u-Hsi, afraid of the reforms the emperor was contemplating, seizes power for herself.

1900 Ghanaian soldier Yaa Asantewaa leads troops against the British in the Anglo-Ashanti War.

June 1900 Tz'u-Hsi supports the Boxer Rebellion. On June 21, she declares war on all foreign powers in China. Later in the summer, she flees with the emperor to Xi'an in a cart, taking with her $70 million worth of royal treasure.

Literature and the Visual Arts

1896 Japanese author Higuchi Ichiyo (b. 1872) dies.

1896 U.S. author Sarah Orne Jewett publishes her most famous short story collection, *The Country of the Pointed Firs*.

1897 New novels include South African Olive Schreiner's pro-Boer *Trooper Peter Halket of Mashonaland*, Italian Grazia Deledda's *Tesoro*, and American Ellen Glasgow's (April 22, 1874–1941) novel, *The Descendant*.

1897 Archaeologists unearth papier-mâché coffins, in whose materials they find scraps of long-lost poetry by Sappho of Lesbos.

1897 English traveler Gertrude Bell, who has taught herself Persian, translates and publishes a collection of poems, *Poems from the Divan of Hafiz*.

1897 U.S. painter Cecilia Beaux (May 1, 1855–September 12, 1942) has the first of fourteen one-woman shows and wins the Carnegie Institute's gold medal. She won the Carnegie bronze last year, and next year she will win a gold medal from the Pennsylvania Academy of Fine Arts. In 1900 she will take a gold at the Paris Exposition.

1898 German artist Käthe Kollwitz (July 8, 1867–April 22, 1945), famous for her etchings, lithographs, woodcuts, and sculpture, wins a gold medal for her print cycle *Revolt of the Weavers*, but the medal is withheld because of the prints' politically controversial message and will not be awarded until 1900.

1898 U.S. journalist Winifred Black interviews Mormon women in an effort to bring an end to polygamy in Utah.

1898 U.S. sculptor Meta Vaux Warrick Fuller (June 6, 1877–March 13, 1968) creates the metal *Crucifixion of Christ in Agony*.

1898 Norwegian-Danish novelist Bertha Skram completes her best-known work, the tragic tetralogy *Hellemyrsfolket*.

July 20, 1898 U.S. journalist Marie Manning (Jan. 22, 1873?–November 28, 1945) begins writing the country's first syndicated romantic advice column, signing herself "Miss Beatrice Fairfax."

1899 French painter Rosa Bonheur (b. 1822) dies. She was noted almost as much for her life-style (she wore men's clothes and never married, preferring a forty-year companionship with the artist Natalie Micas) as for her powerful and accurate depictions of animals. To make sure her knowledge of animal anatomy was sound, she frequented slaughterhouses and dissected animal parts acquired from butchers.

1899 U.S. author Kate Chopin (February 8, 1851–August 22, 1904) publishes the novel *The Awakening*, in which an unhappy wife discovers her individuality but cannot gain her freedom and commits suicide. Controversial, the novel is met with shocked horror across the country and banned by the public library in St. Louis (Chopin's hometown). The St. Louis Fine Arts Club bans Chopin from membership, and she writes little else.

1899 Polish author Gabriela Zapolska (pseudonym of Gabriela Kerwin-Piotrowska) publishes the novel *Z pamietrikow mlodej mezatki* (*Memoirs of a Newly-Wed Woman*).

1899 Beatrix Jones Farrand cofounds the American Society of Landscape Architects.

1900 Award-winning Polish architect Helena Syrkius is born.

1900 Greek writer Sappho Leontias (b. 1832), who ran her own literary magazine, *Euridice*, and advocated the use of modern Greek in schools and literature, dies.

1900 Anna Golubkina is the first Russian artist to glorify the common worker in sculpture.

1900 U.S. author Natalie Clifford Barney (b. October 31, 1876) publishes a poem collection, *Quelques portraits-sonnets des femmes*.

1900 Novels published this year include *Il vecchio della montagna*, by Italian Grazia Deledda (1871–1936), author of thirty-two other novels; Englishwoman Mary Elizabeth Braddon's *The Infidel*; and English romantic novelist Marie Corelli's *The Master Christian*.

1900 Kate Chopin publishes her last story, "Charlie," about a tomboy who rejects marriage and a typical "lady's" education to manage her family's plantation.

1900 French author Sidonie Gabrielle Colette (b. January 28, 1873), with some help from her husband, Willy, publishes the first Claudine novel, *Claudine à l'école* (*Claudine at School*).

Jan. 13, 1900 Denver attorney William Anderson shoots two editors of the *Denver Post* who have insulted him; journalist Leonel Ross Campbell (b. 1857), better known as "Polly Pry," grabs the gun barrel, and when he threatens to shoot her, she says, "Go ahead. And then hang." He does not shoot.

Sept. 1900 Winifred Black, disguised as a boy, is the first outside reporter in Galveston, Texas, after it is devastated by a storm and tidal wave that killed more than 7,000 people. She is the only woman journalist to cover the story.

Performing Arts and Entertainment

1896 Hungarian opera singer Katharina Klafsky, noted for her Wagnerian roles, dies.

1896 Composer and pianist Amy Marcy Beach composes her *Gaelic Symphony*, the first symphony written by an American woman. It is performed by the Boston Symphony Orchestra.

1896 Danish ballerina Adeline Genée (1878–1970) performs the role of Swanilda for the first time; this role will become closely identified with her.

1896 French film director Alice Guy-Blaché (1875–1968) makes *La Fée aux Choux*, arguably the first fiction film.

1897 U.S. actress Maude Adams (b. November 11, 1872) achieves stardom in James Barrie's *The Little Minister* and heads her own theatrical company.

1898 Bohemian-American opera singer Ernestine Schumann-Heink joins New York's Metropolitan Opera.

1898 English composer Ethel Smyth (April 24, 1858–1944), England's first major woman composer, composes the opera *Fantasio*.

1899 U.S. actress Lillian Russell (December 4, 1861–June 6, 1922) commands $1,250 a week for music hall performances.

1899 Irish playwright Augusta Gregory (1852–1932) cofounds the Irish Literary Theatre (later the Abbey

Theatre) in Dublin.

Nov. 20, 1900 French actress Sarah Bernhardt arrives in America for first time since 1896, with fifty supporting players and an intention to play the title role in *Hamlet*, which she thinks will not do well in the United States because of "its seriousness."

Athletics and Exploration

Some experts believe that athletic activity draws strength away from a woman's reproductive organs.

1896 French bicyclist Amélie LeGall, who competes under the pseudonym "Lisette," beats Scottish bicyclist Clara Grace in a one hundred-kilometer race with a time of two hours, forty-one minutes, twelve seconds.

1896 Australia's Royal Melbourne Golf Club has 132 female members.

1896 The first modern Olympic games are held; women are not invited to participate.

Apr. 4, 1896 The first women's intercollegiate basketball game is played between women from Stanford University and the University of California at Berkeley.

1897 U.S. mountaineer Annie Smith Peck climbs Mexico's Popocatepetl and sets an altitude record for women in the Americas by climbing 18,314-foot Mount Orizaba. In 1900, she climbs the Fünffingerspitze, Monte Cristallo, and the Jungfrau.

1897-1899 U.S. traveler and mountaineer Fanny Bullock Workman (b. January 8, 1859) bicycles with her husband for 1,800 miles in Ceylon (Sri Lanka), 1,500 miles in Java, Sumatra, and Cochin China (Vietnam), and 14,000 miles in India.

1898 French driver Mme. Laumaillé becomes the first woman auto racer, finishing fourth in a two-day event from Marseilles to Nice.

1899 Crow women participate in bareback horse races.

1899 The Brazilian states of Pará and Amazonas hire French explorer Octavie Coudreau to chart the Amazon area. Already the author of several books on French Guiana and northern Brazil, Coudreau will explore the Amazon for most of the rest of her life.

1899 Fanny Bullock Workman and her husband make the first of seven exploratory expeditions in the Himalayas, during which they will make some of the first maps and scientific observations of this mountain range. On this trip, they explore the Biafo Glacier and reach an altitude of 17,500 feet.

1899 Smith College physical education director Senda Berenson (March 19, 1868–February 16, 1954) draws up the first official rules for women's basketball. The rules, which will remain in force for seventy years, limit a player to three dribbles and three seconds of holding the ball.

1900 British traveler and explorer Mary Kingsley (b. 1862), who published *Travels in West Africa* in 1897, dies. She argued against imposing European culture on Africa.

1900 British mountaineer Elizabeth Le Blond leads what is possibly the first women's mountain-climbing expedition.

1900 At the Olympics, British tennis player Charlotte Cooper wins the first women's gold medal; American Margaret Abbott takes the gold in the nine-hole golf event.

July 8, 1900 Blanche Hillyard wins the Wimbledon singles title.

Activism

Russian feminists express rebellion by wearing plain clothing and hairstyles, smoking, and forming marriages of convenience to get the right to travel, which can be granted only by a father or a husband.

1896 Swedish feminist Ellen Key (1849–1926) publishes *Missbrukad Kvinnokraft* (*The Abuse of Women's Energy*).

1896 U.S. reformer and suffragist Mary Church Terrell becomes president of the NACW.

1897 Russian political prisoner Maria Vetrovna, raped by her guards, burns herself alive. St. Petersburg student Concordia Samoilova organizes a women's demonstration in protest.

1897 U.S. Theosophist Katherine Tingley (July 6, 1847–July 11, 1929) founds the International Brotherhood League to help minorities, laborers, convicts, and women.

1897 Millicent Garrett Fawcett (1847–1929), sister of English doctor Elizabeth Garrett Anderson, becomes president of the National Union of Women Suffrage Societies.

1898-1900 German feminist Lida Heymann (1867–1943) leads a campaign against prostitution and founds the radical Verein Frauenwald (Women's Welfare Association).

1898   The Danish Women's Suffrage Committee is established.

1898   Alexandra Afernuh becomes owner, editor, and publisher of the Egyptian women's journal *Anis al-Galis*.

1898   Chinese revolutionary Ch'iu Chin (b. 1879), with Joan of Arc as her model, joins the revolt against the Manchu dynasty.

Mar. 18, 1898   U.S. feminist Matilda Joslyn Gage (b. March 25, 1826) dies. Her gravestone is inscribed with her motto: "There is a word sweeter than Mother, Home, or Heaven; that word is Liberty."

1899   Susan B. Anthony represents the United States at the conference of the International Council of Women, which she cofounded. U.S. pacifist May Sewall becomes the organization's president.

1899   U.S. militant temperance activist Carrie Nation (November 25, 1846–June 9, 1911) starts her campaign to close the saloons of Kansas, attacking bars with a hatchet.

1899   Italian feminist author Sibilla Aleramo (1876–1960) edits the magazine *L'Italia femminile* (*Female Italy*).

1899   U.S. anarchist Emma Goldman (June 27, 1869–May 14, 1940) is arrested on suspicion of complicity in a plot to kill President McKinley.

1899   Australian feminist Vida Goldstein begins publishing a monthly newspaper, *The Australian Woman's Sphere*.

1899   German feminist Marie Stritt (1856–1928) replaces Auguste Schmidt as president of the Bund Deutscher Frauenverein (Federation of German Women's Associations).

Mar. 1899   Korean women form Yo-u-hoe (the Association of Women Friends) to oppose concubinage. They stage a sit-in in front of Toksu Palace.

1900   Nigerian feminist Fumilayo Ransome-Kuti, fighter for women's legal and economic rights, is born.

1900   Argentina's Socialist Feminist Center is founded to work for protective labor laws for women.

1900   U.S. journalist and civil rights activist Ida Wells-Barnett becomes the first president of the Negro Fellowship League.

1900   In the United States, the all-black Women's Era Club, led by Josephine St. Pierre Ruffin, is accepted by the General Federation of Women's Clubs, then rejected on the basis of race. Ruffin herself is offered a seat as a delegate on behalf of two other organizations, but she refuses in protest.

1900   Susan B. Anthony steps down as head of NAWSA and is succeeded by Carrie Chapman Catt.

1900   Argentina's first woman doctor, Cecilia Grierson, founds the feminist National Women's Council.

1900   German feminists Anita Augsburg (1857–1943) and Minna Cauer establish the Verband fortschritter Frauenvereine (Union of Progressive Women's Associations).

Business and Industry

1897   German manufacturer Melainie Schwarz becomes the first woman to build a rigid airship; it was designed by her husband, David, who died earlier this year.

Aug. 10, 1898   U.S. dress designer Ellen Demorest (b. November 15, 1824), who began her career as a milliner and coinvented (but did not patent) the paper dress pattern, dies. Her patterns were color-coded for easy use and were popularized through "Madame" Demorest's fashion magazine, which featured the first personal advice column. An abolitionist, Demorest hired both black and white seamstresses despite the fact that her policy lost her some customers. She also invented a bosom pad, a shoulder brace, a hoopskirt, a corset, and a "dress elevator" to lift dresses above dirty streets.

1900   U.S. sisters Ada (February 15, 1875–January 3, 1960) and Minna Everleigh (July 13, 1878–September 16, 1948) open a bordello, the $55,000 Everleigh Club in Chicago. Over the next ten years, they will invest $200,000 more in their establishment, building an art gallery, ballroom, and music room. The sisters employ about thirty prostitutes, whose favors cost about twenty-five or fifty dollars, as opposed to the typical two dollars made by most Chicago prostitutes. The Everleighs make a point of wooing journalists and politicians. They are so popular, in fact, with newspapermen that when a story breaks late at night, the city desk staffers of the *Chicago Tribune* automatically phone the Everleigh Club to locate absent reporters and editors. Always practical, the Everleighs expand their clientele by instituting charge and corporate accounts.

1900   In the United States, 8.6 million women are employed outside the home, many in factory jobs that pay as little as $1.56 for a 70-hour week. Fewer are employed than before in domestic service, more in clerical jobs. Ninety percent are crowded into 25 of 252 job types. The work force is 18.1% female, with 14.3%

of all women working for pay.

1900 The Korean government hires women for the first time in the modern era. Several young women take jobs at the royal mint and cut off their long hair as a sign of independence. In the next few years, textile and tobacco plants will begin hiring women as well.

1900 A survey of Paris prostitutes reveals that more than 50% were formerly domestic servants.

Science and Medicine

1896 Geologist Florence Bascom becomes the first female member of the U.S. Geological Survey.

1896 Physician Kim Chom-dong (Esther Pak) becomes the first Korean woman to study in the United States and the first to study Western medicine.

1896 British astronomer Mary Evershed (1867–1949), noted for her work on solar prominences, publishes *Southern Stars: A Guide to the Constellations Visible in the Southern Hemisphere.*

1897 U.S. chemist Florence Seibert, inventor of an improved apparatus for distilling water and isolator of a pure strain of tuberculin, is born.

1897 U.S. nurse Isabel Robb cofounds and becomes the first president of the Nurses' Associated Alumnae of the United States and Canada (later the American Nurses' Association).

1897 U.S. archaeologist Harriet Boyd Hawes (October 11, 1871–March 31, 1945), who caused a stir by riding her bicycle through the streets of Athens, Greece, volunteers for Red Cross nursing duty during the Balkan War between Greece and Turkey. Later, during World War I, she will risk her life in a war zone to deliver food and clothing to Serbian soldiers in Corfu.

1898 U.S. doctor Helen Taussig, a specialist in congenital heart deformities and a pioneer in surgery on cyanotic infants, is born.

1898 U.S. physician Elizabeth Hurdon (d. 1941) becomes the first woman on the staff of Johns Hopkins University's Medical School.

1898 Polish-French physicist Marie Sklodowska Curie (b. 1867), who coined the term *radioactivity*, invents a new method for extracting radioactive material from raw ore and, with her husband, Pierre, discovers element 84, which they name polonium after Marie's native Poland. In December, the Curies announce the discovery of yet another element, radium.

1898 U.S. ornithologist Florence Merriam Bailey publishes *Birds of Village and Field*, one of the first popular American bird guides.

1898 Rabies vaccine is now produced in large quantities, largely due to the efforts of U.S. physician and bacteriologist Anna Williams.

1898 British physicist Hertha Ayrton becomes the only woman in the Institution of Electrical Engineers.

1898 Scottish-American astronomer Williamina Fleming becomes curator of astronomical photographs at Harvard College Observatory, supervising about twelve women. She is the first woman to receive a corporation appointment at Harvard.

1899 British astronomer Elizabeth Brown, who specialized in solar observation, especially sunspots and solar eclipses, dies.

1899 U.S. physicist Marcia Keith cofounds the American Physical Society.

1899 Women are admitted to Cornell University's medical school; pioneering doctor Elizabeth Blackwell, believing that women now have adequate access to medical education, closes her own medical school for women.

1899 U.S. naturalist Anna Comstock, with the rank of assistant professor, becomes the first woman professor at Cornell University. She won't become a full professor until 1920, and then only after a demotion to lecturer to satisfy outraged university trustees.

1899 British physicist Hertha Ayrton presents a paper on the electric arc to the Institution of Electrical Engineers and presides over the physical science division of the International Council of Women in London.

1900 Japanese woman doctor Yoshioka Yayoi (b. 1872) opens the country's first medical school for women.

1900 The United States has about 5,000 women doctors, 1,500 women medical students, and 7 medical schools for women.

1900 U.S. philanthropist Mrs. John C. Whitin builds an observatory at Wellesley College, replacing the scanty equipment there with a state-of-the-art telescope and making the college competitive in the fast-developing field of astronomy.

Oct. 1900 The *American Journal of Nursing* begins publication, with professional nurse Sophia Palmer as its first editor in chief.

Education and Scholarship

Five-sixths of Russian women are illiterate.

1896 U.S. journalist Ida Tarbell (November 5, 1857–January 6, 1944) publishes a biography of French salon hostess Manon Roland.

1897 U.S. social worker Alice McLellan Birney (October 19, 1858–December 20, 1907) founds and becomes the first president of the National Congress of Mothers, later the Parent-Teacher Association (PTA). Two thousand women attend the first meeting. By 1899, the organization will have 50,000 members.

1897 A discussion at England's Cambridge University of the possibility of granting degrees to women leads to riots, in which students hang in effigy a woman riding a bicycle.

1897 The first nonmissionary girls' school in China is established.

1898 Greek writer and educator Elly Alexioy is born.

1898 English socialist and spiritual leader Annie Besant founds the Hindu College in Benares, India.

1898 U.S. economist, author, feminist, and publisher Charlotte Perkins Gilman publishes the widely acclaimed *Women and Economics*, which is quickly translated into seven languages. It argues that the loss of women's valuable work skills hampers the entire economy.

1898 Germany's University of Erlangen reaffirms its resolve to keep women out, on the grounds that their admission would "overthrow all academic order."

Aug. 27, 1898 U.S. educator Mary Sheldon Barnes (b. September 15, 1850), who revolutionized the teaching of history by emphasizing primary sources and class discussion, dies.

Sept. 5, 1898 A women's organization, Ch'anyang-hoe, is founded in Korea to support women's education.

1899 Finnish educator Lucina Hagman founds Helsinki's Finnish New School, serving as its director until 1938.

1899 The Japanese government makes it mandatory to have at least one girls' secondary school in each prefecture.

1900 Important nonfiction works include French feminist and socialist Hubertine Auclert's (1848–1914) *Les femmes arabes en Algérie* (*Arab Women in Algeria*), Swedish reformer Ellen Key's famous work of educational theory, *Barnhets ahrundrade* (*The Century of the Child*), English poet and essayist Alice Meynell's biography of John Ruskin, and Ida Tarbell's *Life of Abraham Lincoln.*

1900 Austrian writer Marie Ebner-Eschenbach becomes the first woman to receive an honorary doctorate from the University of Vienna.

1900 The University of Baden is the first in Germany to admit women.

1900 Alice Tyler begins thirteen years as secretary of the Iowa State Library Commission; during this time she will nearly triple the number of libraries in the state.

1900 U.S. engineer, efficiency expert, and industrial psychologist Lillian Gilbreth (May 24, 1878–January 2, 1972) is the first female commencement speaker at the University of California, Berkeley. She will have twelve children, two of whom will collaborate on two books about the Gilbreth family, *Cheaper by the Dozen* and *Belles on Their Toes.*

Mar. 9, 1900 German women petition the Reichstag for the right to take university entrance tests.

Religion

1896 NAWSA disavows any connection with Elizabeth Cady Stanton's *Woman's Bible*, a decision not supported by Susan B. Anthony, who says, "I shall be pained beyond expression if the delegates here are so narrow and illiberal as to adopt this resolution. If we do not inspire in women a broad and catholic spirit, they will fail, when enfranchised, to constitute that powerful better government which we have always claimed for them."

1896 U.S. Theosophist Katherine Tingley becomes Outer Head of the Esoteric Section of the Theosophical Society in America, an offshoot of Helena Blavatsky's Theosophical Society. She and five other Theosophists tour Europe, the Middle East, India, and Tibet, visiting religious sites and making converts. In 1900 she will found a utopian community at Point Loma, California, famous for its lush gardens, rich cultural life, and encouragement of women's industries.

1897 French Carmelite nun St. Theresa of Lisieux (b. 1873) dies of tuberculosis. She had four sisters who were also nuns. St. Theresa wrote a famous religious autobiography, *Historie d'une âme* (*The Story of a Soul*).

1898 Austrian religious figure Theresa Neuman, who will display stigmata and appear to survive on a sip of water and a communion wafer per day, is born.

1 9 0 1

General Status and Daily Life

England legalizes the use of their birth names by married women.

The vacuum cleaner is invented.

In England, a female office worker earns about six shillings a week; a one-room flat on the third story costs about one shilling, eightpence a week. Water is often not available on upper-story flats and must be carried up. Lower-class housewives devote a day to washing and spend a considerable amount of time each week keeping the outside front step clean, as a sign of respectability. Older daughters are frequently expected to stay home from school to help mind the younger children.

Government, the Military, and the Law

Jan. 22 Queen Victoria dies. For more than sixty years, she ruled possessions ranging from England, Ireland, Wales, and Scotland to Sierra Leone, Nigeria, Kenya, Uganda, Egypt, India, Burma, Hong Kong, and Jamaica. Princess May expresses the feeling of the nation when she says, "The thought of England without the Queen is dreadful even to think of. God help us all!"

Sept. 7 China's dowager empress Tz'u-Hsi returns to power under the aegis of the Western powers attacked in the Boxer Rebellion, provided she puts certain reforms into effect, including the adoption of a constitution, a ban on foot-binding, and access for girls to state schools.

Dec. 21 Norwegian women vote for the first time.

Literature and the Visual Arts

Women's journals are edited in Egypt by Sa'dya Sa'd al-Din (*Shajarat al-Durr*) and Anisa Attallah (*al-Mara'a*).

Australian writer Miles Franklin publishes the autobiographical novel *My Brilliant Career*. Other new novels include Selma Lagerlöf's *Jerusalem*, Colette's *Claudine à Paris*, Sarah Orne Jewett's historical novel *The Tory Lover*, Canadian feminist lawyer Emily Murphy's satire *Janey Canuck Abroad*, and French courtesan Liane de Pougy's (b. August 11, 1870) *Idylle saphique*, a fictionalized account of her seduction by U.S. poet Natalie Clifford Barney.

Japanese poet Akiko Yosano (1878–1942), a specialist in the five-line *tanka* genre, publishes a collection of 400 poems, *Midaregami (Tangled Hair)*.

Performing Arts and Entertainment

English pianist Harriet Cohen is born.

U.S. composer Carrie Jacobs Bond (August 11, 1862–December 28, 1946) composes the sentimental song "I Love You Truly."

U.S. actress Maude Adams stars in James Barrie's *Quality Street*.

Oct. U.S. opera singer Geraldine Farrar makes her first professional appearance, at the Berlin Court Opera as Marguerite in Gounod's *Faust*.

Athletics and Exploration

English golfer Joyce Wethered is born.

British physical educator Constance Applebee (1874–January 26, 1981) introduces field hockey to the United States.

Britain's Ladies' Golf Union is refused permission to hold its national tournament at St. Andrews in Scotland.

Oct. The first women's field hockey magazine, *Hockey Field*, begins publication.

Activism

Japanese feminist and suffragist Kishida Toshiko (b. 1863) dies.

German socialist and feminist Lily Braun publishes *Die Frauenfrage*.

U.S. reformer and suffragist Mary Church Terrell, three-time president of the NACW, is made honorary president for life.

Feb. 15 U.S. temperance activist Carrie Nation leads an army of 500 on a saloon-smashing rampage through Topeka, Kansas. On September 1, she is arrested in New York City after attracting a large crowd on Eighth Avenue.

Dec. A suffrage association in Paris passes a resolution encouraging married women to keep their own names.

Business and Industry

In England, women are 18% of clerical workers, making about half the wages of male clerks.

There are 243,000 English women working as retail clerks.

In England, women are 91.5% of all servants; in France, they are 82.9% of servants.

Science and Medicine

U.S. nurse Clara Maass (b. 1876) dies of yellow fever in an experiment to find the cause of the disease. She volunteers to be bitten by mosquitoes; she contracts the disease as a result and dies, proving its method of transmission and allowing measures to be taken to stop its spread.

British physicist Hertha Ayrton has a paper, "The Mechanism of the Electric Arc," read to the Royal Society. She is not allowed, as a woman, to present the paper herself, but one of the fellows agrees to read it for her.

U.S. archaeologist Harriet Hawes discovers and begins excavating a Minoan Early Bronze Age town at Gournia.

U.S. anatomist and histologist Florence Sabin publishes the popular textbook *An Atlas of the Medulla and Midbrain.*

Education and Scholarship

U.S. philanthropist Jane Stanford completes the endowment of Stanford University with a gift of 100,000 acres of land and $11 million of other assets.

Mary Emma Woolley (July 13, 1863–September 5, 1947) becomes president of Mount Holyoke College, increasing the number of faculty members, building up the graduate program, encouraging greater religious freedom, abolishing secret societies, intiating an honor system, and ending students' required housekeeping duties. She will remain president until 1937.

Japan's first college for women opens.

Sept. 1 U.S. Methodist missionary Isabella Thobrun (b. March 29, 1840) dies. She spent most of her time in India educating girls and founded the forerunner of Lucknow Woman's College, which later became a part of Lucknow University.

Religion

U.S. Methodist Alma White (June 16, 1862-June 26, 1946), the wife of a minister, founds her own church after she is forbidden by the Methodists to hold revival meetings. By 1936, her Pillar of Fire Church will have forty-six congregations, $4 million in assets, and more than 4,000 members. As leader of the Pillar of Fire, White becomes the first female bishop of any Christian church.

1902

General Status and Daily Life

Norway's Penal Code specifies a five-year prison term for rape.

Abigail Roberson, whose image was used by the Rochester Folding Box Company on its flour bags without her permission, takes her case to the New York Court of Appeals. She loses, but public sympathy for her plight results in one of the first U.S. right-to-privacy laws.

Government, the Military, and the Law

Women of European descent get federal voting rights in Australia.

Martha Washington becomes the first American woman pictured on a U.S. postage stamp.

May 5 Prussian women are forbidden to form political associations.

Literature and the Visual Arts

Chinese poet Ping Hsin (Hsieh Wang-Ying) is born.

U.S. painter Lilly Martin Spencer dies. A creator of humorous genre paintings and a portraitist whose sitters included Elizabeth Cady Stanton, she was successful in her career despite bearing thirteen children. This success was due in large part to her husband, who gave up his own career to manage her finances and run the household.

Chinese artist Miao Jiahui, a widow who supports her family by selling paintings of animals, birds, flowers, and plants, paints *Lotus and Insects*. Miao is a ghost painter for the dowager empress Tz'u-Hsi, whose works of art are much sought after. Tz'u-Hsi has other female ghost painters, including Ruan Yufen and Wang Shao, but Miao is her favorite, staying with her "from morning to night." As a reward for her skill, Miao is given a good rank in the palace and a high salary; she is also exempted from the kowtow.

New literature includes English children's author Beatrix Potter's (b. July 28, 1866) *Peter Rabbit* and *The Tailor of Gloucester*, Helen Keller's *The Story of My Life*, Russian-German intellectual Lou Andreas-Salomé's fiction cycle *Im Zwischerland*, Colette's novel *Claudine en ménage*, and Irish playwright Augusta Gregory's translation of *Guchulain of Muirthemne*.

Rujina A'wad edits the Egyptian women's journal *al-Sa'ada*.

Performing Arts and Entertainment

English composer Ethel Smyth composes the opera *Der Wald*.

Athletics and Exploration

British figure skater Madge Syers takes second place in the world championships. She is defeated by Ulrich Salchow, a man; the world championships allow men and women to compete together, though this will not be the case for much longer.

U.S. mountain climber Annie Smith Peck cofounds the American Alpine Club.

U.S. mountain climber Fanny Bullock Workman explores the Himalayan Chogo Lungma Glacier with her husband.

Activism

German feminists Lida Heymann, Helene Stöcker, Anita Augsburg, Marie Stritt, and Minna Cauer, with eight other women, establish the Deutscher Verband für Frauenstimmrecht (German Union for Women's Suffrage). Augsburg becomes the organization's first president.

Austrian feminist Marianne Hainisch establishes the Federation of Austrian Women's Associations, a coalition of one hundred organizations.

Business and Industry

Black American Maggie Walker (b. 1867) establishes the St. Luke's Penny Savings Bank, becoming the first female bank president in the United States. She gets business from the local government and utilities and lends money to fund public schools when banks owned by whites refuse.

Mar. 23 The minimum work age for Italian girls is raised from 11 to 15.

Science and Medicine

British physicist Hertha Ayrton publishes *The Electric Arc*, which quickly becomes the standard text on the subject. She is nominated for membership in the Royal Society but rejected on the grounds of sex.

U.S. philanthropist Mary Anna Palmer Draper cofounds California's Mount Wilson Observatory.

U.S. ethnologist Alice Fletcher cofounds the American Anthropological Association.

Ida Hyde, known for her work on the circulatory, respiratory, and nervous systems, becomes the first woman member of the American Physiological Society.

U.S. anatomist and histologist Florence Sabin (November 9, 1871–October 3, 1953) becomes the first woman faculty member at Johns Hopkins Medical School. She will do her most important work on tuberculosis, the lymphatics, and the development of blood cells in embryos.

U.S. physician and missionary Ida Scudder supervises construction of the Mary Taber Schell Hospital in Vellore, India.

Education and Scholarship

German historian Ricarda Huch publishes the literary study *Ausbreitung und Verfall der Romantik*.

English poet and essayist Alice Meynell becomes the art critic for The *Pall Mall Gazette*.

About 4,000–5,000 girls are enrolled in missionary schools in China.

Religion

Italian martyr and saint Maria Goretti (b. 1890) is stabbed to death by a man who threatened to rape her.

U.S. Baptist leader Lucy Peabody becomes chairman of the new Committee on the United Study of Missions, a position she will hold until 1929.

1903

General Status and Daily Life

Aluminum cookware becomes popular in the United States.

Government, the Military, and the Law

Danish politician Nina Bang (1866–1928) is elected to the Central Board of the Social Democratic party.

Mlle. Dilhan becomes the first woman admitted to the bar in France.

Literature and the Visual Arts

U.S. journalist Margaret Buchanan Sullivan dies; she wrote for the *Chicago Post*, the *North American Review*, *Catholic World*, and various other periodiocals in New York and Chicago, covering topics from politics to medicine. She wrote a book about Mexico and covered the Republican Convention of 1884, the opening of the Gladstone Parliament in 1886, and the Paris Exposition of 1889.

England's Royal Academy holds its first mixed-sex art classes, though male and female students are still separated for figure drawing.

New novels include Colette's last "Claudine" novel, *Claudine s'en va*; Italian Grazia Deledda's *Elias Portolu*; and U.S. children's author Kate Douglas Wiggin's (September 28, 1856–August 24, 1923) most famous and popular novel, *Rebecca of Sunnybrook Farm*.

French poet Marguerite Burnat-Provins (1872–1952), known for her romantic prose poems, publishes *Tableaux valaisans*.

Jan. 1 U.S. art collector Isabella Stewart Gardner (April 14, 1840–1924) opens Fenway Court, the Boston museum she designed and stocked with her personal collection, which includes works by Titian, Rembrandt, and Raphael. Fenway Court also contains Asian art and Impressionist works.

Performing Arts and Entertainment

Polish-American actress Helena Modjeska (October 12, 1840–April 8, 1909) retires officially from the stage.

Athletics and Exploration

British tennis player Dorothea Douglass (1878–1960) wins the singles title at Wimbledon; she will win seven Wimbledon titles in her career.

Irish novelist Edith Somerville becomes the first female Master of Foxhounds.

U.S. mountain climber Fanny Bullock Workman sets a women's altitude record of 21,000 feet.

British motorboat racer Dorothy Levitt wins her first race.

Aug. 1 U.S. frontierswoman Calamity Jane, scout, mail carrier, and expert shot and rider, dies; she is buried next to her friend "Wild Bill" Hickok. Her drunkenness, pugnacity, and disrespect for policemen got her fired from almost every job she held outside the West.

Oct. 25 About 2,500 Parisian shopgirls participate in a footrace from the Place de la Concorde to Nanterre, a distance of twelve kilometers. The winner, Jeanne Cheminel, completes the race in one hour, ten minutes before a crowd of 20,000.

Activism

Russian socialist Concordia Samoilova (1876–1921) begins working undercover as "Natasha" and is jailed soon afterwards. She is sentenced to fourteen months, and sympathetic workers kill the informant who betrayed her.

Oct. 10 British suffragist Emmeline Pankhurst, dissatisfied with Millicent Garrett Fawcett's National Union of Women's Suffrage Societies, which has achieved only local suffrage rights by means of its polite agitation, founds the Women's Social and Political Union (WSPU), to implement "Action not Words." The WSPU, with its motto of "Votes for Women," is cofounded by Emmeline's daughter Christabel Pankhurst (1880–1958).

Business and Industry

The WTUL is founded in the United States, with Mary

Morton Kehew (September 8, 1859–February 13, 1918) as its first president. Led mostly by middle- and upper-class women, it does have some working-class members, like glove maker Agnes Nestor, cap maker Rose Schneiderman (April 6, 1882–August 11, 1972), and shoe worker Mary Anderson (August 27, 1872–January 29, 1964). Mary Kenney O'Sullivan, the AFL's first female organizer, is one of the principal founders. The WTUL works for protective legislation and educational opportunities for women workers as well as for women's suffrage.

At least ten women pass as men in order to find work as agents, switchmen, and cooks with the New York Central Railway.

July U.S. labor leader Mother Jones leads a procession of children maimed in industrial accidents to see President Theodore Roosevelt, though he says he will not receive her or the children at his home.

Nov. 23 U.S. cosmetics entrepreneur and journalist Harriet Hubbard Ayer (b. June 27, 1849) dies. A pioneer in marketing techniques and a beauty reporter for the *New York World*, she advocated beauty through a healthy diet and sensible life-style.

Science and Medicine

Irish writer on astronomy Agnes Clerke and Irish astronomer Margaret Huggins become two of the few female honorary members of the Royal Astronomical Society.

U.S. cytogeneticist Nettie Stevens (July 7, 1861–May 4, 1912) publishes *Further Studies on the Ciliate Infusoria, Licnophora and Boveria*. She will be one of the first two researchers to discover independently that X and Y chromosomes determine sex.

"Typhoid" Mary Mallon (d. 1938), a notorious disease carrier, is identified as the person who has caused several typhoid outbreaks. Upon being told of this, she refuses to believe it and chases away a Health Department official with a rolling pin. Her resistance to quitting her work as a cook will lead to her confinement in 1915.

Dec. 10 Marie Curie shares the Nobel Prize for Physics for the discovery of the radioactive elements polonium and radium; she is the first woman to receive a Nobel. The daughter of a Polish physicist, she had to work as a governess before starting her scientific career, because she simply did not have enough money to study.

Education and Scholarship

U.S. geographer Ellen Semple (January 8, 1863–May 8,

1932) publishes *American History and Its Geographic Conditions*.

Religion

Italian laywoman, stigmatic, and saint Gemma Galgani (b. 1878) dies.

1904

General Status and Daily Life

Women are no longer considered permanent legal minors in France.

Government, the Military, and the Law

Nelly Schreiber-Favre becomes Switzerland's first woman barrister.

Literature and the Visual Arts

Korean novelist Pak Hwa-song and English romance novelist Barbara Cartland are born.

U.S. novelist Gene Stratton-Porter publishes *Freckles*. By the time of her death in 1924, it will have sold over 8 million copies and made her about $2 million.

U.S. architect Louise Bethune codesigns the French Renaissance Hotel Lafayette in Buffalo, New York.

Irish playwright Augusta Gregory translates the Gaelic saga *Gods and Fighting Men* and writes the play *Spreading the News*.

Performing Arts and Entertainment

Czech actress Franusca Janauschek (b. 1830) dies.

Italian soprano Luisa Tetrazzini (February 28, 1882–April 28, 1940) sings in San Francisco.

U.S. opera singer Geraldine Farrar (February 28, 1882–March 11, 1967) stars in *La Bohème* with Enrico Caruso.

English actress Lillie Langtry (1853–1929), known as much for her affair with Edward VII of England as for her acting, causes a scandal when she strips to her slip onstage in *Mrs. Deering's Divorce*.

Oct. 22 Pianist Hazel Harrison, appearing with the Berlin Philharmonic Orchestra, becomes the first American and American-trained artist to play with a European orchestra.

Athletics and Exploration

The only women's event at the St. Louis Olympics is archery, dominated by longtime U.S. national champion Lyda Scott Howell.

Tennis player May G. Sutton wins the U.S. Open women's singles championship.

British tennis player Lottie Dod wins the British Ladies' Golf Championship.

U.S. mountain climber Annie Smith Peck breaks her own altitude record by climbing the previously unscaled Mount Sorata (21,300 feet) in Bolivia.

Gertrud Furkert defeats about seventy other young women in the 500-meter race of Berlin's *Damensportfest*.

Oct. 15 Georgiana Bishop wins the U.S. women's golf championship.

Activism

Irish reformer and feminist Frances Power Cobbe (b. 1822) dies. She was a proponent of women's suffrage, an end to vivisection, and education for the working classes.

German feminist Helene Stöcker quits the Internationale Abolitionistische Föderation Deutscher Zweig (International Federation for the Abolition of State-Regulated Prostitution) and forms the more radical Bund für Mutterschutz und Sexualreform (League for the Protection of Motherhood and Sexual Reform). This new organization advocates free love, eugenics, legal abortion, and contraception.

Sarah Platt Decker becomes president of the German Federation of Women's Clubs.

U.S. feminists Susan B. Anthony and Carrie Chapman Catt establish the International Woman Suffrage Alliance in Berlin. Catt becomes its first president, and German feminist Anita Augsburg becomes vice president. On the same trip, Anthony travels to England and meets suffragist Christabel Pankhurst, who is

saddened and inspired by the awareness that Anthony will die without seeing her dream of women's suffrage realized. Pankhurst says, "It is unendurable . . . to think of another generation of women wasting their lives begging for the vote. We must not lose any more time. We must act."

U.S. public health nurse, settlement house worker, and social reformer Lillian D. Wald, consumer advocate Florence Kelley, and others establish the National Child Labor Committee, an anti-child-labor organization.

U.S. minister and suffragist Anna Howard Shaw succeeds Carrie Chapman Catt as president of NAWSA, a position she will hold until 1915.

U.S. suffragist Ida Husted Harper (February 18, 1851–March 14, 1931) recommends women's suffrage to offset the evil influence of "the majority of negroes, Indians and immigrants." Her nativist and racist attitudes are quite common in many segments of the suffrage movement.

Indonesian feminist and nationalist Raden Ajeng Kartini, the mother of the modern Indonesian women's rights movement, dies in childbirth at the age of twenty-five. The founder of a girls' school and a contributor to a socialist women's magazine, she fought polygyny, forced marriage, and Dutch colonial control.

Feminists in Mexico City begin publishing a women's magazine, *La Mujer Mexicana*, which will survive until 1908.

Business and Industry

English unionist Gertrude Tuckwell becomes president of the WTUL, a position she will hold until its merger with the Trades Union Congress (TUC) in 1921.

Mar. 27 U.S. labor leader Mary Harris "Mother" Jones is ordered to leave Colorado after doing a little "hell-raising" among striking miners.

Science and Medicine

British physicist Hertha Ayrton becomes the first woman to present a paper to the Royal Society.

U.S. astronomer Anna Winlock (b. 1857) dies. She calculated the paths of the asteroids Eros and Ocllo and compiled an important catalogue of the stars near the north and south poles.

Education and Scholarship

U.S. advocate for the handicapped Helen Keller graduates cum laude from Radcliffe College, the first deaf and blind person to accomplish such a feat.

Important nonfiction works published by women this year include Elizabeth Förster-Nietzsche's biography *Das Leben Friedrich Nietzsches* and U.S. journalist Ida Tarbell's indignant attack on John D. Rockefeller's business tactics, *The History of the Standard Oil Company*.

Jan. 16 Educator Ibu Dewi Sartika (1884–1942) establishes the first girls' school in Indonesia. It teaches chiefly domestic skills, reading, and writing.

Oct. U.S. educator and civil rights administrator Mary McLeod Bethune (July 10, 1875–May 18, 1955) starts a Florida girls' school, the forerunner of Bethune-Cookman College, with five pupils and $1.50 in cash. She funds the school by selling pastries to local workers.

1905

Government, the Military, and the Law

English socialist Beatrice Webb (January 22, 1858–April 30, 1943) becomes a member of the Royal Commission on the Poor Laws.

Literature and the Visual Arts

U.S. author Mary Mapes Dodge (January 26, 1831–August 21), author of *Hans Brinker* and founder of a famous children's magazine, *St. Nicholas*, dies.

Russian sculptor Anna Golubkina creates a famous bust of Marx, despite his unpopularity with the monarchy.

U.S. Impressionist painter Mary Cassatt paints *Mother and Child*. Portraits of mothers are a common subject for the childless Cassatt.

U.S. novelist Edith Wharton (January 24, 1862–August 11, 1937) publishes her first novel of manners, *The House of Mirth*. Well received by critics and the public, it is an outcry against the sexual double standard and the restricted place of women in society.

Also published this year is Baroness (Emma Magdalena Rosalia Maria Josepha Barbara) Orczy's (b. September 23, 1865) novel *The Scarlet Pimpernel*, the story of an English nobleman who rescues aristocrats from the guillotine during the French Revolution. Its heroine, Marguerite St. Just Blakeney, is an intelligent and enterprising woman of great bravery. Other new works include English novelist Frances Hodgson Burnett's (b. November 24, 1849) children's book *The Little Princess*.

Performing Arts and Entertainment

German composer Winifried Zillig is born.

Theatergoers can see flamboyant U.S. dancer Isadora Duncan (b. May 27, 1878) in Vienna, Berlin, and St. Petersburg, American actress Annie Russell creating the title role of Shaw's *Major Barbara* in London, and Polish-American actress Helena Modjeska giving her last stage performance, at New York's Metropolitan Opera.

May U.S. actress Ethel Barrymore (August 16, 1879–June 18, 1959) plays Nora in a New York production of *A Doll's House*.

Nov. 6 Maude Adams opens in New York in *Peter Pan*. This summer, she designed a new costume for the title role, featuring a round collar and a peaked cap that quickly become standard attire for the character. She will eventually play Peter more than 1,500 times.

Athletics and Exploration

Forty Oslo women establish Norway's first rowing club.

Tennis player Elisabeth H. Moore wins the U.S. singles title.

British race car driver Dorothy Levitt wins a road race in Brighton, setting a women's speed record of 79.75 miles per hour.

June May Sutton beats Dorothea Douglass in the women's finals at Wimbledon.

Activism

Feminist Mohtaram Eskandari founds Iran's first women's organization, the Union of Patriotic Women. Its first meeting is dispersed by religious leaders who tie the women to trees and burn some of them alive.

English suffragists Christabel Pankhurst and Annie Kenney (1879–1953) are arrested, and their organization, the WSPU, becomes increasingly militant as a result. Local newspapers use the word *suffragette* for the first time.

Indian author Rokeya Sakhawat Hossain publishes the short story "Sultana's Dream," a utopian work about a country where the men, to keep their destructive tendencies in check, are kept in *purdah*, while the women move about freely.

Austrian novelist and pacifist Bertha von Suttner (June 9, 1843–June 21, 1914), who gave Alfred Nobel the idea for the Peace Prize, becomes the first woman to win it.

Russian revolutionary Vera Liubatovich (b. 1854) returns from Siberia after twenty-three years in exile.

Lithuanian feminist Ona Masiotene cofounds the Lietuvous Moteru Susivienijimas (Alliance of Lithuanian Women).

Russian doctor and feminist Anna Shabanova founds and leads the Electoral Department of the Mutual Philanthropic Society; she will agitate steadily for women's suffrage until 1917, rejecting militant tactics.

Marie Popelin (1846–1913) becomes the first president of the Council of Belgian Women.

Apr. 10 The All Russian Union for Women's Equality holds Russia's first major women's political meeting.

Business and Industry

A Russian woman protests the fact that she earns half as much as a man: "When I get hungry and go buy myself a pickle, they don't charge me half a kopek for it, do they? No, I pay the same kopek a man does."

U.S. inventor Mary Greenewalt patents a rheostat.

U.S. entrepreneur Sarah Breedlove ("Madame C. J.") Walker (b. December 23, 1867) develops the "Walker System" of hair care for black women and begins the business that will make her a millionaire.

Korean businesswoman Yi Il-chong starts a store near Anguk-dong to demonstrate that women can be economically independent.

Ellen M. Henrotin becomes president of the WTUL, serving until 1907.

The International Workers of the World (IWW) is established, with the organization of industrial women workers as one of its goals. Most unions until this point have ignored women or actively opposed their involvement in the workplace.

Finnish politician Miina Sillanpåå (b. 1866), a former domestic servant, begins editing the *Servants' Journal*.

Science and Medicine

The first birth control literature is distributed in Russia.

U.S. ethnologist Alice Fletcher is elected president of the American Folklore Society.

Mary Whiton Calkin becomes the first woman president of the American Psychological Association.

U.S. physician and bacteriologist Anna Williams discovers a quick method of identifying Negri bodies, the indicator of rabies. Her method will remain the standard diagnostic tool until 1939. She also becomes assistant director of the New York City Research Laboratories, a position she will hold until 1934, and coauthors the classic text *Microörganisms Including Bacteria and Protozoa*.

Education and Scholarship

German educator Paula Mueller establishes a school of social work for women.

Religion

Rachel Henderlite, the first woman ordained as a minister in the U.S. Presbyterian Church, is born.

1906

General Status and Daily Life

The number of divorces granted in the United States is almost twice what it was ten years ago, leaping from 42,937 to 72,062.

Government, the Military, and the Law

Mar. 7 Finland grants women equal suffrage.

Literature and the Visual Arts

Korean poet Kim O-nam, Japanese poet Nagase Kiyoko, and Finnish textile designer Dora Jung are born.

U.S. journalist Winifred Black covers the San Francisco earthquake after receiving a telegram from publisher William Randolph Hearst that simply reads, "Go."

Novels published this year include Italian feminist Sibilla Aleramo's autobiographical *Una donna* (*A Woman*) and German historian Ricarda Huch's *Vita somnium breve*.

July U.S. author Mary Andrews (April 2, 1860–August 2, 1936) publishes *A Perfect Tribute*, a sentimental fiction based on Lincoln's disappointment at the reception of his Gettysburg Address. It sells more than 600,000 copies.

Performing Arts and Entertainment

Sarah Bernhardt makes her farewell tour of the United States and raises $17,000 for victims of the San Francisco earthquake.

Russian actress Alla Nazimova (June 4, 1879–July 13, 1945) makes her U.S. stage debut in *Hedda Gabler*.

Ethel Smyth composes the opera *The Wreckers*.

Hungarian-British violinist Adila Fachiri makes her debut in Vienna.

French filmmaker Alice Guy-Blaché directs *The Passion*, a movie about the Crucifixion notable for its elaborate sets and experimental close-ups.

Jan. 28 American Ruth St. Denis (January 20, 1879–July 21, 1968), cofounder of the influential Denishawn School, introduces modern dance in the United States with the first performance of her self-choreographed "Radha."

Nov. 26 American opera singer Geraldine Farrar makes her U.S. debut in *Roméo et Juliette* and begins sixteen years as one of the Metropolitan Opera's principal stars.

Athletics and Exploration

Helen Homans wins the U.S. singles tennis title.

U.S. mountain climber Fanny Bullock Workman sets a women's altitude record of 23,300 feet, a record that will stand until 1934.

British figure skater Madge Syers is the first women's world champion; she will repeat her victory in 1907.

British race car driver Dorothy Levitt sets a new women's speed record of 91 miles per hour.

Activism

English philanthropist Angela Burdett-Coutts (b. 1814), who gave away nearly £3 million to support the arts and to assist the needy of England, Ireland, Africa, and Turkey, dies. She invented the famous English combination of fish and chips, as a suggested meal for the poor.

Emmeline Pankhurst, who advocates violent tactics to force the government to grant suffrage, is the most visible English suffragist, but many women are active in the fight for the vote, including Teresa Billington-Greig (1877–1964), who publishes *Towards Women's Liberty*; Clementina Black, who starts a major suffrage petition; feminist and educator Emily Davies, who leads a suffrage deputation to Parliament; unionist Annie Kenney, who becomes the WSPU's London organizer and is arrested for interrupting a speech by the prime minister, and Emily Davison (b. 1872), who, in her campaign of arson, assault, and stone-throwing, will be arrested eight times. In response to her hunger strikes in prison, she will be forcibly fed forty-nine times.

Australian socialist Lizzie Ahern (1877–1969) is arrested for her defense of public free speech.

Russian revolutionary Mariya Spiridonova (b. 1880) assassinates General Luzhenovsky; her subsequent torture after arrest is internationally condemned.

U.S. radical journalist Ella Bloor (b. July 8, 1862) investigates the Chicago meat-packing industry at the urging of her friend Upton Sinclair. Her discoveries lead to reform of food-packing methods. Many women support such reforms, and the WCTU backs the Pure Food and Drug Act of this year; women's clubs are pivotal in the passage of the act. Led largely by Alice Lakey (1857–1935), clubwomen send 100,000 letters to government officials.

Chinese poet Ch'iu Chin establishes a women's newspaper in Shanghai and runs a revolutionary party headquarters.

Mar. 13 U.S. feminist Susan B. Anthony dies. On her eighty-sixth birthday, President Theodore Roosevelt sent his congratulations, and Anthony exclaimed, "When will men do something besides extend congratulations? I would rather have President Roosevelt say one word to

Congress in favor of amending the Constitution to give women the vote than to praise me endlessly." She pays tribute to her reforming predecessors and says, "With such women consecrating their lives—failure is impossible."

Business and Industry

Hungarian-Israeli fashion designer Fini Leithersdorf is born.

An international ban is placed on night-shift work for women.

British unionists Margaret Grace Bondfield (1873–1953) and Mary Reid Macarthur establish the National Federation of Women Workers.

In France, 22% of postal clerks and telegraph operators are women.

Science and Medicine

U.S. ecologist Anne Morrow Lindbergh (June 22) and British epidemiologist Alice Stewart, whose work on low-level radiation will help to encourage caution in nuclear development, are born.

U.S. anarchist Emma Goldman begins editing the journal *Mother Earth*, in which she advocates the use of contraception, a position that will lead to her arrest and imprisonment.

The San Francisco earthquake and fire severely damage the California Academy of Sciences; Canadian-American botanist Alice Eastwood (1859–October 30, 1953) abandons most of her own possessions to save the academy herbarium's important type specimens and records.

June 10 U.S. physician Mary Putnam Jacobi, who wrote over one hundred medical articles, dies. She became chairman of neurology at the New York Academy of Medicine and established the National Consumers' League, the first consumer association in the United States.

Education and Scholarship

Marie Curie becomes the first woman to teach at the Sorbonne.

German historian Ricarda Huch writes about Garibaldi in *Die Geschichten von Garibaldi.*

U.S. rural educator Jessie Field Stambaugh begins establishing her Boys Corn Clubs and Girls Home Clubs, the forerunners of 4-H.

Muslim Indian feminist Begum Abdullah establishes the forerunner of a women's college in Aligarh.

Highborn Korean women establish Yoja Kyoyuk-hoe (The Society for Women's Education). The group holds discussions and debates on various topics, only some of which are directly related to women's education. It agitates politely for the abolition of certain customs, such as the covering of women's faces outdoors, and founds a girls' school and a hospital in 1907.

Only 306 girls are enrolled in nonmissionary schools in China; they are .07% of the nonmissionary student population.

Religion

There are 116 houses of the Order of the Good Shepherd, which houses reformed prostitutes, in Continental Europe.

1907

General Status and Daily Life

Mar. 1 Civil marriage is abolished in Spain.

Government, the Military, and the Law

Mar. 15 Finland becomes the first country to elect women to Parliament with the seating of nineteen, including Miina Sillanpää.

June 14 Norwegian women get limited suffrage in parliamentary elections. All women who pay taxes (or whose husbands pay taxes) may vote.

Literature and the Visual Arts

Norwegian woodworker Hanna Christie Abrahamsen, known for her paper-thin bowls, is born.

German painter Paula Modersohn-Becker (b. 1876),

famous for her still lives, peasant portraits, nude self-portraits, and powerful paintings of mothers and children, dies.

Three poets begin publishing their work: Russian Anna Akhmatova (1889–1966); Uruguayan Delmira Agustini (1890–1914), whose first collection is entitled *El libro blanco*; and American Sara Teasdale (b. August 8, 1884), whose first book is called *Sonnets to Duse, and Other Poems*.

U.S. sculptor Meta Warrick Fuller wins a gold medal for her tableaux of 150 figures from black history.

Novels published this year include Spanish novelist Emilia Pardo Bazán's *Sirena negra*, Colette's *Retreat from Love*, and U.S. author Dorothy Canfield Fisher's (February 17, 1879–November 9, 1958) first novel, *Gunhild*, inspired by her travels in Norway. British novelist Elinor Glyn publishes *Three Weeks*, banned in Boston for its depiction of a three-week love affair and its ostentatious references to sex as "It."

Apr. U.S. reporter Winifred Sweet Black and three other notable women journalists become known as the "sob sisters" after their sentimental coverage of a sensational murder trial.

Performing Arts and Entertainment

American lutenist Suzanne Bloch, chiefly responsible for the repopularization of the lute in the twentieth century, is born.

Norwegian pianist and composer Agathe Backer-Grøndahl (b. 1847), who performed in concerts throughout Europe and composed over 190 songs, dies.

Italian soprano Luisa Tetrazzini makes her Covent Garden debut as Violetta in *La Traviata*.

Athletics and Exploration

Travel books published this year include *The Desert and the Sown*, written by Englishwoman Gertrude Bell about her travels in Syria, and *From Fiji to the Cannibal Islands* and *Vaiti of the Islands*, both by Irish traveler Beatrice Grimshaw.

The Ladies' Alpine Club, an early women's mountain-climbing group, is established.

British auto racer Dorothy Levitt comes in fourth in Germany's Herkomer Trophy Race out of 172 male and female drivers.

Activism

Russian women present a women's suffrage petition with 20,000 signatures to the government.

The National Council of Greek Women's Organizations is established and unites fifty groups within a year.

British suffragists Teresa Billington-Greig, Charlotte Despard, and Edith How-Martyn establish the Women's Freedom League, urging women not to pay taxes until they are allowed to vote.

English social worker and suffragist Emmeline Pethick-Lawrence (1867–1954) begins publishing the suffrage journal *Votes for Women*.

Australian feminist Rose Scott becomes president of the Peace Society.

U.S. philanthropist Margaret Slocum Sage gives $10 million to endow the Russell Sage Foundation for the betterment of U.S. social conditions.

Feb. 13 British suffragists set up an all-female "Parliament" and march on the all-male version at dusk. Attacked by mounted police, they continue to march forward despite injuries to many demonstrators; five hours later, fifteen of the women actually make it to the House of Commons and try to hold a meeting. They and forty-two others (including Christabel Pankhurst) are arrested, a record for a single women's suffrage demonstration.

July 15 Chinese poet, revolutionary, and feminist Ch'iu Chin, who returned to China to organize women after studying in Japan, is beheaded by the Manchu government. One of the first female followers of Sun Yat-Sen, she was a teacher who dressed in men's suits and ran a girls' school. Her poems were used as evidence against her at her trial. Though she was tortured extensively, she refused to confess to her part in an attempted uprising or to denounce others, responding only, "The autumn wind and rain sadden us."

Aug. 18 German communist and feminist Clara Zetkin cofounds the International Socialist Women's Congress. It meets in Stuttgart, Germany and denounces German military buildup and imperialism.

Business and Industry

Most seamstresses in Paris work ten hours a day; many work more than twelve hours a day.

Finnish politician Miina Sillanpää becomes editor of *The Working Woman*, the women's journal of the Social Democratic Party.

There are about 200 brothels in Pittsburgh, Pennsylvania, and 113 in Portland, Oregon.

Science and Medicine

Alma Dea Morani, the first U.S. woman to become a professor of surgery, and U.S. scientist Ruth Patrick, inventor of the diatometer (a device for measuring water pollution) and cofounder of limnology, the study of freshwater ecosystems, are born.

British astronomer Mary Blagg (b. 1858) begins collating and organizing the names of lunar formations, which are currently rather confused and inconsistent.

American chemist Mary Pennington (b. Oct. 8, 1872), who will revolutionize food transport and storage through her work with refrigeration, vastly reducing the incidence of food poisoning, is hired by the Department of Agriculture. She took the civil service exam as "M. E. Pennington" so that no one would know her sex.

Around this time, Austrian physicist Lise Meitner (b. 1878) publishes papers on alpha and beta radiation and sets up a lab at the University of Berlin. However, she is not allowed to be in the presence of the male students, so she is forced to work in the basement for two years until regulations regarding women relax.

The American Red Cross, thanks to the urging of social welfare worker Emily Bissell (May 31, 1861–March 8, 1948), begins selling Christmas seals to raise funds to fight tuberculosis.

Education and Scholarship

U.S. ethnomusicologist Frances Densmore (May 21, 1867–June 5, 1957) begins recording Native American songs, on the theory that transcription alone is inadequate. Eventually she will record almost 2,500 songs from more than thirty tribes, including the Chippewa, Teton Sioux, Mandan, Hidatsu, and Seminole.

Feminist educator Tuba Azmoudeh founds the first girls' school in Iran.

The first public girls' school in China opens.

Educator Maria Montessori begins opening nursery schools in Italy.

Religion

English spiritual leader Annie Besant becomes president of the Theosophical Society.

1908

General Status and Daily Life

Oct. 30 U.S. society hostess Caroline Astor (b. September 22, 1830) dies. The "Four Hundred," the people invited each year to her January ball, were considered the cream of New York society.

Government, the Military, and the Law

Married taxpaying women in Sweden get local suffrage; women over twenty-five and wives of taxpayers get local suffrage in Denmark.

Elizabeth Garrett Anderson becomes the first woman mayor in England.

Germany's Law of Association allows women to join political parties.

Aug. Chinese dowager empress Tz'u-Hsi proclaims a nine-year plan to prepare the nation for a constitutional government. On November 15, she dies one day after the nominal ruler, the reforming Guangxu emperor, whom she has kept in virtual captivity for the past ten years. It is rumored that she poisoned the emperor, who was her nephew and adopted son.

Aug. 18 Esther Vorhees Hasson (d. March 8, 1942) becomes the first superintendent of the U.S. Navy Nurse Corps. She will retire in 1911.

Literature and the Visual Arts

French surrealist Leonor Fini, Portuguese painter Maria Helena Vieira da Silva (d. 1992), and Italian poet Ruth Domino are born.

Australian novelist Henry Handel Richardson (pseudonym of Ethel Roberts, 1870–1946) publishes her first novel, *Maurice Guest*, a landmark in the treatment of homosexuality in English fiction. Other notable novels published this year include Lucy Maud Montgomery's *Anne of Green Gables*, a classic children's book about an energetic, intelligent orphan, and American author Mary Roberts Rinehart's (August 12,

1876–September 22, 1958) *The Circular Staircase*. Rinehart's works, while popular and notable for their strong heroines, will not receive much critical attention.

French artist Sonia Delaunay (1885–1979), creator of textiles, murals, dresses, and abstract paintings, has her first one-woman show.

Irish playwright Augusta Gregory writes *The Workhouse Ward*.

Julia Ward Howe, already the first female member of the 250-member American Institute of Arts and Letters (1907), becomes the first female member of the more prestigious 50-member American Academy of Arts and Letters.

French poet Marguerite Burnat-Provins publishes *Le livre pour toi*.

Performing Arts and Entertainment

Swedish dancer and choreographer Birgit Cullberg is born.

In the world of dance, Isadora Duncan becomes popular in New York and London, Russian ballerina Tamara Karsavina stars in *Les sylphides*, and American Loie Fuller creates her *Ballet of Light* and founds a dance school.

Concert singer Corinne Rider-Kelsey becomes the first American-trained singer to perform a major role with England's Royal Opera. This year also marks the solo debut of German-American soprano Lotte Lehmann (1888–1976), best known for her roles in the operas of Strauss and Wagner, and the New York debut of Italian soprano Luisa Tetrazzini.

U.S. musical comedy actress Nora Bayes stars in the Ziegfeld *Follies of 1908*, scoring a hit with a song she cowrote, "Shine On, Harvest Moon."

Athletics and Exploration

At the Olympic Games, British archer Q. F. Newall takes the gold medal in her sport, with the silver going to versatile English tennis player Lottie Dod. Madge Syers wins the figure-skating gold. Anna Hubler of Germany wins a gold for pairs skating; Syers takes the bronze. In outdoor tennis, Englishwoman Dorothea Chambers wins the gold. In indoor tennis, the winner is Britain's Gwen Eastlake-Smith; Norway's Molla Bjurstedt Mallory takes a bronze.

German swimmer Martha Gerstung sets a women's world record in the one hundred-meter freestyle.

Britain's Ladies' Golf Union is given permission to hold its national tournament at St. Andrews in Scotland, but women are not permitted in the locker rooms or the lounge.

U.S. mountain climber Annie Smith Peck ascends the north peak of Peru's Mount Huascarán and estimates its height at 24,000 feet; its height is later calculated to be 21,812 feet, but this still gives Peck a record climb for any U.S. man or woman in the Western Hemisphere.

Fanny Bullock Workman travels seventy-four miles by ice with her husband, walking along the Himalayan Hispar and Biafo Glaciers.

June 22 Charlotte Sterry, thirty-seven, becomes the oldest winner of the Wimbledon ladies' singles title, defeating Agnes Morton.

Activism

Scottish feminist, pacifist, and lawyer Chrystal Macmillan, appealing unsuccessfully for the vote, is the first woman to speak before the House of Lords.

English novelist Mrs. Humphry Ward becomes the first president of the Anti-Suffrage League.

Russian feminists hold a national conference attended by 1,000 delegates, only 45 of them workers and none of them peasants. The spokeswoman for the workers is Alexandra Kollontai (1872–1952), later one of the few high-ranking Soviet officials to survive the Stalinist purges. Her remarks are met with fifteen minutes of abuse from the audience.

U.S. child welfare worker and juvenile court advocate Hannah Schoff organizes the International Conference on Child Welfare in Washington, D.C.

The All Russian Union for Women's Equality is banned.

Oct. 13 A suffrage mob of 100,000 storms Britain's Parliament; twenty-four suffragists are arrested, and one woman is carried bodily from the House of Commons.

Oct. 24 English suffragist Emmeline Pankhurst (1858–1928), arrested for the first time, is jailed with her daughter Christabel. During their trial, Christabel called the home secretary and the chancellor of the exchequer as witnesses. The Pankhursts' tactics now grow even more militant and include the destruction of property.

Business and Industry

German housewife Melitta Bentz substitutes blotting paper for cloth to hold the grounds in coffee brewing, thus inventing the Melitta coffee filter. She makes her coffee not by steeping the grounds in water, but by pouring boiling water over them and letting the water drain through the paper filter, through a piece of punctured brass, and then into the pot. Within a year she will sell more than a thousand of the new coffee makers, and eventually her method will be used in 150 countries.

The U.S. Supreme Court upholds a law limiting women to a ten-hour workday, thus barring them from many jobs, such as typesetting and transportation. The Court has been reluctant in the past to limit any workers' hours but did so in this case, since women's health "becomes an object of public interest and care to preserve the strength and vigor of the race."

Mary Baker Eddy founds the *Christian Science Monitor*.

Science and Medicine

English zoologist and parasitologist Miriam Rothschild, author of over 200 scientific papers and cataloguer of 10,000 species of fleas, is born.

English doctor Edith Pechey-Phipson, who spent much of her life in India campaigning for better health care for women and working to ban child marriage, dies.

Korea's first nursing school, started by missionary Margaret Edmund, has its first two graduates.

Physician S. Josephine Baker (b. November 15, 1873) establishes New York's Bureau of Child Hygiene and manages, in only a few years, to make New York's infant mortality rate the lowest in the U.S. or Europe.

U.S. psychologist Margaret Washburn publishes her most influential book, *The Animal Mind*.

The chickadee is named *farus gambeli baileyae* in honor of U.S. ornithologist Florence Merriam Bailey.

Education and Scholarship

Elisabeth Luther Cary (1867–1936) becomes the first full-time art critic for the *New York Times*.

Iran launches a campaign to increase women's literacy.

Berlin's University of Prussia, the last major all-male European university, begins admitting women.

Korea's first public school for girls is founded.

Religion

U.S. religious leader Mary Baker Eddy publishes *Unity of Good* and *Rudimental Divine Science*.

1909

General Status and Daily Life

Yamamato Matsuyo, founder of Japan's Home Economics Extension Service, is born.

The average dowry in India is 200 rupees.

Harems are outlawed in Turkey.

Government, the Military, and the Law

Australia's Women's Political Association is founded to educate voters.

Literature and the Visual Arts

Japanese poet Fumi Saito, writer of verses in the five-line *tanka* style and author of several well-received books, is born.

Swedish novelist Selma Lagerlöf wins the Nobel Prize for Literature.

U.S. expatriate author and salon hostess Natalie Clifford Barney establishes a women's poetry prize in memory of one of her lovers, the young poet Renée Vivien.

U.S. writer Gertrude Stein (b. February 3, 1874) publishes *Three Lives*, a collection of three short stories, "The Good Anna," "Melanctha," and "The Gentle Lena."

Performing Arts and Entertainment

Irish playwright Augusta Gregory becomes manager of the Abbey Theatre, a position she will hold until her death in 1932.

U.S. opera singer Mary Garden appears in Strauss' *Salomé* and is censured for her erotic dancing.

Sarah Bernhardt stars in a play she wrote, *Un coeur d'un homme*.

Athletics and Exploration

English archer Alice Blanche Legh wins a record eighth British championship in a row. The previous record of seven consecutive titles was set by Legh in 1892.

U.S. tennis player Hazel Hotchkiss Wightman wins the U.S. singles, doubles, and mixed doubles titles. She will repeat all three victories in 1910.

Canadian traveler Agnes Deans Cameron publishes *The New North*, describing her trip from Chicago to Athabasca, the Arctic Ocean, the Great Slave Lake, the Mackenzie River, Peace River, and the Lesser Slave Lake.

British mountaineer Gertrude Benham becomes the first woman to climb Mt. Kilimanjaro. By the time of her death, she will have walked through Switzerland, South America, and Canada and climbed 300 mountains higher than 10,000 feet.

June 9-Aug. 6 Alice Huyler Ramsey (president of the Women's Motoring Club of New York) and three other U.S. women make a cross-country auto trip from New York City to San Francisco.

July 9 Tennis player Penelope Boothby defeats Agnes Morton to win the Wimbledon singles title.

Activism

Turkish nationalist Halide Adivar (1883–1964) is forced to flee for her life after her feminist views become too unpopular with the new government. She will fight in Turkey's war of independence and become the first woman professor at the University of Istanbul.

Australian socialist Lizzie Ahern founds the Women's Socialist League.

Australian feminist Vida Goldstein begins publishing *The Woman Voter*.

Irish nationalist politician Constance Markiewicz founds the youth movement Na Fianna.

In the Netherlands, the Association for Women's Suffrage has 6,500 members.

The Sri Lanka Tamil Women's Union is founded.

May In the United States, the National Association for the Advancement of Colored People (NAACP) is founded; two of its organizers are civil rights reformer Mary White Ovington (b. April 11, 1865) and antilynching activist Ida Wells-Barnett.

Sept. 18 Two British suffragists who threw stones at Prime Minister Asquith are imprisoned. On September 28, Asquith orders that hunger-striking suffragists be forcibly fed. This entails strapping or holding the woman down and snaking a tube through a nostril into her throat.

Nov. 10 The Pageant of Great Women is produced in London to popularize the suffrage movement. It portrays women like Boadicea (Boudica), Zenobia, and Lakshmi Bai. Fifty-two actresses have roles in the play, with the part of Prejudice being played by a man.

Dec. 19 U.S. socialist women reject the suffrage movement as being concerned only with the middle class.

Business and Industry

U.S. labor organizer Elizabeth Gurley Flynn (b. August 7, 1890) becomes a member of the General Executive Board of the IWW.

Canadian-American cosmetics entrepreneur Elizabeth Arden (December 31, 1878?–October 18, 1966) opens a Fifth Avenue salon with Elizabeth Hubbard.

Sweden passes a law barring women from night work.

Canadian agricultural journalist E. Cora Hind (b. 1861), known for her astute predictions about wheat, estimates that the Canadian wheat crop this year will total 118,109,000 bushels. The actual total is 118,119,000.

In England, elementary school teachers make about ninety pounds a year; high school teachers make ninty to one hundred pounds on average. Women postal clerks start at sixty-five pounds and can rise to a maximum of one hundred. Women journalists make one to three pounds per week. Shorthand stenographers and typists make about one pound a week, assistant hairdressers fifteen shillings, and assistant dressmakers and milliners about ten shillings. A hospital nurse earns about twenty-five pounds a year.

Nov. 24 In New York, about 18,000 women shirtwaist makers from 500 garment shops go on strike. Most make only three to five dollars a week for fifty-six to fifty-nine hours of work. They are sometimes charged as much as $1.50 a week for needles and thread, electricity, chairs, lockers, tardiness, and damage to goods.

Within a week, shirtwaist production in New York is brought to a virtual halt. Labor leader Clara Lemlich calls (in Yiddish, the first language of most of the strikers) for a general strike. By December 22, more than seven hundred picketers will be arrested. Nineteen are imprisoned and the rest fined. The strike is supported by the local chapter of the International Ladies' Garment Workers' Union (ILGWU) and by the WTUL and its socially prominent members, like Alva Belmont, who says, "Women the world over need protection and it is only through the united efforts of women that they will get it." The strike is successful to some extent, with 300 shops recognizing the ILGWU and many shops offering better wages, hours, and working conditions.

Nov. 28 French law gives women eight weeks of maternity leave after childbirth.

Science and Medicine

U.S. physician and missionary Ida Scudder opens a nursing school in Vellore, India.

Education and Scholarship

Italian educator Maria Montessori publishes *Metodo del pedagogica scientifica*.

Oct. 19 U.S. educator Nannie Helen Burroughs (d. May 20, 1961) opens a school for black girls in Washington, D.C., the National Training School for Women and Girls (later the National Trade and Professional School for Women and Girls). The school's motto is, "We specialize in the wholly impossible." Practical skills, such as homemaking, clerical skills, interior decorating, painting, shoe repair, gardening, and hairdressing, are stressed, but black history is a required course, and personal attributes are cultivated as well. Burroughs emphasizes the "three Bs—the Bible, the bath, the broom—clean life, clean body, clean home."

1910

General Status and Daily Life

The U.S. Mann Act, actively supported by the WCTU, prohibits "interstate and international traffic of women for immoral purposes."

Female life expectancy in Great Britain is 52.4 years.

Government, the Military, and the Law

Women in Norway get local suffrage.

Mar. 23 Women run for office in the Canary Islands.

Literature and the Visual Arts

Births in the arts this year include Korean poet Chu Su-won and Russian poet Olga Berggolts, imprisoned for two years under Stalin and best known for her *Leningrad Notebook*.

Polish novelist Eliza Orzeszkowa (b. 1841) dies.

Women's art exhibits include U.S. portraitist Romaine Brooks's (May 1, 1974–December 7, 1970) first one-woman show in Paris, at which she shows the celebrated nude *White Azaleas*; Russian painter Nataliia Sergeevna Goncharova's (1881–1962) one-woman show in Moscow; and U.S. sculptor Malvina Hoffman's (June 15, 1885–July 10, 1966) exhibit of a marble portrait at the National Academy of Design. Hoffman, who studied with Rodin, will create sculptures of Paderewski, Wendell Willkie, and Katharine Cornell. At the Paris Salon, U.S. sculptor Anna Hyatt Huntington (March 10, 1876–October 4, 1973) wins an honorable mention for her equestrian statue of Joan of Arc.

New poetry by women includes Uruguayan poet Delmira Agustini's collection *Cantos de mañana*, Russian poet Marina Tsvetayeva's (b. 1892) *Vecherniy albon* (*Evening Album*), and French poet Marguerite Burnat-Provins's *Cantique d'été*.

Mary A'jami edits the women's journal *al-A'rus* in Damascus, Syria.

Performing Arts and Entertainment

Russian ballerina Galina Ulanova, noted for her performances in the ballets of Lavrovsky and a dominant force in Russian dance through her position as ballet mistress of the Bolshoi, is born.

U.S. composer Carrie Jacobs Bond composes the sentimental song "A Perfect Day." Within about ten years, it will sell 5 million copies in about sixty different arrangements. By 1925, it will have been recorded fifty times.

Russia's ballerinas are busy this year; Anna Pavlova (1882–January 23, 1931) tours the United States for the first time, Tamara Karsavina stars in *The Firebird*, and Lydia Lopokova (1892–1981) joins Dyaghilev's Ballets Russes and stars in the première of *Carnaval*.

Canadian-American actress Mary Pickford (stage name of Gladys Smith, April 18, 1893–May 29, 1979) stars in the silent films *White Roses*, *The Little Teacher*, *Wilful Peggy*, and *Song of the Wild Wood Flute*.

Filmmakers Alice Guy-Blaché of France and Luise Flack of Austria start their own production companies. Guy-Blaché's company is called Solax; in the next four years, she will direct over one hundred films.

U.S. comedian and singer Fanny Brice (b. October 29, 1891) has her first success with the Irving Berlin song "Sadie Salome" and appears in the Ziegfeld *Follies of 1910*, where her first performance earns twelve encores. She will appear in almost all of the Follies until 1923.

Athletics and Exploration

Viola Spencer becomes the first British woman aviator to fly solo. She is killed while parachute jumping a few weeks later.

Mar. 8 French actress and artist Raymonde de Laroche becomes the first woman in the world to earn a pilot's license.

Sept. 2 Blanche Stuart Scott becomes the first American woman to solo in an airplane.

Activism

Suffragists in English prisons go on hunger strikes. One of them, Lady Constance Lytton (1869–1923), describes the force-feeding for the papers: after four days of hunger strike, she was gagged and her mouth forced open with a steel device; a four-foot tube was used to pump liquid nourishment directly into the stomach. In many other cases, the feeding tube is inserted into the esophagus through the nose. Another suffragist making news is Irish educator Margaret Gillespie, later the first woman magistrate in India, who is imprisoned for throwing stones at 10 Downing Street, the prime minister's residence. In the United States, suffragist Harriot Stanton Blatch (d. November 20, 1940) leads New York City's first big suffrage parade, and in Germany, Minna Cauer organizes a massive suffrage demonstration.

In the United States, 1 million women belong to the General Federation of Women's Clubs.

Charlotte Gulich cofounds the Camp Fire Girls, the first national, secular, interracial organization for U.S. girls.

Brazilian feminist Ernestina Lesina publishes *Anima Vita* (*Life Force*), a general call for women to agitate for their rights.

German feminist Marie Stritt is replaced by the more conservative Gertrude Baumer (1873–1954) as head of the Bund Deutscher Frauenverein (Federation of German Women's Associations). Baumer is still progressive enough, however, to frighten some people; during World War II she will be interrogated frequently by the Gestapo because of her views.

Austrian feminist and politician Adele Schreiber founds the German Association for the Rights of Mothers and Children.

Apr. 18 The U.S. Congress receives a petition for women's suffrage signed by 500,000.

Business and Industry

Danish trade unionist Olivia Nielsen dies. She organized women workers at Tuborg Breweries and expanded the union to several branches with more than 2,000 members.

In the U.S., 16.7% of women are in the work force, constituting 20.9% of the total labor force. About 60% of New York City's immigrant women are wage earners. Ninety percent of black employed women in the United States work as domestic servants or agricultural laborers. They will have more variety of employment during World War I, but the proportion of black women in these two occupations will be back to 90% shortly after the war's end. Only 125,000 women belong to unions, because most unions do not want them, perceiving them as low-paid competition.

U.S. lawyer and worker's compensation expert Crystal Eastman (June 25, 1881–July 8, 1928) publishes a widely read book on work-related accidents.

Science and Medicine

Isabel Robb, principal and superintendent of the Johns Hopkins School of Nursing and establisher of uniform standards in nursing in the United States, dies.

U.S. public health nurse Lillian D. Wald founds Columbia University's Department of Nursing and Health.

Russian-German intellectual Lou Andreas-Salomé, knowing little about the subject, attends her first conference on psychoanalysis. She is destined to become not only a psychoanalyst, but one of Freud's most fervent disciples.

British astronomer Fiammetta Wilson, over the next ten years, will observe more than 10,000 meteors.

Education and Scholarship

In the United States, 140,000 women are enrolled in college, 106,000 of them in coeducational institutions. Women are 70% of high school graduates and 44.1% of college graduates.

Egyptian feminist Huda Shaarawi (1879–1947), anti-British demonstrator and founder of the periodical *Egyptian Woman*, opens a girls' school.

U.S. social reformer Jane Addams becomes the first woman awarded an honorary degree from Yale University.

Mar. 8 Royal decree permits Spanish women to attend universities.

Religion

Dec. 3 U.S. religious leader Mary Baker Eddy, founder of Christian Science, dies with a personal fortune of more than $2,500,000.

Dec. 16 U.S. Shaker eldress Anna White (b. January 21, 1831) dies. In addition to performing her religious duties, White supported the Dreyfus cause, international pacifism, women's suffrage, and vegetarianism. In 1904, she coauthored the only history of the Shakers to be written by a member of the sect.

1911

General Status and Daily Life

In the United States and Europe, more women are keeping their birth names for professional purposes. Some go so far as not to change their names at all upon marriage.

Government, the Military, and the Law

Chile's Communist party is founded; it is the only party in the nation's history never to segregate its female members in a separate "women's section." Most Latin American political parties will first include women only as part of female auxiliaries or organizations subordinate to the male membership.

Portugal allows women to enter the civil service. Portuguese heads of family are allowed to vote, so a female head of household, Carolina Beatriz Angelo, votes in a local election; the law is then changed so that only male heads of household have suffrage.

Mar. 17 Anna Rogstadt takes her seat as the first woman member of Norway's Parliament.

May 8 Icelandic women get the vote.

Literature and the Visual Arts

Chinese playwright Yang Jiang, who will translate Cervantes's *Don Quixote* into Chinese, is born.

English novelist Frances Hodgson Burnett publishes *The Secret Garden*, a children's story about a spoiled girl, Mary Lennox, who develops a sunnier personality through her encounters with her invalid cousin Colin, a lower-class boy named Dickon, and a locked garden with a tragic past. Other novels published this year include U.S. novelist Edith Wharton's *Ethan Frome*, the story of a tragic love triangle, and Emilia Pardo Bazán's *Dulci dueno*.

New Zealand author Katherine Mansfield (1888–January 9, 1923) publishes *In a German Pension*, her first collection of short stories.

U.S. lyric poet Sara Teasdale publishes *Helen of Troy, and Other Poems*.

At the Paris Salon, U.S. sculptor Malvina Hoffman wins an honorable mention for *Russian Dancers*.

Performing Arts and Entertainment

English oboist Evelyn Rothwell is born.

Russian choreographer Bronislava Nijinska (1891–1972) joins Dyaghilev's Ballets Russes, the company's only woman choreographer and later its principal choreographer.

English composer Ethel Smyth composes *March of the Women* for the suffrage movement.

Italian soprano Luisa Tetrazzini gives her first performance at the Met, as Violetta.

Moviegoers can see Asta Nielsen (1881–1972) in the

Danish film *The Abyss* and U.S. actress Mary Pickford in *The One She Loved* and *Just Like a Woman*. On stage, Ethel Barrymore plays the liberated typist, Kate, in *The Twelve-Pound Look*, and Maude Adams stars in *Chantecler*, drawing twenty-two curtain calls at the first performance.

American Anna McKnight becomes one of the movie industry's first film editors.

Anna Hoffman-Uddgren, the first woman film director in Sweden and the second woman film director in the world, directs *Blott en Drorn* and *Stockholmdamernas*.

Athletics and Exploration

Travel books include Gertrude Bell's *Amurath to Amurath*, about her travels in Turkey during the Young Turks' rebellion, and Annie Smith Peck's *A Search for the Apex of South America*. This year Peck, sixty-one, climbs Peru's Mt. Coropuna and plants a "Votes for Women" sign at the top.

U.S. tennis players Eleonora Sears (b. September 28, 1881) and Hazel Hotchkiss Wightman (December 20, 1886–December 5, 1974) win the U.S. doubles title. Wightman, who introduced the volleying game to women's tennis and will win a record forty-four national titles, also wins the singles and the mixed doubles.

July 8 American Nan Jane Aspinall completes a trip from San Francisco to New York City on horseback. She began the 4,500-mile trip, the first solo cross-country horseback ride by a woman, on Sept. 1, 1910.

Aug. 1 Harriet Quimby becomes the second woman in the world and the first in the United States to earn a pilot's license. She failed the flying test once, then nearly broke the record for accurate landing on her second attempt. German Melli Beese also earns her pilot's license this year.

Dec. 31 French pilot Hélène Dutrieu wins the Femina aviation cup and sets a women's distance record of 158 miles.

Activism

Chinese actress Jin Jilan is executed for her support of the republican revolution.

U.S. reformer Jane Addams becomes the first leader of the National Federation of Settlements. She also becomes vice president of NAWSA, a position she will hold until 1914.

The English suffrage movement is gaining strength.

Emmeline Pankhurst's tactics are not universally admired within the movement; this year Teresa Billington-Greig publishes *The Militant Suffrage Movement*, in which she advocates more moderate methods. But Pankhurst has plenty of support. Suffragist Emily Davison, imprisoned for her activities, goes on hunger strike. When she is force-fed, she tries to kill herself to publicize the horrors of forcible feeding. Constance Lytton, tired of being released on health grounds whenever she is arrested for her militant activities, disguises herself as a spinster. When arrested for urging people to stone a public building, she gives her name as Jane Wharton, goes on hunger strike, and is forcibly fed. The rough treatment causes a stroke, which leaves her with permanent partial paralysis.

Greek journalist Kalliroe Parren founds the feminist Lyceum of Greek Women.

Japan's first feminist organization, Seitosha, is established by Hiratsuka Raicho. It publishes the progressive journal *Seito* and disbands in 1916.

Tang Junying establishes the Chinese Suffragette Society in Beijing. She leads an attack on the National Assembly and is arrested in 1913.

Kenyan Me Katilili is a principal leader of the Giriama rebellion against British rule. She organizes tax resistance, is arrested, escapes, and is captured again.

French housewives seize food supplies and wave red banners to protest rising food costs.

June 17 An estimated 40,000–60,000 suffragists march through London, some dressed as famous women of the past. Seven hundred who have been jailed carried lances and banners in purple, green, and white. The march ends at Albert Hall, where Emmeline Pankhurst holds a suffrage meeting.

Business and Industry

The Chicago Vice Commission, assisted by reformer Ellen M. Henrotin, issues its report on prostitution, *The Social Evil in Chicago*: "it is a man and not a woman problem which we face today—commercialized by men—supported by men—the supply of fresh victims furnished by men . . . . So long as there is lust in the hearts of men [the Social Evil] will work out some method of expression."

U.S. philanthropist and suffragist Louise deKoven Bowen gets the Pullman Company to improve worker safety and gets International Harvester to grant women employees a minimum wage.

A Japanese law, passed this year and implemented in

1916, limits women's workdays to twelve hours and regulates night work. It applies only to employers of fifteen or more.

In England, 51% of postal clerks and 35.9% of telegraph operators are women.

Mar. 25 In New York City, the Triangle Shirtwaist Company catches fire; 146 workers, mostly young women, die. They cannot escape through the doors, which have been locked to prevent employees from sneaking out, and many leap from the upper stories. The incident stimulates nationwide interest in factory safety, and the Triangle owners are indicted for manslaughter.

Science and Medicine

U.S. astronomer Annie Jump Cannon (December 11, 1863–April 13, 1941) becomes curator of astronomical photographs at Harvard, a position she will hold until 1938. She will become an honorary member of the Royal Society and the first woman recipient of an Oxford honorary doctorate.

U.S. archaeologist Hetty Goldman (December 19, 1881–May 4, 1972) excavates classical and Neolithic ruins in Halae, Greece.

England has 77,000 female nurses.

U.S. ethnologist Alice Fletcher (March 15, 1838–April 6, 1923) publishes the monograph *The Omaha Tribe*.

May 21 Scottish-American astronomer Williamina Fleming (b. May 15, 1857) dies. She discovered over 200 variable stars, as well as ten of the twenty-four novae known before 1911. She also developed seventeen classification categories for stellar spectra, classified 10,351 stars, and may have discovered the binary nature of Beta Lyrae.

Nov. 4 A scandal breaks in the Paris papers, accusing Marie Curie of consorting with a married scientist. Angry crowds surround her house shouting "Husband stealer!" and "Get the foreign woman out!" When, a few days later, she wins the Nobel Prize for Chemistry for her discovery of the elements radium and polonium, jealous colleagues assume that the prize has been awarded out of pity. Three duels erupt over the supposed affair, overshadowing the fact that she is the first person ever to win two Nobels.

Education and Scholarship

New books include Austrian feminist Marianne Hainisch's *Frauenarbeit*, South African Olive Schreiner's influential text *Women and Labor*, and U.S. journalist

Ida Tarbell's *The Tariff in Our Times*.

Greek feminist Avra Theodopoulou founds the School for Working Women.

The first women's agricultural school is founded on New York's Long Island.

England has 183,298 female teachers; 72.8% of all English teachers are women.

Religion

English mystic Evelyn Underhill publishes *Mysticism and The Path of Eternal Wisdom*.

U.S. reformer Vida Scudder cofounds the Episcopal Church Socialist League.

1912

General Status and Daily Life

The two-year Kewpie doll craze begins in the United States; the dolls and stories about them were invented by U.S. author Rose O'Neill (1874–1944), who made $1.5 million from them and lost the entire fortune by 1936.

Government, the Military, and the Law

Jane Addams becomes the first U.S. woman to make a nominating speech at a national political convention.

The Children's Bureau of the U.S. Department of Labor is established, largely due to the efforts of public health nurse Lillian D. Wald. Its first director is reformer Julia Lathrop (June 29, 1858–April 15, 1932).

Literature and the Visual Arts

Korean authors born this year include journalist Yi Son-hi and novelist Ch'oe Chong-hi.

Japanese artist Nakabayashi Seishuku dies.

Afifa Sa'ab edits the women's journal *al-Khadir* in Lebanon.

Literature by women this year includes Turkish

nationalist Halide Adivar's feminist novel *Handan*, Hungarian author Margit Kaffka's (1880–1918) *Szinek és évek* (*Colors and Years*), U.S. writer Gertrude Stein's *Portrait of Mabel Dodge*, and U.S. author Edna Ferber's (August 15, 1885–April 16, 1968) story collection *Buttered Side Down*.

U.S. author Jean Webster (July 24, 1876–June 11, 1916) publishes her most popular children's novel, *Daddy Long-Legs*, the story of a poor orphan girl whose college education is paid for by a wealthy bachelor; the book stimulates improvements in orphanages. Other new U.S. novels include Edith Wharton's *The Reef*, a novel heavily influenced by the style of Henry James; Ellen Glasgow's *Virginia*; and Willa Cather's (December 7, 1873–April 24, 1947) first novel, *Alexander's Bridge*.

U.S. poet Edna St. Vincent Millay (February 22, 1892–October 19, 1950) publishes the poem *Renasence*. Other poetry landmarks this year are American Amy Lowell's (b. February 9, 1874) first collection, *A Dome of Many-Colored Glass*, which is more traditional in style than her later work; Russian Anna Akhmatova's collection *Evening*; Indian politician and feminist Sarojini Naidu's *The Bird of Time*; American Elinor Wylie's first collection, *Incidental Numbers*; and Russian Marina Tsvetayeva's *Volshebny fonar* (*Magic Lantern*).

Concordia Samoilova cofounds the Russian Communist newspaper *Pravda*.

English painter Vanessa Bell (1879–April 7, 1961), sister of author Virginia Woolf and great-niece of portrait photographer Julia Margaret Cameron, exhibits paintings at the Second Post-Impressionist Exhibition, which also includes the work of Picasso, Braque, Matisse, and Cézanne.

Performing Arts and Entertainment

Australian pianist Eileen Joyce is born.

Film aficionados, who now number in the millions, can see French stage legend Sarah Bernhardt in two movies, *La Dame aux Camelias* and *Queen Elizabeth*. Mary Pickford stars in the silent films *Lena and the Geese* and Anita Loos's (d. 1981) *The New York Hat*. Danish actress Asta Nielsen stars in *Das Mädchen ohne Vaterland*. The schedule imposed by the movie studios is demanding; for example, over the next three years, American actress Dorothy Gish will appear in sixty-one films. Gish appears this year with her sister Lillian in *An Unseen Enemy*.

French composer Lili Boulanger (1893–1918) composes *Pour les funérailles d'un soldat*.

U.S. comedian Fanny Brice creates the mischievous infant "Baby Snooks," a character for which she will become especially famous.

Swedish filmmaker Anna Hoffman-Uddgren directs *Systrarna* and *Miss Julie*.

Athletics and Exploration

Mary K. Browne defeats Eleonora Sears to win the U.S. singles tennis title.

Englishwoman Audrey Beaton founds the Ladies' Lacrosse Association. Within a year, it has members at seven clubs and seventy schools.

Apr. 2 Trehawke Davis becomes the first woman to cross the English Channel in a dirigible.

Apr. 16 Harriet Quimby, the first licensed female U.S. pilot, flies the English Channel west to east, but she receives relatively little attention as a result. She dies in a plane crash on July 1.

July 7 Tennis player Ethel Larcombe defeats Charlotte Sterry to win the Wimbledon singles title.

Summer In Stockholm, women's swimming is included in the Olympics for the first time. The 100-meter freestyle is won with a record-breaking time by Australian Fanny Durack (b. 1894), who swims the distance in the same time as the male winner, despite the fact that she is hampered by a long-skirted, wool swimsuit. Over the next six years, Durack will set eight more world records. The silver in the freestyle goes to Wilhelmina Wylie of Australia and the bronze goes to British swimmer Jennie Fletcher. The 4 x 100-meter freestyle relay is won by Great Britain's team of Jennie Fletcher, Bella Moore, Annie Speirs, and Irene Steer.
   In track, the 400-meter relay is won by Great Britain. Greta Johansson of Sweden wins the gold medal in high diving. Marguerite Broquedis of France wins the outdoor tennis singles title, followed by Germany's Dora Koring and Norway's Molla Bjurstedt Mallory. Britain's Ethel Hannam takes the indoor title.

Activism

U.S. journalist Ida Tarbell publishes *The Business of Being a Woman*, in which she claims that marriage and motherhood are more important than public life and are set aside for women not only by society but by nature.

The League for the Prevention of the Emancipation of Women is founded in Germany.

Turkish activist and author Halide Adivar becomes the

only female member of the country's nationalist club, Ojak.

Feminist Alexandra van Grippenberg founds the Finnish National Council of Women.

Indonesian activist Sitti Rohanda begins publishing the first feminist magazine in Sumatra.

National executive members of the new African National Congress (ANC) include Charlotte Maxeke, South Africa's first black woman doctor.

Feb. 24 U.S. Zionist Henrietta Szold (December 21, 1860–February 13, 1945) becomes founding president of Hadassah.

Mar. 12 Juliette Low (October 31, 1860–January 18, 1927) founds the Girl Scouts with eighteen members. By the time of Low's death, every state will have Girl Scout troops with a total membership of more than 140,000.

Business and Industry

Jan. U.S. radical and labor leader Elizabeth Gurley Flynn helps to organize a strike of 20,000 textile workers in Lawrence, Massachusetts. With birth control advocate Margaret Sanger, she arranges to have the children of the striking workers housed in foster homes for the duration of the strike. When she begins to evacuate the children on February 24, police attack the children and their mothers, and public opinion begins to swing toward the workers. The strike ends in March with wage and overtime concessions for the returning workers; much of the credit for the success of the strike is given to the women.

Science and Medicine

Linda Richards (b. 1852), the first nurse in the United States to complete formal training, dies.

Between now and 1949, U.S. botanist Alice Eastwood will add 340,000 specimens to the herbarium at the California Academy of Sciences.

U.S. nurses Mary Gardner and Lillian Wald coestablish the National Organization of Public Health Nursing (NOPHN). Gardner becomes the organization's first secretary and Wald becomes its first president.

María Paz Mendoza-Guazón, already the first Filipina to graduate from high school, becomes the first Filipina doctor. Later she will become the first president of the Philippine Women's Medical Association.

British dentist Fanny Harwood is the first woman licensed as a dental surgeon by the Royal College of Surgeons.

Education and Scholarship

Italian educator Maria Montessori publishes *Autoeducazione*. To help popularize Montessori's method of early childhood education in the United States, American writer Dorothy Canfield Fisher publishes *A Montessori Mother*, the first of several books she will write praising Montessori schools.

Religion

English mystic Evelyn Underhill publishes *The Spiral Way*.

1913

General Status and Daily Life

In England, working-class families often spend twice as much feeding the father as feeding the mother and children combined. When there is not enough food to go around, it is usually the mother who goes without supper.

A five-to-six-room flat costs about fourteen to fifteen shillings per week. The landlady will rent use of the "copper," the fire-stoked washtub, and the washing space is shared by all tenants, which creates special problems. "The downstairs woman hates having the upstairs woman in her scullery, and the upstairs woman hates washing there. Differences which result in 'not speaking' often begin over the copper."

Cooking facilities are often inadequate, and good hygiene is difficult. Many people can afford only twopence worth of soap a week, and this must be used on both the floor and the baby.

Government, the Military, and the Law

Regina Quintanilha becomes the first woman in Portugal to earn a law degree.

June 29 Norwegian women get full suffrage rights.

Literature and the Visual Arts

Swiss artist Meret Oppenheim is born.

Japanese *bunjin* artist Okuhara Seiko, noted for her paintings of bamboo in the Chinese style, dies. She was a talented calligrapher and a student of Chinese literature and philosophy. Masculine in appearance, with short-cropped hair, she was once approached at an exhibition by a man who tried to grab her breasts to see if she was a woman. She seized him and flipped him over the tray in front of her.

U.S. author Eleanor Hodgman Porter publishes the best-seller *Pollyanna*, about an eternally optimistic little girl; it will be translated into several languages and made into a play and two movies. Other novels of this year include Willa Cather's *O Pioneers!* with its powerful heroine, Alexandra Bergson; Edith Wharton's *The Custom of the Country*, which expresses distaste for vulgarity and commercialism; and Italian feminist author Sibilla Aleramo's *II passagio*.

Sraa al-Mihaya edits the women's magazine *Fatat al-Niyl* in Cairo, Egypt.

New verse collections include Uruguayan poet Delmira Agustini's *Los Calizes vacíos* and Russian poet Marina Tsvetayeva's *From Two Books*.

Puerto Rican author María Cadilla de Martínez' (December 21, 1886–August 23, 1951) story *El Tesoro de Don Alonso* wins a prize from the Society of Writers and Artists of Puerto Rico.

French author Colette becomes fiction editor of *Le Matin*, a position she will hold until 1919.

U.S. sculptor Meta Warrick Fuller creates a sculpture of a black boy and girl for the fiftieth anniversary of the Emancipation Proclamation.

Performing Arts and Entertainment

English concert pianist Gina Bachauer (d. 1976) is born.

In the field of musical composition this year, American Marion Bauer (August 15, 1887–August 9, 1955) composes *Up the Ocklawaha*, a tone poem for violin and piano, and *Fair Daffodils*, a trio for women's voices. American Mabel Daniels (November 27, 1878–May 10, 1971) composes the cantata *The Desolate City*, and French composer Lili Boulanger wins the Prix de Rome for her cantata *Faust et Hélène*, making her the first woman ever to win this award.

Danish film actress Asta Nielsen stars in *Die Suffragetten*.

Britain's first famous film star, Alma Taylor, stars in *David Copperfield*.

Russian ballerina Anna Pavlova forms her own company. In the next decade, the troupe will travel about 300,000 miles, give about 3,600 performances, and introduce ballet to Japan, China, India, and Egypt.

Athletics and Exploration

The Oxford and Cambridge women's lacrosse teams play each other for the first time. The Cambridge players wear knickerbockers and knee-length tunics; the Oxford players wear skirts.

U.S. explorer and photographer Mary Akeley (January 29, 1878–July 19, 1966) begins exploring the Canadian Northwest, photographing the landscape and gathering data on the region's geography and botany.

Activism

Texas lawyer and reformer Hortense Ward lobbies successfully for state laws guaranteeing married women's property rights, workmen's compensation, and a fifty-four-hour work week for women. She is so vigorous in her support of the first law, in fact, that it is nicknamed the "Hortense Ward Act."

German feminist Anita Augsburg establishes the Deutscher Frauenstimmrechtsbund (German Women's Suffrage League).

Irish unionist Louie Bennett (1870–1956) cofounds the Irishwomen's Suffrage Federation and becomes its Secretary.

Feb. 8 Suffragists vandalize the London-Glasgow telephone line.

Feb. 24 English suffragist Emmeline Pankhurst is arrested for encouraging people to blow up Exchequer Chancellor Lloyd George's house. Sentenced on April 3 to three years in jail, she stages a hunger strike. However, the government is fighting back. Its new "Cat and Mouse Act" allows hunger strikers to be released just long enough to get their strength back; then they are recaptured and imprisoned. Under the "Cat and Mouse Act," Pankhurst is released whenever her condition becomes life-threatening and rearrested more than ten times.

Mar. 3 U.S. feminist Alice Paul (January 11, 1885–July 9, 1977), head of NAWSA's Congressional

Committee, organizes a huge march for women's suffrage on the day before President Woodrow Wilson's inauguration. The 5,000 marchers, carrying banners that say "Tell your troubles to Woodrow," are attacked by antisuffrage rioters on Pennsylvania Avenue. Wilson's arrival in D.C. is greeted by empty streets as people pour over to the site of the parade.

In April, Paul, frustrated with NAWSA's slow progress, forms her own group, the more militant Congressional Union (CU), with fellow suffragist Lucy Burns (July 28, 1879–December 22, 1966). NAWSA has been agitating on a state-by-state basis, but the CU hopes to focus on a national amendment granting women the vote. In November, Paul begins publishing *The Suffragist.*

Mar. 10 U.S. abolitionist Harriet Tubman (b. 1820?) dies. An escaped slave herself, she returned to the South several times to assist in the escapes of about 300 slaves; she also served as a cook, laundress, nurse, scout, and spy in the Union army during the Civil War.

Apr. 26 The International Women's Peace Conference begins in The Hague, Netherlands.

May 5 U.S. advocate for the handicapped Helen Keller announces, "I am a militant suffragette because I believe suffrage will lead to socialism, and to me socialism is the real cause." In this year she advocates socialism in a collection of essays, *Out of the Dark.*

June 4 English militant suffragist Emily Davison wraps herself in a WSPU flag and throws herself beneath the king's horse during the Epsom Derby. She dies of her injuries four days later and is buried on June 14 as a national martyr. The funeral procession, which stretches more than two miles, is accompanied by an honor guard of suffragists in black and white.

Dec. Russian socialist Concordia Samoilova becomes an editor of the new journal *Rabotnitsa* (*Woman Worker*) with five other women. Five of the six are arrested immediately, but it begins publication anyway.

Business and Industry

Russian factory women are fined for tardiness, poor work, sickness, and laughing. One young weaver states that "the law provides an 11 1/2 hour day, but some stand at the loom 18 hours for 10 or 12 rubles a month. . . . The foremen make young girls sleep with them. And sometimes they do it, they do it out of fear, out of fear to lose even this work which is like that of a prisoner at hard labor, even these miserable pennies."

Many women garment workers in the United States work a nine-hour day and a half day on Saturday.

Science and Medicine

Hungary changes its law restricting women doctors; until now they have been allowed to practice only in association with male doctors.

U.S. public health nurse Lillian D. Wald's Henry Street Visiting Nurses Service has a staff of ninety-two and makes 200,000 home visits each year.

British astronomer Fiammetta Wilson is the first to spot the return of Westphal's Comet.

U.S. geologist Eleonora Knopf (July 15, 1883–January 21, 1974) becomes the first person to discover a deposit of the mineral glaucophane east of the Pacific Coast.

Education and Scholarship

English classicist Jane Harrison publishes *Ancient Art and Ritual.*

Women are admitted in small numbers to Japan's imperial universities.

France has 4,254 female and 37,783 male university students.

Nov. U.S. missionary Matilda Calder Thurston becomes the first president of China's as-yet-unbuilt Ginling College for Women.

Religion

U.S. Baptist leader Helen Barrett Montgomery becomes president of the new Woman's American Baptist Foreign Mission Society.

1914

General Status and Daily Life

May Mother's Day, due to the lobbying of Anna Jarvis (1864–1948), becomes a national holiday in the United States. Every year, Jarvis honors the anniversary of her mother's death by wearing a white carnation and praying.

Government, the Military, and the Law

Natividad Lopez becomes the first woman lawyer in the Philippines. Later she will become the first Filipina judge as well.

English nurse Flora Sandes (1876–1956) tends to the wounded in Serbia during World War I but soon switches from nursing to active fighting. A gallant soldier, she will be wounded in 1916 and decorated for bravery.

July 1 U.S. prison administrator Mary Belle Harris (August 19, 1874–February 22, 1957) becomes superintendent of women and deputy warden at the Workhouse on Blackwell Island, New York. Placed in charge of 700 women in grim, crowded surroundings, she immediately begins reforms, revising rules and providing a library, activities, and outdoor exercise.

Oct. 13 Lawyer and judge Annette Abbott Adams (1877–1956) becomes the first female federal prosecutor in the United States.

Nov. Russian princess Eugenie Shakhovskaya becomes the first female military pilot when she flies reconnaissance missions with special permission from the tsar. Later she will become a member of the Bolshevik Secret Police and chief executioner at Kiev.

Literature and the Visual Arts

Salima Abu Rashid edits the women's journal *Fatat Lubnan* in Lebanon.

Chilean poet Gabriela Mistral (pseudonym of Lucila Godoy y Alcayaga, 1889–1957) publishes *Sonetos de la Muerte* (*Sonnets of Death*), which wins the Chilean National Prize for Poetry. Other new poetry includes Russian Anna Akhmatova's *Beads* (also sometimes translated as *Rosary*), which earns her her first serious recognition, and American Amy Lowell's *Poppy Seed*, which is more experimental than her earlier work.

Russian artist Nataliia Sergeevna Goncharova has a solo show in Petrograd and begins designing Dyaghilev's Ballets Russes.

Egyptian writer 'Aminah Al-Sa'id is born. The first woman elected to the Egyptian Press Syndicate Board, she will be president of the oldest publishing firm in the Arab world and editor of a weekly women's magazine, *Hawa* (*Eve*).

Literature this year includes *Allomasók* (*Stations*) by Hungarian Margit Kaffka, *Tender Buttons* by American Gertrude Stein, and *Seeds of Pine* by Canadian feminist lawyer Emily Murphy.

Mar. U.S. editor Margaret Anderson establishes the monthly critical journal *Little Review*, which covers such subjects as feminism, Nietzsche, psychoanalysis, and Imagist poetry. Over its history, the *Little Review*'s contributors will include Vachel Lindsay, Emma Goldman, Amy Lowell, Sherwood Anderson, Gertrude Stein, Hart Crane, William Carlos Williams, Ernest Hemingway, H. D. (Hilda Doolittle, September 10, 1886–1961), T. S. Eliot, James Joyce, and Ezra Pound.

Performing Arts and Entertainment

Movie fans can see U.S. actresses Marie Dressler (November 9, 1869?–July 28, 1934) and Mabel Normand appearing with Charlie Chaplin in *Tillie's Punctured Romance*, Mary Pickford in *Tess of the Storm Country*, Asta Nielsen in *Zapatas Bande*, and U.S. actress Mae Marsh (d. February 13, 1968), known for her portrayals of victims and orphans, as "Apple Pie Mary" in *Home Sweet Home*. Before the main feature, viewers may see U.S. silent film actress Pearl White, star of the famous twenty-episode serial *The Perils of Pauline*.

American Mamie Wagner becomes one of the movie industry's first film editors, cutting *The Call of the North*, *The Squaw Man*, and *The Virginian*.

On stage, English actress Mrs. Patrick Campbell originates a role written especially for her, Eliza Doolittle in George Bernard Shaw's *Pygmalion*. English actress Sybil Thorndike (1882–1976), known for her Shakespearean work, her portrayal of St. Joan, and her playing of both male and female roles, joins the Old Vic company. French actress Sarah Bernhardt is finally the undisputed queen of tragedy, now that her old rival, Italian tragedian Eleonora Duse, is retiring. On January 14, Bernhardt is awarded the Legion of Honor.

German soprano Lotte Lehmann makes her London debut as Sophie in Strauss's *Rosenkavalier*.

Athletics and Exploration

American Georgia "Tiny" Broadwick makes the first parachute jump from an airplane.

British tennis player Dorothea Douglass (b. 1878) wins her seventh singles title at Wimbledon, breaking the old record of six titles held by Blanche Bingley Hillyard. Douglass's other victories were in 1903, 1904, 1906, 1910, 1911, and 1913.

Jan. 2 British pilot Trehawke Davis is the first woman

to do a "loop-the-loop."

Activism

The German Federation of Women's Clubs has more than 1 million members.

Russian revolutionary Alexandra Kollontai publishes *The Social Foundations of the Women's Question*, in which she accuses feminists of wanting a few specific privileges for women who are already privileged, instead of wanting greater benefits for women in general.

Feb. Suffragists in Britain break windows at the home secretary's office in London and set fire to the Lawn Tennis Club.

Feb. 20 U.S. feminist Fola LaFollette argues that the idea of changing one's name upon marriage is just as silly for women as for men. She offers a variety of strategies for naming the children of dual-name unions and argues against the term *Mrs.*; suffrage leader Carrie Chapman Catt sends an emissary to scold her for this radical position, telling her, "Your speech has put suffrage back twenty-five years."

May 22 U.S. labor organizer Mother Jones tells activist women, "Never mind if you are not ladylike, you are womanlike."

Aug. 29 In New York City, 1,500 women, including economist and feminist Charlotte Perkins Gilman, march for peace on Fifth Avenue.

Sept. 18 Hungarian feminist and pacifist Rosika Schwimmer (b. September 11, 1877) meets with President Woodrow Wilson to present a petition for peace.

Business and Industry

U.S. businesswoman Marjorie Merriweather Post (March 15, 1887–September 12, 1973) inherits her father's Postum Cereal Company, though she is not allowed to sit on the board of directors until 1936; her husband, more acceptable because of his sex, represents her at meetings.

Dishwasher inventor Jacqueline Cochrane, whose company has sold most of its machines to restaurants and hotels, introduces a version for home use; it is not immediately popular, largely due to the lack of abundant hot water in most American homes. Cochrane's company will later merge with another to form the Kitchenaid company.

English unionist and politician Margaret Grace Bondfield

becomes the secretary of the National Federation of Women Workers, which she helped to found.

U.S. inventor Polly Jacob (later known as Caresse Crosby) obtains the first patent for a brassiere; she got the idea one night to attach two handkerchiefs together to form a substitute for the bulky and heavy corset. Sales are slow at best, and within a few years she will sell the rights for $1,500 to a company that will make $15 million from her idea in the next three decades.

Latvian-American labor organizer Dorothy Jacobs Bellanca (August 10, 1894–August 16, 1946) becomes the first woman on the executive board of the Amalgamated Clothing Workers of America.

Sept. 18 U.S. publisher Miriam Leslie (b. June 5, 1836) dies. When her third husband, Frank Leslie, died broke in the 1880s, she took over his failing newspaper empire and made it profitable again, changing her name legally to "Frank Leslie" to maintain her control over his company. She leaves an estate of about $2 million, about of half of which is bequeathed to the women's suffrage movement.

Oct. 12 U.S. inventor Margaret Knight (b. February 14, 1838) dies with a personal fortune of less than $300; she patented twenty-seven inventions, including the first machine to make flat-bottomed paper bags, a safety device for textile mills, a dress shield, a robe clasp, a spit, machines for shoe cutting, a window frame and sash, a numbering machine, and several types of rotary engines and motors.

Science and Medicine

Women in the sciences will find various ways of serving during World War I. English traveler, author, and archaeologist Gertrude Bell joins the Red Cross and traces missing soldiers. Marie Curie will organize a team of X-ray technicians to help at battlefields. Germany's Dr. Clara Immerwahr Haber, the first woman to earn a Ph.D. in chemistry from the University of Breslau, will commit suicide when her chemist husband refuses to abandon his work developing gas weapons.

Mar. U.S. birth control advocate Margaret Sanger (b. September 14, 1879) begins publishing a feminist journal, *The Woman Rebel*, proclaiming that "a woman's body belongs to herself alone." It contains no specific information about contraception, but the Post Office refuses to mail it. After she distributes a pamphlet called *Family Limitation*, which describes the use of sponges and diaphragms, she is indicted under the Comstock Law (which governs the mailing of "obscene" materials). She flees to Canada on October 20, returning about a year later; the government eventually drops the charges.

June At the second annual meeting of the American College of Surgeons, 1,065 new members are admitted, including the society's first two women: Alice Gertrude Bryant and Florence West Duckering.

Education and Scholarship

Russian-American author Mary Antin (June 13, 1881– May 15, 1949) publishes *They Who Knock at the Gates*, a defense of open immigration that says, "What we get in steerage is not the refuse, but the sinew and bone of all the nations." The book follows up on her most successful work, an autobiography called *The Promised Land* (1912), which will sell about 85,000 copies before her death.

There are 4,126 German women in German universities.

U.S. psychologist Augusta Bronner (July 22, 1881– December 11, 1959) studies the relationship between intelligence and delinquency and finds that character, not brainpower, determines behavior.

Notable scholarly publications this year include U.S. anarchist Emma Goldman's discussion of the works of Shaw, Ibsen, and Strindberg, *The Significance of Modern Drama*; German novelist and historian Ricarda Huch's history of the Thirty Years' War, *Der grosse Krieg in Deutschland*; and Polish-German socialist, feminist, and pacifist Rosa Luxemburg's *The Accumulation of Capital*.

May 19 The first philosophy thesis presented by a woman in France is submitted by Leontine Zanta.

Religion

The Quaker Philadelphia Yearly Meeting goes on record as the only U.S. religious body so far to endorse women's suffrage.

1915

General Status and Daily Life

The first electric clothes washers appear; they do not feature timed cycles or good insulation for the motors, and they require the user to add and drain the water by hand.

Last year, European women wore ankle-length skirts, the standard hem length since the thirteenth century. By this winter, skirts have risen ten inches from the ground.

Jan. 15 U.S. cookery writer Fannie Farmer (b. March 23, 1857) dies. She revolutionized American cooking, making it tastier and encouraging specific terminology, clear instructions, uniform results, and good nutrition. She popularized regular measurements to replace the old "pinch," "handful," and "walnut."

Government, the Military, and the Law

Denmark grants women the vote.

English traveler Gertrude Bell becomes a spy in Cairo for the British government, where her self-taught Arabic and extensive experience in the region become invaluable.

Aug. 5 Englishwoman Edith Cavell (b. 1865), who runs a Brussels nursing school where she treats the wounded of both sides in WWI, is arrested for smuggling Allied soldiers out of German-occupied Belgium. Shot by a German firing squad on October 12, she becomes a British national heroine.

Literature and the Visual Arts

Soviet poet To'ushan Esenova is born in Turkmenia. She will escape being sold as a child bride at six only because her head is shaved due to illness, making her unpresentable; her nine-year-old sister will not escape this fate. She will become a journalist, an airplane pilot, and the editor of a newspaper.

Korean novelist Chang Tok-jo, Korean short story author Im Ok-in, Norwegian poet Astrid Hjertanaes Andersen, and German-Israeli potter Hanna Charag-Zuntz are born.

English novelist Mary Elizabeth Braddon (b. 1837) dies. She wrote poetry, nine plays, and over seventy novels, including the famous and sensational *Lady Audley's Secret*.

New novels include English author Virginia Woolf's (b. 1882) first novel, *The Voyage Out*, and Willa Cather's *The Song of the Lark*.

U.S. author, publisher, and economist Charlotte Perkins Gilman publishes *Herland*, a humorous, feminist, utopian novel about a country inhabited by women. The women, who are encountered by three male American aviators, are pacifist, vegetarian, healthy, practical, and intelligent.

New verse includes English poet Edith Sitwell's *Wheels* and *The Mother and Other Poems*, Bulgarian poet Elisaveta Bagryana's *Savremenna misal*, Sara Teasdale's *Rivers to the Sea*, and a collection of poems and drawings called the *Book of Repulsive Women* by U.S. author Djuna Barnes (b. June 12, 1892).

Performing Arts and Entertainment

Three very different films are the subject of controversy this year. Two receive attention for sex, the other for violence. One of the sexy films is *A Fool There Was*, in which American Theda Bara (Theodosia Goodman, July 20, 1885–April 7, 1955) gets her big break as a vampiric seductress. She becomes famous for the line, "Kiss me, my fool!" and the term *vamp* is born.

The second film to cause a scandal over sex was made in 1914, but the controversy is still fresh in people's minds this year. The movie is *Hypocrites*, directed by Lois Weber, the first woman to write, direct, produce, and star in a movie, hired this year by Universal Studios at the astronomical salary of $5,000 a week. *Hypocrites* depicts a minister being stoned to death for exhibiting a statue of "The Naked Truth." Weber herself, according to popular rumor, poses as the statue after being unable to find an actress willing to pose nude on film. Banned in Boston and the subject of riots in New York, the film is an immense commercial success.

The violent film is *The Birth of a Nation*, a movie that glorifies the Ku Klux Klan (KKK) as a chivalric order for the defense of helpless white southern females victimized by freed slaves. Despite its racist message, it draws big crowds and furthers the careers of its female stars, Lillian Gish and Mae Marsh.

Another notable new film is *Les soeurs ennemies*, the first feature film by French journalist and director Germaine Dulac, cofounder the production company Delia Film. U.S. serial star Grace Cunard cowrites and codirects the twenty-two-episode serial *Broken Coin* and directs the short feature *The Campbells Are Coming*. U.S. director Ruth Ann Baldwin directs the short film *The Black Page* for Universal, and Elsie Jane Wilson directs *Dona Perfecta*. Actress Cleo Madison directs the one-reel *Liquid Dynamite* and the two-reel *The King of Destiny* for Universal. Viola Lawrence (d. 1973) becomes the first important female film editor in the United States. She will work with many of Hollywood's top directors, including Orson Welles, Howard Hawks, and John Ford.

Australian-American actress Judith Anderson (1898–1992) makes her stage debut in Sydney.

The "Emma McChesney" stories of Edna Ferber are turned into a Broadway play, *Our Mrs. McChesney*, starring Ethel Barrymore.

U.S. composer Marion Bauer composes *The Lay of the Four Winds*, a quartet for male voices.

Feb. 23 French tragedian Sarah Bernhardt has her right leg amputated. Offered $100,000 to exhibit her leg, she replies, "Which leg?"

Athletics and Exploration

Tennis players Eleonora Sears and Hazel Hotchkiss Wightman win the U.S. doubles title.

May 1 The first French women's track meet is held at the Stade Brançion.

Activism

Jan. U.S. reformers Carrie Chapman Catt and Jane Addams unite several pacifist groups as the Women's Peace party. Addams becomes chairman of the group, which has about 3,000 members.

Jan. Mexico's first feminist conference is held in Mérida.

Apr. 28-May 1 The International Congress of Women meets at The Hague, Netherlands, to discuss approaches to ending World War I. The idea is dismissed by U.S. president Theodore Roosevelt as "silly and base," but Jane Addams, who presides over the meeting, defends the plan: "We do think it is fitting that women should meet and take counsel to see what may be done." The delegates include some of the world's most distinguished reformers, such as Dutch feminist and physician Aletta Jacobs, English social worker and suffragist Emmeline Pethick-Lawrence, German feminist Lida Heymann, U.S. toxicologist Alice Hamilton, and Hungarian feminist and pacifist Rosika Schwimmer. The Congress of Women forms the International Committee of Women for Permanent Peace (later the Women's International League for Peace and Freedom, WILPF).

Nov. 17 Rosika Schwimmer meets with Henry Ford and gets him to sponsor a peace ship, the *Oscar II*, to travel to the warring countries and mediate. The *Oscar II* sets sail on December 4, but the project and Schwimmer are ridiculed by the press and public, and Ford himself abandons the ship when it reaches Norway.

Business and Industry

U.S. labor leader Rose Schneiderman becomes one of the few female national organizers for the ILGWU.

Mar. Glasgow, Scotland, hires two female streetcar conductors.

July 17 Thirty thousand British women stage a demonstration to demand war jobs.

Science and Medicine

Irish astronomer Margaret Huggins (b. 1848) dies. A specialist in spectroscopy, she studied the Orion nebula and Nova Aurigae and wrote biographies of famous scientists. Several prominent American women of science also die this year, including embryologist and comparative anatomist Susanna Phelps Gage (b. 1857), who specialized in the study of the brain and nervous system; physiologist and pathologist Edith Claypole (b. 1870), a specialist in tissue histology and pathology, who dies as a result of her research on the typhoid bacillus; and Susan La Flesche Picotte (b. June 17, 1865–September 15), daughter of an Omaha chief and sister of activist Susette La Flesche Tibbles. She served her tribe as a doctor for twenty-five years, treating almost every person on the reservation and becoming the unofficial leader of her people.

British astronomer Mary Blagg and American Grace Cook are elected to the Royal Astronomical Society.

Venezuelans Virginia Pereira Alvarez and Luisa Martínez become the first female students at the University of Caracas medical school.

U.S. obstetrician and surgeon Bertha Van Hoosen (d. 1952) founds and becomes first president of the American Women's Medical Association.

Education and Scholarship

New scholarly publications include U.S. feminist historian Mary Ritter Beard's *Women's Work in Municipalities*, English unionist Clementina Black's *Married Women's Work*, U.S. poet Amy Lowell's work of literary criticism, *Six French Poets*, U.S. social work educator and social reformer Edith Abbott's *The Real Jail Problem*, and Russian-German psychoanalyst Lou Andreas-Salomé's essay *Anal-und Sexual*, which wins praise from Freud.

Six times as many boys as girls are educated in Ghana.

U.S. educator Martha Carey Thomas establishes the first college school of social work.

U.S. psychology professor Lillien Martin (1851–1943) becomes the first woman department head at Stanford University.

Sept. U.S. missionary Matilda Calder Thurston opens the Ginling College for Women in Nanking, China.

Religion

July 16 U.S. religious leader Ellen Harmon White (b. November 26, 1827), a cofounder of the Seventh-Day Adventist church and the recipient of more than 2,000 religious visions, dies. Her denomination currently has 140,000 worshipers and 2,500 clergy.

Feb. 24 U.S. evangelist and missionary in India and Africa Amanda Berry Smith (b. January 23, 1837), who preached in the United States, Great Britain, Egypt, and India, and founded an orphanage in Chicago, dies.

1916

General Status and Daily Life

In Russia, women are required to live wherever their husbands tell them; if they run away, they can be forcibly returned to their spouses.

The Japanese women's magazine *Fujin Koron* is established.

Government, the Military, and the Law

Irish nationalist Constance Markiewicz leads 120 soldiers in the Easter Rising, barricading a building for three days and kissing her revolver before surrendering it to the authorities. She is sentenced to death, then life imprisonment, and ultimately freed in 1917.

Canadian lawyer Emily Murphy becomes the first woman magistrate in the British Empire; however, in her first case, the defense lawyer denies her right to try the case, since as a woman, she has no legal identity. Her authority is upheld by the Supreme Court of Alberta.

Ethiopian empress Zauditu (b. 1876) succeeds to the throne, but effective power remains in the hands of Ras Tafari (Haile Selassie). She is deposed in 1928 and dies in 1930.

Nov. 7 U.S. pacifist and feminist politician Jeannette Rankin (June 11, 1880–May 18, 1973) is elected to Congress from Montana, the first woman member of the House of Representatives. She campaigned across her state on horseback and defeated her Democratic opponent by 25,000 votes.

Literature and the Visual Arts

Italian novelist and essayist Natalia Levi Ginzburg and Korean journalist, novelist, and short story author Son So-hi are born.

Romanian author Queen Elisabeth (b. 1843) dies. She wrote novels, diaries, and children's literature in four languages under the pseudonym Carmen Sylva. Her lady-in-waiting Mite Kremnitz sometimes worked on the books with her.

U.S. poet Hilda Doolittle becomes editor of *The Egoist* and publishes *Sea Garden*. Other verse collections include American Amy Lowell's *Men, Women, and Ghosts*, Indian feminist Sarojini Naidu's *The Golden Threshold*, and Argentinian Alfonsina Storni's *The Disquiet of the Rosebush*.

Performing Arts and Entertainment

English composer Ethel Smyth's opera *The Boatswain's Mate* opens in London.

Russian ballerina Lydia Lopokova stars in London in Dyaghilev's production of *Les femmes de bonne humeur*.

Filmgoers can see Mary Pickford in *The Foundling* and *Pride of the Clan*, Theda Bara in *Romeo and Juliet* and in *The Darling of Paris* as Esmeralda, Lillian Gish in *Intolerance*, and Mae Marsh in *Intolerance*, *Hoodoo Ann, A Child of the Paris Streets*, and *The Wild Girl of the Sierras*. Women are active behind the camera as well. The subtitles for *Intolerance* are written by screenwriter Anita Loos, and Frances Marion writes the scenario for *The Foundling*. American serial star Grace Cunard cowrites and codirects the serials *The Purple Mask* and *Peg o'the Ring*. One of the most controversial films of the year, Universal's *Where Are My Children?*, was directed by a woman, Lois Weber. *Children* supports contraception but denounces abortion; it cost $12,000 to make and earns a reported $500,000.

Russian filmmaker Olga Preobrazhenskaya directs *Miss Peasant*.

Athletics and Exploration

The Women's International Bowling Congress is established.

Tennis players Eleonora Sears and Molla Bjurstedt Mallory win the U.S. doubles title; Sears and Willis Davis win the mixed doubles title.

Activism

Feminist María Jesús Alvarado Rivera founds Peru's first women's organization, Evolución Femenina.

Englishwoman Annie Besant founds the Home Rule India League.

At the Democratic National Convention, 7,000 women stage a "Walkless-Talkless Parade" in which tableaux depict women in suffrage and nonsuffrage states.

June U.S. suffragist, essayist, and politician Anne Martin becomes chairman of the new National Woman's Party (NWP), founded by Alice Paul's Congressional Union. The NWP demonstrates at the Democratic and Republican national conventions and is met with violence at the former and the support of candidate Charles Evans Hughes at the latter.

Sept. 8 President Wilson tells a suffrage convention that he favors women's suffrage "in a little while." Feminist Anna Howard Shaw responds, "We have waited long enough to get the vote. We want it now."

Business and Industry

Women in England's printing trade make about nine shillings per week.

Irish trade unionist Louie Bennett begins her successful rebuilding of the Irish Women Workers' Union.

German communist and feminist Clara Zetkin cofounds the Spartacus League.

U.S. physician Alice Hamilton (b. February 27, 1869) is now recognized as her country's leading authority on lead poisoning and one of the few experts anywhere in industrial disease.

American Hazel Hook Waltz invents the bobby pin, only to lose a fortune when a large manufacturer patents and markets a slightly different version.

U.S. fashion designer Nell Donnelly begins designing comfortable, cheap, stylish dresses for housewives. She will establish the Donnelly Garment Company with her husband, grossing as much as $3.5 million per year in the 1920s and marking her clothes with the name "Nelly Don." In 1944, she will sell her stock in the company for more than $1 million, and in 1954, she will retire.

Feb. 16 The British government recruits 400,000 women to do the agricultural labor of men who are now at war.

July 3 U.S. financier Hetty Green (b. November 21, 1834), the world's richest woman, dies. Often chastised for her stinginess (which, to her mind, was mere plainness and thrift), "the Witch of Wall Street" turned a $10 million inheritance into a $100 million fortune.

Science and Medicine

U.S. paleontologist Carlotta Maury (1874–1938), sister of astronomer Antonia Maury, organizes and leads an expedition to the Dominican Republic.

British astronomer Fiammetta Wilson (1864–1920), known for her observations of comets, meteors, and the aurora borealis, is elected to the Royal Astronomical Society.

German-American psychoanalyst Frieda Fromm-Reichmann becomes physician-in-charge of the new hundred-bed military hospital at Königsberg.

U.S. civil engineer and architect Nora Stanton Blatch becomes the first woman member of the American Society of Civil Engineers.

U.S. nurse Adah Thoms becomes president of the National Association of Colored Graduate Nurses, a position she will hold until 1923.

Oct. 16 Margaret Sanger and others open America's first birth control clinic at 46 Amboy Street in Brooklyn. More than a hundred women are lined up for the opening, alerted by 5,000 leaflets printed in English, Italian, and Yiddish: "Mothers! Can you afford to have a large family? Do you want any more children? If not, why do you have them?" The clinic is closed by the police within ten days.

Education and Scholarship

The Indian Women's University opens in Bombay.

Girls are 4.35% of students in nonmissionary schools in China; 172,724 girls are so enrolled.

Feb. 20 U.S. art historian Clara Clement Waters (b. August 28, 1834), author of three of the most popular art handbooks of the 1870s–1890s, dies.

Mar. 26 U.S. educator Susan Blow (b. June 7, 1843), who opened the first public kindergarten in the United States, dies.

Aug. Aurelia Reinhardt becomes president of California's Mills College, a women's college in Oakland. She finds it with a minimal reputation, 212 students, 39 faculty members, and 11 buildings; she will leave it in 1943 with a national reputation, a vastly increased student body, 101 faculty members, and 28 buildings.

1917

General Status and Daily Life

In their first few months in power, Russia's Bolsheviks reform marriage laws, grant equal employment and wage rights, and make accommodations for maternity leave. Adultery is no longer a crime; birth control and abortion are legalized. However, few women know of these changes. Three-quarters of the Russian population is illiterate, and most live in rural areas far from the hotbeds of political change.

The Japanese women's magazine *Shufu no tomo* begins publication.

Mexico's constitution affirms the equality of men and women.

Legal age of marriage is set at fourteen for women and sixteen for men in Sri Lanka.

July 18 Cuba passes laws protecting women's child custody, divorce, and property rights.

Government, the Military, and the Law

In the British war effort, women serve as ambulance drivers, nurses, auxiliaries, and workers in war industries. In the United States, some women work for the Red Cross or Women's Committee of the Council of National Defense (led by journalist Ida Tarbell and suffragist Carrie Chapman Catt).

Russian soldier Mariya Bochkareva (b. 1889) organizes a Women's Battalion of Death to fight in World War I. Bochkareva quickly becomes known and feared for her autocratic, harsh style of command, slapping women who flirt and mandating celibacy for the duration of the war, inciting a mutiny that leaves her with only 300 recruits of the original 1,000. The Women's Battalion goes into battle in July, sustaining heavy casualties.

Pakistani nationalist Abadi Begum ("Bi Amma," d. 1924), speaking from behind a veil, becomes the first Muslim woman to address a political party meeting when she talks to the Muslim League.

The U.S. Navy, anxious to send as many men overseas as possible to fight in World War I and in desperate need of people to fill its clerical jobs, enlists women with the same job classifications and pay as men; 12,000 women will serve during this crisis, most for fewer than two years.

A Brazilian court decision allows Maria José de Castro Rebelo to compete for a position in the Foreign Ministry, the first time that a woman has been permitted to do so. She takes first place.

Canadian suffragist Louise McKinney is elected to Alberta's legislature, becoming the first woman in the British Empire to serve in a legislative body.

Feb. Dutch dancer, courtesan, and spy Mata Hari (b. Margarete Zelle in 1876) is arrested for espionage. On July 25, she is sentenced to death, and on October 15, she is executed by a firing squad.

Apr. 2 Pacifist Jeannette Rankin of Montana is sworn in as the first woman in Congress. Four days later, she joins fifty-five others in voting against entry into World War I. "Peace is a woman's job," she says, "because men have a natural fear of being classed as cowards if they oppose war."

Oct. The Bolshevik Revolution takes place in Russia, with women fighting on both sides. Bolshevik Alexandra Kollontai becomes People's Commissar of Social Welfare, making her the world's first woman Cabinet minister. Faced with a strike, Kollontai does exactly what the old government did; she jails the strikers until they comply with her demands. She is now in charge of hundreds of thousands of wounded veterans, the pension system, orphanages, nursing homes, hospitals, artificial-limb factories, playing-card factories, leper colonies, and other facilities.

The Union of Soldiers' Wives serves as the distribution organization for welfare. At first the women are afraid to handle the money for fear they will lose it or count wrong, but soon the union is running child-care facilities and consumer cooperatives. Shortly after the Bolshevik rise to power, Soviet women get the right to vote.

Literature and the Visual Arts

Japanese *bunjin* artist Noguchi Shohin (b. 1847) dies. She was patronized by the imperial family, and her daughter, Iku, also became an artist.

U.S. painter Georgia O'Keeffe (b. November 15, 1887) has her first one-woman show.

New novels include Hungarian author Margit Kaffka's *Hangyaboly* (*Anthill*), Australian novelist Henry Handel Richardson's *Australia Felix*, and Edith Wharton's *Summer*, the story of a young woman's coming-of-age.

U.S. lyric poet Sara Teasdale publishes *Love Songs*, which wins a prize from the Poetry Society of America. Other verse collections by women include Anna Akhmatova's *The White Flock*, French poet Marguerite Burnat-Provins's *Poèmes de la boule de verre*; and Indian feminist Sarojini Naidu's (d. 1949) *The Broken Wing*.

One of Korea's most prominent modern women authors, T'ansil (pseudonym of Kim Myong-sun, b. 1896), wins a prominent literary prize with her first story, "A Girl with Suspicion." It is a realistic story that discusses male treatment of women and a mother's suicide. After this intial success T'ansil becomes a popular and influential author, writing poetry, novels, plays, and translations.

Performing Arts and Entertainment

English singer Vera Lynn, U.S. singer Lena Horne (June 30), and English mediumistic composer Rosemary Brown, transcriber of over 400 works she claims to have received spiritually from great dead composers, are born.

U.S. musical comedy actress Nora Bayes popularizes George M. Cohan's World War I song, "Over There."

English choreographer, dancer, and teacher Marie Rambert (1888–1981) creates the ballet *La pomme d'or*.

U.S. filmmaker Lois Weber, creator of more than 400 films, starts her own movie studio.

U.S. filmmakers direct several movies, including *The Fires of Rebellion* (Ida May Park), *The Woman Who Could Not Pay* (Ruth Ann Baldwin), *The Silent Lady* (Elsie Jane Wilson), *The Black Wolf* (Nell Shipman), and *The Wreck* (Mrs. George Randolph Chester). Lucille McVey coproduces and codirects an almost weekly series of one-reel comedies.

U.S. moviegoers this year can see Theda Bara in *Cleopatra* and Mary Pickford in *The Little Princess*, *Rebecca of Sunnybrook Farm*, *Romance of the Redwoods*, and *A Poor Little Rich Girl*. The scenario for *Poor Little Rich Girl* was written by U.S. screenwriter Frances Marion (November 18, 1888–May 12, 1973), author of more than one hundred scripts and collaborator on many others.

Athletics and Exploration

French athlete Anne Milliat establishes the Fédération Féminine Sportive de France.

Over the next year, U.S. swimmers Charlotte Boyle and Claire Galligan will experiment so successfully with the six-beat crawl that their style, initially ridiculed, is widely imitated.

U.S. mountain climber Annie Smith Peck becomes a fellow of the Royal Geographical Society.

Activism

The All India Women's Conference passes a resolution against polygyny.

Feminist Kimura Komako organizes Japan's first women's suffrage meeting.

Englishwoman Annie Besant becomes the first woman president of the Indian National Congress, a position she will hold until 1923.

Belgian feminist Martha Bol Poel (1877–1956), imprisoned in 1916 for her work against Germany, is traded for an enemy prisoner and exiled to Switzerland.

Not all U.S. women favor entry into World War I; radical and labor leader Elizabeth Gurley Flynn opposes it, and anarchist Emma Goldman is sentenced to five years in prison for opposing the draft. Pacifist Emily Greene Balch cofounds the Emergency Peace Federation.

Jan. U.S. suffragist Alice Paul's Congressional Union begins picketing the White House for suffrage. Sample signs read: "Mr. President, What Will You Do for Woman Suffrage? How Long Must Women Wait for Liberty?" and "Kaiser Wilson." Tensions rise; police arrest 114, starting in June; 66 are jailed, including Paul, who is arrested in October. Some, like Paul, refuse to eat and are force-fed, while outside, more picketers appear in their places. President Wilson pardons them; they refuse to accept it. All of the prisoners are freed in November.

Mar. 8 On International Women's Day, Russian women carry banners that say "Peace and Bread" and "Our Husbands Must Return from the Front." In some places, women are prevented from demonstrating, leading to riots and confrontations with soldiers, who in some cases find themselves sympathetic to the women's cause. *Pravda* calls it "the first day of the revolution. . . . Women, we salute you!"

Apr. Russian women streetcar conductors voluntarily donate three days' pay each to support publication of the radical paper *Rabotnitsa* (*The Woman Worker*). In July, it is the only communist periodical not banned by the provisional government.

Apr. 9 In the largest women's demonstration ever in Russia, 100,000 soldiers' wives march to demand more food.

May 13 Russian revolutionary Catherine Breshkovskaya, imprisoned and exiled for thirty-two years and now free, says, "We women have all the rights we wanted."

Business and Industry

Prostitution is legalized in Sweden, though pimping remains illegal.

During World War I, U.S. women work in iron and steel mills, chemical plants, foundries, lumber mills, munitions factories, and auto factories in greater numbers than ever before.

Since 1909, nineteen U.S. states have passed laws limiting the length of a woman's workday; twenty states have strengthened old protective laws.

Women are 40% of Russian factory workers.

Dec. 4 Anusuyaben Sarabhai (1885–1972) calls the first major trade union strike in India.

Science and Medicine

British physician Elise Ingliss (b. 1867) dies. At the start of World War I, she offered to go to the front with female medical units, organizing fourteen such groups for the Belgian, French, Russian, and Serbian armies. Her own country's War Office, however, told her, "My good lady, go home and sit still."

U.S. government health researcher Alice Evans announces her discovery that human brucellosis and undulant fever, bovine Bang's disease, and Malta fever (a disease found in goats) are all caused by the same organism. She recommends pasteurization of milk to stop transmission of the disease to humans, but her theory and solution are rejected for nearly ten years.

U.S. anatomist and histologist Florence Sabin becomes the first female full professor at Johns Hopkins Medical School.

Austrian physicist Lise Meitner codiscovers the element proactinium.

Education and Scholarship

The first Pulitzer Prize for biography goes to Americans Laura E. Richards and Maude Howe Elliott for *Julia Ward Howe*.

American poet Amy Lowell publishes *Tendencies in Modern American Poetry*.

Religion

Dec. 22 Italian-American saint and founder Mother Frances Xavier Cabrini (b. July 15, 1850) dies. The first American Catholic saint, she founded sixty-seven religious houses on three continents and was so aggressive and determined that others often referred to her in the masculine, calling her "a great man."

1918

General Status and Daily Life

Freedom of divorce becomes part of the new Soviet Union's family law.

Government, the Military, and the Law

Elizabeth P. Hoisington, the first U.S. woman brigadier general and the seventh director of the WACs (from 1966 to 1971), is born. She will call feminists "a bunch of dumb bunnies" and maintain ladylike decorum among her troops by banning slacks, chewing gum, and motorcycles.

Canada, Germany, and Poland grant women the vote. Women in Sweden get equal suffrage in municipal elections.

Mathilde Bajer becomes the first woman elected to the Upper House of the Danish Parliament.

Women over thirty in Great Britain get the vote, and a few women in Great Britain run for Parliament. Irish nationalist Constance Markiewicz, a candidate of the Sinn Fein party, is elected to Parliament from prison, making her the first woman elected to Parliament in Great Britain. However, as a protest, she, like the other Sinn Feiners, refuses to take her seat.

Seven Polish women become cabinet ministers,

including Irena Kosmowska (1879–1945), who becomes vice-minister of social welfare.

German feminist Clara Zetkin cofounds the German Communist Party.

Salote Tupou III (b. 1900) becomes queen of Tonga, ruling until her death in 1965.

Nov. Hungarian feminist and pacifist Rosika Schwimmer is appointed minister to Switzerland, making her the first modern woman ambassador.

Literature and the Visual Arts

Russian abstract painter Olga Vladimirovna Rozanova (b. 1886) dies.

New novels include Willa Cather's *My Antonía*, the story of a pioneer woman that H. L. Mencken will consider the most beautiful romantic novel ever written; Selma Lagerlöf's *Bannlyst*; and *The Return of the Soldier*, by British author Rebecca West (pseudonym of Cicily Fairfield Andrews, b. 1892).

New poetry collections include Argentinian Alfonsina Storni's (b. 1892) *El dulce dano* and American Amy Lowell's *Can Grande's Castle*.

U.S. author Dorothy Canfield Fisher publishes a collection of war stories, *Home Fires in France*.

June U.S. writer Clara Littledale (January 31, 1891–January 9, 1956) goes to Europe to cover the war for *Good Housekeeping* magazine. After six months, she is recalled and replies in a telegram, "Resigning and remaining."

July 4 Twin U.S. advice columnists Ann Landers (Esther Pauline "Eppie" Friedman Lederer) and Abigail Van Buren (Pauline Esther "Popo" Friedman Phillips) are born.

Performing Arts and Entertainment

Elizabeth Sprague Coolidge gives the first music festival at Tanglewood.

Irish dancer and choreographer Ninette de Valois (b. 1898), who will later be instrumental in founding the national ballet companies of Turkey, Britain, Canada, and Iran, becomes the British National Opera's principal dancer.

New films include *When Men Betray* with Tallulah

Bankhead (1902–December 12, 1968), who also makes her stage debut this year; *Carmen / Gypsy Blood* with Pola Negri; *Hearts of the World* with Dorothy Gish (March 11, 1898–June 4, 1968); and *Stella Maris* and *M'liss* with Mary Pickford. Mabel Normand stars in *Mickey*, the movie that will be most closely identified with her. Women are also working behind the camera. This year, U.S. film editor Anne Bauchens coedits *We Can't Have Everything* with Cecil B. DeMille; she will be his only editor for the rest of his career and will edit nearly forty of his films. Pioneering French film director Alice Guy-Blaché directs *The Great Adventure*, and U.S. women also direct several silent movies, including *Broadway Love* (Ida May Park), *New Love for Old* (Elsie Jane Wilson), *Baree, Son of Kazan* (Nell Shipman), and *The Sins of the Mother* (Mrs. George Randolph Chester).

Activism

The Indian National Congress endorses women's suffrage.

Nepal's first women's organization, the Mahila Samiti Women's Committee, is founded by Dibya Koirala, Yogmaya Devi, Mohan Kumari Koirala, and Purna Kumari Adhikari.

German feminists Lida Heymann and Anita Augsburg establish the journal *Die Frau im Staat*, which Heymann will run until the Nazi rise to power in 1933.

Turkish activist Halide Adivar is elected to the council of the Ojak, the Turkish nationalist club.

Russian leader Lenin is wounded by a would-be assassin, known as Dora or Fanny Kaplan, who is executed.

Mar. U.S. socialist Rose Stokes is arrested for espionage for writing a letter to a newspaper that says, "I am for the people, while the Government is for the profiteers." She is sentenced to ten years in prison, though the conviction will be overturned in 1920.

Nov. The first Russia-Wide Congress of Women Workers and Peasants is chaired by Claudia Nikolayeva and attended by more than 1,000 delegates. One reports that her husband threw her out of the house for planning to attend the conference without his permission. She says proudly, "I have thrown off the oppression of my husband." These delegates are exceptions to the rule; communist women have a hard time mobilizing their sisters, who protest that this is the way things have always been, call themselves illiterate and stupid, or laugh at the organizers. Practically all peasant women are beaten by their husbands, and most accept this as their lot in life.

Nov. 4 U.S. philanthropist Margaret Slocum Sage (b. September 8, 1828) dies. She gave away nearly $80 million in her lifetime, including generous gifts to the U.S. Military Academy, Harvard, Yale, a Louisiana bird refuge, the Young Women's Christian Association (YWCA), Syracuse University, Tuskegee Institute, the Metropolitan Museum of Art, the American Museum of Natural History, the New York Botanical Gardens, and the New York Zoological Society. She also established the Russell Sage Foundation and Russell Sage College, a women's vocational school.

Dec. U.S. radical Elizabeth Gurley Flynn establishes the Workers' Defense Union to help dissident immigrants threatened with deportation and to provide immigrants with general financial and legal support.

Business and Industry

France and the Soviet Union mandate equal pay for equal work.

Peru's Civil Code grants working women two hours per day to nurse their infants.

Mar. 29 The U.S. government reports that 1.4 million women are working in war industries; such women are often not admitted to unions. In August, 91% of working women in New York are paid less than men for equivalent work. After the war, women are pushed out of nontraditional jobs and back into the home and their traditional duties. Mary McDowell of the University of Chicago Settlement says, "During the war they called us heroines, but they throw us on the scrapheap now."

Science and Medicine

British botanist Ethel Sargant (b. 1863) dies. The first woman to serve on the council of the Linnean Society, she specialized in the cytology and morphology of plants and proved the existence of the synaptic stage in cell division.

Polish physician Anna Tomaszewicz-Dobroska (b. 1854), the first woman to practice medicine in Poland, dies.

Austrian physicist Lise Meitner becomes head of physics at the Kaiser-Wilhelm Institut für Chimie.

British birth control advocate Marie Stopes (1880–1958) publishes the controversial, million-selling books *Married Love* and *Wise Parenthood*.

July 2 Frances Elliott Davis becomes the first official black American Red Cross nurse. She would like to join the Army Nurse Corps as well, but it admits no black women yet.

Education and Scholarship

U.S. folklorist Elsie Clews Parsons is elected president of the American Folklore Society and becomes the editor of the *Journal of American Folklore*.

Linda Eastman becomes head of the Cleveland Public Library, making her the first U.S. woman to direct a metropolitan library system. During her tenure, she will expand services for the blind, hospital patients, and immigrants.

U.S. educator Mabel Douglass (February 11, 1877–September 21, 1933) founds and becomes dean of the New Jersey College for Women (later, Douglass College), a women's school affiliated with Rutgers.

Religion

Mother Marianne of Molokai (b. 1836) dies. She founded the first U.S. sisterhood to do missionary work abroad and established a home in Hawaii for leper women, after about fifty other religious societies refused.

Evangelist Aimee Semple McPherson (October 9, 1890–September 27, 1944), founder of the Church of the Foursquare Gospel, arrives in Los Angeles with her mother, one hundred dollars, a tambourine, and a car with a sign that says "Jesus Is Coming Soon—Get Ready."

1919

General Status and Daily Life

Russian law grants a widow the right to one-seventh of her late husband's movable property.

Government, the Military, and the Law

Women get the right to vote in Belgium (April 10), Luxembourg (February 6), Great Britain, Austria, the Netherlands, Ireland, and Sweden.

Argentinian feminist Julieta Lanteri (d. 1932) creates the nation's first feminist political party.

Women in New Zealand get the right to stand for Parliament.

Irish nationalist politician Constance Markiewicz (1858–1927) serves as minister of labor in the banned Irish Parliament, the Dail Eireann.

U.S. nurse and military officer Julia Stimson is made head of the Army School of Nursing and the Army Nurse Corps.

French-Russian revolutionary Inesse Armand is made head of the new Soviet Zhenotdel (Women's Department).

English lawyer Helen Normanton (1883–1957) becomes the first woman accepted by the Inns of Court.

U.S. radical journalist Ella Bloor cofounds the American Communist party.

Mar. Hungarian minister to Switzerland Rosika Schwimmer refuses to serve her country's new communist leader and is stripped of her civil rights.

Nov. 28 British politician Lady Nancy Astor (May 19, 1879–May 2, 1964), promoter of temperance, women's rights, and child welfare and sister of the original "Gibson girl" model, wins a seat in the House of Commons. She is the first woman to take a seat in Parliament (on December 1) and the only woman in Parliament from 1919 to 1921. Her twelve-year-old son's opinion of the history-making victory is, "Well done, mum." Less sanguine is Winston Churchill, who says her intrusion into the previously all-male Commons makes him feel as if she has invaded him in the bathroom. She responds, "Winston, you are not handsome enough to have worries of that kind."

Literature and the Visual Arts

Iran's first women's journal, *Zabane Zan* (*Language of Women*), begins publication with Sadigheh Dolat-Abadi as its editor.

In the United States, the Women's National Press Club is founded. Women are not allowed to become members of the male-only National Press Club, founded in 1908.

U.S. wit, poet, and writer Dorothy Parker becomes a drama critic at *Vanity Fair*, though she will be fired within a year for being too biting in her criticism.

New literature includes Austrian-American novelist Vicki Baum's (1896–1960) *Helene Willfuer* and *Menschen im Hotel* (*Grand Hotel*), Uruguayan poet Juana de Ibarbourou's (b. 1895) *Las lenguas de diamante*, American Anzia Yezierska's (d. November 21, 1970) prizewinning short story "The Fat of the Land," U.S.

poet Amy Lowell's *Pictures of the Floating World*, and Brazilian poet, librarian, journalist, comparative literature professor, playwright, and translator Cecília Meireles's (1901–1964) *Spectres*.

Nov. 19 U.S. expatriate Sylvia Beach (March 14, 1887–December 6, 1962) opens the English-language bookstore Shakespeare and Company on Paris's Left Bank. The store serves not only as a shop but as a lending library, post office, bank, and club for expatriate authors, and its customers will include such literary notables as Ezra Pound, Bryher, Gertrude Stein, Sherwood Anderson, Ernest Hemingway, H.D., Janet Flanner (*The New Yorker*'s "Genêt," March 13, 1892–1978), Katherine Anne Porter (May 15, 1890–September 18, 1980), and James Joyce.

Performing Arts and Entertainment

Trinidadian dancer and choreographer Pearl Primus is born.

Theatrical producer Theresa Helburn (January 12, 1887–August 18, 1959) cofounds the Theatre Guild, which eventually will grow from 135 to 25,000 patrons. In her thirty years with the guild, she will become one of the most powerful women in the U.S. theater.

Spanish dancer Carmen Amaya performs at the Barcelona International Exposition.

French composer Elsa Barraine wins the Prix de Rome.

French pianist Marguerite Long performs the première of Ravel's *Tombeau de Couperin*.

New films include *Male and Female*, starring Gloria Swanson (March 27, 1899–April 4, 1983); *Madame du Barry / Passion*, starring Polish actress Pola Negri; and *The Greatest Thing in Life*, *Broken Blossoms*, and *Take Heart Susie*, all starring Lillian Gish (b. 1896).

U.S. filmmakers direct several movies, including *Amazing Wife* (Ida May Park), *Broken Commandments* (Ruth Ann Baldwin), *The Lure of Luxury* (Elsie Jane Wilson), *Vengeance on Demand* (Mrs. George Randolph Chester), *Bunkered* (Lucille McVey), *The Golden Yukon* (Nell Shipman), and *Upstairs and Down* (Lillian Ducey, who also wrote the film).

Czechoslovakian filmmaker Hedvika Raabeova directs the short movie *Ada*.

Apr. 17 Mary Pickford, with Douglas Fairbanks, Charlie Chaplin, and D. W. Griffith, founds United Artists Corporation, a major film studio.

Athletics and Exploration

French pilot Raymonde de Laroche is killed in a crash while riding as a passenger in an experimental plane.

German women form a national rowing association.

Hazel Hotchkiss Wightman wins the U.S. singles tennis title. She also proposes an international women's tournament to rival the men's Davis Cup. The tournament, begun in 1923, will later be named the Wightman Cup Match.

English traveler and journalist Joan Rosita Forbes (1893–1967) publishes *Unconducted Wanderers*, about her travels in Asia with a female companion.

Apr. French pilot Adrienne Bolland, in a single-engine, eighty-horsepower plane, becomes the first woman to fly across the Andes.

June French tennis player Suzanne Lenglen (May 24, 1899–October 28, 1938) begins her domination of Wimbledon with wins in the singles and the doubles (with Elisabeth Ryan). She will win the singles title again in 1920, 1921, 1922, 1923, and 1925. Lenglen will also win the French Open seven times and popularize short sleeves and short skirts on the court.

Activism

Filipina revolutionary Melchora Aquino (b. 1812) dies. Imprisoned for allowing rebels to use her store as a headquarters, she contributed to Philippine independence from Spain.

Polish-German socialist, feminist, and pacifist Rosa Luxemburg, founder of the German Communist Party, is beaten and murdered by a mob of soldiers.

Egyptian women, among them feminist Huda Shaarawi, march in Cairo to protest British occupation.

Chile's National Council of Women is founded to fight for women's civil rights.

English philanthropist Eglantyne Jebb founds the Save the Children Fund.

U.S. civil rights reformer Mary White Ovington becomes chairman of the board of the NAACP.

Japanese feminists Hiratsuka Raicho, Oku Mumeo, and Ichikawa Fusae (b. 1893) establish the Shin Fujin Kyokai (Association of New Women), which works on behalf of women's unions and equal rights.

Several prominent reformers attend the second conference

of WILPF in Zurich, Switzerland, including Americans Jane Addams, Jeannette Rankin, Mary Church Terrell, Alice Hamilton, and Florence Kelley (Sept. 12, 1859-Feb. 17, 1932). Addams is elected president of the conference, and American Emily Greene Balch becomes secretary-treasurer. German Lida Heymann is elected vice-president.

At a St. Louis suffrage convention, the League of Women Voters (LWV) is organized. Maud Wood Park (January 25, 1871–May 8, 1955) becomes its first president.

Jan. 4 Argentinian feminist, doctor, and teacher Elvira Rawson de Dellepiani helps found the Women's Rights Association, an 11,000-member organization dedicated to political equality, access to prestigious jobs, and protective labor legislation for women.

Jan. 10 In the United States, the Republican National Committee endorses women's suffrage.

Feb. 9 U.S. radical suffragist Sue Shelton White is imprisoned for five days for burning a picture of President Wilson.

Mar. 14 Egyptian nationalist Sjafika Mohammed is killed by the British.

Mar. 19 Korean student activist Hwang Ae-dok is arrested and jailed for three years for her part in the movement for independence from Japan. Many women are arrested or killed in this uprising, known as the March First Movement.

Apr. 7 Belgian women present the government with a suffrage petition signed by 160,000.

Business and Industry

The Treaty of Versailles requires that women receive equal pay, but the stipulation is universally ignored or circumvented.

At Macmillan, American editor Louise Seaman starts the United States' first children's book publishing department.

May 25 U.S. millionaire Sarah Breedlove ("Madame C. J.") Walker dies. She sold cosmetics, particularly hair straighteners, to black women and employed 3,000 people, most of them women called the "Walker Agents," who sold her products door-to-door. Walker used her fortune to contribute to the NAACP and establish scholarships for women at the Tuskegee Institute; she also encouraged her agents to do charitable work.

Aug. 26 United Mine Workers (UMW) organi... Fannie Mooney Sellins is shot and killed by guards at the Allegheny Coal & Coke Company while protecting miners' children during a UMW strike.

Science and Medicine

U.S. medical researcher Dr. Louise Pearce (b. 1885) codevelops tryparsamide, the serum that cures African sleeping sickness.

U.S. physician Esther Lovejoy cofounds and becomes the first president of the Medical Women's International Association.

Education and Scholarship

Indian educator Abala Bose (1865–1951) establishes the Nari Shiksha Samiti, dedicated to the education of women throughout India. Bose will found several educational and relief organizations and support self-defense training for women.

Austrian universities, which have been gradually admitting women since 1897, are now universally coeducational.

Religion

Mother Mary Amadeus (b. Sarah Dunne in 1846), Superior of all North American Ursuline convents, dies. She saved a man from drowning, established schools, founded a convent in Alaska, and traveled extensively in all weather, even after a train accident in 1910 left her crippled. She worked with Cheyenne Indians at a mission whose terrified priests had fled and became so well respected that she was known as Great Holy White Chief Woman.

U.S. theologian Mary Lyman (b. November 24, 1887) begins two years at Cambridge, only to find that the university will not issue a theological degree or even a transcript to a woman.

1920

General Status and Daily Life

The average Japanese woman marries at age twenty-one and has five children.

In the United States, life expectancy for women at birth is 54.6 years compared to 53.6 for men. One of every 7.5 marriages ends in divorce. U.S. birth rates will drop throughout the 1920s.

Sweden's new Marriage Code ends guardianship of wives by husbands and makes wives legal adults at age twenty-one. Husbands and wives get equal property rights.

The Soviet Union becomes the first country in the world to legalize abortion on demand.

France outlaws abortion, the sale of contraceptives, and distribution of birth control information.

Female life expectancy in Great Britain is about sixty years.

Makeup use by "respectable" women is now common in the United States.

Government, the Military, and the Law

Dolores Ibarruri (b. December 9, 1895), known as "La Pasionara" and later famous for the Loyalist battle cry "¡No pasaran!" ("They shall not pass!") during the Spanish Civil War, cofounds Spain's Communist party.

German feminist Gertrude Baumer is elected to the Reichstag, where she will serve until her ouster by the Nazis in 1933. Also elected to the Reichstag are socialist Louise Schröder (1887–1957) and communist Clara Zetkin.

Chinese revolutionary Xiang Jingyu, an opponent of foot-binding and a leader of student demonstrations, cofounds the Chinese Communist Party.

Army nurses are given "relative" rank, which entitles them to only some of the privileges of officers; nurse superintendent Julia Stimson becomes the first female major in the U.S. Army.

The first Austrian women are elected to the National Assembly.

Jan. 5 U.S. women demand equal representation at June's Republican party convention. Later in the year, eight women are named to the Republican National Executive Committee, and Harriet Taylor Upton becomes its vice-chairman.

June Annette Abbott Adams becomes the first female assistant attorney general of the United States and campaigns unsuccessfully for the Democratic nomination for vice president.

June 5 Mary Anderson becomes the first director of the Women's Bureau of the U.S. Department of Labor.

Aug. 26 The Nineteenth Amendment, granting U.S. women the vote, is signed into law; representatives of the National Woman's Party are barred from the ratification ceremony, in a move suffragist Abby Scott Baker calls "quite tragic."

Nov. 12 U.S. lawyer Marilla Ricker (b. March 18, 1840), known as the "Prisoner's Friend," dies. In the District of Columbia, she won an end to the practice of holding poor convicts for fines they could not pay and obtained for prisoners the right to send unopened letters to the governor. A suffragist, she protested every year when paying her taxes and tried, in 1910, to run for governor of New Hampshire. She was also a free thinker who, in several books, attacked religion as "mental suicide."

Literature and the Visual Arts

Japanese poet Kiyoko Tsuda and U.S. poet Mary Ellen Solt are born. Solt will be a leading proponent of concrete poetry, in which words form shapes.

English author Mrs. Humphry Ward (b. 1851) dies, shortly after being named one of England's first seven female magistrates. A proponent of higher education for women, she disapproved of suffragists and often criticized them in her books.

Chinese artist Ren Xia (b. 1876) dies. A member of a famous family of artists, she painted to support her family after the death of her father. She was skilled at landscapes, flowers, and figures and became famous in her own right, but she sometimes sold her paintings under her father's name, because paintings by him fetched a better price.

New novels include Edith Wharton's most famous novel, the Pulitzer Prize-winning *The Age of Innocence*; English mystery writer Agatha Christie's (b. September 15, 1890) *The Mysterious Affair at Styles*, her first detective novel; Colette's *Chéri*, the story of an aging courtesan and her young lover; and the first volume of Norwegian Sigrid Undset's (1882–1949) trilogy *Kristin Lavransdatter*, considered by many to be one of the greatest novels of the twentieth century. American Zona Gale (August 26, 1874–December 27, 1938) publishes *Miss Lulu Bett*, a best-selling comic novel about the rebellion of a spinster. The novel becomes a play, which opens in December of this year and wins the 1921 Pulitzer Prize in drama.

The Japanese women's magazine *Fujin Kurabu* begins publication; it will run until 1988.

New poetry includes Italian Sibilla Aleramo's *Momenti lirichi*, American Edna St. Vincent Millay's controversial collection *A Few Figs from Thistles*, Argentinian Alfonsina Storni's *Languidez*, and Edith Sitwell's *The Wooden Pegasus*.

Uruguayan poet Juana de Ibarbourou publishes the prose poem *El contraro fresco*.

New Zealand author Katherine Mansfield publishes *Bliss and Other Stories*.

U.S. expatriate salon hostess and author Natalie Clifford Barney establishes the Académie des Femmes for female authors.

Korean author Kim Won-ju (1896–1971), who writes under the pseudonym Ilyop, becomes editor of the literary magazine *Sin Yoja* (*New Woman*). She and Chongwol (pseudonym of Na Hye-sok, 1885–1946), along with ten men, also establish the literary magaine *P'yeho*.

Performing Arts and Entertainment

U.S. filmmakers direct several silent movies, including *The Butterfly Man* and *The Midlanders* (Ida May Park), *Good Bad Wife* (Vera McCord), and *Slaves of Pride* (Mrs. George Randolph Chester). Actress Lillian Gish makes her only foray into directing with *Remodeling Her Husband*, starring Lillian's sister Dorothy Gish and written by Elizabeth Carter. After making the film, which depicts a wife who humbles and reforms her adulterous husband, Gish decides that directing is "no career for a lady." U.S. filmmaker Lois Weber directs *The Blot*, a movie about a proud, impoverished family, and gets a contract with Paramount entitling her to $50,000 and half the profits of each picture.

Mary Pickford stars in *Pollyanna*, *The Love Light*, and *Suds*. Polish silent film actress Pola Negri becomes a star in Germany with the release of *Sumurun / One Arabian Night*.

U.S. composer Marion Bauer composes *Allegretto giocoso* for eleven instruments.

English theatre manager Lilian Baylis (1874–1937) takes over the Old Vic Theatre.

Danish ballerina Adeline Genée becomes the first president of the Association of Operatic Dancing (later the Royal Academy of Dancing), a position she will hold until 1954.

Athletics and Exploration

At the Olympics, Swedish figure skater Magda Julin-Mauroy wins the women's gold. Theresa Weld of the United States takes the bronze but is reprimanded by the judges for including a salchow jump in her program; such athleticism is deemed unsuited to women's skating. Ludovika Jakobsson-Eilers of Finland, thirty-five years old, wins the gold in pairs skating.

The trap shooting event is open to both sexes, but no woman medals. Two tennis events are reserved for women. Great Britain wins the gold in doubles, and France's Suzanne Lenglen wins the gold in singles. American Ethelda Bleibtrey wins gold medals in all three aquatic events: 100-meter freestyle, 400-meter freestyle, and the 4 x 100 freestyle relay (with Irene Guest, Frances Schroth, and Margaret Woodbridge). Guest and Schroth take silver and bronze in the 100 meters; the 400 meters is another U.S. sweep, with Woodbridge taking silver and Schroth picking up another bronze.

The United States also sweeps the springboard diving medals, with Aileen Riggin, Helen Wainwright, and Thelma Payne taking first, second, and third place; but there are no U.S. medalists in platform diving, where Denmark's Stefani Fryland-Clausen takes the gold.

Activism

South African antiapartheid activist Francina Baard is born.

U.S. civil rights activist Mary McLeod Bethune, despite threats by the KKK, leads a voter registration drive among black women.

Reformer Jane Addams and labor leader Elizabeth Gurley Flynn become founding members of the American Civil Liberties Union (ACLU).

U.S. feminist Alice Paul begins to work for passage of an Equal Rights Amendment (ERA), though supporters of protective labor legislation, including the WTUL, oppose her.

Britain's Rebecca Sieff (d. 1966), Russia's Vera Weizmann (1881–1966), and Hungary's Edith Eder establish the Women's International Zionist Organization (WIZO), the largest Zionist group in the world.

English suffragist Sylvia Pankhurst, sister of Christabel Pankhurst, stows away on a USSR-bound ship and meets Lenin.

Feminist Huda Shaarawi becomes the head of Egypt's first women's association.

Greek feminist Avra Theodopoulou founds the League

for Women's Rights; she will serve as its president for the next thirty-seven years.

Mexican feminist María Ríos Cárdenas founds the liberal journal *Mujer* (*Woman*).

Business and Industry

Indian labor leader Anusuyaben Sarabhai, already the founder of several craft unions, establishes the Textile Labor Association.

In the United States, 17.1% of women are in the work force, constituting 20.4% of the total labor force. Nine percent of married women are employed. Women are 8% of trade union members; only 6.6% of working women belong to unions. Almost half of all clerical employees are women, up from 4% in 1880.

French fashion designer Gabrielle "Coco" Chanel (August 19, 1884–January 10, 1971) introduces the chemise dress. Her textile, perfume, fashion, and jewelry businesses will make Chanel one of the richest couturiers in France.

Welsh publisher Margaret Rhondda founds the influential weekly magazine *Time and Tide*, which lasts thirty years, thanks to subsidies from her personal funds totaling £250,000.

Science and Medicine

Soviet official Yadgar Nasriddinova, the first Uzbek woman civil engineer, is born.

Soviet scientist Bibi Palvanova is born. She will become the first woman in Turkmenia to win the degree of *doktor* and the first to become a member of the Turkmenian Academy of Sciences, even though at ten her father will move her from home to keep her from going to school and despite being sold into marriage at fourteen as a third wife.

Two of the "ENIAC girls," Adele Katz Goldstine and Kathleen (Kay) McNulty Mauchly are born. They will be part of a team of women assigned in the 1940s to program ENIAC, the world's first general-purpose electronic computer. Women programmers will be replaced by men as soon as the work becomes perceived as creative and interesting rather than merely clerical.

U.S. botanist Katharine Brandegee (October 28, 1844–April 3) dies. She co-founded the *Bulletins* of the California Academy of Sciences and the botanical journal *Zoe*; she also had two species of plants named for her.

British physicist Hertha Ayrton cofounds the National

Union of Scientific Workers.

Marie Curie establishes the Curie Foundation to find medical uses for radiation.

German mathematician Emmy Noether coauthors a paper on differential operators that establishes her as an important scholar in algebra. Within ten years she will be the dominant mathematician at the University of Göttingen.

Education and Scholarship

Alice Tyler becomes president of the American Library Association.

Women are first admitted to Chinese colleges.

In the United States, 283,000 women are in college, making up 47.3% of the total enrollment, though they still usually take sex-stereotyped courses of study.

U.S. feminist historian Mary Ritter Beard (August 5, 1876–August 14, 1958) publishes *A Short History of the American Labor Movement*.

New Jersey librarian Sarah Byrd Askew (1877–1942) designs the first bookmobile.

In the United States, Edith Abbott and Sophonisba Breckinridge establish the first graduate school of social work.

Oct. 7 Oxford University admits its first one hundred full-degree women students.

Religion

French saint Joan of Arc is canonized.

Korea's Buddhist Women's Association is founded at the temple of Myosim-sa.

1921

General Status and Daily Life

Thousands of Indian child brides die each year, many as young as seven.

Korea's Civil Code dictates that a woman must have

authorization from her family to act as her child's legal representative.

In Afghanistan, a new Family Code outlaws child marriage and polygamy. The veil is discouraged, and women's education is encouraged. Queén Suraya appears unveiled in public, but the veil will be reinstated in 1929.

Women give birth to 173,000 illegitimate children in Germany, 55,000 in Chile, 49,000 in Italy, and 65,000 in France. There are 39,000 divorces in Germany this year, up from 18,000 in 1913.

Sept. 7 Sixteen-year-old Margaret Gorman of Washington, D.C., wins the first Miss America pageant.

Government, the Military, and the Law

Nigerian lawyer Aduke Alakija, future president of the International Federation of Women Lawyers, is born.

Suffragist and politician Agnes McPhail becomes Canada's first female member of Parliament.

Xiang Jingyu, the first prominent woman in the Chinese Communist party, is elected to the Central Committee. The new party has made a point of espousing women's rights.

England's first woman barrister, Ivy Williams, begins practicing.

Women in China's Hunan Province get the vote.

In the United States, 1,600 women have law degrees.

Grace Abbott (November 17, 1878–June 19, 1939) becomes head of the U.S. Children's Bureau, a position she will hold until 1934. She will fight for laws against child labor and for better health care for children, overseeing the founding of about 3,000 clinics for children and pregnant women.

Madras becomes the first Indian province to give women the vote.

The Peace Preservation Law, which prevented Japanese women from participation in political groups, is repealed.

Jan. Germany's Nazi party excludes women from membership.

Mar. 13 The first woman is elected to Australia's Parliament.

June 20 Congresswoman Alice Robertson of Oklahoma presides over the U.S. House of Representatives for thirty minutes, becoming the first woman to do so.

Literature and the Visual Arts

Swedish glassmaker Ingeborg Lundin and Greek poet Eleni Vakalo, whose works discuss urban life, politics, and family relationships, are born.

Scottish designer Frances MacDonald (b. 1874) dies. MacDonald, with her sister, Margaret (1865–1933), designed architectural ornaments, metalwork, embroidery, and stained glass.

Friends arrange for the publication of American Marianne Moore's (November 15, 1887–February 5, 1972) *Poems*. Other new collections of poetry are Edna St. Vincent Millay's *Second April*, H. D.'s *Hymen*, and American Elinor Wylie's first widely recognized book, *Nets to Catch the Wind*.

U.S. playwright Rachel Carothers (December 12, 1870–July 5, 1958), whose plays often feature strong heroines and question gender roles, writes *Nice People*. When it becomes a movie next year, she will write the screenplay as well.

Feb. 15 U.S. sculptor Adelaide Johnson's seven-ton marble statue, *The Woman Movement*, is dedicated in the first reception for a woman ever given in the U.S. Capitol.

Performing Arts and Entertainment

U.S. women direct several movies this year, including *Puppets of Fate* (Ruth Ann Baldwin), *The Sons of Wallingford* (Mrs. George Randolph Chester), *That Something* (Margery Wilson), and *That Old Broken Bucket* (May Tully). Writer Frances Marion, who often creates screenplays for Mary Pickford and Douglas Fairbanks, directs *The Love Light*. Nell Shipman writes, directs, and stars in her most famous film, *The Girl from God's Country*. Hollywood has more female directors in the period from 1913 to 1927 than at any other time in history.

Mary Pickford stars in the silent films *Through the Back Door* and *Little Lord Fauntleroy*; Mabel Normand stars in *Molly O*.

Czechoslovakian filmmaker Thea Cervenkova directs *Bludicka* and *The Thief*.

French filmmaker Gabrielle Sorère and U.S. dancer Loie Fuller collaborate on the film *Le Lys de la vie* (*The Lily of Life*), which is one of the first to use a negative print to distinguish reality from illusion.

Jan. 13 U.S. opera singer Mary Garden becomes head of the Chicago Opera Company.

Nov. 7 U.S. dancer Isadora Duncan, invited this year to found a school of dance in Moscow, dances to the *Internationale* at the Bolshoi.

Athletics and Exploration

In Tashkent, a Soviet woman is murdered for encouraging Muslim women to take part in an international athletic competition.

Apr. U.S. aviator Phoebe Fairgrave Omlie (b. November 21, 1902) becomes the first woman in the world to parachute from a plane, cut loose the parachute, and use a second parachute for the rest of the way down.

June 5 U.S. aviator Laura Bromwell, who in May set a women's speed record of 135 miles per hour and broke her own record by doing 199 consecutive loop-the-loops, is killed when she loses control of her plane in a loop.

Oct. 31 French athletic organizer Alice Milliat founds the Fédération Sportive Féminine Internationale. Women's games will be held several times in France from 1921 to 1923, putting pressure on the International Olympic Committee (IOC) to relax its restrictions on women in the Olympics.

Activism

Tayyeba Huq, founder of Bangladesh's Housewives Association, is born.

Japanese women socialists establish the Sekirankai (Red Wave Society).

Russian revolutionary Vera Figner, imprisoned for twenty years in tsarist Russia, publishes her memoirs, *Kogda chasy zhizni ostanovalis* (*How the Clock of Life Stopped*).

An Iranian women's magazine, the *Messenger of Happiness*, begins publication.

Pakistani nationalist Abadi Begum ("Bi Amma") publicly unveils.

The Lucy Stone League is founded in the United States to help married women get the legal right to use their birth names for passports, contracts, and other legal documents.

Business and Industry

Since 1905, American women have received 5,016 patents in such diverse areas as agriculture, mining, manufacturing, structural materials, automobile parts, hotel and restaurant equipment, dressmakers' supplies, office supplies, household products, telephone and telegraph equipment, scientific instruments, ammunition, clothing, umbrellas, medical instruments, safety gear, games, and musical instruments.

May 5 French fashion designer Coco Chanel introduces her new perfume, No. 5.

July 19 Eight million women are employed in the United States, 87% of them as teachers or secretaries.

Science and Medicine

U.S. astronomer Henrietta Leavitt (b. 1868) dies. She researched star magnitudes and observed the reddish coloring of fainter stars, but her most significant discovery was the relationship between the brightness and period of cepheid variable stars, yielding a reliable "measuring stick" for determining stellar distances. She also found about 2,400 new variable stars, half of the variable stars known at the time.

Russian botanist Olga Fedchenko (b. 1845), who studied plants in central Asia, the Crimea, the Urals, and the Caucasus, dies.

Ellen Churchill Semple (1863–1932) becomes the first woman president of the Association of American Geographers.

U.S. engineer, efficiency expert, and industrial psychologist Lillian Gilbreth becomes an honorary member of the all-male Society of Industrial Engineers.

U.S. psychologist Margaret Washburn is elected president of the American Psychological Association.

Five percent of U.S. medical students are women, though 92% of U.S. hospitals refuse to accept women as interns.

Mar. 17 Marie Stopes opens England's first birth control clinic.

May French physicist Marie Curie is presented with a gram of scarce radium by U.S. president Warren G. Harding. The price of the radium was raised by U.S. women, led by journalist Marie Mattingly Meloney (d. June 23, 1943), founder of *Kentucky Magazine* (1880), editor of the *Woman's Magazine*, the *Delineator* (1921-1926), and the *New York Herald Tribune* Sunday magazine, and writer for several prominent papers. Curie, upon arrival in the United States, is greeted by U.S. anatomist Florence Sabin.

Nov. 2 Margaret Sanger (d. September 6, 1966) and Mary Ware Dennett establish the American Birth Control League (later the Planned Parenthood Federation of America). Sanger, a midwife and visiting nurse, became an advocate of birth control after seeing many women worn out or killed by bearing too many children.

Education and Scholarship

The first women are admitted to Lebanon's American and French universities.

Religion

U.S. Baptist leader Helen Barrett Montgomery becomes president of the Northern Baptist Convention.

Apr. 26 Korea's Buddhist Young Women's Association is founded. Its opening meeting espouses equal rights for men and women.

Nov. 5 U.S. reformer Antoinette Brown Blackwell, who espoused the causes of suffrage and abolition and became the first ordained woman minister in the United States, dies. She completed Oberlin's theology course in 1850 but was refused a student's preaching license and prevented from graduating.

1922

General Status and Daily Life

Legal age of marriage in Korea is seventeen for boys and fifteen for girls. Divorce by mutual consent is legalized, but the parents must give their permission for the divorce. Polygamy is abolished.

A new type of woman, the "flapper," is emerging in the United States. She binds her breasts, swears, smokes, and sports bobbed hair, knee-length dresses, rouge, lipstick, and silk underwear. The *Pittsburgh Observer*, noting the new trend, complains of "a change for the worse during the past year in feminine dress, dancing, manners and general moral attitudes."

U.S. writer Emily Post (October 27, 1872–September 25, 1960) publishes *Etiquette: The Blue Book of Social Usage*, which sells 650,000 copies in its first twenty years; Post's syndicated column will appear in over 150 newspapers.

Sept. 22 Congress passes the Cable Act, which guarantees that U.S. women married to foreign men can keep their U.S. citizenship.

Government, the Military, and the Law

Marcelle Renson and Paule Lamy become the first Belgian women to take the lawyers' oath.

Women are 8% of Soviet Communist party members.

Chinese government official Xiang Jingyu becomes head of the Communist party Women's Department.

U.S. judge, lawyer, and suffragist Florence Allen becomes the first woman state supreme court judge.

Women get full suffrage rights in Ireland.

Rosa Torres, as president of the Mérida Municipal Council, becomes the first Mexican woman elected to public office.

Rebecca Latimer Felton (June 10, 1835–January 24, 1930) becomes the first woman member of the U.S. Senate. Appointed by the governor of Georgia to replace a dead senator, she serves for only one day.

Literature and the Visual Arts

Anne Nichols's (1891–1966) play, *Abie's Irish Rose*, begins a 2,327-performance run in New York.

U.S. bookstore owner Sylvia Beach agrees to publish a novel by one of her friends after the manuscript is repeatedly rejected by established publishers. The friend is James Joyce; the book is *Ulysses*.

New novels include Virginia Woolf's *Jacob's Room*, Finnish author Kersti Bergroth's *Kiirashnli*, Willa Cather's *One of Ours*, and Venezuelan Teresa de la Parra's *Diario de una señorita que se fastida*.

New short story collections include New Zealand author Katherine Mansfield's *The Garden Party and Other Stories* and British author Vita Sackville-West's (March 9, 1892–June 2, 1962) *The Heir*.

Russian poet Anna Akhmatova publishes *Anno Domini*;

because her work is considered politically questionable, this will be her last published work for eighteen years. Other new poetry includes Chilean poet Gabriela Mistral's first book, *Desolaçion* (*Desolation*), Uruguayan poet Juana de Ibarbourou's *Raíz salvaje*, and Russian Marina Tsvetayeva's *Versty I*. English poet Edith Sitwell publishes *Façade*, a poem sequence set to music and first performed in January. American Genevieve Taggard's *For Eager Lovers* brings her national renown as a lyric poet.

Feb. 5 U.S. publisher Lila Acheson Wallace cofounds *Reader's Digest*.

Performing Arts and Entertainment

English singer Marie Lloyd (b. 1870), who appeared at most of the major music halls of England, the United States, South Africa, and England, dies. She was best known for the songs "Oh Mr. Porter," "My Old Man Said Follow the Van," and "I'm One of the Ruins That Cromwell Knocked Abaht a Bit."

Hungarian-British violinst Jelly d'Arányi (1895–1966) performs the premiere of Bartok's first violin sonata.

At movie theatres, Lillian and Dorothy Gish star in the French Revolution drama *Orphans of the Storm*. Mary Pickford stars in *Rosita*. Poland's Pola Negri stars in *Die Flamme* and accepts an offer to make films in Hollywood, and Denmark's Asta Nielsen stars in *Fraülein Julie*.
    U.S. director Dorothy Arzner (January 3, 1900–October 1, 1979) helps to make the Rudolph Valentino movie *Blood and Sand*, directing a famous bullfight sequence and editing the film as well. U.S. women direct several movies this year, including *Where Is My Wandering Boy Tonight?* (Mildred Webb), *Our Mutual Friend* and *Kisses* (May Tully), *Neptune's Daughter* (Nell Shipman), and *Just Around the Corner* (written and directed by Frances Marion). June Mathis writes the scenarios for *Blood and Sand* and *Ben Hur*.

Athletics and Exploration

Bullfighter Conchita Cintron is born. She will first appear in the ring as a *rejoneadora* (fighter on horseback) at the age of twelve and will kill approximately 800 bulls as a *rejoneadora* and 400 as a *torera* (fighter on foot).

British aviator Lady Sophie Heath founds the Women's Amateur Athletic Association.

English archer Alice Blanche Legh wins the British championship, giving her a total of twenty-three national titles since 1881.

Fifty-two women swimmers race 3.5 miles across New York Bay. The winner is American Gertrude Ederle.

July 10 U.S. aviator Phoebe Fairgrave Omlie parachutes from a plane at 15,200 feet, setting a women's record.

Oct. Lillian Gatlin becomes the first woman to fly across the United States, traveling from San Francisco to Long Island in twenty-seven hours, eleven minutes.

Activism

Brazilian feminist Bertha Lutz (1894–1976), later an agitator for women's rights in the United Nations (UN) and the initiator of the UN Commission on the Status of Women, founds the Brazilian Federation for the Advancement of Women and becomes its president, a post she will hold until her death in 1976.

Egyptian feminist Huda Shaarawi cofounds the Egyptian Feminist Union, a middle-class reform group.

In El Salvador, market women lead a mass demonstration for the release of political prisoners.

Business and Industry

Chinese Women's Banks open in Beijing and Shanghai.

Lillian and Clara Westropp establish the Women's Savings and Loan Company of Cleveland, a bank with no male employees at all; by 1965 it will have assets of $137 million.

Science and Medicine

U.S. zoologist Libbie Hyman publishes *Laboratory Manual for Comparative Vertebrate Anatomy*.

German-American psychologist Charlotte Bühler publishes a study of adolescence, *Das Seelenleben des Jugendlichen*.

Feb. 7 Marie Curie is elected to the French Académie des Sciences.

Education and Scholarship

Poet Gabriela Mistral begins reorganizing Chile's school system.

English historian Eileen Power (1889–1940) publishes *Medieval English Nunneries c.1275–1535*.

A German court justifies unequal pay for male and female teachers on the grounds that male teachers educate useful workers, while female teachers educate mere housewives.

Girls are 6.32% of students in nonmissionary schools in China; 417,820 girls are so enrolled.

Elise Richter becomes the first woman professor in Austria.

Religion

Sept. 17   Women preachers in Korea's Southern Methodist church demand equal pay.

1923

General Status and Daily Life

Grounds for divorce are now the same for both sexes in Great Britain, which means that women may divorce their husbands for adultery.

Government, the Military, and the Law

Sweden admits women to most of its civil service jobs.

Literature and the Visual Arts

Iraqi poet Nazik Al-Mala'ikah, Polish poet Wislawa Szymborska, Indian novelist Shanta Rama Rau (daughter of Indian family-planning advocate Dhanvanthi Rama Rau), and U.S. mystery author Dorothy Gilman (June 25), creator of secret agent Mrs. Emily Pollifax, are born.

U.S. playwright Rachel Carothers writes *Mary the Third*, widely perceived as an attack on marriage.

New poetry includes American Elinor Wylie's *Black Armour*, Edith Sitwell's *Bucolic Comedies*, American Louise Bogan's *Body of This Death*, Marina Tsvetayeva's *Romeslo* (*Craft*), and Edna St. Vincent Millay's Pulitzer Prize-winning *The Harp Weaver*.

New novels include Willa Cather's *A Lost Lady*, Agatha Christie's *The Murder on the Links*, Colette's *Le Blé en herbe*, and English mystery writer Dorothy Sayers' literate, witty *Whose Body?*, the first Lord Peter Wimsey mystery.

French artist Suzanne Valadon paints *The Blue Room*, one of her best-known works.

German artist Käthe Kollwitz completes her woodcut cycle, *War*, a work heavily influenced by the death of her son in World War I.

Performing Arts and Entertainment

Spanish soprano Victoria de Los Angeles, Spanish pianist Alicia de Larrocha (who will make her debut at age five), and U.S. actress and singer Carol Channing (January 31) are born.

Irish dancer and choreographer Ninette de Valois becomes a soloist with Dyaghilev's Ballets Russes.

American Lillian Ducey writes and directs the silent film *Enemies of Children*. U.S. screenwriter Lotta Woods writes *Robin Hood*.

Lillian Baylis rebuilds and opens Sadler's Wells, a famous English theatre.

Russian choreographer Bronislava Nijinska creates the ballet *Les noces*, getting Stravinsky to write the music and Russian artist Natalia Goncharova to design the sets.

Hungarian-British violinist Jelly d'Arányi performs the premiere of Bartok's second violin sonata.

Russian composer Julia Weisberg composes the tone poem *The Twelve*.

Feb.   U.S. blues singer Bessie Smith (b. April 15, 1894) records "Downhearted Blues" (written by Alberta Hunter), "Gulf Coast Blues," and "Tain't Nobody's Bizzness If I Do."

Athletics and Exploration

In the United States, the Amateur Athletic Union (AAU) votes to admit women in the sports of track and field, swimming, gymnastics, basketball, and handball. Committees dealing with women's sports are required to have at least one woman member.

U.S. explorer Grace Gallatin Seton (January 28, 1872–

March 19, 1959) publishes *A Woman Tenderfoot in Egypt*.

U.S. tennis player Helen Wills Moody (b. October 6, 1905), nicknamed "Little Poker Face," defeats Molla Bjurstedt Mallory for the U.S. women's singles title. Moody will win again in 1924, 1925, 1927, 1928, 1929, and 1931; she will win a record eight Wimbledon singles titles, emerging victorious in 1927, 1928, 1929, 1930, 1932, 1933, 1935, and 1938.

Activism

Czech feminist and politician Franciska Plamnikova becomes the first chairman of the Czech Council of Women. In 1925, she will be elected to the Legislative Assembly.

U.S. educator Lucy Slowe cofounds and becomes the first president of the NACW.

Feminist Huda Shaarawi publicly unveils, inspiring many other Egyptian women to do the same.

Eleanor Glencross founds the Australian Federation of Housewives.

July U.S. feminist Alice Paul organizes a seventy-fifth anniversary reenactment of the Seneca Falls convention and formally introduces her version of the ERA, called by her the Lucretia Mott Amendment. It is introduced in Congress in the fall.

Business and Industry

U.S. business executive Ida Rosenthal (January 9, 1886–March 28, 1973), inventor of the bra with cups, cofounds the Maiden Form Brassiere Company. She will become the company's president in 1958 and its chief executive officer (CEO) in 1959.

English unionist Margaret Grace Bondfield becomes the first woman to head the TUC.

Apr. 9 In *Adkins* v. *Children's Hospital*, the U.S. Supreme Court strikes down a District of Columbia law granting a minimum wage to women and children.

Science and Medicine

Russian-American doctor Rachelle Yarros (1869–1946), a former resident of Hull House, opens the United States' second birth control clinic in Chicago.

British birth control advocate Dr. Marie Stopes is accused by Dr. Halliday Sutherland of experimenting on the poor. She sues for libel and suffers vicious attacks on her own morality throughout the long legal ordeal. Also in this year, she publishes *Contraception: Its History, Theory, and Practice*.

U.S. microbiologist Gladys Henry Dick (December 18, 1881–August 21, 1963) isolates the causative agent of scarlet fever; the discovery leads to her development, with her husband, of a test for the disease.

U.S. paleontologist Winifred Goldring (February 1, 1888–January 30, 1971) publishes the monograph *The Devonian Crinoids of the State of New York*, a study of certain echinoderms in the period before the Carboniferous period of the Paleozoic era.

U.S. nurse Mary Roberts becomes editor of the *American Journal of Nursing*, a position she will hold until 1949.

July 31 U.S. research chemist Stephanie Kwolek, inventor of Kevlar, a fiber stronger than steel that is used in tires, bulletproof vests, and airplanes, is born. The synthetic fibers that she will invent will be the basis of a multimillion-dollar industry.

Education and Scholarship

English archaeologist Gertrude Bell founds Iraq's national museum in Baghdad.

U.S. novelist Edith Wharton is the first woman to receive an honorary Litt.D. from Yale.

Folklorist Elsie Clews Parsons is elected president of the American Ethnological Association.

U.S. educator Aurelia Reinhardt, president of Mills College, becomes president of the AAUW, a post she will hold until 1927.

Religion

New U.S. publications include feminist Charlotte Perkins Gilman's *His Religion and Hers*, classicist Lily Ross Taylor's *Local Cults in Etruria*, and minister Anna Garlin Spencer's (April 17, 1851–February 12, 1931) attack on free love, *The Family and Its Members*.

Jan. 1 Angelus Temple, the $1.5 million headquarters of U.S. evangelist Aimee Semple McPherson, opens. It seats 5,000 and has a fifty-piece band and a huge, lighted, rotating cross that can be seen from fifty miles away.

1924

Government, the Military, and the Law

U.S. feminist, writer, and politician Emily Newell becomes the vice president of the Democratic National Committee, its only woman officer.

Nina Bang is appointed minister for education, becoming Denmark's first woman cabinet minister.

Claudia Nikolayeva becomes head of the Zhenotdel, the Working Women's Section of the Central Committee of the Communist Party, becoming the first woman of working-class origins to rise so far in Soviet Russia.

Nov. Texas politician Miriam "Ma" Ferguson (June 13, 1875–June 25, 1961) is elected governor after her husband, Jim, the former governor, is convicted of financial crimes and barred from holding office. The second woman governor in the United States (after Wyoming's Nellie Tayloe Ross), she ran with the slogan "Me for Ma" and positions against the KKK and for Prohibition.

Literature and the Visual Arts

Russian cubist painter, theatrical designer, and textile designer Liubov Serbeevna Popova (b. 1889) and Russian artist, activist, and composer of political operas Valentina Semonovna Serova (b. 1846) die.

American Marianne Moore's *Observations* wins her the prestigious Dial award for "distinguished services to poetry." Other new collections of poetry are H. D.'s *Heliodora*, Edith Sitwell's (d. 1964) *The Sleeping Beauty*, and Gabriela Mistral's *Ternura* (*Tenderness*).

U.S. author Edna Ferber publishes the novel *So Big*, which wins the Pulitzer Prize and sells 300,000 copies. Other new novels include Venezuelan Teresa de la Parra's *Ifigenía* and English novelist Radclyffe Hall's (1886–1943) *The Unlit Lamp*.

U.S. editors Bertha Mahoney Miller and Elinor Whitney establish *Horn Book Magazine*, the first literary magazine for children.

U.S. editor and literary critic Amy Loveman cofounds the *Saturday Review of Literature*, with which she will be associated for thirty years.

U.S. journalist Dorothy Thompson (July 9, 1893–January 30, 1961) becomes head of the *New York Evening Post*'s Berlin office.

U.S. artist Romaine Brooks paints *Una, Lady Troubridge*, one of her most famous portraits.

Performing Arts and Entertainment

U.S. composer and music educator Ruth Crawford-Seeger (July 3, 1901–November 18, 1953) composes *Five Preludes for Piano*.

U.S. musician Ethel Leginska (April 13, 1886–February 26, 1970) serves as a guest conductor in Munich, Paris, London, and Berlin.

Ethel Barrymore receives good reviews for her performance in *The Second Mrs. Tanqueray*.

Russian choreographer Bronislava Nijinska creates the ballets *Les biches* and *Le Train Bleu*.

New films include *Hedda Gabler*, starring Asta Nielsen; *Romola*, starring Dorothy Gish; and *The Story of Gösta Berling*, starring Swedish-American actress Greta Garbo (b. September 18, 1905).

In the United States, successful Broadway author Jane Murfin codirects the films *Flapper Wives* and *Love Master*; Frances Marion directs *The Song of Love*. Screenwriter Agnes Johnson writes *Forbidden Paradise*, and Dorothy Arzner edits *The Covered Wagon*.

Athletics and Exploration

At the first winter Olympics in Chamonix, Austrian figure skater Herma Planck-Szabo wins the gold. Eleven-year-old Norwegian Sonja Henie (b. April 8, 1912) is a competitor, but she will not win a medal until her next Olympics. Helene Engelmann and Alfred Berger of Austria win the gold for pairs skating, followed by Ludovika Jakobsson-Eilers and Walter Jakobsson of Finland; Jakobsson-Eilers is 39 years old.

At the summer Olympics in Paris, the United States dominates the five women's swimming events. Americans Ethel Lackie, Martha Norelius, and Sybil Bauer win the 100-meter freestyle, 400-meter freestyle, and 100-meter backstroke, respectively. The U.S. team of Gertrude Ederle (b. 1906), Euphrasia Donnelly, Ethel Lackie, and Mariechen Wehselau (who also gets the silver in the 100-meter freestyle) also takes the gold in the 400-meter freestyle relay, and the United States sweeps the 100- and 400-meter freestyle events. Ederle wins bronzes in the 100- and 400-meter freestyles in addition to her relay gold. The only non-U.S. swimmer to take a gold medal is Great Britain's Lucy Morton, who wins the 200-meter breaststroke.

The United States also sweeps the springboard diving, with Elizabeth Becker taking the gold and Aileen Riggin (who also won a bronze in the 100-meter backstroke) getting the silver. Another American, Caroline Smith, wins the platform diving competition, in which Elizabeth Becker takes the silver.

Fencer Ellen Osiier of Denmark wins the first women's Olympic individual foil competition. The United States wins the women's doubles tennis gold; American Helen Wills Moody wins the singles competition. Britain's Kitty McKane, Wimbledon singles winner in 1924 and 1926 and a bronze medalist in 1920, comes in third.

Activism

U.S. activist Phyllis Schlafly, opponent of homosexuality, abortion rights, the ERA, divorce, adultery, and socialism, is born.

Chinese women lead demonstrations after the refusal of Sun Yat-Sen's National Congress to grant them suffrage.

Egyptian feminist Huda Shaarawi founds the Women's Federation, which gets the age of marriage for women raised to sixteen.

U.S. educator and civil rights administrator Mary McLeod Bethune becomes president of the NACW.

Japanese feminist Ichikawa Fusae founds the Fusen Kakutoku Domei (Women's Suffrage League).

Dec. Peruvian activist María Jesús Alvarado Rivera is jailed for proposing feminist reform of the Civil Code.

Business and Industry

U.S. fashion designer Gloria Vanderbilt is born.

U.S. businesswoman and inventor Gertrude Muller (1887–1957) founds Juvenile Wood Products to build and market the child's collapsible toilet seat she designed in 1915. The company will eventually make several types of products for children, including an early car seat.

The *New York Tribune* and the *New York Herald* merge as the *New York Herald Tribune*, largely due to the urging of Helen Reid (November 23, 1882–July 27, 1970), an advertising executive at the *Tribune*. Reid will be a vice president of the unified paper for two decades, making a point of hiring women (including Dorothy Thompson) and expanding features directed at women.

China's Xiang Jingyu leads a tobacco workers' strike in Shanghai.

Mar. 10 The U.S. Supreme Court upholds protective legislation forbidding late-night work by women.

Science and Medicine

English feminist Dora Russell (b. 1894) founds the Workers' Birth Control Group.

English physician Christine Murrell is elected to the Council of the British Medical Association.

Family-planning centers are established in Norway by birth-control activist Katti Anker Moller.

British astronomer Mary Evershed becomes a fellow of the Royal Astronomical Society; Verena Holmes becomes the first woman member of Britain's Institution of Mechanical Engineers.

Florence Sabin becomes the first woman president of the American Association of Anatomists.

Education and Scholarship

English historian Eileen Power publishes *Medieval People*.

Girls are only 14% of all Vietnamese schoolchildren.

Religion

May 9 The Methodist Episcopal church approves the ordination of women.

1925

General Status and Daily Life

The right of married women to keep their birth names is recognized by the U.S. State Department.

Government, the Military, and the Law

Yugoslav politician Milka Planinc, first woman prime

minister of a communist country, is born.

U.S. lawyer Hortense Ward becomes chief justice of the Texas Supreme Court for one case after the entire court disqualifies itself from hearing it; two other women are named justices for the duration of the case.

Helena Wiewiorska (1888–1967) becomes Poland's first woman lawyer.

Mar. 12 Prison administrator Mary Belle Harris becomes the first superintendent of the Federal Industrial Institution for Women at Alderson, West Virginia.

Literature and the Visual Arts

U.S. poet Marianne Moore becomes editor of *The Dial*, a prestigious literary magazine.

U.S. writer Anzia Yezierska publishes *Bread Givers*, a novel about a Jewish immigrant family dominated by a demanding father. Irish novelist Edith Somerville publishes *The Big House at Inver* under the names "Somerville and Ross," and U.S. author Ellen Glasgow publishes her best novel, *Barren Ground*. Other new novels include Willa Cather's *The Professor's House*, Selma Lagerlöf's *Charlotte Löwensköld*, Dutch novelist Johanna van Ammers-Küller's *The Rebel Generation*, Henry Handel Richardson's *The Way Home*, English novelist Ivy Compton-Burnett's (d. 1969) *Pastors and Masters*, and Virginia Woolf's *Mrs. Dalloway*, a daring, experimental work notable for its frequent shifts in point of view.

Portraitist Cecilia Beaux becomes the first U.S. woman invited to paint a self-portrait for the Medici Gallery of famous artists.

U.S. archaeologist Gisela Richter (August 15, 1882–December 24, 1972) becomes curator of the classical collection of New York's Metropolitan Musem of Art.

Helen Elna Hokinson becomes a cartoonist for the *New Yorker*.

May 12 U.S. poet and literary critic Amy Lowell dies. She introduced Asian poetic techniques to literature in English and was such an influential part of the Imagist movement that its followers were called "Amygists" by Ezra Pound. She sometimes translated Chinese and Japanese poems with Florence Ayscough. Her collections *What's O'Clock* (1925, Pulitzer), *East Wind* (1927), and *Ballad for Sale* (1927) are published posthumously.

Performing Arts and Entertainment

U.S. dancer Josephine Baker (June 3, 1906–April 12, 1975) becomes an instant hit in Paris with her performance in *La Révue Nègre*.

U.S. blues singer Bessie Smith records "St. Louis Blues" and "Nobody's Blues But Mine."

U.S. actress Helen Hayes (1900–1992) plays Shaw's Cleopatra; U.S. actress Tallulah Bankhead stars in London in Noël Coward's *Fallen Angel*.

Mary Pickford stars in the silent film *Little Annie Roonie*; Theda Bara stars in *The Unchastened Woman*. Greta Garbo stars with German-American actress Marlene Dietrich (d. 1992) in *The Joyless Street*. Pola Negri stars in *The Charmer*, and Clara Bow stars in *The Plastic Age*. Behind the camera in the United States, Frances Marion writes *Stella Dallas*, Frances Nordstrom codirects *Her Market Value*, and Lotta Woods writes *The Thief of Bagdad*.

English composer Ethel Smyth composes an one-act opera, *Entente cordiale*.

U.S. stage and costume designer Aline Bernstein (December 22, 1880–September 7, 1955) designs the first U.S. production of *The Dybbuk*.

Jan. 9 U.S. musician Ethel Leginska conducts the New York Symphony Orchestra.

Athletics and Exploration

Irish pioneer Nelly Cashman dies. The first white woman in British Columbia, she ran a series of boardinghouses, hotels, restaurants, and stores throughout the West. She prospected for gold in Alaska, founded the Midnight Sun Mining Co., the first Catholic church in Tombstone, the Miner's Hospital Association, and the Irish National League in Tombstone. She was greatly respected by miners, who spared the life of a Tombstone mining superintendent at her request.

British motorcyclist Gwenda Stewart, a former World War I ambulance driver, sets a world twenty-four-hour record. Stewart, who also flies planes and races cars, will hold seventy-six records at one point in her career.

Jan. 22 U.S. mountain climber Fanny Bullock Workman dies. The coauthor of several books, she traveled in Africa, Greece, Asia, and the Middle East by bicycle and by foot. She began climbing in the Himalayas at the age of forty, setting many altitude records, surviving a fall into a crevasse, and naming and surveying several mountains. She was a member of the Royal Geographical Society and the Royal Asiatic Society, became the first woman to lecture at the Sorbonne, and was honored by ten European geographical societies. Her will leaves $125,000 to Bryn Mawr, Radcliffe, Smith, and Wellesley.

Activism

Indian educator Abala Bose founds a home for widows. Outliving one's husband, let alone remarrying, is still frowned upon in India; this year only 2,263 widows remarry, and in 1915, only 15 did so.

Sarojini Naidu becomes the second woman president of the Indian National Congress.

Business and Industry

U.S. cattle rancher Henrietta King (b. 1832) dies. She abandoned old-fashioned cattle drives in favor of railroad shipment, found new sources of water, bred racehorses, paid for the construction of a hospital in Corpus Christi, Texas, and helped develop North America's first real new cattle breed, the Santa Gertrudis. Her funeral is attended by 200 King Ranch cowboys; she leaves 1 million acres and an estate worth $5.4 million.

U.S. broadcasting executive Judith Cary Waller, manager of Chicago radio station WMAQ, gets the rights to broadcast all Chicago Cubs home games.

Science and Medicine

Indian zoologist A. R. Kasturi Bai, head of the Zoology Department at the University of Bangalore, specialist in insects such as silkworms and honeybees, and industrial safety expert, is born.

U.S. computer designer Evelyn Berezin, who will design a digital on-line race-track betting system and one of the world's first word processors, is born.

New publications include U.S. toxicologist Alice Hamilton's *Industrial Poisons in the United States*, English botanist Agnes Arber's *Monocotyledons*, and French chemist Hélène Metzger's (b. 1899) *Les concepts scientifiques* (which wins the Prix Bordin).

German chemist Ida Noddack (b. 1896) codiscovers element 75, rhenium.

Polish-American psychoanalyst Helene Deutsch (b. 1884) becomes director of the Vienna Psychoanalytic

Institute, a position she will hold until 1933.

Anatomist Florence Sabin becomes the first woman member of the National Academy of Sciences.

In Kentucky, nurse and midwife Mary Breckinridge founds the Frontier Nursing Service (FNS). Funding it herself for three years, she sets up a network of midwives on horseback who provide help in labor and preventive care. In the first five years, the FNS serves over 1,000 rural families.

Canadian artist Amice Calverly is hired by the British Archaeological Survey to record ancient Egyptian inscriptions at Abydos; she quickly masters and improves upon the methods of transcription, producing such beautiful and accurate work that four volumes of her pictures are published.

American Harriet Chalmers Adams (October 22, 1875– July 17, 1937), a writer for *National Geographic* and a fellow of the Royal Geographical Society, co-founds and becomes first president of the Society of Woman Geographers. The SWG will include among its members Amelia Earhart and Margaret Mead.

Education and Scholarship

Mother Mary Katherine Drexel (1858–1955) founds New Orleans's Xavier University, the only black Catholic college in the United States.

Puerto Rican author María Cadilla de Martínez publishes *Cuentos a Lillian*, a collection of folktales.

Bombay feminist Attiya Faizi forces her way onto the podium at the all-male Mohammedan Education Conference; her actions result in the admission of women to future conventions.

Ewha Woman's College is the first women's college in Korea, with Alice Appenzeller as its first president. It has only two departments: liberal arts and music.

Religion

French saints Mary-Magdalene Postel and Madeleine Sophie are canonized, along with French nun Theresa of Lisieux (1873–1897).

1926

General Status and Daily Life

The first steam irons go on sale for about ten dollars each. They are not popular until the 1940s and the advent of synthetic fabrics.

Turkey outlaws polygamy and the veil.

Sept. 22 Argentina passes legislation giving women equal civil status. Married women may now work, form contracts, and control their wages without their husbands' permission. They also gain rights over their children in case of separation and divorce. The husband's authority over their joint property, however, is maintained.

Government, the Military, and the Law

Miina Sillanpåå becomes Finland's first female Cabinet minister.

Danish politician Nina Bang becomes Minister of Commerce.

India gives women the right to vote in provincial elections.

Literature and the Visual Arts

Willa Cather publishes *Death Comes for the Archbishop*, an unsentimental, lyrical novel about the life of a priest in the American Southwest. Other new novels are Agatha Christie's *The Murder of Roger Ackroyd*, one of her most famous mysteries; Colette's *La fin de Chéri*, a sequel to *Chéri*; U.S. author Edna Ferber's popular *Show Boat*; American Ellen Glasgow's *The Romantic Comedians*; and the feminist *Chagak (Awakening)*, by Korean author Ilyop.

U.S. author Dorothy Canfield Fisher joins the influential selection board of Book-of-the-Month Club, where she will be the only female member for twenty-five years and where she will help to encourage such writers as Pearl S. Buck (June 26, 1892–March 6, 1973), Isak Dinesen (pseudonym of Karen Blixen, 1885–September 7, 1962), and Richard Wright.

Italian novelist Grazia Deledda wins the Nobel Prize for Literature.

British author Vita Sackville-West publishes the long poem *The Land*, and American author Dorothy Parker publishes the verse collection *Enough Rope*, full of dark humor and self-mockery.

U.S. editor Clara Littledale becomes editor of *Parents' Magazine*, a position she will hold until her death in 1956. By 1946, circulation will reach over one million.

U.S. artist Georgia O'Keeffe paints *Black Iris*, one of her most famous works. O'Keeffe's paintings often feature one or two large, sensual blooms that absorb most of the canvas.

June 14 Impressionist Mary Cassatt, the foremost U.S. painter of her generation, and the foremost woman painter of the nineteenth century, dies. Best known for her paintings of mothers and children, she had to stop work in 1914 after her eyesight failed.

Dec. 3 Agatha Christie disappears. She will be found not long afterward, suffering from apparent amnesia, though some claim the entire adventure is a publicity stunt or an attempt at vengeance on her estranged husband.

Performing Arts and Entertainment

At the movies, fans can see Mary Pickford in *Sparrows*, Lillian Gish in *La Bohème* and *The Scarlet Letter*, Theda Bara in *Madame Mystery*, Clara Bow in *Mantrap* and *Dancing Mothers*, Dorothy Gish in *Nell Gwyn*, and Greta Garbo, now making $5,000 a week at MGM, in *Flesh and the Devil* and *The Torrent*.

On stage, British actress Peggy Ashcroft makes her debut at the Birmingham Repertory Theatre, and Irish dancer Ninette de Valois becomes choreographic director at Lilian Baylis's Old Vic Theatre, a position she will hold until 1931. U.S. actress Tallulah Bankhead stars in London in Noël Coward's *They Knew What They Wanted*, and Ethel Barrymore is a success as Constance Middleton in *The Constant Wife*.

In ballet, Russian Alexandra Danilova, a frequent performer with Dyaghilev and Balanchine, dances in *The Triumph of Neptune*, Russian Tamara Karsavina stars in Bronislava Nijinska's *Romeo and Juliet*, and English choreographer, dancer, and teacher Marie Rambert founds her own company.

German film animator Lotte Reiniger (b. 1899) coproduces the first full-length animated film, *The Adventures of Prince Achmed*.

U.S. musician Ethel Leginska founds and conducts the Boston Philharmonic Orchestra and becomes head of the Boston Women's Symphony Orchestra.

U.S. composer and pianist Amy Marcy Beach founds and becomes the first president of the Association of American Women Composers.

German screenwriter Thea von Harbou, wife of director Fritz Lang, writes the screenplay for his film *Metropolis*. Frances Marion writes the screenplay for *The Son of the Sheik*.

Nov. 3 U.S. sharpshooter Annie Oakley dies. She could, when four glass balls were thrown into the air, leap over a table, pick up a gun, and hit all four targets. She shot flames off candles, dimes from people's hands, and apples from her dog Dave's head. She so often shot the centers out of playing cards that punched tickets were referred to as "Annie Oakleys." The winner of more than $100,000 in prizes during her lifetime, she set several records, including one in which she hit, with a .22 rifle, 943 of 1,000 targets thrown into the air. In her thirty years of performing, she fired approximately 1.2 million shotgun shells.

Athletics and Exploration

American Bessie Coleman (b. 1893), the world's first black woman aviator, dies in a plane crash.

U.S. explorer and photographer Mary Akeley goes to Africa as part of a botanical and zoological expedition, serving as the group's administrator and photographer. When the group's leader, her husband Carl Akeley, dies in November, she takes control of the expedition.

French tennis player Suzanne Lenglen wins at Wimbledon for the sixth time. The crowd, resentful at her temper tantrum over the rescheduling of a match for Queen Mary's convenience, greets her win with sullen silence. She defeats Helen Wills Moody at Cannes in "The Match of the Century," the only time they will play each other, and then turns professional, saying, "People will pay to see anybody they hate."

French weightlifter Jane de Vesley lifts 392 pounds.

Aug. 6 Gertrude Ederle becomes the first woman to swim the English Channel, breaking the previous men's record time. She swam on despite two warnings from her coach to give up.

Activism

Amrit Kaur (1889–1964) cofounds the All India Women's Conference.

Business and Industry

In Russia, 2,265,000 women are in the labor force, constituting 23% of the total labor force.

U.S. labor leader Rose Schneiderman becomes president of the national WTUL, a position she will hold until the organization disbands in 1950.

Science and Medicine

U.S. entomologist Annie Slosson (b. 1838), who had several species named for her, dies.

U.S. educational psychologist Leta Stettner Hollingworth publishes *Gifted Children*.

Education and Scholarship

U.S. educator and philanthropist Martha Berry (October 7, 1866–February 27, 1942), founder of two schools for impoverished mountain children, establishes Georgia's Berry College.

U.S. art historian and educator Helen Gardner publishes *Art Through the Ages*, a survey of art history that becomes a standard text in many universities.

Religion

June 24 U.S. evangelist Aimee Semple McPherson, who disappeared from a beach on May 18, turns up in Arizona, claiming that she has been kidnapped, though the physical evidence disputes her claims. It is later proven that she spent the month of her own free will with a married man, and her popularity begins to wane.

July 9 Mother Mary Alphonsa Lathrop, founder of the Dominican Congregation of St. Rose of Lima, dies. Her group ministers to cancer patients.

1927

General Status and Daily Life

Abortion is legalized in Germany in cases where the mother's life or health is threatened.

Government, the Military, and the Law

In China, attacks on communists begin; many communist women, identified by their bobbed hair, are killed. Some are covered in cotton and oil and burned alive. Not all are captured; Li Chen becomes a local party secretary and survives to participate in the 6,000-mile Long March, fight against the government even while pregnant, and become the first Chinese woman major general. Xiang Jingyu becomes the first leader of the party's women's department.

Literature and the Visual Arts

Greek poet and literary critic Lydia Stephanou and Mozambique poet Noemia de Sousa are born.

New novels include Virginia Woolf's *To the Lighthouse*, which continues her experiments with stream-of-consciousness narration; Anglo-Irish author Elizabeth Bowen's (June 7, 1899–February 6, 1973) first novel, *The Hotel*; English mystery novelist Dorothy Sayers's (July 13, 1893–1957) *Clouds of Witness* and *Unnatural Death* (also published as *The Dawson Pedigree*); Chinese novelist Ding Ling's (b. 1902) *Diary of Miss Sophie*; and Italian Sibilla Aleramo's *Amo dunque sono*.

American Edna Ferber writes the play *Show Boat*, based on her own novel of the same title.

Russian sculptor Anna Golubkina creates a famous bust of Leo Tolstoi.

Performing Arts and Entertainment

U.S. filmmaker Lois Weber directs two commerical failures: *The Angel of Broadway*, which deals with prostitution, and *The Sensation Seekers*, which denounces flappers and the loose morality of the Jazz Age. *Angel* is her last silent film.

U.S. filmmaker Dorothy Arzner writes and directs her first movie, *Fashions for Women*, about a lower-class girl who impersonates a famous beauty. Given two weeks to develop the script and film the movie, she completes it ahead of schedule. Later in the year she films *Ten Modern Commandments*, which, like *Fashions*, stars Esther Ralston. She also directs *Get Your Man*, starring U.S. actress Clara Bow (July 29, 1905–September 27, 1965), who is experiencing her first real success in *Wings*, in which she plays a World War I ambulance driver, and *It*, written by Elinor Glyn. "It," a euphemism for sex appeal, becomes associated with Bow, who is known forever after as "The It Girl."

French journalist and filmmaker Germaine Dulac (1882–1942) makes the world's first surrealist film, *La coquille et le clergyman* (*The Seashell and the Clergyman*), an eerie, symbolic film about a clergyman pursuing sexual fantasies in the form of an elusive, white-robed woman. A British censor says of the movie, "If there is a meaning it is doubtless objectionable."

U.S. comedian Mae West (August 17, 1892–November 22, 1980) stars on Broadway in her short-lived play *The Drag*, about homosexuality. Her first play, *Sex*, was eventually closed down by the police, and West was arrested for "corrupting the morals of youth."

Actress Aziza Amir cofounds Egypt's first movie production company. The company's first film, *The Call of God* (also released as *Laila*), portrays the consequences of an unexpected pregnancy for a betrothed village woman.

Russian filmmaker Olga Preobrazhenskaya directs *Women of Ryazan*, about a woman whose soldier husband repudiates her and drives her to suicide for her infidelity while he is away at war. Her death takes place before he realizes that her seducer is his own father.

Film directors Louise Iribe of France and Olga Chekhova of Russia establish their own production companies.

Russian film editor Esther Shub (1894–1959) creates *The Fall of the Romanovs* and *The Great Road*, using archival footage to make these documentaries. In the United States, Irene Morra edits *High Society*, and Eda Warren edits *Hula*.

Czechoslovakian avant-garde filmmaker Zet Molas, a producer, director, screenwriter, and actress, makes the movie *Old House*.

Dinah Shurey, probably England's first woman film director, directs *Carry On*.

Austrian-American singer Lotte Lenya (c. 1900–1981), best known for her work in the *Threepenny Opera*, appears in the première of Weill and Brecht's *Mahagonny*.

Ethel Smyth composes a concerto for violin and horn, a piece inspired by Hungarian-British violinist Jelly d'Arányi.

Spanish dancer La Argentinita (Encarnaçion Lopéz, 1895–1945) establishes the Ballet de Madrid.

Josephine Baker stars in the film *La sirène des tropiques*.

Sept. 14 U.S. dancer Isadora Duncan dies when her long scarf catches in a rear wheel of her chauffeur-driven car, breaking her neck.

Athletics and Exploration

English aviator Sheila Scott, setter of over one hundred records by 1971, governor of the British Ninety-Nines, and founder of the British Balloon and Airships Club, is born.

At the world figure-skating championships in Oslo, Norway, Norwegian skater Sonja Henie takes first place, beating Austrian skater Herma Planck-Szabo. The victory is controversial because the three Norwegian judges all vote for Henie, while the Austrian and German judges give higher marks to Planck-Szabo. This controversy ensures that afterward no country has more than one judge on the panel.

U.S. aviator Ruth Nichols (February 23, 1901–September 25, 1960), the first woman in the world to earn a hydroplane license and a cofounder of the Ninety-Nines, a women's flying group, becomes one of the first two women to get a Department of Commerce transport license.

U.S. mountaineer Miriam Underhill is the first to traverse a pass in the Dolomites, which becomes known as the Via Miriam in her honor.

At the first European Games, English diver Belle White wins the women's high diving competition.

Activism

Indian social worker Dhanvanthi Rama Rau (b. 1893) becomes secretary of the All India Child Marriage Abolition League.

English feminist Dora Russell attacks traditional sexual mores in her book *The Right to Be Happy*.

The National Council of Catholic Women, the YWCA, the National Council of Jewish Women, and the Women's Industrial League unite to protest restrictive U.S. immigration laws.

July Two hundred cars full of women interrupt President Coolidge's vacation in South Dakota to press for passage of the ERA. The caravan, led by lawyer and suffragist Gail Laughlin, receives national publicity.

Business and Industry

U.S. businesswoman Jayne Baker Spain is born. She will inherit control of the Alvey-Ferguson conveyor-system company and will make a special effort to hire blind workers. Eventually, 10% of her employees will be handicapped, with the result that absenteeism is low and morale high.

U.S. efficiency expert Lillian Gilbreth publishes *The Home-Maker and Her Job*.

U.S. businesswoman Caresse Crosby cofounds the Black Sun Press, which publishes high-quality, limited editions of the works of James Joyce, D. H. Lawrence, Hart Crane, and Ezra Pound.

U.S. entrepreneur Alice S. Marriott cofounds a Washington, D.C., restaurant that will grow into a billion-dollar hotel and food service corporation.

U.S. coal-mining executive Josephine Roche becomes the majority stockholder of the Rocky Mountain Fuel Company. She makes a UMW lawyer her company counsel, raises wages, and improves safety. By 1932, she has doubled production and reduced accidents.

Science and Medicine

U.S. psychologist Margaret Washburn (July 25, 1871–October 29, 1939), author of more than 200 publications, becomes vice president of the American Association for the Advancement of Science.

U.S. mathematician Anna Pell Wheeler (May 5, 1883–March 26, 1959) becomes the first woman invited to deliver the American Mathematical Society's prestigious Colloquium Lectures.

German-American paleontologist Tilly Edinger becomes curator of the vertebrate collection at Frankfurt's Senckenberg Museum.

Botanist Kono Yasui becomes the first Japanese woman to earn a Ph.D. in science.

Education and Scholarship

English historian Eileen Power cofounds the *Economic History Review*.

U.S. social work educators Edith Abbott and Sophonisba Breckinridge establish the *Social Science Review*, a well-respected professional journal.

U.S. historian Mary Ritter Beard coauthors the acclaimed *Rise of American Civilization*.

1928

General Status and Daily Life

Canadians Emily Murphy, Nellie McClung, Irene Parlby, Louise McKinney, and Henrietta Muir Edwards petition for an interpretation of the word *persons* as it applies to Senate appointments; the ruling is that "women, children, criminals and idiots are not legally 'persons.'" This ruling is reversed in 1929 by the Privy Council.

Government, the Military, and the Law

Persecution of Chinese revolutionaries ends in the deaths of feminist Chen Tiejun (1904–March), who is arrested, tortured, and executed by the nationalists of Chiang Kai Shek, and revolutionary Xiang Jingyu (1895-May), who started a fashion of bobbed hair among female rebels. Xiang is arrested, tortured, and shot by a firing squad, gagged to prevent her from making a final speech.

Women in Britain get suffrage at age twenty-one; until now only women over thirty have been allowed to vote.

U.S. lawyer Mabel Willebrandt (b. May 23, 1889) becomes the first woman to chair a committee at the Republican National Convention.

The Soviet Union's Central Committee orders the promotion of women to executive positions. Six women are named to high office in the Communist party, one as governor of a province.

Literature and the Visual Arts

Greek poet and children's author Lina Kasdaglis, translator of Gide and Steinbeck into modern Greek, is born.

Bolivian poet Soledad (pseudonym of Adela Zamudio, b. 1854) and British-American photographer Evelyn Cameron, who photographed the homesteaders, ranchers, and townspeople of eastern Montana, die.

U.S. poet Elinor Wylie (September 7, 1885–December 16), who dies this year, publishes *Trivial Breath*. Her last book, *Angels and Earthly Creatures*, will be published posthumously in 1929.

English author Radclyffe Hall publishes a novel about lesbianism, *The Well of Loneliness*, which is suppressed for obscenity despite testimonials from Virginia Woolf and E. M. Forster. Other new novels include Virginia Woolf's *Orlando* (dedicated to British author Vita Sackville-West), English mystery novelist Dorothy Sayers's *The Unpleasantness at the Bellona Club*, and Selma Lagerlöf's *Anna Svärd*.

Norwegian novelist Sigrid Undset wins the Nobel Prize for Literature.

U.S. author Djuna Barnes publishes *Ryder*, a scandalous monologue censored in her own country, and the novel *Ladies' Almanack*, which gently lampoons members of lesbian Paris such as Radclyffe Hall and Natalie Barney.

U.S. author Zelda Fitzgerald (1900–1948) begins writing six short stories about young women. All will eventually be published, but her husband, F. Scott Fitzgerald, will take partial or complete credit for all of them.

New poetry includes Edna St. Vincent Millay's *The Buck in the Snow*, Dorothy Parker's *Sunset Gun*, and Marina Tsvetayeva's *Poste Rossii (After Russia)*.

English architect Elizabeth Whitworth Scott is selected to design the Shakespeare Memorial Theatre in Stratford-upon-Avon.

Performing Arts and Entertainment

English actress Ellen Terry (b. September 27, 1847), best known for her interpretations of Beatrice, Portia, Desdemona, Lady Teazle, and Lady Macbeth, dies.

U.S. dancer and choreographer Helen Tamiris (d. August 5, 1966) is the first woman invited to perform at Austria's Salzburg Festival.

English comedienne and singer Gracie Fields (1898–1979), best known for her renditions of comic songs and sentimental ballads, gives the first of nine Royal Command Performances.

Spanish dancer La Argentina (Antonia Mercé, 1888–1936), known for her traditional Spanish dances, ballet, and famous castanet style, establishes her own dance company.

U.S. lyricist Dorothy Fields (b. July 15, 1904) collaborates with Jimmy McHugh on the songs for her first Broadway play, *Blackbirds of 1928*. It includes two of her best-known songs, "I Can't Give You Anything But Love" and "On the Sunny Side of the Street."

Mae West stars in her latest Broadway play, *Diamond Lil*, in which she purrs, "When women go wrong, men go right after them."

At the movies, U.S. comedian Fanny Brice stars in *My Man*. Lillian Gish stars in *The Wind*, and Pola Negri stars in *Loves of an Actress*, but the Best Actress Oscar goes to Janet Gaynor for *Seventh Heaven*. Behind the camera in Hollywood, Bess Meredyth writes *Wonder of Women*, and Josephine Lovett receives an Academy Award nomination for the screenplay for *Our Dancing Daughters*. Viola Lawrence edits *Awakening*, and Dorothy Arzner directs *Manhattan Cocktail*.

Athletics and Exploration

Britain's Sophie Heath becomes the first aviator to solo from the Cape of Good Hope to Cairo. Touting the reliability of air travel, she proclaims, "it is so safe that a woman can fly across Africa wearing a Parisian frock and keeping her nose powdered all the way."

U.S. mountaineer Miriam Underhill makes the first woman-led crossing of the Grépon.

English pilot Lady Mary Bailey (1890–1960) makes a solo flight from Croydon, England, to Cape Town, South Africa, and back to Croydon. She also becomes the first woman pilot to fly "blind"—that is, on instruments only.

Norwegian Sonja Henie, the youngest Olympian, wins a gold at the winter Olympics with her "Dying Swan" routine. Andrée Brunet-Joly and Pierre Brunet of France, the bronze medalists in 1924, take the gold in pairs skating.

The IOC decides to allow women to participate in two new sports: track and field and team gymnastics. Only five track-and-field events are allowed, however: the 100-meter and 800-meter races, the high jump, the discus throw, and the 4 x 100-meter relay. England's track stars, disappointed at the lack of variety, refuse to participate in protest. Canada's Ethel Catherwood wins a gold medal in the high jump with a record height of 1.59 meters. American Elizabeth Robinson wins the gold in the 100 meters and takes a silver with her team in the relay; the United States is beaten in this race by the Canadian team, which includes Ethel Smith, the bronze medalist in the 100 meters. Halina Konopacka of Poland wins the discus throw with a world record distance of 39.62 meters.

Germany's Lina Radke takes the gold in the 800 meters with a record-breaking time of 2:16.8, but the press is horrified to see some of the competitors lying down breathless after the race. The *New York Times* reports that "eleven wretched women" have suffered in this unfeminine event, and track-and-field events are withdrawn for the next Olympics. However, male AAU president Gustavus Kirby threatens a men's boycott unless the IOC reverses its decision, and the IOC votes seventeen to one in 1930 to include track and field again.

The United States wins five of the six diving medals, with Elizabeth Becker and Helen Meany winning the gold in platform and springboard diving. In swimming, American Albina Osipowich sets an Olympic record in the 100-meter freestyle, followed by her teammate Eleanor Garatti, who will take a bronze in this event in 1932. Dutch swimmer Maria Johanna Braun takes a gold in the 100-meter backstroke and a silver in the 400-meter freestyle, where she is defeated by American Martha Norelius's world record time of 5:42.8. Germany's Hilde Schrader wins the 200-meter breaststroke. The 4 x 100-meter freestyle relay is won with a world record time by the U.S. team of Garatti, Osipowich, Norelius, and Adelaide Lambert.

German fencer Helene Mayer wins the women's individual foil. The Netherlands wins the first women's team gymnastics gold.

Jan. 3 U.S. aviator Ruth Nichols serves as copilot on a record-setting, nonstop flight from New York to Miami.

Activism

The Arab Women's Union is founded.

Women are active participants in India's struggle for independence. In Calcutta, women revolutionaries are organized by the women's student group Chhatri Sangha. Women in this group carry bombs, assassinate British officials, and make raids on British targets.

Sept. 1 Burmese activist Daw Tee Tee Luce founds an orphanage and school in Rangoon for boys abandoned to live in the streets.

Dec. 22 The Indonesian Women's Congress is established to fight "child marriage, polygyny, arbitrary male-initiated divorce, forced marriage, and unequal inheritance laws."

Business and Industry

Sarah Conboy, suffragist, organizer for United Textile Workers of America and its secretary-treasurer since 1916, and the first woman bank director in the United States, dies.

In Shanghai, male textile mill workers make $1.73–$2.76 per week; women make $1.10–$1.78.

Science and Medicine

U.S. computer programmer Ruth M. Davis is born. She will program SEAC, ORD-VAC, and UNIVAC I, three of the world's first digital computers.

New U.S. publications include ornithologist Florence Merriam Bailey's *Birds of New Mexico*, anthropologist Gladys Reichard's *Social Life of the Navaho Indians*, astronomer Dorothea Klumpke Roberts' *Celestial Atlas*, and anthropologist Margaret Mead's (December 16, 1901–November 15, 1978) landmark work, *Coming of Age in Samoa*.

Microbiologist Alice Evans becomes the first woman president of the Society of American Bacteriologists.

Education and Scholarship

English classicist Jane Harrison (b. 1850), author of several books on ancient Greek culture, dies.

Indian poet, politician, and feminist Sarojini Naidu chairs the All India Conference for Educational Reform.

U.S. journalist Anne O'Hare McCormick (b. May 16, 1880) publishes *The Hammer and the Sickle: Communist Russia Enters the Second Decade*.

U.S. anthropologist and author Zora Neale Hurston (January 7, 1901?–January 28, 1960) becomes the first black graduate of Barnard.

María Paz Mendoza-Guazón, the first Filipina doctor, founds the Philippine Association of University Women.

Religion

U.S. Christian Science leader Augusta Stetson (b. October 12, 1842), who in the early twentieth century rivaled Mary Baker Eddy in popularity, dies.

1929

General Status and Daily Life

Many U.S. homes now have electric irons, washing machines, central heating, and hot-water heaters; the housewife, once a producer of cloth, butter, cheese, and other products, is becoming a consumer instead. One in six marriages ends in divorce.

India raises its marriage age to fourteen for women and eighteen for men and prohibits intercourse with a wife under fifteen years of age. The penalty is a maximum of two years in prison. The act owes its passage in part to

the work of Muthulakshmi Reddy, the first woman nominated to a state legislative assembly in India.

Government, the Military, and the Law

Filipina lawyer and feminist Josepha Abiertas (b. 1894), the first woman to graduate from the Philippine Law School, dies.

Women in Ecuador get the vote. Women in Romania and Greece get local suffrage, but the Greek women's age requirement is higher than the men's.

English unionist and politician Margaret Grace Bondfield, as Minister of Labor, becomes Britain's first woman cabinet minister.

Nov.–Dec. Women rebel in southeastern Nigeria in the Igbo *Ogu Umunwanyi*, or Women's War, known to Westerners as the Aba Riots. Tens of thousands of women converge on British government offices, banks, and white-owned stores, chanting, singing, dancing, releasing prisoners from jails, attacking sixteen Native Courts, and demanding that Igbo officials appointed by the British yield their insignias of office. British troops fire on the women, killing more than fifty and injuring about another fifty. The war was started on November 23 by Nwanyeruwa, a woman who feared that the current British census of women and their possessions meant that women and their meager earnings were about to be taxed. She attacked the agent sent to count her goats and sheep and was soon joined by other women.

Literature and the Visual Arts

Julia Peterkin publishes the Pulitzer Prize-winning novel *Scarlet Sister Mary*. Other new novels include American Ellen Glasgow's *They Stooped to Folly*, Venezuelan Teresa de la Parra's (1895–1936) *Memorías de mama Blanca*, and Australian Henry Handel Richardson's *Ultima Thule*.

U.S. sculptor Malvina Hoffman exhibits 105 statues in sixteen different materials in New York City; the popular collection will spend five years touring the United States.

U.S. author Dorothy Parker wins the O. Henry Prize for the short story "Big Blonde."

Georgia O'Keeffe paints *Black Flower and Blue Larkspur* and makes her first visit to New Mexico. She will become fascinated with the Southwest's art and terrain, and desert images will become prominent in her work.

U.S. artist Florine Stettheimer (August 19, 1871–May 11, 1944) paints *Cathedrals of Broadway*.

U.S. photographer Margaret Bourke-White (June 14, 1904–August 27, 1971) shoots the first cover of *Fortune* magazine.

May U.S. philanthropist Abby Aldrich Rockefeller (October 26, 1874–April 5, 1948) holds a luncheon at which she and others, including Grace Rainey Rogers (d. May 9, 1943), Mary Quinn Sullivan, and Lizzie Bliss, agree to establish New York's Museum of Modern Art (MoMA). Rockefeller alone will donate more than 2,000 artworks to the museum.

Performing Arts and Entertainment

U.S. film director Dorothy Arzner directs Paramount's first sound film, *The Wild Party*, starring Clara Bow in her typical flapper role. While filming it, Arzner invents the first overhead microphone by strapping a mike to a fishing pole. She is the first U.S. woman to direct "talkies," and she will direct fourteen more sound films in the 1930s.

English novelist and screenwriter Elinor Glyn directs two films, *Knowing Men* and *The Price of Things*. *Knowing Men* is attacked by critics for depicting "man as possessing one characteristic alone, which compels him to ogle, then maul, every woman he meets."

In the United States, Lillian Ducey writes and directs *Behind Closed Doors*; film editor Viola Lawrence edits Goldwyn's first sound film, *Bulldog Drummond*. Irene Morra edits *Sunny Side Up*, and Eda Warren edits *Dangerous Curves*.

U.S. singer Bessie Smith stars in the film *St. Louis Blues*. Mary Pickford stars in her first talkie, *Coquette* (for which she wins the Best Actress Oscar), and in *Taming of the Shrew* with her husband, Douglas Fairbanks.

U.S. dancer Doris Humphrey choreographs *Life of the Bee*.

U.S. composer Mabel Daniels's *Exultate Deo* is perfomed by the Boston Symphony.

Polish film producer and director Wanda Jakubowska (b. 1907) cofounds the Society of the Devotees of Artistic Film.

The Soviet film classic *Fragment of an Empire* is scripted by Katerina Vinogradskaya.

American Pancho (Florence) Barnes (1901–1974)

becomes the first female motion picture stunt pilot.

Athletics and Exploration

Aviator Phoebe Fairgrave Omlie sets a women's altitude record of 25,400 feet.

French explorer Alexandra David-Neel (1869–1968), the first European woman to visit the city of Lhasa, publishes *Mystère et magique de Tibet*.

Aug. 18 The first women's cross-country air derby in the United States is held. Twenty pilots, including Amelia Earhart, Pancho Barnes, and Ruth Nichols, fly solo from Santa Monica, California, to Cleveland, Ohio, a distance of 2,350 miles. Louise McPhetridge Thaden wins in the heavy-plane division, and Phoebe Fairgrave Omlie wins in the light-plane division. One pilot, Marvel Crosson, dies when her parachute fails to open after she bails out of her crashing plane.

Activism

U.S. antilynching activist Jessie Daniel Ames (November 2, 1883–February 21, 1972) becomes the director of the women's committee of the Commission on Interracial Cooperation.

Feminist Ona Masiotene becomes president of the Council of Lithuanian Women.

May 28 U.S. Republican party official Pauline Sabin establishes the Women's Organization for National Prohibition Reform, which within three years will be triple the size of the WCTU.

Business and Industry

Indian businesswoman Sumati Morarjee becomes co-owner of the Scindia Steam Navigation Co., a large shipping firm.

U.S. businesswoman Marjorie Merriweather Post (March 15, 1887–September 12, 1973), owner of the Postum Cereal Company, fighting strong resistance from her board of directors, acquires Clarence Birdseye's frozen food patents. The move leads to the formation of General Foods Corporation, the country's largest food company.

Sept. 16 U.S. agriculturalist Harriet Strong (b. July 23, 1844), who patented water storage dams and cultivated walnuts, pomegranates, citrus fruits, and pampas grass in California, dies. She was the first female member of the Los Angeles Chamber of Commerce.

Nov. In an Ecuadoran rail strike, Tomasa Garcés blocks trains from leaving their station by lying on the tracks.

Science and Medicine

Birth control advocate Aletta Jacobs dies. The first woman doctor in the Netherlands and a founder of WILPF, she campaigned against regulated prostitution and worked for shorter workdays, protective legislation for women workers, sex education, penal reform, women's suffrage, and marriage law reform.

New publications include German-American paleontologist Tilly Edinger's *Die Fossilen Gehirne* (*Fossil Brains*), volume I of U.S. paleontologist Winifred Goldring's *Handbook of Paleontology for Beginners and Amateurs*, and U.S. physician Dorothy Reed Mendenhall's *Midwifery in Denmark*, which maintains that interference in childbirth usually hurts more than it helps.

Florence Merriam Bailey becomes the first woman fellow of the American Ornithologists' Union; Margaret Ferguson becomes the first woman president of the Botanical Society of America.

Education and Scholarship

South African scholar and activist Fatima Meer, for some time the highest-ranking black academic in South Africa, is born.

Greek teacher and feminist Soteria Aliberty (b. 1847) dies.

English author Virginia Woolf publishes the essay *A Room of One's Own*, a pioneering work of feminist literary criticism.

New U.S. publications by classical archaeologists include Mary Swindler's ambitious and much-respected *Ancient Painting* and museum curator Gisela Richter's *Sculpture and Sculptors of the Greeks*.

The first seventeen women enter Egyptian universities.

Religion

Yugoslavian nun Mother Theresa (Agnes Gonxha Bejaxhia, b. 1910) joins a teaching convent in Calcutta.

1930

General Status and Daily Life

China's Civil Code grants women the right to marry husbands of their own choice, comparable grounds for divorce, and improved property and inheritance rights. Adultery is now punishable for men as well as women.

Government, the Military, and the Law

Lebanese agricultural economist and UN official Aida Eid is born.

Most German political parties vote to fire government-employed women whose husbands have jobs.

White South African women get the vote.

Literature and the Visual Arts

Japanese poet Tada Chimako, translator of the works of Claude Lévi-Strauss, Peruvian poet Lucia Fox, Venezuelan-American pop art sculptor Marisol (Escobar), English sculptor Elizabeth Frink, Canadian architect Eva Vecsei, and Polish weaver Magdalena Abakanowicz are born.

Italian journalist Oriana Fallaci is born. Her career will take her to Vietnam, the Middle East, and South America, and her interview subjects will include Kissinger and Khomeini.

Chinese painter of flowers and landscapes Wu Shujuan (b. 1853) dies.

Novelist Edith Wharton is elected to the American Academy of Arts and Letters.

New literature includes Uruguayan poet Juana de Ibarbourou's *La rosa de los vientos*, Norwegian Sigrid Undset's novel *The Burning Bush*, and English mystery novelist Dorothy Sayers's *Strong Poison*, which introduces the recurring character Harriet Vane, a mystery novelist accused of murdering her fiancé.

May Edward Stratemeyer, creator of Nancy Drew, the Hardy Boys, and the Bobbsey Twins, among other series for children, dies. The business of churning out new books is taken over by his daughter, Harriet Stratemeyer Adams (d. Mar. 27, 1982), who was often discouraged from writing while her father was alive. She becomes the new "Carolyn Keene" (the pseudonym used for the

Nancy Drew books), creating series of her own, such as the Dana Girls series. Many of the early Nancy Drew books, however, were written neither by Edward nor by Harriet Stratemeyer but by a third writer, Mildred Wirt Benson.

Performing Arts and Entertainment

Norma Shearer wins the Best Actress Oscar for her role in *The Divorcee*. Marlene Dietrich stars in *Der blau Engel (The Blue Angel)* and *Morocco*. Greta Garbo stars in her first talkie, *Anna Christie*, written by Frances Marion. Marion also works this year on *Min and Bill* and *The Big House* (written by Blanche Sewell), winning an Oscar for the latter film. Dorothy Arzner directs Ruth Chatterton in *Sarah and Son* and *Anybody's Woman*.

U.S. composer Ruth Crawford-Seeger wins a Guggenheim Fellowship and composes *Chants*, *String Quarter*, and *Piano Study in Mixed Accents*.

Russian ballerina Natalya Dudinskaya (b. 1912) joins the Kirov Ballet as a soloist in her first season.

Indian actress and filmmaker Devika Rani Chaudhury codirects India's first talkie, *Karma*; later she will establish her own studio.

Russian choreographer Bronislava Nijinska becomes ballet mistress of Paris's Opéra Russe.

U.S. dancer and choreographer Martha Graham (1894–1991) creates the dance *Lamentation*.

Holst composes his *Double Concerto* for Hungarian-British violinists Jelly d'Arányi and Adila Fachiri (1886–1962), who are sisters.

British actress Peggy Ashcroft (1907–1991) plays Desdemona to Paul Robeson's Othello.

Feb. 23 U.S. silent film actress Mabel Normand (b. November 10, 1893?), best known for her work in the comedies of Mack Sennett, dies. She sometimes directed films and often costarred with Charlie Chaplin and Fatty Arbuckle. Her career ended in the early 1920s after her peripheral involvement in two scandalous shootings.

Athletics and Exploration

U.S. pilot Pancho Barnes sets a women's speed record of 196.19 miles per hour and becomes the first woman to fly from Los Angeles to Mexico City.

U.S. mountaineer Miriam Underhill skis down 16,217-foot Mount Rosa.

British tennis player Betty Nuthall wins the U.S. Open.

English aviator Amy Johnson makes the first solo flight by a woman from London to Australia.

July 7 U.S. athlete Babe Didrikson Zaharias breaks three world records at the AAU national track championships.

Activism

Indian activist Sarojini Naidu leads protests against the British-imposed Salt Law.

The Sri Lanka Women's Society is founded.

U.S. civil rights activist Jessie Daniel Ames founds the Association of Southern Women for the Prevention of Lynching (ASWPL).

Business and Industry

A Soviet study finds that women workers are more productive and less often absent than men.

In the United States, 17.8% of women are in the labor force, constituting 21.9% of the total labor force. Most are still trapped in sex-segregated jobs; 81% of teachers are women, as well as 95% of telephone operators and 98% of nurses. Most working women (72%) are single, but hard times are pushing many married women into the labor force. Married women are chastised for "holding jobs that rightfully belong to the God-intended providers of the household," but, as desperate as they are for work, men refuse to stoop to feminized occupations.

May 15 Ellen Church becomes the first airline stewardess.

Aug. 1 U.S. heiress Eleanor Patterson becomes editor and publisher of William Randolph Hearst's *Washington Herald*.

Science and Medicine

England's National Birth Control Council (later the Family Planning Association) is established. Gertrude Denman becomes its first chairman.

New publications include *Practical Vertebrate Morphology*, cowritten by English zoologist Sidnie Manton (1902–1979), a specialist in arthropods; U.S.

anthropologist Margaret Mead's *Growing Up in New Guinea*; and *Field Book of Ponds and Streams: An Introduction to the Life of Fresh Water*, by U.S. ecologist Ann Morgan (May 6, 1882–June 5, 1959), an expert on aquatic insects.

U.S. entomologist Edith Patch becomes the president of the American Nature Study Society and the first woman president of the Entomological Society of America.

Education and Scholarship

A National Education Association survey of U.S. school districts reveals that 77% will not hire married women as teachers; 63% fire women if they marry. In London, England, it is standard practice from 1923 to 1935 to fire married women teachers.

The New York Board of Education rules that married teachers must take their husbands' names.

New publications include U.S. philosopher Susanne Knauth Langer's (b. 1895) *The Practice of Philosophy*, Australian radical journalist Ella Winter Stewart's *Red Virtue*, a book about Soviet women, and U.S. classicist Edith Hamilton's (August 12, 1867–May 31, 1963) *The Greek Way*.

Religion

Korea has 12,380 shamans, 8,000 of them women. Most female shamans are thirty-four to fifty years old.

1931

General Status and Daily Life

Peru's Civil Code makes mothers and fathers nominally equal but gives the father precedence in conflicts and makes him the children's legal representative.

Divorce is legalized in Mexico. Abortion is legal only in cases of rape or threat to the mother's life. In other cases, both the abortionist and the woman can be jailed; sentences are lighter in cases of "family honor."

U.S. cookery writer Irma Rombauer (October 30, 1877–October 14, 1962) privately prints the first edition of *The Joy of Cooking*.

Britain's Department of Health authorizes the distribution of birth control to married couples for health reasons.

Married women in the United States, who have sometimes been keeping their birth names, are doing so less frequently. By the end of the decade, name change will be almost automatic and in some cases legally mandated.

The U.S. birthrate falls as people postpone marriage and children due to economic hardship.

Government, the Military, and the Law

Women in Spain get the vote; women over twenty-one in Sri Lanka get the right to vote and to run for public office. Portuguese women with at least a secondary school education get suffrage.

Literature and the Visual Arts

Canadian author Alice Munro, U.S. architect and urban planner Denise Scott-Brown, and Shiraishi Kazuko, one of Japan's leading contemporary poets, are born.

After having her collection of contemporary art (and the offer of a new wing to house it) rejected by the Metropolitan Museum of Art in New York, sculptor Gertrude Vanderbilt Whitney (January 9, 1875–1942) establishes the Whitney Museum of American Art.

U.S. novelist Pearl S. Buck publishes *The Good Earth*; it sells 2 million copies and is translated into more than thirty languages. Other new novels include French author Marguerite Yourcenar's (pseudonym of Marguerite de Crayencour, b. June 8, 1903) *La nouvelle Eurydice*, English author Vita Sackville-West's *All Passion Spent*, Chinese novelist Ding Ling's *Flood*, and English novelist Ivy Compton-Burnett's *Men and Wives*.

U.S. author Dorothy Parker publishes the verse collection *Death and Taxes*.

German novelist and historian Ricarda Huch becomes the first female member of the Prussian Academy of Literature.

Feb. 7 Chinese author Feng Keng is executed.

Performing Arts and Entertainment

U.S. actress Mae Questel is the voice of cartoon

character Betty Boop.

Australian-American actress Judith Anderson plays Lavinia in *Mourning Becomes Electra*.

German film director Leni Riefenstahl (b. August 22, 1902) forms her own production company.

Austrian film director and actress Leontine Sagan makes *Mädchen in Uniform*, the first German film to share profits cooperatively and the first German film directed by a woman. Later banned by Goebbels, it deals with lesbianism in a girls' boarding school and the way that the rigorous conformity demanded in the school squelches the girls' natural personalities. Also in Germany, screenwriter Thea von Harbou writes the screenplay for Fritz Lang's film *M*.

U.S. composer Mabel Daniels's *Deep Forest* is performed by the Boston Symphony.

English soprano and opera producer Joan Cross makes her Covent Garden debut as Mimi in Puccini's *La Bohème*. She then becomes the starring soprano of Sadler's Wells Opera, where she will remain until 1946.

Irish dancer and choreographer Ninette de Valois and English theater manager Lilian Baylis form the Vic-Wells Ballet. De Valois also choreographs *Job* for the Camargo Society.

In the United States, film director Dorothy Arzner directs *Honor Among Lovers*, starring Claudette Colbert and edited by Helene Turner, and *Working Girls*, starring Frances Dee. Irene Morra writes *Connecticut Yankee*. Frances Marion writes the screenplay for *The Champ*, winning an Academy Award. The Best Actress Academy Award goes to Marie Dressler for *Min and Bill*.

French actress Arletty (b. 1898) appears in her first film, *Un chien qui rapporte*.

Marlene Dietrich stars in *Dishonored*; U.S. actress Jean Harlow stars in *The Public Enemy* and *Platinum Blonde*.

Feb. 15 U.S. circus gymnast Lillian Leitzel (b. Leopoldina Alitza Pelikan in 1892) dies when her aerial equipment breaks and sends her plummeting to the floor. From 1915 on she was the star performer for Ringling Brothers.

Athletics and Exploration

German tennis player Cilly Aussem wins the Wimbledon singles title.

U.S. mountaineer Miriam Underhill fails to climb the Matterhorn due to bad weather and climbs the Jungfrau instead.

Between now and 1947, Polish archer Janina Spychajowa-Kurkowska will win a record seven world titles, more than any other archer, male or female.

Teenage minor league pitcher Jackie Mitchell, the first professional woman baseball player in the United States, strikes out Babe Ruth and Lou Gehrig in an exhibition game in Chattanooga, Tennessee.

Mar. U.S. aviator Ruth Nichols sets an altitude record of 28,743 feet. In April, she breaks Amelia Earhart's women's speed record with a speed of 210.754 miles per hour. In June, she crashes while attempting the first transatlantic crossing by a woman, and in October, still injured from her June crash, she sets a women's distance record with her back in a metal brace.

Aug. In a bathysphere, U.S. scientist Gloria Hollister sets a new women's depth record of 1,208 feet.

Activism

Cuban feminist Graciella Barinaga y Ponce de León stimulates the women's movement with her book *Feminism and the Home*.

U.S. reformer Ella Boole, president of the national WCTU from 1925 to 1938, becomes president of the World's WCTU, a position she will hold until 1947.

Dec. 10 Jane Addams shares the Nobel Peace Prize and gives her $16,000 award to WILPF.

Business and Industry

China's Factory Law gives women limited rights to equal pay.

The Widow Chang, a Chinese bandit who terrorized the residents of western Honan, is captured and executed.

French fashion designer Elsa Schiaparelli (d. 1973), known for her early use of knits, zippers, and synthetic fabrics, is the first to introduce shoulder pads.

Irish trade unionist Louie Bennett becomes the first woman president of the Irish TUC.

July 4 Fashion designer Elizabeth Hawes (December 16, 1903–September 6, 1971) becomes the first American to show a collection in Paris.

Science and Medicine

New U.S. publications include archaeologist Hetty Goldman's *Excavations at Eutresis in Boeotia* and developmental psychologist Florence Goodenough's (August 6, 1886–April 4, 1959) *Anger in Young Children* and *Handbook of Child Psychology*.

U.S. ornithologist Florence Merriam Bailey wins the American Ornithologists' Union's Brewster Medal for her book *Birds of New Mexico*. She is the first woman to win this medal.

America's National Academy of Sciences admits psychologist Margaret Washburn (July 25, 1871–October 29, 1939) and awards its Draper Medal to astronomer Annie Jump Cannon.

Dec. 28 French physicist Irène Joliot-Curie reports on her beryllium research to the Académie des Sciences

Education and Scholarship

Helen Kim becomes Korea's first female Ph.D. recipient.

New publications include U.S. congresswoman, diplomat, and lecturer Ruth Bryan Owen's *The Elements of Public Speaking*, U.S. classicist Lily Ross Taylor's *The Divinity of the Roman Emperor*, U.S. geographer Ellen Semple's *The Geography of the Mediterranean Region: Its Relation to Ancient History*, and English traveler and journalist Joan Rosita Forbes' *Conflict*, a study of the Middle East.

Mar. U.S. poet Louise Bogan (1897–1970) begins thirty-eight years as a literary critic for *The New Yorker*.

May 1 U.S. Episcopal missionary and librarian Mary Elizabeth Wood (b. August 22, 1861) dies. She established a school for librarians and a network of fixed and traveling libraries in China.

Religion

The Anglican church authorizes the limited use of birth control.

U.S. theologian Mary Lyman publishes *The Fourth Gospel and the Life of To-Day*.

Sept. 29 The Episcopal church relaxes its attitude toward remarriage.

1932

General Status and Daily Life

In the Soviet Union, an observer describes one village where "the women stood while the men sat down and ate; kept their heads bent and their hands folded, not speaking until they were spoken to. In one hut when I asked the peasant woman a question, the husband repeated it to his wife, the wife answered him, and he repeated the answer to me." Peasant women still weave their own cloth and wear birchbark shoes.

Government, the Military, and the Law

Brazil and Thailand grant women the vote.

U.S. radical journalist Ella Bloor becomes a member of the American Communist party's Central Committee, a position she will hold until 1948.

Jan. 12 Hattie Caraway (February 1, 1878–December 21, 1950) of Arkansas wins a special election to fill the Senate seat of her late husband, becoming the first elected U.S. woman senator. On May 9 she will become the first woman to preside over the Senate. Later she will become the first woman to chair a Senate committee and the first woman to conduct Senate hearings.

Literature and the Visual Arts

Colombian weaver Olga de Amaral and Hungarian-Italian author and concentration camp survivor Edith Bruck are born.

German artist Käthe Kollwitz, head of the Berlin Academy's division of graphic arts since 1928, is dismissed from this position by the Nazis.

U.S. painter Isabel Bishop (b. 1902) attracts her first serious notice with a one-woman show in New York.

New novels include Elizabeth Bowen's *To the North*, American Ellen Glasgow's *The Sheltered Life*, Zelda Fitzgerald's *Save Me the Waltz*, British author Rose Macaulay's *They Were Defeated*, English mystery novelist Dorothy Sayers's *Have His Carcase*, and Sigrid Undset's *Ida Elisabeth*. U.S. children's author Laura Ingalls Wilder (February 7, 1867–February 10, 1957) publishes her first book, *Little House in the Big Woods*.

U.S. author Edna Ferber writes the play *Dinner at Eight*.

Performing Arts and Entertainment

U.S. comedian, actress, and film director Elaine May and Lithuanian-British ballerina Svetlana Beriosova are born.

U.S. theater manager Jessie Bonstelle (b. 1872), who ran Detroit's Playhouse and Garrick Theatre and who discovered Katharine Cornell (February 16, 1898–1974), dies.

U.S. composer Florence Price wins four prizes at the Wanamaker competition, including first place in the symphonic division for her Symphony in E Minor.

The Dagenham Girl Pipers, a famous bagpipe group, is founded.

Dorothy Arzner, the only successful female film director in 1930s Hollywood, directs *Merrily We Go to Hell*.

Film director Leontine Sagan flees to England to escape Nazi persecution.

U.S. musician Ethel Leginska founds the short-lived National Women's Symphony Orchestra in New York.

French pianist Marguerite Long performs the première of Ravel's Piano Concerto in G.

German film director Leni Riefenstahl directs *Das blaue Licht* (*The Blue Light*).

English composer Elisabeth Lutyens (b. 1906), creator of more than 140 works, writes the ballet *The Birth of the Infanta*.

U.S. actress Jean Harlow (b. March 3, 1911) stars in *Red-Headed Woman* and *Red Dust*. Mae Marsh makes her first talkie, *Over the Hill*, and Asta Nielsen stars in her only talkie, *Unmögliche Liebe*. Ethel Barrymore receives $57,000 for appearing as the tsarina in the film *Rasputin and the Empress*. Clara Bow, whose career is having a hard time outlasting the flapper era, stars in *Call Her Savage*. Depression audiences prefer the charm of child star Shirley Temple, now starring in her first film, *The Red-Haired Alibi*.

U.S. actress Bette Davis (b. Apr. 5, 1908) stars in her first successful film, *The Man Who Played God*. Katharine Hepburn (b. Nov. 8, 1909) stars in her first motion picture, *A Bill of Divorcement*. Filmgoers can see established actresses as well, like Marlene Dietrich in *Blonde Venus* and *Shanghai Express*, and Greta Garbo in *Mata Hari* and *Grand Hotel*. The Best Actress Oscar for this year goes to Helen Hayes for *Sin of Madelon Claudet*.

U.S. screenwriter Sarah Y. Mason wins an Academy Award for her screenplay for *Little Women*, beating out another female screenwriter, Frances Marion, nominated for *The Prizefighter and the Lady*. Other screenplays written by U.S. women are Blanche Sewell's *Grand Hotel* and Eda Warren's *The Big Broadcast*.

The first important Soviet children's film, *Broken Shoes*, is filmed by a woman, M. Barskaya.

British actress Peggy Ashcroft plays Juliet to enthusiastic acclaim.

U.S. composer and pianist Amy Marcy Beach composes the opera *Cabildo*.

Feb. 15 U.S. director and actress Minnie Maddern Fiske (b. December 19, 1865), who pushed for greater realism and social conscience in American theater, dies.

Feb. 15 George Burns and Gracie Allen (July 26, 1895–August 27, 1964) debut with their own radio show, "The Adventures of Gracie," on CBS.

Athletics and Exploration

Sonja Henie of Norway wins a gold at the Lake Placid winter Olympics in figure skating. Andrée Brunet-Joly and Pierre Brunet of France take the gold in pairs skating.

Women's speed skating is introduced as a demonstration sport but will not become official until 1960. Jeanne Wilson of Canada wins the 500 meters and takes a silver in the 1,500 meters. U.S. skater Elizabeth Dubois wins gold in the 1,000 meters and silver in the 500, and American Kit Klein wins the 1,500 meters and gets the 500-meter bronze.

At the summer games in Los Angeles, U.S. track athletes Louise Stokes and Tydia Pickett become the first black women in the Olympics. The star of the games, however, is American Mildred "Babe" Didrikson Zaharias (b. June 26, 1911), who is upset that she is permitted to enter only three events; she becomes the only athlete ever to medal in high jump, javelin, and hurdles. Didrikson ties Jean Shiley, described by the *Los Angeles Times* as "the prettiest girl of the American track team," in the high jump, with both women breaking the previous world record. On a question of style, Shiley, who was not permitted to train on the grounds of her alma mater, Temple University, is awarded the gold. Didrikson also ties Evelyne Hall in the 80-meter hurdles, with a record-breaking time of 11.7 seconds. This time she wins the gold medal. She takes a second gold in the javelin.

The 4 x 100-meter relay race is won with a world record time by the U.S. team of Mary Carew, Evelyn Furtsch, Annette Rogers, and Wilhelmina Von Bremen. Lillian Copeland of the United States wins the discus throw with an Olympic record distance of 40.58 meters.

The United States sweeps all the diving medals.

Dorothy Poynton, Georgia Coleman, and Marion Roper take first, second, and third in the platform event, and Coleman wins a second medal, this time a gold, in the springboard event. She is followed by teammates Katherine Rawls and Jane Fauntz.

In swimming, Helene Madison wins the 100-meter freestyle with an Olympic record time. Madison also wins the 400-meter freestyle, this time setting a world record. Australian Claire Dennis sets an Olympic record in the 200-meter breaststroke. The 4 x 100-meter freestyle relay is won by the U.S. team of Josephine McKim (bronze medalist in 1928 in the 400-meter freestyle), Helen Johns, Madison, and Eleanor Saville-Garatti.

U.S. swimmer Eleanor Holm, winner of the backstroke, is lauded as much for her good looks as for her athletic ability. She, too, seems concerned about her appearance, saying, "It's great fun to swim . . . but the moment I find my swimming is making me athletic looking, giving me big, bulky muscles, making me look like an Amazon rather than a woman, I'll toss it to one side."

Austrian fencer Ellen Preis wins the women's individual foil.

Babe Didrikson Zaharias enters eight events at the AAU championships, winning five of them.

Tennis player Helen Hull Jacobs wins the U.S. women's singles. She will win the title again for the next three years and win the Wimbledon singles title in 1936.

May 20 Amelia Earhart (b. July 24, 1898) becomes the first woman to make a solo flight across the Atlantic.

Aug. 12 U.S. mountaineer Miriam Underhill, with Alice Damesme, makes the first all-female ascent of the Matterhorn.

Activism

U.S. educator Mary McLeod Bethune establishes the National Council of Negro Women (NCNW).

The Argentine Association for Women's Suffrage has about 80,000 members.

Cuba's first National Congress of Women is held in Havana.

Business and Industry

U.S. entrepreneur Olive Beech (b. 1903) cofounds the Beech Aircraft Corporation, serving as its secretary-treasurer until 1950. In 1945, the company will gross $122 million.

Science and Medicine

Irène Joliot-Curie (1897–1956) succeeds her fatally ill mother Marie Curie as head of the Radium Institute.

New publications include U.S. astronomer Dorothea Klumpke Roberts's prizewinning supplement to her *Celestial Atlas*, U.S. physician and bacteriologist Anna Williams's *Streptococci in Relation to Man in Health and Disease*, and German-American psychologist Charlotte Bühler's book on developmental psychology, *Der Menschliche Lebenslauf als Psychologisches Problem*.

U.S. psychologist Augusta Bronner becomes president of the American Orthopsychiatric Association.

Canadian-American botanist Alice Eastwood cofounds and becomes editor of the journal *Leaflets of Western Botany*.

U.S. physician Matilda Moldenhauer Brooks becomes the first person to publish findings on the use of methylene blue to treat cyanide and carbon monoxide poisoning in humans.

Education and Scholarship

U.S. linguist and anthropologist Ella Deloria (January 30, 1888–February 12, 1971), a Dakota (Sioux) Indian and a student of Franz Boas and Ruth Benedict, publishes *Dakota Texts*, a collection of myths.

U.S. classicist Edith Hamilton publishes *The Roman Way*.

U.S. classical archaeologist Mary Swindler becomes the first female editor in chief of the *American Journal of Archaeology*.

Apr. 23 The Folger Shakespeare Library, founded by U.S. philanthropist Emily Folger, opens in Washington, D.C.

Religion

May 29 U.S. Methodist educator Jane Bancroft Robinson (b. December 24, 1847), who organized and promoted the efforts of Protestant laywomen known as deaconesses, dies.

1933

General Status and Daily Life

Portugal's new constitution denies women equal rights because of the "differences resulting from their nature and from the interest of the family."

In Nazi Germany, girls are inducted into the Jungmaedel (Young Maidens), the female division of the Hitler Youth. They are indoctrinated in the pleasures of virtue and motherhood. Between the ages of fourteen and eighteen they may belong to the Bund Deutscher Mädchen (League of German Maidens).

May German abortion providers can be sentenced to two years in jail.

Dec. 25 Italian women who have given birth to fourteen to nineteen children are received by Mussolini in a special ceremony.

Government, the Military, and the Law

Canadian politician Mary Ellen Smith (b. 1862), the first woman in the British Empire to hold Cabinet rank, dies.

Women in Turkey get the vote.

Brazil's first woman deputy, Dr. Carlotta Pereira de Queiroz, is elected to the National Assembly.

Feb. Frances Perkins (April 10, 1880–May 14, 1965) becomes secretary of labor, the first woman in the U.S. Cabinet. She serves until 1945 and writes or helps to write several important pieces of legislation, including the Federal Emergency Relief Act, the Civilian Conservation Corps Act, the National Labor Relations Act, the Social Security Act, and the Fair Labor Standards Act.

Apr. 13 Ruth Bryan Owen (1885–1977) becomes the first U.S. woman minister to a foreign country when Franklin Delano Roosevelt appoints her Minister Plenipotentiary to Denmark.

Summer In Germany, most women in law and the civil service are fired.

Literature and the Visual Arts

Hungarian poet, teacher, radio producer, literary magazine editor, novelist, and book editor Agnes Gergely is born.

New literature includes Dorothy Sayers's novel *Murder Must Advertise*, Korean novelist Kang Kyong-ae's (1907–1943) *Ingan munje (Human Problems)*, and Gertrude Stein's *The Autobiography of Alice B. Toklas*.

U.S. editor May Massee arranges for the publication of Marjorie Flack's classic children's book, *The Story About Ping*. Ping is a small duck in China who becomes separated from his family and discovers the variety of life on the Yangtze River.

U.S. journalist, playwright, and politician Clare Boothe Luce (April 10, 1903–1987) becomes managing editor of *Vanity Fair* and writes her first novel, *Stuffed Shirts*.

U.S. author Marjorie Kinnan Rawlings (August 8, 1896–December 14, 1953) publishes the short story "Gal Young Un" and her first novel, *South Moon Under*.

German Jewish photographer Gisele Freund flees Germany; German novelist and historian Ricarda Huch resigns from the Prussian Academy as a protest against Nazism.

Irish novelist Edith Somerville becomes a founding member of the Irish Academy of Letters.

Jan. 29 U.S. lyric poet Sara Teasdale dies of a drug overdose; her best collection, *Strange Victory*, is published posthumously.

June 6 At Chicago's Field Museum of Natural History, U.S. sculptor Malvina Hoffman unveils a collection of more than one hundred heads and figures of different ethnic groups from Africa, Asia, Europe, North America, and the Pacific Islands.

June 30 The Seattle Art Museum, cofounded by Margaret Fuller, opens.

Performing Arts and Entertainment

Japanese singer Yoko Ono is born.

Filmgoers can see U.S. actress May Robson as Apple Annie in Frank Capra's *Lady for a Day*; Katharine Hepburn in *Morning Glory* (for which she wins the Best Actress Oscar), *Christopher Strong* (a box-office flop directed by Dorothy Arzner), and *Little Women*; Mae West in *She Done Him Wrong*, with costumes by legendary designer Edith Head (b. 1907, nominee for thirty-five Oscars and winner of eight); Jean Harlow in *Bombshell* and *Dinner at Eight* (written by Frances Marion); and Greta Garbo in *Queen Christina*. Ginger

Rogers is paired for the first time with Fred Astaire in *Flying Down to Rio*, and Fay Wray is offered a tall, dark leading man by RKO; she is hoping for Clark Gable, but it turns out to be *King Kong*.

U.S. screenplays written by women include Sonya Levien's Oscar-winning *State Fair* and Blanche Sewell's *Tugboat Annie*.

Egyptian actress Assis stars in *Endama Tehobel Meraa* (*When a Woman Loves*), a film made by her own production company. Egyptian actress Bahija Hafez, head of Fanar Film, produces and stars in *El Dohaya* (*The Victims*).

Florence Price's Symphony in E Minor becomes the first symphony by a black woman composer to be played by a major American orchestra.

U.S. blues singer Billie Holliday (b. April 7, 1915) makes her first recording, with clarinetist Benny Goodman.

Russian ballerina Lydia Lopokova begins an association with England's Vic-Wells theatre that will include roles in *Coppelia*, *Twelfth Night*, *A Doll's House*, *Master Builder* and *Le misanthrope*. English dancer Alicia Markova (b. 1910) becomes the first prima ballerina of the Vic-Wells Ballet.

The Nazi rise to power drives away many women in the arts, including German actress and theater director Helene Weigel, who flees with her husband, Berthold Brecht, and Danish film actress Asta Nielsen, who, despite offers from Goebbels, returns to Denmark.

French composer Elsa Barraine composes the symphonic poem *Pogromes*.

Athletics and Exploration

Sixteen-year-old Spaniard Juanita Cruz, the first professional female bullfighter, draws huge crowds to her fights. Wearing a ladylike skirt and calling herself "Señorita X" so as not to embarrass her family, she becomes famous for her capework and her courage, refusing to run even when without her cape and defenseless: "If I were a man, I would run. Most men matadors do. But if I run, someone in the audience will yell that I am running because I am a woman and I am scared—so I will not run."

Activism

The Nazi rise to power forces German feminists Lida Heymann and Anita Augsburg into exile.

Business and Industry

U.S. Populist Mary E. Lease, who urged farmers to "raise less corn and more hell," dies.

The first women's bank in Indonesia is founded.

Egypt's first protective labor legislation for women is passed.

U.S. restaurateur Ruth Wakefield, owner of the Toll House Inn in Whitman, Massachusetts, creates the chocolate chip cookie.

In the United States, all but six states have laws limiting the number of hours women can work.

Jan. 9 U.S. manufacturer Kate Gleason (b. November 25, 1865) dies. The first woman member of the American Society of Mechanical Engineers, she successfully marketed her father's bevel gear planer, which made gears used in bicycles and automobiles. She developed low-cost, high-quality housing and also took a machine shop $140,000 in debt and turned a profit of $3 million in three years.

Science and Medicine

The Nazis oust Jewish academics and most women in medicine, regardless of their religion; paleontologist Tilly Edinger keeps her job at Frankfurt's Senckenberg Museum with the help of the museum director, who takes her name off the door and brings her in each day through a special entrance. Austrian statistician and mathematician Hilda Geiringer is not so lucky and leaves Germany. German mathematician Emmy Noether, who this year publishes the article "Nichtkommutative Algebra," is dismissed from the University of Göttingen. Physicist Lise Meitner is banned from lecturing at the University of Berlin, but, as an Austrian citizen, she is allowed to continue her research.

Swedish birth control activist Elise Ottesen-Jensen founds the Swedish National Association for Sex Information and Education.

Education and Scholarship

German-American political philosopher Hannah Arendt flees Germany after being briefly imprisoned by the Gestapo for amassing information on German anti-Semitism.

New publications include English economist Joan Violet Robinson's *The Economics of Imperfect Competition*; Puerto Rican educator and folklorist María Cadilla de

Martínez' *La Poésia en Puerto Rico*, which becomes a standard text in many parts of Latin America; Australian-American economist and consumer advocate Persia Campbell's *American Agricultural Policy*; and U.S. anthropologist Gladys Reichard's *Melanesian Design*, which wins a prize from the New York Academy of Sciences.

U.S. legislator Crystal Bird Fauset (June 27, 1893–March 28, 1965) cofounds the Swarthmore College Institute of Race Relations.

Religion

U.S. religious writer Dorothy Day establishes the newspaper *Catholic Worker*.

French visionary Bernadette of Lourdes is canonized.

Women in Korea's Presbyterian church agitate for the right to become elders.

1934

General Status and Daily Life

The Nazi government exempts unwed mothers from the tax on single persons. Especially fertile women get discounts on utilities, free theater tickets, and Honor Cards that allow them to go to the fronts of lines in stores and government offices. Abortion is legalized in March for the "health of the nation" if the fetus is at risk for mental illness, physical defects, or alcoholism. A new publication, called *German Women to Adolf Hitler*, objects to the new policies.

Iranian female students and teachers are ordered to stop wearing the veil in public.

May 28 The Dionne quintuplets, Yvonne, Cécile, Annette, Emilie, and Marie, are born. It is only the third case in history of identical quintuplets and the only one in which the babies survived. The quints' existence will bring millions of tourist dollars to Ontario and slow the traditional killing of twins in Nigeria.

Government, the Military, and the Law

Chinese politician Hao Tianx'u is born.

Women in Chile get the right to vote in municipal elections; women in Cuba and Turkey get the vote.

U.S. lawyer Florence Allen (1884–1966) becomes the first woman federal court judge when she is named to the Sixth Circuit Court of Appeals.

Oct. The Long March, one of the most important episodes in twentieth-century Chinese history, begins. Lasting until 1936, it is the 7,775-mile migration of the Red Army from the south of China to the northwest. About fifty women participate, including revolutionary and women's leader Kang Keqing (b. 1910) and feminist and political leader Deng Yingchao (b. 1904).

Literature and the Visual Arts

In the United States, weaver Sheila Hicks and artist Faith Ringgold, creator of masks, murals, and sculpture, are born. Also born this year are Judith Herzberg, the most important Dutch woman poet of her generation; Greek poet Nana Issaia, translator of Sylvia Plath's works into modern Greek; and Argentinian poet Martha Paley Francescato, author of shaped poems that unite disjointed, surreal collections of ideas.

New poetry includes Alfonsina Storni's *Avant-garde el mundo de siete pozos* and Edna St. Vincent Millay's *Wine from These Grapes*. Korean poet Mo Yun-suk (b. 1910) publishes *Pinna nun chiyok (Glorious Land)*, a controversial work about her native country that draws both praise and criticism for its rambling, musical style. New novels include Agatha Christie's *Murder in Three Acts* and Pearl S. Buck's *The Mother*, controversial for its graphic depictions of childbirth and abortion.

U.S. sculptor Augusta Savage becomes the first black member of the National Association of Women Painters and Sculptors.

U.S. children's author Cornelia Meigs wins a Newbery Medal for *Invincible Louisa*, a book about Louisa May Alcott.

Danish author Isak Dinesen publishes *Seven Gothic Tales*.

Oct. U.S. photographer Margaret Bourke-White covers the Dust Bowl for *Fortune* in the article "The Drought."

Oct. 13 U.S. photographer Gertrude Käsebier (b. 1852) dies.

Performing Arts and Entertainment

Chinese film actress Xie Fang is born.

U.S. stage designer Aline Bernstein designs *The Children's Hour*, a drama about the effects of an accusation of lesbianism, written by U.S. playwright Lillian Hellman (June 20, 1907–June 30, 1984).

U.S. big band and scat singer Ella Fitzgerald (b. April 25, 1918) records her first song, "Are You Here to Stay."

U.S. actress Shirley Temple stars in *Stand Up and Cheer*, *Little Miss Marker*, and *Now and Forever*. By the end of the year, she is one of the most popular film stars in America and receives a special Academy Award as "the outstanding personality of 1934." The Best Actress Oscar goes to Claudette Colbert for her portrayal of a spoiled heiress in the romantic comedy *It Happened One Night*. Movie audiences can also see Katharine Hepburn in *The Little Minister*, Bette Davis in *Of Human Bondage*, Betty Grable in *The Gay Divorcee*, and Marlene Dietrich in *The Scarlet Empress*.

Egyptian actress Assis stars in *Eyoun Sahera* (*The Enchanting Eyes*), made by her production company.

U.S. artist Florine Stettheimer designs sets and costumes for the Gertrude Stein-Virgil Thomson opera, *Four Saints in Three Acts*.

German film director Leni Riefenstahl directs the Nazi propaganda film *Triumph des Willens* (*Triumph of the Will*), filmed at a party rally at Nuremberg.

Nila Mack begins producing the U.S. children's radio show "Let's Pretend," which will run for twenty years.

U.S. filmmaker Lois Weber (June 31, 1881–November 13, 1939) makes her last film, *White Heat*, which addresses racism and intermarriage. Dorothy Arzner directs *Nana*. Irene Morra writes the screenplay for *Bright Eyes*. French film editor Marguerite Renoir works on *Madame Bovary*, and American film editor Anne Bauchens receives an Oscar nomination for her work on *Cleopatra*.

U.S. dancer and choreographer Helen Tamiris combines poetry and jazz in her "Walt Whitman Suite."

Athletics and Exploration

German Gisela Maurmayer wins the world's first women's pentathlon.

U.S. women pilots, including Pancho Barnes, band together to provide airborne emergency supplies in disasters. In a demonstration of their skill and efficiency, the pilots drop a crate of eggs 7,000 feet without breaking any.

British tennis player Dorothy Round wins the Wimbledon singles title; she will win again in 1937.

U.S. pilot Jacqueline Cochran (1910–1980) flies to 30,000 meters in an unheated, unpressurized, canvas-winged biplane.

New Zealand pilot Jean Gardner Batten (b. 1909) breaks by four days Amy Johnson's solo record from England to Australia.

Activism

Spanish communist politician Dolores Ibarurri establishes a women's group, the Agrupación de Mujeres Antifacistas.

Black women in Johannesburg, South Africa, stage a nine-day march to protest an increase in bus fares.

Haiti's League Feminine d'Action Sociale (Women's Social Action League) is founded to fight for women's legal rights in the home, schools, and workplace.

German Nazi women's leader Gertrud Scholtz-Klink (b. 1902) is named head of the Nazi Women's Group and given the title *Reichsfrauenführerin* (National Women's Leader). By the end of World War II, her organization will become responsible for publishing propaganda aimed at women, directing women's groups, and, near the end of the war, organizing women's battalions.

Italian women found the antifascist journal *La voce della donne*.

Belgian feminist Martha Bol Poel becomes president of the National Council of Women.

Business and Industry

U.S. secretarial schools founder Katharine Gibbs (b. 1865) dies.

U.S. cannery founder Tillie Lewis (b. 1901), the first person to can tomatoes in their skins, introduces Italian (*pomodoro*) tomatoes to California.

In Cuba, equal pay for equal work becomes law.

U.S. labor leader Rose Pesotta is elected to a vice presidency in the ILGWU; ILGWU policy specifies that only one woman at a time will serve on the governing board, even though 85% of the membership is female.

Dec. 15 U.S. insurance executive Maggie Walker (b. July 15, 1867), who also founded and ran a successful banking business in Richmond, Virginia, dies. The daughter of servants of Civil War spy Elizabeth Van Lew, she became secretary-treasurer of the Independent Order of St. Luke in 1899, when it had 1,000 members and only $31.60 in the treasury. At her death, Walker has a personal fortune of $40,000 and leaves the Order of St. Luke with wealth, real estate holdings, and its own newspaper, which hires black women as clerks.

Science and Medicine

U.S. anthropologist Ruth Benedict (b. June 5, 1887) publishes her most famous and enduring work, *Patterns of Culture*, in which she argues that aggressive, acquisitive masculinity, while valued in Western culture, is possibly no less pathological than paranoia or schizophrenia. The book, which challenges Western readers' perceptions of their own culture, will remain the standard introductory anthropology text for a quarter of a century. Other noteworthy publications this year are American psychologist Florence Goodenough's *Developmental Psychology*, Alice Hamilton's textbook *Industrial Toxicology*, and English botanist Agnes Arber's (1879–1960) *The Gramineae: A Study of Cereal, Bamboo and Grass*.

Austrian physicist Lise Meitner, though she does not realize it at the time, becomes the first person to split an atom.

Jan. Irène and Frédéric Joliot-Curie bombard an aluminum nucleus with alpha particles, creating the first artificially radioactive substance.

July 4 Marie Curie dies. She discovered two elements, studied radioactivity, invented the Geiger counter, and developed the method of chemical analysis known as fractionation or fractional crystallization. Albert Einstein said of her, "Marie Curie is, of all celebrated beings, the only one whom fame has not corrupted." Her later years were difficult; she developed cataracts, kidney problems, pernicious anemia, and other ailments associated with her overexposure to radioactivity, and many male colleagues tried to attribute her best work to her late husband, Pierre.

Education and Scholarship

U.S. urban planner Catherine Bauer publishes *Modern Housing*.

Puerto Rican educator, folklorist, writer, and feminist

María Cadilla de Martínez becomes the only female member of the Puerto Rican Historical Academy.

Religion

Australian aboriginal ritual leader and artist Dolly Granites is born.

Evangeline Booth, daughter of founder William Booth, becomes general of the Salvation Army.

French Daughters of Charity founder Louise de Marillac is canonized and made patron saint of social workers.

1935

General Status and Daily Life

In Germany, midwives' organizations are nationalized, and homes are founded for unmarried mothers of "hereditarily valuable" children.

Thailand makes the husband the head of household; his wife must have his permission to start a business, hold a job, apply for a passport, or conclude a business contract.

Government, the Military, and the Law

María Elena Jiménez de Crovo, Colombia's first woman minister of labor, is born.

Literature and the Visual Arts

Danish poet, teacher, playwright, and novelist Inger Christensen and Greek architect Suzana Antonakakis are born.

Influential Austrian-British potter Lucie Rie (b. 1902) wins a gold medal at the Brussels Exhibition.

German artist Käthe Kollwitz completes her last print cycle, a set of eight lithographs entitled *Death*.

New poetry collections include Marianne Moore's *Selected Poems*, American Muriel Rukeyser's (1913–1980) *Theory of Flight*, and Italian feminist Sibilla Aleramo's *Si alla terra*.

New U.S. children's books include Laura Ingalls Wilder's *Little House on the Prairie*, in which she describes her pioneer childhood, and Carol Ryrie Brink's Newbery-winning *Caddie Woodlawn*, also a novel about a pioneer girl.

New American plays include Clare Boothe Luce's *Abide with Me* and Zoë Akins's Pulitzer-winning *The Old Maid*.

Performing Arts and Entertainment

Billie Holiday sings at the Apollo Theatre.

U.S. author and film critic Iris Barry (1895–December 22, 1969) becomes the first curator of MoMA's film library.

U.S. actress Shirley Temple, now starring in *Curly Top*, begins three years as the biggest box office draw in Hollywood.

U.S. dancer Doris Humphrey begins choreographing a trilogy: *New Dance*, *Theatre Piece*, and *With My Red Fires*.

U.S. lyricist Dorothy Fields writes the lyrics for *Every Night at Eight*, including the lyrics for the song "I'm in the Mood for Love."

U.S. theater educator, administrator, and director Hallie Flanagan (1890–1969) becomes head of the Federal Theatre Project, a position she will hold until 1939. She will be ousted by the House Un-American Activities Committee (HUAC), one of whose members will ask her if *Doctor Faustus*'s author Marlowe is a communist.

U.S. actress Lynn Fontanne (December 6, 1887–July 30, 1983) stars in *Taming of the Shrew* in New York.

Norwegian soprano Kirsten Flagstad (July 12, 1895–1962) makes her New York debut as Sieglinde. Within one season, she is acknowledged as the dominant star in American opera.

Filmgoers can see Bette Davis in *Dangerous* (for which she wins the Best Actress Academy Award), Greta Garbo in *Anna Karenina*, Jean Harlow in *Reckless* and *China Seas*, and Mae West in *I'm No Angel*.

In the United States, screenwriter Margaret Booth writes *Mutiny on the Bounty*, film editor Barbara R. McLean receives an Academy Award nomination for *Les Miserables*, and stage and costume designer Aline Bernstein designs two RKO movies, *She* and *The Last Days of Pompeii*.

Athletics and Exploration

New Zealand aviator Jean Gardner Batten becomes the first woman to fly the South Atlantic from England to Brazil, breaking the men's record time in the process.

British bridge player Rika "Rixi" Markus, the first woman grandmaster of the World Bridge Federation, wins her first European Women's Championship. She will win eleven more championships by 1974.

Tennis player Hilde Sperling wins the French Open. She will repeat her victory in 1936 and 1937.

U.S. explorer Mary Akeley leads an expedition to the African Transvaal for New York's American Museum of Natural History.

U.S. pilot Jacqueline Cochran becomes the first woman participant in the trans-American Bendix Race.

Amelia Earhart becomes the first person to solo from Honolulu, Hawaii, to California.

Activism

U.S. feminist Ruth Woodsmall becomes general secretary of the World's YWCA, a position she will hold until 1947.

American Indian political leader and journalist Alice Jemison (October 9, 1901–1964), editor of the newspaper *The First American*, becomes the spokesperson for the American Indian Federation.

Egyptian feminist Huda Shaarawi calls for an end to polygamy.

Chinese activist Liu Tsui leads a student demonstration against Japan and is beaten by police.

WILPF amasses 8 million signatures on an international peace petition.

Belgian feminist Martha Bol Poel becomes president of the International Council of Women.

Dutch feminist Rosa Manus organizes an International Women's Conference in Istanbul.

Greek communist and resistance fighter Electra Apolstoloy (b. 1912) goes to Paris as the representative of Greek women to the International Conference Against Fascism.

Jan. 15 U.S. clubwoman Mary Sherman (b. December 11, 1862), who fought successfully for the creation of national parks in the Rockies and Grand Canyon and for the creation of the National Park Service, dies.

Dec. Several organizations merge to form the National Council of Negro Women (NCNW); Mary McLeod Bethune becomes the group's first president, a position she will hold until December 1949. Educator and NCNW cofounder Lucy Slowe becomes the group's first secretary.

Business and Industry

Indian educator Abala Bose establishes a Women's Industrial Cooperative Home in Calcutta.

Finnish designer and entrepreneur Armi Ratia (1912–1979) establishes her own weaving company.

Jan. 16 U.S. outlaw Kate "Ma" Barker is killed in a shoot-out with the Federal Bureau of Investigation (FBI).

Sept. 15 Germany outlaws the employment of Aryan women under thirty-five as servants by Jews.

Science and Medicine

French physicist Irène Joliot-Curie shares the Nobel Prize for Physics for her production of artificial radioactivity.

U.S. anthropologist Margaret Mead publishes *Sex and Temperament in Three Primitive Societies*, a work that challenges Western assumptions about masculinity and femininity.

Apr. 12 German mathematician Emmy Noether, after fleeing Germany for America and finding work at Bryn Mawr and Princeton, dies. Her influential approach to algebra, especially noncommutative algebras, inspired the "Noether School" of mathematics.

Education and Scholarship

New publications include Sidney and Beatrice Webb's *Soviet Communism: A New Civilization?*, the result of a trip they took to the Soviet Union in 1932; English suffragist Sylvia Pankhurst's *Life of Emmeline Pankhurst*; U.S. anthropologist Zora Neale Hurston's *Mules and Men*, a collection of folklore from the black cultures of the American South and the Caribbean; and U.S. author Mari Sandoz's biography of her father, *Old Jules*, which wins the $5,000 nonfiction prize from *Atlantic Monthly*.

U.S. educator Mary McLeod Bethune wins the NAACP's Springarn Medal.

Religion

U.S. theologian Georgia Harkness (April 21, 1891–August 21, 1974) publishes *Holy Flame*, a collection of religious poetry.

1936

General Status and Daily Life

India's Parsi Marriage and Divorce Act allows Parsi women to divorce their husbands if the husbands force them into prostitution.

Colombia's Penal Code allows the acquittal of a husband (but not a wife) after the murder of a spouse if the killer is "beside himself with anger and despair" at discovering the spouse has committed adultery.

Stalin virtually outlaws abortion in the Soviet Union.

The *chador*, a black veil that covers a woman's entire body except her face, is outlawed in Iran.

Government, the Military, and the Law

The first women are elected to Cuba's House of Representatives.

Finnish politician and feminist Miina Sillanpää becomes speaker of Parliament, a position she will hold until 1947.

Spanish politician Federica Montseny becomes minister of health.

Jan. First Lady Eleanor Roosevelt (October 11, 1884–November 7, 1962) begins writing a syndicated column, "My Day."

June U.S. educator and civil rights administrator Mary McLeod Bethune becomes head of Negro Affairs in the National Youth Administration (NYA).

July U.S. federal official Helen Woodward becomes director of the Women's and Professional Division of the Works Progress Administration (WPA), in charge of relief programs for women as well as federal arts projects.

Dec. Edward VIII of England abdicates so that he can

marry the twice-divorced American Wallis Warfield Simpson (b. 1896).

Literature and the Visual Arts

Russian poet and translator Natalya Gorbanyevskaya is born. A frequent demonstrator against the government, she will be arrested in 1969, found insane, and not released until 1972. Also born this year is Polish-Israeli textile designer and quilter Shulamit Litan.

Venezuela's first woman journalist, Carmen Clemente Travieso, begins printing cultural columns for women in several newspapers.

U.S. writer and civil rights advocate Lillian Smith (b. 1898) founds the journal *Pseudopodia* (later *South Today*), the first white-run southern magazine to publish black authors' works.

The American Academy of Arts and Letters holds a 171-work retrospective of Anna Hyatt Huntington's sculpture.

U.S. sculptor Adelaide Johnson's sculpture of Susan B. Anthony is used as the model for the three-cent postage stamp.

New poetry includes Estonian poet Betti Alver's (b. 1906) *Dust and Fire* and *Starry Hour*, Marianne Moore's *The Pangolin and Other Verse*, and Dorothy Parker's *Not So Deep as a Well*.

American Margaret Mitchell (November 8, 1900–August 16, 1949) publishes the Pulitzer Prize-winning novel *Gone with the Wind*, which sells a record 1 million copies in six months. A long historical novel, it is set in the South before, during, and after the Civil War. Its heroine, Scarlett O'Hara, is notable for her ruthless self-interest.

Other new novels include U.S. children's author and storyteller Ruth Sawyer's Newbery-winning *Roller Skates*, English mystery novelist Dorothy Sayers's *Gaudy Night*, British author Rebecca West's *The Thinking Reed*, English poet Stevie Smith's *Novel on Yellow Paper*, and U.S. author Djuna Barnes's most famous novel, *Nightwood*, a tale of desperation set in Paris.

Marjorie Kinnan Rawlings publishes the short story "A Mother in Mannville."

British potter Lucie Rie wins a gold medal at the Milan Triennale.

Painter Dame Laura Knight is admitted to the English Royal Academy, which has almost entirely barred women since its founding. However, she will not be invited to the academy's annual banquet until 1967.

German antiwar artist Käthe Kollwitz's work is banned by the Nazis.

New U.S. plays include Edna Ferber's *Stage Door*, Lillian Hellman's *Days to Come*, and Clare Boothe Luce's most famous work, *The Women*.

Alice Trumbull Mason (1904–1971) begins twenty-seven years of leadership in the American Abstract Artists group, which she serves as treasurer, secretary, and, eventually, president.

Feb. U.S. journalist Dorothy Thompson's "On the Record" column begins appearing in the *New York Herald Tribune*; it will eventually be syndicated in over 170 newspapers.

Mar. U.S. photographer Dorothea Lange's (b. May 26, 1895) landmark Depression photograph, "Migrant Mother, Nipomo, California," is run by hundreds of publications throughout the United States.

May 25 U.S. journalist Winifred Sweet Black (b. October 14, 1863), better known by her pen name "Annie Laurie," dies. A favorite employee of publisher William Randolph Hearst's, she wrote for several papers, including the *San Francisco Examiner*, the *New York Journal*, and the *Denver Post*. Stereotyped as a sentimental "sob sister," she covered many stories considered atypical for a woman and was probably the first female reporter to cover a prizefight.

June U.S. journalist Anne O'Hare McCormick becomes the first woman on the editorial board of the *New York Times*; she will remain on the board until her death in 1954.

Nov. 23 The cover of the first issue of *Life* magazine, a photograph of a New Deal engineering project, is by U.S. photographer Margaret Bourke-White.

Performing Arts and Entertainment

U.S. burlesque queen Gypsy Rose Lee (January 9, 1914?–April 26, 1970) and U.S. dancer Josephine Baker appear in the *Ziegfeld Follies*.

Filmgoers can see Hattie McDaniel in *Show Boat*, Jeannette MacDonald (June 18, 1903?–January 14, 1965) in *San Francisco* (written by Anita Loos), Jean Harlow and Myrna Loy in *Libeled Lady*, Shirley Temple in *Dimples*, Ginger Rogers in *Swingtime*, Paulette Goddard in *Modern Times*, and Greta Garbo in *Camille* (written by Margaret Booth). Luise Rainer wins the Best Actress Oscar for *The Great Ziegfeld*, which also stars Fanny

Brice; Swedish actress Ingrid Bergman (August 29, 1915–August 29, 1982) stars in *Intermezzo* and comes to the attention of producer David Selznick, who brings her to Hollywood.

U.S. screenwriter Adele Comandini receives an Academy Award nomination for *Three Smart Girls*. Other movies written by women this year include *Anything Goes* and *The General Died at Dawn* (Eda Warren), *Craig's Wife* (Viola Lawrence), *Pigskin Parade* (Irene Morra), and *Suzy* (Dorothy Parker).

Russian ballerina Natalya Dudinskaya is the first to perform *Laurencia*.

Norwegian soprano Kirsten Flagstad appears to great acclaim at London's Covent Garden.

U.S. film editor Barbara McLean receives an Academy Award nomination for *Lloyds of London*. French film editor Marguerite Renoir works on *Le Crime de Monsieur Lange* and *Les Bas Fonds*.

Spanish filmmaker Rosario Pi directs *The Wild Cat*.

U.S. lyricist Dorothy Fields wins an Oscar for "The Way You Look Tonight."

French singer Edith Piaf (December 19, 1915–October 11, 1963) makes her radio debut.

Lynn Fontanne stars in *Idiot's Delight* on Broadway, Judith Anderson plays Gertrude to John Gielgud's *Hamlet*, and British actress Peggy Ashcroft stars in *The Seagull*.

Athletics and Exploration

Irish athlete Thelma Hopkins, adept at high jumping, hockey, squash, long jumping, and pentathlon, is born.

Aviator Sophie Heath (b. 1896) dies. The first woman pilot hired by Royal Dutch Airlines, she passed a series of tests that forced the licensing of women as commercial pilots.

British bush pilot Beryl Markham (1902–1986) becomes the first person to fly the Atlantic solo from east to west, a harder task than from west to east because of prevailing headwinds.

American Alice Marble wins the U.S. Open. She will repeat her U.S. victory in 1938, 1939, and 1940, and will win at Wimbledon in 1939.

British pilot Amy Johnson (b. 1903) flies from England to Cape Town, South Africa, in three days, six hours, twenty-five minutes. New Zealand pilot Jean Batten flies solo from England to New Zealand in eleven days fifty-six minutes.

At the winter games in Garmisch-Partenkirchen, Norwegian figure skater Sonja Henie wins her third Olympic gold. Germany's Maxi Herber and Ernst Baier take the gold in pairs skating. In combined skiing, a measure of both downhill and slalom skills, Christl Cranz of Germany takes the gold.

At the summer games in Berlin, American Dorothy Poynton wins the platform diving event, and the United States sweeps the springboard diving medals. Marjorie Gestring, only thirteen, wins the gold. Katherine Rawls (a bronze medalist in the 4 x 100-meter freestyle relay) takes the silver, and Poynton picks up a second medal, getting the bronze.

U.S. swimmer Eleanor Holm, a heroine of the 1932 Games and now married, drinks and dances on the ship to Germany and is barred from the team, to the horror of the press. Dutch swimmer Hendrika Mastenbroek wins the 100-meter and 400-meter freestyle and takes a silver in the 100-meter backstroke, setting Olympic records in the first two events. She is defeated in the backstroke by her own teammate, Dina W. Senff. The Dutch are shut out of the medals in the 200-meter breaststroke, which is won by Hideko Maehata of Japan, but they win the 4 x 100-meter freestyle relay. Senff is not on the winning relay team, but Mastenbroek is, along with Johanna Selbach, Catherina Wagner, and Willemijntje den Ouden.

In fencing, Ilona Elek of Hungary wins the individual foil event, followed by Hélène Mayer of Germany and Ellen Preis of Austria. Mayer, half Jewish, raises her hand on the podium in a Nazi salute. The team gymnastics event, not held since 1928, is won by Germany. The Czechoslovakian team takes the silver; at least one of its members, Zdenka Vermirovska, will be on the gold medal team of 1948.

In track and field, high jumper Gretel Bergmann, setter of a national record of 1.60 meters, is kept off the German team because she is Jewish. Hungary's Ibolya Csák wins the high jump after tying with Great Britain's Dorothy Odam. German Gisela Maurmayer sets a discus record of 47.63 meters. German Tilly Fleischer, the bronze medalist in 1932 in her sport, takes the gold in the javelin with a throw of 45.18 meters. Helen Stephens of the United States wins the 100-meter dash and runs on the gold medal 4 x 100-meter relay team. Italy's Trebisonda Valla wins the hurdles.

Activism

French feminist Marguerite Durand (b. 1865), who founded the world's first daily women's newspaper, *La fronde*, dies.

The Argentine Union of Women, led by Victoria Ocampo, is formed. Its goal is to stop a proposed "reform" of the civil code that would again reduce married women to legal minors, unable to control their wages or to work without their husbands' permission.

The Venezuelan Women's Association is founded.

Greek communist and resistance fighter Electra Apostoloy is sentenced to two years in jail for her antifascist activities.

Science and Medicine

U.S. doctor Elise L'Esperance becomes editor of the *Medical Women's Journal*, a position she will hold until 1941.

Birth control information is ruled to be no longer "obscene" under the U.S. Comstock Act.

Lya Imber, Venezuela's first woman doctor, receives her degree.

Education and Scholarship

In Germany, women have been banned from all professorial posts.

Religion

U.S. theologian Mary Lyman publishes *The Christian Epic*.

In Germany, women are barred from the clergy.

U.S. classicist Edith Hamilton publishes *Prophets of Israel*.

1937

General Status and Daily Life

Adultery is decriminalized in Sweden.

In Egypt, abortion is outlawed except in cases of threat to the woman's life or health or a proven fetal defect.

Government, the Military, and the Law

Women's suffrage is legalized in the Philippines.

German feminist politician Marie-Elizabeth Luders is arrested by the Gestapo and exiled.

Sept.   South African politician Margaret Ballinger stands for Parliament at the request of the ANC. She wins and will remain in office for twenty-two years, when she will be ejected by the passage of the Bantu Self-Government Act.

Literature and the Visual Arts

Margaret Bourke-White publishes *You Have Seen Their Faces*, a collection of photos of southern sharecroppers. Her photo of this year, "The Louisville Flood," shows relief lines under a billboard that proclaims: "World's Highest Standard of Living—There's No Way Like the American Way."

U.S. photographer Berenice Abbott (b. 1898) publishes *Changing New York*.

Swiss artist Sophie Taeuber-Arp (1889–1943), noted for her work in abstract painting, decorative arts and relief sculpture, establishes a short-lived art journal, *Plastique*.

The centerpiece of the Soviet exhibit at the Paris World's Fair is an eighty-foot statue of collective farmers, male and female, by Vera Mukhina.

New poetry includes *The Girl's Country*, by Romanian Maria Banus (b. 1914), who published her first work at age fourteen; Edna St. Vincent Millay's *Conversation at Midnight*; Korean poet Mo Yun-suk's love epic *Wren ui aeka* (*Elegy of a Wren*); Sara Teasdale's posthumous *Collected Poems*; Puerto Rican poet Julia de Burgos's first collection, *Poemas Exactos A Mí Misma* (*Exact Poems to Myself*); U.S. poet and critic Louise Bogan's *The Sleeping Fury*; and *A Good Time Was Had By All*, by English poet Florence Margaret "Stevie" Smith (1902–1971).

Danish author Isak Dinesen publishes *Out of Africa*.

U.S. author Zora Neale Hurston publishes her best novel, *Their Eyes Were Watching God*. Its heroine is independent, sensual, sexual, rebellious, and vividly alive. Another notable novel of 1937 is English mystery writer Dorothy Sayers's last novel, *Busman's Honeymoon*, in which Sayers's witty, self-mocking detective, Lord Peter Wimsey, manages to marry his longtime love, the practical, fiercely independent mystery writer Harriet Vane. Other new novels include American author Mari Sandoz's (May 11, 1896–March 10, 1959) *Slogum House* and Italian feminist Sibilla Aleramo's *Il frustino*.

U.S. editor Betsy Talbot Blackwell becomes editor in chief of *Mademoiselle* magazine.

Feb. 22   U.S. science fiction writer Joanna Russ is born.

Performing Arts and Entertainment

American Maude Valérie White (b. 1855), author and composer of about 200 songs, and Russian pianist Annette Essipoff (b. 1855) die. Particularly well known for her interpretations of Chopin, Essipoff was the teacher of several other great musicians, including Prokofiev.

U.S. dancer and choreographer Helen Tamiris becomes the first president of the American Dance Association and explores race relations in her award-winning *How Long, Brethren?*

U.S. stage director Margaret Webster (b. March 15, 1905) directs the first production of *Richard II* since 1878.

French composer, conductor, and music teacher Nadia Boulanger becomes the first woman to conduct a symphony orchestra in London.

Movie audiences can see Hattie McDaniel and "blonde bombshell" Jean Harlow (d. June 7) in *Saratoga*, Joan Crawford (d. 1977) in *The Bride Wore Red* (directed by Dorothy Arzner and edited by Adrienne Fazan), and Luise Rainer as O-lan in *The Good Earth* (for which she wins the Best Actress Oscar). Judy Garland (Frances Ethel Gumm, June 10, 1922–June 22, 1969) sings "You Made Me Love You" in *Broadway Melody of 1938* and stars with Mickey Rooney in *Thoroughbreds Don't Cry*.

In the United States, the Andrews Sisters, a popular singing group, have their first hit, "Bei Mir Bist Du Schon."

Movies written by women include *Dead End* (Lillian Hellman) and *A Star Is Born* (Dorothy Parker). U.S. screenwriters Mildred Cram and Viña Delmar receive Academy Award nominations for *Love Affair* and *The Awful Truth*, respectively.

One of the few women film producers of the 1930s, Fanny Wolfe, produces *Turn Off the Moon* and *Thrill of a Lifetime*.

Egyptian actress Bahija Hafez, head of Fanar Film, produces and stars in *Laila, Bint al Sahra* (*Laila, Daughter of the Desert*).

French film editor Marguerite Renoir works on *Le Grande Illusion*.

Sept. 26   U.S. blues singer Bessie Smith dies after a car accident when a segregated white hospital refuses to accept her as a patient. Nicknamed "the Empress of the Blues," she recorded with Louis Armstrong and Benny Goodman; her first album, *Downhearted Blues*, sold 2 million copies.

Athletics and Exploration

Chilean tennis player Anita Lizana wins the U.S. singles title.

New Zealand aviator Jean Gardner Batten sets a record time from Australia to England.

July 2   U.S. aviator Amelia Earhart, attempting to circumnavigate the globe, disappears somewhere near Howland Island in the Pacific Ocean. Earhart established a women's flying group, the Ninety-Nines.

Sept. 21   U.S. pilot Jacqueline Cochran sets a women's speed record of 292 miles per hour.

Activism

U.S. Zionist Henrietta Szold travels to Germany to further the efforts of Youth Aliyah, which helps Jewish children escape Nazi persecution and flee to Israel.

U.S. pacifist Emily Greene Balch becomes the honorary international president of WILPF.

Business and Industry

U.S. journalist sisters Bess and Lucile Furman establish the free-lance news service Furman Features.

U.S. entrepreneur Margaret Rudkin (September 14, 1897–June 1, 1967) begins baking and selling high-quality bread at her Connecticut home, Pepperidge Farm.

Science and Medicine

The AMA recognizes birth control as legitimate course material for medical schools.

Austrian scientist Marietta Blau (1893–1970) studies cosmic radiation using photographic plates.

Austrian-English psychoanalyst Anna Freud (December 3, 1895–October 9, 1982), daughter of Sigmund Freud, publishes *The Ego and the Mechanisms of Defense*.

German-American psychoanalyst Karen Horney (September 16, 1885–1952) publishes *The Neurotic Personality of Our Time*. She will ultimately reject Freud's theory of penis envy, postulating that the reverse is true and that men actually suffer from "womb envy."

Education and Scholarship

The Nazis ban the use of the title "Frau Doktor" for female doctors or professors. It is now to be used only for the wives of men with advanced degrees.

May 3 U.S. archaeologist Esther Van Deman (b. October 1, 1862), an expert on ancient Roman building techniques, dies. She was the world's first woman Roman field archaeologist.

1938

General Status and Daily Life

Cuba's Social Defense Code outlaws abortion and prostitution and makes sexual harassment punishable by one to six years in jail and sets penalties of four to thirty years or death for various kinds of rape.

In Germany, spouses in mixed marriages are encouraged to divorce each other. Refusal to conceive children or an attempt to seek an abortion is grounds for divorce, as is infertility, but not if the couple has already had children. Divorce by mutual consent is permitted if the couple has been separated for at least three years.

Sweden ends its ban on contraception and sex education. Abortion is legalized in limited circumstances.

Apr. 12 New York becomes the first state to require medical tests for marriage licenses.

Government, the Military, and the Law

Women are admitted to unarmed military divisions in France.

Crystal Bird Fauset of Pennsylvania becomes the first black woman in America elected to a state legislature.

Stella Reading becomes head of Britain's Women's Voluntary Service, which is in charge of rationing and, in air raids, care of victims and evacuation.

Literature and the Visual Arts

New poetry collections include American Muriel Rukeyser's *U.S. 1*, Gabriela Mistral's *Tala (Felling)*, Korean No Ch'on-myong's (1913–1957) *Sanhorim (Red Coral Reef)*, Stevie Smith's *Tender Any to One*, Alfonsina Storni's (d. October 25) *Mascarillo y trébol*, and Puerto Rican poet Julia de Burgos's *Poema en Veinte Surcos (Poem in Twenty Furrows)*.

U.S. painter Loren MacIver (b. 1909), noted for her urban motifs, has her first solo exhibition in New York.

Pearl S. Buck becomes the first U.S. woman to win the Nobel Prize for Literature.

U.S. author Marjorie Kinnan Rawlings publishes the Pulitzer Prize-winning novel *The Yearling*. Other new novels include French novelist Nathalie Sarraute's (b. 1902) *Tropismes*, Elizabeth Bowen's *The Death of the Heart*, Stevie Smith's *Over the Frontier*, Pearl S. Buck's *The Proud Heart*, Daphne du Maurier's *Rebecca*, and Rachel Field's *All This, and Heaven Too*.

July 16 U.S. journalist Leonel Ross Anthony O'Bryan, better known as "Polly Pry" to her Denver readers, dies. She wrote such a good story about a fire that a *New York World* editor who at first threatened to spank her eventually gave her a job. She wrote pulp fiction, championed cannibal Alferd Packer, founded her own outrageous magazine, *Polly Pry*, in which she covered everything from sports to social gossip, and claimed to be the victim of an assassination attempt by the unions she strenuously opposed.

Aug. The entire financial department of the New York *Post* is fired at noon one day. At 4:00 P.M., reporter Sylvia Porter shows up and is given a column in exchange for taking over all the duties of the fired staff. Her byline is S. F. Porter, and she is not revealed as a woman until 1942.

Performing Arts and Entertainment

German *Lieder* singer and Salzburg Festival regular Elisabeth Schwarzkopf (b. 1915) makes her opera debut in *Parsifal* in Berlin.

U.S. actress and theatrical director Antoinette Perry (June 27, 1888–June 28, 1946), namesake of Broadway's Tony Awards, directs the play *Kiss the Boys Goodbye*, written by Clare Boothe Luce.

German film director Leni Riefenstahl makes a two-part documentary about the Berlin Olympics: *Olympiad: Fest der Völker (Festival of Nations)* and *Olympiad:*

Fest der Schönheit (*Festival of Beauty*). Contrary to orders from Goebbels, she features black American athlete Jesse Owens prominently in the first film. The pair of movies wins the Grand Prize at the Venice International Film Festival.

Film actress Hedy Lamarr makes her U.S. debut in *Algiers*, in which Charles Boyer entreats her to "come with me to the Casbah." Other notable films are *The Adventures of Robin Hood*, with Olivia de Havilland as Maid Marian; *Jezebel*, with Bette Davis as a rebellious Southern belle (for which she wins the Best Actress Oscar); *Hôtel du Nord*, with French actress Arletty; and *Bringing Up Baby* and *Holiday*, with Katharine Hepburn. Judy Garland stars in the first of three "Andy Hardy" movies.

At the Academy Awards, U.S. screenwriter Lenore Coffee is nominated for *Four Daughters*, and American film editor Barbara McLean receives nominations for *In Old Chicago* and *Alexander's Ragtime Band*.

French conductor Nadia Boulanger becomes the first woman to give regular subscription concerts with the Boston Symphony Orchestra.

U.S. costume and fashion designer Edith Head becomes the first female chief designer at a major film studio. In the next five years she will work on over 150 movies.

English actress Sybil Thorndike plays Miss Moffat in *The Corn Is Green*.

Apr. 1 In a major challenge to the studio system, which controls stars' social lives, salaries, and choice of roles, Bette Davis is suspended by Warner Brothers for refusing to play a part assigned her.

Nov. 11 On her radio show, U.S. singer Kate Smith becomes the first person to perform Irving Berlin's "God Bless America." She and the song will become closely identified with each other.

Athletics and Exploration

U.S. pilot Jacqueline Cochran wins the trans-American Bendix Race.

U.S. feminist, explorer, and writer Grace Gallatin Seton describes the matriarchal society of Vietnam's Moi tribes in *Poison Arrows*.

July 29 Jenny Kammersgaad becomes the first person to swim the Baltic Sea. She completes the thirty-seven-mile crossing in forty hours.

Activism

Hitler outlaws all independent women's organizations.

Vietnamese communist and feminist Nguyen Thi Kim Anh publishes *The Woman Question*, attacking both sexism and colonialism.

Pakistani political leader Fatima Jinnah leads the All-India Muslim Women's Committee.

Business and Industry

Westinghouse's company manual says that no man, regardless of his position, will be paid less than the highest-paid woman in the company.

The U.S. Fair Labor Standards Act guarantees a minimum wage for many women, although women in jobs like domestic service and agricultural labor are not affected.

Science and Medicine

Geologist Alice Wilson (d. 1964) becomes the first woman member of the Royal Society of Canada.

The United States has 300 birth control clinics.

German paleontologist Tilly Edinger, who has managed surreptitiously, though a Jew, to keep her museum job, is discovered by the Nazis and forced to quit. She will leave Germany next year. Mathematician Hanna von Cammerer Neumann (d. 1971) leaves this year for England; she is an Aryan but wishes to marry a man who is not.

The German Midwives' Law guarantees every pregnant woman care by a midwife. Women in labor are encouraged to call out Hitlerr's name to ease their pain.

U.S. anthropologist Gladys Reichard publishes *Handbook of American Indian Languages*.

Mar. 13 Austria becomes part of the Third Reich, and Austrians in Germany, including physicist Lise Meitner, are now German citizens and subject to anti-Semitic laws. Meitner, who has been trying to immerse herself in work so as not to notice political changes, is now forced to flee. Her coworker Otto Hahn gives her an heirloom diamond ring so that she will have some source of funds, and she escapes into the Netherlands with help from the Dutch government.

May 5 U.S. pathologist and pediatrician Dorothy Andersen (May 15, 1901–March 3, 1963) announces her discovery of cystic fibrosis.

Education and Scholarship

Laimi Leidenius (b. 1877), the first woman full professor at the University of Helsinki and the first president of the Finnish Federation of University Women, dies.

U.S. educator Genevieve Caulfield (b. 1888), blind from infancy, opens a school for the blind in Thailand.

English author Virginia Woolf publishes the feminist, antiwar essay *Three Guineas*, which draws parallels between patriarchy and fascism.

1939

General Status and Daily Life

U.S. housewives listen to an average of 6.6 radio soaps per day.

Nylon stockings and the first fully automatic electric washing machines appear.

Aug. 12 Mother's Day in Germany is now celebrated today, the anniversary of Hitler's mother's birth. Three million women who have borne at least four children are awarded the Honor Cross of the German Mother. They are to be saluted by any members of the Hitler Youth who see them wearing the decoration.

Government, the Military, and the Law

Kenyan social worker and politician Jael Mbogo is born.

In the Soviet Union, 14.5% of the Communist party is female.

Mona James becomes the first native-born woman barrister in Trinidad.

A woman is named head of the Soviet international airline.

Literature and the Visual Arts

Israeli textile designer, painter, potter, and sculptor

Siona Shimshi is born.

Welsh painter Gwen John (1876–September 18) and Korean author Paek Sin-ae (b. 1908) die. Paek's best-known work is "Poverty-Stricken," which describes a virtuous widow struggling to keep her family alive.

Hilla Rebay (May 31, 1890–September 27, 1967), curator of the Solomon R. Guggenheim Foundation, organizes and becomes the first director of the Guggenheim Museum. Later, she will choose Frank Lloyd Wright to design the museum's permanent building.

U.S. sculptor Augusta Savage, the only black woman artist to receive a commission for the New York World's Fair, creates "Lift Every Voice and Sing" for that event.

U.S. photographer Margaret Bourke-White publishes her pictures of Czechoslovakia in *North of the Danube*.

Children's author Elizabeth Enright wins a Newbery Medal for *Thimble Summer*.

German Dadaist artist Hannah Höch (b. 1889), coinventor of the genre of photomontage, is forced into retirement in the countryside by the Nazis.

New novels include Zora Neale Hurston's *Moses, Man of the Mountain*, Laura Ingalls Wilder's *By the Shores of Silver Lake*, and Australian Henry Handel Richardson's *Young Cosima*.

U.S. author Katherine Anne Porter publishes *Pale Horse, Pale Rider: Three Short Novels*.

Oct. A long-lasting feud erupts between rival Hollywood gossip columnists Hedda Hopper (b. May 2, 1885) and Louella Parsons (August 6, 1881–December 9, 1972).

Performing Arts and Entertainment

Brazilian ballerina Marcia Haydée is born.

The biggest movie event of the year is the cinematic version of Margaret Mitchell's novel *Gone with the Wind*. It stars Vivien Leigh (1913–July 8, 1967) as Scarlett O'Hara and Olivia De Havilland as Melanie Wilkes and has strong supporting performances by Hattie McDaniel (June 10, 1895?–October 26, 1952) as Mammy and Butterfly McQueen as Prissy. McDaniel, who will later become famous as radio's and television's "Beulah," wins the Oscar for Best Supporting Actress and thus becomes the first black actor to win an Academy Award. Leigh wins the Best Actress Oscar.

She has some stiff competition. Judy Garland appears in *Babes in Arms* and *The Wizard of Oz*. In the latter movie, she sings the song "Over the Rainbow," which becomes so closely identified with her that she will use it as her traditional concert finale. Greta Garbo stars in *Ninotchka*, in which she plays a stern Soviet official seduced by the decadent pleasures of the West. Bette Davis stars in *Dark Victory* and *The Women*, and Marlene Dietrich stars in *Destry Rides Again*. U.S. actress Rita Hayworth (1918–1987) stars in *Only Angels Have Wings*, and French actress Arletty stars in *Le jour se lève* (*Daybreak*). British actress Ida Lupino (b. 1918), the only major woman film director in 1950s Hollywood, achieves stardom in *The Light That Failed*.

U.S. film editor Barbara McLean receives an Academy Award nomination for *The Rains Came*. Dorothy Spencer receives a nomination for her editing of *Stagecoach*. French film editor Marguerite Renoir works on *La regle du jeu* (*The Rules of the Game*).

Tallulah Bankhead stars in New York as Regina Giddens in Lillian Hellman's *The Little Foxes*, for which American stage and costume designer Aline Bernstein designed the sets.

Betty Grable (b. December 18, 1916) and Ethel Merman (b. January 16, 1909) star on Broadway in *Du Barry Was a Lady*.

Irish dancer and choreographer Ninette de Valois stages a production of *The Sleeping Princess*, with Margot Fonteyn (1919–1991) in the lead role.

Theresa Helburn's Theatre Guild produces *The Philadelphia Story*, which opens on Broadway on March 28, with Katharine Hepburn in the starring role as Tracy Lord, a rich society woman about to embark upon her second marriage.

English composer Elisabeth Lutyens writes her First Chamber Concerto.

French conductor Nadia Boulanger becomes the first woman to give regular subscription concerts with the New York Philharmonic.

Feb. 27 U.S. contralto Marian Anderson (1902–April 1993) is refused permission to sing at Constitution Hall in Washington, D.C., because she is black. She says, "I am shocked beyond words to be barred from the capital of my country after having appeared in almost every other capital in the world." First Lady Eleanor Roosevelt, outraged, resigns from the DAR, which operates Constitution Hall, and arranges for Anderson to sing on the steps of the Lincoln Memorial instead. On Easter Sunday, April 9, Anderson performs before an audience of 75,000.

Dec. 22 U.S. blues singer Gertrude "Ma" Rainey (b. April 16, 1886) dies.

Athletics and Exploration

English cricketer Rachel Heyhoe Flint, pioneering woman sportscaster and eleven-time captain of the English women's cricket team, is born.

Activism

Dolores Ibarruri, Spanish communist and anti-Franco orator, who once cried, "It is better to die on your feet than to live on your knees!" flees Spain.

Business and Industry

A U.S. survey reveals that a majority of insurance, banking, and public utility companies have policies against hiring women.

Dorothy Schiff becomes the first woman newspaper publisher in New York City when she acquires a majority interest in the *New York Post*. She will control the paper until 1976, serving as owner, editor-in-chief, president, and treasurer.

Jan. 28 U.S. newspaper publisher Eleanor Patterson buys the *Washington Herald* and *Times* from William Randolph Hearst. Three days later, she combines them as the *Times-Herald* and soon makes it the best-selling paper in Washington.

Science and Medicine

French militant feminist and physician Madeleine Pelletier (b. 1874), the first woman in France licensed to practice in mental hospitals, editor of *La suffragiste*, and performer of illegal abortions, dies.

Archaeologist Marion Stirling becomes the first woman to conduct a scientific study of Mexico's Olmec civilization.

French physicist Marguérite Perey (1909–1975), a protegée of Marie Curie's, discovers element 87, francium.

Jan. 16 Austrian physicist Lise Meitner publishes the first report of uranium fission.

Sept. 30 U.S. pathologist and medical researcher Martha Wollstein (b. November 21, 1868) dies. She researched malaria, tuberculosis, typhoid fever, the connection between dysentery and infant diarrhea, polio, pneumonia, and mumps. She also published eighty scientific papers and helped to develop a new method for preparing and standardizing antimeningitis serum.

Education and Scholarship

In India, only about 3 million girls are in school (about 2% of the female population).

There are 306,000 girls and 912,067 boys in Korea's elementary schools, 9,537 girls and 19,343 boys in the high schools, and 2,046 women and 30,628 men in colleges, professional schools, and universities.

Australian welfare worker Daisy Bates (1861–1951) publishes *The Passing of the Aborigines*.

Religion

Mar. 29 U.S. nun and hospital administrator Sister Mary Joseph Dempsey (b. May 14, 1856) dies. Dr. William J. Mayo's first surgical assistant, she ran the Rochester, New York, St. Mary's Hospital with humor, strict discipline, and tight economy; if a surgeon tried to throw away a short length of catgut, she rapped his knuckles with a surgical instrument and reminded him that it could still be used.

1940

General Status and Daily Life

At the beginning of World War II, Stalin changes Soviet law so that the state, not fathers, will support illegitimate children. Women call it the "man's law" and clamor for its repeal, but it is not overturned until after Stalin's death.

Government, the Military, and the Law

Zimbabwe politician Naomi Nhiwatiwa, an advocate of banning the bride-price, is born.

The Republican party becomes the first major political party in the United States to support the ERA. Democrats oppose it for fear it would end protective legislation for women workers.

Nov. French resistance member Edwige de Saint-Wexel (b. 1923) takes part in a demonstration against the Nazi occupation. She is arrested by the Gestapo and tortured for three months. She is beaten, burned, starved, isolated, and not permitted to wash. Released in 1941, with an ankle crippled by an untreated dislocation, she returns to resistance work and helps to smuggle Jews and British pilots out of France.

Literature and the Visual Arts

Dorothy Kunhardt (b. 1901) invents tactile children's books with the publication of *Pat the Bunny*.

German poet Nelly Sachs (1891–1970) flees from Nazi Germany to Sweden with the help of novelist Selma Lagerlöf.

Mexican artist Frida Kahlo (1910–July 13, 1954), who takes her dominant images from folk art, paints *Self-Portrait with Cropped Hair*.

June U.S. author Carson McCullers publishes the novel *The Heart Is a Lonely Hunter*.

Oct. U.S. painter Anna Mary Robertson "Grandma" Moses (September 7, 1860–December 13, 1961), creator of about 1,500 paintings, has her first one-woman show in New York.

Performing Arts and Entertainment

English actress Mrs. Patrick Campbell (Beatrice Tanner, b. 1865) dies. She was especially noted for her performances in *Romeo and Juliet*, *Hamlet*, *The Second Mrs. Tanqueray*, *Pygmalion*, *The School for Scandal*, and the plays of Ibsen.

Anne Bauchens, honored for her work on *North West Mounted Police*, becomes the first woman to win an Academy Award for film editing.

U.S. filmgoers can see Mae Marsh in *The Grapes of Wrath*, Mae West in *My Little Chickadee*, Bette Davis in *All This and Heaven Too*, Rosalind Russell in *His Girl Friday* (in which she plays a hard-boiled reporter choosing between suburban marriage and her fast-paced career), Katharine Hepburn in *The Philadelphia Story*, and Joan Fontaine and Judith Anderson in *Rebecca* (written by British screenwriter Joan Harrison). Ginger Rogers wins the Best Actress Oscar for *Kitty Foyle*.

U.S. stage director Margaret Webster directs Helen Hayes in *Twelfth Night*.

Ethel Barrymore stars as Miss Moffat in *The Corn Is Green*; she will play the part for fourteen months in New York and two on tour.

Activism

U.S. radical and labor leader Elizabeth Gurley Flynn, one of the founders of the ACLU, is expelled for her membership in the Communist party.

June 16 Eleven-year-old Pakistani nationalist Saeeda Bano leads a small group of Muslim women in a parade for freedom.

Business and Industry

There are 13,190,000 Russian women in the work force, constituting 39% of the total labor force.

In the United States, 90% of employed women are working in only 11 of 451 job types. Some job types are overwhelmingly female; women are 91.3% of domestic servants, 93.5% of stenographers, typists, and secretaries, 75.7% of teachers, 97.9% of nurses, and 77.5% of apparel and accessories operatives. Conversely, some jobs are completely monopolized by men. There are no female fire fighters, soldiers, sailors, marines, or railroad conductors. About 20% of women are in the labor force, constituting 24.4% of the total labor force. Married women are 35.5% of the female work force.

Sept. 3 The first issue of *Newsday*, published, designed, and co-owned by U.S. journalist Alicia Patterson (d. July 2, 1963), is printed.

Science and Medicine

U.S. folklorist Elsie Clews Parsons is elected president of the American Anthropological Association.

U.S. microbiologist Gladys Hobby becomes part of the first team to treat patients with penicillin. She will later develop another antibiotic, Terramycin.

Sept. 1 U.S. public health nurse, settlement house worker, and social reformer Lillian D. Wald (b. March 10, 1867) dies. She cofounded the Henry Street Visiting Nurses Service in New York, coordinating the work of ninety-two nurses who made 200,000 home visits a year and almost single-handedly inventing the field of public health nursing.

Education and Scholarship

Australian-American economist and consumer advocate Persia Campbell publishes *Consumer Representation in the New Deal*.

Religion

Frenchwoman Euphrasia Pelletier and Italian laywoman Gemma Galgani are canonized.

1941

General Status and Daily Life

In Germany, the production and sale of all contraceptives are banned. Abortion is largely illegal, but about 600,000 abortions are still taking place every year.

Government, the Military, and the Law

Elisa Ochoa becomes the first female member of Parliament in the Philippines.

Three all-female Soviet regiments of pilots are formed. The 586th Women's Fighter Regiment will have a particularly illustrious record, and every member of the regiment will be decorated by war's end.

The Dutch colonial government grants women's suffrage in Indonesia.

The Nazis massacre Russians at Babi Yar; one of the few survivors, Grunie Melamud, climbs from under a pile of corpses and goes on to fight in the Red Army, winning eleven decorations for heroism.

Jan. 6 English aviator Amy Johnson is lost over the Thames Estuary while flying for the Women's Auxiliary Air Force. She was the first woman to fly the Atlantic east to west; she soloed from London to India and broke her own husband's London-to-Cape Town record by ten hours.

Dec. The United States enters World War II; American aviator Ruth Nichols volunteers the services of Relief Wings, an air ambulance service with centers in thirty-six states, to the Civil Air Patrol.

Dec. 8 U.S. pacifist, suffragist, and politician Jeannette Rankin is the only member of Congress to vote against entering World War II.

Literature and the Visual Arts

Japanese poet and translator Takako Lento is born.

Russian poet Marina Tsvetayeva commits suicide. She was silenced during the Stalinist era, and much of her work will not be published until after her death. Other deaths this year include Iranian poet Parvin Etesami (b. 1907); U.S. portraitist Ellen Rand (March 4, 1875–December 18), whose subjects included Franklin Delano Roosevelt, Elihu Root, William James, and Henry L. Stimson; and English author Virginia Woolf, who drowns herself in the River Ouse on March 28.

American Dorothea Lange is one of the first photographers to win a Guggenheim Fellowship.

New novels include Edna Ferber's *Saratoga Trunk*, Laura Ingalls Wilder's *Little Town on the Prairie*, and Virginia Woolf's *Between the Acts*.

Pearl S. Buck becomes a coeditor of *Asia* magazine, a position she will hold until 1946.

New American poetry includes Marianne Moore's *What Are Years* and Louise Bogan's *Poems and New Poems*.

Performing Arts and Entertainment

Canadian Native American folk singer Buffy Sainte-Marie is born.

U.S. composer Marion Bauer's *Symphonic Suite for Strings*, opus 34, premieres.

U.S. stage director Margaret Webster directs her mother, Dame May Whitty, in *The Trojan Women* and Judith Anderson as Lady Macbeth in *Macbeth*.

Filmgoers can see U.S. actress Agnes Moorehead (December 6, 1900–April 30, 1974) in *Citizen Kane*, Ingrid Bergman in *Dr. Jekyll and Mr. Hyde*, Mary Astor in *The Maltese Falcon*, Greta Garbo in her last film, *The Two-Faced Woman*, Rita Hayworth in *Blood and Sand*, Bette Davis in *The Little Foxes* (based on Lillian Hellman's play and screenwritten by Dorothy Parker), British actress Ida Lupino in *Ladies in Retirement*, *High Sierra*, and *The Sea Wolf*, and Joan Fontaine in *Suspicion* (cowritten by Alma Reville and Joan Harrison), for which she wins the Best Actress Oscar.

Activism

China has 317 women's war work organizations in twenty-one provinces.

About 20% of German women belong to the Nazi Women's Association.

Business and Industry

Germany enlists women as train conductors, custodians, and air raid wardens.

Women textile workers organize in Iran.

Dec. Four thousand women are employed in the U.S. aircraft industry.

Science and Medicine

German-American psychoanalyst Karen Horney cofounds the Association for the Advancement of Psychoanalysis and the American Institute of Psychoanalysis.

Education and Scholarship

French literary critic Julia Kristeva is born.

Pearl S. Buck founds a cultural exchange organization, the East and West Association.

U.S. sociologist and demographer Margaret Hagood publishes *Statistics for Sociologists*; the text influences the entire direction of sociology, increasing the tendency toward quantification.

Puerto Rican educator, folklorist, author, and feminist María Cadilla de Martínez publishes *Raices de la Tierra*, a collection of folktales and essays on Puerto Rican customs.

Approximately 30,000 men and forty women are attending Japan's imperial universities.

Ola Elizabeth Winslow wins a Pulitzer Prize for her biography *Jonathan Edwards*.

1942

General Status and Daily Life

U.S. housewives will find new products on store shelves, including Dannon Yogurt and Raisin Bran. However, many staples are being rationed because of the war; sugar, for example, is limited to one pound every two weeks as of May 14. Women's time has the additional demands of air raid drills, blackout drills, and salvage drives for scrap paper, rubber, and metal. Marriage rates rise due to prosperity, the desire to defer the draft by having children, and the desire to marry quickly before the husband is sent overseas. Divorce also increases during the war, and the birthrate rises.

Government, the Military, and the Law

Russian revolutionary Vera Figner (b. 1852) dies. Jailed for twenty years in tsarist Russia, she headed the Amnesty Committee in Soviet Russia and dedicated herself to helping political prisoners.

Spanish communist politician Dolores Ibarruri becomes, in exile, secretary-general of the Spanish Communist party. She will remain secretary-general until 1960.

In the United States, women enter several branches of the armed forces. The WAC (Women's Army Corps, originally Women's Army Auxiliary Corps, or WAAC) is created in May and headed by Oveta Culp Hobby. The WAVES (Women Accepted for Voluntary Emergency Service), the women's branch of the Navy, is created on July 30. Virginia Gildersleeve becomes chairman of the WAVES advisory council, and Mildred Helen McAfee, on August 3, becomes lieutenant commander in immediate command of the WAVES. Between September of this year and December 1944, more than 1,000 women are admitted to the WASPs (Women's Air Force Service Pilots), an elite group founded by pilot Jacqueline Cochran. The WASPs will not receive veterans' benefits until 1977.

Sept. Soviet pilot Valeria Ivanovna Khomyakova shoots down a German plane over the Volga to become the first woman pilot to down an enemy bomber.

Literature and the Visual Arts

Carson McCullers publishes the short story "A Tree. A Rock. A Cloud." and wins a Guggenheim Fellowship.

Pearl S. Buck publishes *Dragon Seed*, a novel about the effect of World War II on China, and a children's book, *The Chinese Children Next Door*.

U.S. novelist Ellen Glasgow receives a posthumous Pulitzer Prize for *In This Our Life*.

New poetry includes Canadian poet Anne Hébert's *Dreams in Suspension*, Edith Sitwell's *Street Song*, and Edna St. Vincent Millay's *The Murder of Lidice*.

Danish author Isak Dinesen publishes *Winter's Tales*.

First novels by U.S. authors include Eudora Welty's (b. April 13, 1909) *The Robber Bridegroom* and Mary McCarthy's (b. 1912) *The Company She Keeps*.

Performing Arts and Entertainment

English actress Marie Tempest (b. 1866) dies. She was skilled at both musical comedy and drama and was best known for playing elegant matrons.

Tallulah Bankhead plays Sabrina in Thornton Wilder's *The Skin of Our Teeth*.

English composer and conductor Ruth Gipps (b. 1921) composes her first symphony.

Swedish actress Anita Björk (b. 1923) appears in her first film, *Himlaspelet (The Road to Heaven)*. Katharine Hepburn stars in *Woman of the Year*, her first film with Spencer Tracy. Greer Garson wins the Best Actress Oscar for her performance in *Mrs. Miniver*, a patriotic film about the hardships suffered by English citizens during the German bombings of their country. Other noteworthy films this year inlcude *Reap the Wild Wind* with Susan Hayward (June 30, 1917–March 14, 1975), *Song of the Islands* and *Footlight Serenade* with Betty Grable, *Me and My Gal* with Judy Garland, *Cover Girl* with Rita Hayworth, and *Road to Morocco* with Dorothy Lamour.

In the United States, the Andrews Sisters have a hit song, "Don't Sit Under the Apple Tree."

Nov. 26 The movie for which Ingrid Bergman is most remembered, *Casablanca*, opens in a Hollywood theatre. It will be generally released in January 1943.

Athletics and Exploration

English missionaries and travelers Mildred Cable and Francesca French publish *The Gobi Desert*, for which Cable is honored by the Royal Central Asian Society.

Since 1936, Danish swimmer Ragnhild Hveger has set forty-two world records.

U.S. tennis players Louise Brough (b. 1923) and Margaret Osborne win the U.S. doubles title. Brough will win the U.S. singles title in 1947 and the Wimbledon singles title in 1948, 1949, 1950, and 1955. Osborne will win Wimbledon in 1947 and the U.S. Open in 1948, 1949, and 1950. U.S. tennis player Pauline Betz wins the U.S. Open women's singles championships. She will repeat her victory in 1943, 1944, and 1946 and win the Wimbledon title in 1946.

Activism

Dutch feminist Rosa Manus and Czech feminist and politician Franciska Plamnikova (b. 1875) die in Nazi concentration camps.

The ASWPL disbands; antilynching activist Jessie Daniel Ames publishes *The Changing Character of Lynching*.

Chinese novelist Ding Ling attacks sexism within the Communist party in the article "Thoughts on March 8th."

Business and Industry

The U.S. National War Labor Board issues General Order 16, which urges voluntary equalization of men's and women's wages.

Science and Medicine

At about this time, U.S. doctors Elizabeth McCoy and Dorothy Fennel are working with penicillin; McCoy discovers a way to increase production of the drug, and Fennel is part of a team that develops a more powerful strain of the drug, *Penicillium fenneliae*.

Education and Scholarship

Elise Richter, Austria's first woman professor, dies in the Nazi concentration camp at Theresienstadt.

Ghanaian educator Rosamund Mancell (b. 1919) founds the first girls' vocational school in Ghana.

Saudia Arabian queen 'Iffat (b. 1910) establishes a government school for boys.

U.S. classicist Lily Ross Taylor becomes president of the American Philological Association.

New U.S. publications include sociologist Jessie Bernard's (b. 1903) *American Family Behavior*, philosopher Susanne Knauth Langer's *Philosophy in a New Key: A Study in the Symbolism of Reason, Rite and Art*, Mari Sandoz's biography *Crazy Horse*, and classicist Edith Hamilton's *Mythology*.

U.S. historian Margaret Leech (1894–1974) wins the Pulitzer Prize for her description of the nation's capital during the Civil War, *Reveille in Washington*.

Religion

Argentine Catholic antifeminist Delfina Bunge de Gálvez makes a radio speech blaming the breakdown of the family on women who work outside the home. She urges people "to fight for what the Pope asks: the return of women to the home."

July 7 St. Peter's Cathedral in Rome breaks tradition and begins admitting women without stockings.

1943

General Status and Daily Life

Allied housewives plant victory gardens and follow the slogan "Use it up, wear it out, make it do, or do without." In the United States, butter is rationed at four ounces per week, cheese at four pounds per week, and meat at twenty-eight ounces per week. Coffee and flour are also rationed. Fabric rationing means dresses are plainer. Each person is allowed three pairs of leather shoes per year. Kitchen fat, metals, paper, nylon, and rubber are recycled.

Government, the Military, and the Law

Russian military pilot Lilya Litvyak, the top-scoring female Soviet flier with twelve kills, is shot down over Kharkov.

D. B. (Adelaide) Sinclair becomes director of the Women's Royal Canadian Naval Service.

Lithuanian physician Genia Sakin becomes the only plastic surgeon in the Allied armies during World War II.

Russian feminist politician Alexandra Kollontai becomes ambassador to Sweden.

Jan. 29 Ruth Cheney Streeter becomes commander of the U.S. Marine Corps Women's Reserve.

Feb. 18 Chinese political figure Madame Chiang Kai-Shek (Soong Mei-ling, b. 1901) addresses the U.S. Congress.

Apr.-Sept. Polish Jews in the Warsaw ghetto revolt

against the Nazis. Among the leaders of the rebellion are Niuta Teitelboim, Mira Fuchrer, Dvorah Baron, Regina Fudin, Pola Elster, and Zivia Lubetkin.

Literature and the Visual Arts

New U.S. novels include Betty Smith's *A Tree Grows in Brooklyn*; Esther Forbes's historical children's novel *Johnny Tremain*, set during the Revolutionary War; and Laura Ingalls Wilder's *These Happy Golden Years*.

U.S. author Shirley Jackson (December 14, 1919–August 8, 1965) publishes the short story "After You, My Dear Alphonse."

U.S. author Eudora Welty publishes *The Wide Net and Other Stories*.

Dec. 22 British children's author Beatrix Potter (b. 1866) dies. She began not as an author but as a botanist and was the first person to establish that lichens are not single plants but coexisting forms of fungus and algae. The skepticism she received, as a woman, from the scientific establishment soured her on botany, and she turned to other pursuits.

Performing Arts and Entertainment

U.S. theatrical producer Theresa Helburn has an idea for a musical based on the play *Green Grow the Lilacs*. To undertake the project, she unites Richard Rodgers and Oscar Hammerstein for their first collaboration—*Oklahoma!*—and saves her Theatre Guild from bankruptcy.

Dorothy Arzner makes her last commercial film, *First Comes Courage*, starring Merle Oberon (February 19, 1911–October 23, 1979). She then turns to making WAC training films for the U.S. Army.

French pianist Marguerite Long, with Jacques Thibaud, founds an international piano and violin competition.

Agnes Moorehead stars in a radio production of "Sorry, Wrong Number," written by Lucille Fletcher (b. March 28, 1912).

French ballerina Yvette Chauviré (b. 1917) stars in *Suite en blanc*.

English soprano and opera producer Joan Cross (b. 1900) becomes the director of Sadler's Wells Opera.

English singer and actress Petula Clark (b. 1934), later known for her Grammy-winning song "Downtown" (1965), gets her own BBC radio show, "Pet's Parlour."

Movies now playing include *Stage Door Canteen* with Katharine Cornell and Katharine Hepburn, *Casablanca* and *For Whom the Bell Tolls* with Ingrid Bergman, and *The Outlaw* with Jane Russell. Jennifer Jones wins the Best Actress Oscar for *The Song of Bernadette*.

Oct. U.S. stage director Margaret Webster's production of *Othello* opens in New York, already controversial because of its casting of a black actor, Paul Robeson, in the title role.

Athletics and Exploration

Chicago Cubs owner Philip K. Wrigley, worried by the war's drain on male athletes, founds the All-American Girls' Baseball League. Attendance eventually reaches 1 million per year, but Wrigley withdraws his support, and the league goes out of business in 1954.

Activism

U.S. philanthropist Anita Blaine gives Soong Mei-ling $100,000 for Chinese war orphans.

Women in Lebanon stage mass demonstrations against the arrest of political leaders by the French.

Business and Industry

Nigerian merchant Omu Okwei (b. 1872) dies. In many parts of Africa, women traditionally ran the marketplaces, and Okwei, chairwoman of the Council of Mothers, was one of the last great female merchants.

About 310,000 women are employed in the U.S. aircraft industry. Propaganda urges women to take wartime jobs; it is made quite clear that their participation will be temporary, though most surveys show that the women want to keep the new jobs.

Ghanaian entrepreneur Esher Ocloo founds a fruit drink and bottling company.

Anne Loughlin becomes president of Britain's Trades Union Congress.

Jan. 18 U.S. labor leader, WTUL cofounder, pacifist, and suffragist Mary Kenney O'Sullivan (b. January 8, 1864) dies.

Science and Medicine

U.S. physicist Elda Anderson (October 5, 1899–April 17, 1961), codeveloper of the atomic bomb and a pioneer in radiation protection, goes to Los Alamos to work on the cyclotron project, measuring neutron cross sections.

American Myra Logan (1908–1977) becomes the first woman surgeon to perform a heart operation.

Soviet physiologist Lina Solomonovna Stern wins the Stalin Prize for her work on cerebrospinal fluid.

New U.S. scientific publications include pediatrician Ethel Dunham's (March 12, 1883–December 13, 1969) pioneering and influential *Standards and Recommendations for the Hospital Care of Newborn Infants, Full Term and Premature*, geologist and stratigraphic paleontologist Julia Gardner's *Correlation of the Cenozoic Formations of the Atlantic and Gulf Coastal Plain and the Caribbean Region*, and industrial toxicologist Alice Hamilton's *Exploring the Dangerous Trades*.

Apr. 4 U.S. marine zoologist Mary Jane Rathbun (b. June 11, 1860) dies. She organized and catalogued marine invertebrates, published 158 works, and was a specialist in the taxonomy of decapod Crustacea like shrimp and crabs.

Education and Scholarship

Nellie Nielson becomes the first woman president of the American Historical Association.

U.S. anthropologist Ruth Benedict coauthors an antiracist pamphlet, *The Races of Mankind*, to combat fascist views of race. Its direct distribution by the army is blocked by irate southern congressmen, but 750,000 copies are given away anyway by private groups.

Ada Comstock Notestein (d. 1973), the first full-time president of Radcliffe College, convinces Harvard to agree to coeducational classes.

Esther Forbes wins a Pulitzer Prize for her history *Paul Revere and the World He Lived In*.

Dec. 25 U.S. librarian Lutie Stearns (b. September 13, 1866), who helped to found one hundred libraries and 1,480 traveling libraries in Wisconsin, dies.

Religion

St. Mary's College in Notre Dame, Indiana, becomes the first U.S. Catholic college to offer a graduate program in theology open to women.

Apr. 8. U.S. missionary Mary Reed (b. December 4, 1854), who worked with lepers in India for nearly fifty years, dies.

1944

General Status and Daily Life

Germany sets the penalty for performing an abortion at death, unless the woman seeking the abortion is a Jew.

Government, the Military, and the Law

Russian communist Claudia Nikolayeva (b. 1893) dies. Banished to Siberia in the Tsarist era, she headed important Soviet organizations and became a member of the Central Committee.

Several World War II resistance leaders are caught and executed this year. One of them is Indian Muslim Noor un Nissa, shot by the Gestapo on September 13. The first British secret agent in the Nazi Reich, she was tortured by the Nazis but refused to reveal information. Known as "Madeleine" to the French Resistance, she becomes, posthumously, the only female recipient of both the George Cross and the Croix de Guerre.
Two Belgian spies are beheaded by the Nazis in 1944: underground newspaper publisher Marie-Louise Henin (b. 1898) and Marguerite Bervoets (b. 1914), who cofounded a Resistance group and served as a guide, courier, and spy. Hungarian Zionist and commando Hannah Senesh (b. 1921) is captured by the Nazis, tortured, and executed on November 7. She emigrated to Israel at the beginning of the war but returned to help other Jews escape from Hungary. Greek communist activist Electra Apostoloy is also tortured and killed by the Nazi-supported Greek secret police.

Marion Mushkat becomes vice president of the Polish Supreme Court, a position she will hold until 1966.

Ana Pauker becomes Romania's minister of foreign affairs.

French Resistance leader Marie Madeleine Fourcade (b. 1909), code-named "Hedgehog," is captured by the Nazis. She escapes and manages to warn her second-in-command by moving through the fields pretending to be a gleaner. Since 1940, Fourcade has been running a network of spies, passing information and downed Allied pilots across the English Channel.

Clare Boothe Luce gives the keynote speech at the Republican National Convention.

Literature and the Visual Arts

French radical feminist novelist Monique Wittig, whose works attack and fragment "male language," is born.

U.S. publisher Helen Valentine founds and becomes editor in chief of *Seventeen* magazine.

U.S. Imagist poet H. D. publishes *The Walls Do Not Fall*, the first book of a poetic trilogy about World War II. Other works of poetry published this year are Marianne Moore's *Nevertheless*, Muriel Rukeyser's *Beast in View*, and Portuguese poet, socialist member of Parliament, children's book author, and translator Sophia de Mello Breyner Andresen's (b. 1919) *Poems*.

U.S. writer and civil rights advocate Lillian Smith publishes the novel *Strange Fruit*, which deals with interracial love. It is banned in Massachusetts for obscenity and refused delivery by the Post Office; the Post Office ban, however, is lifted by Eleanor Roosevelt. Other new novels include Kathleen Winsor's *Forever Amber*, Spanish novelist Carmen Laforet Diaz's *Nada*, a prizewinning novel that makes her famous, and Carson McCullers's (February 19, 1917–September 29, 1967) *The Ballad of the Sad Café*, a tragic novella about the miseries of unrequited passion. McCullers's novels are notable for their skillful portrayals of grotesques and adolescents.

Aug. 1 German diarist Anne Frank (b. 1929), who has been in hiding in the Netherlands for months with her family and others to avoid being deported as a Jew, makes her last diary entry. On August 4, she and the other occupants of the Secret Annexe are arrested. She dies of typhus on March 12, 1945, in the Bergen-Belsen concentration camp.

Performing Arts and Entertainment

French pianist and composer Cécile Chaminade (b. 1857), who wrote over 200 works for piano, dies.

Ethel Barrymore appears in her last Broadway play, *Embezzled Heaven*, and wins an Oscar for Best Supporting Actress for *None But the Lonely Heart*.

U.S. director and producer Margo Jones directs Tennessee Williams's first Broadway play, *The Glass Menagerie*.

U.S. film producer Virginia Van Upp produces the romantic comedy *Together Again*, starring Irene Dunne. Gladys Lehman writes the screenplay for the musical *Two Girls and a Sailor*, and Helen Deutsch cowrites the screenplay for *National Velvet*, starring Elizabeth Taylor and produced by British producer Joy Harrison. Film editor Barbara McLean wins an Oscar for *Wilson*. Adrienne Fazan edits *Anchors Aweigh*, Viola Lawrence edits *Cover Girl*, and Marjorie Fowler edits her first film, *Woman in the Window*.

U.S. comedian Mae West stars in the play *Catherine Was Great*.

English composer Phyllis Tate (b. 1911) composes a concerto for alto saxophone and strings.

U.S. actress and theatrical director Antoinette Perry directs *Harvey*.

Fanny Brice's character Baby Snooks gets her own radio show, which will run until 1951.

English ballerina Beryl Grey (b. 1927) dances *Giselle*.

French actress Maria Casares (b. 1922) stars in Camus's *Le malentendu*.

New movies include *Lifeboat* with Tallulah Bankhead, *Meet Me in St. Louis* with Judy Garland, *Bathing Beauty* with swimmer Esther Williams, *Dragon Seed* with Katharine Hepburn, and Lauren Bacall's first film, *To Have and Have Not*. Ingrid Bergman wins the Best Actress Oscar for her portrayal of a manipulated wife in *Gaslight*.

Athletics and Exploration

Oct. Women's Auxiliary Ferrying Service (WAFS) pilot Ann Baumgartner becomes the first American woman to fly a jet plane.

Activism

Chile holds its first National Congress of Women.

Egyptian feminist Huda Shaarawi coestablishes the All Arab Federation of Women.

U.S. physician and industrial toxicologist Alice Hamilton becomes president of the National Consumers' League.

Mar. 4 U.S. lecturer and clubwoman Fannie Barrier Williams (b. February 12, 1855), the first black member of the Chicago Women's Club, dies. She once kept her first-class train seat by telling the conductor, "Je suis française."

Business and Industry

This year is the first in which more married women than single women are employed in the United States. Before the war, about 800,000 women belonged to labor unions; now 3.5 million do.

Jan. Argentina passes a minimum wage law for piecework done at home; the law primarily benefits women.

Science and Medicine

U.S. geneticist Barbara McClintock becomes a member of the National Academy of Sciences.

British astronomer Mary Blagg dies. She studied various aspects of the binary Lyrae, RT Cygni, V Cassiopeiae, and U Persei, but she was best known for her work standardizing lunar nomenclature. After her death, a lunar crater is named for her.

Feb. French chemist and scientific writer Hélène Metzger is arrested and later sent to Auschwitz, where she dies.

May 3 U.S. physicist Margaret Maltby (b. December 10, 1860), who worked on electrolyte resistances and the conductivity of certain solutions, dies.

Education and Scholarship

French philosopher Simone de Beauvoir (1908–1986) publishes the existentialist *Pyrrhus et Cinéas*.

U.S. biographer Catherine Drinker Bowen publishes *Yankee from Olympus: Justice Holmes and His Family*.

U.S. efficiency expert Lillian Gilbreth describes how tasks can be adapted in *Normal Lives for the Disabled*.

Helen Jarrell, head of the largest American Federation of Teachers (AFT) local in the United States, becomes the first woman superintendent of the Atlanta public schools.

Religion

May 26 The threat of women's publicly unveiling in Syria causes an armed riot of fundamentalist Muslims.

1945

General Status and Daily Life

Since 1910, about 80,000–200,000 Korean women have been kidnapped and forced to serve as prostitutes or "comfort women" to Japanese troops.

New constitutions grant increased rights for women: Ecuadoran women get equal rights within marriage, Guatemalan men over eighteen and literate women over eighteen get citizenship, and Indonesian women get an equal rights clause.

U.S. housewives can now purchase frozen orange juice and frozen dinners.

Government, the Military, and the Law

Mozambique nationalist and freedom fighter Josina Abiathar Muthemba is born.

Resistance worker Germaine Devalet (b. 1898) dies in the Ravensbrück concentration camp for aiding her fellow Belgians against the Gestapo.

Italy, Japan (December 17), France, Hungary, and Yugoslavia grant women the right to vote.

Women in Venezuela get local suffrage.

The U.S. Army includes 99,000 noncombat WACs. Women serve in the Coast Guard and the Marine Corps Women's Reserve (which has 813 officers and 17,714 enlisted women), and the navy and air force also have women's divisions, the WAVES and WASPs. WASPs teach flying, tow aerial targets for gunnery practice, and test military planes.

English unionist, politician, writer, and feminist Ellen Wilkinson becomes minister of education.

Eleanor Roosevelt becomes a delegate to the UN.

Chinese feminist and political leader Deng Yingchao becomes one of only three women on the Communist party Central Committee.

July Queen Wilhelmina (August 31, 1880–November 28, 1962) of the Netherlands, who was forced to flee from the invading Nazi forces in 1940, returns to her country.

Sept. 8 Iva Toguri d'Aquino (b. 1920), the only one

of seven "Tokyo Roses" to be prosecuted, is arrested in Yokohama for extradition to the United States. During World War II, she spoke on radio, urging U.S. soldiers in the Pacific theater to surrender or desert. She will be imprisoned for ten years and finally pardoned by President Gerald Ford.

Literature and the Visual Arts

Women who die this year include Canadian painter Emily Carr (b. 1871); Russian author Zinaida Hippius (b. 1869), who wrote poems, short stories, drama, literary criticism, and memoirs; and German poet Else Lasker-Schüler (b. 1869), who fled her country after her work was banned by the Nazis.

Chilean poet Gabriela Mistral wins the Nobel Prize for Literature.

U.S. author Jade Snow Wong publishes the memoir *Fifth Chinese Daughter*.

Marjorie Kinnan Rawlings' short story "Black Secret" wins the O. Henry Award.

U.S. journalist Doris Fleeson becomes the first woman to have a syndicated political column.

Margaret Bourke-White publishes "The Living Dead of Buchenwald"; she was one of the first photographers allowed into the liberated concentration camps.

Pearl S. Buck publishes *Talk About Russia*, a collection of interviews with participants in the 1917 revolution, and a novel, *The Townsman*, about life in early Kansas.

Romanian poet Magda Isanos (1916–1944) publishes *The Sky of Mountains*. Her other posthumous works will include *The Land of Light* (1946) and *Poem* (1948); her style was greatly affected by her affliction with tuberculosis. Other new works of poetry include *Tribute to the Angels*, the second volume of H. D.'s trilogy about World War II, and American poet Gwendolyn Brooks's (b. 1917) first book, *A Street in Bronzeville*.

Elizabeth Bowen publishes the short story "The Demon Lover."

Simone de Beauvoir publishes the novel *Le sang des autres* (*The Blood of Others*) and a play, *Les bouches inutiles*.

Mary Chase publishes the Pulitzer-Prize-winning play *Harvey*.

Performing Arts and Entertainment

English cellist Jacqueline Du Pré and American ballerina Suzanne Farrell, especially noted for her interpretations of Balanchine, are born.

Japanese dancer Azuma Iv Tokuho inherits her father's Kabuki troupe. Her mother, Maasya Fujima, was also a noted Kabuki dancer.

U.S. blues singer Billie Holiday records "Don't Explain." Ella Fitzgerald records "Flying Home."

U.S. actress Judy Holliday (Judith Tuvim, June 21, 1921–June 7, 1965) makes her stage debut and wins awards with a small part in *Kiss Them For Me*. Later in the year, she joins the cast of the play *Born Yesterday*, replacing Jean Arthur (d. 1991), with only seventy-two hours to learn her part. The role, Billie Dawn, will bring Holliday national fame.

Russian-American filmmaker Maya Deren (April 29, 1917–October 31, 1961) makes *Study in Choreography for Camera*; U.S. film producer Virginia Van Upp produces *She Wouldn't Say Yes*. Harriet Parsons, daughter of gossip columnist Louella Parsons, produces the feature film *The Enchanted Cottage*. Constance Bennett produces and stars in *Paris Underground*, a film about the French Resistance.

Ayn Rand (February 2, 1905–March 6, 1982) writes screenplays for *Love Letters* and *You Came Along*.

Joan Crawford wins the Best Actress Oscar for her performance in *Mildred Pierce*. French actresses Arletty and Maria Casares star in *Les enfants du paradis* (*Children of Paradise*).

Athletics and Exploration

Tennis player Sarah Palfrey Cooke wins the U.S. women's singles championship; she also won it in 1941.

Business and Industry

U.S. business executive Dorothy Shaver becomes president of the Lord & Taylor department store at a salary of $110,000 per year, the highest salary on record for any woman in the United States.

In the USSR, 15,920,000 women are in the work force, comprising 56% of the total work force.

U.S. inventor Dorothy Rodgers, wife of composer

Richard Rodgers, patents the Jonny Mop toilet bowl cleaner.

French publishers Hélène Gordon-Lazareff (b. September 21, 1909) and Françoise Giroud establish the magazine *Elle*. Gordon-Lazareff will remain editor of the magazine until 1973.

During the war, 6 million U.S. women have entered the work force, 75% of them married and more than 60% of them mothers. They have become riveters, lumberjacks, welders, crane operators, keel benders, toolmakers, shell loaders, cattle handlers, blast-furnace cleaners, locomotive greasers, police officers, taxi drivers, and football coaches. More than 400,000 black women have quit domestic service to enter new jobs.

But not all the news is good. Women working in manufacturing make approximately 65% as much as their male counterparts. Factories are sex-segregated and provide no child care or other support services; the government seems unwilling or unable to help. At war's end, despite their desire to continue working, most women are pushed out of nontraditional jobs and encouraged to return to their kitchens.

Science and Medicine

British physicist Kathleen Yardley Lonsdale (1903–1971), a specialist in X-ray crystallography, becomes the first woman fellow of the Royal Society; she will eventually become its vice president.

Alice Wilson becomes the first woman member of the Canadian Geological Survey.

Feb. 22 U.S. doctor S. Josephine Baker (b. November 15, 1873) dies. She worked to license midwives, distribute free milk to poor mothers, and popularize the use of silver nitrate to prevent blindness in infants. Her influence ended New York University's (NYU) policy of banning women from its postgraduate programs.

Education and Scholarship

Puerto Rican folklorist María de Cadilla Martínez publishes *Hitos de la Raza*, a collection of traditional stories.

British educators Margaret Graham and Mary Stewart convince Makerere University in East Africa to admit women.

Religion

U.S. theologian Georgia Harkness explores the spiritual significance of suffering in *The Dark Night of the Soul.*

1946

General Status and Daily Life

Colombian housewives are barred from obtaining insurance for themselves; they must get it instead through their husbands.

Infibulation is outlawed in Sudan, but the law is seldom enforced. Infibulation is the practice of cutting off a woman's clitoris, labia minora, and labia majora, combined with the sewing up of the vulva. Only a small hole is left to permit menstrual blood and urine to escape. The woman is cut open to permit her husband to have intercourse with her; she is further cut to allow childbirth and then resewn after delivery.

The French Constitution stipulates equality of the sexes.

Japan's new civil code, revised by U.S. occupying forces, gives women freedom to choose their own husbands and equal rights in divorce and inheritance.

July 5 In Paris, model Micheline Bernardi models the first bikini bathing suit.

Government, the Military, and the Law

Pakistani politician Taj Bibi, a member of the Sind Assembly from 1972 until General Zia's coup, is born.

Women in El Salvador get the vote, but their age requirement is higher than that for men. Romanian and Venezuelan (March 15) women and Algerian women with French civil status get full suffrage.

María de la Cruz founds the Partido Femenino Chileno (Chilean Women's Party). Short-lived, the party does manage to help Carlos Ibáñez get elected in 1952 before it breaks into two factions.

Maria Ulfah Santoso becomes Indonesia's minister of social affairs.

Felisa Vda. de Gautier becomes the first woman mayor of San Juan, Puerto Rico. She will hold the office until 1968.

Indian politician Vijaya Pandit (b. 1900) becomes the head of the Indian delegation to the UN.

Apr. 10 In Japan's first postwar election, thirty-nine women are elected to Parliament.

Literature and the Visual Arts

U.S. author Carson McCullers publishes her most acclaimed novel, *The Member of the Wedding*.

U.S. photographer Margaret Bourke-White shoots "Gandhi at His Spinning Wheel."

U.S. Imagist poet H. D. publishes *The Flowering of the Rod*, the third book in her poetic trilogy about World War II. Other new poetry includes U.S. objectivist poet Louise Niedecker's *New Goose*, English-American poet Denise Levertov's (b. 1923) first collection, *The Double Image*, American Elizabeth Bishop's (1911–1979) first collection, *North and South*, and Nelly Sachs's *In den Wohnungen des Todes*.

New novels include Eudora Welty's *Delta Wedding*, Pearl S. Buck's *Pavilion of Women*, Simone de Beauvoir's *Tous les hommes sont mortels* (*All Men Are Mortal*), Ding Ling's *Stories of Heroes*, French novelist Violette Leduc's (b. April 7, 1907) *L'asphyxie*, and Gertrude Stein's *Brewsie and Willie*.

July 27 U.S. author Gertrude Stein dies. As an art critic, she helped to popularize the works of Matisse, Picasso, and Juan Gris; as the doyenne of a Paris literary circle, she encouraged and assisted such authors as Sherwood Anderson, F. Scott Fitzgerald, Ezra Pound, and Ernest Hemingway. Her dying words are, "What is the answer?" When no one in the room responds, she asks, "In that case, what is the question?"

Performing Arts and Entertainment

U.S. soprano Camilla Williams, the first black woman to be a regular member of a U.S. opera company, sings Cio-Cio San in *Madame Butterfly*.

U.S. film producer Virginia Van Upp produces *Gilda*, starring Rita Hayworth as the troubled, sensual wife of a Buenos Aires casino proprietor. Portuguese filmmaker Barbara Virginia directs *Three Days Without God*, in which villagers accuse the local schoolteacher of being the devil's agent, and Danish filmmaker Astrid Henning-Jensen codirects *Ditte Menneskebarn* (*Ditte, Child of Man*), which attacks hypocrisy through its portrayal of an unmarried mother. Russian-American filmmaker Maya Deren makes *Ritual in Transfigured Time*, wins a

Guggenheim Fellowship, and shows three films at the first independent art film show in the United States.

American Maria Tallchief becomes prima ballerina of the New York City Ballet.

U.S. theatrical director and producer Margo Jones directs Maxine Wood's *On Whitman Avenue* on Broadway.

U.S. jazz pianist Mary Lou Williams (1910–1981), an arranger for Benny Goodman, Louis Armstrong, Earl Hines, Tommy Dorsey, and Duke Ellington, composes her *Zodiac Suite*.

Georgian actress Vera Andzhaparidzi (b. 1900) is awarded the Stalin Prize.

French ballerina Yvette Chauviré stars in *Dramma per musica* and is awarded the Legion of Honor.

U.S. screenplays are written by Sally Benson (*Anna and the King of Siam*), Frances Goodrich (coauthor of *The Virginian* and *It's a Wonderful Life*, which stars Donna Reed), and Leigh Brackett (coauthor of *The Big Sleep*, which stars Lauren Bacall). British playwright, screenwriter, and director Muriel Box (b. 1905) shares the Oscar for best original screenplay with her husband for *The Seventh Veil*. Films edited by women include *The Secret Heart* (Adrienne Fazan) and *My Darling Clementine* (Dorothy Spencer).

English soprano and opera producer Joan Cross produces *Der Rosenkavalier* at Covent Garden.

Russian ballerina Natalya Dudinskaya stars in the premiere of Sergeyev's version of Prokofiev's *Cinderella*.

Filmgoers can see Judy Garland in *Till the Clouds Roll By*, Ingrid Bergman in *Notorious*, Lauren Bacall in *The Big Sleep*, and Lana Turner in *The Postman Always Rings Twice*. Olivia de Havilland wins the Best Actress Oscar for her performance in *To Each His Own*.

May 16 Ethel Merman opens on Broadway in *Annie Get Your Gun*, a musical based on the life of sharpshooter Annie Oakley.

Athletics and Exploration

U.S. golfer Babe Didrikson Zaharias wins the women's national golf championship, turns professional, and wins seventeen tournaments in a row.

English hockey player Marjorie Pollard (1899–1982) becomes editor of the magazine *Hockey Field*, a position she will hold until 1970.

Dutch athlete Fanny Blankers-Koen (b. 1918) wins gold

medals in the 80-meter hurdles and the 4 x 100-meter relay, only six weeks after the birth of her first child. From 1938 to 1951, she sets records in the 100 yards, 100 meters, 220 yards, 80-meter hurdles, high jump, long jump, and pentathlon.

Activism

Swiss feminist Emilie Gourd (b. 1879), president of the Swiss Women's Association and founder of the newspaper *Le mouvement feministe*, dies.

Queen Homaina founds the Women's Society, the first women's organization in Afghanistan.

Japanese feminist Ichikawa Fusae founds the Women's Suffrage Center.

The Sudanese Women's League, Sudan's first modern women's organization, is founded. It will be replaced in 1951 by the Sudanese Women's Union, which attacks genital mutilation, polygyny, unequal pay, and unfair divorce laws.

U.S. pacifist, reformer, and economist Emily Greene Balch shares the Nobel Peace Prize. She donates her award money to the Friends Service Council of London and the American Friends Service Committee, an organization for conscientious objectors to war.

Indian social worker Dhanvanthi Rama Rau becomes president of the All-India Women's Conference.

Apr. 24 U.S. architectural preservationist Elizabeth Werlein (b. January 28, 1883), who was instrumental in saving the Vieux Carré (French Quarter) of New Orleans, dies.

Business and Industry

An equal pay clause is introduced in the French Constitution.

Female domestic servants in the United States have a median yearly income of $373. Female professionals make $1,501, female sales workers $754, female government workers $1,795, and women in finance, insurance, and real estate $1,301. Male workers in these jobs have median yearly incomes of, respectively, $465, $3,345, $2,142, $2,453, and $2,518.

Science and Medicine

U.S. doctor Elise L'Esperance becomes the first editor of the *Journal of the American Medical Women's Association.*

French physicist Irène Joliot-Curie becomes director of the Radium Institute and a member of the French Atomic Energy Commission.

Education and Scholarship

Finnish coeducation pioneer Lucina Hagman (b. 1853) dies.

U.S. anthropologist Ruth Benedict publishes *The Chrysanthemum and the Sword: Patterns of Japanese Culture*, which argues that peaceful reintegration of Japan into the world community must depend on elements in Japanese culture rather than a wholesale imposition of European values.

Religion

Elsie Dorothea Chamberlain-Garrington becomes the first female chaplain in the British armed forces.

July 7 Italian-American saint and founder Frances Xavier Cabrini is canonized, making her the first U.S. citizen to become a saint. She founded convents and orphanages in France, Spain, England, Italy, and Latin America.

1947

General Status and Daily Life

The new Japanese Constitution guarantees equal rights for women.

Aluminum foil and the food processor are invented.

Government, the Military, and the Law

Indian freedom fighter Rani Gaidinliu is released after fourteen years in jail for her work against the British occupation. At sixteen, she led a team of guerrilla fighters in the Naga Hills and was captured only after the British committed a large number of troops to the task.

In India, a number of women take positions in the new independent government. Amrit Kaur, founder of the Indian Red Cross, becomes minister of health, and

Vijaya Pandit is named ambassador to the Soviet Union.

Bulgaria, Argentina, and China grant women the vote. Women in Mexico win the right to vote in municipal elections.

The Army-Navy Nurse Act authorizes permanent commissions for U.S. military nurses; Florence Blanchfield (April 1, 1882–May 12, 1971) becomes the first woman officer commissioned in the regular army.

Australian politician Annabelle Rankin (b. July 29, 1908) becomes Opposition Whip.

New Zealand politician Mabel Howard becomes minister of health and child welfare, making her the first woman Cabinet minister in New Zealand.

Literature and the Visual Arts

Japanese poet Kanai Mieko, whose works allude to such diverse things as Japanese cosmetics figure Madam Juju and the Beatles song "Strawberry Fields Forever," is born.

New Romanian poetry includes Maria Banus's *Joy*, Veronica Porumbacu's (1921–March 1977) *Dreams of Old Dokia*, and poet, composer, musician, translator, and children's author Nina Cassian's (b. 1924) *On the Scale of One to One*. German poet Nelly Sachs publishes *In the Habitation of Death*.

U.S. children's author Margaret Wise Brown publishes *Goodnight Moon*.

Performing Arts and Entertainment

The U.S. film *Golden Earrings*, written by Helen Deutsch, is edited by Alma Macrorie. Monica Collingwood edits *The Bishop's Wife*. Czechoslovakian filmmaker Hermina Tyrlova, a maker of puppet films for children, directs *Revolt of the Toys*. English film producer Betty Box (b. 1920) produces *Dear Murderer*.

Russian-American filmmaker Maya Deren becomes the first woman and the first American to receive the Cannes Grand Prix Internationale for avant-garde film.

Susan Hayward plays the alcoholic housewife Angie Evans in *Smash-up, the Story of a Woman*, earning an Academy Award nomination. The Oscar, however, is won by Loretta Young for *The Farmer's Daughter*. Other new movies include *Possessed* with Joan Crawford, *Dishonored Lady* with Hedy Lamarr, and *Dark Passage* with Lauren Bacall. French actress Anouk

Aimée (b. 1932) appears in her first film, *La maison sous la mer*.

U.S. soprano Beverly Sills (b. 1929) makes her debut as Micaela in *Carmen*.

U.S. gospel singer Mahalia Jackson (October 26, 1911–January 27, 1972) records the million-selling *Move on Up a Little Higher*.

Greek soprano Maria Callas (1923–September 15, 1977) makes her professional operatic debut in Verona.

Jan. 11 U.S. musical comedy and vaudeville actress Eva Tanguay (b. August 1, 1878) dies. She was best known for the songs "I've Got to Be Crazy," "I Don't Care," "I Want Someone to Go Wild with Me," and "It's All Been Done Before but Not the Way I Do It."

Dec. 4 On Broadway, Jessica Tandy originates the role of Blanche DuBois in *A Streetcar Named Desire*; Kim Hunter plays Stella.

Athletics and Exploration

Spanish bullfighter Juanita Cruz, the first professional female matador, retires from bullfighting after years of performing in Mexico and South America. She fought in Spain until after the civil war, when Franco barred women from the sport.

The thoroughbred Jet Pilot, owned by cosmetics entrepreneur Elizabeth Arden, wins the Kentucky Derby.

Activism

Russian feminist Natalia Malakhovskaya, founder of the illegal women's group Club Maria, is born.

Princess Aicha of Morocco publicly supports feminism and unveils.

U.S. conservationist Marjorie Stoneman Douglas (b. 1890), a lifelong campaigner to save the Everglades, publishes *The Everglades: River of Grass*.

The Adharsa Mahila Sangh (Model Women's Organization) is established in Nepal to fight child marriage and opposition to the remarriage of widows.

Pakistani student Fatima Sughra, during a nationalist demonstration, rushes past police and replaces the British Union Jack over a government building with her own homemade Pakistani flag. She is the first person to raise that banner.

Business and Industry

Italian socialist Teresa Noce founds the journal *La voce dei tessili* (*The Voice of Textile Workers*).

Irish unionist Louie Bennett replaces Helena Molony (1884–1967) as head of the Irish Trades Union Congress (ITUC). It is Bennett's second term as president of the ITUC.

Science and Medicine

Irish astronomer Annie Russell Maunder (b. 1868) dies. Employed at Greenwich Royal Observatory as a "computer," she specialized in sunspots and the relationship between the earth's climate and changes in the sun.

The U.S. government funds a project for research in contemporary cultures headed by anthropologist Ruth Benedict. The irony is that Benedict, passed over repeatedly for promotion and salary increases on the grounds that married women could make do with less, is now in charge of more anthropological research funds than most of her colleagues have ever seen. Not even a full professor, she is now elected president of the American Anthropological Association.

Czech biochemist Gerty Cori (1896–1957) shares the Nobel Prize for Medicine or Physiology for her collaboration on the isolation of glycogen, a starch that metabolizes into sugar as needed.

English biochemist Dorothy Crowfoot Hodgkin is elected to the Royal Society.

Mohawk Indian physician Lillie Rosa Minoka-Hill is named the outstanding American Indian of the Year and made an honorary member of the Oneida tribe for her contribution to its collective health.

U.S. sculptor Alice Chatham designs the helmet worn by X-1 pilot Chuck Yeager; she will continue to work for the National Aeronautics and Space Administration (NASA) for many years, designing helmets for the Mercury astronauts, pressurized suits for experimental chimpanzees, test dummies, a space bed, and various types of restraints and harnesses.

Education and Scholarship

Chilean feminist and government official Ana Figuero (1908–1970) becomes head of Chile's secondary school system.

New publications include Simone de Beauvoir's *Pour une morale de l'ambiguité* (*Ethics of Ambiguity*), French philosopher Simone Weil's (February 3, 1909–August 28, 1943) posthumous *La Pesanteur et la Grâce* (*Gravity and Grace*), U.S. literary critic Rosemond Tuve's *Elizabethan and Metaphysical Imagery*, and Pearl S. Buck's *How It Happened*, a collection of interviews about Germany from 1914 to 1933.

Religion

Saint Teresa of Lisieux (1873–1897) becomes copatroness of France with Joan of Arc.

French Catholic saints Catherine Labouré, a visionary, and Elizabeth Bichier des Ages, founder of a nursing and teaching community, are canonized.

1948

General Status and Daily Life

Japanese wives must have their husbands' permission to obtain abortions.

Government, the Military, and the Law

Sudanese politician Victoria Yar Arol is born.

Ida Gramcko becomes Venezuela's ambassador to the Soviet Union.

Women are granted the vote in the new nation of Israel and in South Korea.

The Women's Armed Sevices Integration Act provides military women with regular and reserve status. Frances Lois Willoughby becomes the first commissioned woman doctor in the regular U.S. Navy Colonel Geraldine P. May becomes the first head of WAF.

Russian-Israeli agriculture expert Mina Ben-Zvi becomes the first commander in chief of the Women's Corps of the Israeli Defense Army.

Jan. 21 Israeli politician Golda Meir (1898–December 8, 1978) makes an influential speech to the Council of Jewish Federations in Chicago that gains $50 million in crucial funding for the new state of Israel. In May, she signs Israel's Declaration of Independence, and in September, she becomes Israel's first minister to the Soviet Union.

Sept. 4 Queen Wilhelmina abdicates the throne of the Netherlands in favor of her daughter Juliana (b. 1909).

Dec. 10 The UN passes the Universal Declaration of Human Rights, largely due to pressure from Eleanor Roosevelt.

Literature and the Visual Arts

Armenian poet, writer, and journalist Siran Seza begins publishing the magazine *Young Armenian Women*.

Alice Dunnigan becomes the first black woman White House correspondent.

New French novels include Nathalie Sarraute's *Portrait d'un inconnu*, Violette Leduc's *L'affamée*, and Simone de Beauvoir's *L'invitée* (*She Came to Stay*).

June U.S. author Shirley Jackson publishes her most enduring and chilling story, "The Lottery," which describes a town clinging by habit to a horrifying tradition.

Performing Arts and Entertainment

U.S. news analyst Pauline Frederick becomes the first woman broadcaster to cover a national political convention.

Cuban ballerina Alicia Alonso (b. 1921) founds her own ballet company.

American Hanya Holm (b. 1898) choreographs the musical *Kiss Me, Kate*; in 1952 she will register her work with the Copyright Office, becoming the first choreographer to do so.

Russian-American costume designer Barbara Karinska (b. 1886), the first costume designer to win a Capezio Dance Award, wins an Oscar for her work on *Joan of Arc*, starring Ingrid Bergman. Choreographer George Balanchine has said of her, "There is Shakespeare for literature and Madame Karinska for costumes."

U.S. dancer Helen Tamiris choreographs the Broadway musical *Annie Get Your Gun*.

Filmgoers can see Katharine Hepburn in *State of the Union*, Judy Garland in *The Pirate* and *Easter Parade*, Lauren Bacall in *Key Largo*, Rita Hayworth in *The Lady from Shanghai*, and Jean Arthur and Marlene Dietrich in *A Foreign Affair*. Jane Wyman wins the Best Actress Oscar for *Johnny Belinda*.

Italian screenwriter Suso Cecchi d'Amico writes the screenplay for *The Bicycle Thief*.

English soprano and opera producer Joan Cross founds the Opera School (later the National School of Opera) and becomes its Director, a position she will hold until 1964.

Athletics and Exploration

U.S. tennis player Louise Brough wins the singles, doubles, and mixed doubles titles at Wimbledon.

U.S. athlete Babe Didrikson Zaharias and five others establish the Ladies Professional Golf Association (LPGA).

Women are 9.4% of Olympic athletes. In women's figure skating at the St. Moritz winter games, Barbara Ann Scott of Canada takes the gold. Belgian Micheline Lannoy takes the gold in pairs. Switzerland's Hedy Schlunegger wins the gold in downhill skiing. Austria's Trude Beiser wins the gold in the combined downhill and slalom and the silver in downhill. Gretchen Fraser, winning the gold in the slalom and the silver in the Alpine combination, becomes the first American skier to medal at the Olympics. She will say later of the gold medal, "It's lovely, but it's too heavy to wear and it won't make a good ashtray."

At the summer games in London, the individual foil competition is won by Hungary's Ilona Elek, who also took the gold at the last Olympics in 1936. One of the new women's sports is rowing, though there is only one rowing event permitted, as compared with four for men. This event, a 1,500-meter kayak race, is won by Karn Hoff of Denmark. The team gymnastics event is won by Czechoslovakia.

Vickie Draves of the United States is the first woman to take both diving golds. Denmark's Greta Andersen, who will later swim the English Channel six times and set a record England-to-France time, wins the 100-meter freestyle. American Ann Curtis, silver medalist in the 100, wins the gold in the 400-meter freestyle, and the silver medalist in the 400, Denmark's Karen-Margrete Harup, wins the 100-meter backstroke with an Olympic record time. Petronella van Vliet of the Netherlands wins the 200-meter breaststroke. The 4 x 100-meter freestyle relay is won by the U.S. team of Curtis, Marie Corridon, Thelma Kalama, and Brenda Helser. The Danes, including Andersen and Harup, take the silver.

The new women's track-and-field events at this Olympics are the 200-meter dash, the shot put, and the long jump. Dutch athlete Fanny Blankers-Koen is the world record holder in the long jump, but athletes can enter only a certain number of events in the games, so she does not compete in the long jump. That event is won instead by Hungary's Olga Gyarmati, with a leap of 18' 8.25" that falls short of Blankers-Koen's record by 20 inches. Blankers-Koen, who was labeled "too old" by the press, is the sensation of these games, even without participating in the long jump. She wins golds in the 100-meter and 200-meter dashes, the hurdles, and the 4 x 100-meter relay, setting an Olympic record in the hurdles.

American Audrey (Mickey) Patterson takes a bronze in the 200-meter run, becoming the first black woman to medal in the games. Tuskegee Institute track-and-field star Alice Coachman wins the high jump, making her the first black woman to win an Olympic gold. Bronze in the high jump goes to French concert pianist Micheline Ostermeyer, who also sets an Olympic record in the shot put and wins the gold in discus. Herma Bauma of Austria wins the javelin gold with an Olympic record distance of 45.57 meters.

Activism

Egyptian feminist Inji Efflatoun publishes *80 Million*, an analysis of the status of Egyptian women.

South African doctor Charlotte Maxeke cofounds the African Women's League, headed by Ida Mntwana.

Korean politician Soon Chan Park (September 10, 1898–January 10, 1983), one of the principal figures in Asian feminism, founds and becomes first president of the Korean National Women's Association.

Aug. 3 Hungarian feminist and pacifist Rosika Schwimmer dies, shortly after being nominated for a Nobel Peace Prize. A lifelong reformer, she cofounded the pacifist organization Feministák Egyesülete, worked for access to birth control, published a collection of Hungarian folk tales, edited the journal *A Nö*, and translated Charlotte Perkins Gilman's *Women and Economics* into Hungarian.

Business and Industry

U.S. newspaper publisher Katharine Graham (b. 1917), with her husband, gains a controlling interest in the *Washington Post*.

India's Factory Law requires employers of more than fifty women to provide day care for children under six.

Gertrude Rogallo designs the first effective hang glider.

Indian business founder Kamaladevi Chattopadhyay (b. 1903) establishes the Indian Cooperative Union to help refugees find work.

English trade unionist Anne Loughlin becomes general secretary of the 100,000-member Tailors and Garment Workers Union, making her the first woman leader of a mixed-sex union.

Science and Medicine

U.S. architect Eleanor Raymond and U.S. chemist-engineer Dr. Maria Telkes invent the first solar-heated house.

U.S. pathologist and biochemist Gerty Cori is elected to the National Academy of Sciences; English zoologist Sidnie Manton becomes a fellow of the Royal Society.

English botanist Agnes Arber wins the Linnean Society's Gold Medal.

Sept. 17 U.S. anthropologist Ruth Benedict dies, shortly after being made a full professor at Columbia. Her fieldwork was done among Native American cultures and resulted in several books and articles, but her most influential and enduring books were on general anthropological theory and its applications to major world conflicts.

Education and Scholarship

Iranian educator Fatima Sayyah (b. 1902) dies. She was Tehran University's first female professor, Iran's first female UN representative, and editor, from 1945, of the women's magazine *Zanane Iran* (*Women of Iran*).

Cambridge University begins granting full degrees to women.

Religion

U.S. Catholic theologian Dorothy Day publishes *On Pilgrimage*.

Yugoslavian nun Mother Theresa founds the Missionaries of Charity in the slums of Calcutta, India.

U.S. educator Nannie Helen Burroughs becomes president of the National Baptist Woman's Convention, which she has served as corresponding secretary since 1900.

1949

General Status and Daily Life

Hungary and Britain give women equal spousal rights.

Britain tries its first marital rape case. The husband and wife in question were separated, and the justice hearing the case feels that the wife was thus no longer obliged to meet her husband's sexual demands, but the jury finds him not guilty anyway.

The United States sees the introduction of prepared cake mixes, the Pillsbury Bake-Off, Sara Lee cheesecake, canasta, and pizza.

Government, the Military, and the Law

Thirty-one of the 409 members of West Germany's Bundestag are women, including socialist Louise Schröder (1887–1957), former deputy mayor of Berlin.

Russian communist Ana Pauker becomes deputy premier of the Soviet Union, a post she will hold until she is purged in 1952.

Great Britain gets its first female king's counselors, Rose Heilbron and Helena Normanton (1883–1957).

Women in Chile and China get the vote.

American political hostess Perle Mesta (b. October 12, 1889) becomes envoy extraordinary and minister plenipotentiary to Luxembourg, which is ruled by a woman, Grand Duchess Charlotte.

German lawyer and politician Hilde Benjamin becomes vice president of the Supreme Court, a position she will hold until 1953.

Indian politician Vijaya Pandit is named ambassador to the United States.

Mar. 10 Axis Sally (Mildred Gillars, 1900–June 25, 1988) becomes the first woman convicted of wartime treason against the United States. The highest-paid radio broadcaster in Germany, she conveyed propaganda to U.S. troops. She is sentenced to thirty years in prison and a $10,000 fine; she serves twelve years, is released, and becomes a kindergarten teacher.

July 26 Argentinian political figure Eva Perón founds the Peronist Feminist party.

Oct. 12 Eugenie Moore Anderson (b. May 26, 1909) becomes the first U.S. woman ambassador when she is named ambassador to Denmark.

Literature and the Visual Arts

Russian abstract artist and theatrical designer Alexandra Exter (b. 1882) dies.

U.S. poet Gwendolyn Brooks's second collection, *Annie Allen*, makes her the first black Pulitzer Prize recipient. She began writing poetry at age seven.

South African writer Nadine Gordimer publishes her first collection of short stories, *Face to Face*.

New poetry includes Edith Sitwell's *The Canticle of the Rose*, Nelly Sachs's *Sternverdunkelung*, and Sibilla Aleramo's *Il mondo e adolescente*.

Georgia O'Keeffe is elected to the National Institute of Arts and Letters.

May 12 U.S. artist Neysa McMein (b. January 24, 1888) dies. She illustrated advertisements for Palmolive soap, Lucky Strike cigarettes, and Betty Crocker foods; drew sophisticated covers for *McCall's*, the *Saturday Evening Post*, *Collier's*, and *Photoplay*; and painted portraits of Presidents Harding and Hoover, Canadian actress Beatrice Lillie (1898–1989), poet Edna St. Vincent Millay, authors Anne Lindbergh and Dorothy Parker, and actor Charlie Chaplin.

Performing Arts and Entertainment

Tanzanian singer Said Tatu is born.

French film director Jacqueline Audry makes *Gigi*, the first of many films she will make based on works by Colette. In *Gigi*, a young woman trained to be a courtesan rejects her upbringing and chooses marriage instead.

Israeli choreographer Sara Levi-Tanai founds the Inbal dance company, which bases its works on folklore and biblical tradition.

Israeli film producer Margot Klausner, who in 1935 helped to make Israel's first film, founds Israel's oldest and largest production company, the Israel Motion Picture Studios.

Polish film director Wanda Jakubowska makes her best film, *The Last Stop*, about the dehumanization of women in the Nazi concentration camps. Jakubowska herself was imprisoned at Auschwitz and Ravensbrück during the war.

U.S. actress Ruth Gordon (b. 1896) coauthors the screenplay for *Adam's Rib*, which stars Katharine Hepburn as a determined attorney and Judy Holliday as her client, a woman accused of assaulting her husband. Clare Booth Luce writes the screenplay for *Come to the Stable*, and Virginia Kellogg writes the violent James Cagney gangster picture *White Heat*. Ayn Rand writes the screenplay for *The Fountainhead*, based on her book of the same title.

Ingrid Bergman leaves her husband, dentist Peter Lindstrom, for Italian director Roberto Rossellini, who worked with her on this year's *Stromboli*. Her reputation suffers, and she is denounced on the floor of the U.S. Congress.

South African-English composer Priaulx Rainier writes a *Barbaric Dance Suite* for piano.

U.S. dancer Helen Tamiris choreographs the Broadway musical *Touch and Go*, winning the Antoinette Perry ("Tony") Award for her work. Stage and costume designer Aline Bernstein also wins a Tony Award for her costumes for the opera *Regina*.

Filmgoers can see Susan Hayward in *Tulsa*, French actress Anouk Aimée in *Les amants de Vérone* (*The Lovers of Verona*), and Swedish actress Harriet Andersson (b. 1932) in her first film, *While the City Sleeps*.

Athletics and Exploration

Bullfighter Conchita Cintron, prevented by Spanish law from fighting bulls on foot, illegally dismounts and executes several skillful passes, then refuses to kill the bull. The enthusiastic crowd, seeing her arrested, successfully demands her release.

Activism

French feminist philosopher Simone de Beauvoir publishes the controversial, influential two-volume treatise *Le deuxième sexe* (*The Second Sex*), the foremost feminist work of the decade.

Pakistani politician and women's leader Begum Liaquat Ali Khan establishes the All Pakistan Women's Association.

U.S. author Pearl S. Buck founds Welcome House, an agency that arranges the adoptions of Asian-American children.

China's central feminist organization, the All China Democratic Women's Federation (ACDWF), is founded. It lobbies for women's rights and publishes *Women in China* magazine, but it chiefly serves as a means of communicating communist party policies to women.

Egyptian feminist Inji Efflatoun publishes *Women with Us*, an analysis of Egyptian women's status.

Business and Industry

Prostitution is outlawed in China, which closes all brothels in major cities, including the 237 in Beijing. Former prostitutes are sent to work in factories, on farms, and, in a few cases, at the Beijing Opera.

Englishwoman Mirabel Topham (d. 1980) purchases Aintree racecourse, home of the famous Grand National steeplechase; she will own and run the course until 1973.

Argentina's 15,000 female textile workers win the legal right to equal pay.

Science and Medicine

U.S. biochemist Rachel Brown (b. 1898) and mycologist Elizabeth Hazen (b. August 24, 1885) isolate the first antifungal antibiotic, Nystatin, which can be used to treat human fungal infections, to restore moldy paintings, and even to attack Dutch elm disease. The two women use the millions of dollars in profit from the drug to establish the Brown-Hazen Fund, which sponsors scientific research.

American Winifred Goldring becomes the first woman president of the Paleontological Society.

English biochemist Dorothy Crowfoot Hodgkin (b. 1910) establishes the molecular structure of penicillin using X-ray crystallography.

Education and Scholarship

Ani Manoppo, Indonesia's first woman lawyer, becomes dean of the law faculty of Medan.

Oct. 9 Harvard Law School authorizes the admission of women.

Religion

U.S. theologian Georgia Harkness publishes her lectures as *The Gospel and Our World*.

1950

General Status and Daily Life

The constitutions of India and Nicaragua grant women equal rights; India's permits affirmative action programs that favor women.

Israel sets the minimum legal age of marriage for women at seventeen except in special circumstances: when the woman has given birth, when she is pregnant with her fiancé's child, or when she is sixteen and "special conditions" prevail.

Apr. The U.S. Census Bureau recognizes a married woman's right to use her birth name.

Government, the Military, and the Law

Ghana's first woman judge, Annie Jiagge, is called to the bar in the Gold Coast.

Women get equal suffrage rights in El Salvador and Ghana; women over twenty-one get the vote in India.

Olga Nuñez de Sasallow, the first woman in Nicaragua to earn a law degree, becomes the deputy minister of public education.

English politician Edith Summerskill becomes minister of national insurance.

Danish lawyer and politician Helga Pedersen (b. 1911) becomes a member of Parliament and is named minister of justice.

Senator Margaret Chase Smith (b. December 14, 1897), a Republican from Maine, issues a "Declaration of Conscience" against the tactics of paranoid communist-hunter Joseph McCarthy: "I don't want to see the Republican Party ride to victory on the four horsemen of calumny—fear, ignorance, bigotry and smear."

French army physician Valérie Andre (b. 1922), later the first woman general in France, is commissioned as a medical helicopter pilot. She will fly approximately 150 missions in Vietnam under combat conditions.

Jan. 8 Madame Chiang Kai-shek (Soong Mei-ling) returns to Taiwan after a visit to the United States, pledging unending war against the communist government of mainland China.

Aug. After the arrest of her husband, Julius, for espionage, U.S. socialist and alleged spy Ethel Rosenberg (b. September 28, 1915) is arrested on rather flimsy evidence. She will be held for eight months without formal charges being filed.

Literature and the Visual Arts

French writer and filmmaker Marguerite Duras (b. 1914) publishes her first important novel, *Un barrage contre la Pacifique*.

Uruguayan poet Juana de Ibarbourou publishes *Perdida* and becomes president of the Uruguayan Society of Authors.

Nigerian potter Ladi Kwali receives her first serious recognition.

July 12 U.S. interior designer Elsie De Wolfe (b. December 20, 1865) dies. Upon seeing the Acropolis in Athens, she cried, "It's beige! My color!"

Performing Arts and Entertainment

Portuguese cellist Guilhermina Suggia (b. 1888) and English music hall singer Kate Carney (b. 1868) die. Carney, known as "the Cockney Queen," was celebrated for her renditions of "Liza Johnson" and "Three Pots a Shilling."

U.S. gospel singer Mahalia Jackson records "Go Tell It on the Mountain."

French film director Jacqueline Audry makes *L'Ingénue libertine*, a movie based on a tale by Colette. It tells the story of a young married woman in the 1890s who has various sexual adventures before determining that her husband is the best lover of all. Ida Lupino directs *Never Fear* and *Outrage*, which both depict women in trouble, one because of polio and the other because of a rape. English playwright and filmmaker Muriel Box directs her first feature film, *The Happy Family*.

U.S. screenwriter Edna Anhalt receives an Oscar for *Panic in the Streets*, which she coauthored. She defeats Frances Goodrich, coauthor of *Father of the Bride* (starring Elizabeth Taylor, b. 1932) and Virginia Kellogg, coauthor of *Caged*.

Tallulah Bankhead becomes the host of NBC's "The Big Show."

British actress Peggy Ashcroft plays Beatrice in *Much Ado About Nothing*.

French composer Elsa Barraine composes the ballet *Claudine à l'école*, based on Colette's novel of the same name.

English soprano and opera producer Joan Cross produces *La Traviata* at Sadler's Wells Opera.

Norwegian soprano Kirsten Flagstad gives the first performance of Richard Strauss's *Vier letzte Lieder*.

English ballerina Alicia Markova cofounds the London Festival Ballet.

The most notable movie of the year is *All About Eve*, which stars Bette Davis as an aging actress being edged out of the limelight by a devious young admirer. The film also features a young starlet named Marilyn Monroe. It earns an Academy Award nomination and an American Cinema Editors (ACE) award for its editor, Barbara McLean, and an Oscar for the costume designer Edith Head.

Other new films include *Samson and Delilah*, with Hedy Lamarr; *My Blue Heaven*, with Betty Grable, whose intense wartime popularity is beginning to fade; *Sunset Boulevard*, with Gloria Swanson in her most memorable role as an insane, egomaniacal, forgotten silent movie star; and *The Golden Salamander*, with French actress Anouk Aimée. Judy Holliday stars in the film version of *Born Yesterday*, playing Billie Dawn, the ditsy character she made famous on stage. Holliday beats Davis and Swanson for the Best Actress Oscar.

"The Kate Smith Hour" debuts on television.

Jan. 5 A well-received dramatic version of Carson McCullers's *The Member of the Wedding* opens in New York, starring Julie Harris and Ethel Waters (b. 1900).

Apr. 4 The Mozart girls' choir of Dresden seeks political asylum in West Berlin.

Oct. Gracie Allen and George Burns start their television sitcom on CBS.

Nov. U.S. stage director Margaret Webster becomes the first woman to direct at New York's Metropolitan Opera Company.

Athletics and Exploration

Romanian table tennis player Angelica Rozeanu wins the world singles title. She will win it again every year from 1951 to 1955.

U.S. athlete Babe Didrikson Zaharias is named the Associated Press Woman Athlete of the Half-Century.

English equestrienne Pat Smythe (b. 1928) sets a women's horse jumping height record of 6', 10 7/8".

U.S. tennis player Louise Brough wins the singles, doubles, and mixed doubles titles at Wimbledon. With Margaret Osborne, she also wins the U.S. doubles title.

U.S. tennis player Althea Gibson (b. 1927) becomes the first black athlete to compete in the U.S. Open.

Figure skater Jeannette Altwegg wins her fourth British championship.

Aug. U.S. swimmer Florence Chadwick breaks the record time for swimming the English Channel.

Activism

Vietnamese politician Nguyen Thi Binh (b. 1927) organizes Saigon's first anti-American demonstration.

U.S. social reformer Josephine Goldmark (b. 1877), who campaigned for child-labor laws, a ten-hour workday, and protective legislation for women, dies.

Punya Prava Dhungana founds the All Nepal Women's Organization, a group that supports women's education.

Business and Industry

Walter Beech, cofounder of the Beech Aircraft company, dies. His widow, Olive, the other company founder, becomes president, chairman of the board, and CEO. She has already been performing the functions of these offices since June 1940, when Walter first fell ill.

There are 19,180,000 women in the Soviet work force, constituting 47% of the total work force.

In China, most working women have a right to eight weeks of paid maternity leave and one hour a day of nursing time for the first year after delivery.

In the United States, 34% of women are in the work force, constituting 27.9% of the total work force; 70% of households have a single income and a male head of household.

Science and Medicine

Indian family planning advocate Dhanvanthi Rama Rau cofounds Planned Parenthood International.

Hattie Alexander and Grace Leidy develop procedures for genetically altering the bacterium that causes influenzal meningitis.

U.S. botanist and conservationist Emma Lucy Braun (April 19, 1889–March 5, 1971), author of more than 180 books and articles, becomes the first woman president of the Ecological Society of America and publishes *Deciduous Forests of Eastern North America*, which quickly becomes a classic.

New publications include Margaret Mead's *Social Anthropology*, German-American psychiatrist Frieda Fromm-Reichmann's *Principles of Intensive Psychotherapy*, and American anthropologist Gladys Reichard's (July 17, 1893–July 25, 1955) best work, *Navaho Religion: A Study of Symbolism*.

U.S. physician Margaret Giannini founds the Mental Retardation Institute of New York Medical College, one of the first clinics in the world devoted to developmental disabilities.

Helen Octavia Dickens (b. 1900) becomes the first black woman fellow of the American College of Surgeons.

Indian social work organizer Amrit Kaur becomes president of the Indian Red Cross, which she founded.

Education and Scholarship

Yoshi Katsurada becomes the first Japanese woman to earn a science doctorate in mathematics.

Olympiada Kozlova is made head of the Moscow Institute of Economist Engineers.

Religion

The Catholic church canonizes several women this year, including Bartholomea Capitanio and Vincentia Gerosa, Italian founders of the Sisters of Charity of Lovere; French queen Joan of Valois; French founder Emily de Rodat; Italian martyr Maria Goretti; and Ecuadoran teacher Mariana Paredes y Flores. Italian-American St. Frances Xavier Cabrini is made the patron saint of immigrants.

July 17 English-American Salvation Army General Evangeline Booth (b. Dec. 25, 1865) dies. The daughter of the Salvation Army's founders, she was a powerful force in the organization, rising to positions of national and international leadership.

1951

General Status and Daily Life

Sri Lanka legalizes the marriage of girls under twelve if approved by a religious court.

Israel's Women's Equal Rights Act bans gender discrimination.

In Canada, Indian women lose their tribal citizenship if they marry non-Indians, thereby prohibiting their children from inheriting reservation land.

Government, the Military, and the Law

Argentinian political leader Evita Perón, wife of President Juan Perón, runs for vice president. Despite the popularity of her Social Aid Fund, her campaign is met with resistance from the military, and she withdraws her candidacy in August.

Chilean feminist and government official Ana Figuero becomes Chile's special envoy to the United Nations, where she becomes the first woman to head a General Assembly Committee.

U.S. diplomat Eugenie Moore Anderson becomes the first woman in a democratic state to sign a treaty between nations.

Irina Yekaterina becomes a member of the Soviet Supreme Court.

Inés Enriquez Frödden becomes first woman *disputado* (congressional representative) in Chile.

Nepal's women win the right to vote and to run for office.

Literature and the Visual Arts

Japanese novelist Hayashi Fumiko (b. 1904) and U.S. advice columnist Elizabeth Meriwether Gilmer (November 18, 1861–December 16), better known as "Dorothy Dix," die. Her column covered Carry Nation, women's issues, and murder trials; at her zenith, Dix received 400–500 letters per week, had sixty million readers, and made $100,000 a year.

U.S. journalist Marguerite Higgins (September 3, 1920–January 3, 1966) publishes *War in Korea: The Report of a Woman Combat Correspondent* and wins the Pulitzer Prize in foreign correspondence.

Marianne Moore publishes her *Collected Poems*, which wins the Bollingen Prize, the National Book Award, and the Pulitzer. Other new U.S. poetry collections include Ruth Stone's (b. 1915) *In an Iridescent Time* and Adrienne Rich's (b. 1929) *A Change of World*.

French author Marguerite Yourcenar publishes the historical novel *Les memoires d'Hadrien* (*The Memoirs of Hadrian*), a vivid evocation of imperial Rome.

Performing Arts and Entertainment

U.S. film editor Adrienne Fazan is nominated for an Academy Award for her work on *An American in Paris*. U.S. editor Dorothy Spencer is nominated for *Decision Before Dawn* and wins an ACE award for that film.

U.S. stage director Margaret Webster directs *Aïda* at the Metropolitan Opera.

"I Love Lucy," a sitcom starring comedian Lucille Ball, makes its television debut.

Polish composer and violinist Grazyna Bacewicz (1909–1969), composer of ballets, symphonies, concertos, and violin pieces and author of short stories, novels, and a television play, wins the International Composers' Competition with her Fourth String Quartet.

French actress Maria Casares stars in Sartre's play *Le diable et le bon Dieu*.

Filmgoers can see Katharine Hepburn in *The African Queen*, Susan Hayward in *David and Bathsheba*, Jane Powell in *Royal Wedding*, Leslie Caron in *An American in Paris*, and Swedish actress Anita Björk in *Miss Julie*. English actress Vivien Leigh wins the Best Actress Oscar for *A Streetcar Named Desire*.

Mar. 29 Gertrude Lawrence opens in the musical *The King and I* on Broadway.

May 29 U.S. comedian and singer Fanny Brice dies. She appeared in nine *Ziegfeld Follies* between 1910 and 1936, performed on radio, and made six movies; she was best known for her renditions of "Second Hand Rose" and "My Man." A skillful parodist, she made fun of Camille, Theda Bara, and classical ballet.

Athletics and Exploration

British figure skater Jeannette Altwegg (b. 1930) wins the European and world titles.

French pilot Jacqueline Auriol (b. 1917), the world's first woman test pilot, flies 507 miles per hour, breaking the previous women's speed record held by Jacqueline Cochran. In the next thirteen years, she will break the speed record five times.

July 6 Doris Hart defeats Shirley Fry in the women's singles final at Wimbledon. Fry will win Wimbledon and the U.S. Open in 1956; Hart will win the U.S. title in 1954 and 1955.

Sept. U.S. swimmer Florence Chadwick, despite heavy fog, sets a record time crossing the English Channel from England to France.

Activism

Iranian feminist and journalist Zand-Dokht Zand (b. 1910), cofounder of the organization Daughters of Iran, dies.

U.S. communist and labor leader Elizabeth Gurley Flynn is arrested for conspiracy to overthrow the government and sentenced to three years in jail.

The German Women's Council, an umbrella organization of feminist, labor, and religious groups, is founded.

Egyptian feminist Dori'a Shafiq leads 1,500 women to Parliament to demand the vote.

Business and Industry

U.S. fashion designer Lane Bryant, who began making maternity clothes and built a chain of stores catering to larger women, dies.

Vivian Yen founds the award-winning Tai Yuen Textile Company, Taiwan's largest textile corporation.

The International Labor Organization (ILO) passes Convention No. 100, endorsing equal pay for work of equal value. It will be ratified by 105 countries by 1985.

In India, 23% of women are employed.

Zeb-Un-Nirsa Hamidullah becomes publisher and editor of the Pakistani magazine *Mirror*.

U.S. housewife Marion Donovan invents the first disposable diaper, the Boater. Donovan, who also invented a zipper pull and a skirt hanger, will eventually sell her diaper company for $1 million.

Finnish designer Armi Ratia cofounds the successful design house Marimekko.

Science and Medicine

U.S. ecologist Rachel Carson publishes *The Sea Around Us.*

Education and Scholarship

U.S. chef Julia Child cofounds the Parisian cooking school L'École des Trois Gourmandes.

New publications include German-American political philosopher Hannah Arendt's (October 14, 1906– December 4, 1975) *The Origins of Totalitarianism*; U.S. poet Louise Bogan's literary critical history, *Achievements in American Poetry, 1900–1950*; and American Catherine Drinker Bowen's *The Writing of Biography*, a collection of essays.

Margaret Louise Colt wins a Pulitzer Prize for her biography *John C. Calhoun: American Portrait.*

Religion

American Paula Ackerman (b. c. 1894) becomes the first woman to serve as a rabbi when she temporarily takes over her late husband's duties.

Apr. 5 U.S. physician and missionary Rosetta Hall (b. September 19, 1865), who established hospitals and a medical college in Korea, dies.

1952

General Status and Daily Life

China's constitution grants women equality and freedom of marriage.

The first domestic microwave oven goes on sale in the United States for $1,295.

Government, the Military, and the Law

Polish spy Christine Granville, Countess Skarbeck (b. 1915), dies. One of the most successful Resistance agents in France during World War II, she often went on missions to Poland and the Balkans. She saved two Resistance workers from being shot by the Gestapo and talked a unit of Polish troops in the German army into surrendering.

Finnish politician and feminist Miina Sillanpää (b. 1866), a member of Parliament for forty years and a former servant who worked for better conditions for domestics and single mothers, dies.

Chilean feminist and government official Ana Figuero becomes the first woman on the UN Security Committee.

Indian doctor Shushila Nayar (b. 1914) begins four years as speaker of the Delhi Legislative Assembly.

U.S. editor Charlotta Bass is the Progressive party's nominee for vice president, becoming the first black woman to run for vice president of the United States.

Lebanese women who have completed elementary school get the right to vote.

Feb. 8 Elizabeth II (b. 1926) becomes queen of England.

May 29 Women get equal suffrage rights in Greece.

July 26 Argentinian political figure Evita Perón (b. 1919) dies. She convinced her husband, Juan, to name seven women to the Senate and twenty-four to deputy posts. She was a champion of women's and workers' rights, but she also embezzled government funds and made use of the tactics of nepotism, torture, and the "disappearances" of those who offended her.

Literature and the Visual Arts

South African writer Nadine Gordimer (b. 1923) publishes *The Soft Voice of the Serpent*, a collection of short stories.

French sculptor Germaine Richier (1904–1959) creates *Devil With Claws*. Richier works in traditional materials like bronze and uses more unusual items like skulls as well.

U.S. journalist Doris Fleeson (May 20, 1901–August 1, 1970), whose political insights are published in more than one hundred papers nationwide, is dubbed the "Capitol's top newshen" by *Newsweek.*

Mexican potter Doña Rosa rediscovers an ancient Zapotec technique for making blackware out of the gray clay near Oaxaca.

New novels include Doris Lessing's (b. October 22, 1919) *Martha Quest*, Edna Ferber's *Giant*, Spanish novelist Carmen Laforet Diaz's (b. 1920) *La isla y los demonios*, and U.S. author Flannery O'Connor's (March 25, 1925–August 3, 1964) *Wise Blood*.

Iranian writer and film maker Furugh Farrukhzad (1935–1967) publishes a collection of poems, *The Captive*.

May 16   U.S. photographer Frances Benjamin Johnston (b. January 15, 1864) dies. Her work included studies of factories and workers, architectural photographs, and portraits of William McKinley, Theodore Roosevelt, Mark Twain, Joel Chandler Harris, and Susan B. Anthony.

Nov. 13   U.S. author Margaret Wise Brown (b. May 23, 1910) dies. She wrote more than one hundred children's books and lyrics for twenty-one children's records.

Performing Arts and Entertainment

English music hall star and male impersonator Vesta Tilley (Matilda Alice Powles, b. 1864) dies. Extremely popular, she was given a souvenir book at her retirement containing the signatures of 2 million fans.

Audrey Hepburn stars in the play *Gigi*.

U.S. composer Ruth Crawford-Seeger composes *Suite for Wind Quartet*.

A pregnant Lucille Ball (b. August 6, 1911) takes her pregnancy on the air in the second season of "I Love Lucy." It is the first time a pregnancy is depicted on television, though the words *pregnancy* and *pregnant* are not allowed on the air.

Filmgoers can see Esther Williams in *Million-Dollar Mermaid*, Grace Kelly (1929–September 10, 1982) in *High Noon*, Ingrid Bergman in *Europa '51*, Doris Day (b. April 3, 1924) in the musical *April in Paris*, and Swedish actress Anita Björk in *Kvinnors Väntan* (*Secrets of Women*). Katharine Hepburn plays a gifted athlete in *Pat and Mike*. Swedish actress Harriet Andersson stars in *Trots* (*Defiance*) and in *Monika*, which Ingmar Bergman wrote especially for her. Egyptian actress Assis stars in *Salaheddin*, a film made by her own production company. Shirley Booth wins the Best Actress Oscar for her performance in *Come Back, Little Sheba*.

U.S. film editor Anne Bauchens (February 2, 1881?–May 7, 1967) receives an Academy Award nomination for her work on *The Greatest Show on Earth*, which also wins her the first ACE Achievement Award. Adrienne Fazan wins an ACE award for her work on *Singing in the Rain*.

Flutist Doriot Anthony Dwyer of the Boston Symphony Orchestra becomes the first woman appointed to first chair in a major orchestra.

Mexican choreographer Amalia Hernández founds Ballet Folklorico de Mexico.

Chinese film editor Shih Mei directs the documentary *Harness the Huai River*.

May 20   The House Un-American Activities Committee has stepped up its investigations of the entertainment world, convinced that Hollywood is riddled with communists. Playwright and screenwriter Lillian Hellman, due to appear tomorrow before HUAC, writes to committee chairman John S. Wood: "I am most willing to answer all questions about myself . . . . But to hurt innocent people whom I knew many years ago in order to save myself is, to me, inhuman and indecent and dishonorable. I cannot and will not cut my conscience to fit this year's fashions."

June 13   U.S. concert and opera singer Emma Eames (b. August 13, 1865) dies. She sang Marguerite in *Faust*, Desdemona in *Otello*, and Elsa in *Lohengrin*; gave private performances for Queen Victoria; and was also noted for her performances in *Aïda*, *Falstaff*, *Il Trovatore*, *Don Giovanni*, *The Magic Flute*, *The Marriage of Figaro*, *Tannhäusen*, and *Die Walküre*.

Nov.   Agatha Christie's play *The Mousetrap* opens. It will be the longest-running play in British history, still being performed in the 1990s.

Athletics and Exploration

German weightlifter Katie Sandwina (b. 1884) dies.

Winter   At the Olympics in Oslo, Nordic skiing is introduced as a women's sport. The Finns sweep the one event, the 10 kilometers, with Lydia Wideman in first place, Mirja Hietamies in second, and Siiri Rantanen in third. In Alpine skiing, Austria's Trude Jochum-Beiser takes the downhill gold. Andrea Mead Lawrence, winning the slalom and giant slalom, becomes the first American skier to earn two gold medals.

In women's figure skating, 1948 bronze medalist Jeannette Altwegg of Great Britain, this year's European champion, takes the gold; Tenley Albright, the U.S. champion, gets the silver. West German Ria Falk takes the gold in pairs skating.

Summer   At Helsinki, four women compete in the equestrian events, which are now open to both sexes. Ida von Nagel of Germany takes a bronze in the team dressage, and Denmark's Lis Hartel, paralyzed from the knees down by polio, takes a silver in individual dressage.

The IOC now allows individual gymnastics events as well as the team competition. Maria Gorokhovskaya of the Soviet Union wins the all-around competition and takes silvers in the uneven parallel bars, the floor exercise, the horse vault, and the balance beam. Her teammate Nina Bocharova takes the silver in the all-around and the gold in the balance beam. The bronze medalist in the all-around, Hungary's Margit Korondi, gets the gold in the bars and bronzes in the floor exercise and balance beam. Another Hungarian, Agnes Keleti, takes the floor exercise gold and the bronze in the parallel bars. The all-around team gold goes to the Soviet Union's team of Gorokhovskaya, Bocharova, Galina Minaicheva (bronze medalist in the vault), Yekaterina Kalinchuk (gold medalist in the vault), Galina Urbanowich, Pelageya Danilova, Galina Schamrai, and Medeja Dzugeli. Hungary's silver-medal team includes Korondi, Keleti, and 1956 team silver medalists Olga Tass, Erzebet Gulyas-Koteles, and Andrea Bodo.

In track and field, Australia's Marjorie Jackson wins the 100-meter and 200-meter dashes, and her teammate Shirley De La Hunty-Strickland, bronze medalist in the 100-meter dash, wins the 80-meter hurdles. The United States wins the 4 x 100-meter relay, making fifteen-year-old runner Barbara Jones the youngest-ever gold medalist in track.

South Africa's Esther Brand wins the high jump, and New Zealand's Yvette Williams wins the long jump, setting an Olympic record. Soviet athlete Galina Zybina wins the shotput gold. The Soviet Union sweeps the discus throw, with Nina Romaschkova, Yelisaveta Bagryantseva, and Nina Dumbadze taking first, second, and third. Czechoslovakia's Dana Zatopkova wins the javelin throw.

The swimming events are dominated by the Hungarians. Katalin Szoke wins the 100-meter freestyle, and Judit Temes gets the bronze. Another Hungarian, Valeria Gyenge, wins the 400-meter freestyle. Her teammate Eva Novak, the 1948 bronze medalist in the 200-meter breaststroke, takes silvers in the 400-meter freestyle and the 200-meter breaststroke; Novak is defeated in the latter race by yet another compatriot, Eva Szekely. Joan Harrison of South Africa wins the 100-meter backstroke. The 400-meter freestyle relay is won, not surprisingly, by the Hungarian team: Temes, Szoke, Eva Novak, and Ilona Novak. American Patricia McCormick wins the gold in both springboard and platform diving.

Irene Camber of Italy wins the foil fencing competition, followed by prewar champion Ilona Elek and Denmark's Karen Lachmann. Sylvi Saimo of Finland wins the 1,500-meter kayak event.

Activism

Japanese feminist and politician Takayama Shigeri (1899–1977) founds Chifuren, a 6-million-member women's and consumers' rights group that she will head until her death in 1977.

Women's Voluntary Services, a charitable group, is founded by Nepal's Queen Rajya Laxmi Rana and Princesses Princep Shah and Helen Shah.

Business and Industry

U.S. madam Polly Adler (April 16, 1900?–June 9, 1962) publishes her autobiography, *A House Is Not a Home*, which is translated into eleven languages and made into a movie.

Women are 23% of the Yugoslavian work force.

Science and Medicine

British cell biologist Honor Fell (b. 1900), an expert on vitamins, hormones, and immunopathology, is made a fellow of the Royal Society.

U.S. doctor Virginia Apgar (June 7, 1909–August 7, 1974) invents the Apgar Score to measure the well-being of newborns.

Margaret Sanger cofounds and becomes first president of the International Planned Parenthood Federation.

Naval officer Grace Hopper writes the first computer compiler, enabling computer programs to be written without having to be built from scratch each time.

Japanese chemist Kimiko Anno, an expert on complex polysaccharides, becomes an instructor at the Ochanomizu Women's University.

America's Society of Women Engineers (SWE) gives its first annual Achievement Award to Hungarian-American chemist Maria Telkes for her work with solar energy.

U.S. medical researcher Dr. Dorothy Horstmann isolates polio virus in its early stages in the victims' bloodstreams, making it easier to develop a vaccine.

Education and Scholarship

Nov. 13 U.S. physical education specialist Jessie Bancroft (b. December 20, 1867) dies. She was the president and founder of the American Posture League, the first woman member of the American Academy of Physical Education, and the first woman executive secretary of the American Association for the Advancement of Physical Education.

Religion

English missionary and traveler Mildred Cable (b. 1878), who cowrote over twenty books, crossed the Gobi Desert five times, and learned several Chinese dialects, dies.

U.S. journalist, playwright, and politician Clare Boothe Luce, a convert to Catholicism, edits the Catholic publication *Saints for Now*.

1953

General Status and Daily Life

Hurricanes begin to be named after women.

Government, the Military, and the Law

Lebanese and Mexican women get the vote.

The first women are elected to Greece's Parliament.

The Danish Crown, a ceremonial post, is now allowed to pass to women as well as men.

U.S. staff sergeant Barbara Olive Barnwell receives the U.S. Navy-Marine Corps Medal for Heroism after rescuing a drowning soldier in 1952. She is the first woman to receive this medal.

Fae Margaret Adams (b. 1918) becomes the first commissioned woman doctor in the regular U.S. Army.

German lawyer and politician Hilde Benjamin becomes minister of justice.

Golda Meir becomes chairman of the Israeli delegation to the UN.

Mar. 3 U.S. journalist, playwright, and politician Clare Boothe Luce is appointed ambassador to Italy. It is the most important diplomatic post ever to be awarded to a U.S. woman.

Apr. 11 Oveta Culp Hobby becomes the first U.S. secretary of the Department of Health, Education, and Welfare (HEW).

June 19 Convicted spy Ethel Rosenberg is electrocuted. The execution is controversial because many believe she has not committed espionage.

Sept. 15 Indian diplomat Vijaya Pandit becomes the first woman president of the UN General Assembly.

Literature and the Visual Arts

New poetry includes English poet Edith Sitwell's *Gardeners and Astronomers*, Belgian Prix Renée Vivien winner Anne-Marie Kegels's (b. 1912) *Nothing but Living*, Canadian poet Anne Hébert's (b. 1916) *Le tombeau des rois* (*The Tomb of the Kings*), El Salvadoran poet Claribel Alegría's *Vigils*, and Austrian poet Ingeborg Bachmann's (1926–1973) *Die gestundete Zeit*.

New novels include British writer Doris Lessing's *Retreat to Innocence*, French novelist Nathalie Sarraute's *Martereau*, and South African writer Nadine Gordimer's first novel, *The Lying Days*. French writer and filmmaker Marguerite Duras publishes the novel *Les petits chevaux de Tarquinia*.

Mexican painter Frida Kahlo has her first major show, in Mexico City.

Performing Arts and Entertainment

U.S. stage and costume designer Aline Bernstein designs her last show, creating the costume for the off-Broadway play *The World of Sholom Aleichem*.

French filmmaker Alice Guy Blaché is awarded the Legion of Honor.

Kinuyo Tanaka becomes Japan's first woman film director.

Australian-American composer Peggy Glanville-Hicks (b. 1912) writes an opera, *The Transposed Heads*.

Filmgoers can see Betty Grable, Lauren Bacall, and Marilyn Monroe in *How to Marry a Millionaire*, Italian actress Sophia Loren in *Aida*, and Marilyn Monroe in *Niagara* and, with Jane Russell, in *Gentlemen Prefer Blondes* (based on the 1925 novel by Anita Loos). Audrey Hepburn wins the Best Actress Oscar for her performance in *Roman Holiday*.

Films directed by women include Polish producer and director Wanda Jakubowska's *Soldier of Victory*, British actress and director Ida Lupino's thriller *The Hitchhiker*, and English playwright, screenwriter, and director Muriel Box's film about policewomen, *Street Corner*.

U.S. screenwriter Betty Comden receives an Oscar nomination for *The Band Wagon*, which she coauthored.

Helen Deutsch's *Lili* is also nominated.

U.S. news analyst Pauline Frederick moves from ABC to NBC, where, as UN correspondent, she will cover events in the Suez, the Congo, Hungary, Cuba, Cyprus, Vietnam, and the Middle East.

Apr. 23 Leontyne Price performs *La Voyante* at the New York Metropolitan Opera.

July 17 U.S. actress Maude Adams dies. Best known for her work in the plays of Sir James Barrie, she created the roles of Peter Pan and Lady Babbie. Later in her career, she became a lighting designer and worked for General Electric, developing a new type of bulb for which she never bothered to secure a patent.

Nov. 3 Lillian Gish opens in New York in *A Trip to Bountiful*.

Athletics and Exploration

U.S. tennis player Maureen "Little Mo" Connolly (b. September 17, 1934–June 21, 1969) becomes the first woman to win a Grand Slam, taking the singles title at Wimbledon (July 4) and at the U.S. (September 7), French, and Australian Opens. She won the U.S. title in 1951 and will win Wimbledon and the U.S. Open again in 1954.

U.S. swimmer Florence Chadwick (b. 1919) completes four record-breaking English Channel crossings in five weeks. On October 7, she swims the Bosporus from Europe to Asia and back.

French mountain climber Claude Kogan (b. 1919) leads the first ascent of Nun, a 23,410-foot peak in the Nun-Kun massif.

Feb. 8 British figure skater Jennifer Nicks wins the world pairs title.

Feb. 15 Tenley Albright, who has fought a six-year battle against poliomyelitis, becomes the first U.S. woman to win the World Amateur Figure Skating Championship.

May 18 U.S. pilot Jacqueline Cochran, in an F-86 Sabre jet, becomes the first woman to break the sound barrier. Her achievement is duplicated on August 29 by French aviator Jacqueline Auriol.

Business and Industry

Dr. Evelyn Amartiefio founds the Federation of Ghana Women, a trade and business association.

Science and Medicine

The SWE gives its Achievement Award to aeronautical engineer Elsie Gregory MacGill (d. 1980), the first woman to design, build, and test her own plane.

Education and Scholarship

Belgian Marie Gevers becomes the first woman president of Brussels University's law school.

British historian Cecil Woodham-Smith publishes *The Reason Why*, a history of the Battle of Balaclava in which she debunks the glamorous myths surrounding the Charge of the Light Brigade. Other new publications include U.S. philosopher Susanne Knauth Langer's *Feeling and Form*, British philosopher Iris Murdoch's *Sartre, Romantic Rationalist*, and U.S. feminist historian Mary Ritter Beard's *The Force of Women in Japanese History*.

1954

General Status and Daily Life

Argentina legalizes divorce, a reform sought for decades by the nation's feminists. The law will be repealed, however, next year.

Sept. 11 The Miss America Pageant becomes the first nationally televised beauty contest.

Government, the Military, and the Law

Women in Colombia get the vote.

Pakistani politician and women's leader Begum Liaquat Ali Khan becomes the first Muslim woman ambassador.

English politician Edith Summerskill becomes chairman of the Labor party.

After protests by women in Nepal over the lack of women in the King's Advisory Assembly, a second assembly is formed, with four female members out of 113: Punya Prava Dhungana, Mangla Devi, Maya Devi Shah, and Prativa Jha.

Soviet official Mariya Kovrigina becomes minister of health; she will almost single-handedly reorganize the

Soviet Health Organization.

Apr. 15 U.S. birth control advocate Margaret Sanger becomes the first woman to address Japan's Diet.

July 26 U.S. Congresswoman, diplomat, and lecturer Ruth Bryan Owen (b. October 2, 1885) dies. In Congress, she pushed protective legislation for citrus farmers and legislation to make the Florida Everglades a national park; in her capacity on the Foreign Affairs Committee, she was the first woman to serve on a major congressional committee.

Literature and the Visual Arts

Chinese poet Jia Jia, author of *River of Female*, is born.

Canadian author Margaret Lawrence (b. 1926) translates *A Tree of Poverty*, the first English-language collection of Somali folktales and poems.

Italian architect Gae Aulenti (b. 1927) becomes one of the editors of *Casabella*.

Spanish poet, editor, librarian, and teacher of literature Gloria Fuertes (b. 1918) publishes her first books, *Anthology of Poetics and Poems of the Slums* and *I Advise Drinking Thread*. Her works deal with love, human rights, and daily life. Other new poetry includes Gabriela Mistral's *Lagar*, Louise Bogan's *Collected Poems, 1923–1953*, Puerto Rican poet Julia de Burgos's (February 17, 1914?–July 6, 1953) posthumous *El Mar y Tú y Otros Poemas*, Romanian poet Nina Cassian's (b. 1924) *Outdoor Performance—A Monograph of Love*, and French poet Yvonne Caroutch's (b. 1937) celebrated collection *Soifs*.

French writer Françoise Sagan (b. 1935) publishes her first novel, *Bonjour tristesse*. A best-seller, it is made into a film, is translated into many languages, and wins the Prix des Critiques. Other new novels include Iris Murdoch's (b. 1919) *Under the Net*, Anaïs Nin's (February 21, 1903–January 14, 1977) *A Spy in the House of Love*, and American Eudora Welty's *The Ponder Heart*.

May 29 U.S. journalist Anne O'Hare McCormick, the first woman to win a Pulitzer prize in journalism (1937), dies. Her column, "In Europe" (later, "Abroad"), was published three times a week in the *Times*; she interviewed Franklin Delano Roosevelt, Winston Churchill, Adolf Hitler, Benito Mussolini, and Josef Stalin.

Aug. 3 French novelist Sidonie Gabrielle Colette dies during a violent thunderstorm, reveling in the lightning outside her window. Her last words, accompanied by a gesture toward the sky, are, "Look, look!" She was the author of over fifty books and was rivaled in importance in twentieth-century French fiction only by Proust. She was the first female member of the Academie Goncourt, a holder of the Grand Cross of the Legion of Honor, and the first Frenchwoman to be given a state funeral.

Sept. 6 *Life* publishes "Three Mormon Towns," a photo essay by Dorothea Lange and Ansel Adams.

Performing Arts and Entertainment

English film animator and producer Joy Batchelor, maker of over 700 educational films, co-owner of her own production company, and coproducer of the feature film *Animal Farm*, is born.

French filmmaker Agnès Varda directs, produces, and writes her trend-setting first film, *La Pointe Courte*. It juxtaposes twin story lines, one fictional, one real. Other films by women include English director and screenwriter Muriel Box's *Both Sides of the Law*, a movie about a female police officer; English producer Betty Box's *Doctor in the House*; Russian-American director Maya Deren's *The Very Eye of Night*; and French director Jacqueline Audry's *Huis clos* (*No Exit*, starring Arletty.

U.S. film editor Alma Macrorie receives an Academy Award nomination for her work on *The Bridges at Toko-Ri*. The film also wins her an "Eddie" Award from the American Cinema Editors. Frances Goodrich and Dorothy Kingsley collaborate with Albert Hackett on the Oscar-nominated screenplay for *Seven Brides for Seven Brothers*.

U.S. choreographer and dancer Doris Humphrey (October 17, 1895–December 29, 1958), a major figure in experimental dance who studied with Ruth St. Denis, wins the Capezio Award.

Marilyn Monroe (stage name of Norma Jean Baker, June 1, 1926–August 5, 1962) stars in *The Seven Year Itch* and tours South Korea performing for U.S. troops; later in the year she moves to New York to study acting at Lee and Paula Strasberg's Actors Studio.

Danish dancer Adeline Genée retires as president of the Royal Academy of Dancing; the new president is English ballerina Margot Fonteyn.

U.S. composer Mabel Daniels's *A Psalm of Praise* is performed by the Boston Symphony, making her the first woman to have three works played by that symphony.

British actress Peggy Ashcroft plays *Hedda Gabler*, a role for which the King of Norway awards her a medal.

Judy Garland earns an Academy Award nomination for *A Star Is Born*. The Oscar for Best Actress, however, goes to Grace Kelly, also appearing this year in the Hitchcock thriller *Rear Window*, for her performance in *The Country Girl*. Italian actress Sophia Loren (b. 1934) stars in *L'oro di Napoli* (*Gold of Naples*).

U.S. costume and fashion designer Edith Head wins an Oscar for *Roman Holiday*.

Oct. 20 U.S. actress Mary Martin opens as *Peter Pan* in New York City. Like the first stage Peter, Maude Adams, Martin will become closely identified with this role.

Athletics and Exploration

French mountain climber Claude Kogan reaches nearly 25,000 feet on the Himalayan mountain Cho Oyo, a record height for a European woman.

Soviet aviator Z. P. Sidorishina, navigator of a plane designed to land on ice floes, becomes the first woman to fly to the north pole.

U.S. tennis player Hazel Hotchkiss Wightman wins her last national title, 45 years after she won her first.

July 3 Maureen Connolly is injured in a riding accident and retires from tennis. In her professional career, she has lost only three matches.

July 3 Babe Didrikson Zaharias wins the Women's Open Golf Championship for the third time.

Activism

The National Federation of Indian Women, a broad-based, moderate feminist group, is established in India.

Business and Industry

Israel bars women from dangerous and nighttime work in most cases. In most cases, a woman cannot be fired while pregnant.

Israeli Labor Ministry official Ruth Dayan (b. March 3, 1917) organizes and becomes head of Maskit, a center for encouraging and marketing Israeli handicrafts.

Science and Medicine

Greek microbiologist Angeliki Panajiotatou (b. 1875) dies. A specialist in tropical diseases, she was driven out of her first teaching position by shouts of "Back in the kitchen, back in the kitchen."

U.S. entomologist Edith Patch (b. 1876), who specialized in Aphidae, dies. She published fifteen books and almost a hundred papers and had one genus and several species named for her.

Sept. 17 U.S. pathologist and cancer researcher Maud Slye (b. February 8, 1869) dies. A poet as well as a scientist, she was most significant for her breeding and tracking of 150,000 laboratory mice; early in her career, when money was scarce, she deprived herself of food in order to feed her mice.

English birth control advocate Margaret Pyke becomes chairman of the Family Planning Association.

Italian neurobiologist Rita Levi-Montalcini discovers the mechanism that stimulates nerve cell growth.

America's Society of Women Engineers gives its Achievement Award to Edith Clarke (d. 1959), the first woman fellow of the American Institute of Electrical Engineers, for her work on stability theory and circuit analysis.

Education and Scholarship

U.S. author Mari Sandoz publishes the history *The Buffalo Hunters*.

Religion

Italian saint Mary di Rosa is canonized.

1955

General Status and Daily Life

Abortion is made free and legal on demand in China.

Soviet abortion law is liberalized, but the procedure remains legal in most cases only through the first trimester. Divorce on demand is also restored, but twenty years of illegality have left both abortion and divorce somewhat stigmatized.

India outlaws polygyny for Hindus, but Muslim men may still marry up to four women. Men and women may sue for divorce on the grounds of adultery, desertion, physical or mental cruelty, religious conversion, insanity, leprosy, sexually transmitted disease, disappearance for seven years, or persistent and long-term refusal of "conjugal rights." Women may also sue for divorce from a husband found guilty of rape, sodomy, or bestiality. Women who marry before fifteen have until the age of eighteen to divorce their husbands, as long as the marriage is not consummated.

Government, the Military, and the Law

Zimbabwe guerrilla fighter Joyce Nhongo is born.

Swedish politician Alva Myrdal becomes ambassador to India, Burma, and Ceylon, a position she will hold until 1960.

Women in Nicaragua, Peru (September 7), and Indonesia get the vote.

May Frances G. Knight becomes head of the U.S. Passport Office. In her twenty-two years in that position, she will become known for her willingness to use the office to keep tabs on dissident citizens and to restrict the travel rights of communists and other persons deemed dangerous by the government.

Literature and the Visual Arts

U.S. poet H. D. completes her 1,400-line epic, *Helen in Egypt*. Other new poetry includes Elizabeth Bishop's Pulitzer-winning combined collection *North & South and A Cold Spring*, American Adrienne Rich's *The Diamond Cutters*, Australian Rosemary Dobson's (b. 1920) *Child with a Cockatoo*, and Spanish poet Gloria Fuertes's *Piruli*.

New U.S. short story collections include Eudora Welty's *The Bride of Innisfallen* and Flannery O'Connor's *A Good Man Is Hard to Find*.

Caro Brown of Texas's *Alice Daily Echo* becomes the first woman to win a Pulitzer Prize in local reporting.

U.S. poet Marianne Moore publishes the essay collection *Predilections* and becomes one of the fifty members of the American Academy of Arts and Letters.

New novels include Finnish author Kersti Bergroth's *Balaisuntemme*, U.S. author Mary McCarthy's *A Charmed Life*, French novelist Violette Leduc's *Ravages*, Agatha Christie's *Witness for the Prosecution*, Marguerite Duras's *Le square*, and British philosopher and novelist Iris Murdoch's *The Flight from the Enchanter*.

Performing Arts and Entertainment

U.S. dancer Ruth Page founds the Chicago Ballet.

U.S. screenwriter Sonya Levien wins an Oscar for the screenplay for *Interrupted Melody*, which she wrote with William Ludwig. She defeats U.S. screenwriters Betty Comden, coauthor of *It's Always Fair Weather*, and Isobel Lennart, coauthor of *Love Me or Leave Me*. U.S. screenwriter Phoebe Ephron coauthors the screenplays for *There's No Business Like Show Business* and *Daddy Long Legs*.

English filmmaker and screenwriter Muriel Box directs *Simon and Laura*, a movie about a couple whose marriage is in trouble but who play a loving husband and wife on television.

New movies include *The Seven Year Itch*, with Marilyn Monroe, *Les grands manoeuvre* (*The Grand Manoeuvre*) with French actress Brigitte Bardot, and *Rebel Without a Cause* with American Natalie Wood. Italian actress Anna Magnani wins the Best Actress Academy Award for *The Rose Tattoo*.

Jan. U.S. producer and director Margo Jones (December 12, 1912–July 24, 1955), an advocate of theater-in-the-round who has directed several plays by Tennessee Williams, presents a new play she has discovered and will later coproduce on Broadway: Jerome Lawrence and Robert E. Lee's *Inherit the Wind*.

Jan. 7 U.S. contralto Marian Anderson, in *Un ballo in Maschera*, becomes the first black singer to perform at New York's Metropolitan Opera.

May 5 Gwen Verdon opens in *Damn Yankees*.

Athletics and Exploration

U.S. tennis players Louise Brough and Margaret Osborne win the U.S. doubles title.

U.S. explorer Louise Arner Boyd (1887–1972) becomes the first woman to pilot a plane over the north pole.

French mountain climber Claude Kogan makes the first ascent of 24,300-foot Ganesh Himal.

Russian gymnast Larissa Latynina (b. 1935), the most successful gymnast of all time, male or female, wins five gold medals at the European Championships.

Activism

Bharatiya Grammen Mahila Sangh, an Indian women's group devoted to organizing family planning, maternity and child care, and vocational training for women, is founded.

White South African women form Black Sash, a group that protests government policies of racial discrimination.

Dec. 1 Rosa Parks is arrested in Montgomery, Alabama, for refusing to give up her seat on a bus to a white man. The arrest sparks a boycott of buses by blacks, who make up 75% of the ridership.

Business and Industry

Japanese fashion designer Hanae Mori, the first Japanese designer of Western-style clothes, opens her first store in Tokyo.

American Florence Eiseman (b. 1899) becomes the first children's-wear designer to receive the Neiman-Marcus Award.

Britain's Employment Protection Act guarantees women twenty-nine weeks of maternity leave, six of them at 90% salary.

There are 23,040,000 Russian women in the work force, constituting 46% of the total work force.

Women workers in the United States make 63.9% as much as men.

Science and Medicine

U.S. cytologist, geneticist, and zoologist Alice Boring (b. 1883) dies. She was especially noted for her work with amphibian and reptile taxonomy and worked for much of her life in China, facilitating exchanges between Eastern and Western scientists.

U.S. programmer Lois M. Haibt becomes one of the developers of the early computer language FORTRAN. Also in this year, Grace Elizabeth "Libby" Mitchell, who will join the FORTRAN project in 1957, designs the IBM 704 operating system, the ancestor of all computer operating systems.

Dorothy Hodgkin identifies the composition of vitamin B_{12}, which can be used in treating pernicious anemia.

French sociologist, feminist, and journalist Evelyne Sullerot founds the French family planning movement.

America's Society of Women Engineers gives its Achievement Award to Margaret Hutchinson, the first woman graduate in chemical engineering from MIT, for her work in developing the first commercial penicillin production plant.

Emma Sadler Moss becomes the first U.S. woman to head a major medical society when she is elected president of the American Society of Clinical Pathologists.

Education and Scholarship

In Japan, 15% of girls and 21% of boys go to college; 47% of girls and 56% of boys go beyond the nine years of compulsory education.

U.S. classicist Edith Hamilton is elected to the American Institute of Arts and Letters.

Religion

U.S. Catholic founder Mother Mary Joseph Rogers (b. October 27, 1882), who established a missionary order, the Maryknoll Sisters of St. Dominic, dies.

May 23 The U.S. Presbyterian Church sanctions the ordination of female ministers.

Aug. 2 Mrs. Sheldon Robbins of Oceanside, New York, becomes Judaism's first female cantor.

1956

General Status and Daily Life

India outlaws sati, reaffirms the father's right to custody of his children, gives Hindu sons and daughters equal inheritance rights, allows women to adopt children, and gives adopted sons and daughters equal rights.

In Israel, a married woman may keep her own name, take her husband's, or combine the two.

Government, the Military, and the Law

In an abortive rebellion in Cuba, revolutionary and feminist Vilma Espín (b. 1930) organizes women's combat units.

Women in Pakistan and Senegal get full suffrage. Egyptian women get the vote and the right to run for public office.

During Egypt's war with Britain over the Suez Canal, women are trained to fight and nurse the wounded by the Popular Committee of Women's Resistance.

Golda Meir, formerly Israel's minister of labor and social insurance, becomes the minister of foreign affairs, a post she will hold until 1965. She is the only woman in the Cabinet.

East German women are admitted to all parts of the military except combat duty.

Seventy-eight of India's 5,755 lawyers are women.

Peruvian liberal politician Magda Portal, who fought against women's suffrage because she feared women would vote conservatively, publishes a novel criticizing unequal opportunities for women in the left-wing party of which she is a member.

Soviet politician Ekaterina Furtseva becomes the first woman member of the Praesidium.

Indian politician Indira Gandhi (b. 1917) becomes a member of the Central Parliamentary Board and president of the All India Youth Congress.

English lawyer Rose Heilbron becomes Great Britain's first woman recorder (chief magistrate).

Literature and the Visual Arts

New poetry includes Gwendolyn Brooks's *Bronzeville Boys and Girls*, Austrian Ingeborg Bachmann's *Anrufung des Grossen Bären*, Uruguayan Juana de Ibarbourou's *Oro y Tormento*, and Iranian Furugh Farrukhzad's *The Wall*.

Canadian author Mavis Gallant (b. 1922) publishes the short story collection *The Other Paris*.

New children's novels include Mari Sandoz's *The Horsecatcher* and Dodie Smith's *The Hundred and One Dalmatians*.

English artist Barbara Hepworth (1903–1975) sculpts *Orpheus*.

Grace Metalious publishes the best-selling novel *Peyton Place*.

Aug. 23 U.S. art patron Marion MacDowell (b. November 22, 1857) dies. Her MacDowell Colony nurtured the careers of Aaron Copland, Willa Cather,

Thornton Wilder, and Edwin Arlington Robinson.

Performing Arts and Entertainment

Two notable Hollywood weddings take place this year; Marilyn Monroe, currently starring in *Bus Stop*, converts to Judaism and marries Jewish playwright Arthur Miller on June 29. Even the marriage of America's favorite sex goddess, however, pales in comparison to the fervor surrounding the so-called fairy-tale wedding of actress Grace Kelly to Prince Rainier of Monaco on April 19.

U.S. film editor Barbara McLean becomes 20th Century-Fox's supervising editor, a position she will hold until 1969.

American Hanya Holm (b. 1898) choreographs the musical *My Fair Lady*.

French filmmaker Claudine Lenoir directs *L'Aventurière des Champs-Élysées* (*The Adventuress of the Champs-Élysées*).

U.S. film editor Anne Bauchens receives an Academy Award nomination for her work on *The Ten Commandments*; she selected the final 12,000 feet of film from the 100,000 that director Cecil B. De Mille shot. Sonya Levien wins an Oscar for the screenplay for *Oklahoma!*, which she wrote with William Ludwig.

U.S. actress Judy Holliday stars in the stage musical *Bells Are Ringing*.

Greek soprano Maria Callas performs for the first time at New York's Metropolitan Opera.

U.S. stage director Margaret Webster directs *The Merchant of Venice* at Stratford-upon-Avon.

Irish dancer and choreographer Ninette de Valois establishes Britain's Royal Ballet.

U.S. actress Susan Hayward wins an award at Cannes for her performance in *I'll Cry Tomorrow*. Ingrid Bergman stars in *Elena et les hommes* and wins the Best Actress Oscar for her performance in *Anastasia*. Brigitte Bardot stars in *Et Dieu créa la femme* (*And God Created Woman*), and Sophia Loren stars in *La fortuna di essere donna* (*Lucky to Be a Woman*).

Jan. 10 U.S. editor Edith Isaacs (b. March 27, 1878) dies. For decades she edited the influential *Theatre Arts* magazine, helping to bring such artists as Eugene O'Neill, Thornton Wilder, and Martha Graham to prominence.

Mar. 15 English actress and singer Julie Andrews opens on Broadway as Eliza Doolittle in *My Fair Lady*.

Athletics and Exploration

U.S. tennis player Althea Gibson wins the French and Italian singles titles and the Wimbledon doubles title.

Winter At the Olympics, figure skater Tenley Albright (b. July 18, 1935) becomes the first U.S. woman to win a gold medal in figure skating. American Elisabeth Schwarz takes the gold in pairs. Madeleine Berthod of Switzerland wins the downhill; another Swiss skier, Renee Colliard, wins the slalom, and West German Ossi Reichert wins the giant slalom. In Nordic skiing, Lyubov Kosyreva of the Soviet Union wins the 10-kilometer race; as Lyubov Baranova-Kosyreva, she will take silvers in the 10-kilometers and 4 x 5-kilometer relay in 1960. The Finnish team of Sirkka Polkunen, Mirja Hietamies, and Siiri Rantanen wins the 4 x 5-kilometer relay; Rantanen will be on the bronze-medal team in 1960.

Summer At the Melbourne Olympics, the kayak event is won by Yelisaveta Dementyeva of the Soviet Union. In fencing, the women's individual foil is won by Britain's Gillian Sheen.

U.S. diver Patricia McCormick, the Associated Press's (AP) Athlete of the Year, repeats her double win of 1952, taking the gold medals in both platform and springboard diving. McCormick is the first woman to win four gold medals in Olympic diving and the first to sweep both events in two successive Olympics.

The IOC adds a 100-meter butterfly race to the women's swimming events; it is won by U.S. swimmer Shelley Mann. Australian swimmer Dawn Fraser (b. 1937), setter of more than thirty world records, wins the gold medal in the 100-meter freestyle, setting a world record of sixty-two seconds in the process, and takes a silver in the 400 meters. Her teammate Lorraine Crapp gets the 100-meter freestyle silver and wins the 400-meter freestyle gold. Australia, in fact, sweeps the 100-meter freestyle medals, with Faith Leech taking the bronze, and wins the 4 x 100-meter freestyle relay as well with its team of Leech, Fraser, Crapp, and Sandra Morgan. However, not all of the swimming medals go to the Australians. Great Britain's Judith Grinham wins the 100-meter backstroke, and Ursula Happe of West Germany wins the 200-meter breaststroke, followed by Hungary's Eva Szekely. The U.S. team, which includes Shelley Mann, gets the relay silver.

West Germany's team of Liselott Linsenhoff, Hannelore Weygand, and Anneliese Kuppers takes the silver medal in dressage, and Linsenhoff wins a bronze in individual dressage. Silver in the individual event is won by Lis Hartel of Denmark. Great Britain's bronze-medal show jumping team also includes a woman, Patricia Smythe.

The star of the gymnastics competition is Hungarian Agnes Keleti, who finishes her Olympic career with a total of five gold medals, four silver, and one bronze. Five of those medals come in this Olympics; she wins the floor exercise, balance beam, and uneven bars and takes a silver in the individual and team all-around competitions. The sport's rising star is Larissa Latynina of the Soviet Union, who by 1968 will have won eighteen medals. She wins gold medals in the individual all-around, horse vault, and team events and silvers in the floor exercise and uneven bars. The other members of the first-place Soviet team are Sofia Muratova, the bronze medalist in the all-around and uneven bars; Tamara Manina, who also takes a bronze in the beam and a silver in the vault; Ljudmila Yegorova; Polina Astakhova; and Lydia Kalinina.

Australia gives a strong performance in the track events. Betty Cuthbert wins the 100- and 200-meter dashes, Shirley De La Hunty-Strickland wins the hurdles, and the team of De La Hunty-Strickland, Cuthbert, Norma Croker, and Fleur Mellor wins the 4 x 100-meter relay. The U.S. team, which includes 1960's track sensation, Wilma Rudolph, comes in third.

American Mildred McDaniel wins the high jump, and Poland's Elzbieta Krzesinska wins the long jump, setting a world record. Tamara Tyshkevich of the Soviet Union wins the shot put, followed by teammmate Galina Zybina. Soviet athlete Inese Jaunzeme takes the gold in javelin. Olga Fikotova of Czechoslovakia wins the discus throw, and the bronze in this event goes to Nina Ponomaryeva-Romaschkova of the Soviet Union, who will take the gold in 1960.

Sept. 27 U.S. athlete Babe Didrikson Zaharias dies. Setter of records in the 80-meter hurdles, high jump, javelin, and broad jump, she made $1 million from her athletic abilities during her lifetime. A skilled golfer, she was the first woman to break seventy and a cofounder of the LPGA; she was also adept at basketball, baseball, tennis, bowling, and diving.

Activism

Norwegian politician Eva Kolstad becomes president of the Norwegian Association for the Rights of Women, a position she will hold until 1968.

South African activist Lilian Ngoyi (b. 1911), recently elected president of the Federation of South African Women, is arrested with Helen Joseph and Dorothy Nyembe for burning their passes (identification documents that must be carried by blacks over sixteen and presented on demand to officials). Ngoyi will remain in solitary confinement during a trial that will last until 1961.

Business and Industry

In the United States, 21,500,000 women are in the work force, constituting 32.3% of the total work force. A survey of 188 unions reveals that 51 have no women members and 54 have fewer than 10% female membership.

Feb. 22 Austrian-American fashion designer and entrepreneur Hattie Carnegie (b. March 15, 1886?), whose designs included movie costumes, the WAC uniform, and a new habit for Carmelite nuns, dies. At her death, her various businesses employ over 1,000 workers and are worth an estimated $8 million.

Science and Medicine

German-American nuclear physicist Maria Goeppert-Mayer (b. June 22, 1906) is elected to the National Academy of Sciences.

Chinese-American physicist Chien-Shiung Wu (b. 1912), who will be elected to the National Academy of Sciences in 1958, disproves the concept of conservation of parity (the theory that atomic particles behave symmetrically), radically changing the field of nuclear physics.

America's Society of Women Engineers gives its Achievement Award to Elise F. Harmon (d. 1985) for her work on component and circuit miniaturization.

Egypt's Supreme Council of Family Planning is established.

Austrian conservationist Joy Adamson (1910–1980) begins working with Elsa, a lioness whom she hopes to be able to retrain for life in the wild. Her efforts will result in several books, most notably *Born Free* (1960).

German-Scottish geneticist Charlotte Auerbach (b. 1899), discoverer of mustard gas and expert on mutagens, publishes *Genetics in the Atomic Age*.

Education and Scholarship

Saudi Arabian queen 'Iffat, wife of King Faisal, establishes a government school for girls.

Sociologist Rose Hum Lee (August 20, 1904–March 25, 1964) is named chairman of the sociology department at Chicago's Roosevelt University, becoming the first Chinese-American to chair an American university department.

Feb. 7 Riots erupt at the University of Alabama over the enrollment yesterday of Autherine Lucy, the university's first black student. The university responds by suspending her, only to have its decision overturned by a court order.

Religion

M. E. Tower becomes the first woman Presbyterian minister.

1957

General Status and Daily Life

Abortion is legalized in Romania.

Government, the Military, and the Law

Shi Liang becomes China's minister of justice.

Colombia, Lebanon, and Haiti grant women the vote.

German feminist and politician Marie-Elizabeth Luders becomes honorary president of the Federal Democratic party.

Literature and the Visual Arts

U.S. sculptor Meta Warrick Fuller makes a series of ten models of famous black American women for the NCNW.

New poetry includes Swedish poet Sonja Åkesson's (d. 1977) *Situations*, English poet Stevie Smith's *Not Waving But Drowning*, Nelly Sachs' *Und niemand weiss weiter*, and Iranian Furugh Farrukhzad's *Rebellion*.

New novels include Iris Murdoch's *The Sand Castle*, Ayn Rand's *Atlas Shrugged*, and Ding Ling's *The Sun Shines Over the Sangkan River*.

Feb. 2 U.S. architect Julia Morgan (b. January 26, 1872), the first woman in California to get an architect's license, dies. Best known for her design of Hearst Castle (1919), she was also responsible for several University of California and Mills College buildings, the Asilomar Conference Center near Monterey, the rebuilt Fairmont Hotel, St. John's Presbyterian Church in Berkeley, the Berkeley City Club, and a number of YWCA buildings.

Performing Arts and Entertainment

U.S. musician Ethel Leginska conducts the premiere of her opera *The Rose and the Ring*.

U.S. film editor Viola Lawrence is nominated for an Academy Award for her work on *Pal Joey*. Phoebe Ephron coauthors the screenplay for *Carousel*.

Films made by women include Chinese director Wang Ping's *Story of Liupao Village*; French director Jacqueline Audry's *La Garçonne* (*The Bachelor Girl*), a film adaptation of a 1920s story about a woman who wants a man's life, and *L'École des cocottes* (*School for Strumpets*); English producer Betty Box's *A Tale of Two Cities*; and English director Muriel Box's *A Novel Affair*, in which a writer's chauffeur tries to seduce her after discovering her latest manuscript and becoming convinced it reveals her secret love for him.

Filmgoers can see Marilyn Monroe in *The Prince and the Showgirl*, Cyd Charisse in *Silk Stockings*, Doris Day in *The Pajama Game*, and Katharine Hepburn as a computer-phobic librarian in the romantic comedy *Desk Set*. Joanne Woodward wins the Best Actress Oscar for her performance in *The Three Faces of Eve*.

U.S. lighting designer Jean Rosenthal designs the lighting for *West Side Story*.

U.S. stage director Margaret Webster directs *Measure for Measure* at the Old Vic.

The Leningrad ballet school is renamed the Vaganova School in honor of Russian ballet teacher Agrippina Vaganova.

Athletics and Exploration

English athlete Mary Rand (b. 1940) sets a British record in the pentathlon.

American Althea Gibson wins the U.S. Open and, on July 6, becomes the first black tennis player to win the Wimbledon singles title. She will win both titles again in 1958.

Activism

Korea's first woman lawyer, Lee Tai Young, opens the Korean Legal Aid Center for Family Relations. Through it, she helps women, often assisting them in getting divorces.

English consumer advocate Eirlys Roberts (b. 1911)

founds the Consumers' Association.

July 28 U.S. reformer Edith Abbott (b. September 26, 1876) dies. She worked at Hull House, supported women's suffrage and a ten-hour workday for women, wrote more than one hundred books and articles, and defended child labor laws and the rights of immigrants.

Business and Industry

Canadian gold rush pioneer, sawmill manager, author, and second female member of Parliament Martha Black dies.

French vintner Lalou Bize-Leroy takes over her ailing father's vineyards; within twenty years her Romanée-Conti will be featured by all three-star restaurants.

In Mao's "Great Leap Forward," Chinese rural women are encouraged to devote themselves to agricultural labor. To free them for this work, cooking, sewing, and child care are collectivized. This plan has almost universally failed by the 1960s, but women are left with some gains, including the right to set up neighborhood workshops.

Austria gives women sixteen weeks of paid maternity leave, eight before and eight after delivery. Women may also take one year of unpaid leave.

May 10 U.S. entrepreneur and philanthropist Annie Turnbo-Malone (b. August 9, 1869), whose hair-care product business, Poro, created jobs for 75,000 women around the world, dies.

Science and Medicine

Soviet professor Alla Masevich becomes chief of a network of about a hundred tracking stations monitoring all equipment in space, including thousands of astronomers, three tracking ships, operating crews, and hundreds of associated scientists.

The Indonesia Planned Parenthood Federation is founded.

U.S. plant morphologist Katherine Esau (b. 1898) is elected to the National Academy of Sciences.

America's Society of Women Engineers gives its Achievement Award to metallurgist Rebecca Sparling.

Education and Scholarship

New publications include English philosopher Gertrude Anscombe's (b. 1919) *Intention*, Simone de Beauvoir's discussion of China, *La longue marche* (*The Long March*), and American literary critic Rosemond Tuve's *Images and Themes in Five Poems by Milton*.

U.S. biographer and essayist Catherine Drinker Bowen (b. January 1, 1897) publishes *The Lion and the Throne: The Life and Times of Sir Edward Coke, 1552–1634*. The book, which will win a National Book Award in 1958, is based on her research at Cambridge, where she encountered strong resistance to her presence. "Even Bluebeard," she says, "did not consider women more expendable than does a Cambridge don."

U.S. classicist Edith Hamilton is elected to the American Academy of Arts and Letters and made an honorary citizen of Athens.

Bayan Vedida Pars becomes the first woman president of the Turkish National Education Association.

Religion

English author Dorothy Sayers writes the religious play *The Zeal of the House*.

1958

General Status and Daily Life

Afghanistan's prime minister calls for women to reject the veil.

In South Korea, the minimum age at marriage is sixteen for women and eighteen for men. Both spouses keep their family names, but in most cases the woman becomes part of her husband's family. Property of uncertain ownership belongs to the husband.

Government, the Military, and the Law

Liberian lawyer and diplomat Angie Brooks-Randolph (b. 1928), holder of 18 honorary doctorates and foster mother to forty-seven children, becomes Assistant Secretary of State.

U.S. contralto Marian Anderson becomes a delegate to the UN.

Barbara Castle becomes the leader of England's Labor party.

Aug. 8 Sweden's Agda Rössel (b. 1910) becomes the first woman to head a permanent UN delegation.

Oct. 21 Britain's House of Lords gets its first two female members.

Literature and the Visual Arts

Deaths this year include British neo-plastic artist Marlow Moss (b. 1890) and Irish storyteller Peig Sayers, who preserved over 375 stories and forty folk songs for the Irish Folklore Commission and whose autobiography is a classic of Irish literature.

Puerto Rican poet Elsa Tió (b. 1950) publishes her first collection of poetry at the age of eight. Other new poetry includes Muriel Rukeyser's *Body of Waking*, English-American poet Denise Levertov's *Overland to the Islands*, and Brazilian poet Cecília Meireles's *Collected Works*.

U.S. photographer Diane Arbus (March 14, 1923–July 27?, 1971) begins taking pictures on the New York streets, concentrating on people of unusual appearance. This subject matter is more to her liking than the fashion photography she abandoned a year ago.

British author Mary Renault (pseudonym of Mary Challans, September 4, 1905–December 1983) publishes *The King Must Die*, a convincing historical novel based on the ancient Greek legend of Theseus. Other new novels include New Zealand author Sylvia Ashton-Warner's (b. 1905) first novel, *Spinster*, Lebanese author Layla Ba'labakki's (b. 1936) first novel, *I Live*, and French novelist Christiane Rochefort's (b. 1917) *Le repos du guerrier*. Spanish novelist Ana Maria Malute (b. 1926) becomes famous after the publication of her award-winning story of the civil war, *Los hijos muertos*.

Performing Arts and Entertainment

U.S. film editor Adrienne Fazan wins an Academy Award and an ACE award for her work on *Gigi*. Editor Alma Macrorie wins an ACE award for her work on *Teacher's Pet*, which also earns an Oscar nomination for its coauthor, U.S. screenwriter Fay Kanin.

British screenwriter Joan Harrison begins producing the television series "Alfred Hitchcock Presents."

Chinese actress and filmmaker Wang Ping directs *Constant Beam*. French film director Jacqueline Audry makes *C'est la faute d'Adam* (*It's All Adam's Fault*) and *Mitsou*, which is based on a story by Colette. In *Mitsou*, a kept woman convinces her wealthy lover to teach her the social skills she needs to win the love of a lieutenant. Russian filmmaker Yulia Solntseva directs *Poem of the Sea*.

Susan Hayward stars in *I Want to Live*, winning an Academy Award for her performance. Other new films include Muriel Box's *The Truth About Women*, starring Swedish actress Mai Zetterling (b. 1925); *Cat on a Hot Tin Roof*, starring Elizabeth Taylor; *Les amants* (*The Lovers*), starring French actress and film director Jeanne Moreau (b. 1928); *Vertigo*, starring Kim Novak; *Desire Under the Elms*, starring Sophia Loren; and *Inn of the Sixth Happiness*, a film based on the life of missionary Gladys Aylward, starring Ingrid Bergman. Allison Hayes stars as the irradiated Nancy Archer in the cult classic *Attack of the 50-Foot Woman*.

U.S. dancer and choreographer Martha Graham creates *Clytemnestra*.

Polish composer and violinist Grazyna Bacewicz wins the International Rostrum of Composers' orchestral award for *Muzyka*.

Retired Norwegian soprano Kirsten Flagstad directs the new Norwegian State Opera.

Athletics and Exploration

Jamaican table tennis player Joy Foster, age eight, wins the national singles and mixed doubles titles.

U.S. aviator Ruth Nichols sets a women's speed record of over 1,000 miles per hour and a women's altitude record of 51,000 feet.

Russian gymnast Larissa Latynina wins five gold medals at the World Championships.

Activism

U.S. consumer advocate Mildred Edie Brady (June 3, 1906–July 27, 1965) becomes editorial director and senior editor of *Consumer Reports*.

Business and Industry

In the United States, 22,100,000 women are in the work force, constituting 32.7% of the total work force.

Makiko Yamamoto (b. 1920) becomes director of the

Women's Division of the General Council of Trade Unions of Japan, a position she will hold until 1976.

Women in Pakistan are entitled to twelve weeks' paid maternity leave, half before and half after delivery.

Mar. 22 U.S. fashion designer Claire McCardell (b. May 24, 1905), inventor of the stretch leotard, dies. In the 1930s, she created the first sportswear "separates," and during World War II, she created the bodysuit. Her moderately priced, ready-to-wear clothes popularized the use of wool jersey and cotton for non-casual fashions, and she won many awards, including the American Fashion Critics Award and the Neiman-Marcus Award.

Science and Medicine

U.S. biochemist Arda A. Green, who helped to isolate the nervous system regulator serotonin and who discovered the enzymes that make fireflies glow, dies.

English microchemist Rosalind Franklin (b. 1920), who researched viruses and examined carbon structures with X-ray diffraction, dies. In 1951, she was the first researcher to describe the helical structure of the DNA molecule, but her contributions were belittled (and simultaneously exploited) by her male colleagues, who refused to let her attend their meetings and passed her discoveries on to her competitors. After her death, her work, vital to the discoveries made by Watson and Crick, will remain unrecognized.

Turkish astronomer Nuzhet Gökdogen becomes the head of the observatory at Istanbul University.

America's Society of Women Engineers gives its Achievement Award to Mabel M. Rockwell (d. 1979) for her work on electrical control systems.

The Nepal Family Planning Association is founded.

Nigeria's first birth control clinic opens.

Education and Scholarship

U.S. educator Genevieve Caulfield opens an elementary school for blind children in Saigon, Vietnam.

Iranian educator Parvin Birjandi becomes the first Dean of Women at the University of Tehran.

Bibi Palvanova becomes the first woman university president in the Soviet Union.

Religion

The Swedish Lutheran church begins ordaining women as ministers.

1959

General Status and Daily Life

Polish law requires doctors to provide contraceptives to new mothers and abortion recipients.

Hawaii, in its admission to the United States, becomes the first state to pass a law requiring married women to take their husbands' names. It is simply a new version of an existing law from 1860, passed by whites to force the native islanders to conform to white custom; before 1860, Hawaiian island women did not change their names upon marriage.

Government, the Military, and the Law

South African politician Helen Suzman (b. 1917) cofounds the Progressive party.

Israel's Defense Service Law drafts women age eighteen to twenty-six (eighteen to thirty-four for reserves) unless they are married, pregnant, or conscientious or religious objectors.

Laili Rusad becomes Indonesia's ambassador to Belgium and Luxembourg.

Women in Morocco get the vote.

Feb. 2 Indira Gandhi is elected the leader of India's Congress party.

Literature and the Visual Arts

New poetry includes Marianne Moore's *O to Be a Dragon*, English-American poet Denise Levertov's *With Eyes at the Backs of Our Heads*, Lithuanian-Israeli poet, children's author, translator, and comparative literature professor Leah Goldberg's (1911–1970) *The Love of an Orange*, Spanish poet Julia Uceda's (b. 1925) *Butterfly in Ashes*, Mexican poet Isabel Fraire's (b. 1936) first book, *15 Poems of Isabel Fraire*, Peruvian Blanca Varela's (b. 1926) first collection, *This Port Exists*, German Hilde Domin's (b. 1912) *Nur eine Rose als Stütze*, and Nelly Sachs's *Flucht und Verwandlung*.

Mary Lou Werner of the *Washington Evening Star* wins a Pulitzer Prize for local reporting.

New York Herald Tribune columnist Marie Torre becomes the first woman jailed for refusing to reveal a news source.

United Press International (UPI) reporter Helen Thomas, who will cover every president from Kennedy to Reagan, becomes president of the Women's National Press Club.

Japanese novelist Ariyoshi Sawako (1931–1984) publishes *Kinokawa* (*The River Ki*), a novel about four generations of women in Kii Province (Wakayama Prefecture). Other new novels include French novelist Nathalie Sarraute's *Le planétarium*, French writer Françoise Sagan's *Aimez-vous Brahms?*, and American author Flannery O'Connor's second novel, *The Violent Bear It Away*.

U.S. painter Helen Frankenthaler (b. 1928) wins first prize at the Paris Biennale.

Lillian Hellmann publishes the play *Toys in the Attic*.

Feb. 27 U.S. landscape architect Beatrix Jones Farrand dies. Her clients included J. P. Morgan, Abby Alrich Rockefeller, Vassar College, Oberlin College, Princeton, Yale, and the University of Chicago.

Performing Arts and Entertainment

Polish harpsichordist Wanda Landowska (b. 1879) and Russian actress Olga Knipper-Chekova (b. 1870) die. Knipper-Chekhova starred in the Chekhov plays *The Seagull*, *Uncle Vanya*, *Ivanov*, *Three Sisters*, and *The Cherry Orchard*.

Cuban ballerina Alicia Alonso becomes director and prima ballerina of the Ballet Nacional de Cuba.

U.S. screenwriter Leigh Brackett coauthors the screenplay for *Rio Bravo*; French writer and filmmaker Marguerite Duras writes the screenplay for the acclaimed film *Hiroshima mon amour*. Chinese actress and filmmaker Wang Ping directs *Battle of Shanghai*; East German filmmaker Katja Georgi directs the animated movie *The Princess and the Pea*.

Spanish dancer Carmen Amaya (1913–1963) performs in London.

U.S. lyricist Dorothy Fields wins a Tony and a Grammy for her work on the Gwen Verdon vehicle *Redhead*.

Filmgoers can see Marilyn Monroe as a Prohibition-era singer in *Some Like It Hot*, Sandra Dee in *Gidget*; Eva

Marie Saint in the Hitchcock thriller *North by Northwest*, Audrey Hepburn (b. 1929) in *Green Mansions*, Doris Day in *Pillow Talk*, French actress and film director Jeanne Moreau in *Les Liaisons dangereuses*, and Katharine Hepburn and Elizabeth Taylor in *Suddenly, Last Summer*. Simone Signoret wins the Best Actress Oscar for her performance in *Room at the Top*.

Mar. 11 U.S. playwright Lorraine Hansberry's (May 19, 1930–January 12, 1965) *A Raisin in the Sun* opens; it is the first play by a black woman to be produced on Broadway. It will run for 530 performances and lead to a film and a stage tour.

July 17 U.S. blues singer Billie Holiday (b. April 7, 1915?) dies after being arrested in her sickbed on a drug charge. Known as "Lady Day," she toured with Count Basie and Artie Shaw and was most closely associated with the songs "God Bless the Child" and "Strange Fruit" (an antilynching song).

Athletics and Exploration

Czech gymnast Vera Caslavska (b. 1942), winner of twenty-two European, world, and Olympic titles, wins the European gold in the balance beam.

Russian athlete Irina Press (b. 1939), setter of six hurdles records, sets one of eight records in the pentathlon.

Brazilian tennis player Maria Bueno (b. 1939) wins the singles title at Wimbledon and the U.S. Open. She will win again at Wimbledon in 1960 and 1964 and will win the U.S. title in 1963, 1964, and 1966. She will win the Wimbledon doubles five times and the U.S. doubles four times.

July French mountain climber Claude Kogan leads the international all-female Expédition Feminine au Nepal in a climb of 26,700-foot Cho Oyo. In October, she and three other women are killed in an avalanche during an attempted ascent of Cho Oyo.

Business and Industry

U.S. toy designer Ruth Handler, vice president and cofounder of Mattel, Inc., invents the Barbie doll. Named after Handler's daughter, Barbie is the first teenage doll not made out of paper; $500 million worth of Barbies and accessories are sold within five years.

Women are 34.1% of the British labor force.

In Egypt, married women are entitled to fifty days of maternity leave at 70% pay.

About one-third of Soviet crane, forklift, and derrick operators are female; women are most of the public streetcar, bus, and subway operators.

The British Street Offences Act makes it illegal for a woman to work as a prostitute if she "loiters or solicits in a street or public place" to get customers. She can, however, make appointments over the phone quite legally.

June 28 U.S. business executive Dorothy Shaver (b. July 29, 1897) dies. Through her work at Lord & Taylor, she helped to make New York a fashion capital and promoted American designers, including Claire McCardell, Lilly Daché, Anne Fogarty, Rose Marie Reid, and Pauline Trigère.

Science and Medicine

U.S. pathologist and physician Louise Pearce (March 5, 1885–August 10), who helped to develop a treatment for African sleeping sickness, dies.

America's Society of Women Engineers gives its Achievement Award to Désiree LeBleu, an expert on rubber reclamation.

U.S. surgical pathologist and medical educator Virginia Kneeland Frantz (1896–1967) publishes the monograph *Armed Forces Atlas of Tumor Pathology*, a standard reference work for many years.

July In Tanzania's Olduvai Gorge, British paleontologist Mary Leakey (b. 1913) discovers a fossil Australopithecus skull that revolutionizes ideas of the antiquity of humans.

Oct. English astronomer Margaret Burbidge (b. 1920) coauthors the article "Synthesis of the Elements in Stars," which wins the Warner Prize.

Education and Scholarship

U.S. historian Margaret Leech wins the Pulitzer Prize for *In the Days of McKinley*, which is lauded as "a first-rate study of a second-rate President." Jean Schneider also wins a Pulitzer for *The Republican Era, 1869–1901*, a history that she cowrote with Leonard D. White.

German-American political philosopher Hannah Arendt becomes the first woman full professor at Princeton University.

Austrian author Ingeborg Bachmann becomes the University of Frankfurt's first professor of poetics.

Religion

Spanish saint Joaquina is canonized.

Egyptian scholar and author Aisha Abdel Rahman (b. c. 1920), an expert on the women associated with Muhammad, publishes *The Wives of the Prophet*. Abdel Rahman sometimes uses the pseudonym Bint-al-Shah.

1960

General Status and Daily Life

Britain's minimum age of marriage is raised to sixteen for both sexes.

The Sudan requires that both parties consent to any marriage.

May 9 The first commercial birth control pill, Enovid, is approved by the Food and Drug Administration (FDA); its development was funded after the early 1950s by U.S. philanthropist and feminist Katharine Dexter McCormick (b. August 27, 1875).

Dec. 15 The first Teflon-coated pans go on sale in America, after enjoying a few years of success in France.

Government, the Military, and the Law

Esmeralda Arboleda de Cuevas Cancino, Colombia's first woman senator, becomes minister of transport. Later she will serve as ambassador to Austria and Yugoslavia.

Signe Ryssdal becomes Norway's first woman counselor-at-law.

Nigerian independence brings new interest in traditional roles, and the office of *omu*, or women's leader, begins to regain some of the power it lost under British colonial rule. Women, however, will gain ground mostly at a village level; national politics will continue to be dominated by men for at least the next two decades.

Japan gets its first woman Cabinet minister, the minister of health and welfare.

English politician Shirley Williams (b. 1930) becomes general secretary of the Fabian Society, a position she will hold until 1964.

Spanish politician Dolores Ibarurri becomes president of the exiled Spanish Communist party.

Soviet politician Ekaterina Furtseva becomes minister of culture.

Ghanaian lawyer Annie Jiagge becomes chairman of the UN Commission on the Status of Women.

Mar. 6 Swiss women get municipal voting rights.

June 20 U.S. lawyer and federal official Frieda Hennock (b. September 27, 1904) dies. She was the first woman on the Federal Communications Commission, where she fought for strict control of children's programming and for the setting aside of channels for noncommercial, educational purposes.

July 21 Sirimavo Bandaranaike, leader of the Sri Lanka Freedom party, is sworn in as prime minister of Sri Lanka. She is the world's first democratically elected woman head of state.

Sept. Canadian-American physician and FDA official Florence Oldham Kelsey receives an application for the licensing of the tranquilizer thalidomide. Seeing that the drug appears to cause different reactions in animals and humans, she rejects that application and withstands increasing pressure over the next year to reconsider her decision. She is vindicated when the drug proves to cause devastating birth defects in countries where it has been approved for human use.

Literature and the Visual Arts

Mexican poet Isabel Fraire becomes editor of the influential magazine *Revista Mexicana de Literatura*.

Carolina Maria de Jesús, a poor, black resident of a São Paulo, Brazil, *favela* (squatter village), publishes her diary. A detailed and sensitive account of *favela* life, it becomes a best-seller and allows her to escape her life of poverty.

Miriam Ottenberg of the *Washington Evening Star* wins a Pulitzer Prize for local reporting.

U.S. poet Anne Sexton (November 9, 1928–October 4, 1974) publishes her first collection, *To Bedlam and Part Way Back*. Other new works of poetry include Gwendolyn Brooks's *The Bean Eaters*, American Carolyn Kizer's (b. 1925) *The Ungrateful Garden*, French surrealist Joyce Mansour's (b. 1928) *Rapaces*, Canadian Anne Hébert's *Poems*, and American confessional poet Sylvia Plath's (b. Oct. 27, 1932) first collection, *The Colossus*.

U.S. author Harper Lee publishes one of the most

significant novels of the decade, the Pulitzer Prize-winning *To Kill a Mockingbird*, an adept piece of southern local color and a powerful indictment of racism.

Performing Arts and Entertainment

Romanian pianist Clara Haskil (b. 1895) and Spanish opera star Lucrezia Bori (December 24, 1887–May 14) die.

Films made by women include Polish producer and director Wanda Jakubowska's *It Happened Yesterday*; Danish director Annelise Hovman's *Fridehens pris* (*The Price of Freedom*), about anti-Nazi resistance in World War II; English producer Betty Box's *The 39 Steps*; Venezuelan filmmaker Margot Benaceraf's documentary *Araya*, about the inhabitants of the Venezuelan salt desert, which wins a prize at Cannes; and Russian screenwriter and director Marija Andjaparidze's *Aniuta*.

In the United States, Hanya Holm choreographs the musical *Camelot*, and Jean Rosenthal (March 16, 1912–May 1, 1969) designs the lighting for *Becket*.

Indian Sundari Shridharani is directing a school of traditional Indian dance and music which she founded in the 1950s.

U.S. singer Joan Baez (b. January 9, 1941) sings at the Newport Folk Festival and records her first album.

French actress and film director Jeanne Moreau stars in Marguerite Duras's *Moderato Cantabile*. Elizabeth Taylor wins the Best Actress Oscar for her performance in *Butterfield 8*, and Italian actress Sophia Loren stars in *The Millionairess*. Other new films include *The Apartment* with Shirley MacLaine, *Psycho* with Janet Leigh as the victim in Hitchcock's famous shower scene, *Lola* and *La dolce vita* with French actress Anouk Aimée, and *La vérite* (*The Truth*) with French actress Brigitte Bardot (b. 1934).

Athletics and Exploration

Russian-British engineer Dr. Barbara Moore (b. Anya Cherkasova) becomes, at fifty-six, the first woman to walk across the United States.

Winter At the Winter Olympics in Squaw Valley, women's speed skating becomes an official event. East Germany's Helga Haase wins the 500-meter race and gets a silver in the 1,000 meters. Klara Guseva of the Soviet Union wins the 1,000 meters. Guseva's teammate Lydia Skoblikova wins the 1,500 (with a world record time of 2:25.2) and the 3,000 meters. Carol Heiss of the U.S.,

the 1956 silver medalist, wins the gold in women's figure skating, followed by Sjoukje Dijkstra of the Netherlands. Canadian Barbara Wagner takes the gold in pairs.

West Germany's Heidi Biebl wins the downhill; Canada's Anne Heggtveit wins the slalom. Yvonne Ruegg of Switzerland wins the giant slalom. In Nordic skiing, the Soviet Union's Maria Gusakova wins the 10-kilometer race. In the 4 x 5-kilometer relay, the Swedish team of Britt Strandberg, Irma Johansson, and Sonja Ruthstrom-Edstrom takes first place.

Mar. 4 U.S. figure skater Carol Heiss wins the women's world title for the fifth time in a row.

Summer Canoe events for women are expanded at the Rome Olympics. Antonina Seredina of the Soviet Union wins the 500-meter kayak singles and the 500-meter pairs (with Maria Chubina). Fencing events are also expanded; there is now a team foil event as well as the individual competition. The Soviet foil team of Tatiane Petrenko, Valentina Rastvorova, Ljudmila Schishova, Valentina Prudskova, Aleksandra Zabelina, and Galina Gorokhova wins the gold; Rastvorova takes the individual silver. The second-place Hungarian team includes Ildiko Rejto, who as Ildiko Ujlaki-Rejto will medal in the next two Olympics; Italian fencer Irene Camber, a gold medalist in the individual competition in 1952, takes a bronze in the team event. First place in the individual foil goes to West Germany's Heidi Schmid.

West Germany's Ingrid Krämer wins the springboard and the platform diving golds. New to this Olympics is the 4 x 100-meter swimming medley relay, won by the U.S. team of Lynn Burke (gold medalist in the 100-meter backstroke), Patty Kempner, Carolyn Schuler (gold medalist in the 100-meter butterfly), and Christine von Saltza. The United States also wins the 4 x 100 freestyle relay, with a team composed of Joan Spillane, Shirley Stobs, Carolyn Wood, and Von Saltza. Australian swimmer Dawn Fraser (who takes silvers in both relays) wins the gold medal in the 100 meter freestyle, followed by Von Saltza, who wins the 400-meter freestyle. English swimmer Anita Lonsbrough (b. 1941) wins the gold in the 200-meter breaststroke.

The team gymnastics event is won by the Soviet team of Larissa Latynina, Sofia Muratova, Polina Astakhova, Margarita Nikolayeva, Lydia Ivanova-Kalinina, and Tamara Lyukhina. The second-place Czech team includes Vera Cáslavská and balance beam gold medalist Eva Bosáková. Latynina wins the all-around competition and the floor exercise and takes a bronze in the horse vault and silvers in the uneven parallel bars and balance beam. Muratova gets silvers in the all-around and vault and a bronze in the beam. Astakhova, in addition to her team gold, wins one of each type of medal: gold in the uneven bars, silver in the floor exercise, and bronze in the all-around. Lyukhina wins bronzes in the uneven bars and floor exercise. Nikolayeva, completing the Soviet domination of gymnastics this year, wins the gold medal in the vault.

The star of the track events is American Wilma Rudolph (b. 1940), who sets a U.S. women's record by winning three gold medals in one Olympics. She wins the 100 meters, the 200 meters, and the 4 x 100-meter relay (with teammates Martha Hudson, Lucinda Williams, and Barbara Jones). After thirty-two years, the IOC restores the 800-meter race as a women's event; it is won by Lyudmila Shevtsova of the Soviet Union. Shevtsova's teammate Irina Press wins the gold in the hurdles.

Romanian athlete Iolanda Balas (b. 1936), a fourteen-time world record holder, wins the Olympic gold medal for the high jump, setting a new Olympic record in the process. She is the first woman to jump over six feet, and she will set fourteen world records in the next ten and a half years. Soviet athlete Vyera Krepkina sets an Olympic record in the long jump. Tamara Press (b. 1937), Irina's sister and a setter of twelve world records in shotput and discus, wins a gold medal in the former and a silver in the latter. The discus gold goes to Soviet athlete Nina Ponomaryeva-Romaschkova. Elvina Ozolina of the Soviet Union wins the javelin throw, followed by Czechoslovakia's Dana Zatopkova.

Activism

Minerva, Patria, and María Teresa Mirabal, opponents for twenty years of the Dominican Republic's Trujillo regime, are killed by government assassins.

English suffragist Sylvia Pankhurst (b. 1882), the most radical of the Pankhursts, dies. The daughter of Emmeline and the sister of Christabel, she was arrested thirteen times and forcibly fed after staging hunger strikes; her later life was spent fighting fascism.

Vilma Espín, sister-in-law of Cuban leader Fidel Castro and the only female member of the Cuban Politburo, founds and becomes the first president of the Federation of Cuban Women, which fights illiteracy, educates rural women, and promotes communist doctrine.

Business and Industry

Chilean feminist and government official Ana Figuero becomes the first woman assistant director general of the ILO.

Premila Wagle (b. 1920), daughter of Indian family-planning advocate Dhanvanthi Rama Rau, founds a successful clothing export business.

In Russia, 29,250,000 women are in the work force, constituting 47% of the total work force.

In the United States, 23,200,000 women are in the work force, constituting about 33% of the total work force. Two-fifths of all women under thirty are in the labor force.

Women are 60% of Ghana's traders.

U.S. bakery entrepreneur Margaret Rudkin sells her profitable Pepperidge Farm company, which has annual sales of $32 million, to Campbell's Soup Company for about $28 million of Campbell's stock. She remains president of Pepperidge Farm and becomes a director of Campbell's.

Science and Medicine

English zoologist Jane Goodall (b. 1934) begins studying chimpanzees, living among them and becoming accepted in their social structure.

Mary Leakey codiscovers the first remains of *Homo habilis*, which flourished about 1.5–2 million years ago.

U.S. bionicist Dr. Mildred Mitchell guides the isolation tests on the Mercury astronaut candidates.

U.S. astronomer Nancy G. Roman becomes director of the astronomy and astrophysics satellite and sounding rocket program for NASA.

U.S. computer programmer Phyllis Fox, a codeveloper of the artificial intelligence language LISP, writes its official programmers' manual.

America's Society of Women Engineers gives its Achievement Award to solid state researcher Esther Conwell.

Jan. 30   The Soviet Union has 110,000 women scientists, 233,000 women engineers, and 300,000 women doctors; women are 85% of Soviet physicians.

Mar. 20   American Carolyn Van Blarcom (b. June 12, 1879), the first U.S. nurse to earn a midwife's license, and a leading reformer of midwives' training and practice, dies.

Nov. 15   U.S. geologist and stratigraphic paleontologist Julia Gardner (b. January 26, 1882), an expert on gastropod fossils, dies. During World War II she worked with the USGS Military Geology Unit doing tactical analyses of maps; she also identified the secret location of a Japanese bomb launch site by studying the sand particles found in the bombs.

Education and Scholarship

New publications include English economist Joan Violet Robinson's *Exercises in Economic Analysis*, U.S. classicist Lily Ross Taylor's *The Voting Districts of the Roman Republic*, and U.S. sociologist Rose Hum Lee's *The Chinese in the United States of America*.

Kuwait's first six female college graduates earn their degrees from Cairo University.

Saudi Arabia's first girls' schools are opened.

Argentinian educator Elsa Tabernig de Pucciarelli becomes head of the Institute of Foreign Languages at La Plata.

Jan. 30 *Izvestia* reports that there are 1,283,000 women teachers in the Soviet Union.

Religion

Three women become ministers in the Swedish Lutheran Church.

U.S. journalist Fayvelle Mermey (1916–March 1977) becomes the first woman president of a synagogue.

1961

General Status and Daily Life

The housekeeping tips column "Hints from Heloise," written by Heloise Bowles (d. 1977), goes into national syndication. Her 1963 book, *Heloise's Household Hints*, will sell more than 500,000 hardback copies.

U.S. chef Julia Child (b. August 15, 1912) publishes volume 1 of *Mastering the Art of French Cooking*, a book that quickly becomes a classic.

India provides a 5,000-rupee fine and six-month prison sentence for anyone paying a dowry. Gifts, however, do not count as dowry under the law, a fact that effectively nullifies the statute. The law is rather poorly enforced, and if the husband's family is not satisfied with the dowry paid, the bride will often be beaten or even killed.

Hindu and Muslim men in Pakistan may have up to four wives but must ask a wife's permission before taking a new wife. A Muslim man may divorce his wife by notifying her in writing, registering his intentions with the government, and waiting ninety days, during which

time he must continue to support her financially.

Government, the Military, and the Law

Paraguay becomes the last republic in the Americas to grant women the vote.

Annie Jiagge becomes a member of the Ghanaian High Court.

Peruvian politician Cármen Leguía La Riviere founds the Movimiento Social Democrático del Perú, a workers' party that will never manage to attract many members.

Health Minister Elisabeth Schwarzhaupt is West Germany's first woman Cabinet minister.

Mar. U.S. radical and labor leader Elizabeth Gurley Flynn becomes the first woman national chairman of the Communist party.

Literature and the Visual Arts

Russian abstract painter Nadezhda Udaltsova (b. 1885) and Korea's Kim Mal-bong (b. 1901), author of thirty novels, seventy short stories, and forty essays, die.

U.S. author Shirley Jackson's short story "Louisa, Please" wins the Edgar Allan Poe Award.

Austrian author Ingeborg Bachmann wins the Berlin Critics Prize for her collection of short stories, *Das dreissigste Jahr*.

French novelist Christiane Rochefort's *Les petits enfants du siècle* wins the Prix Populiste.

New poetry includes Romanian poet Nina Cassian's *Everyday Holidays*, English-American poet Denise Levertov's *The Jacob's Ladder*, Marianne Moore's *A Marianne Moore Reader*, El Salvadoran poet Claribel Alegría's *Guest of My Time*, and Portuguese poet Sophia de Mello Breyner Andresen's *O Vagabond Christ*.

Performing Arts and Entertainment

Russian ballerina Natalia Makarova (b. 1940) appears in *Giselle* at Covent Garden, London.

Mary Tyler Moore stars on television as housewife Laura Petrie on "The Dick Van Dyke Show."

Hit songs in the United States include "Will You Love

Me Tomorrow" by the Shirelles and "Please Mr. Postman" by the Marvelettes.

Filmgoers can see Audrey Hepburn playing the irresponsible, waiflike Holly Golightly in *Breakfast at Tiffany's*; Marilyn Monroe in her last complete film, *The Misfits*; Natalie Wood (d. 1981) and Rita Moreno in the musical *West Side Story*, based on Shakespeare's *Romeo and Juliet*; Natalie Wood in *Splendor in the Grass*; Swedish actress Harriet Andersson in *Through a Glass Darkly*; and Jeanne Moreau in *Jules et Jim*. Judy Garland plays a nonsinging role as a German housewife in *Judgment at Nuremberg*, earning an Oscar nomination for Best Supporting Actress. Sophia Loren wins the Best Actress Oscar for her performance as a mother struggling to survive in postwar Italy in *Two Women*.

Bulgarian filmmaker Binka Zheljazkova directs the feature film *We Were Young*. French film director Jacqueline Audry makes *Cadavres en vacances* (*Corpses on Holiday*) and *Les petits matins* (*Early Mornings*). Lillian Hellman writes the screenplay for *The Children's Hour*.

Apr. 23 Judy Garland sings at Carnegie Hall in New York City; the resulting album, *Judy at Carnegie Hall*, wins two Grammy Awards and becomes the first two-album set to sell more than 1 million copies.

Athletics and Exploration

Tennis player Darlene Hard wins the U.S. women's singles title for the second year in a row.

Romanian high jumper Iolanda Balas breaks the women's record with a jump of 1.84 meters (6' 3 1/4").

July 7 Angela Mortimer wins the Wimbledon singles title.

July 19 U.S. runner Wilma Rudolph sets a new record of 0:11.2 in the 100-meter dash.

Activism

French lawyer and feminist Gisèle Halimi (b. 1927), as counsel for the Algerian National Liberation Front, defends Algerian nationalist Djamila Boupacha (b. 1942) in an internationally celebrated human rights case that attracts the attention and support of many in France, including Simone de Beauvoir. Boupacha was imprisoned, tortured, and sexually assaulted by agents of the French colonial government.

The Federación de Mujeres Dominicanas (Federation of Dominican Women) is established to work for the sovereignty of the Dominican Republic.

English reformer Eirlys Roberts becomes editor of the consumer magazine *Which?*, a position she will hold until 1977, when the periodical's circulation will be about 7 million.

Women Strike for Peace is organized when housewives across America go on strike, calling for the government "to end the arms race, not the human race." American lawyer and politician Bella Abzug (b. July 24, 1920) becomes the group's national legislative director, a position she will hold until 1970.

Spring U.S. civil rights activist Rubye Doris Smith Robinson (April 25, 1942–October 7, 1967) participates in the Freedom Rides, which challenge segregation on transportation lines; she is arrested and jailed for using a white rest room.

Business and Industry

Women from twenty-three African and Asian countries meet in Haifa, Israel, to found the Mount Carmel International Center for Community Training. Inspired by Golda Meir's desire to help rural women in underdeveloped countries, it offers agricultural and business training for women. Its first director is Russian-Israeli agriculture expert Mina Ben-Zvi.

Science and Medicine

U.S. zoologist Libbie Hyman (December 6, 1888–August 3, 1969), a specialist in the taxonomy and anatomy of invertebrates, is elected to the National Academy of Sciences.

America's Society of Women Engineers gives its Achievement Award to space biologist Laurel van der Wal.

U.S. botanist Agnes Chase (1869–1963), an expert on grasses, becomes a fellow of the Linnean Society.

Education and Scholarship

New publications include Egyptian scholar Aisha Abdel Rahman's *New Values in Arabic Literature*, British philospher Gertrude Anscombe's *Three Philosophers*, and American Mari Sandoz's children's nonfiction book *These Were the Sioux*.

Cuban Methodist minister, children's book author, and literature professor Luisa Gonzalez cofounds Alfalit, an organization that encourages literacy in Latin American countries.

Religion

Italian nun and saint Bertilla Boscardin (1888–1922) is canonized. A peasant girl who became a nun in 1904, she worked as a kitchen maid and laundress before being assigned to her true work as a nurse in the children's ward.

1962

General Status and Daily Life

English needlework instructor Erica Wilson publishes *Crewel Embroidery*, which sells 500,000 copies.

U.S. journalist Helen Gurley Brown publishes the best-seller *Sex and the Single Girl*.

Brazil's constitution gets an equal rights amendment; married women are no longer considered permanent minors.

Government, the Military, and the Law

Eugenie Moore Anderson becomes the envoy to Bulgaria, making her the first U.S. woman ambassador to a communist country.

Muslim women get the vote in Algeria.

Australian-American economist and consumer advocate Persia Campbell is appointed to President Kennedy's Council of Economic Advisers. She will remain on the council during the Johnson administration.

Indian diplomat and politician Vijaya Pandit becomes governor of Maharashtra. Shushila Nayar becomes minister of health.

Sri Lanka's Women Lawyers Association and the Indian Federation of Women Lawyers, which provides legal aid and education to women in India, are founded.

English diplomat Barbara Salt becomes the first British woman ambassador.

Swedish politician Alva Myrdal is elected to the Swedish Upper House and becomes a Cabinet minister.

Literature and the Visual Arts

German painter Gabriele Munter (b. 1877) dies.

New poetry includes Romanian Veronica Porumbacu's *Poems, Retrospective Selection*, Russian Bella Akhmadulina's (b. 1937) first collection, *String*, Spanish poet Julia Uceda's *Strange Childhood*, and American Anne Sexton's second collection, *All My Pretty Ones*.

U.S. fashion journalist Diana Vreeland, author of the famous "Why Don't You?" column in *Harper's Bazaar*, moves to *Vogue* magazine, where she will be editor in chief until 1971.

U.S. author Madeleine L'Engle publishes the science-fiction children's novel *A Wrinkle in Time*.

U.S. author Hortense Calisher (b. 1911) publishes *Tales for a Mirror*, a collection of stories.

British author Doris Lessing publishes her most famous work, the experimental novel *The Golden Notebook*. Other new novels include American Katherine Anne Porter's *Ship of Fools* and English historical novelist Mary Renault's *The Bull from the Sea*, a sequel to her novel about Theseus, *The King Must Die*.

Mar. 26 U.S. sculptor Augusta Savage dies. When she was a child, her father punished her for making "graven images" out of red clay, but she persisted; her subjects included W.E.B. DuBois, Marcus Garvey, Frederick Douglass, and W. C. Handy.

Performing Arts and Entertainment

Films made by women include French director Agnès Varda's *Cléo from Five to Seven*, which depicts two hours in the life of a singer waiting for the results of a cancer test; Chinese director Wang Ping's *Locust Tree Village*; American Shirley Clarke's (b. 1925) first feature film, a cinéma vérité work called *The Connection*; and Czech director Vera Chytilová's (b. 1929) prizewinning films *Ceiling* and *A Bagful of Fleas*, which depicts a group of women textile workers.

U.S. screenwriter Eleanor Perry receives an Academy Award nomination for *David and Lisa*; Leigh Brackett writes the screenplay for *Hatari!* Film editor Anne Coates wins an Oscar for *Lawrence of Arabia*.

Shelley Fabares, who will later star in the long-running television sitcom "Coach," records the hit song "Johnny Angel." Other popular U.S. songs include the Shirelles' "Soldier Boy" and Little Eva's "The Loco-Motion."

South African-English composer Priaulx Rainier composes an oboe quartet, *Quanta*.

U.S. ballerina Suzanne Farrell dances her first solo role in *Serenade*, with the New York City Ballet.

English actress Vanessa Redgrave (b. January 30, 1937) plays Rosalind in *As You Like It*.

Filmgoers can see Bette Davis and Joan Crawford in *Whatever Happened to Baby Jane*, Katharine Hepburn in *Long Day's Journey into Night*, and French actress Brigitte Bardot in *La vie privée* (*A Very Private Affair*). Anne Bancroft and Patty Duke star as Anne Sullivan and Helen Keller in *The Miracle Worker*, with Bancroft winning the Best Actress Academy Award for her work.

Athletics and Exploration

At the European championships, Russian athlete Tamara Press wins gold medals in both shot put and discus.

July 7 U.S. tennis player Karen Susman defeats Vera Sukova in the women's singles final at Wimbledon.

July 23 Australian Dawn Fraser becomes the first woman to swim one hundred meters in under a minute.

Activism

Austrian conservationist Joy Adamson establishes the World Wildlife Fund.

Guinean diplomat Jeanne-Martin Cissé (b. 1926) becomes the secretary-general of the Conference of African Women.

U.S. civil rights leader Fannie Lou Hamer (1918–1977), being treated in a hospital, is given a hysterectomy without her consent. Outraged, she attempts to regain control over her life by registering to vote and is fired as a result from her job at a Mississippi plantation.

Algerian feminist Fadéla M'rabet publishes *La femme algérienne*.

The U.S. State Department revokes the passport of radical Elizabeth Gurley Flynn; she wins it back in a case that goes all the way to the Supreme Court.

Nepalese feminist Bimala Maskey is elected chairman of the All Nepal Women's Organization.

Business and Industry

Prostitution is outlawed in Thailand, largely due to the agitation of Pierra Hoon Veijjabu, Thailand's first woman doctor.

Edith Nelson becomes Jamaica's first female general secretary of a labor union.

There are 24 million women in the U.S. work force, constituting 34.0% of the total work force. Women are 3% of mail carriers, 4% of butchers, 10% of insurance agents, 11% of bartenders, and 12% of bus drivers.

German-British entrepreneur Stephanie "Steve" Shirley founds Freelance Programmers, Ltd., a successful, multinational computer firm.

Science and Medicine

In the United States, women are 1% of all engineers and 6% of physicians.

America's Society of Women Engineers gives its Achievement Award to metallurgist Laurence Pellier. She has worked extensively with materials for chemical plants, especially stainless steels and titanium alloys.

French physicist Marguérite Perey, discoverer of the element francium, becomes the first woman member of the Académie des Sciences in its 200 years.

U.S. ecologist and author Rachel Carson (1907–April 14, 1964) publishes *Silent Spring*, an indictment of the irresponsible use of pesticides. The book popularizes and invigorates the ecology movement.

German-American psychologist Charlotte Bühler publishes *Psychologie im Leben unserer Zeit*. English childbirth educator Sheila Kitzinger (b. 1929) publishes *The Experience of Childbirth*, which advocates reducing pain through knowledge and relaxation rather than drugs.

Education and Scholarship

Saudi Arabian women are admitted to universities.

U.S. historian Barbara Tuchman publishes the best-seller *The Guns of August*, which wins the Pulitzer Prize for general nonfiction. Other new publications include U.S. economist Juanita Kreps's (b. 1921) textbook *Principles of Economics*, Joan Violet Robinson's *Essays in the Theory of Economic Growth*, and English economist Barbara Ward's (1914–1981) *The Rich and Poor Nations*.

In the United States, women are 12% of college teachers.

Religion

Austrian religious figure Theresa Neuman, who displayed stigmata and appeared to survive on a sip of water and a communion wafer per day, dies.

1963

General Status and Daily Life

Over 1 million U.S. women are using birth control pills.

The young women's magazines *Josei sebun* and *Yangu redi* begin publication in Japan.

Government, the Military, and the Law

Women in Iran, Kenya, and Libya get the vote.

Forty-four of the 500 members of West Germany's Bundestag are women.

Tanzanian economist and political scientist Dorah Bantu (b. 1941) becomes Tanzania's first woman foreign service officer.

Apr. 6 U.S. lawyer Mabel Willebrandt dies. A strong defender of Prohibition, she argued more than forty cases before the U.S. Supreme Court, founded the women's penitentiary in Alderson, West Virginia, and served as counsel to Clark Gable, Jean Harlow, and the Screen Directors Guild.

Literature and the Visual Arts

U.S. poet and surrealist painter Kay Sage (June 25, 1898–January 8) and U.S. poet and novelist Sylvia Plath (February 11) commit suicide. This January, Plath published her only novel, *The Bell Jar,* under the pseudonym Victoria Lucas. Largely autobiographical, it describes the descent into insanity of an ambitious young woman.

New poetry includes Romanian poet Maria Banus's *Metamorphosis*, Romanian poet Constanta Buzea's (b. 1941) *From the Earth*, Swedish poet Sonja Åkesson's *Peace in the House*, Gwendolyn Brooks's *Selected Poems*, French poet Thérèse Plantier's (b. 1911) *Chemin d'eau*, Lebanese poet, journalist, and dramatist Nadia

Tuéni's (b. 1935) *Blond Texts*, Peruvian Blanca Varela's *Daylight*, and Adrienne Rich's *Snapshots of a Daughter-in-Law*.

New novels include East German Christa Wolf's *Der geteilte Himmel* (*Divided Heaven*), Christiane Rochefort's *Les stances à Sophie*, American Mary McCarthy's *The Group*, Iris Murdoch's *The Unicorn*, Ivy Compton-Burnett's *A God and His Gifts*, U.S. novelist Joan Didion's (b. 1934) *Run River*, and English novelist Margaret Drabble's (b. 1939) first novel, *A Summer Birdcage*.

Georgia O'Keeffe is elected to the American Academy of Arts and Letters.

U.S. author Joyce Carol Oates (b. 1938) publishes the short story collection *By the North Gate*.

Performing Arts and Entertainment

U.S. country singer Patsy Cline, best known for the songs "Crazy" and "Leavin' on Your Mind," dies in a plane crash at the age of thirty-one.

U.S. rock singer Janis Joplin (January 19, 1943–October 4, 1970) is voted "Ugliest Man on Campus" at the University of Texas (Austin).

Hit songs in the U.S. include the Chiffons' "He's So Fine," Lelsey Gore's "It's My Party," and the Angels' "My Boyfriend's Back."

U.S. actress Agnes Moorehead begins playing Endora on "Bewitched," a role she will retain until 1971, earning four Emmy nominations.

Films by women include American Shirley Clarke's *The Cool World*, the first movie ever shot in Harlem; *I basilischi* (*The Lizards*), written and directed by Italian film director Lina Wertmuller (b. 1928); and Czechoslovakian director Vera Chytilová's *O Necem Jinem* (*Something Different*), in which a gymnast (played by Olympic gold medalist Eva Bosáková) and a housewife (played by Vera Vzelacova) yield to others' expectations.

U.S. chef Julia Child gets her own television show, "The French Chef."

Alicia Markova becomes director of the New York Metropolitan Opera Ballet; Yvette Chauviré becomes the Paris Opéra's artistic and technical adviser.

French composer, conductor, and music teacher Nadia Boulanger becomes the first woman to conduct the Hallé Orchestra.

U.S. film editor Dorothy Spencer is nominated for an Oscar for her work on *Cleopatra*, which stars Elizabeth Taylor.

Movie audiences can see Ursula Andress in the James Bond film *Dr. No*, French actress Anouk Aimée in *8 1/2*, Swedish actress Harriet Andersson in *A Sunday in September*, Audrey Hepburn in *Charade*, Sophia Loren in *Ieri, oggi e domani* (*Yesterday, Today and Tomorrow*), and French actress Catherine Deneuve (b. October 22, 1943) in *La vice et la vertu* (*Vice and Virtue*) and *Les parapluies de Cherbourg* (*The Umbrellas of Cherbourg*). Patricia Neal wins the Best Actress Oscar for her performance in *Hud* (written by Harriet Frank, Jr.).

Athletics and Exploration

U.S. golfer Mickey Wright wins thirteen tournaments and scores a record low score of 62 for eighteen holes.

June 16-19 Soviet cosmonaut Valentina Tereshkova (b. March 6, 1937), aboard *Vostok 6*, becomes the first woman in space. She circles the globe forty-eight times.

July 6 Australian tennis player Margaret Smith Court (b. July 16, 1942) defeats Billie Jean King in the Wimbledon singles final. Court will win the Wimbledon title again in 1965 and 1970 and the U.S. Open in 1962, 1965, 1969, 1970, and 1973.

Activism

U.S. feminist and writer Betty Friedan (b. February 4, 1921) publishes *The Feminine Mystique*, in which she identifies and condemns the means by which women are conditioned to accept domesticity as their only role. The publication of this book rejuvenates the U.S. feminist movement.

South African activist Dorothy Nyembe is arrested and banned.

Sept. 15 Four black girls—Addie Mae Collins, Denise McNair, Carole Robertson, and Cynthia Wesley—are killed when a bomb explodes in a Birmingham, Alabama, church that is sometimes used for civil rights meetings.

Business and Industry

U.S. woman workers earn 63% as much as men.

U.S. newspaper publisher Katharine Graham becomes president of the company that owns the *Washington Post* and *Newsweek*.

U.S. entrepreneur Mary Kay Ash founds Mary Kay Cosmetics, which will gross about $35 million per year in the 1970s.

Ella Jensen (b. 1907) is elected head of the Tobacco Workers Union, making her the first woman in Denmark to chair a dual-sex labor union.

American Jean Nidetch (b. October 12, 1923) founds Weight Watchers, Inc., the world's most commercially successful diet group.

Science and Medicine

German-American physicist Maria Goeppert Mayer shares the Nobel Prize for Physics for her work on a shell model of atomic nuclear structure.

German-American paleonotologist Tilly Edinger becomes president of the Society of Vertebrate Paleontology.

U.S. scientist Mary Petermann, discoverer of ribosomes (which play an important role in protein synthesis), becomes the first woman member of the Sloan-Kettering Institute for Cancer Research.

America's Society of Women Engineers gives its Achievement Award to Beatrice Hicks (d. 1979) for her work on the performance of sensing devices under extreme environmental conditions.

English zoologist Sidnie Manton wins the Linnean Gold Medal.

Indian social worker Dhanvanthi Rama Rau becomes head of the International Planned Parenthood Association, a position she will hold until 1971.

Education and Scholarship

Egyptian scholar Aisha Abdel Rahman publishes *Contemporary Arab Women Poets* and *The Daughters of the Prophet*.

Finnish criminologist Inkeri Antilla (b. 1916) becomes director of the Institute of Criminology at Helskini University.

New Zealand author and educator Sylvia Ashton-Warner publishes *Teacher*, an explication of her experimental teaching techniques.

Ellen Ash Peters becomes the first tenured woman professor at Yale Law School.

Alice Shalvi becomes the first female head of the Institute of Languages and Literatures at Hebrew University in Jerusalem.

Constance McLaughlin Green wins a Pulitzer Prize for her history *Washington: Village and Capital, 1800–1878.*

Religion

"Dominique," sung by Dominican nun Jeanine Deckers, becomes a hit in the United States, earning Deckers $100,000. She gives her profits to the Dominican order.

U.S. religious writer Dorothy Day publishes *Loaves and Fishes.*

Nov. 2 The pope allows five women delegates to attend the Vatican II conference.

1964

General Status and Daily Life

Sweden adopts the title "Fru" for all adult women.

Government, the Military, and the Law

Pakistani politician Fatima Jinnah (1893–1967), the founder of a women's medical college who is known as *Mader-i-Millat* (Mother of the Nation), runs unsuccessfully for president.

Women in the Sudan get the vote; Fatma Ahmed Ibrahim becomes the first woman elected to Parliament.

Danish lawyer and politician Helga Pedersen becomes a justice of the Supreme Court.

Indian leader Jawaharlal Nehru dies; his daughter Indira Gandhi takes his seat in Parliament and becomes minister of information and broadcasting.

English politician Barbara Castle becomes minister of overseas development.

Liberian attorney and diplomat Angie Brooks-Randolph becomes president of the International Federation of Women Lawyers.

Jan. 27 U.S. senator Margaret Chase Smith tries to capture the nomination for president at the Republican National Convention, securing the second largest number of delegate votes.

Sept. 5 American Communist party leader, radical, and labor leader Elizabeth Gurley Flynn dies. She is given a state funeral in Moscow's Red Square.

Literature and the Visual Arts

U.S. journalist Hazel Brannon Smith wins a Pulitzer Prize for editorial writing.

Joanne Greenberg, under the pseudonym Hannah Green, publishes an autobiographical work about insanity, *I Never Promised You a Rose Garden*; the character of Dr. Fried is a representation of the theories of U.S. psychiatrist Frieda Fromm-Reichmann (October 23, 1889–April 28, 1957), a pioneer in the treatment of schizophrenic patients.

Gossip columnist Louella Parsons retires; Sheilah Graham becomes the top gossip columnist in the United States, with 178 papers running her column.

East German novelist Christa Wolf wins her country's National Prize for Art and Literature.

English architect Alison Smithson (b. 1928) codesigns London's Economist Building.

Japanese poet Yoshihara Sachiko's (b. 1932) first collection, *Litanies of Infancy*, wins the Muro Saisei Prize. Other new poetry includes Romanian Ileana Malancioiu's (b. 1940) *Beheaded Bird* and American Maxine Kumin's (b. 1925) *The Privilege.*

Canadian novelist and critic Jane Rule (b. March 28, 1931) publishes her first novel, *The Desert of the Heart*, which shocks some readers with its lesbian subject matter.

French artist Sonia Delaunay becomes the first woman in history to have an exhibition at the Louvre in her lifetime.

Louise Fitzhugh publishes the children's novel *Harriet the Spy*, about a sixth-grade girl whose penchant for jotting down everything she sees convinces her parents she needs psychiatric help.

Performing Arts and Entertainment

U.S. singer and actress Barbra Streisand (b. April 24,

1942) stars in the play *Funny Girl*, which is based on the life of comedian Fanny Brice.

U.S. lighting designer Jean Rosenthal designs the lighting for *Hamlet*, *Hello Dolly!*, and *Fiddler on the Roof*.

U.S. film editor Anne Coates is nominated for an Oscar for her work on *Becket*.

Hit songs in the United States include Dionne Warwick's "Walk On By" and Martha and the Vandellas' "Dancing in the Street."

Filmgoers can see Sophia Loren in *Matrimonio alla italiana* (*Marriage Italian Style*), Audrey Hepburn as flower seller-turned-society belle Eliza Doolittle in the musical *My Fair Lady*, Bette Davis, Olivia de Havilland, and Agnes Moorehead in the thriller *Hush, Hush, Sweet Charlotte*, and Swedish actress Harriet Andersson in *All These Women*. English actress and singer Julie Andrews stars in *The Americanization of Emily* and wins the Best Actress Oscar for her portrayal of the magical nanny *Mary Poppins*.

South African-English composer Priaulx Rainier (b. 1903) composes a cello concerto.

Nov. 9 Judy Garland and her daughter Liza Minnelli (b. March 12, 1946) give a joint concert in London.

Athletics and Exploration

Soviet jockey Maria Burda wins the Trotting Derby, equivalent in importance to America's Kentucky Derby. Her career will include over 500 victories.

U.S. aviator Jacqueline Cochran breaks the women's speed record, flying at 1,429 miles per hour.

Winter At the Innsbruck Olympics, Russian figure skater Lyudmila Belousova (b. 1935), winner of four European and four world pairs titles, wins the gold medal for pairs skating with her husband, Oleg Protopopov. They influence ice skating with their passionate style, which is heavily influenced in turn by ballet. Inventors of the death spiral, they win the gold this year. Sjoukje Dijkstra of the Netherlands takes the gold medal in women's skating.

East German Ortrun Enderlein takes the gold in women's luge. Austria sweeps the downhill medals, with Christl Haas winning the gold, Edith Zimmermann the silver, and Traudl Hecher the bronze. France's Christine Goitschel takes the slalom gold and giant slalom silver, while Marielle Goitschel takes the slalom silver and giant slalom gold.

In cross-country skiing, Claudia Boyarskikh of the Soviet Union takes first place in the new 5-kilometer event, followed by Finland's Mirja Lehtonen and the Soviet Union's Alevtina Kolchina. Boyarskikh takes a second gold in the 10 kilometers, this time in a Soviet sweep: Eudokhia Mekshilo gets the silver and Maria Gusakova the bronze. The Soviet team of Kolchina, Mekshilo, and Boyarskikh wins the 4 x 5-kilometer relay, followed by Sweden's team of Britt Strandberg, Toini Gustafsson, and Barbro Martinsson.

In speed skating, Lydia Skoblikova of the Soviet Union becomes the first person to win four gold medals in one Olympics; she wins the 500, 1,000, 1,500, and 3,000-meter races, setting Olympic records in the first three.

Apr. 16 German pilot Geraldine Mock becomes the first woman to complete a solo flight around the world.

Summer At the Tokyo Olympics, Australian swimmer Dawn Fraser finishes her Olympic career with a total of eight gold and silver medals. Her gold medal in the 100-meter freestyle makes her the only person to win golds in the same event in three successive Olympic Games. She also wins a silver medal in the freestyle relay. She is then suspended for ten years for wearing a nonregulation suit and marching in the opening ceremonies rather than resting as ordered. She also tries to steal a Japanese flag from Emperor Hirohito's palace.

The IOC introduces a new women's swimming event, the 400-meter individual medley, won by American Donna de Varona. American Virginia Duenkel (bronze medalist in the 100-meter backstroke) takes the gold in the 400-meter freestyle. The only Soviet gold medalist in swimming is Galina Prozumenshikova, who wins the 200-meter breaststroke, followed by Claudia Kolb of the United States.

The U.S. team of Cathy Ferguson (gold medalist in the backstroke), Cynthia Goyette, Sharon Stouder, and Kathleen Ellis wins the medley; Stouder and Ellis are also members of the gold-medal freestyle relay team, which also includes Donna de Varona and Lillian "Pokey" Watson. In addition to her relay medals, Stouder wins the 100-meter butterfly and takes a silver in the 100-meter freestyle; Ellis takes bronzes in those two races. West German diver Ingrid Engel-Krämer, a double gold medalist in the last Olympics, holds on to her springboard championship, but she is forced to settle for a silver in the platform event behind Lesley Bush of the United States.

Japan wins the women's volleyball title, followed by the Soviet Union and Poland. Two members of the Soviet team, Ljudmila Buldakova and Inna Ryskal, will also play on the gold medal team in 1968.

Switzerland's Marianne Gossweiler wins a silver in team dressage, which is open to both sexes. The 500-meter kayak single event is won by the Soviet Union's Lyudmila Khvedosyuk. The pairs race is won by West Germans Roswitha Esser and Annemarie Zimmermann.

The team foil gold goes to Hungary's fencers, Ildiko Ujlaki-Retjo (gold medalist in the individual foil),

Katalin Juhasz-Nagy, Lidia Sakovics-Domolky, Judit Mendelenyi-Agoston, and Paula Marosi. The second-place Soviet team includes Galina Gorokhova, Tatiane Samusenko, Valentina Prudskova, Ljudmila Schishova, and Valentina Rastvorova.

Soviet gymnast Larissa Latynina, competitor in three consecutive Olympic Games, ends her Olympic career with more total medals than any other athlete ever, male or female. She is on the first-place team, which also includes Polina Astakhova, Yelena Volchetskaya, Tamara Manina (the silver medalist in the balance beam), Tamara Zamotailova-Lyukhina, and Ljudmila Gromova. Latynina takes a gold medal in the floor exercise, silvers in the all-around and horse vault, and bronzes in the uneven bars and beam. Her teammate Polina Astakhova is almost as impressive, winning a gold in the uneven bars, a silver in the floor exercise, and a bronze in the all-around. The rising gymnastic star, however, is not a Soviet, but a Czechoslovakian, Vera Cáslavská, who in this Olympics and the next will win seven individual golds and four silvers. She wins the individual all-around title as well as gold medals in the beam and vault and a silver medal in the team event.

The IOC introduces two new women's track-and-field events, the 400-meter foot race, which is won by Australia's Betty Cuthbert, and the pentathlon, which is won by Russian athlete Irina Press. Wyomia Tyus of the United States wins the 100-meter dash, followed by American Edith MacGuire and Poland's Eva Klobukowska (who will later be barred from a meet for failing a sex test). MacGuire wins the 200-meter dash. Great Britain's Anne Packer wins the 800 meters and takes a silver in the 400, and her teammate Mary Rand, the pentathlon silver medalist, executes a record-breaking series of long jumps, winning the gold. Even the worst of her jumps breaks the previous record. Rand is the first British woman to win a gold medal in track and field.

Karin Balzer of West Germany wins the hurdles, followed by silver medalist Teresa Ceipla of Poland. Ceipla is a member of Poland's gold medal 4 x 100 relay team, which also includes Klobukowska and Irena Kirzenstein, silver medalist in the 200 meters and the long jump. Second place in the relay goes to the U.S. team, which includes Tyus, MacGuire, and Willye White, a medalist in the 1956 games. Great Britain's third-place team also includes a previous Olympic medalist, Dorothy Hyman, as well as Mary Rand.

Russian athlete Tamara Press wins gold medals in the shot put and discus. Romanian high jumper Iolanda Balas sets an Olympic record, winning the gold medal in her event. Galina Zybina of the Soviet Union takes the bronze in the shot put. Romania's Mihaela Penes wins the javelin throw.

Activism

The Nepal Women's Organization opens the Women's

Legal Aid Services Project to provide free legal assistance to battered, abandoned, and sexually assaulted women.

The first battered women's shelter in the United States opens.

Middle-class Brazilian women organize a march of 800,000 people against President João Goulart.

U.S. civil rights leader Stokely Carmichael, leader of the Student Non-Violent Coordinating Committee (SNCC), is asked what he thinks is the position of women in the movement. He responds, "The only position for women in SNCC is prone."

Business and Industry

There are 25,400,000 women in the U.S. work force, constituting 34.8% of the total work force.

The U.S. Civil Rights Act is passed. Title VII prohibits sex discrimination in the workplace, though not until the very last minute; the addition of women to the list of protected classes is introduced on the day the bill passes the House, presumably to kill the legislation. However, it passes and gives women substantial legal protection. Title VII makes most forced pregnancy leaves illegal and outlaws sex discrimination in hiring unless sex is a bona fide occupational requirement.

Science and Medicine

Soviet engineer Sophia Belkin wins the Lenin Prize, a rough equivalent of the Nobel.

U.S. surgeon Patricia Donahoe gets her M.D.; she will do important research on treating reproductive cancers with the hormone that causes male fetuses to develop male genitalia.

America's Society of Women Engineers gives its Achievement Award to computer programmer Grace Murray Hopper.

U.S. pediatrician and microbiologist Hattie Alexander (April 5, 1901–June 24, 1968), best known for her work on influenzal meningitis, becomes the first woman president of the American Pediatric Society.

English biochemist Dorothy Crowfoot Hodgkin wins the Nobel Prize for Chemistry.

July 31 U.S. physician Dorothy Reed Mendenhall (b. September 22, 1874) dies. She researched Hodgkin's disease, proving that it was not a form of tuberculosis and discovering a type of cell (the Reed cell) associated with it. She also studied infant mortality, after her newborn daughter died due to bad obstetrical care, working to reduce infant deaths through the establishment of new clinics.

Education and Scholarship

German-American political philosopher Hannah Arendt publishes *Eichmann in Jerusalem: A Report on the Banality of Evil*, an account of the trial of a famous Nazi war criminal.

Religion

Pope Paul VI gives Mother Theresa his limousine; she uses it as a raffle prize and uses the raffle proceeds to build a home for lepers.

1965

General Status and Daily Life

East Germany sets the minimum age of marriage at eighteen for both sexes and legalizes divorce by either spouse if a court determines that the union has "lost all meaning." Women have equal child custody and property rights. Abortion, legal since 1950 for medical or eugenic reasons, is now allowed in cases where the woman's social circumstances make it desirable.

Guatemala's constitution forbids discrimination on the basis of sex.

Israel entitles the widow of an intestate man to their car and 50% of his estate if they have had children together. If he has children by another marriage, she gets only 25%.

June 7 The U.S. Supreme Court declares bans on birth control unconstitutional.

Government, the Military, and the Law

Karimah Al-Sa'id becomes Egypt's first woman minister of education.

Israeli politician Golda Meir becomes secretary-general of the Labor party.

Women get the vote in Afghanistan; Kobra Nourzai becomes minister of public health.

Marguerite de Reimacker-Legot becomes Belgium's first woman Cabinet minister.

Elizabeth Lane becomes Britain's first woman High Court judge; Barbara Castle becomes minister of transport.

Princess Lalla Aicha, sister of King Hassan of Morocco, is made ambassador to London.

Finnish criminologist Inkeri Antilla becomes chairman of the government's commissions on juvenile crime and abortion.

Jan. The U.S. Army's first two women in Vietnam, Major Kathleen Wilkes and Master Sergeant Betty Adams, become advisers to Vietnam's new Women's Armed Forces Corps.

Jan. 4 Patsy Mink (b. December 6, 1927), the first Japanese-American woman elected to Congress, takes her seat.

Jan. 8 U.S. judge Lorna Elizabeth Lockwood becomes the first woman state supreme court chief justice.

Oct. 6 U.S. lawyer Patricia Harris takes office in Luxembourg, becoming the first black U.S. ambassador.

Literature and the Visual Arts

South African poet Ingrid Jonker (b. 1933), who clashed with the government over her opposition to apartheid, commits suicide.

Katherine Anne Porter publishes her *Collected Stories*, which wins the National Book Award, the Pulitzer Prize, and a gold medal from the National Institute of Arts and Letters.

U.S. poet Mary Oliver (b. 1935) publishes *No Voyage and Other Poems.* Other new poetry includes Romanian poet Gabriela Melinescu's *Winter Ceremony*, American Elizabeth Bishop's *Questions of Travel*, Australian Mary Dobson's *Cock Crow*, Lebanese poet Vénus Khoury-Gata's (b. 1937) *Unfinished Faces*, Sylvia Plath's posthumous *Ariel*, Hilde Domin's *Ruckkehr der Schiffe*, and Gloria Fuertes's *With Neither Bullet or Poison or Blade.*

American Helen Gurley Brown (b. 1927) becomes editor in chief of *Cosmopolitan* magazine.

Canadian journalist Renaude Lapointe (b. 1912) becomes

the first woman on the editorial board of Montreal's *La Presse*.

New short story collections include Eudora Welty's *Thirteen Stories*, Doris Lessing's *A Man and Two Women*, and Flannery O'Connor's posthumous *Everything That Rises Must Converge*.

Oct. 11 U.S. photographer Dorothea Lange dies. She recorded images of the Depression and the internment of Japanese-Americans during World War II; her photographs of the latter were so sympathetic to the internees that they were confiscated by the government.

Performing Arts and Entertainment

Deaths this year include English pianist Myra Hess (b. 1890) and U.S. theater columnist Dorothy Kilgallen (b. 1913). Kilgallen became nationally famous in 1949 as a panelist on the television game show "What's My Line?" She appeared on the show for sixteen years and invented the question, "Is it bigger than a bread box?"

Dorothy Fields writes the lyrics for the musical *Sweet Charity*, starring Gwen Verdon. Jean Rosenthal designs the lighting for the Broadway play *The Odd Couple*.

Canadian filmmaker Beryl Fox produces and directs the award-winning Vietnam documentary *The Mills of the Gods* and the thirty-minute documentary *Summer in Mississippi*, about a black voter registration drive. Other films by women include French director Agnès Varda's *Le Bonheur*, which wins Best Film at Cannes, and Soviet director Yulia Solntseva's (b. 1901) *The Enchanted Desna*.

The television show "I Dream of Jeannie," starring Barbara Eden as a subservient but mischievous genie, first airs. During its run, which lasts until 1970, NBC forbids Eden to show her navel.

Julie Christie wins the Best Actress Oscar for her performance in *Darling*. Other new films include *The Sound of Music*, starring Julie Andrews as the singing nun and governess Maria von Trapp; *Cat Ballou*, a Western parody starring Jane Fonda (b. December 21, 1937); and *Repulsion*, starring French actress Catherine Deneuve.

English composer and conductor Ruth Gipps composes her third symphony; Australian-American composer Peggy Glanville-Hicks composes the opera *Sappho*.

Athletics and Exploration

English croquet player Dorothy Steel (b. 1884) dies.

She won thirty-one titles, including four Open Croquet Championships and fifteen Women's Championships.

English aviator Sheila Scott sets a 31,000-mile, 189-hour record for the longest consecutive solo flight.

U.S. sailor Peggy Slater, winner of 600 sailing trophies, is the only woman to race in this year's Transpacific Yacht Race.

Czech gymnast Vera Cáslavská wins a gold medal in every event at the European championships.

Activism

White American civil rights activist Viola Liuzzo, a Detroit housewife, is murdered in Alabama for driving freedom marchers from Selma to Montgomery. On December 3, three members of the KKK are found guilty of her murder; a mistrial is declared, and a new trial, with only one defendant, results in an acquittal from an all-white jury.

Haitian activist Casserne Dessalines, an opponent of the Duvalier regime and a member of Femmes Patriots, has her breasts cut off with whips by Duvalier's torturers.

Mar. 10 U.S. civil rights reformer, suffragist, and community leader Daisy Lampkin dies. As a high-ranking officer of the NAACP, she substantially increased membership.

Mar. 17 Seventy-two-year-old American Alice Hertz immolates herself in an anti-Vietnam War protest.

Business and Industry

Spanish courtesan Caroline Puentovalga, better known as La Belle Otero (b. 1868), dies. Her lovers allegedly included King Edward VII of England, Kaiser Wilhelm, Alfonso XIII of Spain, French prime minister Aristide Briand, and author Gabriele d'Annunzio.

Guatemala's constitution guarantees equal pay for equal work.

Americans Mary Draper Janney and Jane Phillips Fleming organize Washington (later Wider) Opportunities for Women (WOW), which helps women get job skills, find jobs, train as inner-city teachers, break into nontraditional fields, and locate day care.

In Japan, 19,030,000 women are in the work force, constituting 39.8% of the total work force. In Russia, there are 37,680,000 Russian women in the work force, constituting 49% of the total work force.

In the United States, 54% of male managers and 50% of female managers say they believe women do not want or expect power.

U.S. filmmaker Susan Wayne becomes the owner of Gotham Film Productions, which will make corporate films for companies like J. C. Penney, Renault, and AT&T.

Apr. 1 U.S. cosmetics entrepreneur Helena Rubinstein (b. December 25, 1870), whose businesses currently employ about 30,000 people, dies.

Science and Medicine

English biochemist Dorothy Crowfoot Hodgkin becomes the first woman since Florence Nightingale to receive the Order of Merit.

German-American psychologist Charlotte Bühler becomes president of the new Association for Humanistic Psychology.

U.S. astronomer Elizabeth Roemer, expert on asteroids and periodic comets and sighter of seventy-nine returning comets between 1953 and 1976, has a minor planet named Roemera in her honor.

U.S. marine biologist Eugenie Clark becomes the founding director of the world's leading shark study institute.

America's Society of Women Engineers gives its Achievement Award to engineer, educator, and combustion expert Martha J. Thomas.

Education and Scholarship

French sociologist, feminist, and journalist Evelyne Sullerot publishes *Demain les femmes*.

U.S. journalist Marguerite Higgins, well known for her work as a war correspondent in Korea, publishes *Our Vietnam Nightmare*.

Religion

Fifty-three percent of U.S. Catholics use birth control.

1966

General Status and Daily Life

Abortion, which has been legal on request in Romania since 1957, is restricted to cases of rape, incest, the life or health of the mother, and congenital disease.

Sri Lanka's new Penal Code outlaws sexual harassment; it can be penalized by whipping, a fine, and a maximum of two years in jail. Rape is punishable by a fine and up to twenty years in jail.

British model Twiggy (Leslie Hornsby) is popularizing the miniskirt, designed by fellow Briton Mary Quant (b. February 11, 1934).

Government, the Military, and the Law

Grete Rehor (b. June 30, 1910), as minister of social administration, becomes the first woman Cabinet minister in Austria.

Fijian politician Adi Losalini Dovi, who began her career in government as a stenographer, becomes a member of the Legislative Council, a post she will hold until 1970.

Lusibu Z. N'Kanza, twenty-six, becomes minister of state for social affairs of Zaïre.

Princess Nakatindi becomes Zambia's first female member of Parliament.

Thirty-eight members of West Germany's Bundestag are women.

U.S. lawyer and political official Patricia Harris becomes a delegate to the UN.

Finnish criminologist Inkeri Antilla begins four years as chairman of the Finnish commission on women's rights and three years as head of the commission on sexual crimes.

Swedish politician Alva Myrdal (b. 1902) becomes minister for disarmament.

Chinese political leader Jiang Qing (b. 1914) becomes cultural adviser to the People's Liberation Army.

English politician Judith Hart becomes minister of state for Commonwealth affairs.

Jan. Indira Gandhi runs for prime minister of India

against male candidate Morarji Desai; crowds awaiting the results outside Parliament shout, "Is it a boy or a girl?" Gandhi wins and becomes her country's third prime minister and the second female elected leader in modern history. She will hold this post until 1977.

Jan. 26 Australian politician Annabelle Rankin becomes minister of housing, making her the first woman to head an Australian federal department.

Apr. 21 Britain's Parliament is opened on television for the first time by Queen Elizabeth II.

Aug. 30 Constance Baker Motley (b. September 14, 1921) becomes the first black woman U.S. federal judge.

Literature and the Visual Arts

U.S. journalist and defender of labor Mary Heaton Vorse (October 9, 1874–June 14) and Finland's first woman architect, Wivi Lönn (b. 1872), die.

U.S. poet Carolyn Kizer becomes the first director of the National Endowment for the Arts' (NEA) Literary Program.

German-Swedish poet Nelly Sachs shares the Nobel Prize for Literature.

Japanese novelist Ariyoshi Sawako publishes *Hanaoka Seishu no tsuma (The Doctor's Wife)*, a historical novel about the loyal wife of an eighteenth-century surgeon. Other new novels include Hilde Domin's *Hier*, American Jacqueline Susann's *Valley of the Dolls*, Mary Renault's *The Mask of Apollo*, and British author Rebecca West's *The Birds Fall Down*. Nigerian novelist Flora Nwapa (b. 1931) publishes *Efuru*, which focuses on clashes between city and village life.

New poetry includes Romanian poet Gabriela Melinescu's *The Abstract Beings*, Marianne Moore's *Tell Me, Tell Me*, Spanish poet Julia Uceda's *Without Much Hope*, Anne Sexton's Pulitzer-winning *Live or Die*, and U.S. poet Adrienne Rich's *The Necessities of Life*. Canadian author Margaret Atwood's (b. 1939) collection *The Circle Game* wins the Governor-General's Award.

The work of U.S. photographer Dorothea Lange is featured in a posthumous exhibit at MoMA.

British novelist Jean Rhys (pseudonym of Gwen Williams, 1894–1970) publishes her best-known work, *The Wide Sargasso Sea*, which retells the story of Charlotte Brontë's *Jane Eyre* from the point of view of Bertha Rochester.

East German novelist Christa Wolf publishes *Nachdenken über Christa T (The Quest for Christa T)*,

which is banned for five years because its criticism of East German society.

Canadian journalist and politician Jeanne Sauvé (b. 1922) becomes general secretary of the Union des Artistes et Auteurs de Canada.

U.S. diarist and novelist Anaïs Nin begins publishing the six volumes of her diary.

Feb. 1 U.S. journalist Hedda Hopper, whose gossip column ran in 85 metropolitan daily papers, 3,000 smaller papers, and 2,000 weekly papers, dies. Politically conservative, she wielded enormous power in Hollywood and engaged in a long-running feud with rival columnist Louella Parsons.

Dec. 24 U.S. editor May Massee (b. May 1, 1881) dies. As an editor of children's books at Doubleday and Viking, she encouraged many prominent authors and artists, including Ludwig Bemelmans of *Madeline* fame.

Performing Arts and Entertainment

Czech film director Véra Chytilová's makes the surreal comedy *Daisies*, and Bulgarian director Nevena Toshevas films the documentary *Bulgaria: Land, People, Sun*.

British film editor Thelma Connell works on *Alfie*.

The Finnish government establishes a grant program for women filmmakers.

U.S. stage lighting designer Jean Rosenthal designs the lighting for the musical *Cabaret*.

U.S. choreographer Twyla Tharp (b. 1942) creates the dance *Re-moves*.

U.S. rock singer Grace Slick becomes the lead singer for Jefferson Airplane. Popular songs include "You Can't Hurry Love," sung by Diana Ross and the Supremes, and "These Boots Are Made for Walkin'," sung by Nancy Sinatra.

French writer and filmmaker Marguerite Duras writes a play, *La musica*, publishes a novel, *Le vice-consul*, and begins directing experimental films.

U.S. singer Aretha Franklin (b. March 25, 1942) records *Never Loved a Man*.

English mezzo-soprano Janet Baker makes her Covent Garden debut in Britten's *A Midsummer Night's Dream*.

Elizabeth Taylor wins the Best Actress Oscar for her performance in *Who's Afraid of Virginia Woolf?* Other new films include *Morgan*, for which English actress Vanessa Redgrave gets an Oscar nomination; *Persona*, starring Norwegian actress Liv Ullmann; and *Un homme et une femme* (*A Man and a Woman*), starring French actress Anouk Aimée.

Feb. 9 U.S. entertainer Sophie Tucker (b. January 13, 1884), "The Last of the Red-Hot Mamas," dies. Despite being what one stage manager called "big and ugly," she made a career of singing boisterous songs full of double entendres. Her theme song was "One of These Days (You're Gonna Miss Me, Honey)."

Athletics and Exploration

British pilot Anne Burns becomes the first woman to win the British Gliding Championship.

Feb. 27 American Peggy Fleming wins the world figure-skating championship. She will repeat her victory in 1967 and 1968.

Activism

Shulamit Aloni (b. 1931) becomes head of the Israeli Consumer Council.

U.S. feminist Betty Friedan founds the National Organization for Women (NOW), serving as its first president until 1970. The organization's members, including United Auto Workers representative Dorothy Haener (b. 1917), vow to oust any public official who "ignores the principle of full equality between the sexes."

South African civil rights activist Winnie Mandela (b. 1934) is arrested and sentenced to a year in jail after continuing to speak on behalf of the banned ANC.

Summer U.S. civil rights activist Rubye Doris Smith Robinson becomes executive secretary of SNCC.

Business and Industry

In the United States, 27,300,000 women are in the work force, constituting 36% of the total work force.

Japanese clerical worker Setsuko Suzuki, fired from the Sumitomo Cement Company because she married, wins her job back in a landmark court case.

U.S. advertising executive Mary Lawrence Wells turns down a multimillion-dollar offer and starts her own agency, Wells, Rich, Greene Inc., of which she becomes chairman and CEO.

June 4 U.S. editor and publisher Blanche Knopf (b. July 30, 1894), wife and partner of Alfred A. Knopf, dies. A principal director of their publishing house, she was responsible for convincing many prominent authors, including Sigmund Freud, André Gide, Thomas Mann, Jean Paul Sartre, Albert Camus, Simone de Beauvoir, Dashiell Hammett, and Raymond Chandler, to bring their work to her.

Science and Medicine

America's Society of Women Engineers gives its Achievement Award to space engineer Dorothy Martin Simon.

Sri Lankan physician Siva Chinnatamby, founder of the Association of Medical Women of Ceylon and the Association of Obstetricians and Gynecologists of Ceylon, becomes a member of the American College of Surgeons.

Virginia Johnson coauthors *Human Sexual Response*, for many years the definitive work on human sexuality.

Austrian physicist Lise Meitner becomes the first woman to win the Atomic Energy Commission's Fermi Award.

There are about 500 birth control clinics in Britain.

Education and Scholarship

New publications include U.S. sociologist Bettina Aptheker's (b. 1944) *Big Business and the American University*, U.S. critic Susan Sontag's (b. 1933) *Against Interpretation*, English economist Barbara Ward's *Spaceship Earth*, and U.S. historian Barbara Tuchman's *The Proud Tower*, an analysis of European society on the brink of World War I.

Judge and legal scholar Margarita Arguas becomes a full professor, after becoming the first woman in Argentina to serve on the National Court of Civil Appeals and the Supreme Court, the first woman member of the Academy of Law and Social Sciences, and the first woman president of the International Law Association.

Religion

Egyptian scholar Aisha Abdel Rahman, an expert on the women associated with Muhammad, publishes *The Mother of the Prophet*.

1967

General Status and Daily Life

In Britain, 20,000 legal and 30,000 illegal abortions are performed yearly; 2,500 women are hospitalized each year after botched abortions. In July, abortion laws are liberalized in England, Scotland and Wales. Two doctors must certify that the procedure results from a birth defect or from a physical or mental risk to the woman or her existing children. In the next few years, deaths from illegal abortions will drop from twenty a year to about one a year, and infanticide rates will also plummet.

Contraception is legalized in France, and Indonesia accepts birth control access as a basic human right.

Hungary passes a law giving women who stay home with children a monthy pension for three years.

Government, the Military, and the Law

France's 283-member senate includes five women; its 487-member assembly has eleven female members.

English politician Shirley Williams becomes minister of state for education and science, a position she will hold until 1969. Judith Hart becomes minister of social security.

Aborigines of both sexes get the vote in Australia.

Bibi Palvanova, who in 1971 will call the yashmak and veil "the symbol of our silence," becomes minister of education for Turkmenia in the USSR.

Literature and the Visual Arts

French poet Anne-Marie Albiach (b. 1937), who also works in the fields of literary theory and semiotics, publishes *Flammigère*. Other new poetry includes Denise Levertov's *The Sorrow Dance*, Belgian Anne-Marie Kegels's *Twelve Poems for a Year*, and Lebanese poet Vénus Khoury-Gata's *Stagnant Lands*.

U.S. author Katherine Anne Porter publishes her *Collected Stories*, winning a Pulitzer Prize.

The work of U.S. photographer Diane Arbus is featured in an exhibition at MoMA.

U.S. poet Gwendolyn Brooks is named a member of the National Institute of Arts and Letters.

June 7 U.S. poet, short story author, and critic Dorothy Parker dies, leaving most of her estate to Martin Luther King, Jr. She was known for her caustic wit and biting sarcasm. When a haughty young man said, "I'm afraid I simply cannot bear fools," Parker responded, "Your mother could, apparently." At a Yale prom, she surveyed the women present and said, "If all those sweet young things were laid end to end, I wouldn't be a bit surprised."

Performing Arts and Entertainment

U.S. jazz singer Ida Cox (b. 1889) and American-Scottish soprano Mary Garden (February 20, 1874–January 3) die. Garden sang Charpentier's *Louise* more than one hundred times and played at least one tenor role, but she was best known as Mélisande in Debussy's *Pellias et Mélisande*.

Tunisian filmmaker Najet Mabaouj directs a film about a forced *Marriage*. Other new films directed by women include Ghanaian Efua Sutherland's *Araba: The Village Story*, which depicts village life from a young girl's perspective; French director Nelly Kaplan's sixty-minute film, *Le Regard Picasso* (*The Picasso Look*), which wins the Golden Lion at the Venice Film Festival; Hungarian Márta Mészáros's (b. 1931) *The Girl*, about a woman born illegitimate who comes to terms with her past; Indian director Manju Dey's *Abhisapta Chambal* (*Accursed Chambal Valley*), which follows a woman through her transformations from dancing girl to bandit to virtuous woman; and American Shirley Clarke's *A Portrait of Jason*, an interview with a male prostitute.

U.S. film editor Marjorie Fowler is nominated for an Oscar for her work on *Dr. Doolittle*. Dede Allen edits *Bonnie and Clyde*, starring Faye Dunaway.

Scottish composer and conductor Thea Musgrave (b. 1928) composes a clarinet concerto.

South African-English composer Priaulx Rainier composes the orchestral suite *Aequora lunae*.

Canadian singer Joni Mitchell (b. 1943) records *Songs to a Seagull*.

French film actress Catherine Deneuve stars in *Belle du jour* and *Les demoiselles de Rochefort* (*The Young Girls of Rochefort*). *The Graduate* stars Katherine Ross and Anne Bancroft; Ross also appears in *Guess Who's Coming to Dinner?*, for which Katharine Hepburn wins the Best Actress Academy Award.

June 17 Barbra Streisand gives a free concert in Central Park, New York; 135,000 attend.

Athletics and Exploration

The Boston Marathon will not accept a woman runner, so American Kathrine Switzer registers as K. Switzer. When she shows up at the race, officials try to keep her from starting, even attempting to rip the number from her back. She finishes anyway and in 1972 becomes the first woman to run officially in the Boston Marathon.

Since 1954, U.S. badminton player Judy Devlin has won ten singles titles at the All England Championships.

Anglers Jane Haywood and Martha Webster each catch record-breaking 410-pound blue sharks.

Czech gymnast Vera Cáslavská wins a gold in every event at the European championships.

English cyclist Beryl Burton (b. 1937), holder of over sixty British cycling titles, seven world titles, and seven silver and bronze medals from international competitions, breaks the British men's record for the twelve-hour time trial by 5 3/4 miles (9.2 kilometers).

U.S. mountain climber Arlene Blum (b. 1945) climbs Mount Pisco, Peru, despite a fall into a crevasse.

Activism

The All Nepal Women's Organization prints a guide to women's legal rights.

Feb. 15 In a demonstration organized by Women Strike for Peace, 2,500 angry women storm the Pentagon, demanding to see "the generals who send our sons to die."

Oct. 15 California antiwar protester Florence Beaumont (b. c. 1912) burns herself to death to protest U.S. involvement in Vietnam.

Dec. 28 U.S. philanthropist Katharine Dexter McCormick dies. She helped birth control pioneer Margaret Sanger to smuggle diaphragms into the country from Europe during the 1920s, built housing for 342 women at MIT to eliminate its ostensible reason for not admitting more women, and financed the development of the birth control pill. At her death, she leaves $5 million to Planned Parenthood.

Business and Industry

U.S. stockbroker Muriel Siebert becomes the first woman to own a seat on the New York Stock Exchange.

Ghana's Labor Decree grants women twelve weeks of maternity leave at half salary, six weeks before and six weeks after delivery. Women are guaranteed job security if they take maternity leave, and women who nurse their babies are given nursing breaks.

In the United States, women with four years of high school make less money than men with fewer than eight years of elementary school; women with four years of college education make less than men with one to three years of high school.

Sex discrimination by U.S. government contractors is banned.

U.S. interior design firm executive Flora Adriana Scalamandrè (b. 1907) of Scalamandrè Silks wins the American Institute of Interior Designers' award. Her firm, founded by her husband, produces reproduction fabrics and wallpapers for period homes. Her daughter, Adriana Scalamandrè Bitter (b. 1934), is also active in the business.

Greek newspaper owner Helene Vlachou closes her two papers rather than submit to military censorship.

Science and Medicine

English astronomer Margaret Burbidge publishes her work on quasars in *Quasi-Stellar Objects*.

U.S. anatomist Berta Vogel Scharrer is elected to the National Academy of Sciences.

The SWE gives its Achievement Award to Marguerite Rogers (d. 1989) for her work on air-delivered tactical weapons.

May 27 German-American vertebrate paleontologist Tilly Edinger (b. November 13, 1897) dies. She was a pioneer in the field of paleoneurology and did the first systematic work on cranial casts (interior models of fossil skulls) to study brain development.

Aug.-Nov. British graduate student Jocelyn Bell (b. 1943) discovers pulsars, though her professor, Antony Hewish, identifies them and gets the credit.

Education and Scholarship

French scholar Hélène Ahrweiler (b. 1916), an expert in Byzantine social history, becomes the first woman to head the Sorbonne's history department.

Saudi Arabian queen 'Iffat founds the College of Education to train women as teachers.

Japanese mathematician Yoshi Katsurada becomes the first woman full professor at Hokkaido University.

Mary Gambrell (d. August 1974) becomes the first U.S. woman president of a major coeducational college when she is named head of Hunter College of the City University of New York.

July 13 Educator Ethel Andrus (b. September 21, 1884), the first woman high school principal in California, founder of the National Retired Teachers Association, and founder and first president of the American Association of Retired Persons (AARP), dies.

Religion

English economist Barbara Ward becomes a member of the Vatican Commission for Justice and Peace.

U.S. theologian Rosemary Radford Reuther publishes *The Church Against Itself.*

1968

General Status and Daily Life

Canada legalizes divorce in many cases, mostly for sexual irregularities, cruelty, desertion, and similar causes.

Use of the contraceptive intrauterine device (IUD) is authorized in the USSR.

Dec. 4 Twenty-year-old Franca Viola flies in the face of Sicilian custom, which dictates that a woman "ruined" by being raped must marry her rapist. Raped by a rejected suitor, she today weds a less violent man. Italy's president attends the wedding.

Government, the Military, and the Law

Argentinian revolutionary Tamara Bunke is killed fighting for Che Guevara in Bolivia.

Barbara Castle becomes Britain's secretary of state for employment and productivity. Judith Hart becomes paymaster-general.

Only 7 of the Japanese Diet's 467 members are women.

Ingrid Gärde Widemar becomes the first woman on Sweden's twenty-four-member Supreme Court. She will serve on the court until 1980 and be replaced by another woman, Berit Palme.

Iranian politician Farrokhrou Parsa, one of the first six women in the Iranian Parliament in 1964, becomes her country's first female Cabinet minister when she is named minister of education.

Republican official Ivy Baker Priest (September 7, 1905–June 23, 1975), nominating Ronald Reagan at the national convention, becomes the first woman to nominate a candidate for president. Priest was the second woman treasurer of the United States.

Vietnamese politician Nguyen Thi Binh, as a member of the Central Committee of the National Liberation Front, leads the delegation to the Paris peace conference.

Botswanan diplomat and politician Gaositwe Keogakwa Tibe Chiepe becomes her country's director of education.

July 7 Charlene Mitchell is named the U.S. Communist party's candidate for President.

Nov. 5 U.S. politician Shirley Chisholm (b. November 30, 1924) becomes the first black woman elected to Congress.

Literature and the Visual Arts

U.S. poet Jane Cooper (b. 1924) publishes her first collection, *The Weather of Six Mornings,* which wins an award from the Academy of American Poets. Other new poetry includes Louise Bogan's *The Blue Estuaries: Poems 1923–1968,* Muriel Rukeyser's *The Speed of Darkness,* Gwendolyn Brooks's *In the Mecca,* American Marge Piercy's (b. 1936) *Breaking Camp,* American Louise Niedecker's *North Central,* French poet Yvonne Caroutch's *Lieux probables,* Spanish poet Julia Uceda's *Poems of Cherry Lane,* and Portuguese poet Sophia de Mello Breyner Andresen's *Selected Works.*

French journalist Francine Lazurick (b. 1909) becomes editor and publisher of the daily *L'Aurore.*

German-American sculptor Eva Hesse has her first one-woman show.

U.S. science fiction and fantasy author Ursula K. LeGuin (b. 1929) publishes *A Wizard of Earthsea,* the first book in a trilogy. It tells the story of a young wizard named Ged who must fight a mysterious shadow. American novelist Anne McCaffrey publishes *Dragonflight,* the first in her immensely successful "Dragonriders of Pern" fantasy books.

Other new books include French novelist Nathalie

Sarraute's *Entre la vie et la mort*, Marguerite Yourcenar's *L'oeuvre au noir*, Françoise Sagan's *La Garde du coeur*, and Muriel Spark's *The Prime of Miss Jean Brodie*.

Feb. 23 U.S. writer Fannie Hurst (b. October 18, 1889), one of the highest-paid novelists in the United States during the 1920s, 1930s, and 1940s, dies. Her works advocated help for Eastern European Jews, gay rights, equal pay, and a woman's right to keep her birth name.

Performing Arts and Entertainment

German opera singer Margarette Klose (August 6, 1902–December 14) and French organist and composer Jeanne Demessieux (b. 1921), the first woman to play in Westminster Abbey and Westminster Cathedral, die.

Women working in film include U.S. film editor Eve Newman, nominated for an Oscar for *Wild in the Streets*, France's Mag Bodard, producer of *Je t'aime, je t'aime* (*I Love You, I Love You*), and dancer and choreographer Ellida Geyra, the first woman in Israel to direct a film, *Before Tomorrow*.

U.S. country singer Tammy Wynette (b. 1942) records *Stand By Your Man*.

Women are about 12% of the Soviet Union's 1,700 composers.

Katharine Hepburn stars in *The Lion in Winter*, for which she earns a record eleventh Oscar nomination. She ties with Barbra Streisand (in *Funny Girl*, written by Isobel Lennart) for the Best Actress Academy Award and becomes the first person, male or female, ever to win four Oscars in the leading-actor category.

Filmgoers can see teenager Olivia Hussey playing the doomed Capulet in Zeffirelli's *Romeo and Juliet*, Joanne Woodward in *Rachel, Rachel*, Jane Fonda in the science fiction adventure *Barbarella*, Norwegian actress Liv Ullmann (b. 1939) in *Hour of the Wolf* and *Shame*, Catherine Deneuve in *Benjamin*, and English actress Vanessa Redgrave in an Oscar-nominated performance in *Isadora*.

Feb. U.S. rock singer Janis Joplin makes her New York City debut in a performance described as "a frantic, sweating, passionate, demanding sexual act." In this year she also appears at the Newport (Rhode Island) Folk Festival and releases her million-selling first album, *Cheap Thrills*.

Athletics and Exploration

British tennis player Virginia Wade, who will win the Wimbledon singles title in 1977, wins the singles title at the U.S. Open.

Kathy Kusner becomes the first licensed woman jockey in the United States.

Winter The Grenoble Olympics are the first Olympic Games to sex-test female athletes. Figure skater Peggy Fleming wins the only U.S. gold medal of the winter games. Russians Ludmila Belousova and Oleg Protopopov, well known for their death spirals and overhead lifts, win the gold in pairs. The gold in luge is won by Erica Lechner of Italy.

Austria's Olga Pall wins the downhill, and France's Marielle Goitschel wins the slalom. Canada's Nancy Green wins the giant slalom and takes the slalom silver. Sweden's Toini Gustafsson wins the 5-kilometer cross-country race, followed by Galina Kulakova and Alevtina Kolchina, both of the Soviet Union. Gustafsson takes another gold in the 10-kilometer race, and Norway's Berit Mordre and Inger Aufles get the silver and bronze. Aufles, Mordre, and Babben Enger-Damon wins the 4 x 5-kilometer relay; Sweden's Gustafsson, Britt Strandberg, and Barbro Martinsson get the silver; and Soviet skiers Kolchina, Kulakova, and Rita Aschkina get the bronze.

Soviet speed skater Lyudmila Titova wins the 500 meters. Dutch skater Carolina Geijessen wins the 1,000 meters with an Olympic record time; Titova takes silver. Finland's Kaija Mustonen wins the 1,500 meters, also setting an Olympic record; Geijessen comes in second. In the 3,000 meters, Dutch skater Johanna Schut sets an Olympic record to capture the gold; Mustonen gets the silver.

Mar. 26 U.S. athlete Eleonora Sears dies. She was adept at tennis, sailing, golf, swimming, trapshooting, football, baseball, and ice hockey. A horse owner and breeder, she was the first woman polo player in the United States and a financial supporter of the U.S. Equestrian Team, sometimes lending her own horses for its use during the Olympics. She popularized squash for women, captained the international team, and won the first women's national squash championship. Her achievements in long-distance walking included walking 108 miles in nineteen hours, fifty minutes.

Summer In Mexico City, the Soviet Union's Lyudmila Pinayeva-Khvedosyuk wins the 500-meter Olympic kayak singles and earns bronze in the 500-meter pairs with Antonina Seredina. West Germans Roswitha Esser and Annemarie Zimmermann win the pairs gold.

In the equestrian events, which are open to both sexes, West Germany's Liselott Linsenhoff wins a gold medal in team dressage; Yelena Petushkova of the Soviet

Union takes a silver, and Marianne Gossweiler of Switzerland gets a bronze. Marion Coakes of Great Britain wins a silver in show jumping.

Yelena Novikova of the Soviet Union wins the individual foil fencing competition. Her team, which also includes Aleksandra Zabelina, Galina Gorokhova, Tatiane Samusenko, and Svetlana Chirkova, wins the team foil gold as well. The individual bronze medalist, Ildiko Ujlaki-Retjo, is also on the silver-medal Hungarian team.

First place in volleyball goes to the Soviet Union; players Ljudmila Buldakova, Tatiana Sarycheva, Nina Smoleeva, Inna Ryskal, Galina Leontieva, and Roza Salikhova will also be on the 1972 gold-medal team.

The all-around team gymnastics gold goes to the Soviet Union's team of Sinaida Voronina (silver medalist in the all-around and bronze medalist in the uneven bars and vault), Natalia Kuchinskaya (bronze medalist in the all-around and floor exercise and gold medalist in the beam), Larissa Petrik (bronze medalist in the beam), Olga Karasseva, Lyudmila Tourischeva, and Lyubow Burda. Second place is captured by the Czech team, which includes Vera Cáslavská. The Czech victory is particularly emotional, as resistance in that country to Soviet occupation was crushed not long before the Olympics. Cáslavská in particular becomes a national symbol, winning golds in the all-around individual competition, the uneven parallel bars, the floor exercise (where she ties with Petrik), and the horse vault and silver in the balance beam.

In swimming, the United States sweeps three events: the 100-meter freestyle, where Jan Henne, Susan Pedersen, and Linda Gustavson come in first, second, and third; the 200-meter freestyle, with Debbie Meyer, Henne, and Jane Barkman taking the medals, and the 200-meter individual medley, in which Claudia Kolb gets the gold, Pedersen the silver, and Henne the bronze. Meyer also wins gold medals in the 400-meter and 800-meter freestyles. Gustavson takes a silver in the 400-meter freestyle, and Kolb wins the 400-meter individual medley. The 100-meter breaststroke is won by Yugoslavia's Djurdjica Bjedov, followed by Galina Prozumenshikova of the Soviet Union and Sharon Wichman of the United States. The same three swimmers medal in the 200-meter breaststroke, but this time Wichman is first, Bjedov second, and Prozumenshikova third.

American Kaye Hall, bronze medalist in the 200, takes the gold in the 100-meter backstroke. The 200-meter backstroke is won by American Lillian "Pokey" Watson. Australia's Lynette McClements, a silver medalist in the 4 x 100 medley relay, wins the 100-meter butterfly, and Ellie Daniel of the United States, the bronze medalist in the 200-meter butterfly, gets the silver. Ada Kok of the Netherlands, who won two silvers in 1964, wins the 200-meter butterfly. The 4 x 100-meter freestyle relay is won by the U.S. team of Barkman, Gustavson, Pedersen, and Henne. The 4 x 100-meter medley relay is also won by the U.S. team,

which includes Hall, Daniel, Pedersen, and Catie Ball. Sue Gossick of the United States wins the springboard diving event; Czechoslovakia's Milena Duchkova wins the platform diving gold.

Polish runner Irena Szewinska-Kirzenstein wins the 200-meter race with a world record time of 22.5 seconds and wins a bronze in the 100-meter dash. She is the first woman to medal in three Olympics in a row and the first to medal in five different events. In the 1970s she will set world records of 49.9 and then 49.29 seconds in the 400 meters.

American Wyomia Tyus wins the 100 meters; she is the first athlete of either sex to win this event in two consecutive Olympics. Colette Besson of France wins the 400 meters and Madeleine Manning of the United States the 800. Maureen Caird of Australia wins the hurdles, and a world-record-setting runner from Taiwan, Chi Cheng, gets the bronze in this event. The 4 x 100-meter relay is won by the U.S. team of Barbara Ferrell (silver medalist in the 100 meters), Margaret Bailes, Mildred Netter, and Tyus.

Czechoslovakia's Miloslava Rezkova wins the high jump; Romania's Viorica Viscopoleanu sets a world record in the long jump to win the gold. The shot put is won by East Germany's Margitta Gummel-Helmboldt, and the pentathlon is won by West Germany's Ingrid Becker. Angela Nemeth of Hungary takes gold in the javelin, and Lia Manoliu of Romania wins the discus throw to become, at thirty-six, the oldest woman Olympic champion. Manoliu also ties the women's record for the longest Olympic career; she participated in her first games in 1952.

Activism

Peggy Charren, Evelyn Kaye Sarson, Lillian Ambrosino, and Judith Chalfen establish Action for Children's Television (ACT), which works for less violence, fewer commercials, and bans on the advertisement of certain products during children's viewing hours.

Japanese author Michiko Ishumure begins a nationwide movement against pollution with her book *Kukai Jodo (Sea of Suffering)*, which documents the nervous system disorders caused by the dumping of mercury into Minamata Bay.

U.S. pacifist and feminist Jeannette Rankin leads an antiwar march on Washington.

Civil rights activist Anne Moody publishes her autobiography, *Coming of Age in Mississippi*.

Feminists picket the Miss America pageant, tossing false eyelashes, pornography, girdles, and curlers into a trash can.

Apr. 8 U.S. civil rights activist Coretta Scott King (b. 1922) leads a memorial march in Memphis for her husband, Martin Luther King, Jr., who was assassinated on April 4.

Business and Industry

In the United States, 45% of families have two income earners; 29,200,000 women are in the work force, constituting 37.1% of the total work force.

Elizabeth Malaise becomes the first woman director of the Belgian National Bank.

Women are 20% of the members of Britain's Trades Union Congress.

U.S. inventor and businesswoman Bette Nesmith Graham's Liquid Paper, Inc. produces more than 10,000 bottles per day and grosses more than $1 million. Graham, a former secretary, invented the popular correcting fluid in 1951.

Science and Medicine

Sri Lanka's Medical Women's Association is founded.

Drought strikes countries near the Sahara Desert; in Senegal, food technologist Marie-Thérèse Basse eases the food crisis by developing *pain de mil*, a bread that uses millet rather than expensive imported wheat.

U.S. neurobiologist Rita Levi-Montalcini is elected to the National Academy of Sciences.

The SWE gives its Achievement Award to Isabella Karle, discoverer of a revolutionary new method of crystal structure analysis.

Oct. 27 Austrian nuclear physicist Lise Meitner dies. When she said she wanted to study physics, her father made her get a teaching certificate first so she would have something to fall back on; she was only the second woman to earn a Ph.D. at the University of Vienna. Meitner discovered nuclear fission with Otto Hahn; he received the Nobel for that achievement in 1944, but she was never so honored, nor did she seek recognition for a discovery that was adapted for such violent purposes.

Education and Scholarship

U.S. historians Will and Ariel Durant win a Pulitzer Prize for general nonfiction for *The Story of Civilization*.

New publications include South African politician Margaret Ballinger's history of her country, *From Union to Apartheid: A Trek to Isolation*; American sociologist Jessie Bernard's *The Sex Game*, and French sociologist, feminist, and journalist Evelyne Sullerot's *Histoire et sociologie du travail féminin*.

Women are 46.1% of students at the University of Chile.

Nov. 14 Yale announces that it will begin admitting women.

Religion

U.S. feminist theologian Mary Daly (b. 1928) publishes *The Church and the Second Sex*.

Jan. 4 U.S. missionary and social reformer Donaldina Cameron (b. July 26, 1869) dies. She attacked and helped destroy San Francisco's Chinese slave trade, fighting it in the courts, through brothel raids, and by sheltering women sold as slaves.

1969

General Status and Daily Life

Canada legalizes advertising for contraceptives and, on May 14, legalizes abortion in cases where the woman's life or health is jeopardized; the procedure must be approved by three doctors.

A "malaria control" program is used as an excuse to sterilize peasant women in Ecuador.

Minimum legal age of marriage is eighteen for both sexes in Sweden.

In Kenya, a law requiring men to support their illegitimate children is repealed.

Government, the Military, and the Law

This year sees the election or appointment of Jordan's first woman ambassador, Laurice Hlass; Ecuador's first woman senator, Isabel Robalino; Venezuela's first woman Cabinet minister, Aura Celina Casanova, minister of development; South Africa's first woman judge, Leonora Neethling; and Puerto Rico's first woman

Cabinet member, Secretary of Labor Julia Rivera de Vincenti.

Jiang Qing, wife of Mao Zedong, is elected to the Politburo of the Chinese Communist party.

Vietnamese politician Nguyen Thi Binh becomes foreign minister for the National Liberation Front's provisional government.

Judith Hart becomes Britain's minister of overseas development, a post she will hold until 1970 and then again from 1974 to 1975 and from 1977 to 1979.

U.S. president Richard Nixon appoints Nancy Hanks as director of the NEA. During the Nixon and Ford administrations, she will secure increased funding for the arts.

German politician Katherina Focke (b. 1922), a Social Democrat, is elected to the Federal Bundestag; forty-three members of West Germany's Bundestag are women.

Ghanaian lawyer Annie Jiagge becomes a judge of the Court of Appeal.

U.S. actress and diplomat Shirley Temple Black becomes a UN representative.

Angie Brooks-Randolph, Liberia's first woman lawyer, becomes the second woman president of the UN General Assembly.

Irish politician Bernadette Devlin McAliskey (b. April 23, 1947), arrested and sentenced this year to six months in jail for anti-British riots, becomes, at twenty-one, one of the youngest people ever elected to Parliament.

Mar. Golda Meir becomes the first woman prime minister of Israel after the death of Levi Eshkol. In October, she wins the office in her own right.

Literature and the Visual Arts

U.S. poet Elizabeth Bishop's *Complete Poems* wins the National Book Award. Other new poetry includes Romanian Ana Blandiana's (b. 1942) *The Third Mystery*, Sonja Åkesson's *Streetballads*, Bella Akhmadulina's *Music Lessons*, Gwendolyn Brooks's *Riot*, American Jayne Cortez's (b. 1936) *Piss-stained Stairs and the Monkey Man's Wares*, Marge Piercy's *Hard Loving*, American Lucille Clifton's (b. 1936) *Good Times*, Adrienne Rich's *Leaflets*, American Louise Glück's (b. 1943) *Firstborn*, French surrealist Joyce Mansour's *Phallus et momies*, Egyptian poet, novelist, essayist, and dramatist Andrée Chedid's (b. 1921) *Contre chant*, Mexican poet Isabel Fraire's *Only This Light*, El Salvadoran poet Claribel Alegría's *Long Distance Call*,

Italian feminist Sibilla Aleramo's *Luci della mia sera*, and German poet and translator Petra von Morstein's (b. 1941) *To All*.

Russian author Natalia Baranskaia publishes the short story "Nedelia kak nedelia" ("A Week Like Any Other"), dramatizing women's double burdens at work and at home.

French novelist, academic, and feminist Hélène Cixous cofounds the magazine *Poétique*.

New York's MoMA buys the statue *Repetition Nineteen* by German-American sculptor Eva Hesse (January 11, 1936–May 29, 1970).

English poet Stevie Smith wins the Queen's Gold Medal for Poetry.

U.S. science fiction author Ursula K. LeGuin publishes *The Left Hand of Darkness*, set on a planet on which every person is both male and female. Other new novels include Joyce Carol Oates's *Them*, Elizabeth Bowen's last novel, *Eva Trout*, Christiane Rochefort's *Printemps au parking*, Margaret Atwood's *The Edible Woman*, and Mary Renault's *Fire from Heaven*.

Apr. 12 U.S. editor Charlotta Bass (b. October 1880?) dies. For more than forty years, she edited *The California Eagle*, attacking the KKK (who sued her unsuccessfully for libel), atomic weapons, the film *Birth of a Nation*, and the Scottsboro, Alabama, trial of nine black men.

May 12 U.S. journalist Bess Furman (b. December 2, 1894), who covered national politics for such prestigious organizations as the *New York Times* and AP, dies. She covered the White House, where she was so well received that Eleanor Roosevelt knitted her baby a blanket, and was the first woman regularly assigned by AP to the House of Representatives.

Performing Arts and Entertainment

U.S. television producer Joan Ganz Cooney (b. 1929), founder and executive director of the Children's Television Workshop, airs "Sesame Street" for the first time.

Films directed by women include Bulgarian Lada Boyadgieva's *I Dissent*; Hungarian Judit Elek's first film, *The Lady from Constantinople*, about an old woman moving to a new apartment; French writer and film maker Marguerite Duras's *Détruire dit-elle* (*Destroy She Said*); and U.S. critic Susan Sontag's *Duet for Cannibals*, which she also writes. French director Nelly Kaplan makes her first feature film, *La fiancée du pirate*, in which the gypsy Marie exposes a town's hypocrisy by seducing most of the men and one woman.

Maggie Smith (b. 1934) wins the Best Actress Oscar for her performance in *The Prime of Miss Jean Brodie*, screenwritten by Jay Presson Allen. Movie audiences can also see Jane Fonda in *They Shoot Horses, Don't They?*, Barbra Streisand in *Hello Dolly!*, Liv Ullmann in *The Passion of Anna*, Petula Clark in *Goodbye Mr. Chips*, Katherine Ross in *Butch Cassidy and the Sundance Kid*, and Anita Björk in *Adalen 31*.

Apr. 28 U.S. pianist Hazel Harrison (b. May 12, 1883) dies. She was well received in Europe, but the fact that she was black hampered her career in the United States.

Dec. Rock singer Janis Joplin performs at Madison Square Garden in New York City.

Dec. 18 Katharine Hepburn opens on Broadway in the musical *Coco*, a critical failure but a popular success.

Athletics and Exploration

U.S. jockey Diane Crump becomes the first woman to ride at a major track.

In the Syracuse, New York, public schools, boys' sports have a $90,000 budget as compared with the girls' sports budget of $200. Later, the girls' budget is cut entirely. A similar state of affairs can be found in most school districts and at most universities.

May 12-July 25 Sharon Sites Adams (b. c. 1930) becomes the first woman to sail across the Pacific alone.

July 5 British tennis player Ann Haydon Jones defeats Billie Jean King at Wimbledon.

Oct. 12 Norwegian figure skater Sonja Henie dies. Best known for her three Olympic gold medals and her ten consecutive world championships in skating (more than any other skater, male or female, except Ulrich Salchow of Sweden), she was also a film actress, tennis player, and auto racer. She won more than 1,400 skating prizes.

Activism

The General Union of Palestinian Women, a branch of the Palestine Liberation Organization (PLO), is formed.

Venezuela's first feminist group, the Movimiento de Liberación de la Mujer (Women's Liberation Movement), is founded.

South African civil rights activist Dorothy Nyembe is sentenced to fifteen years in jail.

Feb. 2 Arab girls riot in Israel; ninety are wounded in the police suppression of the rebellion.

Business and Industry

Women are 37.2% of the British work force.

Women workers in Italy make 70% as much per hour as men.

In the United States, Equal Employment Opportunity Commission (EEOC) revisions make it illegal to advertise many jobs under "male" and "female" headings.

U.S. inventor Pansy Ellen Essman patents a sponge pillow to hold babies safely still while they are bathed; the invention will earn her more than $2 million.

Science and Medicine

British entomologist Evelyn Cheeseman dies. She collected 42,000 insect specimens in New Guinea and also traveled to the New Hebrides, Melanesia, the Marquesas Islands, and the Galapagos Islands in search of new species.

The SWE gives its Achievement Award to Alice Stoll for her development of fire-resistant fibers and fabrics.

The United States has 650 female veterinarians.

Swiss-American psychiatrist Elisabeth Kübler-Ross publishes her classic work, *On Death and Dying*, which states that terminally ill people pass through five classic attitude stages: denial, anger, bargaining, depression, and acceptance.

The Lebanon Family Planning Association is founded.

In the United States, 99% of 1,000 engineering consulting firms surveyed say they hire no women engineers.

Ukrainian doctor Esther Minuhin is honored by her republic for her work with tuberculosis patients.

Education and Scholarship

English historian Lady Antonia Fraser publishes the biography *Mary, Queen of Scots*. Other new publications include U.S. feminist and sociologist Bettina Aptheker's bibliography *Higher Education and the Student Rebellion in the United States* and British author Rebecca West's *McLuhan and the Future of Literature.*

Princeton University begins admitting women undergraduates.

Cornell University offers the first accredited women's studies course.

U.S. academic Angela Davis (b. January 26, 1944) is fired from her teaching position at UCLA for being a communist.

Oct. 2 U.S. educator May Arbuthnot (b. August 27, 1884), coauthor of the "Dick and Jane" readers, dies.

Religion

Mary H. Looram (b. 1899) dies. For thirty-five years, she headed the Motion Picture Committee of the International Federation of Catholic Alumnae, known as the toughest censorship board in the country.

Swedish politician Alva Myrdal becomes minister for church affairs, a position she will hold until 1973.

American Cynthia Wedel becomes the first woman president of the National Council of Churches.

Mar. 16 U.S. civil rights activist Coretta Scott King becomes the first woman to speak from the pulpit of St. Paul's Cathedral in London.

1970

General Status and Daily Life

During this decade, most U.S. states retreat from a general policy of requiring women to take their husbands' names.

Denmark makes both partners responsible for the family's financial support and recognizes the value of housework. Property purchased during the marriage belongs to the partner who pays for it. Children may bear either parent's surname; women may keep their birth names, and husbands may take their wives' names if they choose.

The average Dutchwoman has 2.6 children.

The concept of "head of household" is abolished in France; women receive equal parental control over their children.

Divorce is legalized in Italy.

The Austrian government begins addressing all female employees as "Frau" to end confusion over married or unmarried status.

Government, the Military, and the Law

Ragnhild Selmer becomes Norway's first woman Supreme Court judge.

New Jersey lawyer Anne Thompson becomes the United States' first black woman prosecutor.

Sri Lankan politician Sirimavo Bandaranaike (b. 1916) is reelected prime minister after five years out of office. She will remain prime minister until 1977.

Botswana's Gaositwe Keogakiwa Tibe Chiepe is appointed high commissioner to the United Kingdom and to Nigeria.

Korean feminist politician Soon Chan Park becomes secretary-general of the Democratic party.

Women are allowed to enlist in the Tanzanian army.

In the United States, women earn 8% of all law degrees.

Feb. 23 American Emma Miller (b. July 6, 1874) dies. She was a longtime member of the Democratic National Committee who said at ninety-two, "They can throw me out but I will not resign."

June Indian prime minister Indira Gandhi takes over the Home Ministry, giving her direct control of three departments; she already holds the atomic energy and planning portfolios.

She then "derecognizes" the ancestral privileges of former maharajas, stripping them of the financial and legal benefits awarded them at national independence. When her plan does not pass through the Council of State with the needed two-thirds majority, she simply overrules its decision and enacts the plan on her own authority. On December 15, the Supreme Court rules her action against the princes unconstitutional, and some of her own ministers resist the reform.

June 11 Army Colonel Anna Mae Hays, director of the Army Nurse Corps, and Elizabeth Hoisington, director of the WAC, become the first women brigadier generals in the United States.

Aug. 21 Maria Teresa Carcomo Lobo becomes the

first woman in Portugal to hold a Cabinet-level post when she is named undersecretary of state for welfare.

Literature and the Visual Arts

New poetry includes Romanian Constanta Buzea's *Hills*, Ana Blandiana's *Fifty Poems*, Romanian poet, children's author, and painter Gabriela Melinescu's (b. 1942) *The Disease of Divine Origin*, U.S. objectivist Louise Niedecker's (d. 1970) *My Friend Tree* and *My Life by Water*, Ruth Stone's *Topography and Other Poems*, Gwendolyn Brooks's *Family Pictures*, Maxine Kumin's *The Nightmare Factory*, Margaret Atwood's *Procedures for Underground*, American Sandra McPherson's (b. 1943) *Elegies for the Hot Season*, Greek poet Eva Mylonás's (b. 1936) first collection, *Voyage*, Swiss poet Monique Laederach's (b. 1938) *Penelope* and *The Tin, the Stream*, and Italian Maria Luisa Spaziani's (b. 1924) *The Eye of the Cyclone*.

Ghanaian author Ama Ata Aidoo publishes a play, *Anowa*, and a collection of short stories, *No Sweetness Here*.

U.S. autobiographer, poet, and playwright Maya Angelou (b. 1928) publishes *I Know Why the Caged Bird Sings*. U.S. author Toni Morrison (b. 1931) publishes *The Bluest Eye*, a novel about a black girl named Pecola Breedlove who wishes she had blue eyes like white girls. Raped by her alcoholic father, Pecola associates whiteness with beauty and finally goes insane. Other new novels include Italian Rossana Ombres's *Principessa Giacinta*, U.S. author Alice Walker's (b. February 9, 1944) first novel, *The Third Life of Grange Copeland*, Nigerian novelist Flora Nwapa's *Idu*, New Zealand novelist Sylvia Ashton-Warner's *Three*, Eudora Welty's *Losing Battles*, Violette Leduc's *La folie en tête*, and Iris Murdoch's *A Fairly Honorable Defeat*.

Georgia O'Keeffe wins the National Institute of Arts and Letters gold medal for painting.

Chinese novelist Ding Ling is imprisoned during the Cultural Revolution. She will spend the next five years in solitary confinement and be exiled to a remote village thereafter.

Performing Arts and Entertainment

U.S. screenplays include Eleanor Perry's *Diary of a Mad Housewife*, Marguerite Roberts's *True Grit*, and Carole Eastman's *Five Easy Pieces*. Films edited by U.S. women include Margaret Booth's *The Owl and the Pussycat*, Dede Allen's *Little Big Man*, and Marion Rothman's *Beneath the Planet of the Apes*.

U.S. feminist Kate Millett (b. September 14, 1934) films *Three Lives*, a documentary about three different women: independent Mallory, bisexual Robin, and Lillian, an older Italian woman reflecting on the sexism of her childhood.

Japanese film director Toshie Tokieda releases a well-received documentary, *Report from China*, which assesses the state of communist China's industry, education, and home life. Colombian producer Gabriela Samper wins the Maltese Cross at Argentina's Cordoba Film Festival for her film *The Salt Man*, and Czech film director Véra Chytilová makes *Fruit of Paradise*.

Lauren Bacall stars in the play *Applause*, for which she wins a Tony Award.

U.S. singer and actress Barbra Streisand stars in the film *On a Clear Day You Can See Forever*. Other new films include *Airport*, for which Helen Hayes receives the Best Supporting Actress Oscar; *Tristana*, starring Catherine Deneuve; *Love Story*, starring Ali McGraw as a woman with a terminal illness; and *Women in Love*, for which British actress Glenda Jackson (b. May 9, 1936) receives the Best Actress Oscar.

Apr. American Helen Thompson becomes manager of the New York Philharmonic.

Athletics and Exploration

Billie Jean King, outraged at the inequity of men's and women's tennis prizes (at the Italian championships this year, for example, she won $600 while the men's winner got $3,500), calls for a boycott of tournaments; meeting with resistance from the U.S. Lawn Tennis Association, she helps Gladys Heldman to organize the Virginia Slims Circuit. Within a few years the women's circuit plays in twenty-two cities with prizes totaling $775,000.

U.S. sharpshooter Mary DeVito sets a record unmatched by any woman or man; in bench rest shooting, her shots vary by only 7.68" at 1,000 yards.

Australian Margaret Smith Court wins tennis's Grand Slam—the singles titles at Wimbledon, the U.S. Open, the French Open, and the Australian Open.

Soviet engineer Svetlana Savitskaya becomes the first female pilot to win the World Aerobatics Championship.

U.S. mountain climber Arlene Blum takes part in the first all-woman ascent of Alaska's Mount McKinley.

May 2 Diane Crump becomes the first woman jockey in the Kentucky Derby; she finishes twelfth.

June 30 American Mary Bacon becomes the first female jockey to win one hundred races.

Activism

The umbrella group CARIWA, the Caribbean Women's Association, is established.

Palestinian Leila Khaled becomes the first woman to hijack an airplane.

Nyfeministene (New Feminists), a Norwegian women's group, is formed.

Irish women in Belfast hold a protest march in which they deliberately break the British curfew.

New feminist publications include American Robin Morgan's (b. January 29, 1941) *Sisterhood Is Powerful*, a collection of feminist documents; American Kate Millett's influential *Sexual Politics*; Australian Germaine Greer's (b. January 29, 1939) *The Female Eunuch*; and Canadian Shulamith Firestone's (b. 1945) *The Dialectic of Sex: The Case for Feminist Revolution*.

U.S. academic and radical Angela Davis is charged with murder, kidnapping, and criminal conspiracy. She was not present when the crimes were committed, but she is accused of buying a shotgun used in a bloody attempt to free radical prisoners. She will be acquitted in 1972.

May 4 Nineteen-year-old Allison Krause is shot and killed at a Kent State anti-war demonstration, with three others, by National Guardsmen.

Aug. Marie Cox founds the first national Native American women's group, the North American Indian Women's Association.

Aug. 26 In New York City, 50,000 march down Fifth Avenue to mark the fiftieth anniversary of women's suffrage. Betty Friedan, Gloria Steinem (b. 1934), Kate Millett, and Bella Abzug address the crowd on the need for day care, nonsexist advertising, and Social Security reform. Friedan says, "Man is not the enemy. Man is a fellow victim."

Business and Industry

In the United States, women earn 3% of all M.B.A.s. Working women make 57.2% as much as men; 31,500,000 women are in the work force, constituting 38.1% of the total work force.

Women are 25% of Chile's manufacturing workers, 39.3% of Japan's work force, and 51% of Russia's work force.

U.S. labor organizer Dolores Huerta (b. 1930) becomes vice-president of the United Farm Workers.

In Libya, employed women receive a pay bonus upon marriage. A new law mandates equal pay for women but also imposes protective measures: women are not to hold jobs deemed "dangerous or toilsome," to work at night in most cases, or to work more than forty-eight hours per week.

British politician Barbara Castle gets an Equal Pay Act passed by Parliament, but employers circumvent it by giving women different job titles.

Mexico passes an equal pay law.

Polish crane operator Anna Walentynowicz, a worker at the Gdansk shipyard, leads strikes over food prices; she will later contribute to the foundation of the Solidarity labor union.

English millionaire businesswoman Margery Hurst (b. 1914), founder of the successful Mayfair temporary employees' agency, becomes one of the first women underwriters at Lloyds.

Women in South Africa hold 68.5% of service jobs but only 6% of administrative and managerial jobs.

Science and Medicine

In the United States, women earn 10% of all medical degrees and about 26% of B.S. degrees.

The Boston Women's Health Book Collective publishes the first edition of *Our Bodies, Ourselves*, a pioneering work that encourages women to become comfortable with their bodies and assertive about finding good health care. The first commercial edition appears in 1973.

U.S. biologist and ecologist Ruth Patrick and U.S. bacteriologist Rebecca Craighill Lancefield are elected to the National Academy of Sciences.

German-American engineer Irmgard Flügge-Lotz, an expert in fluid mechanics, becomes the second woman fellow of the American Institute of Aeronautics and Astronautics and wins the SWE's Achievement Award.

June 26 The AMA sanctions abortions performed for social or economic reasons.

Education and Scholarship

New publications include Hannah Arendt's *On Violence*,

British novelist and philosopher Iris Murdoch's *The Sovereignty of Good*, and French sociologist, feminist, and journalist Evelyne Sullerot's *La femme dans le monde moderne*.

The first Kuwaiti woman to complete a graduate program earns her degree in nuclear physics.

Ada Louise Huxtable of the *New York Times* wins the Pulitzer Prize for criticism or commentary.

Aisha Rateb becomes Cairo University's first professor of international law.

U.S. educator Brenda Jubin becomes the first woman resident dean at Yale University.

Women are 25% of U.S. 825,000 higher education faculty.

Sept. 22 U.S. physician, social reformer, and industrial toxicology pioneer Alice Hamilton dies. The first woman professor at Harvard, she was not allowed to march in the school's commencement processions, to enter the Harvard Club, or to receive the traditional faculty allotment of football tickets.

Religion

English-Chinese missionary Gladys Aylward (b. 1903) dies. During her long residence in China, she helped the government to enforce bans on foot-binding, the practice of breaking and confining girls' feet to produce a prized and crippling mark of beauty. Aylward was best known, however, for her conduct during World War II, when she led one hundred children on a march away from the invading Japanese.

U.S. theologian Rosemary Radford Reuther publishes *The Radical Kingdom*.

Della Lowe founds the first union for Native American ceremonial performers.

St. Catherine of Siena and St. Teresa of Avila are the first two women named Doctors of the Church, an honor that recognizes their significant contributions to Catholic doctrine.

Mar. 11 U.S. religious leader Edith Lowry (b. March 23, 1897), noted for her work among migrant farm workers, dies.

1971

General Status and Daily Life

The National Commission on the Status of Women in India is formed. Female mean age at marriage is seventeen in India; 5.8% of Hindu marriages and 5.7% of Muslim marriages are polygynous. Only 0.5% of the Indian female population is separated or divorced.

Dowry is outlawed in Afghanistan, but the practice continues anyway.

The open sale of birth control is outlawed in Argentina.

Two women die every week in Bogotá, Colombia, from complications resulting from botched abortions; abortion is illegal in Colombia. In China, abortion still requires the husband's consent; until about 1973, it will also require the consent of the husband's parents.

In Nepal, the consent of both parties is required for a valid marriage. The bride must be at least sixteen and the groom eighteen with parental consent, eighteen and twenty-one without. Because of strong traditions against widows remarrying, the bride and groom must be fewer than twenty years apart in age. In Nepal, 2.4% of females age six to nine are married. By age 24, 92% of women are married. In at least one region, women practice polyandry.

A study of women in Shiraz, Iran, reveals that veiled and unveiled women are subjected to equal verbal and physical harrassment.

Merna Ellentuck of Roosevelt, New Jersey, is forbidden to vote without putting "Mrs." before her name.

In the United States, crime rates are rising much faster for women than for men.

Government, the Military, and the Law

Women appointed to cabinet posts this year include Egyptian Minister of Social Affairs Aisha Rateb, Chinese Vice Minister of Economic Relations with Foreign Countries Chen Muhua, Norwegian Minister of Family and Consumer Affairs Inger Vall, and Danish Minister for Social Affairs Eva Gredal.

Mexican lawyer María Patricia Kurczyn Villalobos becomes director of the Women's Federal Prison in Mexico City.

Helga Pedersen of Denmark becomes the first woman

judge on the European Court of Human Rights.

Gertrude D. T. Schimmel is the first woman in the New York Police Department to be promoted to captain. She was also the NYPD's first woman lieutenant and will be its first inspector.

Air Force Reserve Officer Training Corps (ROTC) student Leslie Halley becomes the first woman to receive a commission through ROTC.

U.S. feminists Gloria Steinem, Betty Friedan, Fannie Lou Hamer, and Congresswoman Bella Abzug announce the formation of the National Women's Political Caucus to help women get elected at all levels of government.

Annabelle Rankin becomes Australia's first woman ambassador.

U.S. politician Anne Armstrong (b. 1927) becomes the first female cochairman of the National Republican Committee.

Feb. 7 Swiss women get the vote.

Apr. 7 Mozambique nationalist and freedom fighter Josina Abiathar Muthemba dies.

Literature and the Visual Arts

American Marcia Gillespie becomes editor in chief of *Essence* magazine.

Ghanaian journalist Kate Abbam becomes publisher and editor of *Obaa Sima* (*Ideal Woman*) magazine.

Lucinda Franks of UPI wins a Pulitzer Prize for national reporting.

Nigerian author Flora Nwapa publishes *This Is Lagos*, a short story collection.

New poetry includes Romanian Veronica Porumbacu's *Circle*, Anne Sexton's *Transformations*, Carolyn Kizer's *Midnight Was My Cry*, American Diane Wakoski's (b. August 3, 1937) *The Motorcycle Betrayer Poems*, Adrienne Rich's *The Will to Change*, and French experimental poet Anne-Marie Albiach's epic *Etat*.

Jan. The National Press Club votes to admit women. Until now, women have been able to cover speeches made at the club, but they must sit in the balcony and cannot use the club's wire machines. This is a serious disadvantage, as the club is often the site of major speeches and announcements by U.S. and foreign officials. U.S. journalist Esther Van Wagoner Tufty, a war correspondent in World War II, Korea, and Vietnam, is the first woman elected to the National Press Club.

Performing Arts and Entertainment

U.S. jazz pianist, composer, and singer Lil Armstrong (b. 1900) dies onstage at a concert celebrating the work of her ex-husband, Louis Armstrong. During her career, she led both all-female and all-male bands.

Peggy Lenore Williams joins the Ringling brothers, Barnum and Bailey Circus, becoming the first female circus clown in the United States.

Films made by women include U.S. director Eve Arnold's *Beyond the Veil*, a documentary about contemporary harem life in Arabia, and French director Nadine Marquand Trintigant's *Ca n'arrive qu'aux autres*, starring Catherine Deneuve. France's Nelly Kaplan directs *Papa, les petits bateaux*, in which an apparently empty-headed blonde named Cookie is kidnapped, but defeats her captors and takes the ransom for herself.

British screenwriter Penelope Gilliat writes the screenplay for *Sunday, Bloody Sunday*.

U.S. art critic and journalist Aline Saarinen becomes head of NBC's Paris bureau, making her the first woman in charge of an overseas television news department.

Popular songs in the United States include Janis Joplin's "Me and Bobby McGee" and Carole King's "It's Too Late."

Jane Fonda wins the Best Actress Oscar for her performance in *Klute*.

Athletics and Exploration

English aviator Sheila Scott makes the first solo equator-to-equator flight over the North Pole in a light aircraft.

German sprinter Renate Stecher wins the 100 and 200 meter races at the European Games.

Austrian skier Annemarie Proell Moser (b. 1953) wins the World Cup downhill championship. French skier Britt Lafforgue wins the World Cup slalom.

Seven percent of U.S. high school girls are involved in interscholastic sports.

British sailor Nicolette Milnes-Walker becomes the first woman to make a solo nonstop sail across the Atlantic Ocean. She travels from east to west in the 33' yacht *Aziz* in 44 1/2 days.

U.S. aviator Jacqueline Cochran becomes the only living woman in the American Aviation Hall of Fame.

U.S. tennis player Billie Jean King (b. November 22, 1943), winner of a record twenty Wimbledon doubles, singles, and mixed doubles titles, becomes the first woman athlete to earn $100,000 in one year.

Australian tennis player Evonne Goolagong (b. July 31, 1951) wins the Wimbledon singles title. She will win it again in 1980.

Apr. 26 Sylvia Cook begins a trip with John Fairfax; when the journey is completed on Apr. 22, 1972, she will be the first woman to row across the Atlantic.

Activism

Aileen Hernandez becomes the first black president of NOW.

Housewife Erin Pizzey (b. 1939) founds Women's Aid, Britain's first battered women's shelter.

Mexican feminists establish the National Women's Movement to work for reproductive rights and an improved image of women in the media and in school curricula.

The Israeli feminist group Nilachem (We Shall Fight) is founded.

French lawyer and feminist Gisèle Halimi founds the abortion-rights group Choisir. It publishes the *Manifeste des 343*, a document in which 343 notable women admit to having had abortions despite France's restrictive abortion law. Among the signatories is Simone de Beauvoir.

In Chile, women rebel over lack of food, staging a "March of the Empty Pots"

Business and Industry

U.S. restaurant proprietor Alice Waters opens the celebrated restaurant Chez Panisse in Berkeley, California.

Washington Post publisher Katharine Graham holds fast throughout the Watergate scandal, despite sexist, violent threats against her for printing stories about government corruption.

In India, 12% of women are employed.

Women are 36% of the British work force.

Mary Andrews Ayres becomes the first woman head of the American Association of Advertising Agencies, founded 34 years ago.

Workers at Dong-il, a major Korean textile firm, elect a female union president.

Science and Medicine

U.S. chemist Mildred Cohn and U.S. psychologist Eleanor Jack Gibson are elected to the National Academy of Sciences.

The SWE gives its Achievement Award to Alva Matthews, a designer of helicopter blades, thin shell concrete, and telstar tracking antennas, for her work in engineering mechanics and applied mathematics.

Education and Scholarship

Educator and home economist Pamela Thompson-Clewry, the first woman in Sierra Leone to earn a science degree, becomes the first woman department head at Sierra Leone University.

U.S. historian Barbara Tuchman publishes *Stilwell and the American Experience in China*, which wins the Pulitzer Prize for general nonfiction in 1972. Other new publications include French feminist Xavière Gauthier's (b. 1942) *Surréalisme et sexualité* and English economist Joan Violet Robinson's *Economic Heresies*.

Religion

Mother Theresa wins the $25,000 Pope John XXIII Peace Prize.

English economist Barbara Ward is the first woman to speak before the Vatican Council.

U.S. Presbyterian elder Lois Stair becomes the first woman moderator of that denomination's General Assembly.

Nov. Chinese deacon Jane Hwang Hsien Yuen and English deacon Joyce Bennett become the first female Anglican priests.

1972

General Status and Daily Life

The Indian Penal Code allows a man to press charges against his wife's adulterous lover; no charges, however, may be filed against the wife, since she is deemed incapable of responsibility for her own actions. Abortion, previously legal in India only to save the life of the woman, is now legalized in cases of rape or failure of contraception.

Canada's first homes for battered women are opened.

East Germany legalizes free abortion on demand in the first trimester.

In Libya, a woman cannot be legally forced to marry against her will, but neither can she legally marry without the consent of her male guardian. Women are entitled to own houses as a place to "menstruate, give birth, and care for their offspring." Divorce may take place by mutual consent, by judicial order, or by *talaq* (unilateral divorce by the male). Financial settlements after divorce usually favor the husband.

In Romania, abortion on demand is legalized for women over forty and women with four or more children.

The U.S. Congress approves the ERA, which, if added to the Constitution, would empower the government to ensure that rights are not abridged on the grounds of sex. The proposed amendment now goes to the states for possible ratification, but despite an extension of the time limit, it will not achieve the required passage by two-thirds of state legislatures.

Nancy Allyn of California and Donna Brogan of Georgia are refused permission to register to vote if they use "Ms." as their title.

Government, the Military, and the Law

Chinese revolutionary Ho Hsiang-ning (b. 1879), director of the women's department of the Kuomintang, dies.

Finland's Helvi Sipilä becomes assistant secretary-general of the UN; it is the highest UN post held by a woman to date.

Women are one third of Soviet judges.

Josephine Abayah becomes the first woman member of

Parliament in Papua New Guinea.

Margit Bigler-Enggenberger becomes Switzerland's first woman federal court judge.

Captain Arlene B. Duerk becomes the U.S. Navy's first woman admiral.

Ghanaian diplomat Amonno Williams becomes Ambassador to Luxembourg.

Elaine Noble of Massachusetts becomes the first openly gay or lesbian politician to be elected to statewide office.

In Norway, Inger Vall becomes minister of government administration, and Eva Kolstad (b. 1918) becomes minister of consumer affairs. Canadian journalist and politician Jeanne Sauvé becomes secretary of state for science and technology. German politician Katherina Focke becomes minister for youth, family affairs and health, a position she will hold until 1976.

Jan. 15 Margrethe II becomes Denmark's first queen in her own right since the fifteenth century.

Jan. 25 U.S. politician Shirley Chisholm, who serves this year on the Democratic National Committee, announces that she will run for president.

Nov. 15 Jeanne Martin Cissé (b. April 1926) of Guinea becomes the first woman to preside over the UN Security Council.

Dec. 13 Annemarie Renger (b. 1919) becomes the first woman president of the West German Bundestag, the second highest political office in the nation.

Literature and the Visual Arts

New poetry includes Maria Banus's *Anyone and Something*, Ana Blandiana's *October, November, December*, American Ruth Stone's *Cheap*, Gwendolyn Brooks's *Aloneness*, Denise Levertov's *Footprints*, American Mary Oliver's *The River Styx, Ohio and Other Poems*, Lucille Clifton's *Good News About the Earth*, Blanca Varela's *Waltzes and Other False Confessions*, and Anne Sexton's *The Book of Folly*.

Anne De Santis of the *Boston Globe* wins a Pulitzer Prize for local reporting.

The work of U.S. photographer Diane Arbus is featured at a posthumous exhibit at MoMA. The exhibit will later tour the United States and Europe. Arbus is also the first U.S. photographer included in the Venice Biennale.

The Guggenheim Museum holds a memorial exhibition

of the works of German-American sculptor Eva Hesse; it is the first Guggenheim retrospective for a woman artist.

Japanese novelist Ariyoshi Sawako publishes *Kokotsu no hito*, a novel about the plight of senior citizens. Other new novels include U.S. science fiction novelist Ursula K. LeGuin's *The Farthest Shore*, the third book in her Earthsea fantasy trilogy; Lebanese author Vénus Khoury-Gata's *Maladjusted*; Christiane Rochefort's feminist utopia *Archaos ou le jardin étincelant*; Tillie Olsen's (b. 1913) *Tell Me a Riddle*; Nathalie Sarraute's *Vous les entendez*; and Margaret Atwood's *Surfacing*, which portrays a Canadian woman escaping into nature from the negative influences of Americans and men.

Feb. 2 U.S. expatriate author Natalie Clifford Barney dies. Barney's Paris salon drew such intellectual celebrities as Anatole France, Gertrude Stein, Edith Sitwell, Auguste Rodin, Maria Rainer Rilke, Gabrielle D'Annunzio, Sinclair Lewis, Marcel Proust, Paul Valéry, Colette, Ford Madox Ford, and Guillaume Apollinaire.

Spring Portuguese authors Maria Isabel Barreno (b. 1939), Maria Teresa Horta, and Maria Velho da Costa, known as "the three Marias," publish a collection of their works, *New Portuguese Letters*. It is denounced as obscene, and all three are arrested. Their trial begins in October and ends in April 1974 with the dropping of the charges and the declaration that the book is a work of literary merit.

Performing Arts and Entertainment

Polish-American actress in Yiddish theatre Berta Gersten (August 20, 1896?–September 10), who played more than 150 roles, including Yiddish versions of Shakespeare, Shaw, and Ibsen, and appeared onstage every season from 1918 to 1972, dies.

Helen Reddy records "I Am Woman," which becomes an anthem of the feminist movement.

U.S. screenwriter Jay Presson Allen writes the screenplay for *Cabaret*, which wins a Best Actress Oscar for singer and actress Liza Minnelli, who plays a vulnerable young singer in prewar Berlin.

U.S. screenwriter Suzanne De Passe writes the screenplay for *Lady Sings the Blues*, which stars U.S. pop singer Diana Ross as blues legend Billie Holiday. Other U.S. films edited by women include *Play It Again, Sam*, edited by Marion Rothman; *What's Up, Doc?* (starring Barbra Streisand), edited by Verna Fields; and *Slaughterhouse Five*, edited by Dede Allen, who "pestered" her way into the business and then "carried more film and swore more than anyone else" until she

was accepted by her male colleagues.

French West Indian-Angolan filmmaker Sarah Maldoror directs *Sambizanga*, a movie that depicts a woman's political awakening after the torture and execution of her husband by Portuguese authorities.

U.S. dancer Judith Jamison (b. 1943) becomes the first woman, first dancer, and first black artist elected to the Board of the National Endowment for the Arts.

Italian film director Lina Wertmuller wins the best director award at Cannes for *Mimi metallurgio ferito nell'onore*.

English composer and conductor Ruth Gipps composes her fourth symphony.

Belgian filmmaker Chantal Akermann (b. 1950) makes her first movie, *Hotel Monterey*.

British guitarist and singer Joan Armatrading (b. 1947) records *Whatever's for Us*.

Liv Ullmann and Harriet Andersson star in *Cries and Whispers*; Arletty stars in *Les volets fermés*.

Roberta Flack records the popular song "The First Time Ever I Saw Your Face"

Athletics and Exploration

Austrian skier Annemarie Proell wins the World Cup downhill championship. French skier Britt Lafforgue wins the World Cup slalom, becoming the first woman to win that event twice.

The first Women's World Cup match in cricket is held. England, captained by Rachel Heyhoe Flint, wins.

The Soviet Union's Trotting Derby is won by jockey Alla Polzunova.

U.S. tennis player Billie Jean King becomes *Sports Illustrated*'s first female Athlete of the Year.

U.S. thoroughbred racing jockey Robyn Smith finishes the year placing seventh in international jockey standings.

Title IX of the U.S. Education Amendments bans sex discrimination in educational programs receiving federal funds. Women's sports programs benefit a great deal from Title IX, though even by the 1990s, funding for men's and women's sports will not be equal.

Winter At the winter Olympics in Sapporo, Japan, Alpine skier Barbara Cochran becomes the first U.S.

gold medalist in her sport in twenty years, winning the slalom and defeating the silver medalist, France's Danielle Debenard, by a mere 0.02 seconds. The downhill and giant slalom golds both go to Swiss skier Marie-Theres Nadig; the silvers in these events go to Austria's Annemarie Proell Moser.

Austrian Beatrix "Trixie" Schuba wins the gold in skating despite a lackluster free skate; free skating becomes worth more in comparison to compulsory exercises in future Olympics. Soviet skaters Irina Rodnina and Alexei Ulanov win the gold in pairs skating.

East Germany's Anna-Maria Muller wins the gold in luge. In Nordic skiing, the Soviet Union's Galina Kulakova wins the 5-kilometer race, followed by Marjatta Kajosmaa of Finland. Kulakova also wins the 10-kilometer race, in which Kajosmaa picks up a bronze; silver goes to Soviet skier Alevtina Oljunina. In the relay, Kulakova wins a third gold medal with the Soviet team, which also includes Oljunina and Lyubov Mukhatcheva. The Finnish team of Kajosmaa, Hilkka Kuntola, and Helena Takalo comes in second, and Norway's team of Inger Aufles, Aslaug Dahl, and Berit Lammedal-Mordre takes the bronze.

Speed skater Dianne Holum, a silver medalist in the 3,000 meters and a double medalist in 1968, wins the 1,500 meters with an Olympic record time, giving her the first American gold medal of the 1972 games and the first gold for any U.S. woman speed skater. Holum's teammate Anne Henning sets an Olympic record in the 500 meters and wins the gold, followed by Vera Krasnova and Lyudmila Titova of the Soviet Union. Henning must settle for a bronze in the 1,000 meters, behind Olympic record setter Monika Pflug of West Germany. Dutch skater Christina Baas-Kaiser wins the 3,000 and takes a silver in the 1,500.

Summer At the summer Olympics in Munich, Yulia Ryabchinskaya of the Soviet Union wins the kayak 500-meter singles. The kayak pairs event is won by the Soviet team of Lyudmila Pinayeva-Khvedosyuk and Jekaterina Kuryshko.

In the equestrian events, Yelena Petushkova is a member of the Soviet Union's gold-medal dressage team; Liselott Linsenhoff and Karin Schluter of West Germany are on the silver-medal West German team; Sweden's third-place team includes Ulla Hakansson, Ninna Swaab, and Maud van Rosen. Ann Moore of Great Britain wins a silver in individual show jumping, and American Kathy Kusner wins a silver in team show jumping. Britain's Mary Gordon-Watson and Bridget Parker win golds in the team three-day event. In individual dressage, Linsenhoff takes the gold, and Petushkova takes the silver.

In fencing, Antonella Lonzi-Ragno of Italy takes the gold, and Galina Gorokhova of the Soviet Union gets a bronze. The team foil event is won by the Soviets: Aleksandra Zabelina, Yelena Belova-Novikova, Gorokhova, Tatiane Samusenko, and Svetlana Chirkova.

The USSR wins the volleyball gold; team members Nina Smoleeva and Inna Ryskal will be on the silver medal team in 1976. Japan takes second place, and its players Takako Iida, Takako Shirai, and Mariko Okamoto will remain on the team in 1976 to take the gold. Women's archery is included once more in the Olympics, largely due to the lobbying of Inger Frith, Danish president of the International Archery Foundation. Doreen Wilber of the United States wins the gold.

Australian swimmer Shane Gould (b. September 4, 1956) wins five medals: golds in the 200-meter and 400-meter freestyle with world record times, another world record gold in the 200-meter individual medley, a bronze in the 100-meter freestyle, and a silver in the 800-meter freestyle. Her teammate Beverly Whitfield wins the 200-meter breaststroke with an Olympic record time and gets a bronze in the 100-meter breaststroke, and another Australian, Gail Neall, wins the 400-meter individual medley with a world record time.

Japan's Mayumi Aoki wins the 100-meter butterfly. Galina Stepanova-Prozumenshikova of the Soviet Union takes a silver in the 100-meter and a bronze in the 200-meter breaststroke; East German Kornelia Ender, who will dominate the 1976 games, takes silvers in the 200-meter individual medley and the 4 x 100 freestyle and medley relays.

The United States has the most successful swim team. Sandra Neilson wins the 100-meter freestyle with an Olympic-record time. Shirley Babashoff wins the 200-meter freestyle and takes a silver in the 100. Keena Rothhammer wins the 800-meter freestyle with a world-record time and takes a bronze in the 200. In the 100-meter breaststroke, Catherine Carr sets another world record, and Melissa Belote sets an Olympic record in the 100-meter backstroke and a world record in the 200-meter backstroke. The United States sweeps the 200-meter butterfly, with Karen Moe, Lynn Colella, and Ellie Daniel taking first, second, and third; Moe sets a world record. The United States wins both relays with world record times. The 4 x 100 freestyle team includes Neilson, Jennifer Kemp, Jane Barkman, and Babashoff; the medley team includes Belote, Carr, Deena Deardurff, and Neilson. American Micki King wins the springboard diving event, followed by Sweden's Ulrika Knape, who wins the platform event.

In track and field, British pentathlete Mary Peters wins the gold medal, followed by West German Heidemarie Rosendahl (the gold medalist in the long jump) and East German Burglinde Pollak. The hurdle race, expanded by the IOC from 80 to 100 meters, is won with an Olympic record time by East Germany's Annelie Ehrhardt. A new race, the 1,500 meters, is won with a world record time of 4:1.4 by Soviet runner Ludmilla Bragina, and another new event, the 4 x 400-meter relay, is won by the East German team of Dagmar Kasling, Rita Kuhne, Helga Seidler, and Monika Zehrt. Zehrt also gets a gold medal in the 400-meter race, setting an Olympic record.

East German sprinter Renate Stecher (b. 1950), the first woman in the world to run 100 meters in under eleven seconds, wins the 100- and 200-meter races and runs on the silver-medal 4 x 100 relay team. Her teammate Ruth Fuchs wins the javelin gold. Irena Szewinska-Kirszenstein of Poland, a longtime Olympian, gets a bronze in the 200 meters. Nadezhda Chizova of the Soviet Union wins the shot put, and her teammate Faina Melnik wins the discus.

The West Germans acquit themselves well. Hildegarde Falck wins the 800 meters and runs on the third-place 4 x 400 team. The West German team of Christiane Krause, Ingrid Mickler, Annegret Richter, and Rosendahl wins the 4 x 100 relay, and Ulrike Meyfarth wins the high jump.

The most celebrated athlete of the 1972 games is Soviet gymnast Olga Korbut (b. 1955). Although she does not win any of the all-around medals, which go to Soviet Lyudmila Touritscheva, East German Karin Janz (the 1968 silver medalist in the uneven parallel bars), and Soviet Tamara Lazakovitch, Korbut captures all the press with her vulnerable, childlike appeal. She wins three gold medals (in the floor exercise, beam, and team events) and a silver (in the uneven bars), becomes the first person to perform a back somersault on the uneven parallel bars in competition, becomes the first woman to perform a backflip on the balance beam, charms the crowd, and inspires thousands of would-be gymnasts. The trend toward elfin, juvenile gymnasts will continue into the 1990s, with coaches increasingly searching for flexibility and fearlessness and the media searching for endearing children to laud.

The team competition in gymnastics is won by the Soviets: Touritscheva (silver medalist in the floor exercise and bronze medalist in the vault), Korbut, Tamara Lazakovitch (silver medalist in the beam and bronze medalist in the floor exercise), Lyubow Burda, Elvira Saadi, and Antonina Koshel. East Germany's second-place team includes Janz, who also wins the bars and vault and takes a bronze in the beam.

Aug. 12 U.S. runner Kathy Hammond, an Olympic relay silver medalist, sets a new women's world record in the 440-yard race.

Activism

The National Conference of Puerto Rican Women is founded.

Egyptian feminist Nawal El Saadawi publishes *Women and Sex*, addressing women's position in the Arab world, especially with regard to chastity.

Americans Brenda Feigen Fasteau and Ruth Bader Ginsburg establish the ACLU Women's Rights Project.

Japanese feminist Enoki Misako (b. 1939) leads the

militant group Chupiren (Pink Panthers). The organization, in existence for only about five years, fights wife beating and supports contraception, abortion rights, and equal hiring practices.

July The first issue of *Ms.* magazine, cofounded by U.S. feminist Gloria Steinem, is distributed.

Oct. French teenager Marie-Claire Chevalier is tried for procuring an abortion in a celebrated case that helps lead to the legalization of abortion. She is defended by noted feminist lawyer Gisèle Halimi.

Business and Industry

Countess Marion Gräfin Dönhoff, chief editor of the German political weekly *Die Zelt* since 1968, becomes its publisher.

The Soviet magazine *The Woman Worker* reaches a circulation of 12 million, the third highest in the world.

In the United States, 33,300,000 women are in the work force, constituting 38.5% of the total work force. Women with college degrees often earn less than men with eighth grade educations.

Jan. 20 U.S. economist and politician Juanita Kreps becomes the first female director of the New York Stock Exchange.

Sept. 20 U.S. businesswoman and textile designer Dorothy Liebes (b. October 14, 1897) dies. Known as "the mother of modern weaving," she revolutionized the industry, using unusual colors and materials such as beads, bamboo, cellophane, metal, leather, and straw. Her clients included King Ibn Saud of Saudi Arabia, Yosemite Valley's Ahwanee Hotel, the San Francisco Stock Exchange Club, ocean liners, airplanes, theaters, hotels, and private homes; at her height she created 2,500 designs per year.

Dec. 15 Australia mandates equal pay for women.

Science and Medicine

U.S. physicist Gertrude Scharff Goldhaber and U.S. geneticist Elizabeth Shull Russell are elected to the National Academy of Sciences.

British astronomer Margaret Burbidge becomes the first woman director of the Royal Greenwich Observatory, but she is denied the traditional title, astronomer royal.

America's SWE gives its Achievement Award to thermal engineer Nancy Fitzroy.

In India, women are 1% of engineering students.

Tunisian health administrator Saida Agrebi (b. 1945) becomes director of field-workers for the Tunisian family planning agency.

Feb. 20 German-American physicist Maria Goeppert-Mayer dies. Her work with benzene was the first attempt to predict the electron spectrum of a complex molecule. She was also part of the team that first isolated the radioactive isotope uranium-235.

Education and Scholarship

New publications include Margaret Atwood's *Survival: A Thematic Guide to Canadian Literature*, U.S. sociologist Jessie Bernard's *The Future of Marriage*, and English landscape architect Sylvia Crewe's (b. 1901) *Gardens of Moghul India*.

Women are 21% of Pakistani university students.

Apr. 28 Five Oxford colleges decide that they will begin admitting women in 1974.

Religion

Japanese religious ascetic and poet Mitsuhashi Takajo (b. 1899) dies.

American Sally Preisand becomes the world's first woman rabbi.

Dominican nun Elinor Rita Ford (b. 1931) becomes superintendent of schools for the New York Archdiocese, which includes 314 schools and 184,000 students. She is the first nun and the first woman to hold such a position in a major city's Catholic school system.

U.S. theologian Arlene Anderson Swidler, cofounder of the *Journal of Ecumenical Studies*, publishes the book *Woman in a Man's Church*.

Apr. 30 Seven nuns are arrested in a New York protest against U.S. involvement in Vietnam.

1973

General Status and Daily Life

Abortion up to twenty-eight weeks is legalized in South

Korea for cases of rape, incest, danger to the mother's health, or evidence of fetal abnormality. The woman and the abortionist are subject to a one-year prison term in cases of illegal abortion.

Sex discrimination by savings and loans is banned in the United States.

Denmark legalizes first trimester abortion on demand.

An Italian court fixes the value of a housewife's work at $6.25 a day.

Minimum age of marriage in Senegal is sixteen for women and twenty for men; the consent of both bride and groom is necessary for a legal ceremony. Polygyny is legal, but if a man wishes to have more than one wife, he must state this desire at the time of his first marriage. Most women are given a dowry at marriage. Divorce by mutual consent is legal, and there are ten acceptable causes for contested divorce.

Jan. 22 Abortion is illegal under all circumstances in thirty-one U.S. states; about 1 million illegal abortions are performed every year. On this date, in a case known as *Roe* v. *Wade*, the Supreme Court strikes down all laws preventing women from obtaining abortions in the first trimester; limited protection is provided for later abortions. Sarah Weddington (b. 1945) is the lawyer for "Jane Roe" (Norma McCorvey), a Texas woman seeking an abortion.

Government, the Military, and the Law

Irish diplomat Mary Tinney becomes ambassador to Sweden.

Ilona Burka, at twenty, becomes Hungary's youngest member of Parliament (MP). One-quarter of Hungary's 352 MPs are women.

Women in Jordan get the vote.

Judge Jochiko Mibuchi, as head of the Niiyata Court of Family Affairs, becomes the first woman head of a Japanese court.

Women are admitted to the U.S. Navy's pilot training program.

Tanzanian Julia Manning becomes the first woman High Court judge in East and Central Africa.

Malayan Tan Sri Fatimah, as head of Social Welfare, becomes Malaya's first woman Cabinet minister.

Chinese politician Chen Muhua becomes a member of the Chinese Communist party Central Committee.

Argentinian political leader Isabel Perón (b. 1931), second wife of Juan Perón, becomes vice president.

The number of women law students in the United States has quadrupled since 1969.

Air Force officer Jeanne Holm (b. 1921) becomes the first U.S. woman major general.

Pakistani politician and women's leader Begum Liaquat Ali Khan becomes governor of Sind, making her the first Pakistani woman to govern a province.

Politician Shulamit Aloni establishes Israel's Civil Rights party.

Apr. Lelia Kasensia Smith Floey of Taft, Oklahoma, becomes the first black woman mayor in the United States.

Literature and the Visual Arts

Lebanese poet Nadia Tuéni wins the Prix de l'Académie Française.

U.S. author Erica Jong (b. 1942) publishes *Half Lives*, a collection of poems. However, it is her female picaresque novel of this year, *Fear of Flying*, that brings her fame.

Grace Mirabella becomes editor in chief of *Vogue* magazine.

Zivia Cohen becomes editor of Israel's *Na'amat*, a magazine aimed at working women.

New poetry includes Ileana Malancioiu's *Lilies for Miss Bride*, Maxine Kumin's Pulitzer-winning *Up Country*, Marge Piercy's *To Be of Use*, Diane Wakoski's *Dancing on the Grave of a Son of a Bitch*, American Kathleen Spivack's (b. 1938) *Flying Inland*, Rosemary Dobson's *Selected Poems*, Japanese poet Sachiko Yoshihara's *Hirugao*, Anne-Marie Kegels's *The Roads Are on Fire*, and Adrienne Rich's *Diving into the Wreck*.

New U.S. novels include Toni Morrison's *Sula* and Rita Mae Brown's (b. November 28, 1944) *Rubyfruit Jungle*.

Performing Arts and Entertainment

U.S. gospel singer Rosetta Tharpe Morrison (b. 1916) and German dancer and choreographer Mary Wigman (b.

1896), a major influence in European modern dance, die.

U.S. filmmaker Sarah Kernochan coproduces and codirects *Marjoe*, a portrait of a cynical evangelist that wins the Academy Award for Best Documentary. U.S. screenwriter Eleanor Perry cowrites and coproduces *The Man Who Loved Cat Dancing*. Other films made by women include director and producer Cinda Firestone's award-winning documentary *Attica*, a history of the 1971 prison riot; Turkish producer Turkan Soray's *Going Back*, about a village woman returning to her home after several years in Istanbul; and Italian director Lina Wertmuller's *Film d'amore e d'anarchia* (*Love and Anarchy*). East German filmmaker Gitta Nickel wins a first prize at the Leipzig International Film Festival for her Vietnam documentary, *Tay Ho, the Village in the Fourth Zone*.

Roberta Flack records the hit song "Killing Me Softly."

American Gloria Katz coauthors the screenplay for *American Graffiti*, edited by Verna Fields and Marcia Lucas. Fields also edits *Paper Moon*, starring Tatum O'Neal, and Dede Allen edits *Serpico*.

U.S. choreographer Twyla Tharp creates *Deuce Coupe* for the Joffrey Ballet.

Glenda Jackson wins the Best Actress Oscar for her performance in *A Touch of Class*. Filmgoers can also see Linda Blair in the horror movie *The Exorcist*, Liv Ullmann in *Scenes from a Marriage*, Barbra Streisand in *The Way We Were*, Jane Fonda in *A Doll's House*, and Brigitte Bardot in *Si Don Juan était une femme*.

Joan Baez records the album *Diamonds and Rust*.

English ballerina Alicia Markova is named governor of the Royal Ballet.

U.S. costume and fashion designer Edith Head wins an Oscar for *The Sting*.

July 2 U.S. actress Betty Grable dies. In the mid-1940s, her salary of $300,000 per year was the highest for a woman in the United States; at the height of her popularity in World War II, 60,000 copies of her pinup picture were mailed in one week.

Oct. Universal's Pamela Douglas becomes the first black woman producer at a major motion picture studio.

Dec. 22 U.S. radio and television soap opera writer Irna Phillips (b. July 1, 1901), creator of "The Guiding Light," the longest-running soap opera in history, dies. She also wrote for "Another World," "The Days of Our Lives," "As the World Turns," and "Peyton Place."

Athletics and Exploration

Women are finally allowed to fight on foot as toreras in Spanish bullrings. Maria de Los Angeles and Angela Hernández quickly take advantage of the opportunity.

Linda Meyers becomes the first U.S. archer to win a world championship.

Austrian skier Annemarie Proell Moser wins the World Cup downhill championship and wins eleven consecutive downhill competitions.

U.S. swimmer Lynne Cox sets a new women's record, crossing the English Channel in nine hours, thirty-six minutes, only one minute slower than the men's record.

Largely due to the agitation of Billie Jean King, the U.S. Lawn Tennis Association agrees to grant equal prizes of $25,000 to the male and female winners at its annual tournament. Previously, the male winner made more money. Also in this year, King wins the women's singles at Wimbledon and founds the Women's Tennis Association, which is joined by Martina Navratilova and Chris Evert.

Russian gymnast Ludmila Touritscheva (b. 1952) wins the gold medal in every apparatus and in the combined exercises at the European championships. She was also the world champion in 1970 and 1971.

German sprinter Renate Stecher sets records of 10.8 seconds in the 100 meters and 22.1 seconds in the 200 meters.

Sept. 20 Billie Jean King defeats male player Bobby Riggs 6-4, 6-3, 6-3 in a much-publicized "Battle of the Sexes" before 30,000 spectators and about 40 million television viewers.

Activism

Mothers of political prisoners stage a hunger strike in Nicaragua.

The first National Lesbian Feminist Conference is held in Los Angeles, California.

A midwest group of volunteers has performed 11,000 safe illegal abortions since 1969. The volunteers' numbers are listed under "Jane How" in the phone book, since "Jane" can tell you "how" to get an abortion. The organization charges an average of $45; the usual going rate for an illegal abortion at this time is $2,000.

American Margo St. James founds a prostitutes' rights group, COYOTE (Call Off Your Old Tired Ethics).

Lakota Sioux Indians Lorelei Means and Madonna Gilbert, two of the leaders of the armed takeover of Wounded Knee in February, establish the "We Will Remember" Indian Survival School in Rapid City, South Dakota.

ALIMUPER, the Alliance for the Liberation of Peruvian Women, is formed.

Dec. Menominee Indian Ada Deer establishes the National Committee to Save the Menominee People and Forests, which manages to return the Menominee land to reservation status after its nearly disastrous conversion to an ordinary Wisconsin county.

Business and Industry

Anthea Gaukroger, Audrey Geddes, Susan Shaw, and Muriel Wood are the first women brokers admitted to the London Stock Exchange. Ingrid Elgenmann becomes Switzerland's first woman stockbroker.

The most common job for women in Colombia is domestic service; the average servant works twelve to fifteen hours a day for a salary of twenty-five dollars a month plus room and board.

Barbara Grier and Donna McBride establish Naiad Press, a successful publisher of lesbian fiction; Virago, the world's largest feminist press, is also established.

Women make 63.1% as much as men in Austria, 70% as much in Australia, 79.2% as much in Denmark, 70.3% as much in West Germany, 84.1% as much in Sweden (for manual labor), 62.5% as much in Great Britain, and 56.6% as much in the United States.

In the United States, only 0.7% of apprentices are women. Women are found in only 70 of the 450 jobs that accept apprentices.

American Leslie Arp becomes the first woman chef at New York's Waldorf Astoria Hotel.

Self-Employed Women's Association (SEWA) is founded in India. Its members include street vendors, pieceworkers, and manual laborers.

Women are 10% of Peruvian agricultural laborers and 51% of the total Russian work force.

Marianne Burge becomes the first woman partner of a Big Eight accounting firm when she becomes a partner at Price, Waterhouse & Company.

Jan. Emily Howell, employed by Frontier Airlines, becomes the first commercial airline pilot in the United States.

July 7 England's highly successful Virago Press, which specializes in books by and about women, is established by Australian publisher Carmen Callil.

Science and Medicine

French feminist psychoanalyst Luce Iragaray (b. 1939) publishes *Le Langage des déments*.

Women are 70% of Soviet doctors, but they tend to be concentrated in specialties that have lower status and pay; they are 90% of pediatricians, for example, but only 6% of surgeons.

U.S. inventor and computer entrepreneur Patricia Wiener patents one of the first memory systems to be contained on a single silicon computer chip.

Three U.S. women are elected to the National Academy of Sciences: medical geneticist Beatrice Mintz, hemoglobin biologist Helen M. Ranney, and pediatric cardiologist Helen Brooke Taussig.

Japanese scientist Katsuko Saruhashi becomes head of the Meteorological Research Institute's geochemistry laboratory.

The SWE gives its Achievement Award to electrical engineer Irene Carswell Peden, who in 1975 will become first woman on the Board of Directors of the Institute of Electrical and Electronics Engineers (IEEE).

Education and Scholarship

Women are 35.9% of university students in Indonesia.

July 23 U.S. historian Beatrice Hyslop (b. April 10, 1899) dies. She was made a Chevalier of the Legion of Honor in 1961 for her work on the history of France.

Nov. 1 U.S. biographer and essayist Catherine Drinker Bowen dies. Asked why she had never written a woman's biography, she responded, "a woman's biography—with about eight famous historical exceptions—so often turns out to be the story of a man and the woman who helped his career."

Religion

U.S. feminist theologian Mary Daly publishes *Beyond God the Father*.

In the United States, the abortion rights group Catholics for a Free Choice is founded.

1974

General Status and Daily Life

In South Korea, 35% of women age fifteen to forty-nine in union use contraception, with most favoring the pill and the IUD.

Mexico's Civil Code grants women equal rights in marriage. Minimum legal age of marriage is eighteen for both men and women. Women may own property, and both partners in a marriage choose the couple's place of residence.

Australia's first rape crisis center opens in Sydney.

Federally funded birth control is approved in Austria.

Hungary limits abortion on demand to unwed teens, single, divorced, separated, and widowed women, women over thirty-five, and women who have three children or two children and another "obstetrical event." All other abortions must be for one of the approved reasons: health of the woman, birth defects, rape, incest, or inadequate housing.

Denmark's government begins subsidizing day care.

Abortion is legal in Nicaragua only when the woman's life is threatened.

In Nepal, married women have limited rights over property. For example, she may not dispose of more than half of her share of the couple's assets without permission from her husband or sons.

The IUD is approved for use in Japan.

Indonesia's age of consent for marriage is sixteen for women and eighteen for men with parental consent, or twenty-one for both sexes without parental consent. Muslim men must go through the courts in order to obtain permission for polygyny. The Muslim man's right to divorce his wife at will (*talaq*) is also restricted and must be subject to both a religious and civil court proceeding. Some groups in Indonesia are patrilineal, some are matrilineal (with the bride retaining her birth name after marriage), and most are bilateral, with each partner remaining a member of his or her own clan after marriage.

The top U.S. best-seller is Marabel Morgan's *Total Woman*, which advises women to flatter men, obey them, and keep them constantly aroused.

California legalizes use of the title "Ms." Many feminists prefer this title to "Miss" or "Mrs.," since, like "Mr.," it does not indicate marital status.

Kathryn Kirschbaum, mayor of Davenport, Iowa, is denied a credit card without her husband's signature. This situation is remedied by the U.S. Equal Credit Opportunity Act, which allows women to borrow money and get credit cards on the same basis as men.

May 15 A. H. Robins agrees to discontinue marketing of the Dalkon Shield IUD, noted for its high failure rate and link to uterine infections, from which seven women have died.

May 31 U.S. food writer Adelle Davis (b. February 25, 1904) dies. Her books on nutrition, such as *Let's Cook It Right* (1947), were riddled with inaccuracies but popularized the idea of a balanced diet.

Government, the Military, and the Law

New women Cabinet ministers include Britain's secretary of state for social security Barbara Castle and secretary of state for prices and consumer protection Shirley Williams; Portugal's first woman minister of social welfare, Maria de Lourdes Pintassilgo; Canada's minister of environment Jeanne Sauvé; and France's first secretary of state for women's affairs, Françoise Giroud.

María Eugenia Rojas de Moreno runs unsuccessfully for president in Colombia.

The Merchant Marine Academy becomes the first U.S. service academy to admit women.

Norwegian politician Eva Kolstad becomes president of the Liberal party.

Diplomat Gwendoline Konie begins three years as Zambian ambassador to Sweden, Norway, Denmark, and Finland.

U.S. film actress Shirley Temple Black (b. April 23, 1928) becomes ambassador to Ghana.

More women run for office in the United States than at any previous time. Mary Louise Smith becomes the first woman chair of the Republican party.

Zambian lawyer Lombe Phyllis Chibesakunda joins Zambia's male-dominated diplomatic corps.

Israeli politician Shulamit Aloni becomes a minister without portfolio and pushes for passage of the Civil Marriage Bill.

Apr. 10 Israeli prime minister Golda Meir resigns.

May 28 Lawyer Simone Veil (b. 1927) becomes the first woman Cabinet minister in France when she is appointed Minister of Health and Social Security. She will hold this post until 1979. On June 28, she obtains passage of liberalized contraception laws, and on November 29, she obtains the legalization of abortion after a thirty-hour debate in the National Assembly.

July 1 Vice President Isabel Perón of Argentina becomes the world's first woman president after the death of her husband, President Juan Perón.

Sept. Gail A. Cobb of Washington, D.C., becomes the first U.S. policewoman killed in the line of duty.

Sept. 16 Renaude Lapointe becomes the first woman speaker of Canada's Senate.

Nov. 5 U.S. politician Ella Grasso (May 10, 1919–February 5, 1981) of Connecticut becomes the first woman governor of a state not elected in succession to her husband.

Dec. Elizabeth Domitien becomes the first woman prime minister of the Central African Republic.

Literature and the Visual Arts

Mexican poet, novelist, and ambassador to Israel Rosario Castellanos (b. 1925) dies.

New novels include Spanish author Ana Maria Malute's *Olvidado Rey Gudu* and Japanese novelist Ariyoshi Sawako's antipollution *Fukugo osen*.

New poetry includes American Jane Cooper's *Maps & Windows*, Lucille Clifton's *An Ordinary Woman*, American Kathleen Spivack's *The Jane Poems*, Anne Sexton's *The Death Notebooks*, Margaret Atwood's *You Are Happy*, Thérèse Plantier's *Jusqu'à ce que l'enfer gêle*, and Rossana Ombres's *The Bestiary of Love*. French poet Yvonne Caroutch wins the Cocteau Prize for her *La voie du coeur de verre* (1972).

Sarah Rippin becomes chief editor of *AT*, Israel's only monthly magazine.

Performing Arts and Entertainment

U.S. pop singer and member of The Mamas and the Papas Cass Elliot (b. 1943) dies.

U.S. actress Marlo Thomas creates the children's television special "Free To Be . . . You and Me," which celebrates nontraditional roles for men and women.

American Anita Kerr becomes the first woman to compose, arrange, and conduct a feature film score.

Antonia: A Portrait of the Woman is the most successful full-length documentary of the year. Produced by folksinger Judy Collins and directed by U.S. filmmaker Jill Godmilow, it is a movie about the daily activities of conductor Antonia Brico.

U.S. actress Cicely Tyson (b. 1933) stars in the television movie *The Autobiography of Miss Jane Pittman*.

Italian director Liliana Cavani directs *The Night Porter*, a disturbing film about a sadomasochistic relationship.

French writer and filmmaker Marguerite Duras makes a film called *Les parleuses*, a series of conversations with feminist critic Xavière Gauthier.

Ellen Burstyn wins the Best Actress Oscar for *Alice Doesn't Live Here Anymore*. Several women are involved in the making of the film, including production designer Toby Rafelson, editor Marcia Lucas, coproducer Audrey Maas, and associate producer Sandy Weintraub.

U.S. film producer Julia Miller coproduces the Academy Award-winning movie *The Sting*.

Belgian filmmaker Chantal Akermann makes *Je, tu, il, elle*.

Ingrid Bergman stars in *Murder on the Orient Express*, winning her third Oscar for the performance; Lauren Bacall also stars in *Orient Express*. Faye Dunaway stars in *Chinatown*, and Mia Farrow stars in *The Great Gatsby*.

Mar. 28 U.S. lyricist Dorothy Fields, who collaborated with Jerome Kern, Albert Hague, and her own brother on some of the most popular shows on Broadway, dies. With her brother, she wrote the book for *Annie Get Your Gun*; in 1971, she was the first woman elected to the Songwriters' Hall of Fame.

Athletics and Exploration

Carol Polls becomes the first licensed woman boxing judge in the United States.

Austrian skier Annemarie Proell Moser wins the World Cup downhill championship; U.S. freestyle skier Julie Meissner wins the first international women's championship.

Lanny Moss of the Portland Mavericks becomes the first woman manager of a minor league baseball team.

Girls are admitted to Little League baseball teams. Eleven-year-old Bunny Taylor becomes the first Little League girl to pitch a no-hitter.

Japanese tennis player Kazuko Sawamatsu becomes the first woman professional player in Japan and the first Japanese player to win a major Wimbledon title in forty-one years. She has won 192 consecutive Japanese tournaments.

The first national girls' basketball league in the United States, the All-American Girls' Basketball Conference, is founded.

English sailor Clare Francis (b. 1946), maker of a thirty-seven-day solo voyage across the Atlantic, comes in third in the Round Britain Race.

July 6 U.S. tennis player Chris Evert (b. 1954) wins the Wimbledon singles title. She will win it again in 1976 and 1981 and will win the U.S. Open in 1975, 1976, 1977, 1978, 1980, and 1982.

Activism

The WILPF opens a branch in Sri Lanka.

Six Dutch women in Amsterdam begin a movement to shelter battered women, called Bliijf van Mijn Lijf (Hands off My Body).

French philosopher and feminist Simone de Beauvoir becomes president of the League for the Rights of Women.

Feb. U.S. publishing heiress Patty Hearst is kidnapped by the radical Symbionese Liberation Army (SLA). In April, Hearst announces that she will stay with the SLA and fight for "the freedom of oppressed people." On April 15, she helps SLA members to rob a bank, perhaps under duress; she will be found guilty of armed robbery in 1976.

May 7 The League of Women Voters begins admitting men.

Nov. 13 U.S. nuclear plant worker Karen Silkwood is killed in a car crash on her way to talk to a *New York Times* reporter about safety violations at the Kerr-McGee Cimarron Facility near Oklahoma City. Her notebook, documenting the infractions, is never found, and some suspect foul play. Her death leads to a congressional investigation of nuclear safety.

Business and Industry

Uruguayan unionist Nibuya Sabalsajaray (b. 1951) dies

after being arrested and tortured.

Women are 39.4% of the U.S. work force and 36% of office workers in Ecuador.

In the United States, the Coalition of Labor Union Women (CLUW) is established.

Cuba's 590,000 employed women get the right to sixteen weeks of paid and one year of unpaid maternity leave.

Ireland's Equal Pay Act gives women the right to equal pay for equal work and protects women who file discrimination suits from retribution.

In Thailand, women industrial workers make 67% as much as their male counterparts.

Mar. 20 U.S. fashion designer Anne Klein (b. Hannah Golofski in 1921) dies.

Science and Medicine

U.S. geneticist Catherine H. Bailey, developer of thirty-nine new hybrid fruit varieties, presents the paper "Genetics and Plant Breeding" at a horticultural congress in Warsaw, Poland.

Two U.S. women are elected to the National Academy of Sciences: research botanist Estella Bergere Leopold and biochemist Sarah Ratner.

The SWE gives its Achievement Award to Barbara Crawford Johnson, supervisor of support programs for the Apollo missions, Skylab, Apollo-Soyuz test programs, and the space shuttle program.

May 22 German-American engineer and mathematician Irmgard Flügge-Lotz (b. July 16, 1903), whose theory of discontinuous automatic control made possible the development of jet planes, dies. She produced more than fifty technical papers on such subjects as aerodynamics, navigation, flight controls, and flight dynamics.

Education and Scholarship

Emily Genauer of *Newsday* wins the Pulitzer Prize for criticism or commentary.

German-American historian Hanna Gray (b. 1930) becomes the first woman provost of Yale University and the first provost without a Yale degree. Later, acting in an interim capacity, she becomes the first woman president of Yale, and eventually she will become the president of the University of Chicago.

The world's oldest known tune, a Mesopotamian melody for an eleven-string lyre, is performed for the first time in 3,400 years after being deciphered by U.C. Berkeley Assyriologist Anne D. Kilmer.

New publications include French feminist and psychoanalyst Luce Iragaray's *Speculum de l'autre femme*, British feminist Juliet Mitchell's (b. 1940) *Psychoanalysis and Feminism*, American biographer Catherine Drinker Bowen's posthumous *The Most Dangerous Man in America: Scenes from the Life of Benjamin Franklin*, and English feminist sociologist Ann Oakley's (b. 1944) *Housewife* and *The Sociology of Housework*.

Pauline Jewett becomes Canada's first woman college president.

Mar. 11 U.S. parent educator Sidonie Matsner Gruenberg (b. June 10, 1881), author of several popular and influential guides to child care, dies.

Religion

U.S. feminist theologian Mary Daly publishes *Beyond God the Father*.

U.S. theologian Rosemary Radford Reuther edits the book *Religion and Sexism*.

Eleven women are ordained as Episcopal priests without church sanction; the ordinations will be recognized in 1976. One of the eleven, Alison Cheek, becomes the first woman to celebrate the Eucharist in the U.S. Episcopal church.

1975

General Status and Daily Life

In Thailand, 40% of women age fifteen to forty-nine in union use some form of contraception, with the pill being the most popular method. By comparison, only 7% of Pakistani women in the same age group use contraception, with abstinence and condoms being the preferred methods. In the Netherlands, 75% of married women under forty-five use contraception, with the pill being by far the most popular method.

Sweden legalizes free abortion on request, with a doctor's consultation, during the first trimester. From the first trimester until the eighteenth week, a social worker must be consulted as well. From weeks eighteen to twenty-eight, the woman must have the approval of the National Board of Health, and after week twenty-eight, abortion is permitted only to save the woman's life.

First-trimester abortion is legalized in Austria; minors still need parental consent. Indian abortion law is liberalized to allow the procedure on request through the twentieth week. A woman may get an abortion without her husband's permission.

Iranian law requires a man to have his first wife's consent before taking a second wife. This law will later be reversed under the Khomeini regime.

Minimum legal age at marriage is eighteen for both sexes in Kenya, although some exceptions are permitted. Some girls are married as young as ten years old. The groom usually pays a bride-price to the woman or her parents. Minimum legal age of marriage is sixteen for women and eighteen for men in Italy, and sixteen for both sexes with parental consent in Ireland (but until this year the ages were twelve for women and fourteen for men with consent). Irish couples may marry at twenty-one without parental consent.

In Nicaragua, 48% of families are headed by women.

Adultery is decriminalized in France; divorce is legal by mutual consent or in cases of mental illness, six-year separation, or misconduct by one party.

Cuba's Family Code recognizes the equality of spouses, the economic value of domestic tasks, and the duty of both husband and wife to contribute to housework.

Apr. A royal decree bans contraceptives in Saudi Arabia.

Government, the Military, and the Law

The U.S. Supreme Court rules that women cannot be excluded from juries on the basis of sex.

In the United States, Congress orders military academies to begin admitting women, and Specialist Fourth Class Debra Houghton becomes the army's first female tank driver. Female participation in the military is at an all-time high, with women making up 4.5% of the U.S. Army. West Germany admits women to its military medical corps. In Finland, women are 1.3% of the military, and in Israel, Ruth Muscal becomes the director of the Israeli Defense Force and the Cheil Nashim (Women's Army).

Women are 16% of judges in Indonesia and 2% of lawyers and judges in Thailand.

Seven of the twenty-three paramount chiefs in the Cook Islands are women.

Canadian politician and journalist Jeanne Sauvé becomes minister of communications, a position she will hold until 1979.

Irish politician Bernadette Devlin McAliskey cofounds Ireland's Independent Socialist party.

The Central African Republic's Elizabeth Domitien becomes that country's figurehead prime minister; she will be removed from office next year.

Liberian lawyer and diplomat Angie Brooks-Randolph becomes a permanent representative to the UN and ambassador to Cuba.

Zambian lawyer and diplomat Lombe Phyllis Chibesakunda is named ambassador to Japan.

The highest Communist party official in Tajikistan is a woman, Ibodat Rahimova. The vice president and vice premier are also women.

Feb. 11 Margaret Thatcher becomes the first woman leader of Britain's Conservative party. She says, "I am very, very thrilled." In the same year, Baroness Janet Young becomes the Conservative party's vice-chairman.

Mar. U.S. lawyer Carla Anderson Hills becomes secretary of the Department of Housing and Urban Development (HUD).

June 12 Indian Prime Minister Indira Gandhi, indicted on 52 individual charges, is found guilty of two counts of campaign malpractice. She is barred from holding public office for six years. On June 26, she declares a state of emergency and gives herself dictatorial powers, suspending habeas corpus, censoring the press, jailing subversives, restricting air traffic, and increasing military activity. Thousands of political prisoners are arrested by August. On July 4, twenty-six opposition political organizations are banned.

Aug. 22 Mauritanian feminist Toure Aissata Kane becomes her country's first female Cabinet minister when she is appointed minister for the protection of the family and for social affairs.

Sept. 5 Manson "family" member Lynette Alice "Squeaky" Fromme tries to assassinate President Gerald Ford in Sacramento.

Sept. 22 Sara Jane Moore tries to assassinate President Ford in San Francisco.

Dec. Maria Isabel Carmelo Rosa becomes Portugal's secretary of state for consumer protection.

Literature and the Visual Arts

Lynn Young becomes the first woman senior editor at *Newsweek*.

Caroline Kismaric becomes managaing editor of the photography magazine *Aperture*.

New poetry includes Denise Levertov's *The Freeing of the Dust*, Maxine Kumin's *House, Bridge, Fountain, Gate*, American Shirley Williams's (b. 1944) *The Peacock Poems*, Louise Glück's *The House on Marshland*, American Maura Stanton's (b. 1946) *Snow on Snow*, Eva Mylonás's *Clear Metal*, Thérèse Plantier's *La loi du silence*, Nadia Tuéni's *Dreamers of the Earth*, and Vénus Khoury-Gata's *South of Silence*. Anne Sexton's *The Awful Rowing Toward God* is published posthumously.

U.S. journalist Helen Thomas, White House bureau chief for UPI, becomes the first woman president of the White House Correspondents Association.

Robin Herman becomes the first woman sports reporter for the *New York Times*.

Agatha Christie publishes *Curtain*, the last Hercule Poirot novel. Nigerian novelist Flora Nwapa publishes *Emeka*. U.S. author Ntozake Shange publishes *For Colored Girls Who Have Considered Suicide When the Rainbow Is Enuf*.

Nov. Joan Beck becomes the first woman on the editorial board of the *Chicago Tribune*.

Performing Arts and Entertainment

U.S. journalist May Craig (December 19, 1888–July 15) dies. A Washington insider and a tough questioner, she had her own radio program, "Inside Washington."

Scottish composer and conductor Thea Musgrave composes *Orfeo*.

French film technician Babette Mangolte, who was once refused membership in a cinematographic organization because of her sex, wins the Prix de la Lumière at the Toulon film festival for her photography in Yvonne Rainer's *Film About a Woman Who . . .* and in her own version of *What Maisie Knew*.

New albums include Carly Simon's (b. 1945) *The Best of Carly Simon*, which contains the song "You're So Vain," Joni Mitchell's *The Hissing of Summer Lawns*, and Jefferson Starship's *Red Octopus*, with lead singer Grace Slick.

U.S. choreographer Twyla Tharp creates *Ocean's Motion*.

Belgian filmmaker Chantal Akermann makes *Jeanne Dielman, 23 quai du Commerce, 1080 Bruxelles*, about a day in the life of a housewife/prostitute. Films directed by Frenchwomen include Jeanne Moreau's *La Lumière* and Marguerite Duras's *India Song*.

The movie *Jaws* is edited by Verna Field.

U.S. comedian Lily Tomlin stars in the film *Nashville*, written by Joan Tewskbury. Other new movies include *Hustle*, starring Catherine Deneuve; *The Stepford Wives*, starring Katherine Ross; and *The Story of Adele H*, starring Isabelle Adjani. Louise Fletcher wins the Best Actress Oscar for her performance as a sadistic nurse in *One Flew Over the Cuckoo's Nest*.

Veronika Dudarova conducts the Moscow Symphony Orchestra; Dilbar Abdurakhmanova conducts the Tashkent Theatre of Opera and Ballet.

Nov. Kathleen Nolan becomes the first woman president of the Screen Actors' Guild.

Athletics and Exploration

West German bowler Annedore Haefker sets a world record to win the women's world championship, downing 4,615 pins in twenty-four games.

U.S. boxer Marion Bermudez becomes the first woman to box in the Golden Gloves tournament.

At the Pan-American Games, U.S. sharpshooter Margaret Murdock defeats all her male competitors to win the overall gold.

Austrian skier Annemarie Proell Moser wins the World Cup downhill championship.

Norweigan ski jumper Anita Wold sets a record distance of 321', 5".

U.S. swimmer Diana Nyad becomes the first person to swim the thirty-two miles across Lake Ontario. On October 6, she swims around Manhattan Island in seven hours, fifty-seven minutes.

At the European Cup finals, Romanian shot putter Valentina Cioltan becomes the first woman athlete to be disqualified from a competition for steroid use.

U.S. tennis player Billie Jean King founds the World Team Tennis League and the Women's Professional Softball League.

Mar. 29 Soviet speed skater Tatiana Averina sets a world record in the 1,000 meters, only eighteen days after setting a world record in the 1,500 meters.

May 16 Japanese mountain climber Junko Tabei (b. 1939) becomes the first woman and the 36th person to reach the top of Mount Everest.

July 17 U.S. aviator Phoebe Fairgrave Omlie, the first woman to earn a federal pilot's license, the first woman to earn an aircraft mechanic's license, cofounder of the first airport in Tennessee, and founder of flight schools, dies.

Activism

Egyptian feminist Dori'a Shafiq (b. 1910) dies. A guerrilla fighter against the British and the holder of a doctorate from the Sorbonne, she championed the cause of women's suffrage and established the feminist group Bint-E-Nil (Daughters of the Nile).

In Mexico City, the International Women's Year World Conference outlines a ten-year plan for the improvement of women's lot around the world.

U.S. feminist Susan Brownmiller publishes the landmark study *Against Our Will: Men, Women, and Rape*.

U.S. teacher Bonita Bergin founds Canine Companions for Independence, an organization that teaches dogs to help the disabled.

Gloria Dean Scott becomes the first black president of the Girl Scouts of America.

U.S. attorney Margaret Bush Wilson becomes the first black chairwoman of the NAACP.

Norwegian lesbians form Lesbisk Bevegelse (the Lesbian Movement) to fight for gay rights.

South African scholar and activist Fatima Meer becomes head of the Black Women's Federation.

Business and Industry

The First Women's Bank opens in New York City.

U.S. inventor and businesswoman Bette Nesmith Graham's Liquid Paper, Inc. produces 25 million, sells its product in thirty-one countries, and employs 200 people. Graham resigns as chairman of the board; in 1979, Gilette will buy the company for nearly $50 million plus royalties until the year 2000.

India mandates equal pay for equal work, but the law will be only sporadically enforced. Many women are classified as "temporary" workers, which exempts them from protection. India's Factory Law, requiring employers of more than fifty women to provide day care for children under six, is extended to all employers of more than thirty women.

Women make 64.4% as much as men in Austria, 83.2% as much in Denmark, 72.3% as much in West Germany, 80% as much in Italy (for manual labor), 85.2% as much in Sweden (for manual labor), 67.6% as much in Great Britain, and 57% as much in the United States. Italian women agricultural workers make 91.8% of men's wages.

Rose Totino becomes the first woman corporate vice president in Pillsbury's 106 years in business when the corporation buys out her Totino's pizza business.

Women are 37.3% of the Japanese work force and 76.6% of Finland's textile workers. In France, women are 38% of the total work force, 14% of upper managers, 19% of middle managers, 61% of clerical workers, 24% of skilled blue-collar workers, 30% of agricultural laborers, 50% of sales workers, and 66% of clerical workers. In the USSR, women are three-quarters of service workers, one-quarter of construction and transportation workers, more than 80% of food and textile workers, more than 90% of garment workers, and 49% of manufacturing workers. In Great Britain, women are 9.7% of managers, 71.3% of clerical workers, 7.3% of farm workers, 0.2% of construction workers, and 72.1% of service workers.

Three times as many women as men in Thailand own businesses or sell wares in the marketplaces.

Britain's Employment Protection Act grants women maternity leave and protects them from being fired for becoming pregnant. Companies with fewer than six employees are exempt from the new Sex Discrimination Act, which prevents companies from discriminating on the basis of marital status and bars bias in hiring, training, and promotion.

In the United States, 21% of families are supported financially by women.

Science and Medicine

Five U.S. women are elected to the National Academy of Sciences: statistician Gertrude Mary Cox, anthropologist Frederica Annis de Laguna, psychologist Dorothea Jamison, anthropologist Margaret Mead, and medical physicist Rosalyn S. Yalow.

The SWE gives its Achievement Award to aeronautical

engineer Sheila Widnall.

In Finland, women are 5.1% of physicists, 29.5% of doctors, and 98% of nurses. In Hungary, they are 40.8% of doctors and 85% of industrial designers. Women are 16.9% of Thailand's doctors and 9% of U.S. doctors.

In the USSR, women are 50% of scientists, 40% of engineering students, and 84% of public health and social welfare workers. Most Soviet doctors are women; the Belorussian Psychoneurological Center and the leading eye hospital are both headed by women, Efrosina Breus and Nadezhda Puchkovskaya.

Canadian photographers Leone Pippard and Heather Malcolm begin the first extensive study of beluga whales in the wild. Pippard repeats her studies in 1977 and becomes a campaigner for a clean enivronment for the whales on the St. Lawrence River.

U.S. women earn 28.5% of all bachelor's degrees, 18.97% of computer science bachelor's degrees, 9.7% of physics bachelor's degrees, 22.4% of chemistry bachelor's degrees, and 41.96% of math bachelor's degrees.

The All India Institute of Medical Sciences stops performing amniocentesis after discovering that it is being used to identify and abort female fetuses.

South African doctor and activist Mamphela Ramphele founds the Zanempilo Health Clinic in King William's Town.

June 24 U.S. microbiologist and mycologist Elizabeth Hazen dies. With Rachel Brown, she discovered the antifungal antibiotic nystatin, which has been used to combat vaginal yeast infections, intestinal infections, skin and mucous membrane diseases, fungus in livestock feed, and mold that developed on artworks after a flood in Florence, Italy. Shortly before her death, Hazen, with Brown, became one of the first two women to win the American Institute of Chemists' Chemical Pioneer Award.

July 13 U.S. physiologist Judith Pool (b. June 1, 1919), specialist in muscle physiology and blood coagulation, dies. Her work on cold precipitation of AHF (antihemophilic factor) helped to change the treatment of hemophilia.

Sept. 5 U.S. microbiologist Alice Evans (b. January 29, 1881) dies. Though she never earned an M.D. or Ph.D., she discovered the cause of brucellosis and proved that it could be carried in cows' milk.

Education and Scholarship

About 5% of women and 33% of men in Nepal are literate.

Historian Carroll Smith-Rosenberg publishes the influential essay "The Female World of Love and Ritual," which examines passionate relationships between women in nineteenth-century America. Other historical publications include English historian Eileen Power's *Medieval Women* and American historian Sarah Pomeroy's *Goddesses, Whores, Wives, and Slaves: Women in Classical Antiquity*.

Mary McGrory of the *Washington Star* wins the Pulitzer Prize for criticism or commentary.

Alice Frey Emerson becomes the first woman president of 141-year-old Wheaton College in Massachusetts; Jill Ker Conway becomes the first woman president of Smith College.

Women are 44% of France's professors and teachers, 85% of Hungarian teachers, and 73% of Soviet teachers. Women are 1.4% of U.S. high school principals, down from over 50% in 1950. The number of U.S. women in college, however, has risen 45% since 1970.

In most countries, more boys than girls are in school, especially at the secondary level.

Religion

Canada's Anglican church approves the ordination of women priests.

Four women are ordained as Episcopal priests; the earlier ordination of eleven other women is repudiated.

Jan 10 Bernadette Olowo of Uganda is the first female ambassador to the Vatican.

Sept. 14 U.S. laywoman Elizabeth Ann Bayley Seton becomes the first native-born U.S. Catholic saint.

1976

General Status and Daily Life

West Germany legalizes abortion up to the twenty-second week for eugenic reasons or to preserve the physical or mental health of the woman; abortion is legalized up to the twelfth week for pregnancies resulting from rape or incest.

In England and Wales, 77% of women under age forty-five use contraception. Three percent of married Nepalese women age fifteen to forty-nine use contraception; in Mexico, 35% of women fifteen to forty-nine in union use contraception, favoring the Pill.

Civil marriages may now be dissolved by divorce in Colombia; women, but not men, must wait 270 days before remarrying.

Afghanistan's Civil Code dictates that the legal age of marriage is sixteen for girls and eighteen for boys. However, girls can marry legally at fifteen if they have parental consent. A man may divorce his wife in writing or by speaking a traditional form called the *talaq*; a woman must go through the courts to divorce her husband. Divorced women get custody of boys until age seven and of girls until age nine; divorced men can get custody of their children earlier than these ages if the mother remarries or behaves immorally.

In Japan, women do an average of 26.3 hours of housework per week; men do 1.5 hours.

The U.S. Congress limits Medicaid funding of abortions to those intended to save the life of the woman and those resulting from rape or incest.

Sweden makes voluntary sterilization legal and free on request for those over twenty-five. Those between eighteen and twenty-five years of age must apply for permission to be sterilized.

In Thailand, men and women must be at least seventeen years old to marry with the consent of both parents or twenty to marry without parental consent. The groom sets aside *khongman*, or bridal property, for his wife on the day of their engagement; it becomes hers at marriage, and whatever she owned before marriage remains hers. Widows must wait 310 days before remarrying in most cases. Many wives control the family finances and contribute more income to the household than their husbands.

In Kenya, a law banning wife beating is defeated in Parliament. One member is quoted as saying, "If you do not slap a woman her behavior will not appeal to you. Just slap her and she will know you love her."

Abortion is legalized in Israel in the cases of incest, threat to the life of the mother or her physical or mental health, or the unsuitable age of the mother (over forty or under seventeen). The procedure must be approved by a panel of three, and the woman must be warned of the "physical risk and mental anguish."

Government, the Military, and the Law

Women newly appointed to high office include Sudan's minister of social affairs, H.E. Fatima Abdel Mahmoud; Shirley Temple Black, the first female chief of protocol to a U.S. president; English paymaster general Shirley Williams; France's first secretary of state for universities, Alice Saunier-Seite, and minister of culture Françoise Giroud; unified Vietnam's first education minister, Nguyen Thi Binh (b. 1927); and Portugal's secretary of state for finance, Maria Manuela Morgado.

Sakado Ogata becomes Japan's first woman diplomat of ministerial rank.

The U.S. Army, Navy, Air Force, and Coast Guard academies begin admitting women.

Rear Admiral Fran McKee becomes the first woman line officer (rather than nurse) to be promoted to admiral in the U.S. Navy.

Major Eva Berg becomes chief of the Joint Norwegian Military Nursing Services.

Australia has 3,500 women in its military, Belgium 600, Canada 3,450, Taiwan 12,500, Denmark 550, Israel 8,000, Japan 2,300, the Netherlands 1,900, New Zealand 750, Norway 1,250, the Philippines 450, the Soviet Union 10,000, Turkey 100, the U.K. 14,700, the United States 108,800, and Yugoslavia 2,600. In most countries, women are 5% or less of the total military force. Greece, Italy, and Portugal have no women at all in the military.

Women in Portugal get full political rights. Since 1968, women have had the vote, but only "heads of families" have been allowed to elect or be elected to local councils. Until now, wives have also been legally obligated to display obedience to their husbands.

Jan. 14 Norwegian politician Gro Harlem Bruntland (b. 1939) becomes minister of the environment. Ruth Ryste (b. 1932) becomes minister of social affairs. Annemarie Lorentzen becomes minister of consumer affairs and government administration. Inger Louise Andvig Valle (b. 1921) becomes minister of justice.

Mar. Argentinian president Isabel Perón is deposed by the military and imprisoned for five years for corruption; her fall from power is followed by general persecution of feminists.

July U.S. politician Barbara Jordan (b. February 21, 1936), the first black woman elected to Congress from the Deep South, becomes the first black and the first woman to give the keynote speech at the Democratic National Convention. The convention is chaired by

Lindy Boggs, the first woman elected to Congress from Louisiana and the first woman to chair the national convention of a major U.S. political party.

July 30 Labor minister Tina Anselmi (b. 1927) becomes the first woman in the Italian Cabinet.

Oct. 8 Karin Söder (b. 1928) becomes Sweden's first female minister for foreign affairs. Elvy Olsson (b. 1923) becomes minister of housing and physical planning; Britt Mogård (b. 1922) becomes deputy minister of education and cultural affairs; Birgit Friggebo (b. 1941) becomes deputy minister of housing and physical planning; and Ingegerd Troedsson (b. 1929) becomes deputy minister of health and social affairs.

Dec. Captain Vittoria Renzullo becomes the first woman to command a police precinct in New York City.

Literature and the Visual Arts

Irish architect and designer of furniture and carpets Eileen Gray (b. 1879) dies.

English mystery writer Agatha Christie dies. The creator of legendary fictional detectives Hercule Poirot and Miss Marple, she published seventy-eight crime novels, six romances under the name Mary Westmacott, four nonfiction works, twenty plays, and about 150 short stories.

U.S. photographer Imogen Cunningham (b. 1883) dies. Her portrait subjects included Martha Graham and Gertrude Stein.

U.S. poet Grace Schulman (b. 1939), poetry editor of *The Nation*, publishes *Burn Down the Icons*. Other new American U.S. includes Muriel Rukeyser's *The Gates*, Audre Lorde's (1934–November 17, 1992) *Coal*, Adrienne Rich's *Of Woman Born*, Elizabeth Bishop's *Geography III*, Anne Sexton's posthumous *45 Mercy Street*, Tess Gallagher's (b. 1943) *Instructions to the Double*, Ellen Bryant Wright's (b. 1943) *Claiming Kin*, Carolyn Forche's (b. 1950) *Gathering the Tribes*, and Diane O'Hehir's *Summoned*. New poetry from elsewhere includes Egyptian Andrée Chedid's *Cerémonial de la violence* and *Fraternité de la parole*, and German Karin Kiwus's (b. 1942) first book, *On Both Sides of the Present*.

U.S. novelist Toni Morrison publishes *Song of Solomon*, whose heroine, Pilate, stabs a man who beats her daughter. Maxine Hong Kingston publishes her autobiographical novel, *The Woman Warrior*, which describes her childhood efforts to reconcile the conflicts of being Chinese-American. American Anne Rice publishes the novel *Interview with the Vampire*, a sexually charged exploration of the vampire myth.

Other new novels include Alice Walker's *Meridian*, Christa Wolf's *Kindheits-muster*, Nathalie Sarraute's *Disent les imbeciles*, and Margaret Atwood's *Lady Oracle*.

Nov. British journalist Anthea Disney becomes the first North American bureau chief for the *London Daily Mail* when she is named to head the New York office.

Performing Arts and Entertainment

Egyptian popular singer Oum Koulsoum, who performed hundreds of songs and became known as "the People's Artist," dies. Other performers who die this year include Russian-American pianist and teacher Rosina Lhévinne (b. 1880), French-American coloratura soprano Lily Pons (April 12, 1904–February 13), and U.S. actress Rosalind Russell (b. 1991), noted for playing strong women like the nonconformist free spirit Auntie Mame.

U.S. choreographer Twyla Tharp creates *Push Comes to Shove* for the American Ballet Theatre.

Italian film director Lina Wertmuller directs *Pasqualino settebellezze*. French writer and film director Nelly Kaplan makes *Néa*, and Belgian filmmaker Chantal Akermann directs *News from Home*.

Filmgoers can see Liv Ullmann in *Face to Face*, Audrey Hepburn as the middle-aged and war-weary Maid Marian in *Robin and Marian*, Talia Shire as a working-class wallflower in *Rocky*, Jodie Foster and Cybill Shepherd in *Taxi Driver*, Jessica Lange re-creating Fay Wray's damsel-in-distress role in a remake of *King Kong*, Sissy Spacek as a scorned and destructive adolescent in *Carrie*, French actress Anouk Aimée in *Si c'était à refaire*, and Lauren Bacall in *The Shootist*. Faye Dunaway wins the Best Actress Oscar for her performance as a cold, ambitious television reporter in *Network*.

Jan. 13 American Sarah Caldwell (b. 1928) becomes the first woman conductor of the Metropolitan Opera. She is invited to do so when Beverly Sills refuses to sing there unless she conducts.

Oct. Jane Pauley replaces Barbara Walters (b. 1931), cohost since 1974, on NBC's morning news program, the "Today Show," after Walters accepts a $1 million offer from ABC.

Oct. 6 U.S. broadcast journalist Pauline Frederick bcomes the first woman to moderate a presidential debate.

Athletics and Exploration

Australian squash player Heather McKay wins the Women's World Open Championship and her fourteenth consecutive British Women's Open. She also won the Australian Women's Open every year from 1960 to 1973.

American Janet Guthrie becomes the first woman to compete in the Indy 500.

Of 125 sailors in the Royal Western Singlehanded Transatlantic Race, four are women. The only woman to finish the race is English sailor Clare Francis, who sets a women's record of twenty-nine days despite rough seas and icebergs.

U.S. mountaineer Arlene Blum climbs Mount Everest.

U.S. stuntwoman Kitty O'Neil sets a new women's land speed record of 612 miles per hour.

U.S. drag racer Shirley "Cha Cha" Muldowney wins the NHRA (National Hot Rod Association) Spring Nationals.

American Sue Fish wins the National Women's Motocross Championships.

Japanese golfer Chako Higuchi, seven-time national champion in her own country, wins the European Women's Championship.

South African golfer Sally Little wins the first Women's International tournament.

U.S. golfer Judy Rankin becomes the first woman player to surpass $100,000 in earnings and is named the LPGA Player of the Year.

Feb. 4 The winter Olympics opens in Innsbruck, Austria. American Dorothy Hamill wins the gold in figure skating. In pairs, Soviet skater Irina Rodnina takes the gold for the second Olympics in a row, this time with her new partner, Alexander Zaitsev. In its first year as an Olympic sport, ice dancing is won by Soviets Ljudmila Pakhomova and Alexander Gorshkov.

Slalom skier Hanni Wenzel wins a bronze, becoming Liechtenstein's first medalist, male or female. The slalom event is won by West Germany's Rosi Mittermaier, who also wins the downhill and takes a silver in the giant slalom. Kathy Kreiner of Canada wins the giant slalom. East German Margit Schumann takes the gold in luge.

In the 5-kilometer cross-country ski race, Finland's Helena Takalo gets the gold, followed by Raisa Smetanina and Nina Baldycheva of the Soviet Union. Smetanina wins the 10 kilometer race, followed by Takalo and Soviet skier Galina Kulakova. The Soviet team of Baldycheva, Zinaida Amosova, Kulakova, and Smetanina wins the 4 x 5-kilometer relay, followed by the Finnish team of Liisa Suihkonen, Marjatta Kajosmaa, Hilkka Kuntola, and Takalo. East Germany's team, which includes 1980 medalists Barbara Petzold and Veronika Schmidt, takes the bronze.

Speed skater Sheila Young of the United States wins three medals, a gold in the 500 (with an Olympic-record time), a silver in the 1,500, and a bronze in the 1,000. Tatiana Averina of the Soviet Union sets Olympic records in the 1,000 and 3,000 meters and adds two bronzes, in the 500 and 1,500, to her two golds. Her teammate Galina Stepanskaya sets an Olympic record to win the 1,500.

May 19 Women get the right to play at Lord's Cricket Ground in London, an all-male institution since 1787.

Summer At the Montreal Olympics, the IOC adds basketball and team handball to the list of women's sports and adds six rowing events. Women are 20.6% of Olympic athletes this year. Soviet-bloc athletes win forty-four of the forty-nine women's medals. Princess Anne, daughter of Britain's Queen Elizabeth II, is the only female athlete not to be sex-tested.

The 500-meter kayak singles event is won by East Germany's Carola Drechsler-Zirzow. The 500-meter pairs event is won by Soviets Nina Popova and Galina Kreftes. Bulgaria's Svetla Ozetova and Zdravko Yordanova-Barboulova take the gold in double sculls; their teammates Siika Kelbecheva-Barboulova and Stoyanka Grouicheva win the coxless pair. East Germany wins the quadruple sculls, the coxed four, and the eight oars. Another East German, Christina Scheiblich, wins the single sculls.

Switzerland's Christine Stueckelberger wins the individual dressage competition, and several women are on the medals stand for team dressage, including West Germany's Gabriela Grillo (gold), Switzerland's Stueckelberger and Doris Ramseier (silver), and Hilda Gurney, Dorothy Morkis, and Edith Master of the United States (bronze). Mary Anne Tasukey of the United States is on the gold-winning three-day event team.

In fencing, Italy's Antonella Lonzi-Ragno wins the individual foil. The Soviet team of Yelena Belova-Novikova, Olga Kniazeva, Valentina Sidorova, Nailia Guiliazova, and Valentina Nikonova wins the team foil, followed by France's team (which includes 1980 gold medalists Brigitte Latrille, Christine Muzio, and Veronique Trinquet). American Margaret Murdock takes the silver medal in men's small-bore rifle, three-position, becoming the first woman to medal in an Olympic shooting event.

The Soviet Union takes the team handball gold, followed by East Germany and Hungary. Japan wins the volleyball gold, followed by the USSR and North Korea. Soviet player Lyudmila Chernysheva will be on the gold medal team in 1980; her teammate Inna Ryskal is the first woman to win four Olympic volleyball medals.

Luann Ryon of the United States wins the archery gold. The Soviet Union wins the gold in basketball, followed by the United States (including Nancy Liebermann and Charlotte Lewis). Of the Soviets, Angele Rupshene, Iuliyana Semenova, Nelly Feriabnikova, and Olga Sukharnova will remain on the team to medal again in 1980.

The swimming events are hotly contested; a rivalry arises between East German Kornelia Ender and American Shirley Babashoff, and Babashoff makes controversial accusations of steroid use (later substantiated) by the East German team. Ender wins individual golds in the 100-meter freestyle, the 200-meter freestyle, and the 100-meter butterfly; Babashoff wins silvers in the 200, 400, and 800-meter freestyles and the 4 x 100 medley relay.

Ender is not the only East German powerhouse; Petra Thuemer wins the 400- and 800-meter freestyles, Hannelore Anke wins the 100-meter breaststroke, Ulrike Richter wins the 100- and 200-meter backstrokes, Ulrike Tauber wins the 400-meter individual medley and takes a silver in the 200-meter butterly, and Andrea Pollack wins the 200-meter butterfly and takes a silver in the 100. East Germany also wins the 4 x 100 medley with its team of Richter, Anke, Pollack, and Ender and silvers in the 4 x 100-meter freestyle relay with a team composed of Ender, Pollack, Petra Priemer (silver medalist in the 100-meter freestyle), and Claudia Hempel.

Few medals are left for anyone but the East Germans, but Soviet swimmer Marina Koshevaia gets a bronze in the 100-meter breaststroke and wins the 200. The U.S. team of Babashoff, Kim Peyton, Wendy Boglioli (bronze medalist in the 100-meter butterfly), and Jill Sterkel wins the freestyle relay. The springboard diving gold goes to American Jennifer Chandler; Soviet Elena Vaytsekhovskaia wins the platform event, in which Swedish diver Ulrika Knape gets the silver.

West German runner Annegret Richter wins the 100-meter dash and takes silvers in the 200 meters and 4 x 100 relay. East German Bärbel Eckert Wockel wins the 200 meters and runs on the gold-medal 4 x 100 relay team with Marlies Oelsner, Carla Bodendorf, and Renate Stecher, who also wins a silver in the 100 and a bronze in the 200. East German Johanna Schaller wins the 100-meter hurdles, and her teammate Angela Voigt wins the long jump. In Montreal, Polish runner Irena Szewinska-Kirszenstein sets a world record in the 400 meters. Another East German, Rosemarie Ackermann, wins the high jump, becoming the first woman to jump 2 meters over her own height. Second place in the high jump goes to Sara Simeoni of Italy.

Soviet runner Tatiana Kazankina wins the 800 and 1,500-meter races. Poland's Irena Szewinksa-Kirszenstein wins the 400 meters, setting a world record. East Germany's team of Doris Brachmann Maletzki, Brigitte Koehn Rohde, Christina Lathan Bremer, and Ellen Streidt wins the 4 x 400 relay. Ivanka Hristova wins Bulgaria's first gold track-and-field medal in the

shot put; silver in this event goes to the Soviet Union's Nadezhda Chizhova. The discus winner, Poland's Danuta Rosani, is disqualified for steroid use, so the gold goes to East Germany's Evelin Schlaak. Ruth Fuchs of East Germany wins the javelin gold, and her teammates Sigrun Siegl and Burglinde Pollak win gold and bronze, respectively, in the pentathlon.

The star of the gymnastics competition is Romanian Nadia Comaneci (b. 1961). On July 18, on the uneven bars, she becomes the first Olympic gymnast to score a perfect ten. She goes on to score six more perfect tens and takes the gold medals in the bars, beam, and individual all-around, as well as a silver in the team event and a bronze in the floor exercise. Her strongest competition comes from Soviet gymnast Nelli Kim, who wins the floor exercise and the vault and comes in second in the all-around. Past stars Lyudmila Touritscheva and Olga Korbut are members of the gold-medal team but win no golds on their own; Touritscheva gets silvers in the floor exercise and vault and a bronze in the all-around, and Korbut's only other medal is a silver in the balance beam. The other members of the gold-medal Soviet team are Kim, Svetlana Grozdova, Elvira Saadi, and Marija Filatova.

Aug. Russian runner Lyudmilla Bragina (b. 1943) breaks her own world record in the 3000 meters with a time of 8 minutes, 27.1 seconds.

Activism

Twenty feminists establish the Women's Union of Greece; by 1982 it will have 10,000 members.

U.S. feminists protest *Snuff*, a film that presents the dismemberment and murder of a woman as pornography.

The Spanish feminist journal *Vindicación Feminista* begins publication.

The All Nepal Women's Organization, the umbrella group for all feminist groups in Nepal, has more than 60,000 members.

An important Mexican feminist journal, *Fem*, begins publication; it is edited by Mexican feminist Margarita García Flores and Guatemalan feminist Alaíde Foppa.

Aug. In northern Ireland, three children are killed in fighting between British troops and the Irish Republican Army; Betty Williams and Mairead Corrigan establish the Peace People's Movement, a joint Catholic-Protestant pacifist organization. In December, they are awarded the Nobel Peace Prize, but in January 1977, the movement collapses due to conflicts between the leaders and attacks on its demonstrators by angry partisans.

Business and Industry

Ten female chefs establish the Association des Restauratrices-Cuisinières (ARC) after they are barred from France's national chefs' association. Gisele Berger becomes the ARC's president.

Women are 40.5% of the U.S. work force, 51% of the Russian work force, 90% of Korea's clerical workers, and 38.8% of Nepalese agricultural laborers.

American Sylvia Porter's syndicated financial column, "Your Money's Worth," is read by more than 40 million readers.

Husbands in West Germany can no longer control decisions about their wives' employment.

Brazil's Labor Ministry reports that women are paid less than men, despite regulations requiring equal pay.

Women textile workers go on strike in Colombia.

British cosmetics entrepreneur Anita Roddack founds the Body Shop. She sells products from the Third World made with natural ingredients, paying more than necessary for these products to stimulate local economies. None of the products are tested on animals, and old containers are refilled to save money and to reduce waste. The Body Shop makes no promises of youth or beauty and discloses all of its ingredients, something not required by British law. All of the franchises are expected to be involved in charity work.

A Japanese court makes it illegal for men and women to have separate pay scales for the same work; most companies, after the ruling, simply change women's job titles and continue to pay them less.

In Chiengmai province, Thailand, 72% of women contribute more money than their husbands to the family finances.

Flora Nwapa founds the first Nigerian book publishing company run by a woman.

In the United States, 90% of 9,000 women surveyed claim they have been sexually harassed at work.

In Japan, pregnant women are often involuntarily "retired" from their jobs.

Tunisian Saida Agrebi becomes head of the Working Women's Committee of the Arab League Agency.

Science and Medicine

The American Astronomical Society, the American Chemical Society, and the American Graphical Society get their first women presidents or directors: Margaret Burbidge, Anna Harrison, and Sarah Kerr Myers, respectively.

U.S. anthropologist Margaret Mead becomes president of the American Association for the Advancement of Science.

Many pregnant women in Sri Lanka are anemic, due to taboos that prevent them from eating high-protein foods like fish, meat, and eggs during menstruation, pregnancy, and lactation.

In Kenya, women are fewer than 5% of doctors and engineers and 90% of nurses.

In southern Sudan, there is only one midwife per 18,251 people, and 97% of women are anemic.

Oncologist Charlotte Friend and mathematician Julia Robinson are elected to the U.S. National Academy of Sciences.

The SWE gives its Achievement Award to Ida Pressman for her work on power control systems.

Education and Scholarship

French scholar Hélène Ahrweiler becomes the first woman president of the seven-hundred-year-old Sorbonne.

French sociologist, feminist, and journalist Evelyne Sullerot publishes *Histoire et mythologie de l'amour*.

In Kenya, there are fifty-four boys', thirty-one girls', and fifteen coeducational secondary schools. Women are 30% of primary and secondary school teachers.

Art historians Ann Sutherland Harris and Linda Nochlin publish *Women Artists 1550–1950*, a survey of the principal women artists in the Western tradition.

Religion

U.S. evangelist and faith healer Kathryn Kuhlman (b. 1910?) dies.

Sept. 16 The Episcopal church formally approves the ordination of women as priests.

Oct. Joan Martin, once the first black woman student at Princeton Theological Seminary, becomes the first black woman minister of the United Presbyterian church.

1977

General Status and Daily Life

Contraceptive use rates vary; 71% of Norwegian women under forty-five in union use contraception, with most preferring the IUD and the condom. In Peru, 36% of women age fifteen to forty-nine in union use contraception, with 35% of those using the rhythm method. In Spain, 51% of women under forty-five in union are using contraception; the most popular methods are withdrawal, the pill, and the rhythm method. In China, 84% of couples of childbearing age use contraception. In Colombia, 46% of women age fifteen to forty-nine in union use contraception, and in Finland, 80% of women under forty-five do so.

Abortion is legalized in New Zealand for the first twenty weeks of pregnancy, only in cases of incest, threat to the mental or physical health of the mother, or abnormality of mother or fetus. Restrictions are tighter for abortions performed after twenty weeks.

Australia has seventy-two battered women's shelters.

In Brazil, one divorce per person is legalized, as long as there has first been a legal separation.

Of 9,000 rapes reported in West Germany this year, 850 result in convictions. Wives are beaten in an estimated 5 million families.

Canada bans discrimination on the basis of sex or marital status.

Afghanistan's constitution grants men and women equal legal rights.

New York City weatherman Tex Antoine is fired for commenting that women should "relax and enjoy it" if rape is inevitable.

Mean age at marriage for Japanese women is twenty-five. Wife battery is the second largest cause of divorce. Tokyo's Women's Counseling Center, with a capacity of thirty, is established this year to house battery victims and their children. In its first year, 6,000 women apply for shelter, and 919 are accommodated.

In the United States, 1,200,000 abortions are performed, 400,000 of them on teenagers.

Romanian mothers of four or more children receive Maternity Medals.

Libya has three women's "rehabilitation centers" for unwed mothers, rape or assault victims, prostitutes, victims of forced marriage, and divorcées without support. No medical personnel are available at the centers; no distinction is made between criminals and victims. The "rehabilitation" consists of classes in housework and sewing.

Legal age at marriage for Portuguese women is raised to sixteen.

Sweden's first rape crisis center opens in Stockholm.

There is one divorce for every two marriages in the United States.

Government, the Military, and the Law

Women hold fewer than 7% of all elected offices in the United States.

Women in Nigeria get the vote.

Lawyer and politician Elisabeth Blunschy-Steiner (b. July 13, 1922) becomes the first woman president of Switzerland's National Council.

Korea's first woman lawyer, Lee Tai Young, is arrested and disbarred when her politics are considered dangerous to President Park Chung Hee.

An Israeli women's party is formed.

In the Indonesian government, women are only 6.2% of Assembly and 7.2% of House members.

Saudi Arabian Princess Misha is executed for marrying a man of her own choice rather than one of her father's.

Economist and politician Juanita Kreps becomes the first female U.S. secretary of commerce; Patricia Harris becomes the first black woman in the Cabinet when she is appointed secretary of HUD.

Radical feminist Miswo Enoki establishes an unsuccessful Japan Woman's party.

Chinese politician Chen Muhua becomes minister of economic relations with foreign countries and is named to the Politburo, one of only two women members of that powerful body.

Feb. 25 Danish prime minister Anker Jørgenson names three women to his cabinet: Ritt Bjerregaard (b. 1941), minister for education; Eva Gredal, minister for social affairs; and Lise Østergaard, minister without portfolio in the ministry of social affairs.

Mar. Indian prime minister Indira Gandhi calls an early

election, loses, and is ejected from Parliament, arrested, and jailed.

Mar. U.S. lawyer Eleanor Holmes Norton (b. 1937) becomes the first woman to head the EEOC.

Mar. 25 Maria Manuela Morgado, already Portugal's secretary of state for finance, is named to the additional post of secretary of state for treasury.

May 13 After the death of Spanish dictator Francisco Franco, communist leader Dolores Ibarruri, exiled for thirty-eight years, returns to a triumphal welcome. In June she is reelected to the Parliament.

May 15 Pirkko Annikki Työläjärvi becomes Finland's minister of social affairs and health.

Literature and the Visual Arts

Hungarian poet Anna Hajnal (b. 1907) dies. A prominent author of thirteen books, she translated Shakespeare into Hungarian and cofounded a Budapest literary magazine in the 1930s.

Katharine White, the *New Yorker*'s first fiction editor, dies.

New poetry includes Diane Wakoski's *Spending Christmas with the Man from Receiving at Sears*, American Heather McHugh's (b. 1948) *Dangers*, Julia Uceda's *Bells of Sansueña*, and Maria Luisa Spanziani's *Passage with Chains*.

U.S. author Maxine Hong Kingston publishes *China Men*, a novel that attacks U.S. policies on Chinese immigration.

U.S. poet Judith Viorst wins the Georgia Children's Storybook Award for *Alexander and the Terrible Horrible No Good Very Bad Day*.

Chilean poet and literary critic Marjorie Agosin (b. 1955) publishes *Chile: Gemidos y Cantares*, a collection of poetry.

Margo Huston of the *Milwaukee Journal* wins a Pulitzer Prize for local reporting.

Colleen McCullough publishes the best-seller *The Thorn Birds*.

Performing Arts and Entertainment

Scottish composer and conductor Thea Musgrave composes the opera *Mary, Queen of Scots* for the Scottish Opera.

Chinese-American theatre director Tisa Chang founds the award-winning Pan Asian Repertory Theatre in New York City.

American Perry Miller Adato becomes the first woman to win the Directors Guild of America Award, for her television documentary *Georgia O'Keeffe*.

French filmmaker Agnès Varda directs *One Sings, the Other Doesn't*, about a long-standing friendship between two women.

English actress Vanessa Redgrave wins the Best Supporting Actress Academy Award for her potrayal of a political activist in *Julia*, which also stars Jane Fonda as playwright Lillian Hellman. American Diane Keaton wins the Best Actress Oscar for the title role in *Annie Hall*; her baggy menswear in the film starts a brief, sporadically revived fashion trend. Other new films include *A Star Is Born*, with Barbra Streisand, and *Star Wars*, with Carrie Fisher as the feisty damsel-in-distress Princess Leia.

U.S. singer Debby Boone has a pop hit with "You Light Up My Life."

Violette Verdy (b. Nelly Guillerm 1933) becomes the first woman director of the Paris Opera Ballet.

Swiss composer Tona Schercher-Hsiao (b. 1938) composes *L'invitation au voyage*, the wind quintet *Ziguidor*, and the orchestral work *Oeil de chat*.

Chinese conductor Zeng Xiaoying (b. 1929), China's first woman orchestra conductor, becomes head conductor at Beijing's Central Opera Theatre.

Mar. Bette Davis becomes the first woman to win the American Film Institute's Life Achievement Award.

Nov. 6 U.S. broadcast journalist Jessica Savitch becomes anchor of the Sunday "NBC Nightly News."

Athletics and Exploration

Soviet archer Rustamowa Zebinisso scores a world record 1,285 points out of a possible 1,440.

Romanian runner Natalia Maracescu sets world records in the mile and the 5,000 meters. French runner Chantal Langlace sets a women's world marathon record. East German runner Marlies Oelsner sets a world record in the 100 meters. Her compatriots Karin Rossley and Rosemarie Ackermann set new world records in the 400-

meter hurdles and the high jump, respectively. Czech shot putter Helena Fibingerova sets a world record distance of 73', 2 3/4", and American Kate Schmidt sets a record in the javelin throw.

American Peggy Steding wins her fourth U.S. Ladies' Professional Racquetball Championship.

Fourteen-year-old U.S. tennis player Tracy Austin becomes the youngest competitor in Wimbledon history.

U.S. diver Cynthia Potter McIngvale becomes the first woman to complete a three-and-a half somersault off a three-meter board in competition.

In the United States, the Women's Basketball League is formed; it will dissolve in 1981 after the founding of more than twelve professional teams.

Pioneering American professional baseball umpire Pam Postema graduates from umpire school.

Marie Ledbetter becomes the first woman to win the World Accuracy Title for parachuting. She jumps eight times from 2,500 feet, missing the targets by an accumulated distance of only 3 1/3".

Canadian Cindy Nicholas makes the first round-trip, nonstop English Channel swim by a woman.

Activism

In El Salvador, women establish the Committee of Mothers of Political Prisoners and the democratic activist group, Frente Femenino (Women's Front). The latter group will have 150,000 members within a decade.

Eleanor Smeal (b. 1939) becomes the first paid president of NOW, with a salary of $17,500 per year. She will hold this post until 1982.

There are 6,800 women's groups in Kenya.

In Rome, 10,000 women demonstrate against rape, starting a campaign to revise rape laws that will succeed in 1982.

Women in Peru agitate for the right to abortion on demand.

South African activists Helen Joseph, Ilana Kleinschmidt, Jacqueline Bosman, and Barbara Waite are arrested for refusing to testify against ANC activist Winnie Mandela.

Mar. In Argentina, fourteen mothers of "disappeared" political prisoners begin holding weekly vigils. They are jailed and harassed, but 2,500 more women join the crusade.

Business and Industry

Women are 13.4% of the Libyan agricultural work force. Ninety percent of these women are unpaid family workers. Libyan women are 7.2% of the manufacturing work force. They are 1% of all petroleum industry workers, 0.25% of construction workers, and 30% of health service workers.

Japanese fashion designer Namiko Mori opens a store from which to sell her fashions for the handicapped. Easy to get into and out of, her clothes are displayed low for easy wheelchair access.

Britain bans discrimination on the basis of sex or marital status, except in the military.

Women are 33.7% of the Indonesian labor force; many earn as little as seventeen cents a day.

U.S. inventor Ann Moore patents the Snugli baby carrier, which she developed with Lucy Aukerman and which is based on the slings she saw African women using during her tenure in the Peace Corps.

Women make 63.1% as much as men in Austria, 82% as much in Australia, 85.2% as much in Denmark, 72.7% as much in West Germany, 58.75% as much in Sweden, 58.9% as much in the United States, 41.4% as much in Bombay, India, and 71.9% as much in Great Britain.

In the Netherlands, women are 43.3% of clerical workers and 64.7% of service workers.

Norway's Working Environment Act gives workers a year of parental leave, with eighteen weeks of it at full salary; six weeks of this must be taken by the mother after delivery, and the rest of the time may be divided between the parents in any way they choose.

Apr. Jane O'Grady becomes the American Federation of Labor-Congress of Industrial Organizations' (AFL-CIO) first woman lobbyist.

Science and Medicine

Shere Hite publishes *The Hite Report*, a best-selling analysis of women's sexuality based on 3,000 questionnaires.

Indian mathematical genius Shakuntala Devi solves the following problem in less than twenty seconds:
$$(25{,}842{,}278 + 111{,}201{,}721 + 370{,}247{,}830 + 55{,}511{,}315) \times 9{,}878 = 5{,}559{,}369{,}456{,}432$$

Four U.S. women are elected to the National Academy of Sciences: anthropologist Elizabeth Florence Colson, biochemist Elizabeth Fondal Neufeld, and geneticists Ruth Sager and Evelyn Maisel Witkin.

Egyptian family-planning activist Assiza Hussein becomes president of International Planned Parenthood. There are 3,438 government-run family planning centers in Egypt.

America's Society of Women Engineers gives its Achievement Award to electrical engineer Mildred Dresselhaus, the first woman chair (in 1972) of MIT's department of electrical engineering.

Women are 2.7% of U.S. engineers, 22% of Irish medical students, and fewer than 3% of Kenya's engineering students.

U.S. bioengineer Thelma Estrin, one of the first people to analyze the human nervous system with computers, becomes a fellow of the IEEE.

Women are 0.95% of Nepal's engineers, 8% of scientific and technical workers, 13.33% of doctors, and 75% of nurses.

U.S. researcher Rosalyn Yalow wins the Nobel Prize for medicine for her invention of radioimmunoassay (RIA). RIA has revolutionized medical diagnosis; it is used to analyze hormones, vitamins, enzymes, and toxins and to diagnose diabetes, thyroid disease, hypertension, infertility, cancer, and hepatitis.

The U.S. Department of Defense names a new computer language ADA, in honor of pioneer computer programmer Ada Lovelace (1815–1852).

Education and Scholarship

Reading Is FUNdamental (RIF), founded by American Margaret McNamara, has more than 600 projects in forty-eight states.

Women are 25.8% of Indonesia's government university teachers and 100% of kindergarten teachers. They are 32% of U.S. higher education faculty.

The first female Rhodes scholars are selected.

Sociologist Suzanne Keller becomes Princeton's first tenured woman professor; Joan Girgus becomes the first woman undergraduate dean.

Mary R. Lefkowitz and Maureen B. Fant publish *Women in Greece and Rome*, a sourcebook of historical documents translated into English. The book covers women's roles in medicine, athletics, religion, business, and daily life.

Women are 39% of university students in Chile, 25% in El Salvador, 20% in the Sudan, 43% in Ireland, 41% in Italy, and 38.7% in Greece.

In most countries, more men than women are literate. In some places, the gap is huge, as in Morocco, where 10% of women and 34% of men are literate, or India, where 19% of women and 47% of men are literate. In other countries, however, including Hungary, Norway, and Austria, literacy rates are equal.

Religion

The Vatican denies women the right to become priests.

American Rosalie Muschal-Reinhardt becomes the first married woman to complete all the academic requirements for the Catholic priesthood.

Jan. American Jacqueline Means becomes the first officially ordained woman Episcopal priest. In the first dual-sex ordination ceremony in the Episcopal Church, Dr. Pauli Murray becomes the church's first black woman priest.

July Cora Sparrowk becomes the first woman head of the American Baptist Churches.

1978

General Status and Daily Life

The typical Sri Lankan woman lives in the country, wakes at 3 A.M. to fetch water, gather fuel, and cook breakfast, goes to a paid job, returns at 7 P.M., and continues her housework until late at night. It is considered shameful for a man to do housework.

One rape occurs every hour in London, England.

The legal period for abortion in Finland is reduced from sixteen to twelve weeks.

In Greece, 45 legal and about 500,000 illegal abortions are performed.

Austria's first battered women's shelter opens in Vienna.

The sale of girls is outlawed in Afghanistan.

The mean age at marriage for a Sudanese woman is 21.3.

Most marriages are arranged, some at birth. Brides are purchased by the groom's family for as much as a hundred cattle. Polygyny is common, and a marriage involves long and complex ceremonies, sometimes lasting as long as forty days. Chiefs have been known to have as many as one hundred wives. In some groups, a woman may marry another woman (or women) by paying the bride-price and can be considered the "father" of the wife's children. In some groups a woman is considered married even after her husband's death and must obtain a divorce if she wishes to remarry.

Polygyny is legal but discouraged in Libya.

In Romania, 58% of women in union under age forty-five are using some form of contraception, but since the pill, IUDs, and diaphragms are illegal or unavailable, most women use withdrawal or the rhythm method.

The average Senegalese family (which may be polygynous) has seven children. Only 4% of women age fifteen to forty-nine in union use some form of contraception, with abstinence being the most common method.

In Spain, female adultery is decriminalized.

The average Dutch woman has 1.6 children.

In Morocco, average age at marriage for a rural woman is 14.5.

In Israel, about 60,000 cases of wife beating are reported; only two men go to jail for the crime.

Age of consent for civil marriage in India is raised to eighteen for women and twenty-one for men. Religious marriage may take place at fourteen for women and eighteen for men.

Italy repeals a long-standing law that allows a rapist to go unpunished if his victim agrees to marry him. Law 194 legalizes first-trimester abortions for women over eighteen in many cases. Later abortions may be performed only in cases of threat to the woman's health or deformity of the fetus. Medical practitioners may refuse to perform abortions if the procedure violates their principles. Before the passage of this law, about 3 million illegal abortion were performed each year in Italy, killing about 20,000 women.

Feb. 1 The first U.S. stamp honoring a black woman, Harriet Tubman, is issued.

July 25 Englishwoman Lesley Brown gives birth to the world's first test-tube baby, Louise Brown.

Dec. 27 John Rideout, the first man indicted in the United States for marital rape, is acquitted, although he admits to having beaten Greta, his wife. At least 14% of U.S. wives are raped by their husbands.

Government, the Military, and the Law

Australia establishes a National Women's Advisory Council to advise the Ministry for Home Affairs and Environment.

Chinese politician Chen Muhua becomes vice premier, eventually taking charge of health care, birth control, and the 1982 census.

Italian politician Tina Anselmi becomes Italy's minister of health.

In Israel, women are 44% of civil service workers, but only 19% of senior civil service personnel.

Egyptian politician Aisha Rateb becomes minister of foreign affairs.

Indian politician Indira Gandhi is released from prison and resigns from the Congress party, forming a new party, the India National Congress.

May Margaret A. Brewer becomes the first woman brigadier general in the U.S. Marine Corps.

Literature and the Visual Arts

Women sportswriters in the U.S. get the right to enter major league baseball locker rooms.

New American poetry includes Muriel Rukeyser's *Collected Poems*, Denise Levertov's *Life in the Forest*, Audre Lorde's *The Black Unicorn*, Adrienne Rich's *The Dream of a Common Language*, and Tess Gallagher's *Under Stars*.

U.S. humorist and housewife Erma Bombeck sells the paperback rights to her book about the suburbs, *If Life Is a Bowl of Cherries—What Am I Doing in the Pits?* for $1 million. She celebrates by not doing her laundry for three days.

South African writer Nadine Gordimer publishes the novel *Berger's Daughter*.

Jan. 1 The new head of the London bureau, Bonnie Angelo, becomes *Time* magazine's first woman foreign bureau chief.

Performing Arts and Entertainment

Liza Minnelli wins her third Tony Award for *The Act*.

Kay Gardner founds the New England Women's Symphony.

Journalist Charlayne Hunter Gault, one of the first two black students at the University of Georgia, joins PBS's *MacNeil-Lehrer Report*.

English director Tina Packer cofounds Shakespeare & Company, a group that performs for schools, trains professional actors, offers support for teachers of Shakespeare, and gives thirty students a year a thorough education in Shakespearean acting.

Filmgoers can see U.S. pop singer Diana Ross (b. 1944) in *The Wiz*, Australian singer Olivia Newton-John playing a sweet and proper high school student in love with a "greaser" in the film musical *Grease*, Maureen Stapleton and Diane Keaton in *Interiors*, and Ingrid Bergman and Liv Ullmann in *Autumn Sonata*. Bergman receives an Oscar nomination, but Jane Fonda wins the Best Actress Oscar for her performance in *Coming Home*.

Athletics and Exploration

(Carol) Blaze Blazejowski wins the first Margaret Wade Trophy for best U.S. woman college basketball player. She scored 3,199 points in her college career and a record 52 points in one game.

In the United States, the Women's Basketball League (WBL) is founded, but salaries are low, attendance is poor, and two of the eight teams fold before the end of the first year. New franchises replace the old ones, but by 1981 only three teams will be left in viable condition, and the WBL will fold.

Russian figure skater Irina Rodnina (b. 1949), winner of more pairs skating titles than anyone in history, male or female, wins the world pairs skating title with Alexander Zaitsev for the sixth time in a row. She has won this title every year since 1969, the first four times with Aleksei Ulanov.

U.S. mountain climber Arlene Blum organizes and leads the American Women's Himalayan Expedition. Two members of the party, Irene Miller and Vera Komarkova, become the first women and the first Americans on the summit of Annapurna, the tenth highest mountain in the world.

June English sailor Naomi James becomes the first woman to sail around the world alone.

June East German runner Ulrike Bruns sets a world record in the 1,000 meters.

Activism

Polish peasant women wielding sickles protest a farmers' retirement tax, then stage a widespread milk strike, refusing to deliver the milk produced on their farms.

Sicilian women demonstrate in favor of abortion rights and are beaten, arrested, and pelted with stones.

South African politician Helen Suzman wins the UN Human Rights Award for her work against apartheid.

Israel has its first national feminist conference.

Demonstrations by Kuwaiti women put an end to a proposed law banning women from office work.

San Francisco holds the first Take Back the Night march. These marches, which will soon number in the hundreds, protest pornography and violence against women.

The ACDWF is reestablished after being banned during the Cultural Revolution; revolutionary and women's leader Kang Keqing becomes its head.

Dec. A National Women's Congress is held in Medellín, Colombia. Nineteen women's groups meet to discuss abortion and the abuse of sterilization procedures.

Business and Industry

In the United States, 42 million women are in the work force. A survey of 208 unions reveals that 18 have no women members, and 60% have fewer than 10% women members.

New York City admits women to its fire-fighting ranks, as long as they can pass the physical tests to which male fire fighters are subjected; seventy-nine women take the fire fighters' test, and all fail. One of the women, Brenda Berkman, sues successfully for a more reliable test.

Women are 47% of the Thai labor force. They are 16.5% of managers and administrators, 43.6% of clerical workers, and 60% of sales workers.

In Israel, women are 61% of professional and technical workers.

In Japan, 91% of companies have jobs inaccessible to women; 73% start male and female employees at different salaries; 52% do not promote women; 78% do not hire women university graduates; and 77% have different retirement plans for men and women. Only 1.7% of Japanese companies have child-care facilities.

In Austria, working women make 72% as much as men.

The United States outlaws discrimination against women in hiring, firing, forced leave, or benefits for pregnancy or childbirth.

Denmark bans sex discrimination in hiring, promotion, and training. Women are not to be fired for pregnancy.

Women are 49.1% of the agricultural force and 39.2% of the industrial work force in Poland.

Apr. 25 The U.S. Supreme Court rules that women may not be charged more than men for the same pension benefits.

Science and Medicine

Swedish midwives get the right to prescribe oral contraceptives.

The Society of Women Engineers gives its annual Achievement Award to chemist Giuliana Cavaglieri Tesoro for her work on polymers, textiles, and flame-resistant fibers.

Women are 18.3% of Dutch doctors.

Astronomer Margaret Burbidge, anthropologist Mary Haas, chemist Isabella Karle, and biochemist Mary Osborne are elected to the National Academy of Sciences.

Education and Scholarship

U.S. librarian Alicia Page (b. 1921) designs a computing system for interlibrary loans; by 1985, her company will be doing $6 million in sales per year.

U.S. historian Barbara Tuchman publishes *A Distant Mirror*, which uses the story of one nobleman as a focus for various forces at work in the fourteenth century, from the bubonic plague to the Hundred Years' War. Other publications include English childbirth educator Sheila Kitzinger's cross-cultural study *Women as Mothers* and American author and critic Susan Sontag's essay collection *Illness as Metaphor*.

Women are 32.1% of U.S. higher education faculty.

Women are 33% of university students in Iran, 22% in Kenya, and 39% in Austria and 37.7% in of all higher

education students in Sri Lanka.

In South Korea, women are 30% of undergraduate and 16% of graduate students.

Religion

Barbara Andrews (b. c. 1934), who became the first woman minister in the American Lutheran church in 1970, dies.

Norway's Equal Status Act prohibits sexual discrimination in all but religious communities.

U.S. feminist theologian Mary Daly publishes *Gyn/Ecology: The Metaethics of Radical Feminism*. Daly's work breaks down the very structure of words as she tries to create new ways of looking at language, religion, and feminism.

Apr. U.S. Episcopal priest Mary Michael Simpson (b. 1926) becomes the first woman to preach in London's Westminster Abbey.

1979

General Status and Daily Life

In Canada, 59.5% of single or widowed women over sixty-four live at or below the poverty level.

Danish birth control clinics begin distributing contraceptives free of charge.

Egypt's Decree Law 44 requires that wives obey their husbands. President Sadat, influenced by his wife Jihan, decrees that a woman may file for divorce if her husband decides to take a second wife; 3% of Egypt's marriage are polygamous.

The United States introduces a new coin, the Susan B. Anthony dollar, which is withdrawn two years later.

The U.S. National Weather Service begins naming half of all tropical storms and hurricanes after men.

Abortion is legalized on demand in France up to the tenth week after a one-week waiting period. It is also legal when the physical or mental health of the woman will be jeopardized by the pregnancy or when the fetus's health is in question.

A sample of 14,586 marriages in China's Anhui

province reveals that 15% were by free choice, 75% were arranged and agreed to by the bride and groom, and 10% were arranged against the will of the couple.

There are 121,000 day-care centers in England and Wales.

Pakistan passes four laws called the Hadood Ordinances, which govern adultery, fornication, rape, and prostitution. The ordinances ban the testimony of women in certain types of serious criminal trials, such as those for theft, murder, adultery, and rape. A woman must have four adult male Muslim witnesses to prove rape. If the accused rapist is not convicted, the woman can be sentenced to eighty lashes for "false testimony" under the Qazf Ordinance.

Sex-based discrimination is banned by the Nigerian Constitution.

Abortion on demand in the first twelve weeks is legalized in Norway.

In Sweden, 33% of children are born to single or cohabiting mothers; in Norway the percentage is 13.1%. Female mean age at marriage in Norway is twenty-three.

In South Korea, women under twenty-three and men under twenty-seven must have parental consent to marry.

Life expectancy in Japan is 78.9 years for women and 73.4 for men.

In Italy, 78% of women under forty-five in union are using contraception.

The average U.S. marriage lasts 6.6 years.

July 2 The U.S. Supreme Court decision strikes down a law requiring parental consent for minors' abortions.

Government, the Military, and the Law

Of the top 2,147 civil service workers in Switzerland, 1% are women.

Women are 16.1% of Dutch barristers and solicitors.

Spain's Feminist party is formed.

Lea Guido becomes Nicaragua's minister of social welfare.

Women are 49 of the 179 members of Denmark's Folketing (Parliament). In Britain, 51 of the 1,107 members of the House of Lords are women, as are 19 of the 635 members of the House of Commons. The United States has 1 woman senator out of 100 and 16

women representatives out of 435.

Women are 5.9% of the Canadian military; two-thirds of noncombat jobs are open to women.

In Argentina, the marines begin accepting women as cadets.

Three women are elected to Zimbabwe's Parliament.

Pakistani politician and women's leader Begum Liaquat Ali Khan receives the UN's Human Rights Award.

Chinese politician Hao Tianx'u becomes vice-minister of the textile industry.

Jan. The first 1,500 women volunteers join Greece's military.

Apr. 3 Jane Byrne (b. 1934) is elected mayor of Chicago.

May Margaret Thatcher (b. October 13, 1925) becomes Britain's first woman prime minister.

July 19 Maria de Lourdes Pintassilgo becomes Portugal's first woman prime minister.

Aug. 3 U.S. lawyer and politician Patricia Harris, former dean of Howard University Law School and ambassador to Luxembourg, and current secretary of HUD, becomes secretary of HEW. When the department splits into Education and Health and Human Services (HHS), she remains secretary of HHS until 1981.

Dec. Farrokhrou Parsa, Iran's first woman Cabinet minister, is executed by a firing squad for her feminist views, including her belief that schoolgirls should not have to wear the veil and her advocacy of nonsexist teaching materials.

Literature and the Visual Arts

U.S. author Erica Jong publishes *Fanny*, a parody of the novel *Fanny Hill*.

U.S. sculptor Louise Nevelson is elected to the American Academy of Arts and Letters.

Judy Chicago (b. Judy Gerowitz 1939) unveils her massive feminist artwork *The Dinner Party*. The room-sized sculpture features a forty-six-foot triangular table, set with symbolic runners and thirty-nine plates for 39 prominent women throughout history, and a floor decorated with the names of 999 notable women.

New poetry includes American Mary Oliver's *Twelve Moons*, Alice Walker's *Good Night Willie Lee, I'll See*

You in the Morning, American Diana O'Hehir's *The Power to Change Geography*, and Israeli Dahlia Ravikovitch's (b. 1936) *A Dress of Fire*.

U.S. novelist Toni Morrison publishes *Tar Baby*. Other new novels include Italian journalist Oriana Fallaci's *Un uomo* (*A Man*) and Canadian Margaret Atwood's *Life Before Man*.

Performing Arts and Entertainment

French composer, conductor, and music teacher Nadia Boulanger (b. 1887) dies. A holder of multiple doctorates and winner of numerous awards, including a commandership of the Legion of Honor, she taught music at Radcliffe, Wellesley, Juilliard, and the Paris Conservatoire, numbering such notable composers as Aaron Copland and Lennox Berkeley among her pupils.

Belgian filmmaker Chantal Akermann makes *Les rendezvous d'Anna*, which will win the Best Director awards at the 1980 Paris and Chicago film festivals.

Portuguese journalist Maria Antonia Palla is acquitted of "outrage against public morals" and "incitement to crime" after producing a television documentary on abortion.

Italy's only women's radio station, Rome's Radio Donna, is bombed by neofascists.

Swiss composer Tona Schercher-Hsiao composes *Lo* for trombone and strings.

Sally Field wins the Best Actress Oscar for her performance in *Norma Rae*. Other new movies include *Anna*, starring Harriet Andersson; *The Rose*, starring American pop singer Bette Midler (b. 1945) as a self-destructive rock singer; *Revenge*, directed by Lina Wertmuller and starring Sophia Loren; *The China Syndrome*, starring Jane Fonda as a television reporter uncovering safety hazards at a nuclear power plant; *Manhattan*, starring Diane Keaton and Meryl Streep (b. June 22, 1949); *Kramer vs. Kramer*, starring Streep as a mother who leaves her family; *10*, starring Bo Derek and Julie Andrews; and *Alien*, starring Sigourney Weaver as a resourceful crew member on a space vessel attacked by monsters.

Athletics and Exploration

U.S. runner Joan Benoit (b. May 16, 1957) wins the women's section of the Boston Marathon.

June 16 American Evelyn Ashford becomes the first woman to run the 100-meter dash in under eleven seconds.

July 7 Czech-American tennis player Martina Navratilova defeats Chris Evert at Wimbledon. Navratilova, who won the title in 1978 as well, will win it again every year from 1982 to 1987 and in 1990 as well. She will also win the U.S. Open in 1983, 1984, 1986, and 1987.

Aug. 20 U.S. swimmer Diana Nyad swims from the Bahamas to the United States, a distance of 60 miles.

Sept. 9 U.S. tennis player Tracy Austin wins the U.S. Open. She will win it again in 1981.

Oct. 21 Grete Waitz wins the women's section of the New York Marathon.

Activism

U.S. folk singer Joan Baez cofounds the human rights commission Humanitas.

U.S. feminist Kate Millett visits Iran to work for women's rights under the Khomeini government but is expelled from the country.

Egyptian feminist Nawal El Saadawi (b. October 27, 1930) publishes *The Hidden Face of Eve: Women in the Arab World*, which discusses rape, female genital mutilation, emphasis on virginity and family honor, and women in Arab history, religion, and literature.

Simone de Beauvoir, Christine Delphy, and Monique Wittig establish the journal *Questions feministes*.

The Lesbian Feminist Alliance is founded in Kansai, Japan.

Women's groups in Indonesia operate 299 orphanages.

Brazil's day-care movement begins at the First Congress of São Paolo Women.

The Afghanistan Women's Revolutionary League begins working against Soviet occupation.

Mar. 8 Six thousand women march in Tehran, Iran, to protest the oppressive policies of the new leader, Ayatollah Ruhollah Khomeini. They chant, "In the dawn of freedom, there is no freedom." On March 10, 15,000 women seize Iran's Palace of Justice to protest the loss of their rights, and on March 13, two women attack Khomeini's spokesman, one with a gun and one with a knife.

Business and Industry

Women are 13.8% of the work force in Guatemala. They are 34% of clerical workers and 40% of professional and technical workers.

Cindy Pawlcyn cofounds Real Restaurants, a company that owns several restaurants in the San Francisco Bay area, including Fog City Diner and Mustards. Other notable Bay area restaurants, including China Moon and Greens, have been or will be founded by women.

Women make 84.7% as much as men in Denmark, 76% as much in Australia, 57.6% as much in Ireland, 72.6% as much in West Germany, 89.3% as much in Sweden (for manual labor), 70.7% as much in Great Britain, and 59.7% as much in the United States.

Austria and Sweden pass equal pay laws.

In the United States, 24,000 of the 1,500,000 building trades union members are women.

United Airlines is ruled discriminatory in its weight guidelines for flight attendants.

Women are more than 41% of the British work force but only 13% of employers and managers and only 9% of skilled manual laborers.

In Israel, women hold 9% of managerial, 28% of sales, and 57% of clerical positions.

Two hundred Korean women workers go on a fast and occupy the YH textile plant in Seoul to protest the company's plan to relocate. In the resulting police assault on the plant, one protester, Kim Kyong Suk, is killed, prompting nationwide outrage and rioting.

In Afghanistan, women are 1.5% of sales workers, 8.5% of clerical workers, and 13.5% of professional and technical workers.

Women are 33.4% of the El Salvadoran work force. They are 16% of administrators and managers, 40.6% of clerical workers, 42.8% of professional and technical workers, and 69% of sales workers.

Women are 28.3% of Denmark's agricultural laborers; 81% of these are unpaid family laborers. Women are also 69% of Danish textile and garment workers. They are 21% of Australia's agricultural laborers, 24.5% of the Mexican labor force, and 51% of the Russian work force.

In Poland, 60% of working women work in service, clerical, or sales jobs.

Ninety percent of female textile workers in Lebanon are paid less than the minimum wage.

Science and Medicine

U.S. physicist Katherine Blodgett, who invented the nonreflecting glass used in camera lenses, picture frames, and various scientific disciplines, dies.

Women are 19.25% of doctors in India and 93% of nurses in Australia.

The Society of Women Engineers gives its annual Achievement Award to U.S. public works manager Jessie Cambra, head of the Road Department of Alameda County, California, with its 547 miles of roads and $12 million budget. She is the first woman to graduate in engineering from the University of California, Berkeley, and the first woman director of the American Public Works Association.

French engineer Henriette Magna copatents a computer data-carrier for recording information.

Nine Soviet engineers, including three women (Elena Kistova, Natalya Lukicheva, and Elena Jurova), patent a pressure-sensitive semiconductor structure.

The IEEE has only six women fellows.

Five family-planning centers open in Greece, bringing the national total to seven.

Mar. 21 English paleontologist Mary Leakey is reported to have discovered the world's oldest biped footprints in an ancient lava field.

Dec. England has 1,743 family-planning centers for National Health Service patients.

Education and Scholarship

Women are 70% of teachers in Poland, 71% in Sri Lanka (but only 2.5% of professors), and 60% in Australia. Women are 33.3% of U.S. higher education faculty.

Women are 46.7% of university students in Egypt.

In Indonesia, 49% of women and 70.9% of men are literate; 31% of Palestinian women in refugee camps are illiterate.

In Saudi Arabia, 19% of women and 48% of men are literate. Women are not permitted to study engineering at universities; at many universities, women are allowed to use the library only one day a week, when men are not admitted. Some schools teach women via closed-circuit television to maintain strict segregation of the sexes.

U.S. women earn 95.1% of college degrees in home economics and 94.6% of those in library science. This is the first year that more U.S. women than men have entered college.

Religion

U.S. religious scholar Elaine Pagels publishes *Gnostic Gospels*.

U.S. Mormon Sonia Johnson is excommunicated for criticizing her church's antifeminist stance.

Dec. 10 Yugoslavian nun Mother Teresa accepts the Nobel Peace Prize; she founded a religious order in India that now controls 700 shelters and clinics.

1980

General Status and Daily Life

The use of oral contraceptives by women under sixteen is banned in Hungary.

Patria potestas, the supreme authority of the male head of household, is abolished in Nicaragua.

In Brazil, 25% of hospital beds are occupied by women suffering complications after illegal abortions. There are approximately 3 million illegal abortions per year. In Colombia, 280,000 illegal abortions are performed; one-fourth of Egyptian pregnancies are illegally aborted. In Canada, abortions must be approved by a medical panel, but only 30% of public hospitals have abortion approval committees. In the United States, 1,553,890 abortions are performed, 91% of them in the first trimester. In India, a woman dies about every ten minutes from a botched abortion. Abortion is legal in India in many cases, but many women in rural areas have no access to clinics.

In the United States, 18.4% of births are to unwed mothers, and 40.8% of births are to mothers under age twenty.

Divorce by mutual consent is legalized in China. Reconciliation is encouraged if only one spouse wants a divorce. Men are usually not permitted to divorce their wives during a pregnancy or the year after delivery.

In a landmark decision, an English court of appeals awards custody to a lesbian mother.

A Greek woman attacks and wounds her rapist; he is sentenced to 5 1/2 months in jail, while she is sentenced to three years.

The FBI estimates that a rape occurs every six minutes in the United States, noting that many rapes are not reported and neglecting to include marital rape in its statistics. At least half of all rape victims are attacked by people they know. Arrests are made in 38% of reported rape cases.

Sweden has the highest incidence of reported rape in Scandinavia, 15.8 per 100,000 population. This year, 885 rapes are reported to the police. Two thousand rapes are reported in Indonesia, and 973 rapes are reported in Mexico City alone. About 7,000–10,000 sexual assaults occur in Israel.

Saudi Arabia's King rules that brides and grooms must be permitted to meet each other before the wedding. Most women marry by age sixteen and are bought by the groom with a bride-price.

In Indonesia, 66% of women and 5% of men marry before age seventeen.

Mexico's first crisis center for women opens.

An Italian man is acquitted on the grounds of self-defense after shooting a lesbian. He claims that her very existence threatens him.

Summer The U.S. Supreme Court upholds limits on Medicaid funds for abortions, even when the abortions are medically necessary.

Nov. Contraception is legalized in Ireland for use by married couples.

Government, the Military, and the Law

South African politician Margaret Ballinger (b. 1894) dies. A member of Parliament for twenty-two years, she helped to form South Africa's Liberal party in 1953.

In Austria, twelve of the fifty-eight Bundesrat members, ten of the fifty-seven National Assembly members, and twenty-one of one hundred provincial leaders are women.

Republican party co-chair Mary Crisp refuses to attend the national convention after her party withdraws its support for the ERA.

Princess Victoria becomes heir to the throne of Sweden after the Act of Succession gives the monarch's firstborn child of either sex the right to rule.

Women are 6% of Spain's lawyers.

Senegal gets its first nine female police officers and inspectors.

Nobuko Takahashi becomes Japan's first female ambassador when she is posted to Denmark.

Vigdis Finnbogadottir (b. 1930) becomes Iceland's first woman president.

Women in the Israeli military are permitted in only 270 of 850 job categories, none of them involving combat. Half of the categories open to women are clerical, and two—typing and folding parachutes—are exclusively female.

Canadian journalist and politician Jeanne Sauvé becomes speaker of the House of Commons.

In the United States, women earn 48% of law degrees, but a study of Harvard Law School graduates seven years after their graduation finds that 25% of the men but only 1% of the women are partners in their firms.

Women are 9.5% of the army and 5% of the navy in Greece.

Indira Gandhi is reelected prime minister of India after being out of office since 1977.

Apr. 30 Queen Juliana of the Netherlands abdicates in favor of her daughter Beatrix (b. 1938).

Sept. Sri Lankan prime minister Sirimavo Bandaranaike is found guilty of misconduct and cast out of Parliament.

Literature and the Visual Arts

New poetry includes Lucille Clifton's *Two-Headed Woman*, Diane Wakoski's *Cap of Darkness*, Chilean Marjorie Agosin's *Conchali*, and American Rita Dove's (b. 1952) *The Yellow House on the Corner*.

Mar. 6 French novelist Marguerite Yourcenar becomes the first female member of the Académie Française in its 345-year history. The Académie is charged with preserving the purity of the French language.

Performing Arts and Entertainment

New movies include *Urban Cowboy*, with Debra Winger; *Private Benjamin*, with Goldie Hawn as a pampered woman who joins the army; and *Coal Miner's Daughter*, with Sissy Spacek giving an Oscar-winning performance as country singer Loretta Lynn (b. 1935). One of the great comic triumphs of the year is *9-5*, starring Jane Fonda, Dolly Parton, and Lily Tomlin as office workers plagued by a "sexist egotistical lying hypocritical bigot"; they get even with him and feminize their workplace.

A women's film group, Cine Mujer, is founded in Colombia.

English composer and conductor Ruth Gipps composes her fifth symphony.

Athletics and Exploration

U.S. mountain climber Arlene Blum leads a joint Indian-American women's expedition to Gangotri Glacier and publishes *Annapurna: A Woman's Place*.

Jan. 26 American Mary Decker (b. August 4, 1958) becomes the first woman to run a mile in under 4 1/2 minutes.

Winter At the Lake Placid Olympics, the pairs figure skating gold goes to Irina Rodnina and Alexander Zaitsev; Rodnina has now won this event for three Olympics in a row. Soviet skaters Natalia Linichuk and Gennadi Karponosov take the gold in ice dancing, and East German Annette Potzsch wins the women's event. In luge, Vera Zozulia of the Soviet Union takes the gold. In downhill skiing, Annemarie Proell Moser of Austria takes the gold, followed by Hanni Wenzel of Liechtenstein, who wins the slalom and giant slalom.
In Nordic skiing, Raisa Smetanina of the Soviet Union wins the 5-kilometer race, followed by Finland's Hilkka Riihivuori and Czechoslovakia's Kvetoslava Jeriova. Barbara Petzold of East Germany wins the 10-kilometer race; Finns Riihivuori and Helena Takalo take silver and bronze. The 4 x 5-kilometer relay is won by the East German team of Marlies Rostock, Carol Anding, Veronica Hesse-Schmidt, and Petzold; the Soviet team of Nina Baldycheva, Nina Rocheva, Galina Kulakova, and Smetanina takes the silver, and Norwegians Inger Helene Nybraaten, Anne Jahren, Brit Pettersen, and Berit Aunli take the bronze.
East Germany's Karin Enke wins the 500-meter speed skating race with an Olympic record time of 41.78 seconds. The 1,000 is won by Soviet skater Natalia Petruseva, who also takes a bronze in the 500. Annie Borckink of the Netherlands wins the 1,500 meters, and Norway's Bjoerg-Eva Jensen wins the 3,000.

Summer Several nations, led by the United States, refuse to attend the Moscow Olympics as a protest against the Soviet Union's occupation of Afghanistan.
The field hockey gold is won by the team from Zimbabwe. The Soviets win the basketball, volleyball,

and team handball golds; Soviet handball players Lyubov Berezhnaya, Zinaida Turchina, Tatiana Makarez, Ljudmila Bobrus, Aldona Chesaitite, and Larissa Karlova were also on the gold medal team of 1976. Some members of the second-place Yugoslav team, including Mirjana Ognjenovic, Svetlana Anastasovski, Svetlana Kitic, Biserka Visnjic, and Jasna Merdan, will remain on their team to take the gold in 1984.

In rowing, the single scull is won by Romania's Sanda Toma, and the double sculls are won by Soviets Yelena Khloptseva and Larissa Popova. East Germany wins the quadruple sculls, coxed four, and eight oars, as well as all the other races: Birgit Fischer wins the 500-meter kayak singles, and Carsta Genauss and Martina Bischof win the 500-meter kayak pairs. The coxless pair gold goes to Ute Steindorf and Cornelia Klier.

In the equestrian events, which are open to both sexes, Austria's Elisabeth Theurer wins the gold for individual dressage. The Soviet team dressage gold medalists include a woman, Vera Misevich. Anna Casagrande and Marina Sciocchetti are on the silver-medal Italian three-day event team.

Keto Losaberidze of the Soviet Union wins the women's archery competition. France's Pascale Trinquet-Hachin wins the individual foil fencing gold; her team, which also includes Brigitte Latrille-Gaudin, Christine Muzio, Veronique Brouquier, and Isabelle Regard, wins the team foil gold as well. Second place in the team event goes to the Soviet team, which includes 1976 medalists Yelena Belova-Novikova, Valentina Sidorova, and Nailia Guiliazova.

The Soviet Union wins the gymnastics gold with its team of Yelena Davydova, Marija Filatova (bronze medalist in the uneven bars), Nelli Kim, Yelena Naimuschina, Natalia Shaposhnikova, and Stella Zakharova. Davydova wins the all-around and takes a silver in the balance beam; Kim wins the floor exercise, and Shaposhnikova wins the vault, takes a bronze in the beam, and ties for a bronze in the floor exercise with East German Maxi Gnauck. Gnauck wins the bars and takes a silver in the all-around. The sensation of the 1976 games, Romanian Nadia Comaneci, the European champion in 1975, 1977, and 1979, wins only one event, the beam, and takes silvers in the team competition and floor exercise and a bronze in the all-around.

In track and field, Soviet runner Lyudmila Kondratyeva wins the 100-meter dash, followed by East Germans Marlies Gohr and Ingrid Auerswald. Another East German, Bärbel Eckert Wockel, wins the 200 meters. East German Marita Koch takes gold in the 400 meters and runs on the silver-medal 4 x 400-meter relay team. Soviet Nadezhda Olizarenko sets a world record in the 800 meters and takes a bronze in the 1,500, a race won by her teammate Tatiana Kazankina. Another Soviet, Vera Komisova, wins the 100-meter hurdles with an Olympic record time and runs on the second-place 4 x 100-meter relay team.

The 4 x 100-meter relay is won by the East German

team of Auerswald, Gohr, Eckert Wockel, and Romy Muller. The Soviets win the 4 x 400; this time the team is composed of Tatiana Prorochenko (a bronze medalist in the 4 x 100 in 1976), Tatiana Goishchik, Nina Zyuskova, and Irina Nazarova.

Sara Simeoni of Italy wins the high jump, setting an Olympic record. Another Olympic record is set by long jump gold medalist Tatiana Kolpakova, whose winning jump is nine inches farther than her personal best. East Germans Ilona Slupianek and Evelin Jahl-Schlaak win the shot put and discus. Cuba's Maria Colon wins the javelin, and Soviet athlete Nadejda Tkachenko wins the pentathlon.

The swimming events are dominated by East Germany. Barbara Krause wins the 100- and 200-meter freestyles. Caren Metschuk wins the 100-meter butterfly and takes silver in the 100-meter freestyle. Petra Schneider wins the 400-meter individual medley and takes a silver in the 400-meter freestyle. Ute Geweniger wins the 100-meter breaststroke, and Rica Reinisch wins the 100- and 200-meter backstrokes. Ines Geissler wins the 200-meter butterfly. Freestyle swimmer Ines Diers has plenty of medals to take home: a bronze in the 100 meters, silvers in the 200 and 800, and a gold in the 400. In fact, only two individual swimming golds go to non-East Germans. Australia's Michelle Ford wins the 800-meter freestyle (and takes a bronze in the 200-meter butterfly), and Soviet swimmer Lina Kochushite wins the 200-meter breaststroke.

The East Germans also win the two relays. Krause, Metschuk, Diers, and Sarina Hulsenbeck win the 4 x 100 freestyle relay, and Reinisch, Geweniger, Metschuk, and Andrea Pollack (the silver medalist in the 200-meter butterfly) win the medley. Soviet diver Irina Kalinina wins the springboard gold, and East German Martina Jaschke emerges victorious in the platform competition.

Activism

After two women are murdered by their husbands, Brazilian feminists establish the Center for the Defense of the Rights of Women.

María Magdalena Henriquez, cofounder of the Comisión de Derechos Humanos de El Salvador (El Salvador Human Rights Commission), is assassinated.

Shramik Stree Mukti Parishad, an organization that fights economic discrimination, wife beating, and traditional oppression in India, is formed.

An "underground railroad" is formed in Israel by Arab, Jewish, and Christian feminists to rescue young women threatened with murder to protect "family honor."

The Native American feminist group Ohoyo ("woman" in Choctaw) holds a national meeting in Albuquerque.

In the United States, the first conference of the National Coalition Against Domestic Violence is held.

Russian feminist Natalia Malakhovskaya, artist Tatyana Mamanova, and poet Julia Voznesenskaya write *Women and Russia*, a document critical of the Soviet Union's sexism. They smuggle it out of the country and are later banished.

Jan. Women demonstrate for abortion rights in Brazil.

Apr. 27 Naheed, an Afghani schoolgirl, leads a children's protest against the Soviet occupation of her country; seventy children are killed.

Business and Industry

U.S. secretary Bette Nesmith Graham (b. March 23, 1924), inventor of Liquid Paper, dies, leaving a personal fortune of $50 million. She leaves half of it to charity and half to her only child, ex-Monkee Michael Nesmith.

Women are 40.5% of the labor force in Portugal (11.9% of clerical workers and 74% of unpaid family workers), 12.9% in Kuwait (77.6% of them non-Kuwaiti), 31% in Cuba (14.8% of agricultural workers and 93% of tobacco workers), and 29.8% of agricultural laborers in Norway (68.7% of them unpaid family laborers).

Women are 37.6% of the labor force in South Korea. They are 32% of professional and technical workers, 32.7% of clerical workers, and 58% of service workers. Many women in manufacturing jobs earn about sixty-three cents an hour.

Women are 19% of the work force in Afghanistan, 7% in Algeria, 26% in Argentina, 40% in Australia, 23% in Brazil, 36% in Chile, 38% in China, 25% in Colombia, 38% in Denmark, 26.6% in Ecuador, 8% in Egypt, 47.1% in Finland, 44% in France, 42% in Ghana, 33% in Greece, 32% in India, 14% in Iran, 36% in Israel, 29% in Italy, 33% in Kenya, 5.7% in Libya, 16% in Morocco, 30.4% in the Netherlands, 39% in Nepal, 22% in Nicaragua, 40% in Nigeria, 11% in Pakistan, 46% in Poland, 45% in Romania (40.3% of industrial laborers), 5% in Saudi Arabia, 38% in Senegal, 35% in South Africa, 25% in Sri Lanka (90% of tea pickers), 11% in Sudan, 44.2% in the United States, 51% in the USSR, and 38% in West Germany.

Women agricultural workers make half as much as men in Ghana and 40% as much in El Salvador. In nonagricultural jobs, Danish women earn 84% as much as men, and Egyptian women earn 63% as much.

West Germany, Sweden, and the Netherlands pass laws banning gender discrimination in the workplace.

American Michaela Walsh founds Women's World Banking to provide loans to women with no credit or collateral; by 1991 the organization will have helped 500,000 women entrepreneurs worldwide.

In the United States, women earn 21% of M.B.A.s.

New EEOC guidelines ban sexual harassment.

U.S. fashion designer Jhane Barnes (b. March 4, 1954) becomes the first woman to win the Coty Award for menswear.

A survey of 400 Dutch women finds that 90% have been sexually harassed at work.

In Gdansk, Poland, 3,000 women defy a row of tanks to hand out flowers and Solidarity literature.

About 40% of working women in the Bangkok, Thailand, area are prostitutes.

Women workers make 69% as much as men in France, 78% as much in Israel, 50% as much in Peru, and about 85% as much in Norway.

Jan. In the Soviet Union, 460 occupations are closed to women on the grounds that the jobs are too dangerous, although many hazardous traditional occupations are left open to them.

Jan. Women are 17.8% of Hungarian construction workers.

Mar. 20 Linda Eaton, Iowa City's first woman fire fighter, is awarded damages after a legal battle over whether she can breast-feed her baby at work.

July 3 Two accused prostitutes in Iran are buried up to their necks and stoned to death.

Dec. Polish labor organizer Halina Bortnowska leads a steelworkers' strike in Cracow.

Science and Medicine

U.S. hematologist and geneticist Eloise Giblett is admitted to the National Academy of Sciences.

In South Korea, women are 13.6% of doctors.

The SWE gives its annual Achievement Award to metallurgist Carolyn Preece.

In the United States, women earn 33% of medical degrees.

Women in Senegal get the right to train as civil

engineers at the Polytechnic School.

U.S. computer programmer Dona Bailey goes to work for Atari and codesigns the arcade game "Centipede." Other arcade games designed by women include "Joust," whose graphics were created by Janice Hendricks.

Sept. 22 Procter and Gamble announces the recall of Rely tampons after tampon use is linked to Toxic Shock Syndrome (TSS), a potentially fatal condition. On October 20, the FDA calls for warning labels about TSS on tampon packages.

Education and Scholarship

U.S. feminist critics Sandra Gilbert (b. 1936) and Susan Gubar publish an important study of women's literature, *The Madwoman in the Attic*.

In Japan, women are 22% of university students and 88.1% of junior college students. Women are 17% of university students in Libya, 46% of full-time university students in Canada, and 30% of university students in Switzerland.

In South Korea, women are 15.2% of university professors and 28.7% of teachers. Women are 4% of Danish university professors and 79% of Swedish teachers.

In Kuwait, 28.91% of women over twenty have university degrees, but more than 80% of those are non-Kuwaiti; 50.4% of Kuwaiti women and 77.1% of non-Kuwaiti resident women are literate, compared with 77.39% and 75% for men.

Saudi Arabia has 11,847 female teachers in government schools.

Women are 33.3% of the United States' 1,127,000 higher-education faculty.

One-fourth of China's college graduates are women.

Religion

American Dorothy Day (b. 1897) dies. She worked for pacifism, civil rights, tolerance of Jews, and rights for migrant workers, being jailed more than once for her activism, but she is best known for the newspaper she founded, the *Catholic Worker*.

July 5 Iranian women protest Islamic dress codes in Tehran.

July 17 Marjorie Matthews becomes the first woman bishop of the American Methodist church.

Dec. 4 Four U.S. nuns helping El Salvadoran rebels are killed by the government.

1981

General Status and Daily Life

Eight million women are raising children alone in the United States; only 59% are entitled to child support, and only 72% of those have received any payment at all. Most of those who have received payment have not received the full amount.

A Finnish study shows that women and girls do twice as much housework as men and boys.

In Guatemala, 18% of women age fifteen to forty-four in union use contraception.

Greece's Ministry of Social Welfare runs 1,026 day-care centers which serve 60,000 children. Norway has 78,189 day-care slots, or about one for every four children under age seven.

One-third of Canadian and one-half of Swedish marriages end in divorce.

The U.S. Congress withdraws Medicaid funding for abortions to end pregnancies caused by rape or incest.

About 2,500–3,000 cases of domestic violence are reported to Swedish police; an estimated 99% of such crimes go unreported.

Sweden begins providing government funds to women's shelters.

The average woman in India has eight pregnancies between the ages of fifteen and forty-five. About 3.5 million women are sterilized each year in India.

Two Javanese women are sentenced to eight months in jail and twenty months on probation for lesbian acts; one of them is subjected to surgical and medical treatment to "cure" her.

Abortion is legalized in the Netherlands during the first two trimesters. Approval by two doctors and a five-day waiting period are required. Most women who have abortions in Dutch clinics are actually from other countries with more restrictive abortion laws.

Kenya's Law of Succession gives women equal inheritance rights.

Seventy percent of Italian voters favor keeping abortion legal.

Iran makes lesbians subject to execution after three warnings.

Sixty percent of Irish women in union age fofteen to forty-four use contraception; 50–80% of pharmacists refuse to sell contraceptives.

Life expectancy in most parts of the world is higher for women than for men. However, in India, it is 51.6 years for women and 52.6 for men.

In Peru, about 80% of reported injuries each day are the result of wife battering.

This year, 20,500 Spanish women seeking abortions travel from Spain, where abortion is punishable by up to six years in prison, to Great Britain, where the procedure is legal.

The European Court of Justice upholds a British law giving the father no right to determine whether or not a baby shall be carried to term.

Mar. 23 The U.S. Supreme Court upholds a law requiring doctors to notify a minor's parents before performing an abortion.

Government, the Military, and the Law

Chinese revolutionary and political leader Soong Ching-ling (b. 1893), sister of Soong Mei-ling, dies.

Two of the fifteen members of Italy's supreme court, the Consiglio Superiore della Magistratura, are women.

In Nicaragua, 30% of the Sandinista army is female.

In the Soviet Union, 26.6% of Party Congress delegates and 3.1% of Politburo members are women.

Gro Harlem Bruntland becomes Norway's first female prime minister.

Italian Diadora Bassani's effort to enroll in the Naval Academy ends in a court decision barring women from the military.

Women are 40% of government employees in Sudan.

French politician Yvette Roudy becomes secretary of state for women's rights.

Jan. 25 Mao's widow, "Gang of Four" member Jiang Qing, arrested on October 12, 1976, is sentenced to death

for persecuting 700,000 and executing 35,000 during China's Cultural Revolution. She is dragged from the room, screaming, "It is right to rebel! Making revolution is no crime!" On January 25, 1983, her sentence is commuted to life imprisonment.

July 29 In the most talked-about royal wedding of the decade, perhaps of the century, Britain's Prince Charles and Lady Diana Spencer marry at St. Paul's Cathedral. The marriage will produce two sons but result in a separation much covered in the tabloids.

Sept. 25 U.S. judge Sandra Day O'Connor (b. 1930), nominated July 7, becomes the first woman justice of the U.S. Supreme Court.

Oct. Greek film actress Melina Mercouri (b. 1923) becomes Greece's minister of culture and sciences, a post she will hold until 1989. She begins fighting an unsuccessful battle to get the British to return the Elgin marbles, Greek carvings and statues pillaged and sent to Britain in the early nineteenth century.

Literature and the Visual Arts

In the United States, women are 50.2% of reporters and editors.

Joyce Carol Oates publishes the short story collection *A Sentimental Education.*

New U.S. poetry includes Gwendolyn Brooks's *To Disembark*, Linda Gregg's (b. 1942) *Too Bright to See*, Heather McHugh's *A World of Difference*, and Adrienne Rich's *A Wild Patience Has Taken Me Thus.*

Beth Henley publishes *Crimes of the Heart.*

Performing Arts and Entertainment

English ballerina Margot Fonteyn, at sixty-two, dances the part of Lady Capulet in Nureyev's *Romeo and Juliet* at Milan's La Scala.

Tyne Daly and Sharon Gless debut as television cops in "Cagney & Lacey."

English filmmaker Sally Potter makes her first movie, *The Gold Diggers*, starring Julie Christie.

Brazil's first television program produced by and for women, "TV Mulher," debuts.

Elizabeth Taylor stars on Broadway in a revival of Lillian Hellman's *The Little Foxes.*

Diane Keaton and Maureen Stapleton (as U.S. anarchist Emma Goldman) star in *Reds*. Other new films include *Raiders of the Lost Ark*, starring Karen Allen; *The French Lieutenant's Woman*, starring Meryl Streep; and *On Golden Pond*, starring Katharine Hepburn and Jane Fonda. Hepburn wins the Best Actress Oscar for *Pond*.

Popular songs in the United States include Kim Carnes's "Bette Davis Eyes."

Mar. 26 U.S. comedian Carol Burnett wins $1.6 million in a libel suit against *The National Enquirer*. She donates the money to charity.

Athletics and Exploration

Spanish bullfighter Juanita Cruz, the first professional female matador, dies.

The all-male Explorers Club, which has included such notable men as Theodore Roosevelt, Roald Amundsen, and Sir Edmund Hillary, decides to admit women as members.

U.S. golfer Pat Bradley wins the U.S. Open.

U.S. tennis player Billie Jean King is sued by a former lover, Marilyn Barnett, and admits publicly that she is bisexual.

Since 1974, the number of U.S. schools offering women's athletic scholarships has risen from 60 to 500.

Apr. 4 Susan Brown, coxswain, is first woman to compete in the tradition-laden Oxford-Cambridge rowing match on the Thames.

Activism

U.S. radical feminist Andrea Dworkin (b. September 26, 1946) publishes *Pornography: Men Possessing Women*.

Italian activist Teresita de Angelis founds the National Association of Housewives to work for pensions for housewives over fifty-five.

The first lesbian feminist magazine in Athens, Greece, *Labyris*, begins publication.

An Afghanistan Women's Revolutionary League leader, Farida Ahmadi, is captured and tortured by the Soviets but escapes.

Thai activist Kanitha Wichiencharoen opens the country's first battered women's shelter.

Gloria T. Hull, Patricia Bell Scott, and Barbara Smith edit *All the Women Are White, All the Blacks Are Men, But Some of Us Are Brave: Black Women's Studies*.

Mar. 8 Colombia's Women's Center opens in Bogotá.

Mar. 31 Dutch women go on strike to protest the waiting period and two-doctor approval clauses in their country's new abortion law.

July Colombia hosts the first All Latin American Women's Conference, which has 250 delegates from twenty-five countries.

Aug. 26 To mark the anniversary of women's suffrage and to show support for the ERA, women chain themselves to the White House fence.

Sept. Egyptian feminist Nawal El Saadawi is arrested for publishing articles that criticize President Sadat's policies; she is one of many feminists arrested at about this time. She is imprisoned for eighty days and released only after Sadat's assassination.

Oct. 14 Polish women seize factories to protest food shortages.

Nov. Peruvian feminists march to protest pornography and violence against women.

Dec. South African civil rights activist Winnie Mandela is banned for the fifth time.

Business and Industry

In the United States, 25% of families are supported by women.

In the United States, women are 98.4% of kindergarten and preschool teachers, 45.4% of sales workers, 80.5% of clerical workers, 61% of textile workers, 97.6% of in-home child-care workers, 19.1% of janitors, 47.3% of bartenders, 97.2% of dental assistants, 89.3% of hairdressers and cosmetologists, and 25.5% of farm laborers. Thirty percent of employed women work part-time. Female elementary school teachers make 82% as much as men; female lawyers make 71% as much as male lawyers; female engineers make 68% as much as male engineers; female sales workers make 52% as much as their male counterparts.

Women make 84.5% as much as men in Denmark, 75% as much in New Zealand, 61% as much in Finland, 72.5% as much in West Germany, 69.5% as much in Britain, 85% as much in Italy, and 59.2% as much in the United States. Women migrant workers in Ecuador make half as much as men.

Americans Caroline Leonetti Ahmanson (b. 1918) and

Jean A. Crockett (b. c. 1919) become the first two women to chair regional Federal Reserve Banks.

In Brazil, 27% of working women are domestic servants; 9% are elementary school teachers; 6% are seamstresses.

A survey of Japanese businesses hiring university graduates reveals that 24% hire both sexes, 5% hire women only, and 71% hire men only. Of those that hire both, 39% give different training to men and women; 21% give women no training at all. Two percent force women to retire if they marry, become pregnant, or give birth. Nineteen percent have different retirement ages for men and women, and 45% do not offer promotions to women. Eighty-three percent of the businesses have male-only positions, from which women are barred for reasons ranging from physical weakness and "lack of skill" to "lack of good judgment."

In Finland, 76% of mothers with preschool children are employed.

In China, women are generally assigned jobs worth fewer work points, such as tea picking and weeding, while men are assigned higher-value jobs like plowing and harvesting. Maternity leave with full pay ranges from fifty-six days to six months; retirement age for women is five years earlier than for men.

Women are 24.2% of the work force in New Zealand, 36.7% in Yugoslavia, 40.7% in Canada, 25% in Lebanon, and 28.5% in Peru. They are 79% of India's agricultural workers.

Soviet women are entitled to 112 days of paid maternity leave, an additional two weeks of paid leave for difficult pregnancy or labor, a year of leave at partial pay, and up to two years in some cases of leave with no pay. Women lose no seniority if they take maternity leave.

The Japanese Supreme Court bans discriminatory pension plans.

Women are 28% of Japanese union members. They are 38.7% of the labor force, 80.7% of the unpaid labor force, and 52.3% of clerical workers.

Women are 25.3% of the Moroccan agricultural work force, 30% of scientific workers, 69% of textile workers, and 90.6% of domestic servants.

An estimated 80% of women workers in New Zealand are victms of sexual harassment.

Science and Medicine

The Society of Women Engineers gives its annual Achievement Award to biomedical engineer Thelma Estrin, the first woman to be certified as a clinical engineer, for her work applying computer analysis to neurophysiological research. Estrin has been the president of the Biomedical Engineering Society and executive vice president of the IEEE.

Three U.S. women join the National Academy of Sciences: molecular biologist and immunologist Marian Elliott Koshland, astronomer Vera Rubin, and biochemist Thressa Campbell Stadtman.

U.S. artist Nancy Burson copatents a computer process and apparatus for altering and "aging" pictures of faces. This technique will be used by plastic surgeons and by law enforcement agencies.

Women are 25% of Algeria's doctors and 34.3% of Cuba's public health workers.

In the United States, women earn 37% of B.S. degrees and fewer than 5% of engineering doctorates.

Education and Scholarship

Elaine Marks and Isabelle de Courtivron edit New French Feminisms, a collection of texts from the contemporary women's movement in France.

Women are 55% of university students in Sweden.

Girls in China are educated less than boys; most girls receive about a sixth grade education.

In U.S. higher education, women are 10% of full professors, 21% of associate professors, 36% of assistant professors, and 51% of instructors and lecturers. Only the first two groups have tenure; 60% of male faculty members are tenured. Women are 33.5% of higher education faculty.

Simone de Beauvoir publishes a controversial book about her longtime companion Jean Paul Sartre, Les cérémonies des adieux.

Religion

U.S. theologians Rosemary Radford Ruether and Rosemary Skinner Keller edit Women and Religion in America, volume 1. The second volume will be issued in 1988. Other works of religious scholarship include Blu Greenburg's On Women and Judaism: A View from Tradition, Christine Downing's The Goddess: Mythological Images of the Feminine, Jean McMahon Humez's Gifts of Power: The Writings of Rebecca Jackson, Black Visionary, Shaker Eldress, and Judith Ochshorn's The Female Experience and the Nature of the Divine.

1982

General Status and Daily Life

The average U.S. woman is 22.3 years old at her first marriage; 56% of women ages fifteen to forty-four are in union. Cohabitation is becoming more common.

A study of 2,500 women in Quebec reveals that 70% have experienced sexual harassment.

Adultery is decriminalized in Greece.

In Hungary, working women spend four times as much time on housework as men do.

In the United States, 3.3 million women have unintended pregnancies (1.5 million of them due to lack of contraceptive use), and 1.6 million have abortions; 92% of women age fifteen to forty-nine use some form of contraception. The most common methods are the pill and sterilization; low-income women are more likely to be sterilized. Forty-one percent of Native American women have been sterilized, sometimes without their consent.

A Peruvian report estimates that 10–15% of the women in its prisons have been jailed for obtaining or performing abortions. Peru's death rate from abortion (50 in 10,000 women) is ten times that of most industrialized nations. Most abortions are punishable by jail for both the doctor or midwife and the woman who chooses to abort.

Norway has twenty-one women's crisis centers and twenty-six telephone hot lines for rape and battery victims.

Twenty percent of urban Mexican households are headed by women.

An estimated 80,000 rapes occur yearly in Mexico, 10,000 in Mexico City alone. Few of these rapes are reported.

Kuwait becomes the first Arab nation in the Persian Gulf region to legalize abortion. Abortion is allowed within the first four months if the mother's life is threatened or if the fetus is seriously brain-damaged.

About 40% of Japanese marriages are arranged.

Israeli law permits conviction of sex offenders on the victim's testimony alone, without corroboration.

Contraceptives are difficult to obtain in Iran except through the black market.

Average dowry in India (despite the fact that dowry is technically illegal) is 10,000 rupees.

The Indian government launches a pro-contraceptive campaign. Women are paid twenty-two dollars to be sterilized. (Men are paid fifteen dollars.)

In Indonesia, 75% of Muslim women marry by the age of eighteen.

Mar. The minimum legal age of execution in Iran is lowered to ten years for girls and sixteen years for boys.

July 26 Traditional genital mutilation of women is outlawed in Kenya.

Aug. Pakistan's Islamic Ideology Council proposes a Law of Evidence, making a woman's testimony worth half as much as a man's and recommending that women murder victims' lives be valued at half as much as men's.

Dec. Marital, anal, and oral rape are outlawed in Canada.

Government, the Military, and the Law

French pilot, feminist, and antiprostitution activist Marthe Ricard (b. 1889) dies. Her spy work during World War I won her the Legion of Honor, and in her fifties she worked with the French Resistance.

Zhor Ounissi becomes Algeria's secretary of State for Social Affairs; she is the first woman Cabinet minister since independence was achieved in 1962.

Women are 15.5% of U.S. lawyers.

Argentina's infantry and air force begin accepting women as cadets.

In Ghana, Ama Ata Aidoo becomes secretary of education, and Joyce Aryee becomes secretary for information.

Women are 2% of the military in Denmark, 4.7% in Britain (5.6% of the air force, 3% of the army, and 5% of the navy), 6.4% in Australia, and 8.55% in New Zealand.

Nicaragua has two women on its Supreme Court.

Dutch lesbian Evelien Eshuis is elected to Parliament.

Women are 27.5% of the Swedish Riksdag (Parliament).

Forty-five women have served in South Korea's National Assembly since 1948.

The U.S. Army bans women from twenty-three jobs it claims are combat related and closes forty-nine other specialties to women.

Spring Bertha Wilson becomes Canada's first woman Supreme Court judge.

Mar. Women are 9% of U.S. military personnel. Of these 191,340 women, 39.8% are in the army and 4.2% are in the marines. Thirteen percent of them are officers.

Apr. Carmen Grez becomes the first head of Chile's Ministry of the Family.

Aug. 6 Colombia's ministries of education, development, health, labor, communications, energy, justice, and public works have female heads.

Literature and the Visual Arts

Burmese leftist author Ma Ma Tay dies.

British potter Lucie Rie has a retrospective exhibition at the Victoria and Albert Museum.

New U.S. poetry includes Denise Levertov's *Candles in Babylon*, Audre Lorde's *Chosen Poems: Old and New*, Diane Wakoski's *The Magician's Feast Letters*, Carolyn Forche's *The Country Between Us*, Susan Howe's *Pythagorean Silence*, and Katha Pollitt's *Antarctic Traveller*.

Alice Walker publishes the Pulitzer Prize-winning epistolary novel *The Color Purple*. Set in the South during the early twentieth century, it tells the story of Celie, who overcomes abuse to find love with a blues singer named Shug Avery. Popular with critics and the general public, the novel addresses sexism in America and Africa.

Joyce Carol Oates publishes the novel *A Bloodsmoor Romance*, set in the nineteenth century with multiple points of view and overlapping narratives.

U.S. novelist Anne McCaffrey publishes *The Crystal Singer*, a science fiction novel about an arrogant young woman who achieves fulfillment as an elite member of a dangerous profession.

U.S. mystery novelist Sara Paretsky publishes *Indemnity Only*, the first V. I. Warshawski mystery. Other novels featuring the tough, conscientious detective will include *Deadlock* (1984), *Killing Orders* (1985), *Bitter Medicine* (1987), *Blood Shot* (1988), *Burn Marks* (1990), and *Guardian Angel* (1992).

Performing Arts and Entertainment

Filmgoers can also see French film actress Catherine Deneuve in *Le Choc*, Sally Field as a misguided newspaper reporter in *Absence of Malice*, and Hungarian actresses Jadwiga Jankowska-Cieslak and Grazyna Szapolowksa as journalists who fall in love with each other in *Another Day*. Meryl Streep wins the Best Actress Oscar for her performance as a Polish concentration camp survivor in *Sophie's Choice*; Jessica Lange wins the Best Supporting Actress Oscar for *Tootsie*.

Perry Miller Adato wins the Directors Guild of America Award for her *Echoes and Silence*, a documentary about poet Carl Sandburg.

Barbara Vielle founds France's Compagnie de Barbarie, an all-female circus.

Athletics and Exploration

The Soviet Union wins the women's basketball World Championship. After this game, however, the U.S. team will dominate international competition until 1991.

U.S. cyclist Connie Paraskevin-Young (b. July 4, 1961) wins the World Match Sprint title. She will repeat her victory in 1983.

June Women are banned from most Iranian sports events.

Sept. U.S. runner Joan Benoit wins a marathon just months after Achilles tendon surgery, breaking the U.S. women's record by two minutes.

Activism

South African author and activist Ruth First is killed by a letter bomb.

West German women's groups have established 120 shelters for battered women.

Egyptian feminist Nawal El Saadawi founds an international Arab women's organization, the Association of Women's Solidarity.

Dec. 11 Twenty thousand British women form a nine-mile human chain around a military base at Greenham Common in an effort to halt proposed storage of Cruise and Pershing missiles there.

Business and Industry

In Portugal, female agricultural laborers earn 35.7% as much as their male counterparts; in industry they make 52.8% of men's wages.

Women are two-thirds of Peru's 75,000 street vendors.

Women are 43% of the U.S. labor force. They are 99% of secretaries, 92% of telephone operators, 92% of bank tellers, 17% of mail carriers, 16% of butchers, 24% of insurance agents, almost 50% of bartenders, and 47% of bus drivers. Most U.S. women work in jobs that are 75% female; 22% work in jobs that are 95% female.

Women are 29% of the work force in Spain, 46% in Sweden, 36% in China, 50.2% in East Germany, and 42.4% in Britain. In Britain, women are 7% of managers, 77.2% of clerical workers, 10% of farm workers, 0.2% of construction workers, and 76.2% of service workers.

In Mexico, 36% of employed women work in the textile industry. Many women in factories earn less than a dollar an hour.

Poland's Solidarity labor union is 50% female but has only one female member on its national council.

France's Ministry for Women's Rights creates centers to train women in male-dominated manual jobs such as metalwork.

Women are 70% of domestic servants in El Salvador.

Ten percent of British women report that they have been sexually harassed at work.

May British nurses strike for higher wages.

Fall K. Kokkta becomes the first woman manager of the Bank of Greece.

Science and Medicine

Polish-American psychoanalyst Helene Deutsch dies. One of Freud's first four women anaylsands, she became one of his most fervent disciples, best known for her two-volume *Psychology of Women*. She was the second woman to gain membership in the Vienna Psychoanalytic Society.

Nicaraguan Lea Guido becomes the first woman president of the Pan-American Health Organization.

Agricultural scientist Mary-Dell Chilton, paleoecologist Margaret Davis, physiologist Martha Vaughan, and biochemist Marianne Grunberg-Manago are elected to the National Academy of Sciences in the United States.

In East Germany, women are 72% of students in engineering and technical colleges.

Canada cuts federal aid to family-planning centers by over 60%.

The Society of Women Engineers gives its annual Achievement Award to American electrical and computer engineer Harriett Rigas (d. 1989).

In the United States, women are 4% of engineers and 14.6% of doctors and dentists.

French astronomy student Martine Kempf (b. 1958) designs a fast, lightweight voice-recognition system; within four years it will be used in voice-controlled wheelchairs and surgical microscopes.

Education and Scholarship

A female teacher in Iran is jailed for her association with a woman who refuses to wear the *chador*; the teacher is executed after she is found to possess books by Flaubert, Zola, and Rousseau.

Chinese women must now score higher than men on entrance exams in order to get into college.

In Italy, women are 66% of elementary and secondary teachers and 47.5% of college teachers. Women are 30% of teachers in Pakistan and 70% in El Salvador.

U.S. historian Laurel Thatcher Ulrich publishes *Good Wives*, which discusses the everyday lives of women in New England from 1650 to 1750.

Argentinian poet, translator, and feminist Leonor Calvera publishes *El Género Mujer* (*The Woman Gender*), an analysis of women's history from the Paleolithic period to the present.

Women are 27% of higher education students in Mexico, 26.3% in Morocco, 44% in Switzerland, 52.5% in East Germany, and 49.8% in Hungary. Women are 34% of graduate students in Egypt.

In the United States, women are 55% of two-year college students, 53% of four-year college and university students, and 39% of graduate students.

Religion

Caroline Walker Bynum publishes *Jesus as Mother: Studies in the Spirituality of the High Middle Ages.*

Susannah Heschel publishes *Towards a Feminist Rejuvenation of Judaism.*

1983

General Status and Daily Life

Ten percent of French families are solely supported by women.

A new French law offers 70% repayment for abortions.

Greece's new Family Law makes both spouses equal in decision making, gives women the right to keep their birth names after marriage, outlaws dowry, legalizes divorce by mutual consent, and abolishes a wife's need to get her husband's permission to conduct business, remove her children from the city, or put them in a school.

China's "one family, one child" policy is contributing to increased female infanticide and abuse of women who give birth to daughters. Some rural women are sterilized without their consent to reduce the birthrate.

Iranian law bars women from the judiciary, the military, and the police force. Women are required to dress modestly in public. Women are not permitted to use public transportation, cafeterias, movie theaters, and beaches.

Saudi Arabia has approximately 200 day-care centers nationwide for a total national population of over 4 million.

In Britain, 75% of women use some form of birth control.

The U.S. Supreme Court overturns legislation requiring preabortion counseling, parental consent, and waiting periods.

Swedish wives can keep their birth names; husbands may apply to take their wives' last names if they wish.

Half of the black children in the United States live in female-headed households.

In the United States, a woman is hospitalized every eighteen seconds because of a beating by her husband or sexual partner.

The contraceptive pill is still not legal in Japan; 81.1% of couples using some form of contraception use condoms; 1.1% use diaphragms.

There are about 500–800 battered women's shelters in the United States, and about 700 rape-crisis programs.

Sixty-five percent of women over eighteen in Mexico have children. Although abortion is illegal in most cases, about 1.6 million abortions are performed yearly, 92% of them under unsanitary conditions. About 100,000 women die each year from botched abortions.

The Dutch constitution prohibits discrimination on the grounds of sex.

Mar. 6 The contraceptive sponge wins FDA approval.

Apr. The *chador* is made mandatory for all Iranian women; appearing unveiled will result in a prison sentence of one month to one year.

Apr. An antiabortion amendment guaranteeing "the equal right to life of the unborn" passes the Irish Parliament; approximately 5,000 Irishwomen per year obtain abortions by traveling to England for the procedure. In September, the antiabortion amendment passes a national referendum.

May Controversy erupts in Brazil after a woman is sentenced to fourteen years for killing her husband, while a man who killed his wife is given a two-year suspended sentence on the grounds that he was "defending his honor."

Sept. 17 Vanessa Williams becomes the first black Miss America. Shortly afterward, the revelation that she once posed for pornographic pictures forces her to step down, but she goes on to a career as a singer and MTV veejay.

Government, the Military, and the Law

El Salvadoran professor and lawyer Mélida Anaya Montes, second-in-command of the Popular Liberation Forces, is assassinated.

Nicaragua's chief press censor is a woman, Lieutenant Nelba Blandón. Women are 47% of Nicaragua's militia.

Susan Ryan becomes Australia's minister for education and youth affairs.

Austria has two woman mayors and three women cabinet ministers, Family Affairs Minister Elfriede Karl, Women's Affairs Minister Johanna Dohnal, and Construction Minister Beatrix Eypeltauer.

Ester Figueiredo becomes Brazil's minister of federal

culture and education.

In China, 21.2% of the delegates to the Sixth National People's Congress are women. Women are 11 of the 210-member Central Committee of the Communist party.

There are twelve women in the Peruvian legislature.

Lebanon appoints its first woman ambassador, Sameera Al-Daher.

Women are 22% of the West German Bundesrat and 10% of its Bundestag, 27% of Hungary's National Assembly, 5.7% of France's National Assembly and 3% of its Senate, 8% of Senegal's National Assembly, 1.8% of Japan's House of Representatives and 7.2% of its House of Councillors, and 25.8% of the Norwegian Storting (Parliament).

Sixty-seven of Mexico's 350 Parliamentary deputies are women. One of Mexico's fifty-seven senators is female. One woman, Griselda Alvarez Ponce de León, is a state governor.

The Indonesian civil service is 32% female, but only 5% of those in positions of authority are women.

In Portugal, women are 9% of the diplomatic service and 7.2% of the National Assembly (June 1); no women are in the Cabinet (Apr.).

Margaret Heckler becomes the U.S. secretary of health and human services; she will hold this post until 1985. Elizabeth Dole becomes secretary of transportation, serving until 1987.

Apr. Elda Pucci of Palermo, Sicily, becomes the first woman mayor of a major Italian city.

Nov. 11 Englishwoman Mary Donaldson becomes the first woman lord mayor of London in the 800 years of that office's existence.

Literature and the Visual Arts

Alice Walker publishes *In Search of Our Mothers' Gardens*, a collection of essays about racism, body image, creative expression, and "womanism."

American Josephine Miles (1911–1985) publishes her *Collected Poems*. Other new American poetry includes Mary Oliver's Pulitzer-winning *American Primitive*, Rita Dove's *Museum*, Susan Howe's *Defenestration of Prague*, and Ellen Bryant Wright's *The Forces of Plenty*.

Aboriginal women in Australia's Northern Territory band together to sell their traditional art.

Nepalese journalist and feminist Manjula Giri founds a monthly women's magazine, *Gargi*.

Mar. Soviet poet Irina Ratushinskaya is jailed for her writings.

Performing Arts and Entertainment

U.S. songwriter Diane Warren writes pop singer Laura Branigan's hit "Solitaire."

Bonnie Bedelia stars as three-time world champion hot rod racer Shirley "Cha-Cha" Muldowney in the movie *Heart Like a Wheel*.

Cyndi Lauper (b. 1953) records *She's So Unusual*, the first album by a woman to contain four Top Ten hits. It sells 4.5 million copies and wins a Grammy. Among its songs are "She Bop," "Girls Just Want to Have Fun," and "Time After Time."

Shirley MacLaine wins the Best Actress Oscar for her performance in *Terms of Endearment*, in which she plays Debra Winger's mother. The Best Supporting Actress Oscar goes to Linda Hunt for her portrayal of a man in *The Year of Living Dangerously*. Meryl Streep and Cher star in *Silkwood*, written by Nora Ephron.

Irene Cara records the hit song "Flashdance."

Aug. 8 Christine Craft is awarded $500,000 in damages after KMBC-TV in Kansas City, Missouri, fires her from her position as news anchor for being "too old, unattractive, and not deferential enough to men." The award is overturned by a higher court on October 31, and in 1984 the award is amended to $325,000.

Athletics and Exploration

British dart player Sandy Reitan is named the Number One Woman's Dart Player by the World Dart Federation.

U.S. middle-distance runner Mary Decker holds records in every distance between 800 and 10,000 meters. She wins the 3,000 meters and the 1,500 meters at the World Championships.

Apr. 18 U.S. runner Joan Benoit wins the women's section of the Boston Marathon with a record time.

June 18–24 Physicist Sally Ride, aboard the *Challenger*, becomes the first U.S. woman in space.

Activism

An Iranian female political prisoner is raped in jail by twenty men; her sister later approaches a religious leader with grenades strapped to her body and kills him and herself.

Marianela García Villas, cofounder of the Comisión de Derechos Humanos de El Salvador, is assassinated.

Women lawyers in Pakistan protest the proposed Law of Evidence, which makes a woman's testimony in court worth half as much as a man's. The demonstrators, including attorney Asma Jahangir, are teargassed and beaten by police; Jahangir is arrested.

Gloria Anzaldua and Cherrie Moraga edit *This Bridge Called My Back: Writings by Radical Women of Color.* The contributions include poetry, essays, and letters on feminism, racism, homophobia, religion, self-awareness, and the search for role models. Contributors include Jo Carrillo, Chrystos, Cheryl Clarke, Genny Lim, Naomi Littlebear Morena, Audre Lorde, Barbara Noda, Beverly Smith, and Nellie Wong.

East German pacifists Barbel Bohley and Ulricke Poppe are arrested for nuclear disarmament activism.

American Donna Brazile organizes a convergence of 500,000 people on Washington, D.C., for the twentieth anniversary of Martin Luther King's civil rights march there.

Iranian editor of the left-wing young women's newspaper *Azzaraksh* Zohreh Ghaeni is arrested. Several other female left-wing leaders are also arrested, including translator and author Mariam Firouz, president of the Democratic Women's Organization of Iran; journalist Malakeh Mohammadi, editor of the Tudeh party newspapers *Mardom* and *Donya*; physicians Mitra Ameli and Fatemeh Izadi; and educator Zohreh Tonekaboni. They will all be held until at least 1990 without a fair trial and often without access to necessary medical care.

Norwegian feminist Bente Volder wins a lawsuit against pornographer Leif Hagen, who is found guilty of slandering all women.

Jan. Twenty Italian women block the entrance to a Sicilian missile base as part of a pacifist demonstration.

Feb. 14 Indian outlaw Phoolan Devi, known as the "Bandit Queen," surrenders to authorities after evading government forces for two years. Perceived by some as a criminal guilty of robbery, kidnapping, and murder and by others as a warrior on behalf of women and the lower castes, she was married at eleven to a man in his thirties, sold by him for a cow, and advised to commit suicide by her own mother. She will be held without trial for

eleven years until the Indian Supreme Court orders her release on February 18, 1994.

Dec. The Multisectorial de Mujeres, a coalition of women's groups, is established in Argentina.

Business and Industry

In Russia, 58,910,000 women are in the work force, constituting 51% of the total work force.

Yugoslavia extends maternity leave from 180 to 270 days.

Women are 43.5% of the British work force and 60% of Chinese textile workers.

French law provides for fines or imprisonment for employers who violate equal pay laws, but such laws do not apply to part-time workers, who are 82% women.

In Hungary, women earn 20–30% less than men who hold the same jobs.

Wendy Strothman becomes head of Beacon Press and saves it from bankruptcy.

Until this year, Kenyan women have needed male cosigners to get loans.

Median annual income for women over sixty-five in the United States is $5,600.

In the United States, 53% of women are in the work force. Women are 70% of sales clerks and 32% of managers and executives. On average, female college graduates earn $14,679 per year; male high school dropouts earn $12,117 per year. Women with high school diplomas earn less, on average, than men with fewer than four years of elementary school.

In America, 52.9% of women work outside the home, forming 43% of the work force. Nine thousand are carpenters; 29,000 have become truck drivers since 1970.

In Japan, women's wages are 53% of men's.

July The French Parliament passes the "Roudy Law," which protects women workers from discrimination in wages, hiring, job assignment, promotion, relocation, or qualifications; businesses with fewer than fifty employees are exempt. The law is named for its chief proponent, Women's Rights Minister Yvette Roudy.

Science and Medicine

U.S. physician Barbara McClintock (b. June 16, 1902)

wins the Nobel for Physiology or Medicine for her 1951 discovery that genes can "jump" randomly between cells. For many years, her discovery brought her only derision and neglect from the scientific community.

Women are 40% of Romania's physicians.

U.S. biologist Lynn Margulis, author of *The Origin of Eukaryotic Cells*, is elected to the National Academy of Sciences (NAS). She theorized correctly that cells with nuclei form through the synthesis of nonnucleated cells (such as microbes), a hypothesis that originally met with extreme skepticism, even hostility, from male scientists. Her views on symbiosis have changed the entire scientific view of cell development. Also elected to the NAS this year are biochemist Joan A. Steitz and geneticist Mary-Lou Pardue.

The Society of Women Engineers gives its annual Achievement Award to environmental engineer Joan B. Berkowitz for her work on hazardous waste management.

U.S. computer programmer Roberta Williams's (b. 1953) company, Sierra On-Line, is doing $10 million in sales per year. Williams is the creator or co-creator of several computer games, including "Mystery House," "The Wizard and the Princess," "Time Zone," "Zork," and "King's Quest."

In China, women are 33% of scientists and technicians and 58% of medical workers.

Jan. American-Belizean biologist and conservationist Sharon Matola founds the Belize Zoo with twenty animals left over from a British wildlife film. The first and only zoo in Belize, it will have 120 animals, a full staff, a children's outreach program, and a weekly radio show by 1992.

Education and Scholarship

Women are 42% of higher education students in Romania, 34% in Ecuador, and 33% in the Netherlands.

U.S. economist Elizabeth Bailey, a former trustee of Princeton University, becomes dean of the Graduate School of Industrial Administration at Carnegie Mellon University. She is the first woman to head a major graduate business school.

In the United States, about 70% of male and 50% of female higher education faculty members have tenure.

In China, women are 25% of university faculty and 100% of early childhood educators.

Religion

More than 20,000 Iranian women and girls have been executed for "anti-Islamic" activities.

American Rosemary Radford Ruether publishes *Sexism and God-Talk*, an important work of feminist theology. Other religious publications include Elaine Sommers's *Mennonite Women: A Story of God's Faithfulness, 1683–1983*, Susannah Heschel's *On Being a Jewish Feminist*, and Nancy A. Falk and Rita M. Gross's *Unspoken Worlds: Women's Religious Lives in Non-Western Cultures*.

May Franciscan nuns in Warsaw, Poland, are beaten and arrested by the government for allegedly shielding the families of imprisoned labor leaders.

June 18 Ten Iranian Baha'i women, including a pianist, a nurse, college students, the former personnel director of Iran Television, and the first Iranian woman physicist, are executed for refusing to convert to Islam.

Oct. 14 The National Council of Churches issues a translation of the Bible in which God is gender-neutral. Lutheran and Greek Orthodox churches reject the new translation.

1984

General Status and Daily Life

Polygyny is legal in Afghanistan; daughters inherit half as much as sons.

The Reagan administration denies U.S. funds worldwide to any family-planning program that provides abortions or abortion information. As a result, sixty-seven developing nations where abortion is legal are unable to offer this service. About 200,000 women die of botched abortions as a result.

In Algeria, men can divorce by *talaq*, a simple verbal declaration. A woman who divorces her husband forfeits her dowry. Women are made permanent legal minors on June 9.

In Egypt, men can divorce by *talaq*. A woman cannot get a divorce for battery or adultery if she has tolerated it earlier in the marriage. Marital rape is legal, and women have lesser inheritance rights. Arranged marriage is common.

Australia outlaws sexual harassment.

In the United States, twenty-nine abortion clinics are bombed or set on fire. Eighteen doctors who perform abortions report receiving death threats. In all, 131 acts of vandalism and violence against abortion providers are reported.

Jan. Abortion laws in Portugal are relaxed somewhat. Until now, abortion has been illegal, with a jail term of two to eight years for performing or receiving an abortion; rates of illegal abortion are high, averaging 100,000-200,000 per year, and about 2,000 women per year die as a result. Now abortions will be legal in cases of rape, fetal deformity, or danger to the life of the mother, but three physicians must give their approval, and only first-trimester abortions are permitted.

Aug. 16 The United States legalizes withholding from the paychecks of fathers whose child support checks are at least thirty days overdue.

Government, the Military, and the Law

Britain has twenty-three women in the House of Commons and forty-three women in the House of Lords.

CBS News employee Peggy Noonan becomes a speech writer for U.S. president Ronald Reagan. She teaches Reagan handlers to use a "sound bite" in each speech—a quick, catchy phrase that will make a good thirty-second clip on the evening news. Later she will write George Bush's pivotal "thousand points of light" speech that turns the tide in his favor in the 1988 presidential race.

Jeanne Sauvé becomes the first woman governor-general in Canada.

U.S. philanthropist Ellen Malcolm founds EMILY's (Early Money Is Like Yeast) List to coordinate political contributions to female candidates.

July 20 Democrat Geraldine Ferraro becomes the first woman nominee for vice president for a major political party.

Oct. 31 Indian prime minister Indira Gandhi is assassinated.

Literature and the Visual Arts

New U.S. poetry includes Denise Levertov's *Oblique Prayers*, Adrienne Rich's *The Fact of a Doorframe*, Maura Stanton's *Cries of Swimmers*, Louise Erdrich's (b. 1954) *Jacklight*, and Diane Wakoski's *The Collected Greed*.

U.S. feminist Audre Lorde publishes *Sister Outsider: Essays and Speeches*.

U.S. journalist Olive Ann Burns publishes her first novel, *Cold Sassy Tree*. Set in 1906, it is narrated by a boy named Will Tweedy and focuses on the quirky patriarch of a southern town and his new wife, the much younger Love Simpson.

Performing Arts and Entertainment

U.S. dancer Judith Jamison's first ballet, *Divining*, is performed.

U.S. jazz pianist Toshiko Akiyoshi (b. Dec. 18, 1929) begins leading her own orchestra.

Daryl Hannah stars as a mermaid in the movie *Splash*. Karen Allen is a widow romanced by an alien in *Starman*. Lily Tomlin and Victoria Tennant star in the comedy *All of Me*. Dame Peggy Ashcroft wins the Best Supporting Actress Oscar for *A Passage to India*, and Sally Field wins the Best Actress Oscar for *Places in the Heart*.

Jan. U.S. talk-show host Oprah Winfrey becomes host of "AM Chicago," later called "The Oprah Winfrey Show."

Athletics and Exploration

The National Collegiate Athletic Association (NCAA), which often lobbies against the Title IX education act (mandating equal treatment for men's and women's sports in federally funded schools), rules that schools out of compliance with Title IX will receive suspensions from national competition—for the women's teams.

People Express pilot Betsy Carroll becomes the first woman to fly a transatlantic jumbo jet.

Winter At the winter Olympics in Sarajevo, East German skater Katarina Witt, this year's world champion, wins the gold in women's figure skating. Soviets Elena Valova and Oleg Vasiliev, coached by Tamara Moskvina, win the gold in pairs. Britain's Jayne Torvill and Christopher Dean take the gold in ice dancing with a sensual performance to Ravel's "Bolero," followed by Soviets Natalia Bestemianova and Andrei Boukine.
    Finnish skier Marja-Liisa Hämäläinen wins the 5-kilometer and 10-kilometer cross-country races, becoming the first double gold medalist of this games. She also wins the 20-kilometer race, a new event. Raisa Smetanina of the Soviet Union, a medalist in past

Olympics, gets silvers in the 10- and 20-kilometer races. The 4 x 5-kilometer relay is won by the Norwegian team of Inger Helene Nybraaten, Anne Jahren (bronze medalist in the 20-kilometer race), Brit Pettersen (bronze medalist in the 10-kilometer race), and Berit Aunli (silver medalist in the 5-kilometer race). Third place goes to the Finnish team, which includes Hämäläinen and 1988 gold medalist Pirkko Maatta.

Switzerland's Michela Figini, seventeen, wins the Olympic downhill, becoming the youngest skier ever to win a gold medal. In the slalom, Paoletta Magoni of Italy wins the gold. American Debbie Armstrong wins the giant slalom. East Germany sweeps the women's luge medals, with Steffi Martin, Bettina Schmidt, and Ute Weiss taking first, second, and third.

East German speed skater Karin Kania-Enke wins the 1,000 and 1,500 meters with Olympic record times and takes silvers in the 500 and 3,000. Her teammate Christa Rothenburger sets another Olympic record in the 500 meters to win the gold, and another East German, Andrea Schoene, wins the 3,000 with an Olympic record time and takes silvers in the 1,000 and 1,500. Soviet skater Natalia Petruseva, a gold medalist in 1980, cannot repeat her victory and settles for bronzes in the 1,000 and 1,500.

Summer The Soviets stay home this year in retaliation for the U.S. boycott of the 1980 games. In Los Angeles, American runner Joan Benoit wins the first Olympic women's marathon only a few weeks after knee surgery; her Scandinavian rival Grete Waitz (the silver medalist) is hampered by the California heat. Portugal's Rosa Mota takes the bronze. Swiss runner Gabriela Anderson-Schiess, dehydrated, staggers doggedly toward the finish line and collapses after crossing it in thirty-seventh place. Although she recovers fully a few hours later, the media make outraged noises over the officials' refusal to prevent her from continuing.

American Evelyn Ashford wins the 100-meter dash with an Olympic record time, followed by teammate Alice Brown. American Valerie Brisco-Hooks makes history twice with her wins in the 200- and 400-meter races; she sets an Olympic record in the 200 and becomes the only Olympic athlete of either sex to win both these events. Second place in the 400 goes to a woman who will make big news in 1988, Florence Griffith Joyner (b. December 21, 1959).

Romania's Doina Melinte wins the 800 meters and earns a silver in the 1,500. Her teammate Maricica Puica, the bronze medalist in the 1,500, wins the 3,000 meters in its first time as a women's Olympic event; the two favorites in this race, Zola Budd (b. 1966) of South Africa and Mary Decker of the United States, collide during the race and knock each other out of contention. Decker is sidelined with a hip injury, and Budd finishes seventh. The 1,500 is won by Italy's Gabriella Doria.

American Benita Fitzgerald-Brown wins the 100-meter hurdles, and the 400-meter hurdles, a new event, is won by Nawal El Moutawakel, who gives Morocco its

first-ever Olympic gold medal. The U.S. team of Alice Brown, Jeannette Bolden, Chandra Cheeseborough (the silver medalist in the 400 meters), and Ashford wins the 4 x 100 relay. The United States also wins the 4 x 400 relay with its team of Lillie Leatherwood, Sherri Howard, Brisco-Hooks, and Cheeseborough.

Ulrike Mayfarth of West Germany wins the high jump and sets an Olympic record; Italy's Sara Simeoni comes in second. The long jump is won by Romania's Anisoara Cusmir-Stanciu. Claudia Losch of West Germany wins the shot put, and Ria Stalman of the Netherlands wins the discus. Great Britain's Tessa Sanderson takes the gold in javelin. The pentathlon is replaced by the heptathlon, and Australia's Glynis Nunn wins the gold, followed by American Jackie Joyner Kersee (b. March 3, 1962).

Separate women's shooting events are held for the first time at the Olympics. Linda Thom of Canada wins the sport pistol event. American Pat Spurgin wins the air rifle competition. Xiao Xuan Wu of China, bronze medalist in the air rifle, takes a gold medal in the small-bore rifle, three-position.

U.S. cyclist Connie Carpenter-Phinney wins the first women's Olympic road race. She is the only woman so far to compete in both the summer and winter Olympics; she was also at the Sapporo winter games in 1972. North Korea's Hyang-Soon Seo wins the individual archery event. Yugoslavia wins the team handball gold, and China wins the gold in volleyball; Chinese team members Xilan Yang, Huijuan Su, Ying Jiang, Xiaojun Yang, and Meizhu Zheng will also be on the bronze medal team in 1988.

The Netherlands wins the gold in field hockey. The basketball gold is won by the United States; team members Teresa Edwards, Cynthia Brown, Anne Donovan, and Lynette Woodard were also members of the silver-medal 1976 team.

In the rowing events, Sweden's Agneta Andersson gives an impressive performance, winning the 500-meter kayak singles, the 500-meter kayak pairs (with Anna Olsson), and a silver in the kayak fours (with Olsson, Eva Karlsson, and Susanne Wiberg). Romania wins the kayak fours, double sculls, coxless pair, quadruple sculls, and coxed four. Romanian Valeria Racila wins the single sculls. The only event not won by Andersson or the Romanians is the eight oars, which is won by the United States.

Olympic veteran Christine Stueckelberger of Switzerland takes a silver in team dressage; another woman, Amy Catherine De Bary, is also on the Swiss team. The third-place Swedish team has three women: Ulla Hakansson, Ingamay Bylund, and Louise Nathhorst. Denmark's Anne Grethe takes the silver in individual dressage, and Switzerland's Heidi Robbiani takes the bronze in individual show jumping. The U.S. gold-medal show jumping team includes Melanie Smith. American Karen Stives is the silver medalist in the individual three-day event, and Britain's Virginia Holgate gets the bronze. Stives is also on the gold-medal three-day event team. Holgate picks up a silver with her team, which also includes Diana Clapham and Lucinda Green. West Germany's bronze-medal team includes one woman, Bettina Overesch.

China's Jujie Luan wins the individual foil fencing gold; the team gold is won by the West Germans: Cornelia Hanisch, Christiane Weber, Sabine Bischoff, and Zita Funkenhauser. France's third-place team includes three gold medalists from 1980: Pascale Trinquet-Hachin, Brigitte Latrille-Gaudin, and Veronique Brouquier.

Synchronized swimming makes its debut as an Olympic sport. The U.S. team of Candy Costie and Tracie Ruiz takes the gold in the duet. Ruiz also captures the gold in the solo event, followed by Canada's Carolyn Waldo. China's Jihong Zhou wins the platform diving gold, and Canada's Sylvie Bernier wins the springboard event. Silver in the springboard goes to American Kelly McCormick, daughter of 1952 and 1956 champion Pat McCormick.

Without the East Germans present, the United States dominates the swimming events. Nancy Hogshead and Mary Wayte win the 100- and 200-meter freestyles, respectively. Tiffany Cohen wins the 400- and 800-meter freestyles. Theresa Andrews wins the 100-meter backstroke. Mary T. Meagher wins the 100- and 200-meter butterfly, and Tracy Caulkins (b. January 11, 1963), the only swimmer of either sex to have set U.S. records in every stroke, wins the 200- and 400-meter individual medleys. The United States also wins the freestyle relay with its team of Hogshead, Carrie Steinseifer, Dara Torres, and Jenna Johnson (silver medalist in the 100-meter butterfly) and the medley relay with its team of Andrews, Caulkins, Meagher, and Hogshead.

Only three swimming gold medals go to other nations: the 100-meter breaststroke, won by Petra Van Staveren of the Netherlands; the 200-meter breaststroke, won by Canada's Anne Ottenbrite (the silver medalist in the 100); and the 200-meter backstroke, won by Jolanda de Rover of the Netherlands, the bronze medalist in the 100-meter backstroke.

Romania's team of Simona Pauca, Mihaela Stanulet, Cristina Grigoras, Laura Cutina, Lavinia Agache, and Ecaterina Szabo wins the team gymnastics gold, followed by the United States and China. Szabo wins golds in the vault and floor exercises and silvers in the all-around and beam. Pauca wins the beam and takes a bronze in the all-around, and Agache comes in third in the vault. American Mary Lou Retton (b. 1968) performs a full-twisting double layout Tsukuhara, a move only a few men have completed successfully. She wins the all-around gold, a silver in the vault, and bronzes in the floor exercise and uneven bars. Canada's Lori Fung wins the gold in a new event, rhythmic gymnastics.

Oct. 11 Kathryn Sullivan becomes the first American woman to walk in space.

Activism

U.S. feminist Robin Morgan publishes *Sisterhood Is Global*, an analysis of the position of women in dozens of countries.

Business and Industry

Women workers make 58.6% as much as men in the United States, 80.7% as much in Sweden, 76.8% as much in the Netherlands, 76.5% as much in Australia, 74.3% as much in Austria, 73.5% as much in France, 66% as much in Canada, and 65.7% as much in Great Britain.

Business Week estimates that in the United States, women hold only 2% of the top 50,000 management jobs. The top 1,300 public companies have a total of 367 women and 15,500 men on their boards; women hold only 2.8% of directorships in Fortune 500 companies.

The Association of Flight Attendants becomes the only AFL-CIO union led by a woman. One-third of U.S. union members are women.

Of 6 million employers in the United States, 1,800 offer child care, three times as many as in 1982.

In Egypt, a woman must have her husband's permission to work outside the home; if she does not obtain it, he can legally withdraw financial support.

Science and Medicine

The Society of Women Engineers gives its annual Achievement Award to environmental engineer Geraldine V. Cox for her work on water pollution.

Education and Scholarship

U.S. feminist theologian Mary Daly publishes *Pure Lust*, a work of feminist philosophy.

Religion

U.S. inventor Helen G. Gonet patents an electronic Bible.

Muslim women in Egypt cannot marry non-Muslims, though Muslim men may.

Twenty-six U.S. nuns from fifteen orders sign a pro-choice declaration in the *New York Times*. Most are subsequently harassed by the church to retract, and some resign from their orders.

Feminist theologian Elizabeth Schüssler Fiorenza, who argues that women can reconcile feminism and Christianity, publishes *Bread Not Stone: The Challenge of Feminist Biblical Interpretation*.

1985

General Status and Daily Life

In Japan, the average age at marriage for women is 25.5 years (compared with 28.2 for men); the average woman has two children.

In the United States, 149 acts of vandalism and violence against abortion providers are reported.

Aug. 25 Thirteen-year-old American Samantha Smith, a peace ambassador to Soviet Union, dies in a plane crash. Her heartfelt letter to Soviet leader Mikhail Gorbachev led to a visit to the USSR and helped to create amity between the two nations.

Oct. Britain's House of Lords determines that girls under sixteen can obtain birth control pills without notification of their parents.

Government, the Military, and the Law

Penny Harrington of Portland, Oregon, becomes the first woman chief of a major U.S. police department.

Sept. Iranian women are trained to handle automatic weapons and mortars in special camps. A woman officer, Showkat Abbassian, says, "We are only waiting for Imam Khomeini's orders to go to the front."

Literature and the Visual Arts

U.S. artist Judy Chicago unveils *The Birth Project*, a multimedia presentation about the birth experience.

American Rita Dove publishes the short story collection *The Fifth Sunday*.

U.S. poet Anne Winters (b. 1939), who also translates from French, German, Italian, Latin, ancient Greek, and

Hebrew, publishes *The Key to the City*, which wins the National Book Critics Circle Award. Other new U.S. poetry includes Tess Gallagher's *Willingly*, Linda Gregg's *Alma*, Brenda Hillman's (b. 1951) *White Dress*, and Jane Miller and Olga Broumas's prose-poem collection, *Black Holes, Black Stockings*.

Anne Rice publishes *The Vampire Lestat*.

Performing Arts and Entertainment

Filmgoers can see Meryl Streep playing Danish author Isak Dinesen in *Out of Africa*, Kathleen Turner as an assassin and Anjelica Huston as a scheming woman in love in *Prizzi's Honor*, Sonia Braga in *Kiss of the Spider Woman*, Demi Moore and Ally Sheedy in *St. Elmo's Fire*, and U.S. actress Kelly McGillis as an Amish widow in *Witness*. Jane Fonda, Anne Bancroft, and Meg Tilly star in the film *Agnes of God*, in which questions of faith are addressed during an investigation of a saintlike young nun. Tilly gets an Oscar nomination. Talk-show host Oprah Winfrey is also nominated for her portrayal of a strong woman nearly broken by racism in *The Color Purple*, which also stars Whoopi Goldberg, Margaret Avery, and Rae Dawn Chong. The Best Actress Oscar, however, goes to Geraldine Page for *The Trip to Bountiful*, and the Best Supporting Actress Award goes to Anjelica Huston for her role as a ruthless would-be Mafia bride in *Prizzi's Honor*.

Films directed by women include Indian Mira Nair's *India Cabaret*, a movie about Bombay strippers; Polish filmmaker Agnieszka Holland's *Angry Harvest*, and French filmmaker Agnès Varda's *Vagabond*, a movie about the death of a female vagrant.

U.S. pop singer Suzanne Vega records a self-titled album that features the song "Marlene on the Wall."

Athletics and Exploration

American Barbara Perez becomes one of boxing's few women judges.

U.S. sailor Peggy Slater becomes the first woman member of the prestigious Transpac Yacht Club.

Thirty-five percent of U.S. high school girls are involved in interscholastic sports.

U.S. basketball player Lynette Woodard becomes the first woman member of the Harlem Globetrotters.

U.S. golfer Danielle Ammaccapane wins the NCAA tournament.

Martina Navratilova is the highest-paid woman in tennis, with earnings of $1,328,829.

Fencer Molly Sullivan wins the U.S. women's foil championship.

Czechoslovakian tennis player Hana Mandlikova wins the U.S. Open.

Activism

Eleanor Smeal, after three years out of office, becomes president of NOW, serving until 1987.

Apr. A sixteen-year-old girl from the terrorist National Lebanese Resistance kills two Israeli soldiers in a suicide detonation of a car bomb.

Sept. 19 American Tipper Gore urges Congress to mandate labels for record albums containing "offensive lyrics."

Business and Industry

In the United States, 50% of the 46,000,000 working women hold jobs in only 20 of 441 possible categories, mostly in positions with lower pay; 80% are in feminized jobs—jobs almost entirely filled by women, such as clerical work, sales, teaching, nursing, and waitressing.

Fewer than 15% of U.S. families have a single income and male head of household.

In the United States, 47% of male managers and 82% of female managers say they would feel comfortable working for a female boss, up from 27% and 75% in 1965.

In Japan, 23,670,000 women are in the work force, constituting 39.7% of the total work force.

Greta Marshall becomes investment manager of the California Public Employees' Retirement System, the nation's second largest pension fund at $40 billion.

Science and Medicine

Primatologist Dian Fossey is murdered, probably by poachers whom she tried to keep away from the endangered mountain gorillas she studied.

U.S. women earn 39.2% of all bachelor's degrees, 36.9% of computer science bachelor's degrees, 13.6% of physics bachelor's degrees, 36.4% of chemistry bachelor's

degrees, and 46.1% of math bachelor's degrees.

The Boston Women's Health Book Collective publishes *The New Our Bodies, Ourselves*.

The Society of Women Engineers gives its annual Achievement Award to Y.C.L. Susan Wu for her research in electrofluid dynamics and her work in education.

Astronomer Sandra M. Faber becomes a member of the National Academy of Sciences.

Education and Scholarship

U.S. historian Carroll Smith-Rosenberg publishes *Disorderly Conduct: Visions of Gender in Victorian America*.

U.S. literary critic Susan Howe publishes *My Emily Dickinson*.

Social psychology professor Berit Ås founds the Kvinneuniversitetet (Women's University) in Loten, Norway.

Religion

Conservative Judaism decides to accept women as rabbis.

1986

General Status and Daily Life

In Italy, 12% more rapes are reported than last year, but 69% in Rome and 95% in Sicily go unsolved.

A Ugandan judge says of wife beating, "It is better for one person to suffer rather than risk a complete breakdown of family life."

The *New York Times* begins using "Ms." as a title for women.

In the United States, 133 acts of vandalism and violence against abortion providers are reported.

The last three Playboy clubs in the United States close for lack of profits. The clubs were notorious for their "bunnies," attractive young waitresses dressed in tight, skimpy costumes with floppy ears and fuzzy tails.

A Philadelphia judge is forced to apologize after he calls the victim in a rape case "coyote-ugly" and tells the defendant, "This was an unattractive girl and you are a goodlooking [sic] fellow. You did something to her which was stupid."

The U.S. Supreme Court overturns a law requiring preabortion counseling.

Iranian and Pakistani women are sometimes stoned to death for adultery.

Government, the Military, and the Law

Takako Doi becomes head of the Socialist party, making her the first woman leader of a major Japanese political party.

Barbara Mikulski is elected to the U.S. Senate, doubling women's representation there; the other woman senator is Nancy Kassebaum, elected for the first time in 1978.

Philippine leader Corazon Aquino ousts President Ferdinand Marcos.

Apr. Dissident politician Benazir Bhutto (b. 1953) returns to Pakistan after being jailed and then exiled after her father's execution by the Zia regime.

Literature and the Visual Arts

New U.S. poetry includes Audre Lorde's *Our Dead Behind Us*, Diane Wakoski's *The Rings of Saturn*, and Rita Dove's Pulitzer-winning *Thomas and Beulah*.

American Louise Erdrich publishes the novel *The Beet Queen*.

Canadian author Margaret Atwood publishes *The Handmaid's Tale*, a chilling novel about a repressive government that uses religion to make women the enslaved breeders for powerful men.

U.S. novelist Margaret George publishes *The Autobiography of Henry VIII*.

Performing Arts and Entertainment

U.S. singer Anita Baker's debut album, *Rapture*, wins a Grammy and sells 5 million copies.

"The Oprah Winfrey Show" begins national syndication.

Meryl Streep stars in *Heartburn*, a movie written by Nora Ephron and based on the marriage and divorce of Ephron and journalist Carl Bernstein. Filmgoers can also see Bette Midler and Helen Slater in the comedy *Ruthless People*, Demi Moore (b. November 11, 1963) and Elizabeth Perkins as single women looking for relationships in *About Last Night . . .*, Sigourney Weaver reprising her role as the giant-bug-killer Ripley in *Aliens* (produced by Gale Anne Hurd), Ellen Barkin in *The Big Easy*, and Whoopi Goldberg as a bank employee-turned-amateur spy in *Jumpin' Jack Flash* (directed by Penny Marshall). Marlee Matlin wins the Best Actress Oscar for her role in the romantic drama *Children of a Lesser God*. Dianne Wiest wins the Best Supporting Actress Oscar for *Hannah and Her Sisters*.

U.S. comedian and actress Lily Tomlin wins a Tony award for her performance in Jane Wagner's play, *The Search for Signs of Intelligent Life in the Universe*. In this one-woman show, Tomlin plays characters who include a bag lady who talks to aliens, a teenage performance artist who thinks of people as "specks," a male weightlifter and sperm donor, a rich lady with a bad haircut, and a middle-aged feminist with hyperactive twins, a leaky geodesic dome house, a frustrating job, a divorce, and a doctor who is convinced that all her problems are the result of premenstrual syndrome (PMS).

American Peggy Miller Adato wins a Directors Guild of America Award for her documentary *Eugene O'Neill: A Glory of Ghosts*.

U.S. comedian Ellen DeGeneres (b. January 1, 1958) makes her first appearance on *The Tonight Show*.

Athletics and Exploration

U.S. explorer Ann Bancroft (b. 1955), starting on Ward Hunt Island in Canada, becomes the first woman to walk to the North Pole.

U.S. golfer Pat Bradley is the top women's money winner and Player of the Year.

U.S. figure skater Debi Thomas wins the world championship; East German Katarina Witt comes in second.

U.S. jockey Julie Krone wins a race at Monmouth Park. One of the losing jockeys, Miguel Rujano, whips her across the face; she punches him. A brawl ensues, and both are fined. Rujano is suspended from racing for five days.

Jan. 28 Astronaut Judith Resnick and teacher Christa McAuliffe die in the explosion of the *Challenger* space shuttle.

Activism

Nov. U.S. activist Amy Carter, daughter of former President Jimmy Carter, is arrested in a demonstration against Central Intelligence Agency (CIA) recruitment at the University of Massachusetts at Amherst.

Business and Industry

Only one state, Connecticut, has a woman president of its state AFL-CIO federation.

Women are 33% of the presidents and 50% of the officers of the 3,500 locals of the American Federation of State, County, and Municipal Employees (AFSCME).

In the United States, 5.9% of women are self-employed.

June Two women and four men in Iran are found guilty of involvement in prostitution and stoned to death.

July 2 The U.S. Supreme Court upholds affimative action on the basis of race and gender.

Science and Medicine

U.S. archaeologist Diane Chase, with her husband, Arlen, discovers the tomb of a seventh-century Maya woman in Belize. The height of the pyramid that contains the tomb, and the elaborate nature of the burial chamber itself indicate that the woman's status was very high indeed. The discovery leads some archaeologists to reconsider their assumption that women were held in low esteem among the Maya.

DNA research suggests that all humans may be descended from one African female ancestor.

The Society of Women Engineers gives its annual Achievement Award to American chemist Yvonne C. Brill for her work on rocket and satellite propulsion.

Geologist Susan W. Kieffer, geneticist Liane B. Russell, and mathematician Karen K. Uhlenbeck are inducted into the National Academy of Sciences.

U.S. physicist Leona Libby, the only woman officially assigned to the Manhattan Project, dies. Despite a hint from one colleague that she "go back to pots and pans," she was instrumental in the development of the A-bomb, codesigning the first nuclear reactor, working on the first thermal column, and inventing the rotating neutron spectrometer. She also invented a method of tracking climatic changes by measuring the amounts of isotopes found in tree rings.

Education and Scholarship

American Tess Gallagher publishes *A Concert of Tenses: Essays on Poetry*.

Gerda Lerner publishes *The Creation of Patriarchy: Women and History*.

Religion

New works of religious scholarship include Catherine Keller's *From a Broken Web: Separation, Sexism, and Self*, Mercy Amba Oduyoye's *Hearing and Knowing: Theological Reflections on Christianity in Africa*, Paula Gunn Allen's *The Sacred Hoop: Recovering the Feminine in American Indian Traditions*, and Elizabeth A. Petroff's *Medieval Women's Visionary Literature*.

1987

General Status and Daily Life

Ten women are killed in the United States every day by their batterers. On October 30, Karen Straw is acquitted on grounds of self-defense after killing her abusive husband.

Mar. 3 The West German fashion magazine *Buda Moden* begins distribution in the USSR.

Sept. *Izvestia* reports that abortion is a standard means of birth control in the Soviet Union.

Dec. A Sicilian man beats his thirteen-year-old sister to death for wearing makeup and staying out till 8:00 P.M.; he is given only a mild sentence, since "family honor" is involved.

Government, the Military, and the Law

Britain's House of Commons has 41 women and 609 men.

Arizona Republican Donna Carlson blows the whistle on her boss, Governor Evan Mecham. Her grand jury testimony and the resulting death threat she receives from a Mecham associate lead to impeachment proceedings against Mecham and six felony indictments. Meanwhile, a recall campaign is being led by Gray Panther and retired professor Naomi Harward. Ousted,

Mecham is officially replaced by Secretary of State Rose Mofford on April 5, 1988.

Verna Williams becomes the first woman governor of New Mexico's largest pueblo, Isleta.

Jan. 27 Sheila Hellstrom becomes the first Canadian woman brigadier general.

Apr. 4 Iceland's Women's Alliance becomes part of the ruling coalition of parties.

Apr. 18 Annette Strausse becomes the first woman mayor of Dallas. Texas has other women mayors at this time, including Betty Turner of Corpus Christi, Janice Coggeshall of Galveston, and Kathryn Whitmire of Houston.

June 8 U.S. secretary Fawn Hall becomes the only woman to testify in the Iran-Contra hearings; she describes how Lt. Col. Oliver North shredded incriminating documents.

July Wilma Mankiller becomes the first woman leader of the Cherokee Nation.

Aug. 28 Philippine president Corazon Aquino suppresses a soldiers' rebellion.

Literature and the Visual Arts

U.S. author Fannie Flagg publishes *Fried Green Tomatoes at the Whistle Stop Café*, a novel about the deep love between two southern women, Idgie and Ruth, and the way in which their story of defiant independence and fierce loyalty awakens the inner strength of another woman, Evelyn Couch.

Artist Susan Rothenberg's *Three Trees* sells for $209,000, the most ever paid for a work by a contemporary woman artist.

American Nancy Fried sculpts *Hanging Out*, a statue of a headless woman standing casually with with thumbs in skirt waistband, one breast—and one diagonal mastectomy scar—exposed.

Washington, D.C.'s, National Museum of Women in the Arts opens to the public.

New U.S. poetry includes Tess Gallagher's *Amplitude*, Susan Howe's *Articulation of the Sound Forms in Time*, Ellen Bryant Wright's *The Lotus Flowers*, and Jane Miller's *American Odalisque*.

Apr. 7 Katherine Fanning, editor of the *Christian Science Monitor*, becomes the first woman president of the American Society of Newspaper Editors.

Dec. 3 U.S. feminist cartoonist Nicole Hollander, creator of the "Sylvia" strip, publishes the collection *Never Take Your Cat to a Salad Bar*.

Performing Arts and Entertainment

Filmgoers can see Ann Magnuson as a woman who finds the perfect (albeit artificial) man in *Making Mr. Right* (directed by Susan Seidelman), Bette Midler and Shelley Long as very different actresses in the buddy comedy *Outrageous Fortune*, Debra Winger and Theresa Russell in the thriller *Black Widow*, and Faye Dunaway in *Barfly*. Glenn Close and Anne Archer star in the thriller *Fatal Attraction*; Close creates controversy as Michael Douglas's psychotic, obsessive one-night stand, as many feel that her character stereotypes single women as obsessive and desperate. Cher wins the Best Actress Oscar for her portrayal of a young widow rediscovering love in *Moonstruck*; Olympia Dukakis wins the Best Supporting Actress Oscar for her role in the same film.

U.S. pop singer Whitney Houston records the album *Whitney*.

U.S. movie executive Dawn Steel becomes president of Columbia Pictures, a position she will hold until 1991.

Indian filmmaker Mira Nair directs *Children of Desired Sex*, about the use of amniocentesis to select the sex of a child.

U.S. broadcast journalist Linda Ellerbee establishes her own production company.

U.S. singer Aretha Franklin is inducted into the Rock and Roll Hall of Fame.

Athletics and Exploration

U.S. swimmer Janet Evans (b. August 28, 1971) sets world records in the 1,500-meter and 800-meter freestyle.

German tennis player Steffi Graf (b. 1969) defeats Martina Navratilova to win the French Open. Graf will win the Wimbledon singles title in 1989 and 1991 and the U.S. Open in 1988 and 1989.

Tania Aebi becomes the first American woman to sail alone around the world.

The Deutscher Sportsbund (German Sports Federation) has 20,043,290 members, 36.3% of them female.

Spanish bullfighter Maribel Atiénzar retires at the age of twenty-eight after thirteen years as a matador, angry at the sex bias which she says led promoters to boycott her.

All-America forward Shelly Pennefather goes to Japan to play basketball for $200,000 a year. Opportunities for women in professional basketball remain more promising for women in countries outside the United States, so many U.S. players choose to go abroad to play.

U.S. jockey Julie Krone wins 324 races for more than $4.5 million in purses. This makes her the sixth most productive jockey in the country.

The Tennessee Lady Vols win the NCAA women's basketball title.

East German swimmer Silke Horner sets a women's world record of 1:07.91 in the 100-meter breaststroke.

Mar. 18 Susan Butcher becomes the second person to win the Iditarod dogsled race more than once. T-shirts in Alaska read, "Alaska: Where Men Are Men and Women Win the Iditarod."

June 5 Dr. Mae Jemison becomes NASA's first black woman astronaut.

June 12 Nancy Lieberman and Lynette Richardson of the U.S. Basketball League are the first two women to play in the same game in a mostly male professional league.

July 24 American Hulda Crooks, ninety-one, becomes the oldest woman to scale Japan's Mt. Fuji.

Nov. 1 British runner Priscilla Welch wins the women's division of the New York Marathon; she is the oldest winner ever at forty-two.

Activism

American Rosalie Maggio publishes *The Nonsexist Word Finder*, which helps writers find alternatives to false generics like "mankind." It is expanded in 1992 as *The Bias-Free Word Finder*.

U.S. litigant Beulah Mae Donald (1920–1988) destroys a branch of the KKK with a $7 million judgment in the lynching of her son.

Aug. 18 Molly Yard becomes president of NOW.

Aug. 26 Ex-president of NOW Eleanor Smeal is arrested while demonstrating for gay and lesbian rights at the Vatican Embassy.

Oct. 11 Gay rights activist Virginia Apuzzo speaks to

500,000 before the Capitol building in Washington, D.C.

Business and Industry

Women own 30% of U.S. businesses.

Stockbroker Elaine Garzarelli becomes Wall Street's top guru after predicting the October 19 market crash.

American Cathleen Black is making $435,000 a year as publisher of *USA Today*, the best-read newspaper in the United States with a paid circulation of 1.6 million. Previously, she worked in ad sales for *Travel & Leisure*, *New York* magazine, and *Ms*.

Lenore Miller, President of the Retail, Wholesale, and Department Store Union, is elected to the AFL-CIO's Executive Council; she is one of three women on the council, which has thirty-eight members.

Jan. 13 The U.S. Supreme Court upholds a California law requiring maternity leave and job security upon return.

Aug. 16 In Spain, 84% of women workers report that they have been sexually harassed.

Science and Medicine

The Society of Women Engineers gives its annual Achievement Award to American research manager Nancy Dicciani for guiding the development of new industrial products, including a catalyst to assist benzene production, a product to separate air into nitrogen and oxygen, and a technique for recovering and purifying landfill gas.

Italian neurobiologist Rita Levi-Montalcini wins the Nobel Prize for Medicine or Physiology.

U.S. anthropologist Jane E. Buikstra and British paleontologist Mary Leakey are inducted into the National Academy of Sciences.

Mar. 2 For the first time, the first- and second-place awards in the Westinghouse Science Talent Search go to girls: Louise Chia Chang and Elizabeth Lee Wilmer.

Oct. 10 The *New York Times* reports that a team led by Dr. Helen Donis-Keller has mapped all twenty-three pairs of human chromosomes, a move that will allow location of specific genes for prevention and treatment of genetic disorders.

Religion

Self-proclaimed priestess Alice Lakwena leads a rebellion in Uganda.

Monica Sjöö and Barbara Mor publish *The Great Cosmic Mother: Rediscovering the Religion of the Earth*.

Feb. 5 The Jewish Theological Seminary of America announces that it will begin certifying women as Conservative cantors.

Apr. 4 Catholic bishops release a gender-inclusive New Testament.

Aug. 24 U.S. United Methodist minister Reverend Rose Mary Denman is suspended for lesbianism; she joins the Unitarian Universalist church, which permits gay clergy.

1988

General Status and Daily Life

Indiana teenager Rebecca Bell becomes the first known U.S. woman to die because a parental consent law kept her from access to a safe, legal abortion.

RU486, a chemical abortifacient that is highly effective in the first weeks of pregnancy and makes surgical abortions less necessary, is legalized for sale in France.

Jan. The Canadian Supreme Court rules that Canada's old abortion law, which permitted only hospital committee-approved "therapeutic" abortions, unconstitutionally limits a woman's control of her own body.

Feb. The Boy Scouts of America, after fourteen years of lobbying by Catherine Pollard, allows women to become scoutmasters.

Apr. Zana Muhsen is allowed to leave Yemen. In June 1980, at the age of fifteen, she was tricked into leaving Great Britain for Yemen by her father, who had secretly sold her into marriage for £1,300 ($2,340). Her fourteen-year-old sister, Nadia, was also sold. They were denied the right to leave Yemen and forced to act as wives to the men who bought them. Nadia remains in Yemen, fearing her daughter will be sold into marriage at the age of nine if she is left behind.

Government, the Military, and the Law

Congress authorizes a memorial for female Vietnam veterans.

Lenora Fulani of the New Alliance party is the first female and the first black presidential candidate to get on the ballot in all fifty states.

Texas politician Ann Richards gives the keynote speech at the National Democratic Convention.

In the United States, the manager of the Dukakis presidential campaign, named to the post in 1987, is Susan Estrich.

Brigadier General Gail Reals becomes the first woman to command a marine base.

Brenda Burns becomes the first woman warden of a U.S. men's prison.

Kvennalistinn (Women's Alliance), a women's political party founded in Iceland in 1983, is now, with 31.3% support, the nation's most popular party.

Ann Dore McLaughlin replaces William Brock as secretary of labor, the first woman head of that department since Frances Perkins.

Jan. Margaret Thatcher becomes Britain's longest-serving twentieth-century prime minister.

Jan. 10 Rosario Ibarra de Piedra becomes Mexico's first woman candidate for president.

Sept. Chinese political official Chen Muhua becomes head of the ACDWF.

Literature and the Visual Arts

Anne Tyler publishes the novel *Breathing Lessons*, which follows one day in the life of a middle-aged married couple.

New York Times columnist Anna Quindlen publishes a collection of her work, *Living Out Loud*. The essays cover topics ranging from abortion, religion, and politics, to child raising and sibling rivalry.

Anne Rice publishes her third vampire book, *Queen of the Damned*.

U.S. artist Mary Cassatt's *The Conversation* sells for $4.5 million, the highest price ever paid for a painting by a woman.

New U.S. poetry includes Maura Stanton's *Tales of the Supernatural*, Heather McHugh's *Shades*, Diana O'Hehir's *Home Free*, and Cathy Song's (b. 1955) *Frameless Windows, Squares of Light*.

Mar. 31 U.S. novelist Toni Morrison wins the Pulitzer Prize for *Beloved*.

Apr. 20 U.S. sculptor Louise Nevelson (b. September 23, 1900) dies. Her last major outdoor sculpture, the thirty-foot steel *Sky Horizon*, is installed at the National Institutes of Health this year.

Performing Arts and Entertainment

American Penny Marshall directs the hit film *Big*.

American Tracy Chapman records a self-titled folk-rock album that includes the songs "Talkin' 'Bout a Revolution," "Why?" and "Mountains of Things." The album's lyrics denounce sexism, racism, and materialism.

Filmgoers can see Lily Tomlin and Bette Midler in the mistaken-identity comedy *Big Business*, Diane Keaton as a woman fighting for her daughter's custody in *The Good Mother*, Christine Lahti as a 1960s radical on the run underground in the 1980s in *Running on Empty*, Jodie Foster in an Oscar-winning performance as a working-class rape victim and Kelly McGillis as her lawyer in *The Accused*, Sigourney Weaver as primatologist Dian Fossey in *Gorillas in the Mist*, Debra Winger as an undercover FBI agent infiltrating a white supremacist group in *Betrayed*, Susan Sarandon as a baseball groupie in *Bull Durham*, Holly Hunter in *Broadcast News*, Sigourney Weaver as a sneaky boss and Melanie Griffith as an exploited secretary in *Working Girl*, Michelle Pfeiffer as a Mafia widow trying to escape her past in the romantic comedy *Married to the Mob*, and Bette Midler, Barbara Hershey, and Mayim Bialik in the sentimental *Beaches*. German actress Marianne Sagebrecht stars as a woman who sets up shop at the *Bagdad Cafe*. American Geena Davis wins the Best Supporting Actress Academy Award for her portrayal of a dog trainer in *The Accidental Tourist*.

Dana Delaney stars on television as a Vietnam War nurse in the dramatic series "China Beach."

Indian filmmaker Mira Nair directs *Salaam Bombay*, a critically acclaimed film about homeless children.

Oprah Winfrey stars in a television movie version of Gloria Naylor's *The Women of Brewster Place*.

South African singer Miriam Makeba records *Sangoma* and tours the United States.

U.S. pop singer Paula Abdul releases *Forever Your Girl*, which includes the songs "Opposites Attract" and "Cold-Hearted Snake."

U.S. opera singer Renée Fleming makes her first appearance as Countess Almaviva in *The Marriage of Figaro*, the role with which she will become most closely identified.

Oct. U.S. singer Anita Baker's second album, *Giving You the Best That I've Got*, is released; by year's end it will sell more than 3 million copies.

Athletics and Exploration

U.S. pilot Jennifer Hudgens becomes, at eleven, the youngest woman to fly a plane cross-country.

American Susan Butcher wins Alaska's Iditarod dogsled race for the third year in a row.

German tennis player Steffi Graf wins a Grand Slam—the singles titles at Wimbledon, the U.S. Open, the French Open, and the Australian Open.

French cyclist Jeannie Longo wins the Tour de France for the second year in row, riding 524 miles in 22:41.38.

U.S. stunt pilot Joann Osterud makes continuous outside loops for more than two hours, breaking the old record.

Ann Meyers and Nera White become the first female players nominated to the Basketball Hall of Fame.

Grete Waitz wins the New York City Marathon.

U.S. runner Gail Devers sets a U.S. record in the 100-meter hurdles.

Winter At the Calgary Olympics, figure skater Katarina Witt of East Germany, world champion in 1983 and 1985, takes the gold, followed by Canadian Elizabeth Manley and American Debi Thomas. Witt is the first women's double gold medalist since Sonja Henie won in 1928 and 1932. Thomas is the first black athlete to medal in a winter games.
Soviets win the gold and silver medals in pairs skating, with Ekaterina Gordeeva and Sergei Grinkov in first and Elena Valova and Oleg Vassiliev in second. Their teammates Natalia Bestemianova and Andrei Boukine take the gold in ice dancing. East Germany sweeps the women's luge medals, with Steffi Walter-Martin, Ute Oberhofner, and Cerstin Schmidt taking first, second, and third.
West German Marina Kiehl wins the gold in women's downhill. Swiss skier Vreni Schneider wins the slalom and giant slalom. In super giant slalom,

Austrian Sigrid Wolf takes the gold. Austria's Anita Wachter wins the combined downhill and slalom gold. U.S. Virgin Islands skier Seba Johnson, at fourteen, is the youngest competitor and the Olympics's first black Alpine skier.

In Nordic skiing, Finland's Marjo Matikainen wins the 5-kilometer race and takes a bronze in the 10 kilometers. Soviet skier Vida Ventsene wins the 10 kilometers and takes the 5 kilometers bronze. Her teammate Raisa Smetanina, an Olympic veteran, takes bronzes in the 10 and 20 kilometers to bring her medal total to nine since 1976. A third Soviet, Tikhonova, wins the 20 kilometers, followed by a fourth Soviet medalist, Anfisa Reztsova. The Soviet team of Svetlana Nagueikina, Nina Gavriliuk, Tikhonova, and Reztsova wins the 4 x 5-kilometer relay, followed by the Norwegians (Turde Dybendahl, Marit Wold, Anne Jahren, and Marianne Dahlmo) and the Finns (Pirkko Maatta, Marja Liisa Kirvesniemi, Matikainen, and Jaana Savolainen).

U.S. speed skater Bonnie Blair breaks East German Christa Rothenburger's old record and wins the 500 meters. Rothenburger comes in second, and East German Karin Kania-Enke takes third. Blair also takes a bronze in the 1,000, becoming the only U.S. competitor to win two medals at this Olympics. Dutch skater Yvonne van Gennip wins the 1,500, the 3,000, and (in its first year as a women's event) the 5,000 meters. Kania-Enke takes silvers in the 1,000 and 1,500, and Rothenburger wins the 1,000, setting Olympic and world records in the process.

Apr. U.S. mountain climber Helen Thayer, fifty-one, becomes the first woman to ski alone to the North Magnetic Pole.

Summer In Seoul, Monique Knol of the Netherlands wins the bicycle road race. Soviet cyclist Erika Saloumiae wins the match sprint, and bronze medalist Connie Paraskevin-Young, world match sprint champion in 1984, brings home the only U.S. women's cycling medal of this Olympics.

South Korea sweeps the women's archery medals: first, second, and third go to Soo-nyung Kim, Hee-kyung Wang, and Young-sook Yun, who are also the three gold medalists in team archery. West Germany's Anja Fichtel wins the individual foil gold, followed by her teammates Sabine Bau and Zita Funkenhauser; not surprisingly, the West German team, composed of Fichtel, Bau, Funkenhauser, Christiane Weber, and Annette Klug, wins the team gold.

The basketball gold goes to the U.S. team. Australia wins the field hockey gold, followed by South Korea and the Netherlands. The Dutch team includes several of the 1984 gold medalists: Carina Benninga, Bernadette De Beus, Anneloes Nieuwenhuizen, Martine Ohr, Marieke Van Doorn, Arlette Van Manen, Sophie Von Weiler, and Laurien Willemse. South Korea wins the team handball gold, and the Soviet Union wins the gold in volleyball.

Yugoslavia's Jasna Sekaric wins the women's air pistol event and takes a bronze in the sport pistol. Nino Saloukvadze of the Soviet Union gets a gold in the sport pistol event and silver in the air pistol. Soviet shooter Irinia Chilova wins the air rifle competition; Silvia Sperber of West Germany wins the small-bore rifle, three-position and takes the silver in air rifle. South Korea wins all of the women's Taekwondo golds, except in the welterweight division, where American Arlene Limas takes first place.

Table tennis makes its debut as an Olympic sport. South Korea's Jung-Hwa Hyun and Young-Ja Yang win the doubles, followed by China's Jing Chen and Zhimin Jiao. Chen wins the gold in singles, followed by teammates Huifen Li and Zhimin Jiao. Another new event is the women's 470 class in yachting, won by Americans Allison Jolly and Lynne Jewell.

In the equestrian events, which are open to both sexes, women sweep the individual dressage medals. First place goes to West Germany's Nicole Uphoff, second to France's Margitt Otto-Crepin, and third to Switzerland's Christine Steuckelberger (a silver medalist in team dressage this year). West Germany wins the gold in team dressage; its team includes Uphoff, Ann Kathrin Linsenhoff, and Monica Theodorescu. Canada's third-place team includes Cynthia Ishoy, Eva Maria Pracht, and Gina Smith. Lisa Jacquin and Anne Kursinski are on the silver-medal U.S. show jumping team, and Virginia Leng (bronze medalist in the individual three-day event) and Karen Straker of Great Britain win silvers in the team three-day event.

West Germany's Steffi Graf wins the tennis singles gold, followed by Argentina's Gabriela Sabatini and, in third place, American Zina Garrison and Bulgarian Manuela Maleeva. Garrison wins the doubles gold with Pam Shriver; silver goes to Czechoslovakia's Jana Novotna and Helena Sukova, and Graf ties for bronze with her partner, Claudia Kohde-Kilsch, and with the Australian team of Elizabeth Smylie and Wendy Turnbull.

In the rowing events, Bulgaria's Vania Guecheva wins the kayak 500-meter singles and takes a silver in the 500-meter kayak pairs with Diana Palliska and a bronze in the kayak fours with Palliska, Ogniana Petkova, and Borislava Ivanova. East Germany's Birgit Schmidt wins the kayak pairs with Anke Nothnagel, wins the kayak fours with Nothnagel, Ramona Portwich, and Heike Singer, and takes a silver in the kayak singles. East German Jutta Behrendt wins the single sculls, and her teammates Birgit Peter and Martina Schroeter win the double sculls. Romania's Rodica Arba and Olga Homeghi win the coxless pair gold. East Germany wins the quadruple sculls, the coxed four, and the eight oars.

The Canadian team of Michelle Cameron and Carolyn Waldo takes the gold in the synchronized swimming duet. Waldo wins the solo event, followed by Tracie Ruiz-Conforto of the United States. China's Xu Yanmei wins the platform diving event, and her teammate Gao

Min wins the gold in the springboard. East Germany's Kristin Otto wins the 50-meter and 100-meter freestyles, the 100-meter backstroke, and 100-meter butterfly; she also takes a gold medal in the 4 x 100 freestyle relay, with Katrin Meissner (bronze medalist in the 50 meters), Daniela Hunger (winner of the 200-meter medley and bronze medalist in the 400-meter medley), and Manuela Stellmach (bronze medalist in the 200-meter freestyle). East Germany also wins the 4 x 100 medley relay with its team of Otto, Birte Weigang (silver medalist in the 100- and 200-meter butterfly), Meissner, and Silke Hoerner (winner of the 200-meter breaststroke and bronze medalist in the 100 meters). East Germany's Heike Friedrich wins the 200-meter freestyle and takes a silver in the 400, and her teammate Kathleen Nord wins the 200-meter butterfly.

U.S. swimmer Janet Evans wins three gold medals (in the 400- and 800-meter freestyles and 400-meter individual medley) and sets one Olympic and one world record. Bulgaria's Tania Dangalakova wins the 100-meter breaststroke. Hungary's Krisztina Egerszegi wins the 200-meter backstroke and takes a silver in the 100 meters. Three former U.S. medalists return to the victory platform; Mary T. Meagher takes a bronze in the 200-meter butterfly, Dara Torres and Mary Wayte, members of the 1984 gold medal team, take bronzes in the freestyle relay, and Wayte wins a silver in the medley relay.

In a new women's track-and-field event, the 10,000-meter race, Russia's Olga Bondarenko takes the gold. Rosa Mota of Portugal wins the women's marathon. American Florence Griffith-Joyner wins the 100-meter and 200-meter races and the 4 x 100-meter relay (with Alice Brown, Sheila Echols, and 100-meter dash silver medalist Evelyn Ashford). She also wins a silver in the 4 x 400 relay. Other U.S. medalists include Louise Ritter, who wins the gold with an Olympic record high jump, and "Flo-Jo"'s sister-in-law, Jackie Joyner-Kersee, who wins the long jump and the heptathlon.

The East Germans win several medals. Sigrun Wodars wins the 800, Martina Hellmann the discus, and Petra Felke the javelin. The Soviet Union wins golds in the 400 (Olga Bryzguina), the 3,000 (Tatiana Samolenko, the bronze medalist in the 1,500), the shot put (Natalia Lisovskaya), and the 4 x 400 relay, whose team includes Bryzguina. Paula Ivan of Romania wins the 1,500 and takes a silver in the 3,000. Jordanka Donkova of Bulgaria wins the 100-meter hurdles, and Australia's Debra Flintoff-King wins the 400-meter hurdles.

In team gymnastics, the gold goes to the Soviets: Svetlana Baitova, Elena Chevtchenko, Olga Strajeva, Svetlana Boguinskaia, Natalia Lachtchenova, and Elena Shoushounova. Romania gets the silver. Shoushounova wins the all-around, takes a silver in the beam, and wins a bronze in the uneven bars, but it is Romanian Daniela Silivas, silver medalist in the all-around, who shines in the individual apparatus events, winning the beam, parallel bars, and floor exercises and

taking a bronze in the vault. Third place in the all-around goes to Svetlana Boguinskaia, who wins the vault and takes a silver in the floor exercise. Her teammate Marina Lobatch wins the gold in rhythmic gymnastics.

Activism

Sept. Florida real estate agent Sheelah Ryan wins $55 million in the lottery and uses much of it to fund the Ryan Foundation, which helps homeless and battered women and single mothers.

Business and Industry

U.S. fashion designer Jhane Barnes's design firm has retail sales of $20 million.

British cosmetics entrepreneur Anita Roddack's Body Shop has 300 stores in thirty-four countries.

Soviet publisher Yelena Korenevskaya begins publishing *Soviet Culture*, an English-language travel guide and the USSR's first private travel magazine.

At about this time, Della Femina, Travisano & Partners, the eighteenth-largest advertising agency in the United States, becomes the first ad agency in the country to add a woman's name. It becomes Della Femina, McNamee WCRS to recognize its president and chief operating officer, Louise R. McNamee.

Science and Medicine

Gertrude Elion wins the Nobel Prize for Medicine or Physiology for her work on leukemia, herpes, and heart transplants.

The Society of Women Engineers gives its annual Achievement Award to American Roberta Nichols for her research into alternative fuels for transportation.

Psychologist Frances K. Graham, neurobiologist Carol A. Gross, anthropologist Patty Jo Watson, and entomologist Mary Jane West-Eberhard become members of the National Academy of Sciences.

Education and Scholarship

Lambda Delta Lambda, the United States' first primarily lesbian sorority, is founded at UCLA.

Joan Konner becomes the first woman dean of Columbia's Graduate School of Journalism.

Bonnie Anderson and Judith Zinsser publish *A History of Their Own*, a two-volume work that chronicles the lives of everyday and extraordinary European women from prehistory to the twentieth century.

Religion

American Barbara Harris becomes the first woman Episcopal bishop.

American Catharine Burroughs is the first Western woman named a *tulku* or reincarnated lama of Tibetan Buddhism.

Winter Jewish women read the Torah at Jerusalem's Wailing Wall; they are accosted by outraged traditionalists who shout, "I forbid it!" "The Torah is not for women," and "Women with the Torah—this is like pigs at the Wall!"

1989

General Status and Daily Life

U.S. women's right to legal abortion is undermined by the Supreme Court in *Webster* v. *Reproductive Health Services*, which upholds restrictions on abortion at public facilities or facilities receiving public funds.

A pregnant Florida cocaine addict is convicted of transmitting drugs to a "minor"—her fetus.

In Japan, the average age at first marriage is 25.8 for women and 28.5 for men.

Government, the Military, and the Law

Kristin Baker becomes the first female captain of the West Point Corps of Cadets.

Burmese pacifist and political prisoner Aung San Suu Kyi, jailed when her National League for Democracy party threatened military rule by winning 81% of the vote in an election, goes on a hunger strike. She is the first Burmese woman to run for high political office.

U.S. actress and diplomat Shirley Temple Black becomes ambassador to Czechoslovakia, a position she will hold until 1992.

Thanks to a lawsuit filed in 1981 by Isabelle Gauthier, Canadian women now have access to all combat positions in the military except submarine duty.

Literature and the Visual Arts

U.S. author Amy Tan publishes *The Joy Luck Club*, which tells the stories of two generations of Chinese-American women.

Alice Walker publishes *The Temple of My Familiar*, which continues the stories of her characters from *The Color Purple*.

New U.S. poetry includes Dolores Kendrick's (b. 1927) *The Women of Plums: Poems in the Voices of Slave Women*, Emily Hiestand's (b. 1947) *Green in the Witch-Hazel Wood*, Brenda Hillman's *Fortress*, Rita Dove's *Grace Notes*, Louise Erdrich's *Baptism of Desire*, and Mary Jo Salter's *Unfinished Painting*.

U.S. Hopi artist Linda Lomahaftewa draws *Blue Cloud Maiden*, an oil pastel portrait that draws on traditional, stylized representations.

Fourteen-year-old Chinese artist Wang Yani becomes the youngest person to have a one-woman show at the United States' Smithsonian Institution. She began painting at the age of two and a half and had her first show in Shanghai at age four. By age six, she had painted 4,000 pictures.

Fall The Civil Rights Memorial in Montgomery, Alabama, is dedicated. It was designed by U.S. architect Maya Lin, who also designed the Washington., D.C., Vietnam War Memorial.

Performing Arts and Entertainment

U.S. blues singer Bessie Smith is inducted posthumously into the Rock and Roll Hall of Fame.

U.S. comedians Kathy Najimy and Mo Gaffney have an off-Broadway hit, *The Kathy and Mo Show: Parallel Lives*, which discusses everything from menstrual periods to hairspray to God.

Canadian country and western singer k.d. lang records *Absolute Torch and Twang*.

Isabelle Adjani is nominated for an Oscar for her work in *Camille Claudel*. Julia Roberts is nominated for her portrayal of a diabetic daughter in *Steel Magnolias*. Brenda Fricker wins the Best Supporting Actress Oscar for *My Left Foot*, and Jessica Tandy wins the Best

Actress Award for her portrayal of a cranky, mentally faltering Southern matriarch in *Driving Miss Daisy*. Meg Ryan stars in the movie *When Harry Met Sally . . .*, written by Nora Ephron.

Athletics and Exploration

U.S. tennis player Chris Evert retires with a world record 157 tournament wins.

Spanish bullfighter Angela Hernández is gored through the knee by a bull, leaving the bottom half of her leg attached by a single tendon. Carried from the plaza and fitted with an artificial knee, she will try in later years to make a comeback but will be paid a fraction of her former fees.

Midori Ito becomes the first Japanese woman figure skater to win a world championship.

Swiss slalom skier Vreni Schneider wins a record fourteen World Cup races in one season. She also wins the World Cup overall slalom title and will repeat her victory in 1990.

U.S. speed skater Bonnie Blair wins the World Sprint Championship.

The Tennessee Lady Vols win the NCAA basketball championship.

China's Huang Zhihong becomes the first Asian to win a World Cup track-and-field event when she wins the gold in the shot put.

Soviet gymnast Svetlana Boguinskaya wins the all-around world title.

Feb. U.S. golfer Dottie Mochrie wins her first tournament; in 1992 she will win $690,000.

Activism

NOW has more than 200,000 members.

Science and Medicine

The Society of Women Engineers gives its annual Achievement Award to American metallurgist Doris Kuhlmann-Wilsdorf, a pioneer in the study of solids under conditions of erosion, friction, and other deformation-creating forces.

Economist Ester Boserup, psychologist Marianne Frankenhauser, biologist N. M. Le Douarin, biologist

Philippa Marrack, social scientist Jane Menken, and anthropologist Barbara H. Partee are elected to the National Academy of Sciences.

Greek archaeologist Liani Souvaltzi excavates sites in the Siwa Oasis, believing that the tomb of Alexander the Great lies there.

Education and Scholarship

In Japan, women are 91% of junior college and 26% of four-year college students.

Religion

Feminist theologian and Episcopal priest Isabel Carter Heyward publishes *Touching Our Strength: The Erotic as Power and the Love of God*.

1990

General Status and Daily Life

The FDA approves Norplant, a device that, implanted under the skin of a woman's arm, releases hormonal contraceptives slowly for a long period of time.

In Japan, the average woman lives 81.8 years and may well be one of the 300 million readers of the nation's sixty-nine women's magazines. When she marries, her wedding will cost ¥5.7 million (US$39,000). If she works outside the home, she will spend about two and a half hours each weeknight on housework, compared with her husband's eight minutes.

In the United States, the Department of Health and Human Services handles 18 million cases of delinquent child support payments; only 18% result in collection.

Ohio governor Richard Celeste grants clemency to twenty-six women convicted of killing or assaulting their batterers.

Oct. Aminata Diop, a citizen of Mali, seeks political asylum in France to avoid traditional genital mutilation. Her appeal is rejected.

Government, the Military, and the Law

Japan's Diet has forty-six women members.

Violeta Chamorro (b. 1929) becomes president of Nicaragua.

Ann Richards becomes governor of Texas.

Sharon Pratt Dixon of Washington, D.C., becomes the first black woman mayor of a major U.S. city.

Federal judge Kimba Wood sentences junk bond broker Michael Milken to ten years in prison.

Pakistani prime minister Benazir Bhutto is dismissed and imprisoned.

Sahana Pradhan becomes Nepal's Minister of Industry and Commerce for Interior Government.

Kuwaiti women cannot vote.

Literature and the Visual Arts

U.S. author Bettina Flores self-publishes *Chiquita's Cocoon*, described as "a combination of autobiography, self-help book and Latina feminist manifesto."

Mexican screenwriter Laura Esquivel (b. 1950) publishes *Como agua para chocolate* (*Like Water for Chocolate*), which becomes the number-one best-selling novel that year. Translated into English in 1992, the novel tells the story of Tita, who is forced by tradition to give up her lover so that she may tend to the needs of her aging mother. The heartbroken Tita pours all of her emotion into her cooking, and her food magically transforms those who eat it.

U.S. author Audre Lorde publishes the performance poem *Need: A Chorale for Black Woman Voices*.

U.S. artist Jane Ash Poitras paints *Wounded OKA*, which commemorates the successful fight to keep a golf course from being constructed on sacred Mohawk land.

U.S. poet Joy Harjo (b. 1951) publishes *In Mad Love and War*.

Dec. 31 British mystery novelist P. D. (Phyllis Dorothy) James is made a baroness. Her novels include *The Black Tower* (1975), *Devices and Desires* (1989), and *The Skull Beneath the Skin* (1982).

Performing Arts and Entertainment

U.S. producers Wallis Nicita and Lauren Lloyd produce the comedy *Mermaids*; both women are casting legends. Nicita cast Kathleen Turner in *Body Heat* and cast all of Lawrence Kasdan's films, *Missing*, and *The Witches of Eastwick*; Lloyd cast Haing S. Ngor in *The Killing Fields*. Nicita and Lloyd are also the producers of *The Butcher's Wife*, which stars Demi Moore as a southern psychic searching for love in New York.

New films include *The Handmaid's Tale*, a dramatization of Margaret Atwood's dark, futuristic novel that stars Natasha Richardson as Offred; *Mermaids*, starring Cher and Winona Ryder; *Dick Tracy*, starring Madonna; *White Palace*, starring Susan Sarandon as a middle-aged burger waitress in love with a much younger man; *Edward Scissorhands*, with Winona Ryder; *Green Card*, with Andie MacDowell; *Hamlet*, with Glenn Close as Gertrude and Helena Bonham Carter as Ophelia; *The Long Walk Home*, a movie about the 1955 Montgomery bus boycott starring Sissy Spacek and Whoopi Goldberg; *Postcards from the Edge*, starring Meryl Streep and based on a book by Carrie Fisher; *I Love You to Death*, starring British comedian Tracey Ullman as a woman determined to kill her two-timing husband; *Henry and June*, based on the diaries of Anaïs Nin and starring Uma Thurman and Maria de Medeiros; and *Pretty Woman*, a popular romantic comedy starring Julia Roberts as a prostitute-Cinderella.

Yolanda Toussieng designs the bizarre hairstyles for *Edward Scissorhands*. She will later win an Oscar for 1993's *Mrs. Doubtfire*.

Joanne Woodward wins the New York Film Critics Circle Best Actress Award for *Mr. and Mrs. Bridge*, written by Ruth Prawer Jhabvala. Jhabvala will be nominated for an Oscar in 1993.

U.S. blues singer "Ma" Rainey is inducted into the Rock and Roll Hall of Fame.

In the United States, women direct 23 of the year's 406 feature films. Ellen Lewis casts the mob movie *Goodfellas*.

U.S. songwriter Diane Warren writes Michael Bolton's hit song "When I'm Back on My Feet Again" in ten minutes. Warren, also the author of Cher's hit "If I Could Turn Back Time," has written eighteen top-ten songs and had seven songs on the Billboard singles chart simultaneously.

Canadian director Deepa Mehta makes a film about male bonding, *Sam and Me*, which wins an award at Cannes in 1991.

New albums include Suzanne Vega's *Days of Open Hand*, Whitney Houston's *I'm Your Baby Tonight*, and *Mariah Carey*.

The Best Actress Oscar goes to Kathy Bates for her portrayal of a demented romance-novel fan in *Misery*; the Best Supporting Actress Oscar goes to Whoopi Goldberg for her portrayal of a psychic in *Ghost*, which also stars Demi Moore.

May 21 Polish actress Krystina Janda wins the Best Actress Award at Cannes for *The Interrogator*.

Athletics and Exploration

Susan Butcher wins the 1,168-mile Iditarod dogsled race, which runs from Anchorage to Nome, for the fourth time, setting a record time.

Figure skater Kristi Yamaguchi wins the U.S. pairs championship with partner Rudi Galindo.

Chinese diver Fu Mingxia, eleven, becomes the youngest world champion in any sport. Fear that such young divers will injure themselves leads the sport's governing body to restrict those under fourteen from entering major competitions.

Soviet gymnast Svetlana Boguinskaya wins or ties every event at the European Championships and scores perfect tens in the floor exercise and the balance beam. Her teammate Natalia Kalinina ties her on the beam and the uneven parallel bars.

Long- and middle-distance runner Francie Larrieu Smith (b. November 23, 1952) becomes the top-ranked woman marathoner in the United States.

Yugoslav tennis player Monica Seles wins the French Open; Argentina's Gabriela Sabatini wins the U.S. Open.

Activism

Three hundred women are arrested and six killed in pro-democracy demonstrations in Nepal.

Botswanan Unity Dow files a successful lawsuit challenging her nation's unequal 1984 Citizenship Act.

Nov. Argentinian Lidia Otero, Venezuelan Evangelina García Prince, and Brazilian Marta Alvarez establish the Latin American Network of Feminist Political Women.

Nov. 6 In Riyadh, Saudi Arabia, forty-seven women drive cars to protest a law preventing women from operating vehicles. They are briefly imprisoned and called "corrupters of society" by religious leaders. They

are fired from their jobs; some have their lives or families threatened.

Business and Industry

Japan has 10,600,000 wives who work outside the home and 14,800,000 who do not. There are 25,930,000 women in the work force, constituting 40.6% of the total work force; 34.4% of women employees (not including family workers and the self-employed) are clerical workers, and 12.5% are sales workers.

Science and Medicine

The SWE gives its annual Achievement Award to U.S. electrical engineer Lynn Conway (b. 1938) for her work with very large scale intergrated (VLSI) circuit and system design.

Engineer Esther Conwell, physiologist Gertrude Elion, agricultural scientist Nina Fedoroff, anthropologist Sarah Blaffer Hrdy, mathematician Cathleen Morawetz, German biologist Christiane Nusslein-Volhard, and neurobiologist P. S. Goldman-Rakic become members of the U.S. National Academy of Sciences.

Marine scientist Sylvia Earle (b. 1935) wins a gold medal from the Society of Woman Geographers.

Education and Scholarship

In Japan, 96% of girls attend some high school; 37% go on to college, as compared with 35% of boys, but most girls go to junior colleges so as not to be better educated than their husbands.

U.S. historian Laurel Thatcher Ulrich publishes her Pulitzer Prize-winning history, *A Midwife's Tale*. The book uses details from the diary of Maine midwife Martha Ballard to depict the society of New England in the late eighteenth and early nineteenth centuries.

Susie Tanhu and K. Lalita publish *Women Writing in India 600 B.C.–20th Century*.

In China, one third of college graduates are women.

Religion

The United Methodist church finds that 41% of its female clergy have been sexually harassed by colleagues.

Oct. Suzan Johnson becomes the New York Police Department's first female chaplain.

1991

General Status and Daily Life

More adult women in the United States are injured by battery than any other cause.

Brazil abolishes "defense of honor" as a legitimate cause for killing an allegedly adulterous wife.

In the Dominican Republic, about 200 beauticians dispense contraceptives and family-planning advice. Women find the beauty parlor more convenient and private than a clinic.

The U.S. Supreme Court upholds a ban on all-male eating clubs at Princeton University; the case was started by feminist Sally Frank in 1979, who tried to join an all-male club and was harassed by the members.

U.S. etiquette expert Judith Martin publishes *Miss Manners' Guide to Excruciatingly Correct Behavior*, which contains such gems as, "Q. 'I am embarrassed when a woman I am lunching with grabs the check. . . . What is the woman's real objective here—to prove she's my equal?' A. 'Yes.'"

The average age at marriage for Japanese women is 25.9.

Mar. Great Britain repeals an eighteenth-century law sanctioning marital rape.

July Great Britain legalizes RU486 up to the ninth week of pregnancy; surgical abortions are legal up to the twenty-eighth week.

July 13 In Kenya, 303 schoolboys attack a girls' dormitory after the girls refuse to join a protest against the headmaster. They kill nineteen and rape seventy-one. A deputy principal says, "The boys never meant any harm against the girls. They just wanted to rape."

Sept. France becomes the first country to recognize female genital mutilation as a form of persecution under the Geneva Convention. More than 80 million African women have been genitally mutilated.

Dec. Poland's medical society begins ousting doctors who perform abortions except in cases of rape or where the woman's life is threatened, even though the procedure is legal.

Government, the Military, and the Law

University professor Lale Aytaman becomes Turkey's first woman provincial governor.

Gloria Molina becomes the first Latina on the powerful Los Angeles County Board of Supervisors.

U.S. Army Reserves Captain Yolanda Huet-Vaughn is the only Gulf War resister to refuse to fight on the grounds of international law; she claims the war violates the UN charter.

Islamic law (Shariah) is adopted in Pakistan; it limits women's rights as witnesses, judges, and lawyers.

The Minnesota Supreme Court now has a female majority.

U.S. soldier Donna Jackson comes out as a lesbian before being shipped to the Persian Gulf, saying, "I want everyone to know that there's nothing wrong with being gay and serving my country with pride."

Women are 22% of U.S. lawyers and judges.

In some cases in Sudan, one man's testimony in court is equal to two women's.

Anna Popowicz, a former lawyer for Solidarity, becomes Poland's minister of women's and family affairs; a proponent of sex education and family planning, she will be ousted by February 1992 for her progressive policies.

Apr. Hanue Kitamura of Ashiya City becomes the first woman mayor in Japan. Japan's first woman vice-governor is also elected this year.

May Edith Cresson, appointed by President François Mitterand, becomes France's first woman prime minister.

May Former Chinese political leader Jiang Qing commits suicide.

June Of 5,078 candidates for office in Algeria, only 70 are women.

Oct. Anita Hill testifies before the Senate Judiciary Committee that she was sexually harassed by Supreme Court appointee Clarence Thomas. The testimony generates controversy, discussion of sexual harassment nationwide, and increased political activity by women angry at Hill's reception by the Senate.

Literature and the Visual Arts

Bosnian ten-year-old Zlata Filipovic begins keeping a diary in which she details the horrors of war in the former Yugoslavia. The diary, which will be published in 1994, is likened by many to Anne Frank's.

Barbara Brandon becomes the first black woman syndicated cartoonist when her strip, "Where I'm Coming From," is picked up by Universal Press Syndicate.

South African Nadine Gordimer wins the Nobel Prize for Literature.

Amy Tan publishes the novel *The Kitchen God's Wife*.

Egyptian feminist Nawal El Saadawi publishes the novel *Searching*.

Jan. 3 Art director Cipe Pineles Burtin dies. The first woman member of the Art Directors Club, the first woman member of its Hall of Fame, and the only woman in the Hall of Fame from 1975 until 1990, she designed the look of several prominent magazines, including *British Vogue*, *Seventeen*, and *Mademoiselle*.

Performing Arts and Entertainment

Pratibha Parmar makes the film *Khush* (*Pleasure*) about South Asian gays and lesbians. Indian director Mira Nair directs *Mississippi Masala*, about the love affair between a black American and a woman of Indian descent. Sagarai Chabbra makes *Now, I Will Speak*, India's first documentary about rape.

U.S. rock singer Tina Turner is inducted into the Rock and Roll Hall of Fame.

U.S. rapper Yo Yo releases her feminist, assertive debut album, *Make Way for the Motherlode*.

Polish filmmaker Agnieszka Holland directs *Europa, Europa*, an acclaimed film about a Jewish boy who pretends to be a Nazi in order to escape the Holocaust.

Filmgoers can see Mia Farrow, Judy Davis, Judith Ivey, Bernadette Peters, Cybill Shepherd, and Gwen Verdon in *Alice*, Elizabeth Perkins in *He Said, She Said* (codirected by Marisa Silver), Meg Ryan in *The Doors* (costume design for 10,000 cast members by Marlene Stewart), Mary Elizabeth Mastrantonio as a corporate lawyer in *Class Action*, Ellen Barkin as a male chauvinist-turned-woman in *Switch*, Pamela Reed in *Kindergarten Cop*, and Madonna (b. 1959) in *Truth or Dare*. Jodie Foster stars as a novice FBI agent in *Silence of the Lambs* (for which she wins the Best Actress Oscar) and directs and stars in *Little Man Tate*, with Dianne Wiest. Laura Dern and Diane Ladd star in the film *Rambling Rose*, directed by Martha Coolidge; Dern and Ladd will both be nominated for Oscars, becoming the first mother and daughter nominated in the same year. Sally Field stars

as a U.S. woman held prisoner in Iran in *Not Without My Daughter*. Geena Davis and Susan Sarandon star as rebellious women on the run in the controversial film *Thelma and Louise*. Many claim the movie bashes men; others retort that it's merely a response to hundreds of misogynist films. Suzana Peric does the music editing for *Silence of the Lambs*, as she has for *Something Wild*, *Married to the Mob*, *Dead Ringers*, and *Postcards from the Edge*.

U.S. opera singer Renée Fleming makes her Metropolitan Opera debut.

Athletics and Exploration

Swiss skier Vreni Schneider wins the World Cup giant slalom; Yugoslavia's Natasa Bokal wins the slalom.

At the World Cup speed skating races, American Bonnie Blair wins the 500 meters, and German skater Gunda Kleemann wins the 1,500.

The Tennessee Lady Vols win the NCAA basketball title.

Gymnast Kim Zmeskal becomes the first American to win the world all-around championship. Soviet gymnast Svetlana Boguinskaya comes in second. Romanian Cristina Bontas ties for first place in the floor exercise.

Chinese athlete Huang Zhihong wins the world championship in the shot put.

U.S. kick boxer Kathy Long becomes the first martial artist named to the *Black Belt* and *Inside Kung-Fu* halls of fame in the same year.

Yugoslav tennis player Monica Seles wins the French Open.

U.S. basketball player Bridgette Gordon leads her Italian team to a national championship, cheered on by her own fan club, the Boys of Bridgette.

U.S. golfer Pat Bradley wins her thirtieth career tournament.

Judy Sweet becomes the first female president of the NCAA.

Hungarian swimmer Kristina Egerszegi breaks a world backstroke record at the European Championships.

Austrian Petra Kronberger (b. February 21, 1969) wins the World Cup slalom title, single-handedly besting ten national teams in Nations Cup scoring. Vreni Schneider of Switzerland wins the giant slalom title, followed by Austria's Anita Wachter. Austrian Sabine Ginther and

French skier Florance Masnada tie for the combined World Cup title. U.S. freestyle skier Ellen Breen wins the World Cup ski ballet championship.

U.S. figure skaters Kristi Yamaguchi, Tonya Harding, and Nancy Kerrigan finish first, second, and third at the World Championships.

Jan. At the world swimming championships, China's Qian Hong wins the 100-meter butterfly, and Australia's Linley Frame wins the 100-meter breaststroke.

Jan. In thirty-eight days, between December of last year and now, Austrian skier Petra Kronberger, winner of fifteen World Cup races, wins a race in every major ski event: slalom, giant slalom, Super G, downhill, and combined.

Feb. U.S. figure skater Tonya Harding wins the national women's title. During the event, she becomes the second woman in the world (after Japanese skater Midori Ito) to land a triple axel in competition.

Apr. U.S. runner Francie Larrieu Smith sets a record in the 10,000 meters.

June 8 U.S. jockey Mary Bacon (b. 1948) commits suicide after an illness leaves her unable to continue her racing career. She rode in 3,526 races, taking first 286 times, second 310 times, and third 323 times and winning approximately $1 million.

Aug. British runner Liz McColgan, the silver medalist in the 10,000 meters in Seoul in 1988, wins the world championship in this event. Soviet runner Tatyana Ledovskaya wins the 400-meter hurdles, and German sprinter Katrin Krabbe wins the 100- and 200-meter dashes. Algerian runner Hassiba Boulmerka wins the world championship in the 1,500 meters; she is the first woman world champion from Algeria. Her country awards her the Medal of Merit, but Muslim fundamentalists issue a statement attacking her for running in the meet unveiled, with her face and legs exposed.

Oct. Spanish bullfighter Cristina Sánchez is chosen as the best student at the Tauromaquia de Madrid bullfighting school. As a female matador, she faces serious sexual discrimination, even though she has fought well enough to be awarded the bull's ears and tail. She says, "Those who scream at me to go to the kitchen have to know that they strengthen me and motivate me to fight bulls with even more anger, with more desire to demonstrate that women, just as men, deserve an opportunity . . . I want to make the *machistas* eat their words. Sometimes I even throw the ears directly to them."

Nov. The first World Championship for Women's

Soccer is held in Guangzhou, China.

Activism

Stanford University medical school professor Frances Conley resigns her post to protest sexual harassment, then returns to the school to fight the harassment from within.

Cuban poet, human rights leader, and dissident Maria Elena Cruz Varela is arrested, beaten, and forced to eat parts of her manuscripts.

Burmese opposition leader Aung San Suu Kyi wins the Nobel Peace Prize.

Jan. Ten thousand Sri Lankan women protest political violence in their country.

Sept. Minnesota high school student Katy Lyle wins a suit against her school, which did not defend her from sexual harassment. Sexual graffiti about her was removed only after sixteen complaints from her parents. She gets a settlement of $15,000 and a guarantee of programs at the school to address the issue of harassment.

Sept. Women in Colombia push for the criminalization of incest and marital rape.

Nov. Veena Hayat, a friend of Pakistani opposition leader Benzir Bhutto, and Khursheed Begum, another political activist, are attacked and raped by government-hired assailants. Rape is used in many parts of the world as a means of suppressing politically active women.

Business and Industry

Japan's Child Care Leave Law allows either parent to take a leave of absence from work until the child's first birthday.

In the United States, child care workers earn five to seven dollars an hour; journeyman electricians earn four or five times as much. Few women are training for male-dominated jobs such as plumber, electrician, machinist, or auto mechanic. Women are only 2% of building trades workers.

France criminalizes sexual harassment in the workplace.

After a lawsuit, Continental Airlines is forced to rehire Terri Fischette, whom it fired for not wearing makeup.

In the United States, 7% of employed women are self-employed.

The EEOC receives 6,883 complaints of sexual harassment.

Feminist bookstores gross $30 million in the United States.

June More than 400,000 Swiss women stage a one-day strike for equal pay.

Science and Medicine

The Society of Women Engineers gives its annual Achievement Award to American physicist Julia Weertman for her work on material failure at high temperatures.

Biochemist Jane S. Richardson, anthropologist Victoria Bricker, biochemist Mary Edmonds, physicist Mary Gaillard, and physiologist Susan Leeman are elected to the National Academy of Sciences.

Women are 18% of U.S. doctors.

Education and Scholarship

Women are 59.5% of graduate students in Cuba.

June In the Philippines, where 98% of teachers are women, the government concludes that lack of contact with male teachers "could lead to the children becoming weaklings and sissies."

Religion

New publications include Mary Hunt's *Fierce Tenderness: A Feminist Theology of Friendship*, Norwegian Kari Elisabeth Børresen's *Image of God and Gender Models in Judaeo-Christian Tradition*, Fatima Mernissi's *Women and Islam: An Historical and Theological Enquiry*, and I. Julia Leslie's *Roles and Rituals for Hindu Women*.

1992

General Status and Daily Life

Maryland rape victim Lynn Groff is sentenced to fourteen days in jail for "filing a false rape charge" because she agreed to have sex with her attacker after he threatened to kill her and her child.

The forty-five-year-old Miss Canada beauty pageant is ended.

In the United States, 186 acts of vandalism and violence against abortion providers are reported.

Feb. U.S. boxer Mike Tyson is found guilty of raping a beauty pageant contestant, Desiree Washington. The case generates controversy because of Tyson's fame and focuses attention on the pervasiveness of acquaintance or "date" rape. Some reports estimate that as many as one in four women will be raped in their lifetimes, most often by people they know.

June East and West Germany, in reunification, compromise on abortion; the procedure has been legal in the East and illegal in the West except in cases of rape, incest, or threat to the woman's health. In unified Germany, abortion will be legal in the first trimester, following counseling. The compromise is immediately challenged by conservatives.

June 29 The U.S. Supreme Court rules to uphold *Roe* v. *Wade* in determining the constitutionality of a Pennsylvania law but also upholds certain restrictions on abortion. Justices Blackmun, O'Connor, Stevens, Kennedy, and Souter agree that women should be able to have abortions before fetal viability "without undue interference from the state" but that later abortions can be restricted. The opposing justices, Rehnquist, White, Scalia, and Thomas, write, "We believe Roe was wrongly decided, and that it can and should be overruled."

The court rules that mandatory counseling, waiting periods, minor-consent laws, and record keeping on abortions by doctors are legal; it strikes down a provision requiring the husband's consent for married women, noting that "a state may not give to a man the kind of dominion over his wife that parents exercise over their children."

July The state of Washington mandates twice as many women's toilets as men's in places of public assembly.

Aug. Saudi Arabian refugee Nada (a pseudonym) goes into hiding after being refused political asylum in Canada. She fled her country after being persecuted for appearing unveiled and unchaperoned in public; Canadian authorities advised her "to comply with the laws" of Saudi Arabia and to "show consideration for the feelings of her father." Most countries still do not consider gender-based discrimination valid cause for political asylum.

Nov. In an Irish referendum, free access to abortion information and the right to obtain abortions outside the country are approved by a 3-1 margin.

Dec. Hungary passes a restrictive abortion law, which requires women seeking first-trimester abortions to receive counseling, wait three days, and get permission from a committee. Women who get abortions after the first trimester are subject to a three-year jail term, as are the medical personnel providing the service.

Government, the Military, and the Law

China has no women in the Politburo, 10 women on the 177-member Central Committee, 3 women of 39 national ministers, and 150 women among its 3,000 mayors and vice-mayors.

The new German Bundestag has 136 women among its 662 members.

In Brazil, where abortion is almost always illegal and contraception is largely unavailable, women sell their votes to politicians in exchange for access to sterilization.

About twenty-six women are assaulted, grabbed, and undressed on hallway gauntlets by male officers at the U.S. Navy Tailhook Convention in Las Vegas. Complaints about the harassment, at first ignored, result in an investigation and demands for the resignation of senior navy officers. Admiral Kelso, present at Tailhook, is accused of tampering with the investigation; he will retire early in 1994.

Three women—Yetunde Braimah, Catherine Wayas, and Sarah Jibril—run with forty-two men for president of Nigeria.

Black women are 48.7% of U.S. Army women, 26.8% of enlisted women in the navy, 28.5% of enlisted women in the marines, and 23.7% of enlisted women in the air force.

Jan. Poet and dissident Blaga Dimitrova becomes vice president of Bulgaria. Dimitrova, whose works were sometimes banned by the old communist regime, wrote some works that defend the rights of Turkish residents of Bulgaria.

Jan. 16 Ten Salvadoran guerrilla leaders sign their nation's peace accords, including Nidia Díaz, who in 1985 was shot five times, captured, and released in a prisoner exchange.

Apr. Labor MP Betty Boothroyd becomes the first woman speaker of Britain's House of Commons.

Nov. Women's representation in Ireland's 166-member Dàil (Parliament) goes from thirteen to twenty members.

Dec. German women in Parliament ensure that rape victims from Bosnia-Herzegovina can still seek asylum in Germany, despite the nation's increasing desire to halt the incoming flow of refugees.

Dec. Taiwanese feminist and dissident Hsiu-lien Lu, an essayist, novelist, publisher, and founder of Taiwan's National Organization for Women, is elected to the national legislature.

Literature and the Visual Arts

Portuguese poet Natalia Correia dies.

U.S. novelist Toni Morrison publishes *Jazz*.

Alice Walker publishes *Possessing the Secret of Joy*, a novel that discusses the genital mutilation of Tashi, a character from Walker's novel *The Color Purple*.

Performing Arts and Entertainment

U.S. film actress Lillian Gish dies, leaving an estate of $10 million. Some of her fortune is used to endow an award in the performing arts. Other U.S. deaths this year include actress Gracie Lantz, the voice and coinventor of cartoon character Woody Woodpecker; jazz guitarist Mary Osborne, the first professional woman electric guitarist; and screenwriter Helen Deutsch.

At the movies, Sharon Stone stars in the controversial and confusing thriller, *Basic Instinct*. Rebecca DeMornay delivers a chilling performance as a psychotic nanny in *The Hand That Rocks the Cradle*. Jessica Tandy, Kathy Bates, Mary Stuart Masterson, and Mary-Louise Parker star in *Fried Green Tomatoes*, based on a book by Fannie Flagg. British actress Emma Thompson wins the Best Actress Oscar for *Howard's End*, which also stars Helena Bonham-Carter and Vanessa Redgrave.

Indian filmmaker Deepa Dhanraj directs *Something Like a War*, about family-planning experiments conducted on Indian women.

Irish pop singer Sinead O'Connor records *Am I Not Your Girl?*

Mexican screenwriter Laura Esquivel writes the screenplay for the movie *Como agua para chocolate* (*Like Water for Chocolate*), which is based on her novel of the same name. It wins eleven Ariel Awards from the Mexican Academy of Motion Pictures.

Penelope Spheeris directs the film *Wayne's World*. Nora Ephron directs *This Is My Life*, starring Julie Kavner and coauthored by Ephron and her sister, Delia Ephron.

Athletics and Exploration

Red Sox owner Jean Yawkey dies at age eighty-three.

Russian runner Olga Markova wins the Boston Marathon, setting the fastest women's marathon time since 1985.

Yugoslav tennis player Monica Seles beats German Steffi Graf to win the French Open. She is the first woman to win three straight French Opens since 1937.

Lisa Raymond wins the NCAA women's tennis title.

Canada beats the United States in the women's world hockey championship. Notable players include American forward Cammi Granato, who scored eight goals and two assists, and Canadian goalie Manon Rheaume, who is making news as a professional player.

Swiss skier Vreni Schneider has more World Cup races—thirty-eight—any other active skier, male or female. Only three skiers in history have won more.

Cincinnati Reds owner Marge Schott comes under fire for racist remarks and hiring practices.

Stanford wins the women's NCAA basketball title.

The first high school varsity football game takes place in which two girls play on opposing teams. Split end Sarah Price is already playing on the Chamblee (Georgia) High team when Seneca (South Carolina) High coach Tom Bass names April Smith to his team as a receiver. Smith acquits herself well during the game, and Bass awards her the game ball, then kicks her off the team, saying, "I don't think the girls are capable of playing football. They have the heart, but they don't have the physical tools. April played as well as she could play tonight, but now she's history."

Despite Title IX-mandated equity in sports programs supported by federal funds, women get only one-third of sports scholarship dollars in the United States. Women are only 31% of student athletes. They are 48% of coaches and 17% of administrators of women's teams; women's-team coaching jobs still pay about half as much as coaching jobs on men's teams.

In one notorious case, the University of Massachusetts cuts the women's tennis, volleyball, and lacrosse teams, despite the tennis team's willingness to raise funds to pay for its program. The women's tennis team costs only $14,000 a year, compared with men's basketball, which gets annual funding of $750,000. Bad courts are cited as a reason for discontinuing tennis, though the courts are used by summer sports campers, who pay $170 each for the privilege. The school also has plans to offer men's hockey, a very expensive sport, starting in 1994, with no new women's sports planned.

Yugoslavian tennis player Monica Seles wins the U.S. Open, defeats Mary Joe Fernandez to win the Australian Open, and rejects Jimmy Connors's challenge to a $2 million "battle of the sexes."

Golfer Patty Sheehan wins the U.S. Women's Open.

Tammy George becomes the women's world bull-riding champion.

U.S. caver Jeanne Gurnee becomes the first woman president of the National Speleological Society.

U.S. golfer Pat Bradley becomes the twelfth member of the LPGA Hall of Fame. In the last eighteen years, she has finished in the top ten in 55.9% of her 485 tournaments, a record for consistency unmatched by any currently active male or female player. She has qualified for the Hall of Fame by winning thirty tournaments.

U.S. tennis player Tracy Austin, at twenty-nine, becomes the youngest person ever invited to join the Tennis Hall of Fame.

Hungarian chess player Judit Polgar becomes the youngest international grandmaster ever, beating Bobby Fischer's record by one month.

U.S. athletes Lusia Harris and Nera White become the first women inducted into the Basketball Hall of Fame.

U.S. swimmer Jenny Thompson sets a world record of 54.48 seconds in the women's 100-meter freestyle.

Jan. Kristi Yamaguchi wins the U.S. women's figure skating title, landing a troublesome triple Salchow. April Sargent-Thomas wins the ice dancing title only three weeks after emergency ovarian surgery. Calla Urbanski, a waitress supposedly "too old" at thirty-one to win a championship, takes the pairs title.

Winter At the Albertville Olympics, U.S. speed skater Bonnie Blair, in the 500 meters, wins the first gold medal for the United States in the 1992 games. She is followed by China's Ye Qiaobo and Germany's Christa Rothenburger Luding. In the 1,000, Blair takes gold again, followed by Ye Qiaobo. Blair will win more gold medals in the 1994 games, finishing her career with a total of five and the all-time record for gold medals by a U.S. woman in any sport. U.S. short-track speed skater Cathy Turner gets a team silver in the 3,000 meters and an individual gold in the 500 meters.

Canadian skier Kerrin Lee-Gartner wins the women's downhill gold. Austrian Petra Kronberger wins the gold in the combined. American Donna Weinbrecht takes the gold in freestyle mogul skiing in its first year as a regular Olympic event.

Russian skaters Marina Klimova and Sergei Ponomarenko take first in ice dancing. The Russians also take gold and silver in pairs: Natalia Mishkutienok and Artur Dmitriev in first and Elena Bechke and Denis Petrov in second, both teams coached by Tamara Moskvina. American Kristi Yamaguchi takes the women's gold, followed by Midori Ito of Japan and Nancy Kerrigan of the United States; Ito lands the only triple axel in the women's competition at the Olympics.

The most gold medals won by a woman at the games are three taken by Russian cross-country skier Lyubov Egorova, who wins golds in the 15-kilometer race, pursuit, and 4 x 5-kilometer relay. She also wins silvers in the 5 kilometers and 30 kilometers.

Feb. U.S. golfer Dottie Mochrie brings her total career winnings to more than $1 million. In April, her rival Danielle Ammaccapane will achieve the same feat.

Feb. Martina Navratilova beats Jana Novotna at the Virginia Slims of Chicago, winning her 158th tournment and breaking the previous record of 157 wins set by Chris Evert.

Summer U.S. gymnast Shannon Miller wins two silver and three bronze medals at the Olympics in Barcelona, the most medals for any U.S. athlete at the summer or winter 1992 games. One of her silvers is in the all-around, which is won by Russia's Tatyana Gutsu.

American Gail Devers wins the 100-meter dash, followed by Jamaica's Juliet Cuthbert and Russia's Irina Privalova. Jackie Joyner-Kersee wins the heptathlon; former decathlon gold medalist Bruce Jenner calls her "the greatest mutlievent athlete ever, man or woman." American Gwen Torrence wins the 200-meter dash. Russia wins the 4 x 400 relay, followed by the United States. The United States wins the 4 x 100.

Paraskevi Patoulidou wins the 100-meter hurdles, becoming the first Greek track-and-field medalist since 1896 and the first-ever Greek woman track-and-field medalist. Algeria's Hassiba Boulmerka wins the 1,500. Ethiopia's Derartu Tulu wins the 10,000, followed by South Africa's Elana Meyer. German Heike Drechsler wins the long jump, followed by Russia's Inessa Kravets and America's Jackie Joyner-Kersee.

In swimming, American Summer Sanders wins the 200-meter butterfly. Qian Hong of China wins the 100-meter butterfly, and American Crissy Ahmann-Leighton gets the silver. Hungarian Krisztina Egerszegi wins the 400-meter individual medley and sets Olympic records in the 100- and 200-meter backstrokes. China's Zhuang Yong wins the 100-meter freestyle, followed by American Jenny Thompson. China's Lin Li wins the 200-meter individual medley. Germany's Dagmar Hase wins the 400-meter freestyle, and American Janet Evans wins the 800. The U.S. team of Thompson, Anita Nall (silver medalist in the 100- and 200-meter breaststroke), Ahmann-Leighton, and Lea Loveless wins the 4 x 100 medley relay, breaking East Germany's 1984 record. Nicole Haislett of the United States wins the 200-meter freestyle. Japan's Kyoko Iwasaki wins the 200-meter

breaststroke.

New Zealand's Barbara Kendall wins the sailboarding gold. Russia wins the gold in team handball and basketball. China's Zhang Shan wins a gold in skeet shooting, becoming the only woman in Olympic history to win a dual-sex shooting event. She sets an Olympic record of 223 out of 225 possible points. American Launi Meili wins the three-position rifle gold, setting an Olympic record of 684.3 points. South Korean Yeo Kab Soon wins the air rifle event, followed by Bulgaria's Vesela Letcheva and Yugoslavia's Aranka Binder.

Catherine Fleury of France wins the women's judo, 134.5-lb. class. Yael Arad of Israel takes the silver, becoming the first-ever Israeli Olympic medalist. South Korean archer Cho Youn Jeong wins two gold medals. American Jennifer Capriati defeats Steffi Graf to win the singles tennis gold. The doubles gold is won by Americans Mary Joe Fernandez and Gigi Fernandez.

Activism

U.S. activist Shirley Berman dies at fifty-five. She had a child born with Down Syndrome and worked successfully for the passage of a law that requires doctors to inform women if their fetuses will be retarded.

Guatemalan Indian human rights advocate Rigoberta Menchu is awarded the Nobel Peace Prize.

Patricia Ireland succeeds Molly Yard as president of NOW.

Women in Zimbabwe protest violence against women, using the slogan, "It's your mother, it's your daughter, it's your sister."

Jan. 16 A women's caravan leaves for Baghdad to bring food, vitamins, and medicine to Iraqi children harmed by the Gulf War.

Mar. Fifty Kenyan women demonstrate for the release of political prisoners. The women, some over seventy, are attacked by police with batons and tear gas; four, including environmentalist and feminist Wangari Maathai, are knocked unconscious.

Apr. 5 More than 500,000 demonstrate for women's reproductive rights in Washington, D.C.

Business and Industry

The EEOC receives 10,532 sexual harassment complaints, 90% of them from women.

Women own 28% (or 5.4 million) of U.S. businesses.

U.S. advertising executive Charlotte Beers becomes CEO and chairwoman of Ogilvy & Mather Worldwide, one of the largest advertising agencies in the world.

May Afghanistan's religious affairs minister announces on television that women who work outside the home must wear head scarves, gloves, and long skirts.

Science and Medicine

U.S. mathematician, naval officer, and computer pioneer Grace Hopper (b. 1906) dies. One of the first computer programmers in the world, she worked on the early Mark I and UNIVAC computers, on the first compiler, and on the language known as COBOL. She was one of the first few women admitted to the Institute of Electrical and Electronic Engineers and the National Academy of Engineers.

Currently, U.S. astronomer Carolyn Shoemaker is credited with the most discovered comets. She has found twenty-six with her husband, Gene, and one on her own. One of her discovered comets will strike Jupiter in the summer of 1994, resulting in rare opportunities for scientific observation.

The Society of Women Engineers gives its annual Achievement Award to engineer Evangelia Micheli-Tzanakou for her models of the visual system, which have enabled developments in a variety of fields from digital signal processing to pattern recognition systems.

Physicist Margaret Geller, geneticist Carol Gross, anthropologist Olga Linares, geophysicist Susan Solomon, and biochemist JoAnne Stubbe are elected to the National Academy of Sciences.

Education and Scholarship

Women are 70% of China's 4 million adult illiterates.

Religion

Amy Ogden Welcher, U.S. founder and first president of Church Women United, dies.

U.S. theologian Mary Daly publishes *Outercourse*, in which she describes herself as a pirate smuggling theological treasures hidden from women.

Religious leaders in Algeria blame women for unemployment, boys' failure in school, housing problems, and crime.

July Nigerian religious leaders blame "indecent"

women for a drought, resulting in attacks on women wearing nontraditional dress, protests by women, and the burning of the offices of the Association des Femmes Nigeriennes.

1993

General Status and Daily Life

Croatian and Muslim women are systematically raped by Serbs in what was once Yugoslavia. Some attacks are filmed as pornography.

Approximately 10,000 women and girls are imported from Burma to Thailand each year and sold into slavery in brothels. The Thai government's response to this traffic is the arrest of the women, while the brothel owners and traffickers (who deceive the girls, some as young as twelve, with promises of good jobs across the border) go free.

The female condom is on the market in Austria, Holland, Switzerland, and Great Britain, with final tests taking place in the United States.

Mar. The UN Commission on Human Rights condemns gender-based human rights violations.

Government, the Military, and the Law

U.S. president Bill Clinton names Joycelyn Elders as his surgeon general (replacing the first woman Surgeon General, Antonia Novello), Donna Shalala as secretary of HHS, Madeline Albright as UN ambassador, Alice Rivlin as deputy director of the Office of Management and Budget, Hazel O'Leary as secretary of energy, Carol Browner as administrator of the Enivronmental Protection Agency, Laura Tyson as chair of the Council of Economic Advisers, and Janet Reno as attorney general. Reno is the first woman to hold her office; she was Clinton's third nominee. Nominees Kimba Wood and Zoe Baird were withdrawn from consideration, amid cries of sexism, after questions arose over their payments to child-care providers.

Canadian politician Kim Campbell is chosen to lead the Conservative party.

Ruth Bader Ginsburg, the first tenured woman professor at Columbia Law School, becomes the second woman on the U.S. Supreme Court.

Jan. Interior Ministry official Charatsri Teepirat becomes the first woman to govern a province in Thailand.

Mar. The Italian Senate determines that 30% of all candidates for local councils must be women. In May, Judge Gabriella Riello throws out election results in fourteen towns because the 30% requirement has not been met.

Apr. In South Africa, twenty-six parties meet to plan postapartheid strategies. Each group is required to involve women in its discussions, and women are about 16% of the delegates.

June Tansu Ciller becomes Turkey's first female prime minister.

Sept. 28 U.S. First Lady Hillary Rodham Clinton pitches the Clinton administration's health reform plan to Congress; it is the first time a First Lady, rather than a cabinet member, has made such a Congressional presentation.

Literature and the Visual Arts

U.S. mystery novelist Sue Grafton publishes *"J" Is for Judgment*. Her other novels, which feature female detective Kinsey Millhone, are *"A" Is for Alibi* (1982), *"B" Is for Burglar* (1985), *"C" Is for Corpse* (1986), *"D" Is for Deadbeat* (1987), *"E" Is for Evidence* (1988), *"F" Is for Fugitive* (1989), *"G" Is for Gumshoe* (1990), *"H" Is for Homicide* (1991), and *"I" Is for Innocent* (1992).

German author Christa Wolf publishes *What Remains and Other Stories*.

Oct. 7 U.S. novelist Toni Morrison wins the Nobel Prize for Literature.

Dec. 21 U.S. sculptor Mary Tarleton Knollenberg dies at eighty-eight. The winner of a Guggenheim Fellowship, she studied in Paris and was noted for her female forms in bronze and stone.

Performing Arts and Entertainment

U.S. film actress Myrna Loy dies.

French filmmaker Agnès Varda directs *Jacquot*, a biography of her late husband, director Jacques Demy. Polish filmmaker Agnieszka Holland directs *The Secret Garden*, a lush movie version of Frances Hodgson Burnett's children's novel. U.S. filmmaker Jennifer Lynch directs *Boxing Helena*, about an obsessed surgeon who imprisons his female patient (Sherilyn Fenn) by cutting off her arms and legs.

Belgian a cappella group Zap Mama, which uses lyrics in French, English, Zulu, and Arabic, records *Zap Mama: Adventures in Afropea 1*.

Filmgoers can see Diane Keaton as a bored wife convinced she has uncovered a murder and Anjelica Huston as a sharp-witted, sensual, poker-playing author in *Manhattan Murder Mystery*. Huston also appears as Morticia Addams in *Addams Family Values*. Meg Ryan stars in the successful romantic comedy *Sleepless in Seattle* (cowritten by Nora Ephron, who receives an Oscar nomination for Best Screenplay), and Michelle Pfeiffer and Winona Ryder star in a film version of Edith Wharton's *The Age of Innocence*. Jane Campion wins the Oscar for Best Screenplay and is nominated for Best Director for the romance *The Piano*; the stars of *The Piano*, Holly Hunter and eleven-year-old Anna Paquin, win Best Actress and Best Supporting Actress, respectively, and the film's producer, Jan Chapman, is nominated for an Oscar. British actress Emma Thompson stars in *Much Ado About Nothing*.

English filmmaker Sally Potter directs the film *Orlando*, a dramatization of Virginia Woolf's novel about androgyny, starring Tilda Swinton.

Several popular shows now on television have been created or produced by women, including "Evening Shade," created by Linda Bloodworth-Thomason, who also created "Designing Women"; "Roseanne" and "Grace Under Fire," produced by Marcy Carsey; and "Murphy Brown" and "Love & War," created by Diane English.

Amy Tan's *The Joy Luck Club* becomes a film.

Jan. 28 U.S. composer Kay Swift (b. April 19, 1897) dies. Her popular songs included "Can This be Love," "Can't We Be Friends," "Who Could Ask for Anything More," and "Fine and Dandy." Her 1930 musical *Fine and Dandy* was the first for which all the music was composed by a woman.

Mar. Lea DeLaria, on "The Arsenio Hall Show," becomes the first openly lesbian stand-up comic to perform on a late-night talk show.

Athletics and Exploration

U.S. Olympic athlete Evelyne Hall and Russian aviator Valentina Grizodubova, a World War II combat pilot, die.

Hungarian Judit Polgar, sixteen years old, becomes the first woman chess player to reach the interzonal stage, an important landmark on the road to a shot at the world championship. The sister of two other notable women chess players, Zsuzsa and Zsofia Polgar, Judit is ranked fifty-third in the world and this year defeated former world champion Boris Spassky.

U.S. jockey Julie Krone wins the Belmont Stakes to become the first female victor in a Triple Crown race.

American "Grandma" Jan Youren, forty-nine, is inducted into the National Cowgirl Hall of Fame. A rider for thirty-six years, she has twice won the world bareback bronc championship and is the mother of six-time world bull-riding champion Tonya Stevenson.

The SWG gives a gold medal to American Kathryn Sullivan, a three-time space shuttle astronaut named this year to head the National Oceanographic and Atmospheric Administration (NOAA). The SWG's Outstanding Achievement Award goes to UCLA professor Patricia Anawalt, an expert on Aztec clothing and textiles who coedited a reprint of the *Codex Mendoza*, a study of Aztec pictographs.

Apr. *Discovery* space shuttle crew member Ellen Ochoa, an electrical engineer, becomes the first Latina in space.

Activism

Nancy Gruver and Joe Kelly cofound *New Moon*, a feminist magazine for preteen and adolescent girls. The magazine's twenty-five-member editorial board is composed of girls eight to fourteen, including Gruver and Kelly's twin daughters, Nia Kelly and Mavis Gruver.

May In Argentina, 300 women seize bridges to protest a proposed privatization of roads.

May The World Health Organization condemns the genital mutilation of women, due in part to years of lobbying by Ghanaian-British feminist Efua Dorkenoo.

June Sunera Thobani replaces Judy Rebick as head of an influential Canadian feminist group, the National Action Committee (NAC) on the Status of Women.

Business and Industry

Feb. Responding to the fact that 70% of postcommunist Russia's unemployed are women, Labor Minister Gennady Melikyan says, "Why should we employ women when men are unemployed? It's better that men work and women take care of children."

May More than 200 workers, mostly women, die in Thailand in the world's worst factory fire. The death toll is increased by locked exits and an absence of alarms and fire escapes; the women are told to keep working even after the fire is detected.

July U.S. department store executive Sue Kronick, an executive vice president of Bloomingdale's, becomes president and chief operating officer of Rich's/Goldsmith's.

Science and Medicine

The SWE gives its annual Achievement Award to U.S. chemist Elsa Reichmanis, holder of ten patents and member of the American Association for the Advancement of Science, for her work developing polymer resist systems for integrated circuits.

Martha Sloan becomes the IEEE's first woman president.

The U.S. National Academy of Sciences inducts eight women: molecular biologists Elizabeth Blackburn and Christine Guthrie, agricultural scientist Adrienne Clarke, bacteriologist and geneticist Sydney Kustu, geneticist Nancy Kleckner, psychologist Eleanor Maccoby, geologist Alexandra Navrotsky, and mathematician Marina Ratner.

Feb. Pamela Maraldo replaces Faye Wattleton as head of the Planned Parenthood Federation of America.

Education and Scholarship

Sylvia A. Boone, a specialist in African and women's art, and the first tenured black woman professor at Yale, dies at fifty-two.

MIT labor economist Phyllis A. Wallace dies at sixty-nine.

Gerda Lerner publishes *The Creation of Feminist Consciousness: From the Middle Ages to 1870*.

Religion

Arlene Swidler publishes *Homosexuality and World Religion*.

Women can be Shinto priests and shrine maidens in Japan. Shinto has an important female deity, Amaterasu Omikami.

June About 800 women are arrested in Tehran, Iran, for violating Islamic dress codes. The laws require women to cover all but their hands and face in public, even when they are passengers in cars. Some of those arrested are sentenced to be flogged.

Select Bibliography

Anderson, Bonnie S., and Judith P. Zinsser. *A History of Their Own*. New York: Harper and Row, 1988.

Attwater, Donald. *The Penguin Dictionary of Saints*. Harmondsworth, England: Penguin, 1983.

Bacon, Margaret Hope. *Mothers of Feminism: The Story of Quaker Women in America*. San Francisco: Harper and Row, 1986.

Barnstone, Aliki, and Willis Barnstone, eds. *A Book of Women Poets*. New York: Shocken, 1992.

Bernstein, Gail Lee, ed. *Recreating Japanese Women, 1600–1945*. Berkeley: University of California Press, 1991.

Bird, Caroline. *Enterprising Women*. New York: W. W. Norton, 1976.

Bresler, Fenton. *Sex and the Law*. London: Muller, 1988.

Brunn, Emilie Zum, and Georgette Epiney-Burgard. *Women Mystics in Medieval Europe*. New York: Paragon House, 1989.

Bush, Barbara. *Slave Women in Caribbean Society*. Kingston: Heinemann, 1990.

Carruth, Gorton. *The Encyclopedia of American Facts and Dates*. 8th ed. New York: Harper and Row, 1987.

Cary, M., and H. H. Scullard. *A History of Rome Down to the Reign of Constantine*. New York: St. Martin's, 1975.

Cott, Nancy F., and Elizabeth H. Pleck. *A Heritage of Their Own*. New York: Simon and Schuster, 1979.

Cunnington, C. Willett, and Phillis Cunnington. *The History of Underclothes*. New York: Dover, 1992.

Duberman, Martin Bauml, Martha Vicinus, and George Chauncey, Jr., eds. *Hidden from History: Reclaiming the Gay and Lesbian Past*. New York: New American Library, 1989.

Duby, Georges, ed. *A History of Private Life*. Cambridge, MA: Belknap, 1988.

Dunn, C. J. *Everyday Life in Imperial Japan*. New York: Dorset, 1989.

Durant, Will. *The Story of Civilization*. New York: Simon and Schuster, 1934.

Ehrenreich, Barbara, and Deirdre English. *For Her Own Good: 150 Years of the Experts' Advice to Women*. Garden City, NY: Anchor Books, 1979.

Fairbank, John King. *China: A New History*. Cambridge, MA: Belknap, 1992.

Fister, Patricia. *Japanese Women Artists 1600–1900*. New York: Harper and Row, 1988.

Fraser, Antonia. *Mary Queen of Scots.* New York: Delacorte, 1969.

————. *The Warrior Queens.* New York: Vintage Books, 1990.

————. *The Weaker Vessel.* New York: Vintage Books, 1985.

Gallagher, Catherine, and Thomas Laqueur, eds. *The Making of the Modern Body.* Berkeley: University of California Press, 1987.

Gies, Frances, and Joseph Gies. *Life in a Medieval Castle.* New York: Harper and Row, 1974.

————. *Women in the Middle Ages.* New York: Harper and Row, 1978.

Green, Rayna. *Women in American Indian Society.* New York: Chelsea House, 1992.

Grun, Bernard. *The Timetables of History.* New York: Simon and Schuster, 1979.

Guttmann, Allen. *Women's Sports: A History.* New York: Columbia University Press, 1991.

Hafkin, Nancy J., and Edna G. Bay, eds. *Women in Africa: Studies in Social and Economic Change.* Stanford, CA: Stanford University Press, 1976.

Hahner, June, ed. *Women in Latin American History: Their Lives and Views.* Los Angeles: UCLA, 1980.

Harris, Ann Sutherland, and Linda Nochlin. *Women Artists: 1550–1950.* New York: Alfred A. Knopf, 1989.

Hibbert, Christopher. *The Virgin Queen.* Reading, MA: Addison-Wesley, 1991.

Hiley, Michael. *Victorian Working Women.* Boston: David R. Godine, 1979.

Hudson, M. E., and Mary Clark. *Crown of a Thousand Years.* New York: Crown, 1978.

James, Edward T., ed. *Notable American Women: A Biographical Dictionary.* Cambridge, MA: Belknap, 1971.

Japan: An Illustrated Encyclopedia. Tokyo: Kodansha, 1993.

Kenneally, James J. *The History of American Catholic Women.* New York: Crossroad, 1990.

Kim, Yung-Chung. *Women of Korea: A History from Ancient Times to 1945.* Seoul, Korea: Ewha Woman's University Press, 1982.

King, Margaret L. *Women of the Renaissance.* Chicago: University of Chicago Press, 1991.

Köhler, Carl. *A History of Costume.* New York: Dover, 1963.

Lefkowitz, Mary R., and Maureen B. Fant. *Women's Life in Greece and Rome.* Baltimore, MD: Johns Hopkins University Press, 1982.

Lister, Margot. *Costume: An Illustrated Survey from Ancient Times to the Twentieth Century.* Boston: Plays, 1968.

Loewe, Michael. *Everyday Life in Early Imperial China During the Han Period 202 B.C.–A.D. 220.* London: B. T. Batsford, 1968.

Longford, Elizabeth. *Queen Victoria: Born to Succeed.* New York: Pyramid Books, 1966.

Mandel, William M. *Soviet Women.* New York: Anchor Press, 1975.

Markale, Jean. *Women of the Celts.* Rochester, VT: Inner Traditions International, 1986.

McCall, Andrew. *The Medieval Underworld.* New York: Dorset Press, 1979.

Miles, Rosalind. *The Women's History of the World.* Topsfield, MA: Salem House, 1989.

Miller, Francesca. *Latin American Women and the Search for Social Justice.* Hanover, NH: University Press of New England, 1991.

Moffat, Mary Jane, and Charlotte Painter, eds. *Revelations: Diaries of Women.* New York: Vintage Books, 1975.

Morgan, Robin. *Sisterhood Is Global.* Garden City, NY: Anchor Books, 1984.

Murray, Janet. *Strong-Minded Women and Other Lost Voices from 19th Century England.* New York: Pantheon Books, 1982.

Neumann, Erich. *The Great Mother.* Princeton, N.J.: Princeton University Press, 1974.

Norton, Mary Beth, et al. *A People and a Nation: A History of the United States.* 2nd ed. Boston: Houghton Mifflin, 1986.

Ogilvie, Marilyn Bailey. *Women in Science.* Cambridge, MA: MIT Press, 1991.

Olsen, Kirstin. *Remember the Ladies: A Woman's Book of Days.* Pittstown, NJ: Main Street, 1988.

O'Neill, Lois Decker. *The Women's Book of World Records and Achievements.* Garden City, NY: Anchor Press, 1979.

Osen, Lynn M. *Women in Mathematics.* Cambridge: MIT Press, 1990.

Pescatello, Ann, ed. *Female and Male in Latin America.* Pittsburgh: University of Pittsburgh Press, 1973.

Pisan, Christine de. *The Book of the City of Ladies.* New York: Persea Books, 1982.

Plutarch. *Makers of Rome: Nine Lives by Plutarch.* Trans. by Ian Scott-Kilvert. New York: Penguin Books, 1965.

Posner, Alice. *Women in Engineering.* Skokie, IL: VGM Career Horizons, 1981.

Power, Eileen. *Medieval Women.* Cambridge: Cambridge University Press, 1975.

Pritchard, James B. *The Ancient Near East.* Vol. 1. Princeton, NJ: Princeton University Press, 1958.

Read, Phyllis J., and Bernard L. Witlieb. *The Book of Women's Firsts.* New York: Random House, 1992.

Reeves, Minou. *Female Warriors of Allah: Women and the Islamic Revolution.* New York: E. P. Dutton, 1989.

Seagraves, Anne. *Women Who Charmed the West.* Lakeport, CA: Wesanne, 1991.

Siraisi, Nancy G. *Medieval and Early Renaissance Medicine: An Introduction to Knowledge and Practice.* Chicago: University of Chicago Press, 1990.

Smith, Sharon. *Women Who Make Movies.* New York: Hopkinson and Blake, 1975.

Sorel, Nancy Caldwell. *Ever Since Eve: Personal Reflections on Childbirth.* New York: Oxford University Press, 1984.

Stannard, Una. *Mrs Man.* San Francisco: Germainbooks, 1977.

Stone, Lawrence. *The Family, Sex and Marriage in England 1500–1800.* New York: Harper and Row, 1979.

Suetonius. *The Twelve Caesars.* Harmondsworth, England: Penguin, 1985.

Tacitus. *The Annals of Imperial Rome*. Harmondsworth, England: Penguin, 1985.

Tannahill, Reay. *Sex in History*. New York: Stein and Day, 1982.

Trevor-Roper, H. R. *The European Witch-Craze of the Sixteenth and Seventeenth Centuries*. New York: Harper and Row, 1956.

Uglow, Jennifer S. *The International Dictionary of Women's Biography*. New York: Continuum, 1985.

Ulrich, Laurel Thatcher. *Good Wives*. New York: Oxford University Press, 1983.

Vare, Ethlie Ann, and Greg Ptacek. *Mothers of Invention: From the Bra to the Bomb, Forgotten Women and Their Unforgettable Ideas*. New York: Quill, 1987.

Views from Jade Terrace: Chinese Women Artists 1300–1912. New York: Rizzoli, 1988.

Woloch, Nancy. *Women and the American Experience*. New York: Alfred A. Knopf, 1984.

Wolpert, Stanley. *A New History of India*. New York: Oxford University Press, 1977.

Index

AARP. *See* American Association of Retired Persons
AAU. *See* Amateur Athletic Union
AAUW. See American Association of University Women
Abakanowicz, Magdalena, 230
Abayah, Josephine, 323
Abbam, Kate, 321
Abbasa, 34
Abbasian, Showkat, 371
abbesses, 30, 32, 33–34, 35, 37, 41–42, 43, 46–47, 55, 66, 70, 73. *See also* abbeys; convents; nuns
abbeys, 30, 31, 32, 38, 39, 46, 47; founded by women, 41. *See also* abbesses; convents; nuns, Catholicism
Abbey Theatre, 166–67, 184. *See also* theaters
Abbott, Berenice, 246
Abbott, Edith, 199, 211, 225, 287
Abbott, Emma, 146
Abbott, Grace, 212
Abbott, Margaret, 167
ABC, 279, 339
Abd ar-Rahman, 35, 36
Abdel Mahmoud, H. E. Fatima, 338
Abdel Rahman, Aisha, 292, 296, 300, 308
abdications, 33, 45, 54–55, 62, 83, 90, 137, 243–44, 267, 354
abduction, 136, 223, 332
Abdul, Paula, 378
Abdulhamid I (Ottoman sultan), 96
Abdullah, Begum, 180
Abdurakhmanova, Dilbar, 335
Abelard, 41–42
Abella, 105
Abhisapta Chambal, 309
Abide With Me, 242
Abiertas, Josepha, 228
Abie's Irish Rose, 214
abolitionists, 102, 106, 113, 115, 118, 124, 127, 130, 134, 142, 161, 168, 214; conflicts of, with suffragists, 138; lectures and speeches of, 113, 118, 127; periodicals of, 120, 123, 143;

statues of, 133; writings by, 80, 97, 110, 112, 115, 118, 130. *See also* Civil War; reformers
aborigines, 163, 241, 309, 365
abortifacients, 17, 18, 85, 377. *See also* abortion; contraception
abortion, 8, 78, 128, 154; access to information about, 388; activism for right to, 176, 322, 326, 330, 345, 348, 356, 359, 391; adolescents and, 361; age a factor in access to, 323, 330, 338, 347; attitude toward, 78, 281, 351, 358, 370–71, 388; as birth control, 374; in books, 239, 377; casualties from botched, 82, 309, 320, 353, 361, 364, 367, 368, 377; Christianity and, 23, 40, 59; committee approval of, 333–34, 338, 353, 377, 388–89; cost of, 329; counseling before, 333–34, 338, 364, 373, 388–89; criminalization of, 103, 114, 209, 243, 248; on demand, 209, 281, 306, 323, 327, 330, 333–34, 349, 350; demographics of, 82, 103, 114, 323; of female fetuses, 337; first-trimester, 40, 281, 323, 327, 333–34, 337–38, 343, 346, 347, 349, 350, 353, 357, 361, 368, 385, 388–89; government commission on, 304; government funding of, 323, 338, 357, 364, 367, 381; as grounds for divorce, 28, 248; husband's consent for, 266, 320, 334, 388; illegal, 320, 327, 329, 364, 389; in-laws' consent for, 320; legal after failure of contraception, 323; legal after rape or incest, 232, 306, 327, 330, 337–38, 343, 357, 368; legal for risk of alcoholism, 239; legalized, 201, 223, 232, 237, 248, 281, 286, 326, 327, 331, 334, 338, 343, 347, 349, 350, 357, 361, 368; legal to prevent birth defects, 239, 246, 304, 306, 309, 327, 330, 337–38, 343, 347, 349,

361, 368; legal to save the woman's life, 223, 232, 246, 306, 314, 323, 330, 333–34, 338, 361, 368; legal to save the woman's mental or physical health, 223, 246, 304, 306, 309, 314, 327, 330, 337–38, 343, 347, 349; legal when housing is inadequate, 330; legal when the woman's social circumstances are a factor, 304; loosening of restrictions on, 116, 281, 323, 334; marital status a factor in access to, 330; medical associations and, 319, 385; methods of, 14, 18, 103; number of previous children a factor in access to, 323, 330; numbers of, 114, 309, 361, 346, 353; numbers of illegal, 253, 309, 327, 346, 347, 353, 364, 368; opponents of, 200, 219; parental consent for, 334, 350, 358, 364, 377, 388; penalties for, 6, 11, 22, 57, 114, 232, 237, 258, 327, 358, 388–89; physicians' consent for, 309, 314, 333–34, 357, 359, 368; providers of, 251, 329; second-trimester, 327, 333–34, 337–38, 343, 357, 361, 385; terrorism against providers of, 368, 371, 372, 388; third-trimester, 333–34; tightening of restrictions on, 306, 346; travel abroad for, 357, 358, 364, 388; waiting period for, 349, 359, 364, 388–89. *See also* abortifacients; birth control clinics; contraception; fetus; infanticide
About Last Night . . ., 373
Abraham, 105
Abrahamson, Hanna Christie, 180
Abrégé de l'art des accouchements avec plusiers observations sur des cas singuliers, 93
"Abroad," 280
Absence of Malice, 362
absenteeism of women workers, 231

Claudine en ménage, 173
Claudine s'en va, 174
Claudius (Roman emperor), 18, 19, 20
Claypole, Edith, 199
cleaning: chemicals for, 154; devices for, 145, 157, 171; by domestic servants, 50, 134; as women's work, 25, 43, 64, 82, 90. *See also* housework; laundry
Clear Metal, 335
Clélie, 75
Clemencia, 126
Cléo from Five to Seven, 297
Cleopatra (Egyptian alchemist), 24
Cleopatra VII (Egyptian queen), 16–17, 75, 220
Cleopatra (film), 202
Cleopatra (film, 1934), 240
Cleopatra (film, 1963), 300
Clepsydra, 13
clergy: aboriginal and Native American, 241, 320; Anabaptist, 65; Anglican, 322, 337; Buddhist, 11, 381; cantors, 283, 377; Cathar, 42, 47; Catholic, 346; chaplains, 132, 264, 384; Congregational, 127, 129; defenders of, 77–78, 131–32; Episcopal, 333, 337, 342, 346, 349, 382; goddess priestesses, 6, 7, 14, 23, 26; heretic ministers, 52; hierarchies of, 53; lesbian, 377; Lutheran, 290, 295, 349; Methodist, 145, 216, 296; Methodist Episcopal, 141, 219; Methodist Protestant, 149; *omu*, 154; pagan priestesses, 6, 10, 21, 26, 31; prejudice against, 65, 124, 214, 246; Presbyterian, 239, 283, 286; privileges of, 14; Protestant, 132, 178, 217; Quaker, 78, 102, 105, 109; rabbis, 275, 327, 372; sacred prostitutes, 6; selection of, 14; sexual harassment of, 384; Shaker, 102; shinto, 69, 73, 394; as suffragists, 176; synagogue presidents, 295; Ugandan priestess, 377; Unitarian Universalist, 377; United Methodist, 377; United Presbyterian, 342. *See also* abbesses; bishops; deacons; evangelists; missionaries; mystics; nuns; obeah; popes; prophets; religious founders and leaders; saints; shamans; Vestal Virgins
clerical workers, 348, 375; income of, 133, 172, 185; as inventors, 314, 356; in the military, 202, 354; number of, 135, 143, 148, 168, 172, 211, 213, 253, 333, 336, 341, 345, 348, 352, 356, 359, 360, 363, 384;

stenographers, 20, 137, 185; training of, 131, 186. *See also* typists
Clerke, Agnes, 153, 175
Clifton, Lucille, 315, 323, 331, 354
Cline, Patsy, 299
Clinton, Bill, 392
Clinton, Hillary Rodham, 393
Cliquot, Nicole-Barbe, 100
clitoridectomy. *See* genital mutilation
clitoris, 262
Clive, Kitty, 98
Cloelia, 8
cloistering of nuns, 46, 47
Close, Glenn, 375, 383
cloth, manufacture of. *See* spinning; textile industry; weaving
Clothilde (Frankish queen, wife of Clovis I, 27
clothing, manufacture of. *See* sewing
Clotild (Frankish princess and nun), 30
Clouds of Witness, 224
Clough, Anne Jemima, 109
Clovis I (Frankish king), 27, 28
Clovis II (Frankish king), 31
clowns, 321
clubwomen, 138, 152, 162, 168, 176, 177, 242
Clytemnestra, 5
Clytemnestra (film), 289
Cnut, 37, 38
"Coach," 297
Coachman, Alice, 268
Coakes, Marion, 313
Coal, 339
Coal Miner's Daughter, 354
Coast Guard (U.S.), 260, 338
Coates, Anne, 297, 302
Coatlícue, 41. *See also* goddess worship
Cobb, Gail A., 331
Cobbe, Frances Power, 147, 176
cobblers. *See* shoemaking
COBOL, 392
Cochran, Barbara, 324
Cochran, Jacqueline, 240, 242, 249, 255, 322; speed records of, 247, 274, 279, 302
Cochrane, Josephine, 157, 196
Cock Crow, 304
cockfighting, 25
Coco, 316
Cocteau, Jean, 151
Code of Hammurabi, 4
Codex Mendoza, 394
Codines, Geralda, 51
Cody, William "Buffalo Bill," 151, 155, 161
coeducation. *See* higher education; women's schools, colleges, and universities
Coelebs in Search of a Wife, 105
coemptio, 11

Coggeshall, Janice, 375
Coffee, Lenore, 249
coffee, 92
Coffin, Keziah, 101
Cofitachique, Lady of, 61
cohabitation, 3, 4, 11, 15, 35, 126, 350, 361
Cohan, George M., 202
Cohen, Harriet, 171
Cohen, Tiffany, 370
Cohen, Zivia, 328
Cohn, Mildred, 322
coinage, 12, 17, 19, 24, 33, 68
Colbert, Claudette, 233, 240
"Cold-Hearted Snake," 378
Cold Sassy Tree, 368
Colella, Lynn, 325
Coleman, Bessie, 223
Coleman, Georgia, 235–36
Colet, Louise, 129, 142
Colette, Saint, 58
Colette, Sidonie Gabrielle, 193, 280, 324; ballets and films based on the works of, 269, 271, 272, 288; Claudine novels of, 166, 171, 173, 174; other novels of, 181, 209, 216, 222
Coligny, Louise de, 64
Colinet, Marie, 64–65
The Collected Greed, 368
Collected Poems (Bogan), 280
Collected Poems (Céu), 72
Collected Poems (Miles), 365
Collected Poems (Moore), 274
Collected Poems (Rukeyser), 347
Collected Poems (Teasdale), 246
Collected Stories (Porter), 304, 309
Collected Works (Meireles), 288
Collected Works from the Brush-and-Ink Harmony Hall, 110
Colliard, Renee, 285
Collier's, 269
Collingwood, Monica, 265
Collins, Addie Mae, 300
Collins, Judy, 332
Collins, Lottie, 161
Colombia, 354, 359; abortion in, 320, 353; adultery in, 243; cabinet members of, 241, 362; contraception in, 343; diplomats of, 292; domestic servants of, 329; education of women in, 111; film producers of, 318; housewives of, 262; insurance in, 262; marriage, divorce, and remarriage in, 338; military leaders and personnel of, 108; rape in, 387; rebels of, 96, 105, 108; politicians of, 292, 331; seamstresses of, 108; spies of, 108; spouse murder in, 243; strikes in, 342; suffrage in, 279, 286; weavers of, 234; women in the work force of, 356
Colon, Maria, 355

Mary the Jewess, 21
Mary the Third, 216
Mascarillo y trébol, 248
Masevich, Alla, 287
Masham, Abigail, 83
Masham, Damaris, 82
Ma Shouzhen, 69
Masinissa, 12
Masiotene, Ona, 178, 229
Maskey, Bimala, 298
The Mask of Apollo, 307
Masnada, Florance, 387
Mason, Alice Trumbull, 244
Mason, Sarah Y., 235
Massachusetts, 91, 97, 118, 142;
accused murderers of, 159;
adultery in, 71; banning of works
in, 181, 198, 259;
businesswomen of, 73, 95, 238;
colleges in, 161, 337;
colonization of, 68, 69; divorce
in, 94; duties of wives in, 75;
education of women in, 113;
heretics of, 73–74; histories of,
102; inventors of, 238; labor
unions of, 121; lesbians of, 323;
literacy in, 77; midwives of, 73;
military leaders and personnel of,
96; misogyny in, 73; museums
of, 174; orchestras of, 222;
politicians of, 323; prisons of,
120; Quakers in, 78; shoemakers
of, 131; strikes in, 152, 192;
textile industry of, 115, 192;
theologians of, 73–74; wife-
beating in, 71, 141; witch hunts
of, 74, 82; women's income in,
131; women's periodicals of, 112
Massachusetts Institute of
Technology, 141, 149, 283, 310,
346, 394
Massee, May, 237, 307
Massilia (Marseilles), 21
Mass in D, 161
mastectomy, 375. *See also*
gynecological practices
Mastenbroek, Hendrika, 245
Master, Edith, 340
The Master Builder, 238
The Master Christian, 166
master craftsmen, 46. *See also*
apprentices
*Mastering the Art of French
Cooking*, 295
Masters, Sybilla, 84
Masterson, Mary Stuart, 389
Mastrantonio, Mary Elizabeth, 386
matadors. *See* bullfighters
Mata Hari, 235
match makers, 157
Materia Medica for Nurses, 158
Mater Matuta, 14. *See also* goddess
worship
maternity leave, 186, 201, 366, 387;
with job security, 310, 376; paid,

272, 289, 309, 333, 345, 360;
with partial pay, 283, 291, 310,
360; unpaid, 148, 287, 333, 345,
360
mathematicians. See individual
nations under "mathematicians
of" *See also* statisticians
mathematics, 76, 158; study of, 111,
140, 337, 372
Mathews, Ann, 102–3
Mathilde d'Aguilan, 76
Mathis, June, 215
Mathurine, 63
Matilda (regent of Normandy), 38
Matilda (uncrowned queen of
England), 40, 41
Matilda, Saint, 37
Matilda of Tuscany, 38
Matikainen, Marjo, 379
Matisse, Henri, 191, 263
Matlin, Marlee, 373
Matoaka. *See* Pocahontas
Matralia, 14. *See also* goddess
worship
matriarchy, 11, 21, 53, 68, 249
matrilineality, 4, 15, 21, 43, 145,
147, 330
matrilocality, 1, 29, 34, 145
Matrimonial Causes Act (1857), 129
Matrimonio alla italiana, 302
Matronalia, 14. *See also* goddess
worship
Matterhorn, 142, 162, 233, 236
Matthews, Alva, 322
Matthews, Marjorie, 357
Matto de Turner, Colrinda, 155, 160
Mauchly, Kathleen "Kay" McNulty,
211
Maugham, W. Somerset, 151
Maunder, Annie Russell, 266
Mauprat, 117
Maurice Guest, 182–83
Mauritania: cabinet ministers of,
334; feminists of, 334
Maurmayer, Gisela, 240, 245
Maury, Antonia, 158, 201
Maury, Carlotta, 201
Mausolus of Halicarnassus, 13
Mavrogenous, Manto, 122
Mavrokordatu, Alexandra, 81
Mawia, 25
Ma Xianglan. *See* Ma Shouzhen
Maxeke, Charlotte, 192, 268
Maximilian (Holy Roman Emperor),
57
Maximilian II (ruler of Bavaria), 91
Maxims of Ptah Hotep, 3
May (English princess), 171
May, Elaine, 235
May, Geraldine P., 266
Mayan Empire, 1, 4, 28–29, 30, 374;
adultery in, 29; age at marriage in,
29; division of labor in, 28;
divorce in, 29; dowry in, 29;
etiquette in, 29; incest taboos of,

29; marriage in, 29; matrilocality
in, 29; polygyny and
concubinage in, 29; puberty rites
of, 28; rape in, 29; remarriage in,
29; rulers of, 25; slavery in, 29;
virginity in, 28–29
Mayer, Hélène, 227, 245
Mayer, Maria Goeppert, 300
Mayfair agency, 319
Mayfarth, Ulrike, 369
Mayflower, 69
mayors, 182, 262, 269, 328, 331,
350, 365, 375, 383, 385, 389
Mazarin, Cardinal Jules, 71–72
mazeppa, 134
Ma Zu. *See* Tian Hou
M.B.A. degree, 356
Mbogo, Jael, 250
McAfee, Mildred Helen, 255
McAliskey, Bernadette Devlin, 315,
334
McAuliffe, Christa, 373
McBride, Donna, 329
McCaffrey, Anne, 311, 362
McCalla, Sarah, 95
McCall's, 269
McCardell, Claire, 289, 291
McCarthy, Joseph, 271
McCarthy, Mary, 255, 282, 299
McChesney, Emma, 198
McClellan, George, 132
McClements, Lynette, 313
McClintock, Barbara, 260, 366–67
McClintock, Mary, 123–24
McClung, Nellie, 226
McColgan, Liz, 387
McCord, Vera, 210
McCormick, Anne O'Hare, 228, 244,
280
McCormick, Katharine Dexter, 292,
310
McCormick, Kelly, 370
McCormick, Patricia, 277, 285, 370
McCorvey, Norma, 327
McCoy, Elizabeth, 256
McCullers, Carson, 252, 255, 259,
263, 272, 344
McDaniel, Hattie, 244, 247, 250
McDaniel, Mildred, 285
McDowell, Mary, 205
McGillis, Kelly, 371, 378
McGraw, Ali, 318
McGrory, Mary, 337
McHugh, Heather, 344, 358, 378
McIngvale, Cynthia Potter, 345
McKane, Kitty, 219
McKay, Heather, 340
McKee, Fran, 338
McKim, Josephine, 236
McKinley, William, 168, 276
McKinney, Louise, 202, 226
McKnight, Anna, 189
McLaughlin, Ann Dore, 377
McLean, Barbara R., 242, 245, 249,
251, 259, 272, 284

321
Mutiny on the Bounty, 242
Mutual Philanthropic Society, 178
Muzio, Christine, 340, 355
Muzyka, 289
myalism, 89, 102
Myanmar (Burma), 171, 282; authors
    of, 362; pacifists of, 381;
    politicians of, 381, 387; school
    and orphanage founders of, 227;
    traders and merchants of, 37;
    women of, sold into slavery in
    Thailand, 392
My Antonía, 204
My Blue Heaven, 272
"My Boyfriend's Back," 299
My Brilliant Career, 171
mycologists, 337
My Darling Clementine, 263
"My Day," 243
My Emily Dickinson, 372
Myers, Sarah Kerr, 342
My Fair Lady (play), 284, 285
My Fair Lady (film), 302
My Friend Tree, 318
My Left Foot, 381
My Life by Water, 318
My Little Chickadee, 252
Mylonás, Eva, 318, 335
"My Man," 274
My Man, 227
"My Old Man Said Follow the Van,"
    215
Myong-ok, 97
Myrdal, Alva, 282, 297, 306, 317
Myrine, 6
Mysia, 14. *See also* goddess worship
Mystère et magique de Tibet, 229
The Mysteries of Udolpho, 97–98
The Mysterious Affair at Styles, 209
"Mystery House," 367
Mysticism, 190
mystics, 33, 42–43, 47, 52, 55, 58,
    66, 70, 102, 107, 190, 192. *See
    also* prophets; spiritualists;
    stigmatics
Mythology (Hamilton), 256
mythology, 21, 91
Myths of the Iroquois, 153

NAACP. *See* National Association
    for the Advancement of Colored
    People
Na'amat, 328
Nachdenken über Christa T, 307
Nada, 259
Nadig, Marie-Theres, 325
Naehun, 58
Na Fianna, 185
Nagase Kiyoko, 179
Nagel, Ida von, 276
Naguekina, Svetlana, 379
Naheed, 356
Na Hye-sok, 210
Naiad Press, 329

Naidu, Sarojini, 221, 228, 231;
    poetry of, 191, 200, 202
Naimuschina, Yelena, 355
Nair, Mira, 371, 375, 378, 386
Najimy, Kathy, 381
Nakabayashi Seishuku, 190
Nakatindi, 306
The Naked Truth, 198
Nakshedil, 96
Nall, Anita, 391
Nameless and Friendless, 129
names, women's, 59. *See also* birth
    names; married names
Namiko Mori, 345
Nana, 240
Nancy Drew. *See* Drew, Nancy
Nandi, 112
Nanny of the Maroons, 86
Napoleonic Code, 103
Nari Shiksha Samiti, 208
Narodnaya Volya, 147, 151
NASA. *See* National Aeronautics and
    Space Administration
Nashville, 335
Nasriddinova, Yadgar, 211
Nassiba bint Kaab, 31
Natalia (martyr), 26
Natalia (Spanish martyr), 35
Nateham, Josephine, 154
Nathhorst, Louise, 369
Nation, Carrie, 168, 171, 273
The Nation, 339
National Academy of Design, 186
National Academy of Engineers, 392
National Academy of Medicine, 144
National Academy of Sciences (U.S.):
    Henry Draper Medal of, 153, 234;
    members of, 221, 234, 260, 268,
    286, 287, 296, 310, 314, 319,
    322, 326, 330, 333, 336, 342,
    346, 349, 356, 360, 367, 372,
    374, 376, 380, 382, 384, 388,
    392, 394
National Aeronautics and Space
    Administration, xiii, 266, 376
National American Woman Suffrage
    Association, xiii, 170, 193–94;
    officers of, 156, 162, 168, 176,
    189. *See also* American Woman
    Suffrage Association; National
    Woman Suffrage Association;
    suffrage; suffragists
National Anti-Slavery Standard, 120
National Assembly (France), 94, 96,
    99, 122, 103, 159, 331
National Association for the
    Advancement of Colored People,
    xiii, 185, 208, 243; officers of,
    207, 305, 336
National Association of Colored
    Women, xiii, 162, 167, 171, 217
National Birth Control Council
    (Britain). *See* Family Planning
    Association (Britain)
National Book Award (U.S.), 274,

288, 304, 315
National Book Critics Circle, 371
National Catholic Total Abstinence
    Union, 149, 156
National Collegiate Athletic
    Association, 368, 371, 376, 382,
    386, 390
National Commission on the Status
    of Women (India), 320
National Congress of Mothers. *See*
    Parent-Teacher Association
National Consumers' League, 180,
    259
National Council of Churches (U.S.),
    317, 367
National Council of Jewish Women,
    159, 225
National Council of Negro Women,
    xiii, 243, 286
National Education Association
    (U.S.), 232
National Endowment for the Arts
    (U.S.), 307, 315, 324
The National Enquirer, 359
National Geographic, 221
National Hot Rod Association (U.S.),
    340. *See also* race car drivers
National Institute of Arts and Letters,
    269, 318
National Institutes of Health, 378
National Liberation Front (Vietnam),
    315
National Museum of Women in the
    Arts, 375
National Oceanographic and
    Atmospheric Administration, 394
National Organization for Women,
    xiii, 308, 322, 345, 372, 376,
    382, 391
National Park Service (U.S.), 243
National Press Club (U.S.), 206, 321
National Prize for Art and Literature
    (East Germany), 301
National Retired Teachers
    Association (U.S.), 311
National School of Opera (Britain),
    267
National Secular Society (Britain),
    145
National Speleological Society, 390
National Union for the Education of
    Girls, 144
National Union of Scientific
    Workers, 211
National Union of Women Suffrage
    Societies (Britain), 167, 174
National Weather Service (U.S.), 349
National Woman Suffrage
    Association, xiii, 139, 147, 156,
    162. *See also* American Woman
    Suffrage Association; National
    American Woman Suffrage
    Association; suffrage; suffragists
National Women's Party, 200, 209
National Youth Administration

295–96
Wilmer, Elizabeth Lee, 376
Wilson, Alice, 249, 262
Wilson, Bertha, 362
Wilson, Elsie Jane, 198, 202, 205, 207
Wilson, Erica, 297
Wilson, Fiammetta, 188, 194, 201
Wilson, Jeanne, 235
Wilson, Margaret, 82
Wilson, Margaret Bush, 336
Wilson, Margery, 212
Wilson, Sarah, 88
Wilson, Woodrow, 196; and women's suffrage, 193–94, 200, 203, 208
Wilson, 259
Wimbledon, 332, 345; doubles title, 207, 267, 272, 285, 291, 322; mixed doubles title, 267, 272, 322; women's singles title, 151, 156, 161, 167, 174, 177, 183, 185, 191, 195, 207, 217, 219, 223, 233, 236, 240, 245, 255–56, 267, 272, 274, 279, 287, 291, 296, 298, 300, 312, 316, 318, 322, 329, 332, 351, 375, 378
Wimsey, Lord Peter, 216, 246
Winchilsea, Countess of. *See* Finch, Anne
The Wind, 227
Windeyer, Mary, 162
Winebald, Saint, 34
Wine from These Grapes, 239
wine houses, 46
wine makers. *See* vintners
Winfrey, Oprah, 368, 371, 373, 378
Winger, Debra, 354, 365, 375, 378
Wings, 224
Winlock, Anna, 176
Winnemucca, Sarah, 147, 151
Winslow, Ola Elizabeth, 254
Winsor, Kathleen, 259
Winter Ceremony, 304
Winters, Anne, 371
Winter's Tales, 255
Wisconsin, 258, 329
Wise Blood, 275–76
Wise Parenthood, 205
Wise Woman's Prophecy, 36
Wistar, Mary Waln, 110
witches, 25, 52, 58, 65, 66, 78, 88; demographics of, 66; executions of, 52, 54, 58, 65, 66, 74, 78, 81, 82, 93, 102, 103; torture of, 58, 66; trials of, abolished, 85, 103
The Witches of Eastwick, 383
With Eyes at the Backs of Our heads, 290
With My Red Fires, 242
With Neither Bullet or Poison or Blade, 304
Without Much Hope, 307
Witkin, Evelyn Maisel, 346

Witness, 371
Witness for the Prosecution, 282
Witt, Katarina, 368, 373, 378
Wittenmyer, Annie, 143
Wittig, Monique, 259, 351
Wives and Daughters, 133
The Wives of England, 119
The Wives of the Prophet, 292
The Wiz, 348
"The Wizard and the Princess," 367
A Wizard of Earthsea, 311
The Wizard of Oz (film), 251
Wodars, Sigrun, 380
Woffington, Peg, 92
Wold, Anita, 335
Wold, Marit, 379
Wolf, Christa, 299, 301, 307, 339, 393
Wolf, Sigrid, 378–79
Wolfe, Fanny, 247
Wollstein, Martha, 251–52
Wollstonecraft, Eliza, 100
Wollstonecraft, Mary, 98, 100, 102, 114
"Woman" (article), 120
Woman (magazine), 211
A Woman (novel), 179
Woman, Church, and State, 164
The Woman Gender, 363
"Woman Has No Vocation to Public Life," 162
Woman in a Man's Church, 327
Woman in the Nineteenth Century, 121
The Woman in the Window, 259
womanism, 365
The Woman Rebel, 196
The Woman Movement, 212
Woman of the Year, 255
The Woman Question, 249
The Woman's Bible, 164, 170
Woman's Era Club, 162, 168
Woman's Magazine, 213–14
Woman's Mission, 118
The Woman's Sharpe Revenge, 73
A Woman Tenderfoot in Egypt, 216–17
The Woman Voter, 185
The Woman Warrior, 339
The Woman Who Could Not Pay, 202
The Woman Worker, 194, 203, 326
The Women (film), 251
The Women (play), 244
women: as legal minors, 8, 11, 12, 25, 28, 32, 37, 82, 103, 114, 117, 125, 150, 175, 209, 245–46, 297, 323, 367; sale of, 2, 3, 6, 8, 37, 53, 59, 69, 74, 89, 346, 366, 377; value of, 6, 28, 361; willed as property, 1, 11, 30, 54
Women Accepted for Voluntary Emergency Service, xiv, 255, 260. *See also* Navy, U.S.
Women and Economics, 170, 268
Women and Islam: An Historical and

Theological Enquiry, 388
Women and Labor, 190
Women and Religion in America, 360
Women and Russia, 356
Women and Sex, 326
Women and the Times We Live In, 140
Women and Work, 130
Women Artists 1550–1950, 342, 396
Women as Mothers, 349
Wome's Life n in Greece and Rome, 346, 396
Women in Love (film), 318
Women in the Air Force, 266
The Women of Brewster Place, 378
Women of England, 117
Women of Iran, 268
The Women of Plums: Poems in the Voices of Slave Women, 381
Women of Ryazan, 224
Women's Air Force Service Pilots, xiv, 255, 260
Women's Army Auxiliary Corps (US). *See* Women's Army Corps
Women's Army Corps (US), xiv, 204, 255, 257, 260, 286, 317. *See also* Army, U.S.
Women's Auxiliary Air Force (Britain), 253
Women's Auxiliary Ferrying Service (U.S.), 259
Women's Battalion of Death, 201
Women's Christian Temperance Union, xiv, 143, 147, 154, 162, 229, 233; legislation supported by, 179, 186
Women's Corps (Israel), 266
Women's Exponent, 149
Women's Industrial League (U.S.), 225
Women's International League for Peace and Freedom, xiv, 198, 207–8, 230, 233, 242, 247, 332
The Women's Movement, 162
Women's National Press Club, 206, 290
Women's Newspaper, 125–26
women's organizations, 20, 22, 130, 134, 138, 147, 156, 160, 167, 177, 178, 185, 192, 205, 207, 210, 217, 219, 227, 229, 231, 240, 245, 246, 259, 264, 268, 270, 274, 298, 303, 326, 345, 362, 366; abolitionist, 115, 118; abortion-rights, 322; artistic, 150, 239; athletes', 156, 162, 177, 181, 191, 200, 203, 213, 329, 332, 335, 340, 345, 348; banned, 100, 183, 249; black women's, 243, 336; business, 152, 243, 279, 329; charitable, 99, 100, 151, 277, 351; chefs', 342; civil defense or military auxiliary, 201, 202, 248, 254;

women as a percentage of, 140,
148, 152, 157, 168, 187, 211,
231, 223, 253, 272, 277, 283,
286, 289, 291, 294, 298, 303,
305, 308, 314, 316, 319, 322,
326, 329, 333, 336, 342, 345,
348, 349, 352, 356, 360, 363,
366, 372, 384, 387
workhouses, 114
The Workhouse Ward, 183
Working Girl, 378
Working Girls, 233
The Working Woman, 181
Workman, Fanny Bullock, 167, 173,
174, 179, 183, 220
workplace, discrimination in. *See*
discrimination
Works Progress Administration, 243
work week, 163, 168, 185, 193, 319
World Cup (skiing), 321, 324, 329,
332, 335, 382, 386–87, 390
A World of Difference, 358
The World of Sholom Aleichem, 278
World's Anti-Slavery Convention,
118
World's Columbian Exposition, 157,
159, 160, 162
World Health Organization, 394
World Team Tennis League, 335
World War I, 196, 197, 202, 216,
308, 361; ambulance drivers of,
201, 220, 224; military leaders
and personnel of, 201, 202; relief
workers and nurses during, 158,
161, 169, 201, 203; women in
the work force during, 187, 201,
205; women's opposition to,
198, 202, 203
World War II, 187, 252, 253, 261,
294; fashions during, 289;
heroines of, 320; journalists of,
321; literature and films about,
255, 258, 261, 263, 293;
photographers of, 261, 305;
pilots during, 393; pinups of,
328; rationing during, 254, 256;
resistance leaders and spies of,
258–59, 275; surgeons in, 256;
women in the work force after,
262; women's organizations
during, 240
World Wildlife Fund, 298
Wormeley, Katharine Prescott, 134
Wounded Knee, 329
Wounded OKA, 383
WPA. *See* Works Progress
Administration
Wray, Fay, 238, 339
The Wreck, 202
The Wreckers, 179
Wren ui aeka, 246
wrestlers, 8, 9, 138
Wright, Ellen Bryant, 339, 365, 375
Wright, Frances, 113
Wright, Frank Lloyd, 250

Wright, Laura, 158
Wright, Lucy, 102
Wright, Martha C., 123–24
Wright, Mickey, 300
Wright, Rebecca, 102
Wright, Richard, 216
A Wrinkle in Time, 297
writers. See inidividual nations under
"authors of," "essayists of,"
"poets of," etc.
writing, 10, 81, 110, 111, 177
The Writing of Biography, 275
WSPU. *See* Women's Social and
Political Union
WTUL. *See* Women's Trade Union
League
Wu, Chien-Shiung, 286
Wu, Xiao Xuan, 369
Wu, Y. C. L. Susan, 372
Wu (Chinese state), 24
Wu Chao, 31, 33
Wulfrida, 37
Wu Shangxi, 126
Wu Shujuan, 230
Wuthering Heights, 122
Wylie, Elinor, 191, 212, 216, 226
Wylie, Wilhelmina, 191
Wyman, Jane, 267
Wynette, Tammy, 312
Wyoming: governors of, 218;
suffrage in, 137

Xiang Jingyu, 209, 212, 214, 219,
224, 226
Xiang Jianzhang, 110
Xie, Miss, 38
Xie Fang, 240
Xieyunlou ci, 126
Xu Can, 75
Xue Susu, 76
Xue Wu. *See* Xue Susu
Xu Mei. *See* Gu Mei
Xu Yanmei, 379

Yale University, 188, 205, 217, 290,
300, 309, 314, 320, 333, 394
Yalow, Rosalyn S., 336, 346
Yamaguchi, Kristi, 384, 386, 390,
391
Yamamoto, Makiko, 289
Yamamato Matsuyo, 184
Yamazaki Ryu-jo, 83
Yan, Miss, 34
Yang, Xiaojun, 369
Yang, Xilan, 369
Yang, Young-Ja, 379
Yang Guifei, 33
Yang Jiang, 188
Yangu redi, 299
*Yankee from Olympus: Justice
Holmes and His Family*, 260
Yao Yi, 72
Yard, Molly, 376, 391
Yarros, Rachelle, 217
yashmak, 309. *See also* veiling of

women
Yawkey, Jean, 390
Yeager, Chuck, 266
The Yearling, 248
The Year of Living Dangerously, 365
Yegorova, Ljudmila, 285
Yehe Nala. *See* Tz'u-Hsi
Yekaterina, Irina, 273
yellow fever, 152, 172
The Yellow House on the Corner, 354
Yellow Rose of Texas. *See* Emily
(Texas slave)
"The Yellow Wallpaper," 160
Yemen: rulers of, 38; sale of women
in, 377
Yen, Vivian, 274
Ye Qiaobo, 390
Yesterday, Today and Tomorrow, 300
Ye Wanwan, 69
Ye Xiaoluan, 69
Ye Xiaowan, 69
Yezierska, Anzia, 206, 220
Yi, Lady (Korean coruler), 38
Yi, Lady (Korean royal mistress),
136–37
Yichunge yincao, 129
Yiddish, 186, 201, 324
Yi Il-chong, 178
Yi Son-hi, 190
Yoko, Madam, 145, 165
Yolande, 54
Yolande of Flanders, 49
Yong, Zhuang, 391
Yonge, Charlotte, 126
Yordanova-Barboulova, Zdravko,
340
Yoshida Shuran, 137
Yoshihara Sachiko, 301, 328
Yoshioka Yayoi, 169
You Are Happy, 331
You Came Along, 261
"You Can't Hurry Love," 307
You Have Seen Their Faces, 246
"You Light Up My Life," 344
"You Made Me Love You," 247
Young, Ann Eliza, 122
Young, Baroness Janet, 334
Young, Connie. *See* Paraskevin-
Young, Connie
Young, Loretta, 265
Young, Lynn, 335
Young, Sheila, 340
Young Armenian Women, 267
Young Cosima, 250
The Young Girls of Rochefort, 309
Young Women's Christian
Association, xiv, 205, 225, 242,
286
Yourcenar, Marguerite, 232, 274,
311–12, 354
Youren, Jan, 393
"You're So Vain," 335
"Your Money's Worth," 342
Youth Aliyah, 247
Yo Yo, 386

About the Author

KIRSTIN OLSEN is the author of *Remember the Ladies: A Woman's Book of Days* (1989) and other books. She is working on a one-act play about Queen Elizabeth I and a historical novel set in England and France from 1770 to 1792. She has taught high school and middle school English and worked as a free-lance writer.